The Interpersonal Communication Book

The Interpersonal Communication Book

Tenth Edition

Joseph A. DeVito

Hunter College of the City University of New York

Humber College Library

PEARSON

Boston ■ New York ■ San Francisco
Mexico City ■ Montreal ■ Toronto ■ London ■ Madrid ■ Munich ■ Paris
Hong Kong ■ Singapore ■ Tokyo ■ Cape Town ■ Sydney

Vice President, Editor-in-Chief: Karen Hanson
Executive Editor: Karon Bowers
Series Editorial Assistant: Jennifer Trebby
Development Editor: Doug Texter
Marketing Manager: Mandee Eckersley
Production Administrator: Annette Pagliaro
Editorial Production: Nesbitt Graphics, Inc.
Composition Buyer: Linda Cox
Manufacturing Buyer: Megan Cochran
Cover Administrator: Linda Knowles
Photo Researcher: Julie Tesser
Text Design: Glenna Collett
Composition: Publishers' Design and Production Services, Inc.

For related titles and support materials, visit our online catalog at www.ablongman.com

Between the time website information is gathered and then published, it is not unusual for some sites to have closed. Also, the transcription of URLs can result in unintended typographical errors. The publisher would appreciate notification where these errors occur so that they may be corrected in subsequent editions.

Library of Congress Cataloging-in-Publication Data
DeVito, Joseph A.
    The interpersonal communication book / Joseph A. DeVito.—10th ed.
        p.   cm.
    Includes bibliographical references and index.
    ISBN 0-205-36765-8 (pbk.)
    1. Interpersonal communication.   I. Title.
BF637.C45D49 2004
302.2—dc21   2002034543

Printed in the United States of America
10 9 8 7 6 5 4 3 2 1   RRD   08 07 06 04 03

Brief Contents

Contents

| PART TWO | MESSAGES: VERBAL AND NONVERBAL | 133 |

Specialized Table of Contents

A S K *the Researcher*

ETHICS in *Interpersonal Communication*

SELF-TESTS

INTERMEDIA

Increasing Interpersonal Effectiveness

Welcome to *The Interpersonal Communication Book*

It's a great privilege to present this tenth edition of *The Interpersonal Communication Book.* Each revision has enabled me to improve the presentation of interpersonal communication so that it accurately reflects what we currently know about the subject and is as clear, as interesting, and as involving as it can possibly be.

This tenth edition continues to provide in-depth coverage of interpersonal communication, blending theory and research on the one hand and practical skills on the other. Its philosophical foundation continues to be the notion of choice. Choice is central to interpersonal communication; as speaker, listener, and communication analyst, you are constantly confronted with choices at every stage of the communication process, choices that will influence the effectiveness of your messages and your relationships. This text provides you with worthwhile options for a vast array of interpersonal situations and discusses the theory and research evidence bearing on these communication choices. After completing this text, you should be better equipped to make more reasoned, more reasonable, and more effective communication decisions. While the orientation and basic philosophy remain the same, this revision is a major one, introducing a new organization and a variety of new features.

THE TEXT

When the first edition of this book was written, the field of interpersonal communication had no clear and agreed-upon focus and courses varied widely in what they covered. Consequently, a text of numerous short units (the first edition contained 42 units) from which instructors could select and arrange into patterns that made sense for their unique courses seemed the logical way to present interpersonal communication. Gradually, however, the field of interpersonal communication became more focused and, as a result, the basic course became more standardized and came to be built largely around the topics considered here. Further, users of previous editions reported that the chapter format would work better for them and their students. As a result of these changes and preferences, the previous edition's 22 units have been reorganized into 14 chapters. The text continues to be divided into three parts but some material has been rearranged. The following description will further explain the logic of this new organization.

Part One, "Interpersonal Communication Preliminaries," covers the foundation concepts that are basic to all forms of interpersonal communication and relationships.

- Chapter 1, "Universals of Interpersonal Communication," combines the material formerly in Units 1 ("Universals") and 2 ("Axioms"), bringing the fundamental concepts and principles into one introductory chapter.
- Chapter 2, "Culture in Interpersonal Communication," combines the cultural material formerly in Units 1 and 3 into one early chapter on all the cultural founda-

tion material. This chapter also includes the discussion of cultural time, formerly in Unit 13.

- Chapter 3, "The Self in Interpersonal Communication," combines the material from Unit 4 on self-concept, self-esteem, and self-disclosure and the discussion of communication apprehension from Unit 5.
- Chapter 4, "Perception in Interpersonal Communication," is a revision of Unit 6 on perception.
- Chapter 5, "Listening in Interpersonal Communication," is a revision of Unit 7 on listening.

Part 2, "Messages: Verbal and Nonverbal," covers the varied aspects of verbal and nonverbal messages and brings them all together in a discussion of conversation.

- Chapter 6, "Universals of Verbal and Nonverbal Messages," covers the interaction of verbal and nonverbal messages and concepts that are basic to both systems of interaction and is a revision of Unit 9. This chapter also includes the discussion of assertiveness that formerly appeared in Unit 5.
- Chapter 7, "Verbal Messages," covers the verbal message system and combines the material formerly in Units 10 ("Understanding Principles and Pitfalls") and 11 ("Reducing Barriers to Interaction").
- Chapter 8, "Nonverbal Messages," combines the material formerly in Units 12 ("Body and Sound") and 13 ("Space and Time").
- Chapter 9, "Messages and Conversation," is a revision of Unit 14.

Part 3, "Interpersonal Relationships," covers the nature and stages of interpersonal relationships, the major types of relationships, and the central concepts of conflict and power.

- Chapter 10, "Universals of Interpersonal Relationships," a revision of Unit 15, introduces the nature of interpersonal relationships and explains the stages relationships may pass through. The discussion of the developmental approach to interpersonal communication, in Unit 1 in the previous edition, is included here to explain the nature of interpersonal relationships.
- Chapter 11, "Interpersonal Relationships: Growth and Deterioration," combines the material formerly in Units 16 and 17.
- Chapter 12, "Interpersonal Relationships: Friendship, Love, Family, and Workplace," discusses the major types of interpersonal relationships and presents a more streamlined discussion of the material formerly in Units 20 (on friends and lovers), 21 (on families), and 22 (on workplace relationships).
- Chapter 13, "Conflict in Interpersonal Relationships," is a revision of Unit 19.
- Chapter 14, "Power in Interpersonal Relationships," is a revision of Unit 18.

This text is a complete learning package that will provide you with the opportunity to learn about the research and theory in interpersonal communication and to practice the skills necessary for effective interpersonal interaction.

Each chapter opens with a photograph from a film that visually introduces the topic of the chapter. A connecting paragraph then points out the relationship between the film and the chapter contents. In addition, the chapter opener includes a list of the major topics covered in the chapter.

Each chapter has a four-part ending: (1) **Summarizing,** a summary in full-sentence outline form; (2) **Applying,** a series of questions to provide opportunities to apply the material from the chapter; (3) **Experiencing,** a guide to approximately 90 experiential

vehicles designed to help you work with the chapter contents that you can access easily on the text's website (**www.ablongman.com/devito**); and (4) **Researching,** suggestions for researching interpersonal communication using Research Navigator, an extremely powerful and extensive database of popular and scholarly articles that is available with this text for the first time.

A **Glossary of Concepts and Skills** appears at the end of the text. It integrates concepts and skills, providing both definitions of key terms and, where appropriate, the corresponding skills (*in italics*), once again emphasizing the close connection between theory and practice.

FEATURES OF THE INTERPERSONAL COMMUNICATION BOOK

You'll get maximum benefit out of this text if you understand the way the book was written and some of the logic underlying the book's features. Instructors who used the previous edition will find identified here some of the major new and revised features.

Ask the Researcher

A feature introduced in the previous edition, **Ask the Researcher,** is continued in this edition and emphasizes the close connection between theory and research on the one hand and practical skills on the other. Nationally and internationally known theorists and researchers were asked to respond to typical student questions about interpersonal com-

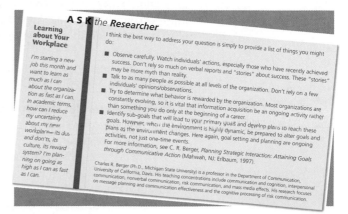

munication. You'll find their responses—22 in all—both provocative and practical. You may find it interesting to read the question and try to answer it yourself. Then you can compare your answer with that provided by the researcher and, in small groups or with the class as a whole, with those of other students. A complete list of these Ask the Researcher items is provided in the Specialized Table of Contents on page xviii.

Ethics in Interpersonal Communication

Each chapter contains an **Ethics in Interpersonal Communication** box (Chapter 6 has two) that presents a brief discussion of an ethical issue related to the chapter content. These ethics discussions cover issues such as ethical listening, keeping secrets, lying, interpersonal silence, your obligation to self-disclose, and workplace ethics. Topics new to this edition include an introductory box on ethical questions, culture and ethics, the ethics of Internet communication, the ethics of pathos, and ethical conflict. In addition to discussing these specific ethical issues, each box contains a related case and asks you to consider how you would respond. A complete list of these Ethics in Interpersonal Communication boxes is provided in the Specialized Table of Contents on page xviii.

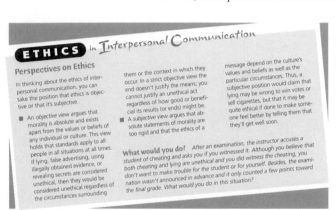

Workplace Communication and Relationships

The previous edition contained a unit on workplace communication. In this edition that material, as well as new examples and new research, has been integrated throughout the text. This change reflects the increasing importance of interpersonal communication to the workplace and the growing concern students have for insights into the ways in which interpersonal communication functions in the business world. For example, romantic relationships in the workplace, mentoring, and networking discussions are now integrated into the relationship chapter.

Culture and Interpersonal Communication

As our knowledge of culture and its relevance to interpersonal communication grows, so must its presence in an interpersonal communication textbook and course. An entire chapter devoted to culture (Chapter 2, "Culture in Interpersonal Communication") is presented early in the text as one of the foundation concepts for understanding interpersonal communication. This chapter covers the relationship of culture and interpersonal communication, the ways in which cultures differ, and intercultural communication and how you can make it more effective. In addition to this separate chapter, the importance of culture to all aspects of interpersonal communication is stressed throughout the text. Here are some of the more important discussions:

- The cultural dimension of context; culture in complementary and symmetrical relationships, in the principle of adjustment, and in ethical questions (Chapter 1)
- The role of culture in the development of self-concept and as an influencing factor in self-disclosure, and its importance in communication apprehension (Chapter 3)
- Culture and schemata, implicit personality theory, the self-serving bias, uncertainty, and developing cultural sensitivity (Chapter 4)
- Listening, culture, and gender (Chapter 5)

- Cultural and gender differences in politeness, directness, and assertiveness (Chapter 6)
- Cultural identifiers, ethnocentrism, racism, sexism, and heterosexism in racist, sexist, and heterosexist listening and language (Chapter 7)
- Culture and body gestures, attractiveness and culture, the influence of culture on facial and eye communication, gender and cultural differences in touch, silence in culture and in a sociopolitical world, culture and space expectations, color and culture, gifts and culture, time and intercultural communication, and culture and immediacy (Chapter 8)
- Conversational maxims, culture, and gender; culture and expressiveness (Chapter 9)
- Relationships in cultural context; positiveness and culture (Chapter 10)
- Attitude similarity and culture; equity, culture, and gender (Chapter 11)
- Cultural differences in friendship, cultural differences in loving, culture and the family (Chapter 12)
- Conflict, culture, and gender; culture and face-saving; culture and equality (Chapter 13)
- The cultural dimension of power, Machiavellianism and culture, culture and the knowledge gap (Chapter 14)

People with disabilities may also be viewed from a cultural perspective, and in this edition four special tables offer suggestions for communication between people with and people without disabilities. These tables provide tips for communication between blind and sighted people (Chapter 1); between people with and people without disabilities, for example, people who have cerebral palsy or who use wheelchairs (Chapter 2); between deaf and hearing people (Chapter 5); and between people with and people without speech and language disorders (Chapter 9).

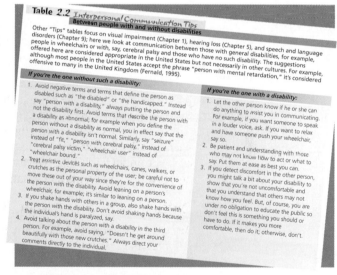

Table 2.2 Interpersonal Communication Tips Between people with and without disabilities

Technology

Technology—the Internet, e-mail, instant messaging, cell phones, and the like—has had a major impact on all aspects of interpersonal communication and interpersonal relationships. As a result, technology and its influence on the world of interpersonal communication is integrated throughout this text. Examples of these technological discussions include e-mail, listservs, and chat groups as forms of interpersonal communication (Chapter 1), cautions to observe in e-mail communication (Chapter 1), lurking as a means of uncertainty reduction (Chapter 4), ethical guidelines for Internet communication (Chapter 6), politeness guidelines for Internet communication (Chapter 6), conversational maxims and e-mail (Chapter 9), opening and closing e-mail conversations (Chapter 9), online relationships (Chapter 10), the Internet and relationship maintenance (Chapter 11), and online conflicts (Chapter 13).

A second way in which technology is integrated is through the use of Research Navigator, a powerful and extensive online database of popular and research articles in communication, as well as in related areas of psychology, sociology, anthropology, education, and business. Each chapter ends with suggestions for researching interpersonal communication using this database. Access to Research Navigator is available in special packages with a new textbook. Instructors should contact their Allyn & Bacon representative for more information.

A third way in which technology is integrated is through the use of an extensive package of electronic supplements that is updated regularly. A listing of available ancillaries may be found at the end of this preface. Updates may be found at **www. ablongman.com/devito**.

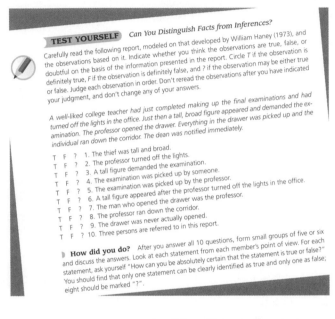

TEST YOURSELF   *Can You Distinguish Facts from Inferences?*

Carefully read the following report, modeled on that developed by William Haney (1973), and the observations based on it. Indicate whether you think the observations are true, false, or doubtful on the basis of the information presented in the report. Circle *T* if the observation is definitely true, *F* if the observation is definitely false, and *?* if the observation may be either true or false. Judge each observation in order. Don't reread the observations after you have indicated your judgment, and don't change any of your answers.

A well-liked college teacher had just completed making up the final examinations and had turned off the lights in the office. Just then a tall, broad figure appeared and demanded the examination. The professor opened the drawer. Everything in the drawer was picked up and the individual ran down the corridor. The dean was notified immediately.

T F ?   1. The thief was tall and broad.
T F ?   2. The professor turned off the lights.
T F ?   3. A tall figure demanded the examination.
T F ?   4. The examination was picked up by someone.
T F ?   5. The examination was picked up by the professor.
T F ?   6. A tall figure appeared after the professor turned off the lights in the office.
T F ?   7. The man who opened the drawer was the professor.
T F ?   8. The professor ran down the corridor.
T F ?   9. The drawer was never actually opened.
T F ?   10. Three persons are referred to in this report.

▶ **How did you do?**   After you answer all 10 questions, form small groups of five or six and discuss the answers. Look at each statement from each member's point of view. For each statement, ask yourself "How can you be absolutely certain that the statement is true or false?" You should find that only one statement can be clearly identified as true and only one as false; eight should be marked "?".

Self-Tests

Twenty-five **Test Yourself** self-tests help personalize the material and are presented throughout the text. Self-tests cover topics such as your cultural beliefs and values, your willingness to self-disclose and reveal who you "really" are, your degree of communication apprehension, and your verbal aggressiveness and argumentativeness. Approximately half of these self-tests are used regularly in interpersonal communication research; the other half were developed to highlight and preview some part of the text material. Two new self-tests are included in this edition: "How Ethnocentric Are You?" in Chapter 7 and "What Do Your Relationships Do for You?" in Chapter 10. New to this edition, each self-test now concludes with a two-part discussion: "How did you do?" contains the scoring instructions and "What will you do?" asks what steps you might consider taking as a result of the insights provided by this self-assessment. A complete list of self-tests appears in the Specialized Table of Contents on page xiii.

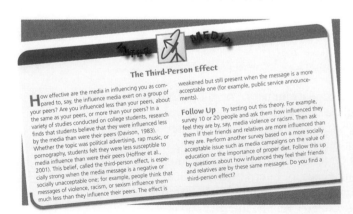

The Third-Person Effect

How effective are the media in influencing you as compared to, say, the influence media exert on a group of your peers? Are you influenced less than your peers, about the same as your peers, or more than your peers? In a variety of studies conducted on college students, research finds that students believe that they were influenced less by the media than were their peers (Davison, 1983). Whether the topic was political advertising, rap music, or pornography, students felt they were less susceptible to media influence than were their peers (Hoffner et al., 2001). This belief, called the third-person effect, is especially strong when the media message is a negative or socially unacceptable one; for example, people think that messages of violence, racism, or sexism influence them much less than they influence their peers. The effect is

weakened but still present when the message is a more acceptable one (for example, public service announcements).

Follow Up   Try testing out this theory. For example, survey 10 or 20 people and ask them how influenced they feel they are by, say, media violence or racism. Then ask them if their friends and relatives are more influenced than they are. Perform another survey based on a more socially acceptable issue such as media campaigns on the value of education or the importance of proper diet. Follow this up by questions about how influenced they feel their friends and relatives are by these same messages. Do you find a third-person effect?

InterMedia

A new feature focusing on the relationship of the mass media to interpersonal communication has been added to this edition. Fourteen **InterMedia** boxes appear throughout the text—one per chapter—identifying areas where interpersonal communication and mass media intersect. Among the issues addressed are cultural imperialism, the third-person effect, cultivation theory, gatekeeping, hate speech, the spiral of silence, parasocial relationships, and violence in the media. The title for these sections is taken from Gary Gumpert and Robert Cathcart, who introduced the term to the field in their *Inter/Media: Interpersonal Communication in a Media World* and who argued for the usefulness of looking at both interpersonal communication and the mass media as closely related and interdependent. A complete list of InterMedia boxes appears in the Specialized Table of Contents on page xiii.

Increasing Effectiveness

In the previous edition, Unit 8 was devoted to the characteristics of effective interpersonal communication. In this edition, this material has been revised, updated, and distributed throughout the text in **Increasing Effectiveness** boxes, one per chapter. Each box contains a discussion of the characteristic of effectiveness and the ways in which you can better communicate with these qualities of effectiveness. A complete list of these Increasing Effectiveness boxes appears in the Specialized Table of Contents on page xiii.

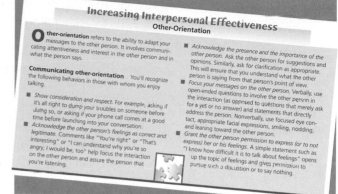

ViewPoint

In the previous editions, the photo captions contained substantive material rather than the typical brief description of the photo. This edition takes this concept a step further and presents each caption as an issue to be discussed with prompting questions. These captions, called **ViewPoint,** appear with all interior photos and should provide a useful stimulus for class discussion.

I SEE

In this edition, new brief interactive experiences (called **I SEE** for *Integrated Self-Exploration Experiences*) have been integrated into the text. These are designed to encourage you to think about the concepts discussed in the text in terms of your own interpersonal experiences. They are identified in the margins by an eyeglasses icon.

CHAPTER-BY-CHAPTER CHANGES

In addition to the new material in the self-tests, the Ask the Researcher items, the Ethics in Interpersonal Communication boxes, and the new InterMedia feature, a variety of new research has been integrated into the text, as have new examples and illustrations. Other material has been added, updated, expanded, or substantially revised; by chapter, the most notable changes are:

■ Chapter 1: Universals of Interpersonal Communication. Among the added or greatly expanded topics are the importance of interpersonal skills, message overload, the axiom of message ambiguity, communicating between blind and sighted persons, and some suggested precautions to take in electronic communication in light of irreversibility.

■ Chapter 2: Culture in Interpersonal Communication. New and expanded topics include enculturation and communication between people with and without disabilities. In addition, cultural time is presented as a basic cultural distinction and the principles for improving intercultural communication have been revised extensively.

■ Chapter 3: The Self in Interpersonal Communication. New or expanded topics include the value of avoiding self-disclosing communication, guidelines for resisting self-disclosure, and the relationship between communication apprehension and dating behavior.

■ Chapter 4: Perception in Interpersonal Communication. Among the new and expanded topics are the implications of the model of perception and research on the Pygmalion effect. In addition, the suggestions for increasing accuracy in interpersonal perception have been thoroughly revised and streamlined.

■ Chapter 5: Listening in Interpersonal Communication. The discussion of communication between deaf and hearing people has been expanded and the section on styles of listening has been thoroughly revised for greater clarity in the ways to use each of these styles.

■ Chapter 6: Universals of Verbal and Nonverbal Messages. The differences between direct and indirect messages have been clarified and the concept of assertiveness has been made more interactive with the new I SEE feature.

■ Chapter 7: Verbal Messages. The concept of ethnocentrism has been expanded with the inclusion of a new self-test.

■ Chapter 8: Nonverbal Messages. This chapter is similar to the previous edition with some new research on smell communication and the incorporation of some material formerly in tables into the text, for example, the factors influencing dyadic distance and the types of territories.

■ Chapter 9: Messages and Conversation. A new discussion of communication between those with and without speech and language disorders and a discussion of dialogic and monologic communication have been added. The discussion of effective excuses has been expanded to a five-part explanation.

■ Chapter 10: Universals of Interpersonal Relationships. The discussion of the advantages and disadvantages of interpersonal relationships has been replaced with a new self-test, "What Do Your Relationships Do for You?" The discussion of the developmental definition of communication, formerly in Unit 1, is now presented here to explain the characteristics of interpersonal relationships.

■ Chapter 11: Interpersonal Relationships: Growth and Deterioration. This chapter streamlines the material from Units 16 and 17 of the previous edition and personalizes the material on romantic rules and repairing relationships.

■ Chapter 12: Interpersonal Relationships: Friendship, Love, Family, and Workplace. This chapter combines and streamlines the material from three separate units in the previous edition, bringing the major kinds of relationships into one cohesive discussion.

■ Chapter 13: Conflict in Interpersonal Relationships. Recent research on cultural differences in conflict has been added, the discussion of ways to define the conflict has been revised for greater clarity, and the issues that people fight about and the suggestions for achieving greater argumentativeness include I SEE interactive experiences.

■ Chapter 14: Power in Interpersonal Relationships. Added or expanded materials include a discussion of the relationship of power to violence and an introduction to the types of power. In addition, the discussion of empowering apprehensives, formerly with communication apprehension in Unit 5, has been combined with the general discussion of empowerment.

ANCILLARIES/SUPPLEMENTARY MATERIALS

Instructor Supplements

Print Supplements

- **Instructor's Manual/Test Bank** by Narissra Punyanunt, Texas Tech University. This Instructor's Manual/Test Bank includes sample syllabi, chapter outlines, classroom activities, discussion questions, and video suggestions. The Test Bank contains over one thousand items including challenging multiple-choice, true-false, and short-answer essay questions along with an answer key that ranks the difficulty level of each item.
- **The Blockbuster Approach: Teaching Interpersonal Communication with Video, 2/e,** by Thomas E. Jewell, Marymount College. This guide provides lists and descriptions of commercial videos that can be used in the classroom to illustrate interpersonal concepts and complex interpersonal relationships. Sample activities are also included.

Electronic Supplements

- **Computerized Test Bank**
  The printed Test Bank is also available electronically through our computerized testing system, TestGen EQ. The fully networkable test generating software is now available on a multiplatform CD-ROM. The user-friendly interface enables instructors to view, edit, and add questions, transfer questions to tests, and print tests in a variety of fonts. Search and sort features allow instructors to locate questions quickly and arrange them in a preferred order.
- **PowerPoint Presentation Package** by Dan Cavanaugh.
  This text-specific package consists of a collection of lecture outlines and graphic images keyed to every chapter in the text. Available at **www.ablongman.com/ppt**.
- **Allyn & Bacon Digital Media Archive for Communication, Version 2.0**
  This CD-ROM offers still images, video clips, and assorted lecture resources that can be incorporated into multimedia presentations in the classroom.
- **Video: Interpersonal Communication with Guidebook**
  Eight interpersonal scenarios examine a wide range of interpersonal issues. An extensive guide provides a script, class discussion questions, and exercises for each of the episodes.
- **Allyn & Bacon Interpersonal Communication Video**
  This interpersonal video contains three scenarios illustrating key concepts in interpersonal communication with a guide featuring transcripts and teaching activities. A separate video guide is available as well.
- **Interpersonal Movie Library**
  This collection is available to adopters and contains popular feature films dealing with a range of interpersonal topics. Contact your Allyn & Bacon representative for ordering information. Some restrictions apply.
- **Allyn & Bacon Communication Video Library**
  A collection of communication videos produced by Films for the Humanities and Social Sciences. Contact your local Allyn & Bacon sales representative for ordering information. Some restrictions apply.
- **VideoWorkshop for Interpersonal Communication Instructor's Teaching Guide** by Lynn Disbrow, Sinclair Community College.
  This guide provides teaching suggestions, quiz questions and answers, and dis-

cussion starters that will help instructors use the VideoWorkshop for Interpersonal Communication CD-ROM in class. A correlation guide helps you relate the materials to your text. The complete CD-ROM and Student Learning Guide are included in the guide. Go to **www.ablongman.com/videoworkshop** for more details.

Student Supplements

Print Supplements

- **Brainstorms** by Joseph A. DeVito.
  A guide to thinking more creatively about communication, or anything else. Students will find 19 practical, easy-to-use, creative thinking techniques along with insights into the creative thinking process.

- **iSearch with Research Navigator for Speech Communication**
  This resource guide for the Internet covers the basics of using the Internet, conducting Web searches, and critically evaluating and documenting Internet sources. It also contains Internet activities and URLs specific to the discipline of speech communication. Access to Research Navigator is included.

Electronic Supplements

- **Companion Website Plus with Online Practice Tests** (**http://www.ablongman. com/devito**) by Joseph A. DeVito and Gary Kuhn, Chemeketa Community College.
  This site includes skill-building exercises and extensions and elaborations on the text. The website also includes an online study guide with practice tests and weblinks.

- **VideoWorkshop for Interpersonal Communication Student Learning Guide** by Lynn Disbrow, Sinclair Community College.
  VideoWorkshop for Interpersonal Communication is a new way to bring video into your course for maximized learning! This total teaching and learning system includes quality video footage on an easy-to-use CD-ROM plus a Student Learning Guide and an Instructor's Teaching Guide—both with textbook-specific Correlation Grids. The result? A program that brings textbook concepts to life with ease and that helps your students understand, analyze, and apply the objectives of the course. VideoWorkshop is available for your students as a value-pack option with this textbook.

- **Research Navigator™**
  Allyn & Bacon's new Research Navigator™ is the easiest way for students to start a research assignment or research paper. Complete with extensive help on the research process and three exclusive databases of credible and reliable source material including EBSCO's ContentSelect Academic Journal Database, *New York Times* Search by Subject Archive, and "Best of the Web" Link Library, Research Navigator™ helps students quickly and efficiently make the most of their research time. Go to **www.researchnavigator.com** for information on accessing Research Navigator.

- **Tutor Center** (Access Code Required)
  www.aw.com/tutorcenter
  Our Tutor Center provides free, one-on-one tutoring for students who purchase a new copy of participating Allyn & Bacon textbooks. Qualified instructors tutor students on all material covered in the texts. The approach is highly interactive, pro-

viding both knowledge of the academic discipline and methods for study of that discipline. Tutoring assistance is offered by phone, fax, Internet and email during Tutor Center hours. For more details and ordering information, please contact your Allyn & Bacon publisher's representative.

ACKNOWLEDGMENTS

I owe a great debt to the many researchers who responded to my call for responses to a variety of questions and whose answers appear in the **Ask the Researcher** feature throughout the text. Without their cooperation, goodwill, and support, this feature could not have been done. I thank them all (in order of appearance): Linda L. Putnam, Michael L. Hecht, Howard Giles, Matt Martin, Sandra Petronio, James C. McCroskey, Charles R. Berger, Andrew D. Wolvin, Rebecca B. Rubin, Thomas M. Steinfatt, Ralph Smith, Russel Windes, Gary Gumpert, Susan Drucker, Marie L. Radford, Fred E. Jandt, Alan M. Rubin, Dan Canary, Steve Duck, Mary Anne Fitzpatrick, Bernard J. Brommel, Jean Civikly-Powell, Andrew S. Rancer, Melanie Booth-Butterfield, and Steven Booth-Butterfield.

I also want to express my appreciation to the many specialists who carefully reviewed the eighth and ninth editions of this text. Your comments resulted in a large number of changes. Thank you: Dianne L. Blomberg, Metropolitan State College of Denver; Karen Desch, Northern Wyoming CC District, Gillette Campus; Donna Goodwin, Tulsa Community College; William D. Harpine, University of Akron; Eileen Hemenway, North Carolina State University; Sally Henzl, University of Wisconsin-Milwaukee; Susan Kline, Ohio State University; Neil Patten, Ferris State University; Donald Polzella, University of Dayton; Jacqueline Ralston, Columbia College; Glen Stamp, Ball State University; and Terri Kelley Wray, George Mason University.

In addition, I wish to express my appreciation to the people at Allyn & Bacon who contributed so heavily to this text. I especially wish to thank Karon Bowers, Executive Editor, who provided support and guidance throughout the revision process; Doug Texter, development editor, who made extensive and valuable suggestions for improving this edition; and Annette Pagliaro, production editor, who oversaw the process of creating this book from manuscript. I would also like to thank Julie Tesser, photo researcher, who found the functional and visually appealing photos; Julie DiSilva, copy editor, who improved the clarity and style of the writing; and Susan McIntyre, project manager at Nesbitt Graphics, who handled the day-to-day details of producing the book.

Joseph A. DeVito
jdevito@hunter.cuny.edu

Universals of Interpersonal Communication

Cast Away (2000)

If you your lips would keep
    from slips
Five things observe with care;
To whom you speak, of whom
    you speak,
And how, and when, and
    where.

—W. E. Norris

Nature of Interpersonal Communication
Elements of Interpersonal Communication
Axioms of Interpersonal Communication

The story of Chuck Noland (Tom Hanks), a FedEx engineer who is marooned on a desert island with no one to talk with, is told in Cast Away. *So great is his need to interact and communicate with another person that Noland turns a volleyball into a companion he names Wilson. Now he has someone to talk to. In this chapter we introduce this quintessential human skill: interpersonal communication. Here we explain what it is, its main elements, and the principles or general axioms that guide how interpersonal communication works.*

Interpersonal communication is something you do every day:

- ■ talking with coworkers
- ■ giving or responding to a compliment
- ■ making new friends
- ■ asking for a date
- ■ communicating through instant messaging
- ■ maintaining and repairing relationships
- ■ breaking off relationships
- ■ applying for a job
- ■ giving directions
- ■ persuading a supervisor

Understanding these interactions is an essential part of your education. Much as an educated person must know geography, history, science, and mathematics, you need to know the how, why, and what of interpersonal communication. It's a significant part of the world in which you live and it's becoming more significant daily.

Moreover, interpersonal communication is an extremely practical art, and your effectiveness as a friend, relationship partner, coworker, or manager will depend largely on your interpersonal skills. For example, in a survey of 1,001 people over 18 years of age, 53 percent felt that a lack of effective communication was the major cause of marriage failure, significantly greater than money (38 percent) and in-law interference (14 percent) (How Americans Communicate, 1999). The relevance of interpersonal communication skills to relationships is, of course, a major theme of this text and will be returned to repeatedly.

In a similar way, interpersonal skills are crucial to professional success, a relationship that has been widely documented (Morreale, Osborn, & Pearson, 2000). Interpersonal skills have become so important that the United States Department of Labor, in its report, "What Work Requires of Schools"—a report based on interviews with managers, employers, and workers who described the skills needed to function effectively at their jobs—identified interpersonal skills as one of five skills essential for a nation and an individual to be economically competitive in the world marketplace (*New York Times,* July 3, 1991, p. A17). In a study conducted by the Collegiate Employment Research Institute of Michigan State University of more than 500 employers, "good oral, written, and interpersonal communication skills were reported among the most notable deficiencies observed in new college graduates" (Scheetz, 1995). Interpersonal skills are considered "key in [the] office of the future" (*TMA Journal,* 1999, p. 53) and a "key career advantage for finance professionals in the next century" (Messmer, 1999). In studies in the health care industry communication skills figure prominently in enabling nurses to rise in the corporate hierarchy and in building patient trust (Nordhaus-Bike, 1999; Titlow, Rackoff, & Emanuel, 1999). Interpersonal skills are also identified as one of six areas that define the professional competence of physicians and trainees (Epstein &

Hundert, 2002). And a study focusing on the education of hotel and restaurant admin-istrators concluded that "communication and interpersonal skills" was one of the three vitally important subjects that need to be emphasized (Dittman, 1997). The importance of interpersonal communication skills seems, then, to extend over the entire spectrum of professions.

Understanding the theory and research in interpersonal communication and mas-tering its skills go hand in hand. The more you know about interpersonal communica-tion, the more insight and knowledge you'll gain about what works and what doesn't work. The more skills you have within your arsenal of communication strategies, the greater will be your options for communicating in any situation. In a nutshell, the greater your knowledge and the greater the number of communication options at your disposal, the greater the likelihood that you'll be successful in achieving your interper-sonal goals.

This book emphasizes your understanding of interpersonal communication: its the-ories and research and its practical skills. Theory-research and skills are considered to-gether as we progress through the elements of interpersonal communication, the ways verbal and nonverbal messages operate in interpersonal encounters, and the ways re-lationships are developed and maintained, repaired, and even dissolved. As a preface to an area of study that will be enlightening, exciting, and extremely practical, examine your assumptions about interpersonal communication by taking the accompanying self-test.

TEST YOURSELF   *What Do You Believe about Interpersonal Communication?*

Respond to each of the following statements with T if you believe the statement is usually true or F if you believe the statement is usually false.

_____ 1. Good communicators are born, not made.
_____ 2. The more you communicate, the better at it you will be.
_____ 3. Opening lines such as "Hello, how are you?" or "Fine weather today" or "Have you got the time?" serve no useful interpersonal purpose.
_____ 4. In your interpersonal communications, a good guide to follow is to be as open, empathic, and supportive as you can be.
_____ 5. When verbal and nonverbal messages contradict each other, people believe the verbal message.
_____ 6. The best guide to follow when communicating with people from other cultures is to ignore the differences and treat the other person just as you'd treat mem-bers of your own culture.
_____ 7. Effective interpersonal communicators do not rely on "power tactics."
_____ 8. Fear of public speaking is detrimental and must be eliminated.
_____ 9. When there is conflict, your relationship is in trouble.
_____ 10. When two people are in a close relationship for a long period of time, one should not have to communicate his or her needs and wants; the other person should know what these are.

▶ **How did you do?**   As you probably figured out, all 10 statements are generally false. As you read this text, you'll discover not only why these beliefs are false but also the trouble you can get into when you assume they're true. For now, and in brief, here are some of the reasons each of the statements is generally false: (1) Effective communication is a learned skill; although some people are born brighter or more extroverted, all can improve their abilities and become more effective communicators. (2) It's not the amount of communication people engage in but the quality that matters; if you practice bad habits, you're more likely to grow less effective than more effective, so it's important to learn and follow the principles of effectiveness. (3) These kinds of messages actually serve the extremely important purposes of opening the channels of communication and letting each other know that the normal rules of communication will operate in this conversation. (4) Each interpersonal situation is unique and therefore the type of communication appropriate in one situation may not be appropriate in another. (5) Whether you believe the verbal or the nonverbal messages depends on the total communication context, but generally research does find that people are more likely to believe the nonverbal messages. (6) This assumption will probably get you into considerable trouble since people from different cultures will often attribute different meanings to a message; members of different cultures also follow different rules for what is and is not appropriate in interpersonal communication. (7) Power is an inevitable part of all interpersonal interactions, so it really can't be eliminated even if you want it to be. (8) Most speakers are nervous; managing, not eliminating, the fear will enable you to become effective regardless of your current level of fear. (9) All meaningful relationships experience conflict; relationships are not in trouble when there is conflict, though dealing with conflict ineffectively can often damage the relationship. (10) This assumption is at the heart of many interpersonal difficulties—people aren't mind readers, and to assume they are merely sets up barriers to open and honest communication.

▶ **What will you do?**   This is perhaps, then, a good place to start practicing the critical thinking skill of questioning commonly held assumptions about interpersonal communication and about yourself as an interpersonal communicator. Consider, for example, what other beliefs you have about communication and about yourself as a communicator. How do these beliefs influence your communication?   ●

NATURE OF INTERPERSONAL COMMUNICATION

We can best understand interpersonal communication by looking at its major characteristics, forms, and purposes.

Characteristics of Interpersonal Communication

Interpersonal communication is the communication that takes place between two persons who have an established relationship; the people are in some way "connected." Interpersonal communication would thus include what takes place between a son and his father, an employer and employee, two sisters, a teacher and a student, two lovers, two friends, and so on.

You could argue that it's impossible to have dyadic (two-person) communication that isn't interpersonal. Invariably, there is some relationship between two people who are interacting. Even the stranger who asks directions of a neighborhood resident has an identifiable relationship with the resident as soon as the first message is sent. This interpersonal (but nonintimate) relationship will then influence how the two individuals interact with each other.

Dyadic Primacy   Even when you have triads (groups of three people), dyads (two-person relationships) are still primary; dyads are always central to interpersonal relationships, a process referred to as **dyadic primacy** (Wilmot, 1999). Consider, for example, the following situation: Al and Bob (a dyad) have been roommates for their first two years of college. Expenses have increased, so they ask Carl to join them and become a third roommate. Now a triad exists. But the original dyad has not gone away; in fact, now there are three dyads: Al and Bob, Al and Carl, and Bob and Carl. Al and Bob are ballplayers and talk a lot about sports. Al and Carl are both studying communication and talk about their classes. Bob and Carl belong to the same religious club and frequently discuss the club's activities. At times, of course, all three interact, but even here the topic of conversation will determine who talks primarily to whom. If the topic is sports, Al and Bob will primarily address each other; Carl will be a kind of outsider. When the topic is classes, Bob is the outsider.

If you examine families, workers in a factory, neighbors in an apartment house, or students in class, you'll find that each large group breaks down at times into a series of dyads. The specific dyad formed naturally depends on the situation, and dyads will probably change over time. As in the case of Al, Bob, and Carl, different dyads will form, depending on the nature of the interaction.

TRY IT!
Apply your knowledge of dyadic coalitions; go to **www.ablongman.com/devito**.

Dyadic Coalitions A **dyadic coalition** is a two-person relationship formed by members of a larger group for achieving a mutually desired benefit or goal (Wilmot, 1999). Coalitions—whether in the family, among friends, or at work—may be productive or unproductive. Two workers may form a coalition to develop a program for improving worker morale. Two teachers may undertake research together. The result of these coalitions will benefit not only the individuals involved but also, eventually, all members of the group.

At other times, coalitions are unproductive. The grandparent who develops a coalition with the grandchild against the child's parent may cause all sorts of family difficulties; parental resentment and jealousy, as well as guilt for the child, are just a few possibilities. A parent experiencing marital difficulties may form a coalition with one of the children. This often results in alienating the left-out parent and preventing the child from benefiting from a close relationship with that parent.

Dyadic Consciousness In addition to what you do and say, your interpersonal relationships depend on what you think about your relationship. As your relationship develops, a **dyadic consciousness** emerges; you begin to see yourself as part of a pair, a team, a couple. It's almost as if a third party enters the picture. No longer is it just you and the other person; it's now you, the other person, and the relationship. As the relationship becomes more involved, this third party takes on greater importance. Often individuals sacrifice their own desires or needs for the well-being of "the relationship."

Forms of Interpersonal Communication

Often interpersonal communication takes place face-to-face: talking with other students before class, interacting with family or friends over dinner, trading secrets with intimates. This is the type of interaction that probably comes to mind when you think of conversation. Because of technological advances, however, much conversation now takes place online. Online communication is becoming a part of people's experience throughout the world. Such communications are important personally, socially, and professionally. The three major online types of conversation—e-mail, the mailing list group, and the chat group—differ from each other and from face-to-face interaction.

In *e-mail,* you usually type your letter in an e-mail program and send it (along with other documents you may wish to attach) from your computer via modem or cable to your server (the computer at your school or at some commercial organization like America Online), which relays your message through a series of computer hookups and eventually to the server of the person you're addressing. Unlike face-to-face communication, traditional e-mail does not take place in real time. You may send your message today, but the receiver may not read it for a week and may take another week to respond. Much of the spontaneity created by real-time communication is lost here. You may, for example, be very enthusiastic about a topic when you send your e-mail but practically forget it by the time someone responds. Instant messaging, on the other hand, does take place in real time (essentially) and so it more closely resembles face-to-face interaction.

E-mail is more like a postcard than a letter and so can be read by others along the route. It's also virtually unerasable. Especially in large organizations, employees' e-mails are stored on hard disk or on back-up tapes and may be retrieved for a variety of reasons. Currently, for example, large corporations are being sued because of sexist and racist e-mail that their employees wrote and that plaintiffs' lawyers have retrieved from archives long thought destroyed. Also, your e-mail can be easily forwarded to other people by anyone who has access to your files. Although this practice is considered unethical, it's relatively common.

The *listserv* or *mailing list group* consists of a group of people interested in a particular topic who communicate with each other through e-mail. Generally, you subscribe to a list and communicate with all other members by addressing your mail to the group e-mail address. Any message you send to this address will be sent to each member who subscribes to the list. Your message is sent to all members at the same time; there are no asides to the person sitting next to you (as in face-to-face groups). The accompanying Web site provides a list of mailing lists categorized by topic.

Chat groups, especially Internet Relay Chat (IRC) groups, have proliferated across the Internet. These groups enable members to converse in real time discussion groups. At any one time, there are thousands of groups, so your chances of finding a topic you're interested in are high. Unlike mailing lists, chat communication lets you see a member's message as it's being sent; there's virtually no delay, and recent innovations now enable you to communicate with voice as well as text. Like mailing lists and face-to-face conversation, the purposes of chat groups vary from communication that simply maintains connection with others (what many would call "idle chatter" or "phatic communion") to extremely significant discussions in science, education, health, politics, and just about any field you can name.

Communication chat groups resemble the conversation you'd observe at a large party. The guests divide up into small groups varying from two on up, and each discusses its own topic or version of a general topic. For example, in a group about travel, five people may be discussing the difficulties of traveling to certain Middle East countries, three people may be discussing airport security systems, and two people may be discussing bargain rates for cruises to Mexico, all on this one channel dealing with travel. Such groups also allow you to *whisper,* to communicate with just one other person without giving access to your message to other participants. So, although you may be communicating in one primary group (say, dealing with airport security), you also have your eye trained to pick up something particularly interesting in another group (much as you do at a party). Chat groups also notify you when someone new comes into the group and when someone leaves. Like mailing lists, chat groups have the great advantage that they enable you to communicate with people you would never meet and interact with otherwise. Because chat groups are international, they provide excellent exposure to other cultures, other ideas, and other ways of communicating.

In face-to-face conversation you're expected to contribute to the ongoing discussion. In chat groups you can simply observe; in fact, you're encouraged to *lurk*—to observe

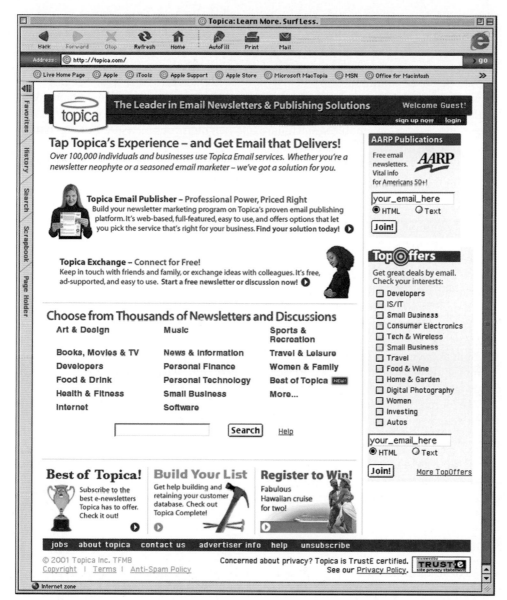

You can explore a wide variety of online newsletters and discussions by visiting the Topica Web site at http://topica.com/. How many newsletters or discussions can you find that might be useful in studying interpersonal communication? (*Source:* Reprinted by permission of Topica Inc.)

the participants' interaction before you say anything yourself. In this way, you'll be able to learn the cultural rules and norms of the group.

Purposes of Interpersonal Communication

Interpersonal communication serves a variety of purposes, for example, to learn, to relate, to influence, to play, and to help. Interpersonal communication enables you to *learn,* to better understand the external world—the world of objects, events, and other people. Although a great deal of information comes from the media, you probably discuss and ultimately learn or internalize information through interpersonal interactions. In fact, your beliefs, attitudes, and values are probably influenced more by interpersonal encounters than by the media or even formal education.

Most important, however, interpersonal communication helps you learn about yourself. By talking about yourself with others, you gain valuable feedback on your feelings, thoughts, and behaviors. Through these communications, you also learn how you appear to others—who likes you, who dislikes you, and why.

Interpersonal communication helps you *relate*. One of the greatest needs people have is to establish and maintain close relationships. You want to feel loved and liked, and in turn you want to love and like others. Such relationships help to alleviate loneliness and depression, enable you to share and heighten your pleasures, and generally make you feel more positive about yourself.

Very likely, you *influence* the attitudes and behaviors of others in your interpersonal encounters. You may wish them to vote a particular way, try a new diet, buy a new book, listen to a record, see a movie, take a specific course, think in a particular way, believe that something is true or false, or value some idea—the list is endless. A good deal of your time is probably spent in interpersonal persuasion.

Talking with friends about your weekend activities, discussing sports or dates, telling stories and jokes, and in general just passing the time are *play* functions. Far from frivolous, this extremely important purpose gives your activities a necessary balance and your mind a needed break from all the seriousness around us.

Therapists of various kinds serve a helping function professionally by offering guidance through interpersonal interaction. But everyone interacts to *help* in everyday encounters: You console a friend who has broken off a love affair, counsel another student about courses to take, or offer advice to a colleague about work. Success in accomplishing this helping function, professionally or otherwise, depends on your knowledge and skill in interpersonal communication.

The purposes of interpersonal communication can also be viewed from two other perspectives (see Figure 1.1). First, purposes may be seen as motives for engaging in

Theories of Media Influence

Media messages have effects on readers, listeners, and viewers. Some messages have obvious influence, for example, the product advertisements on television or on the Internet and the editorials in newspapers. Other media messages influence indirectly, for example, the dramas and sitcoms that influence your view of family, of work and workplace relationships, and of friendship and love.

An early theory, called the one-step theory, argued that the influence of the media was direct and immediate; it occurred in one step—from the media to you. You read a newspaper or watched television and were persuaded by what you read or saw (Schramm & Porter, 1982). As an audience member you were viewed as relatively passive, as a target that could hardly resist being influenced.

A more sophisticated explanation visualizes media influence as a two-step process: First, the media influence opin-

ion leaders (step 1) and second, these opinion leaders influence the rest of the people (step 2). A more current and complicated approach, the multistep theory, claims that media interact with interpersonal channels. So, for example, the media might influence you on a specific issue, then you interact interpersonally with others who influence you to alter your newly formed opinions. You then attend to more media and they influence you in other directions. In this view, media influence combines with interpersonal influence.

Follow Up   Can you identify specific ways in which the media have influenced you? For example, have media messages influenced your buying habits, your view of relationships, or your attitudes toward the opposite sex? What theory seems to best explain how the media influence you?

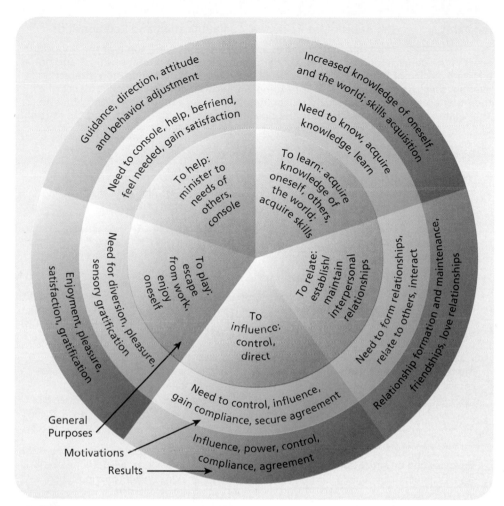

Figure 1.1

Why You Engage in Interpersonal Communication

This figure identifies some of the reasons you listen. The innermost circle contains the general purposes of interpersonal communication. The middle circle contains the motivations that lead you to communicate. The outer circle contains the results that you might hope to achieve by engaging in interpersonal communication. A similar typology of purposes comes from research on motives for communicating. In a series of studies, Rubin and her colleagues (Rubin, Fernandez-Collado, & Hernandez-Sampieri, 1992; Rubin & Martin, 1994; Rubin, Perse, & Barbato, 1988; Rubin & Rubin, 1992; Graham, 1994; and Graham, Barbato, & Perse, 1993) have identified six primary motives for communication: pleasure, affection, inclusion, escape, relaxation, and control. How do these compare to the five purposes discussed here?

interpersonal communication. That is, you engage in interpersonal communication to satisfy your need for knowledge or to form relationships. Second, these purposes may be viewed in terms of the results you want to achieve. That is, you engage in interpersonal communication to increase your knowledge of yourself and others or to exert influence or power over others.

You can gain an additional perspective on interpersonal communication by looking at the major divisions or areas of the field as identified in Table 1.1 on page 10.

Table 1.1   **The Areas of Interpersonal Communication and Relationships**

This table is intended as a guide for identifying some of the important areas in the general topic of "interpersonal communication and relationships" and not as a formal outline of the field. The six areas of interpersonal communication interact and overlap; they're not independent. For example, interpersonal interaction is a part of all the other areas; similarly, intercultural communication can exist in any of the other areas. The related academic areas illustrate the close ties among fields of study and the centrality of communication to all academic areas.

General and Related Areas	*Selected Topics*
Interpersonal interaction: communication between two people *Related areas:* Psychology, Education, Linguistics, Counseling	Characteristics of effectiveness, Conversational processes, Self-disclosure, Active listening, Nonverbal messages in conversation, Online interaction
Health communication: communication between health professional and patient *Related areas:* Medicine, Psychology, Counseling, Health care	Talking about AIDS, Increasing doctor–patient effectiveness, Communication and aging, Therapeutic communication, Communicating safe-sex guidelines
Family communication: communication within the family system *Related areas:* Sociology, Psychology, Family studies, Social work	Power in the family, Dysfunctional families, Family conflict, Heterosexual and homosexual families, Parent–child communication
Intercultural communication: communication among members of different races, nationalities, religions, genders, and generations *Related areas:* Anthropology, Sociology, Cultural studies, Business	Cross-generational communication, Male–female communication, Black–Hispanic–Asian–Caucasian communication, Prejudice and stereotypes in communication, Barriers to intercultural communication, The Internet and cultural diversity
Business and organizational communication: communication among workers in an organizational environment *Related areas:* Business, Management, Public relations, Computer science	Interviewing strategies, Sexual harassment, Upward and downward communication, Increasing managerial effectiveness, Leadership in business
Social and personal relationships: communication in close relationships, such as friendship and love *Related areas:* Psychology, Sociology, Anthropology, Family studies	Relationship development, Relationship breakdown, Repairing relationships, Gender differences in relationships, Increasing intimacy, Verbal abuse

Interpersonal communication is usually motivated by a combination of factors and has a combination of results or effects. Any interpersonal interaction, then, serves a unique combination of purposes, is motivated by a unique combination of factors, and can produce a unique combination of results.

ELEMENTS OF INTERPERSONAL COMMUNICATION

The model presented in Figure 1.2 is designed to reflect the circular nature of interpersonal communication; both persons send messages simultaneously rather than as a linear sequence where communication goes from person 1 to person 2 to person 1 to

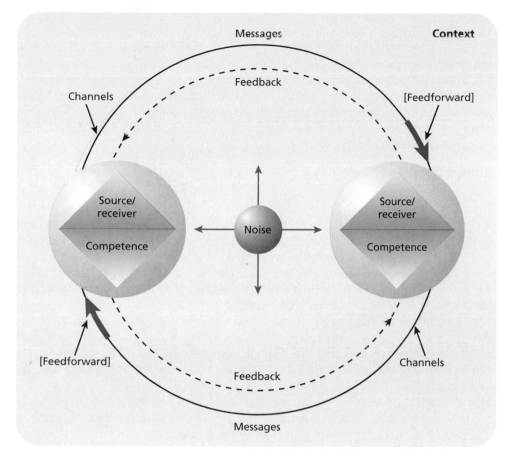

Figure 1.2

A Model of Some Universals of Interpersonal Communication
After you read the section on the elements of interpersonal communication, you may wish to construct your own model of the process. In constructing this model, be careful that you don't fall into the trap of visualizing interpersonal communication as a linear or simple left-to-right, static process. Remember that all elements are interrelated and interdependent. After completing your model, consider, for example: (1) Could your model also serve as a model of *intra*personal communication? A model of small group, public, or mass communication? (2) What elements or concepts other than those noted here might be added to the model?

person 2 and on and on. Each of the concepts identified in the model and discussed here may be thought of as a **universal of interpersonal communication,** in that it's present in all interpersonal interactions.

Source–Receiver

Interpersonal communication involves at least two persons. Each person formulates and sends messages (**source** functions) and also perceives and comprehends messages (**receiver** functions). The term *source–receiver* emphasizes that both functions are performed by each individual in interpersonal communication.

Who you are, what you know, what you believe, what you value, what you want, what you have been told, and what your attitudes are all influence what you say, how you say it, what messages you receive, and how you receive them. Likewise, the person you're speaking to and the knowledge that you think that person has will greatly influence your interpersonal messages (Lau, Chiu, & Hong, 2001). Each person is unique; each person's communications are unique.

Encoding–Decoding

Encoding refers to the act of producing messages—for example, speaking or writing. *Decoding* is the reverse and refers to the act of understanding messages—for example, listening or reading. By sending your ideas via sound waves (in the case of speech) or light waves (in the case of writing), you're putting these ideas into a code, hence *en-coding*. By translating sound or light waves into ideas, you're taking them out of a code, hence *decoding*. Thus, speakers and writers are called **encoders,** and listeners and readers are called **decoders.** The term *encoding–decoding* is used to emphasize that the two activities are performed in combination by each participant. For interpersonal communication to occur, messages must be encoded and decoded. For example, when a parent talks to a child whose eyes are closed and whose ears are covered by stereo headphones, interpersonal communication does not occur because the messages sent are not being received.

Competence

Your ability to communicate effectively is your interpersonal **competence** (Spitzberg & Cupach, 1989). Your competence includes, for example, the knowledge that in certain contexts and with certain listeners one topic is appropriate and another isn't. Your knowledge about the rules of nonverbal behavior—for example, the appropriateness of touching, vocal volume, and physical closeness—is also part of your competence. In short, interpersonal competence includes knowing how to adjust your communication according to the context of the interaction, the person with whom you're interacting, and a host of other factors discussed throughout this text.

You learn communication competence much as you learn to eat with a knife and fork—by observing others, by explicit instruction, by trial and error. Some have learned better than others, though, and these people are generally the ones with whom you find it interesting and comfortable to talk. They seem to know what to say and how and when to say it.

Not surprisingly, there's a positive relationship between interpersonal competence on the one hand and success in college and job satisfaction on the other (Rubin & Graham, 1988; Wertz, Sorenson, & Heeren, 1988). So much of college and professional life depends on interpersonal competence—meeting and interacting with other students, teachers, or colleagues; asking and answering questions; presenting information or argument—that you should not find this connection surprising. Interpersonal competence also enables you to develop and maintain meaningful relationships in friendship, love, family, and work which, in turn, contribute to the lower levels of anxiety, depression, and loneliness observed in interpersonally competent people (Spitzberg & Cupach, 1989).

Messages

Messages—signals that serve as **stimuli** for a receiver—may be auditory (hearing), visual (seeing), tactile (touching), olfactory (smelling), gustatory (tasting), or any combination. You communicate interpersonally by gesture and touch as well as by words and sentences. The clothes you wear communicate to others and, in fact, to yourself as well. The way you walk communicates, as does the way you shake hands, tilt your head, comb your hair, sit, smile, or frown. These signals are your interpersonal communication messages. Interpersonal communication can take place by telephone, through prison cell walls, through web-cams, or face-to-face. Increasingly, it's taking place through computers.

Messages may be intentional or unintentional. They may result from the most carefully planned strategy as well as from the unintentional slip of the tongue, lingering body odor, or nervous twitch.

Messages may refer to the world, people, and events as well as to other messages. Messages that are about other messages are called **metamessages** and represent many of your everyday messages, for example: "Do you understand?" "Did I say that right?" "What did you say?" "Is it fair to say that . . . ?" "I want to be honest." "That's not logical." Two particularly important types of metamessages are feedback and feedforward.

Feedback Messages   Throughout the interpersonal communication process, you exchange **feedback**—messages sent back to the speaker concerning reactions to what is said (Clement & Frandsen, 1976). Feedback tells the speaker what effect she or he is having on listeners. On the basis of this feedback, the speaker may adjust, modify, strengthen, de-emphasize, or change the content or form of the messages.

     Feedback may come from yourself or from others. When you send a message—say, in speaking to another person—you also hear yourself. That is, you get feedback from your own messages: you hear what you say, you feel the way you move, you see what you write. In addition to this self-feedback, you get feedback from others. This feedback can take many forms. A frown or a smile, a yea or a nay, a pat on the back or a punch in the mouth are all types of feedback.

     Feedback can be looked at in terms of five important dimensions: positive–negative; person focused–message focused; immediate–delayed; low monitoring–high monitoring; and supportive–critical. To use feedback effectively, you need to make educated choices along these dimensions (Figure 1.3).

Positive–Negative   Feedback may be positive (you pay a compliment or pat someone on the back) or negative (you criticize someone or scowl). **Positive feedback** tells the speaker that he or she is on the right track and should continue communicating in essentially the same way. **Negative feedback** tells the speaker that something is wrong and that some adjustment should be made.

Person Focused–Message Focused   Feedback may center on the person ("You're sweet" or "You have a great smile"). Or it may center on the message ("Can you repeat that number?" or "Your argument is a good one").

Immediate–Delayed   In interpersonal situations, feedback is often sent immediately after the message is received; you smile or say something in response almost simultaneously with your receiving the message. In other communication situations, however, the feedback may be delayed. Instructor evaluation questionnaires completed at the end of the course provide feedback long after the class began. When you applaud or ask questions of a public speaker at the end of a lecture, the feedback is delayed. In interview situations, the feedback may come weeks afterward. In media situations, some feedback comes immediately through Nielsen ratings, and other feedback comes much later through viewing and buying patterns.

WEB EXPLORATION
To learn more about feedback messages, go to **www.ablongman.com/ devito**.

Positive ___:___:___:___:___:___ Negative
Person Focused ___ : :___:___:___:___ Message Focused
Immediate ___:___:___:___:___:___ Delayed
Low Monitoring ___:___:___:___:___:___ High Monitoring
Supportive ___:___:___:___:___:___ Critical

Figure 1.3

Five Dimensions of Feedback
What kinds of feedback would be exchanged between casual acquaintances? What kinds would be exchanged between two people who disliked each other?

The "feedback theory of relationships" holds that satisfying interpersonal relationships may be characterized by feedback that is positive, person focused, immediate, low monitoring, and supportive, and that unsatisfying relationships are characterized by feedback that is negative, self-focused, nonimmediate, high monitoring, and critical. How effective do you find this theory? How effective is this theory in explaining relationships with which you're familiar?

Low Monitoring–High Monitoring   Feedback varies from the spontaneous and totally honest reaction (low-monitored feedback) to the carefully constructed response designed to serve a specific purpose (high-monitored feedback). In most interpersonal situations, you probably give feedback spontaneously; you allow your responses to show without any monitoring. At other times, however, you may be more guarded, as when your boss asks you how you like your job or when your grandfather asks what you think of his new earring.

Supportive–Critical   Supportive feedback accepts the speaker and what the speaker says. It occurs, for example, when you console another, encourage him or her to talk, or otherwise confirm the person's definition of self. Critical feedback, on the other hand, is evaluative; it's judgmental. When you give critical feedback (whether positive or negative), you judge another's performance, as in, for example, coaching someone learning a new skill.

Feedforward Messages   **Feedforward** is information you provide before sending your primary messages (Richards, 1951). Feedforward reveals something about the messages to come. Examples of feedforward include the preface or table of contents of a book, the opening paragraph of a chapter, movie previews, magazine covers, and introductions in public speeches. Feedforward may serve a variety of functions: to open the channels of communication, to preview the message, to disclaim, and to altercast.

To Open the Channels of Communication   In his influential essay "The Problem of Meaning in Primitive Languages," anthropologist Bronislaw Malinowski (1923) coined the phrase *phatic communion* to refer to messages that open the channels of communication rather than communicate information. Phatic communion is a perfect example of feedforward. It's information that tells you that the normal, expected, and accepted rules of interaction will be in effect. It tells you another person is willing to communicate.

To Preview the Message   Feedforward messages frequently preview other messages. They may, for example, preview the content ("I'm afraid I have bad news for you"), the importance ("Listen to this before you make a move"), the form or style ("I'll tell you all the gory details"), and the positive or negative quality of subsequent messages ("You're not going to like this, but here's what I heard").

To Disclaim   The **disclaimer** is a statement that aims to ensure that your message will be understood as you want it to be and that it will not reflect negatively on you. For example, you might use a disclaimer when you think that what you're going to say may be met with opposition. Thus, you say "I'm not against immigration, but . . ." or "Don't think I'm homophobic, but . . . ." (Disclaimers, as they function to prevent conversational problems, are discussed in Chapter 9.)

To Altercast   Feedforward is often used to place the receiver in a specific role and to request responses in terms of this assumed role, a process called **altercasting** (Weinstein & Deutschberger, 1963; McLaughlin, 1984). For example, you might altercast by asking a friend, "As a future advertising executive, what would you think of corrective advertising?" This question casts your friend in the role of advertising executive (rather than parent, Democrat, or Baptist, for example) and asks that she or he answer from a particular perspective.

Message Overload   **Message overload** (often called **information overload** in business) is one of the greatest obstacles to achieving communication efficiency and has even been linked to health problems in corporate managers (Lee, 2000). The ease with which e-mail and Internet messages can be copied or forwarded to large numbers of people with a few taps of the keyboard has obviously contributed to message overload as has the junk mail and spam that seems to grow every day. Invariably, you must select certain messages to attend to and other messages to ignore. Today, for example, the American worker is exposed to more messages in one year than a person living in 1900 was in his or her entire life. Today, the average employee receives more than 50 e-mails daily. And in one day, the average manager sends and receives over 100 documents.

One of the problems with message overload is that it absorbs an enormous amount of time. The more messages you have to deal with, the less time you have for those messages or tasks that are central to your purposes. Similarly, under conditions of message overload, errors are more likely simply because you cannot devote the needed time to any one item. The more rushed you are, the more likely you are to make mistakes.

Another problem is that the overabundance of messages may make it difficult for you to determine efficiently which messages need immediate attention and which don't, which messages may be discarded and which must be retained. Consider your own ways of dealing with message overload (Uris, 1986).

Do you

I SEE

1. Think before passing on messages, realizing that not all messages must be passed on, that not everyone needs to know everything?
2. Use the messages as they come to you and then throw them out? For example, do you write the relevant dates for a meeting on your calendar and then throw out the announcement or delete the e-mail?
3. Organize your messages? Have you created folders to help you store and retrieve the information you need quickly?
4. Get rid of extra copies? When you receive multiple copies do you get rid of all but the one you need?
5. Distinguish between messages that you should save and messages that are only cluttering up your space?

Channel

The communication **channel** is the medium through which messages pass. It's a kind of bridge connecting source and receiver. Communication rarely takes place over only one channel; two, three, or four channels are often used simultaneously. For example, in face-to-face interaction, you speak and listen (vocal–auditory channel), but you also gesture and receive signals visually (gestural–visual channel), and you emit odors and smell those of others (chemical–olfactory channel). Often you communicate through touch (cutaneous–tactile channel). Another way to think about channels is to consider them as the means of communication: for example, face-to-face contact, telephone, e-mail and snail mail, chat groups, instant messaging, news postings, film, television, radio, smoke signals, or fax.

At times one or more channels may be damaged. For example, in the case of the blind, the visual channel is impaired and so adjustments have to be made. Table 1.2 gives you an idea of how such adjustments between blind and sighted persons can make interpersonal communication more effective.

Noise

Noise interferes with receiving a message someone is sending or with someone receiving your message. Noise may be physical (others talking loudly, cars honking, illegible handwriting, "garbage" on your computer screen), physiological (hearing or visual impairment, articulation disorders), psychological (preconceived ideas, wandering thoughts), or semantic (misunderstood meanings). Technically, noise is anything that distorts the message, anything that prevents the receiver from receiving the message (Table 1.3 on page 18).

A useful concept in understanding noise and its importance in communication is **signal-to-noise ratio.** *Signal* refers to information that you'd find useful, and *noise* refers to information that is useless (to you). So, for example, a mailing list or newsgroup that contains lots of useful information would be high on signal and low on noise; those that contain lots of useless information would be high on noise and low on signal.

Since messages may be visual as well as spoken, noise too may be visual. The sunglasses that prevent someone from seeing the nonverbal messages from your eyes would be considered noise, as would blurred type on a printed page.

Table *1.2* *Interpersonal Communication Tips*
Between blind and sighted people

People vary greatly in their visual abilities; some are totally blind, some are partially sighted, and some have unimpaired vision. Ninety percent of the people who are "legally blind" have some vision. All, however, have the same need for communication and information. Here are some tips for making communication between blind and sighted people more effective.

If you're the sighted person and are talking with a blind person:	*If you're the blind person and are interacting with a sighted person:*
1. Identify yourself; don't assume that the blind person will recognize you by your voice.	1. Help the sighted person meet your special communication needs. If you want your surroundings described, ask. If you want the person to read the road signs, ask.
2. Face the blind person; you'll be easier to hear.	2. Be patient with the sighted person. Many people are nervous talking with people who are blind for fear of offending. Put them at ease in a way that also makes you more comfortable.
3. Don't shout. Don't assume that people who are visually impaired are also hearing impaired. Speak in your normal conversational tone.	
4. Remember that your gestures, eye movements, and facial expressions cannot be seen, so it's necessary to encode into speech all the meanings you wish to communicate.	
5. Use audible conversational turn-taking cues. When you pass the role of speaker to a person who's visually impaired don't rely on nonverbal cues; instead, say something like "Jane, what do you think?" or "Do you agree with that, Joe?"	
6. Use your normal vocabulary and discuss topics that you would discuss with sighted people. For example, don't avoid terms like "see" or "look" or even "blind." Don't avoid discussing a television show or a painting or the way your new car looks; these are normal conversational topics for all people.	
7. In guiding a person who is blind, follow these simple suggestions: a. If you want to offer assistance to a blind person, ask first. Ask, for example, "Would you like me to hold your arm as we go upstairs?" instead of just grabbing the person. b. Identify obstacles before reaching them—"There are three steps coming up" or "We're going to make a right in a short time." c. When you have to leave, make sure the blind person is comfortable where he or she is. For example, ask the person if he or she would like to sit while you get the coffee.	

These suggestions were drawn from the following sources: **http://www.cincyblind.org/what_do_you_do_.htm** and **http://www.rnib.org/uk/wesupply/fctsheet/method.htm** (both accessed 4/5/02).

All communications contain noise. Noise cannot be totally eliminated, but its effects can be reduced. Making your language more precise, sharpening your skills for sending and receiving nonverbal messages, and improving your listening and feedback skills are some ways to combat the influence of noise.

Table 1.3   Four Types of Noise

The ability to both recognize and reduce noise is one of the most essential communication skills. What kinds of noise occur in settings such as the classroom, the workplace, and the family dining room? How can you combat the noise encountered in these settings?

Types of Noise	Definition	Examples
Physical	Interference that is external to both speaker and listener and that prevents accurate transmission of the signal or message	Screeching of passing cars, hum of computer, sunglasses
Physiological	Physical barriers within the speaker or listener	Visual impairments, hearing loss, articulation problems, memory loss
Psychological	Cognitive or mental interference	Biases and prejudices in senders and receivers, closed-mindedness, inaccurate expectations, extreme emotionalism (anger, hate, love, grief)
Semantic	Speaker and listener assigning different meanings	People speaking different languages, use of jargon or overly complex terms not understood by listener, dialectical differences in meaning

Context

Communication always takes place in a **context** that influences the form and content of your messages. At times this context isn't obvious or intrusive; it seems so natural that it's ignored—like background music. At other times the context dominates, and the ways in which it restricts or stimulates your messages are obvious. Compare, for example, the differences among communicating in a funeral home, in a football stadium,

View point A recent study finds that 80 percent of young adult women consider finding a spouse who can communicate his feelings more desirable than finding one who earns a good living (**www.gallup.com/ poll/releases/pr010627b.asp**, accessed June 27, 2001). How important, compared to all the other factors you might take into consideration in choosing a partner, is the ability to communicate? What specific communication skills would you consider "extremely important" in a life partner?

in a formal restaurant, and at a rock concert. The context of communication has at least four dimensions, all of which interact and influence each other.

The *physical dimension* is the tangible or concrete environment in which communication takes place—the room, hallway, or park, the boardroom or the family dinner table. The size of the space, its temperature, and the number of people present in the physical space would also be part of the physical dimension.

The *temporal dimension* refers not only to the time of day and moment in history but also to where a particular message fits into the sequence of communication events. For example, a joke about illness told immediately after the disclosure of a friend's sickness will be received differently than the same joke told in response to a series of similar jokes.

The *social–psychological dimension* includes, for example, status relationships among the participants, roles and games that people play, norms of the society or group, and the friendliness, formality, or gravity of the situation.

The *cultural context* (Chapter 2) refers to the cultural beliefs and customs of the people communicating. When you interact with people from different cultures, you may each follow different rules of communication. This can result in confusion, unintentional insult, inaccurate judgments, and a host of other miscommunications. Similarly, communication strategies or techniques that prove satisfying to members of one culture may prove disturbing or offensive to members of another.

Ethics

Because communication has consequences, interpersonal communication also involves **ethics;** each communication act has a moral dimension, a rightness or wrongness (cf., Jaksa & Pritchard, 1994; Johannesen, 1994, 2001). Communication choices need to be guided by ethical considerations as well as by concerns with effectiveness and satisfaction. Nevertheless, some research finds important cross-cultural similarities; for example, it's been proposed that there are certain universal ethical principles that are held by all cultures such as that you should tell the truth, have respect for another's dignity, and not harm the innocent (Christians & Traber, 1997). Ethics is therefore included as a universal of interpersonal communication and is presented in this text in "Ethics in

ETHICS *in Interpersonal Communication*

Ethical Questions

As a kind of preview, consider just a few of the ethical issues raised in these "Ethics in Interpersonal Communication" boxes.

■ What obligations do you have to keep a secret (Chapter 3)?

■ Are ethical principles objective or subjective? For example, if lying is unethical, is it unethical in all situations or would it depend on the circumstances (Chapter 4)?

■ What are your ethical obligations as a listener (Chapter 5)?

■ What are your ethical obligations when speaking (Chapters 6 and 7)?

■ When do you have an obligation to speak up (Chapter 8)?

■ What information about yourself do you have an obligation to reveal

to friends and romantic partners (Chapter 10)?

■ Are there ethical and unethical ways to engage in conflict and conflict resolution (Chapter 13)?

What would you do? *You want to break up with someone you've been involved with in an office romance for the last 6 months because you've met someone else who you want to date. What common strategies would a man and a woman each use in this situation? Which strategies do you consider fair and ethical? Which would you consider unfair and unethical?*

Interpersonal Communication" boxes. These boxes cover issues such as the differences between subjective and objective approaches to ethics, whether the ends justify the means, the ethical obligations of speakers and listeners, lying, gossip, and unethical speech.

AXIOMS OF INTERPERSONAL COMMUNICATION

Now that the nature of interpersonal communication and its elements are clear, we can explore some of the more specific axioms or principles that are common to all or most interpersonal encounters. These axioms are largely the work of the transactional researchers Paul Watzlawick, Janet Helmick Beavin, and Don D. Jackson, presented in their landmark *Pragmatics of Human Communication* (1967; Watzlawick 1977, 1978).

Interpersonal Communication Is Grounded in Theory and Research

Before you begin reading this section, try taking the self-test "What Do You Know about Research?" It will help clarify some essential concepts in understanding research that you'll encounter in this text as well as in other courses.

TEST YOURSELF   *What Do You Know about Research?*

The following statements raise important issues about the research process, particularly how research should be interpreted. Mark each statement T if you think it's generally true and accurate; mark F if you think it's generally false and inaccurate.

_____ 1. When one event (B) regularly and consistently follows another event (A), we can say that A causes B or that B results from A.

_____ 2. It's important to know the results of research because they will apply to you at some point in your life.

_____ 3. Results from research conducted 20 years ago are generally of only historical interest.

_____ 4. If the same results emerge from several different research studies, we can be pretty sure that the findings are valid.

_____ 5. The only worthwhile research findings are those that are obtained on the basis of experimental research in which all variables are carefully controlled and analyzed with the best statistical techniques.

▶ **How did you do?**   Statement 1 is false and raises the issue of correlation versus causation. When two things occur together (for example, B consistently and reliably accompanies A), it does not mean that one causes the other; in many instances a third variable, C, might be causing both A and B. For example, let's say that fear of communication and low self-disclosure are observed together in a large number of people; those who have great fear of communication also reveal little of themselves and, conversely, those who have little fear of communication reveal a great deal about themselves. Can you conclude that the level of communication fear determines the amount of self-disclosure? The answer is no; a third factor, say self-esteem, may actually cause both the fear of communication and the level of self-disclosure.

Statement 2 is false. Research results, at least in the humanities and social sciences such as communication, are true in a statistical sense; that is, they apply to perhaps 95 percent of the population. You may be in the 5 percent to which the results do not apply. Further, you may be different in crucial respects from the participants sampled in the research study and so the results may not directly apply to you. The vast cultural differences that we're just beginning to understand make it unlikely that research findings obtained from students at a large midwestern university will apply to the farm workers in Guatemala.

Statement 3 is also false. Although research methods are a lot better today than they were 20 years ago, the time during which a research study was conducted is not sufficient reason to consider one worthless and one worthwhile. The value of the research depends on the study and on the specific changes that may have taken place over the 20 years. For example, studies conducted on power in the heterosexual relationship, the role of technology in relationships, or the influence of finances on relationships 20 years ago would have to be examined in light of the tremendous societal changes that have taken place and that affect these issues. Generally, the more recent study will prove the more useful.

Statement 4 involves confusion between validity and reliability—two concepts that are crucial for understanding research findings—and is also false. *Reliability* refers to the consistency of results. It's a measure of how consistently a particular relationship or result is found in research. *Validity,* on the other hand, is a measure of the extent to which an instrument or test measures what it claims to measure. For example, intelligence tests are extremely reliable and you'll obtain essentially the same results on repeated testing. The validity issue, however, is different and asks "Does the intelligence test really measure intelligence?" Similarly, we can measure your degree of romanticism with a simple pencil and paper test and get essentially the same results on repeated testing. But it's quite another issue to claim that the test really measures what we would consider "romanticism." Consistency of findings does not mean that the test is valid, only that it's reliable. Both are important; generally, we want tests and research instruments to be both reliable and valid.

Statement 5 is also false, although not everyone would agree with this. The assumption made in this text is that all research methods are useful for different purposes. Historical research is useful for certain questions, survey research is useful for other questions, and experimental research is useful for still other purposes.

▶ **What will you do?** In this course and throughout your college career (and well into your professional career) you will need to evaluate research, to judge when conclusions drawn from research are warranted and when they aren't. So, keep the few suggestions offered here in mind and supplement them with continued study of research methods and theory.   ●

Throughout this book and throughout your course you'll encounter a wide variety of theories and research findings on interpersonal communication. These theories and research findings constitute what we know about interpersonal communication. They tell you how interpersonal communication works as well as what works effectively. From these theories and research findings you not only come to understand how interpersonal communication works, but you can also derive skills for achieving greater interpersonal effectiveness.

Interpersonal skills exist on two levels: specific and general. Openness and empathy are examples of specific skills. Mindfulness, cultural sensitivity, and flexibility are general skills—or what we call metaskills, skills that help you to regulate or manage your use of the specific skills. For example, cultural sensitivity will help you realize that empathy and openness need to be applied in light of the cultural context in which you find yourself. Both specific and general skills are essential to interpersonal effectiveness.

The skills identified in this book are presented in "Increasing Interpersonal Effectiveness" boxes throughout the text. These skills were identified in a number of research studies conducted largely in the 1970s and 1980s (Gibb, 1961; Hart & Burks, 1972; Hart,

A S K *the Researcher*

The Value of Interpersonal Skills

I'm entering the job market and have been invited to visit several organizations. I want to negotiate the best deal in my first job. Is this course in interpersonal communication going to help me with something like this?

Interviewing and negotiating for a job is a communication process and should center on four major aspects:

■ Manage information. Pose questions about your particular needs; don't just follow the interviewer's questions.

■ Introduce multiple issues into the bargaining mix. This will enhance prospects of reaching a mutually satisfactory agreement. Issues such as job requirements, starting date, promotion opportunities, relocation, training programs, medical benefits, and office support are critical aspects of a job and should be discussed in addition to starting salary.

■ Package issues by trading off options and compensating for relative costs.

■ Go into job negotiations with your "best alternative to a negotiated agreement" (BATNA). If you possess unique skills in a tight marketplace or have multiple job offers, you hold a stronger BATNA and can make use of it in bargaining for higher wages and job benefits.

Your successful completion of these tasks will depend on your interpersonal communication skills, the very skills identified in this book and in this course.

For further information see R. J. Lewicki, D. M. Saunders, & J. W. Minton, *Negotiation,* 3rd ed. (Boston, MA: Irwin-McGraw Hill) and L. L. Putnam, "Bargaining," in *International Encyclopedia of Communication,* Vol. 1, ed. E. Barnouw (Philadelphia, PA: Oxford University Press), pp. 176–178.

Linda L. Putnam (Ph.D., University of Minnesota) is a professor of communication at Texas A&M University and teaches courses in conflict management and organizational communication. She conducts research on language and organizations, managerial negotiation, and environmental conflict management and is the Director of the Program on Conflict and Dispute Resolution at the George Bush School of Government and Public Service. LPutnam@tamu.edu (Reprinted by permission of Dr. Linda Putnam, Department of Communication, Texas A&M University.)

Carlson, & Eadie, 1980; Bochner & Kelly, 1974; Wiemann, 1977; Spitzberg & Hecht, 1984; Rubin & Nevins, 1988; Spitzberg & Cupach, 1984, 1989; Watzlawick, Beavin, & Jackson, 1967; Watzlawick, 1977; Lederer, 1984; Lederer & Jackson, 1968; Kim, 1991). More recent research, cited throughout the text and in the effectiveness boxes, has confirmed these skills as essential to interpersonal effectiveness and has elaborated on and extended their applications. The summaries of these skills presented in the various boxes is a synthesis of this research.

Theory in Interpersonal Communication   A **theory** is a generalization that explains how something works—gravity, DNA identification, interpersonal attraction, or communication, for example. In academic writing the term is usually reserved for a well-established system of knowledge about how something works or how things are related. The theories you'll encounter in this text will vary greatly: communication as a process of adjustment, how we're attracted to some people and not to others, how communication works when relationships deteriorate, or how self-disclosure operates in friendship. In reading about these theories, you may well ask, "Why should I learn this? Of what value is this material to me?" Here are a few answers to these legitimate questions (Griffin, 2000; Infante, Rancer, & Womack, 1993; Littlejohn, 1996).

Theories help you understand how interpersonal communication works. Theories provide general principles that help you understand a great number of specific events—

Increasing Interpersonal Effectiveness
Mindfulness

Mindfulness is a state of awareness in which you're conscious of your reasons for thinking or behaving. It's opposite, **mindlessness,** refers to a lack of conscious awareness of what or how you're thinking (Langer, 1989). To apply interpersonal skills effectively you need to become mindful of the unique communication situation you're in, your available communication options, and the reasons why one option is likely to be better than the others (Langer, 1989; Elmes & Gemmill, 1990; Burgoon, Berger, & Waldron, 2000).

Increasing Mindfulness   To increase mindfulness, try the following suggestions (Langer, 1989).

■ *Create and recreate categories.* Learn to see objects, events, and people as belonging to a wide variety of categories. Try to see, for example, your prospective romantic partner in a variety of

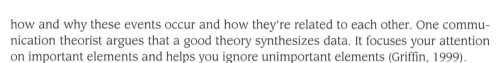

roles—child, parent, employee, neighbor, friend, financial contributor, and so on. Avoid storing in memory an image of a person with only one specific label; if you do, you'll find it difficult to recategorize the person later.

■ *Be open to new information and points of view,* even when these contradict your most firmly held beliefs. New information forces you to reconsider what might be outmoded ways of thinking. New information can help you challenge long-held but now inappropriate beliefs and attitudes. Be willing to see your own and others' behaviors from the viewpoints of people very different from yourself.

■ *Beware of relying too heavily on first impressions* (Chanowitz & Langer, 1981; Langer, 1989). Treat first impressions as tentative, as hypotheses that need further investigation. Be prepared to revise, reject, or accept these initial impressions.

how and why these events occur and how they're related to each other. One communication theorist argues that a good theory synthesizes data. It focuses your attention on important elements and helps you ignore unimportant elements (Griffin, 1999).

Interpersonal communication theories also help you predict future events. The theories summarize what has been discovered in the past and can therefore offer an educated and informed prediction for events in the future. For example, based on the theories of interpersonal conflict resolution, you would be able to predict which conflict strategies will prove effective and which will prove ineffective in resolving differences. Of course, these theories will not provide correct answers 100 percent of the time; but they will offer useful generalizations that are likely to be correct beyond chance.

Interpersonal communication theories also help generate research. For example, if a theory predicts that verbal aggressiveness will lead to physical violence, this suggests to the researcher a variety of important questions that can be subjected to study (Infante, Rancer, & Womack, 1996). For example, the research might ask, "What types of verbal aggressiveness lead to physical violence?" "Are men or women more likely to become physically violent after being verbally aggressive?" "Can we reduce the likelihood of physical violence by teaching people to become less verbally aggressive?" In serving this research-generating function, theories add to our knowledge of interpersonal communication.

Theories reveal some degree of accuracy, some degree of truth, not absolute truth. In the natural sciences such as physics and chemistry, theories have extremely high accuracy. If you mix two parts of hydrogen to one part of oxygen, you'll get water—every time you do it. In the social and behavioral sciences (communication, sociology, psychology), the theories are far less accurate in describing the way things work and in predicting how things will work. One communication theorist offers this summary guidance: "[B]ecause a theory does not reveal truth, does not mean that it fails to communicate a kind of truth. An insight or useful way of classifying or explaining events is a kind of truth. Just don't make the mistake of believing too hard in one theory because every theory has its limits" (Littlejohn, 1996, p. 361).

WEB EXPLORATION
To learn more about research in interpersonal communication, go to **www.ablongman.com/devito**.

Research in Interpersonal Communication   Usually on the basis of some theory and its predictions—though sometimes from a simple desire to answer a question—research is conducted (Clark, 1991). It is conducted so that we can learn more about how interpersonal communication works. On the basis of these research findings, we develop the principles for more effective interpersonal interaction. Research, for example, often tells us what interpersonal strategies work and what strategies don't work. Understanding the research process will help you to better appreciate how we learn about communication as well as better understand the findings, conclusions, and principles that are developed on the basis of this research.

Sometimes the research questions are totally theoretical: "How do listeners deal with ambiguous messages?" Sometimes they're extremely practical, even urgent: "How can children best resist drugs?" Often, of course, practical implications are drawn out of "purely theoretical" research, and theoretical insights are drawn out of "purely applied" research.

It is the research, then, that enables you to answer questions about people's interpersonal communication behavior and helps advance truth about an important aspect of human experience. Let's say you find that total honesty in your romantic relationship is effective and that it creates a strong bond between you and your partner. How useful is that "finding" to other couples? On the one hand, it may be very useful because all couples might respond as you and your partner do. Or it may be of limited usefulness if your relationship is unique and unlike those of most other people. Ideally, research provides us with findings that are applicable to a large percentage of the people.

The "Ask the Researcher" boxes that appear throughout the text highlight this emphasis on research and its implications for everyday interpersonal communication by asking active researchers and theorists to answer specific questions relating theory to practice.

Interpersonal Communication Is a Transactional Process

A **transactional** perspective views interpersonal communication as a process, one whose elements are *inter*dependent. Figure 1.4 visually explains this transactional view and distinguishes it from two earlier views of how interpersonal communication works.

Interpersonal Communication Is a Process   Interpersonal communication is best viewed as an ever-changing process. Everything involved in interpersonal communication is in a state of flux: you're changing, the people you communicate with are changing, and your environment is changing. Sometimes these changes go unnoticed and sometimes they intrude in obvious ways, but they're always occurring.

The process of communication is circular: One person's message serves as the stimulus for another's message, which serves as a stimulus for the other person's message, and so on. Throughout this circular process, each person serves simultaneously as a speaker *and* a listener, an actor *and* a reactor. Interpersonal communication is a mutually interactive process.

Elements Are Interdependent   The elements in interpersonal communication are *inter*dependent. Each element—each part of interpersonal communication—is intimately connected to the other parts and to the whole. For example, there can be no

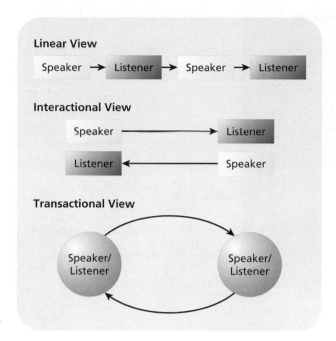

The Transactional View of Interpersonal Communication
The top figure represents a linear view of communication, in which the speaker speaks and the listener listens. The middle figure represents an interactional view, in which speaker and listener take turns speaking and listening; A speaks while B listens and then B speaks while A listens. The bottom figure represents a transactional view, in which each person serves simultaneously as speaker and listener; at the same time that you send messages, you also receive messages from your own communications as well as from the reactions of the other person(s).

source without a receiver; there can be no message without a source; there can be no feedback without a receiver. Because of interdependency, a change in any one element causes changes in the others. For example, you're talking with a group of fellow students about a recent examination, and your teacher joins the group. This change in participants will lead to other changes—perhaps in the content of what you say, perhaps in the manner in which you express it. But regardless of what change is introduced, other changes result.

Interpersonal Communication Is Ambiguous

Some degree of **ambiguity** is present in all interpersonal communication; all messages are ambiguous to some degree. When you express an idea you never communicate your meaning exactly and totally; rather, you communicate your meaning with some reasonable accuracy—enough to give the other person a pretty clear idea of what you mean. Sometimes, of course, you're less accurate than you anticipated and your listener "gets the wrong idea" or "gets offended" when you only meant to be humorous or "misunderstands your emotional meaning." Because of this inevitable uncertainty you may qualify what you're saying, give an example, or ask "Do you know what I mean?" These additional explanations help the other person understand your meaning and reduce uncertainty (to some degree).

   Similarly, all relationships contain uncertainty. Consider your own close interpersonal relationships and ask yourself the following questions. Answer using a 6-point scale with "1" meaning completely or almost completely uncertain and "6" meaning completely or almost completely certain.

   How certain are you about

1. What you can or cannot say to each other in this relationship?
2. Whether or not you and your partner feel the same way about each other?
3. How you and your partner would describe this relationship?
4. The future of the relationship?

View point What kinds of relationship ambiguity do you think are most damaging to a relationship's stability? Are there kinds of ambiguities that you think would solidify a relationship? Are there differences between the ways men and women look at relationship ambiguity?

Most likely your responses weren't all 6s and your relationship partner would be equally unlikely to respond with all 6s. These questions—taken from a relationship uncertainty scale (Knoblock & Solomon, 1999)—and others like it illustrate that you probably experience some degree of uncertainty about the norms that govern your relationship communication (Question 1), the degree to which you each see the relationship in similar ways (Question 2), the definition of the relationship (Question 3), and the relationship's future (Question 4).

The skills of interpersonal communication presented throughout this text may be looked at as a means for reducing ambiguity and making your meaning as clear as possible.

Interpersonal Relationships May Be Symmetrical or Complementary

Interpersonal relationships can be described as either symmetrical or complementary (Bateson, 1972; Watzlawick, Beavin, & Jackson, 1967). In a **symmetrical relationship,** the two individuals mirror each other's behavior (Bateson, 1972). If one member nags, the other member responds in kind. If one member is passionate, the other member is passionate. If one member expresses jealousy, the other member also expresses jealousy. If one member is passive, so is the other. The relationship is one of equality, with the emphasis on minimizing the differences between the two individuals.

Note, however, the problems that can arise in this type of relationship. Consider the situation of a couple in which both members are very aggressive. The aggressiveness of one person fosters aggressiveness in the other, which fosters increased aggressiveness in the first individual. As this cycle escalates, the aggressiveness can no longer be contained, and the relationship is consumed by the aggression.

In a **complementary relationship,** the two individuals engage in different behaviors. The behavior of one serves as the stimulus for the other's complementary behavior. In complementary relationships, the differences between the parties are maximized. The people occupy different positions, one superior and the other inferior, one passive and the other active, one strong and the other weak. At times, cultures establish such relationships—for example, the complementary relationship between teacher and student or between employer and employee.

Early marriages are likely to be complementary relationships where each person tries to complete him- or herself. When these couples separate and form new relationships, these new ones are more likely to be symmetrical and involve a kind of reconfirmation of their own identity (Prosky, 1992). Generally, research finds that complementary couples have a poorer marital adjustment level than do symmetrical couples (Main & Oliver, 1988; Holden, 1991).

Interpersonal Communication Refers to Content and Relationship

Messages may make reference to the real world, for example, to the events and objects you see before you. At the same time, however, they also refer to the relationship between the people communicating. For example, a judge may say to a lawyer, "See me in my chambers immediately." This simple message has both a content aspect, which refers to the behavioral response expected (namely, that the lawyer will see the judge immediately), and a relationship aspect, which says something about the relationship between the judge and the lawyer and, as a result of this relationship, how the communication is to be dealt with. Even the use of the simple command shows that there is a status difference between the two parties. This difference can perhaps be seen most clearly if you imagine the command being made by the lawyer to the judge. Such a communication appears awkward and out of place because it violates the normal relationship between judge and lawyer.

In any two communications, the content dimension may be the same, but the relationship aspect may be different, or the relationship aspect may be the same and the content dimension different. For example, the judge could say to the lawyer, "You had better see me immediately" or "May I please see you as soon as possible?" In both cases, the content is essentially the same; that is, the message about the expected behavioral response is the same. But the relationship dimension is quite different. The first message signifies a definite superior–inferior relationship; the second signals a more equal relationship, one that shows respect for the lawyer.

Similarly, at times the content may be different but the relationship is essentially the same. For example, a daughter might say to her parents, "May I go away this weekend?" or "May I use the car tonight?" The content of the two questions is clearly very different, but the relationship dimension is essentially the same. It clearly reflects a superior–inferior relationship in which permission to do certain things must be secured.

The major implications of these content and relationship dimensions center on conflict and its effective resolution. Many problems between people result from failure to recognize the distinction between the **content and relationship dimensions** of communication. For example, consider the couple arguing because Pat made plans to study with friends during the weekend without first asking Chris if that would be all right. Probably both would agree that to study over the weekend is the right decision. Thus, the argument isn't primarily concerned with the content level. It centers on the relationship level; Chris expected to be consulted about plans for the weekend. Pat, in not doing so, rejected this definition of their relationship. Similar situations occur when one member of a couple buys something, makes dinner plans, or invites a guest to dinner without first asking the other person. Even though the other person might have agreed with the decision, the couple argues because of the message communicated on the relationship level.

Let me give you a personal example. My mother came to stay for a week at a summer place I had. On the first day, she swept the kitchen floor six times, although I repeatedly said that it didn't need sweeping, that I would be tracking in dirt and mud from outside, and that all her effort was just wasted. But she persisted, saying that the floor was dirty and should be swept. On the content level, we were talking about the value of sweeping the kitchen floor, but on the relationship level, we were talking about something quite different: we were each saying, "This is my house." When I realized this (although, I confess, only after considerable argument), I stopped complaining about sweeping a floor that didn't need sweeping. Not surprisingly, she stopped sweeping.

Consider the following interchange:

Dialogue	*Comments*
He: I'm going bowling tomorrow. The guys at the plant are starting a team.	He focuses on the content and ignores any relationship implications of the message.
She: Why can't we ever do anything together?	She responds primarily on a relationship level, ignores the content implications of the message, and expresses her displeasure at being ignored in his decision.
He: We can do something together anytime; tomorrow's the day they're organizing the team.	Again, he focuses almost exclusively on the content.

This example reflects research findings that men generally focus more on the content while women focus more on the relationship dimensions of communication (cf., Pearson, West, & Turner, 1995; Wood, 1994; Ivy & Backlund, 2000). Once you recognize this difference, you may be better able to remove a potential barrier to communication between the sexes by being sensitive to the orientation of the opposite sex. Here is essentially the same situation but with added sensitivity:

Dialogue	*Comments*
He: The guys at the plant are organizing a bowling team. I'd sure like to be on the team. Would it be a problem if I went to the organizational meeting tomorrow?	Although focused on content, he is aware of the relationship dimensions of his message and includes both in his comments—by acknowledging their partnership, asking if there would be a problem, and expressing his desire rather than his decision.
She: That sounds great, but I was hoping we could do something together.	She focuses on the relationship dimension but also acknowledges his content orientation. Note, too, that she does not respond as though she has to defend her emphasis on relationship aspects.
He: How about your meeting me at Joe's Pizza, and we can have dinner after the organizational meeting?	He responds to the relationship aspect—without abandoning his desire to join the bowling team—and incorporates it.
She: That sounds great. I'm dying for pizza.	She responds to both messages, approving of his joining the team and their dinner date.

Arguments over the content dimension are relatively easy to resolve. Generally, you can look up something in a book or ask someone what actually took place. It is relatively easy to verify disputed facts. Arguments on the relationship level, however, are much more difficult to resolve, in part because you may not recognize that the argument is in fact a relational one. Once you realize that, you can approach the dispute appropriately and deal with it directly.

Interpersonal Communication Is a Series of Punctuated Events

Communication events are continuous transactions. There is no clear-cut beginning and no clear-cut end. As participants in or observers of the communication act, you segment this continuous stream of communication into smaller pieces. You label some of these pieces causes or stimuli and others effects or responses.

Consider an example. A married couple is in a restaurant. The husband is flirting with another woman, and the wife is talking to her sister on her cell phone. Both are scowling at each other and are obviously in a deep nonverbal argument. Recalling the situation later, the husband might observe that the wife talked on the phone, so he innocently flirted with the other woman. The only reason for his behavior (he says) was his anger over her talking on the phone when they were supposed to be having dinner together. Notice that he sees his behavior as a response to her behavior. In recalling the same incident, the wife might say that she phoned her sister when he started flirting. The more he flirted, the longer she talked. She had no intention of calling anyone until he started flirting. To her, his behavior was the stimulus and hers was the response; he caused her behavior. Thus, the husband sees the sequence as going from phoning to flirting, and the wife sees it as going from flirting to phoning. This example is depicted visually in Figure 1.5 on page 30 and is supported by research which shows that, among marrieds at least, the individuals regularly see their partner's behavior as the cause of conflict (Schutz, 1999).

This tendency to divide communication transactions into sequences of stimuli and responses is referred to as **punctuation** (Watzlawick, Beavin, & Jackson, 1967). Everyone punctuates the continuous sequences of events into stimuli and responses for convenience. Moreover, as the example of the husband and wife illustrates, punctuation usually is done in ways that benefit the self and are consistent with a person's self-image.

Understanding how another person interprets a situation, how he or she punctuates, is a crucial step in interpersonal understanding. It is also essential in achieving empathy (feeling what the other person is feeling). In all communication encounters, but especially in conflicts, try to see how others punctuate the situation.

Interpersonal Communication Is Inevitable, Irreversible, and Unrepeatable

Interpersonal communication cannot be prevented (is inevitable), cannot be reversed (is irreversible), and cannot be repeated (is unrepeatable). Let's look briefly at each of these qualities and their implications.

Inevitability   Often communication is thought of as intentional, purposeful, and consciously motivated. In many instances it is. But in other instances you're communicating even though you might not think you are or might not even want to be. Consider, for example, the new editorial assistant sitting at the desk with an "expressionless" face,

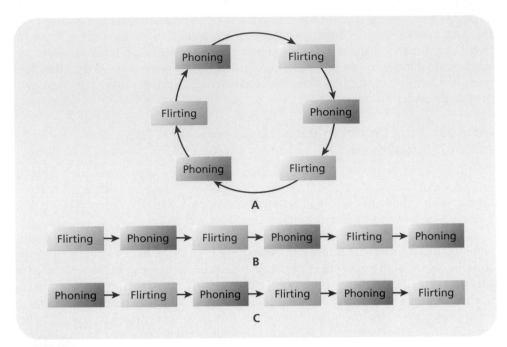

Punctuation and the Sequence of Events
In the figure, (A) shows the actual sequence of events as a continuous series of actions with no specific beginning or end. Each action (phoning and flirting) stimulates another action, but no initial cause is identified. (B) shows the same sequence of events as seen by the wife. She sees the sequence as beginning with the husband's flirting and her phoning behavior as a response to that stimulus. (C) shows the same sequence of events from the husband's point of view. He sees the sequence as beginning with the wife's phoning and his flirting as a response to that stimulus. Try using this three-part figure, discussed in the text, to explain what might go on when a supervisor complains that workers are poorly trained for their jobs and when workers complain that supervisors don't know how to supervise.

perhaps staring out the window. Although this assistant might say that she or he is not communicating with the manager, the manager may derive any of a variety of messages from this behavior—for example, the assistant lacks interest, is bored, or is worried about something. In any event, the manager is receiving messages even though the assistant might not intend to communicate. In an interactional situation, all behavior is potentially communication. Any aspect of your behavior may communicate if the other person gives it message value. On the other hand, if the behavior (for example, the assistant's looking out the window) goes unnoticed, then no communication would have taken place (Watzlawick, Beavin, & Jackson, 1967; Motley, 1990a, 1990b; Bavelas, 1990; Beach, 1990).

Further, when in an interactional situation, your responses all have potential message value. For example, if you notice someone winking at you, you must respond in some way. Even if you don't respond openly, that lack of response is itself a response and it communicates (assuming it is perceived by the other person).

Irreversibility   The processes of some systems can be reversed. For example, you can turn water into ice and then reverse the process by melting the ice. Moreover, you

TRY IT!
Apply your understanding of irreversibility; go to www.ablongman.com/devito.

can repeat this reversal of ice and water as many times as you wish. Other systems, however, are irreversible. In these systems, the process can move in only one direction; it cannot go back again. For example, you can turn grapes into wine, but you cannot reverse the process and turn the wine back into grapes.

Interpersonal communication is irreversible. What you have communicated remains communicated; you cannot *un*communicate. Although you may try to qualify, negate, or somehow reduce the effects of your message, once it has been sent and received, the message itself cannot be reversed. In interpersonal interactions (especially in conflict), you need to be especially careful that you don't say things you may wish to withdraw later. Similarly, commitment messages, such as "I love you," must be monitored lest you commit yourself to a position you may be uncomfortable with later.

Face-to-face communication is evanescent; it fades after you have spoken. There is no trace of your communications outside of the memories of the parties involved or of those who overheard your conversation. In computer-mediated communication, how-ever, the messages are written and may be saved, stored, and printed. Both face-to-face and computer-mediated messages may be kept confidential or revealed publicly. But computer messages may be made public more easily and spread more quickly than face-to-face messages. Written messages provide clear evidence of what you have said and when you said it.

Due to the permanence of electronic communication, you may wish to be cautious in your e-mail messages, probably your most common form of computer communica-tion, though these cautions apply to all forms of electronic communication such as newsgroup postings and website messages as well.

- ■ E-mails are difficult to destroy. Often e-mails you think you deleted will remain on servers and workstations and may be retrieved by a clever hacker.
- ■ E-mails can easily be made public; the ease of forwarding e-mails to others or of posting your comments on websites makes it especially important to consider that what you intend for one person may actually be received by many.
- ■ E-mails are not privileged communication and can easily be used against you, es-pecially in the workplace. Criticism of others may one day be turned against you in accusations of discrimination.
- ■ E-mails provide permanent records, making it impossible for you to say, for ex-ample, "That's not exactly what I said" because exactly what you said will be there in black and white.
- ■ Personal e-mail files can be accessed by someone else—a nosy colleague at the next desk or a visiting neighbor—and then be sent to others.

Unrepeatability   In addition to being inevitable and irreversible, interpersonal communication is unrepeatable. The reason is simple: Everyone and everything is con-stantly changing. As a result, you can never recapture the exact same situation, frame of mind, or relationship dynamics that defined a previous interpersonal act. For exam-ple, you can never repeat the experience of meeting a particular person for the first time, comforting a grieving friend on the death of his or her mother, or resolving a spe-cific conflict.

You can, of course, try again, as when you say, "I'm sorry I came off so forward; can we try again?" But notice that even when you say this, you don't erase the initial im-pression. Instead, you try to counteract the initial (and perhaps negative) impression by going through the motions once more. In doing so, you try to create a more positive im-pression, which you hope will lessen the original negative effect.

REVIEWING Key Terms and Concepts in Interpersonal Communication

This chapter introduced interpersonal communication, its elements, and some of its axioms or basic principles.

Nature of Interpersonal Communication

What is interpersonal communication? At what point does communication become interpersonal?

■ Interpersonal communication is communication between two or more connected individuals that involves dyadic primacy (the two-person unit is of central importance), dyadic coalitions (two-person groups form even in larger groups), and dyadic consciousness (the two persons think of themselves as a pair).

■ Interpersonal communication can take place and interpersonal relationships can develop from face-to-face interactions as well as those you have on the Internet.

■ Interpersonal communication serves a variety of purposes. It enables you to learn, relate, influence, play, and help.

Elements of Interpersonal Communication

What are the essential elements of interpersonal communication?

■ Source–receiver is the person who sends and receives interpersonal messages simultaneously.

■ Encoding–decoding refers to the act of putting meaning into verbal and nonverbal messages and deriving meaning from the messages you receive from others.

■ Competence is the knowledge of and ability to use effectively your own communication system.

■ Messages are the signals that serve as stimuli for a receiver; metamessages are messages that refer to other messages.

   ■ Feedback messages are messages that are sent back by the receiver to the source in response to other messages.

   ■ Feedforward messages are messages that preface other messages and ask that the listener approach future messages in a certain way.

   ■ Messages can quickly overload the channels, making meaningful interaction impossible.

■ Channels are the media through which messages pass and which act as a bridge between source and receiver, for example, the vocal–auditory channel used in speaking or the cutaneous–tactile channel used in touch.

■ Noise is the inevitable physical, physiological, psychological, and semantic interference that distorts a message.

■ Context is the physical, social–psychological, temporal, and cultural environment in which communication takes place.

■ Ethics is the moral dimension of communication, the study of what makes behavior moral or good as opposed to immoral and bad.

Axioms of Interpersonal Communication

What general principles help explain what interpersonal communication is and how it works?

■ Interpersonal communication is grounded in theory and research.

   ■ The theories of interpersonal communication are the organized generalizations about interpersonal communication and the evidence bearing on them.

■ Through theory and research you learn how interpersonal communication works and from this, you can derive principles for achieving more effective interpersonal interaction.

■ Interpersonal communication is a transactional process.

   ■ Interpersonal communication is a process, an ongoing event, in which the elements are interdependent; communication is constantly occurring and changing.

   ■ Don't expect clear-cut beginnings or endings or sameness from one time to another.

■ Interpersonal communication is ambiguous.

   ■ All messages are potentially ambiguous; different people will derive different meanings from the "same" message.

   ■ There is ambiguity in all relationships.

■ Interpersonal relationships may be symmetrical or complementary.

   ■ Interpersonal interactions may stimulate similar or different behavior patterns, and relationships may be described as basically symmetrical or complementary.

   ■ Develop an awareness of symmetrical and complementary relationships. Avoid clinging rigidly to behavioral patterns that are no longer useful and mirroring another's destructive behaviors.

■ Interpersonal communication refers to content and relationship.

   ■ All communications refer both to content and to the relationships between the participants.

   ■ Be aware of and respond to relationship messages as well as content messages.

■ Interpersonal communication is a series of punctuated events.

   ■ Everyone separates communication sequences into stimuli and responses on the basis of his or her own perspective.

   ■ View punctuation as arbitrary, and adopt the other's point of view to increase empathy and understanding.

■ Interpersonal communication is inevitable, irreversible, and unrepeatable.

   ■ When in an interactional situation, you cannot not communicate; you cannot uncommunicate; you cannot repeat exactly a specific message.

   ■ Seek to control as many aspects of your behavior as possible. In listening, seek out nonobvious messages. Beware of messages you may later wish to take back, for example, conflict and commitment messages.

APPLYING Key Terms and Concepts in Interpersonal Communication

1. Can you identify any primary dyads in your extended family? What functions do these dyads serve?

2. How would you explain interpersonal communication or interpersonal relationships in terms of metaphors such as a seesaw, a ball game, a flower, ice skates, a microscope, a television sitcom, a work of art, a long book, a rubber band, or a software program?

3. What kinds of feedforward can you find in this book? What additional feedforward messages would you find useful in a textbook? In a lecture?

4. How does feedback work in conversation between persons with impaired hearing? Between a person with impaired hearing and one with normal hearing? Between persons who are blind? Between a person who is blind and one who has normal vision?

5. What characters in television sitcoms or dramas do you think demonstrate superior interpersonal competence? What characters demonstrate obvious interpersonal incompetence?

6. Visit the website of a professional communication association (try, for example, the National Communication Association at **www.natcom.org,** the International Communication Association at **www.icahdq.org** or the International Listening Association at **www.listen.org**).What kinds of information do these websites provide?

7. How would you describe one of your interpersonal relationships in terms of symmetrical and complementary interactions? For example, is it a relationship defined by the differences or by the similarities between you? Is there equality between you, or is one of you superior? Are you dependent on each other or independent? Is the power shared, or is one person in control?

8. How would you describe the optimum level for relationship ambiguity? For example, would you want to be certain about everything? Be kept in the dark about certain things?

9. How would you describe a recent argument in terms of relationship and content? How did the argument develop? How was it resolved?

10. What explanations might you offer to account for someone sending contradictory messages?

11. Can you recall a recent disagreement in which differences in punctuation figured prominently? What happened? Was the disagreement resolved?

12. How does the principle of inevitability operate in the classroom? In your home? On your job?

13. For what types of messages—in addition to messages of conflict and commitment, noted in the text—is it especially important to remember that communication is irreversible?

14. With very good intentions, you tell your partner: "I guess you'll just never learn how to dress." To your surprise, your partner becomes extremely offended. Although you know you can't take the statement back (communication really is irreversible), you want to lessen its negative tone and its effect on your partner and on your relationship. What can you say?

EXPERIENCING   Key Terms and Concepts in Interpersonal Communication

Go to **www.ablongman.com/devito**.

A variety of exercises will help you gain a deeper understanding of the concepts in this chapter and help you to apply this material to your own interpersonal interactions.

(1) **Models of Interpersonal Communication** asks you to draw a model of interpersonal communication that will visualize and explain a specific interpersonal situation. (2) **How Would You Give Feedback?** and (3) **How Would You Give Feedforward?** provide practice in examining the types of feedback and feedforward you have available. (4) **Ethics in Interpersonal Communication** asks you to consider what you feel is an ethical response in a variety of interpersonal situations. (5) **How Can You Respond to Contradictory Messages?** looks at types of situations that may call for you to respond to their contradictory meanings. (6) **I'd Prefer to Be** is an icebreaker that will help you get to know others in the class and at the same time explore factors that can influence your interpersonal communication. (7) **Applying the Axioms** and (8) **Analyzing an Interaction** provide opportunities to examine how the axioms may be applied to actual interpersonal situations.

RESEARCHING with Research Navigator   Key Terms and Concepts in Interpersonal Communication

Go to **http://www.researchnavigator.com**.

At the end of each chapter you'll find a "Researching with Research Navigator" section that will suggest exercises and experiences for searching the research and for designing research to answer questions about interpersonal communication (and thus get a better understanding of how research works). In each chapter you'll find the following three types of questions: (1) reading an article relating to one of the main topics of the chapter, (2) investigating key terms used in the study of interpersonal communication, and (3) answering questions about

how interpersonal communication works and how it can be used most effectively.

You can accomplish this research activity—as well as a variety of other research tasks—with the help of Research Navigator, one of the best and most technologically sophisticated search systems. You'll find this system useful in this course and in all your courses. It provides you with a database of hundreds of professional and popular publications—many of which you can read online, save to disk, or print in full text form. Log on to **http://www.researchnavigator.com** and follow the directions.

Reading an article.

Read a popular or academic article on the nature, elements, or principles of interpersonal communication. On the basis of this article, what can you add to the discussion presented in this chapter?

Investigating key terms.

Investigate one of the key terms discussed in this chapter (for example, encoding, decoding, competence, messages, feedback, feedforward, channel, noise, context, purpose, ethics, and mindfulness). What additional insights can you provide?

Finding answers.

Try finding answers to any one of the following questions. Use the communication database first and primarily but don't limit yourself. The anthropological, psychological, and sociological databases will also prove helpful. If you can't find answers—after all, research hasn't provided answers to all interesting questions—then try designing a research study that would help you answer the question.

■ Are interpersonal communication skills related to relationship success—for example, to success as a friend, lover, or parent?

■ How is interpersonal communication related to teaching?

■ How is interpersonal communication applicable to your own profession?

■ What are the most important interpersonal skills for success in business?

■ Are competent communicators less anxious and less fearful of communication?

■ Do men and women communicate interpersonally in the same way?

2 Culture in Interpersonal Communication

Crouching Tiger, Hidden Dragon (2000)

No culture can live, if it attempts to be exclusive.

—Mahatma Gandhi

Culture and Interpersonal Communication
How Cultures Differ
Intercultural Communication

*T*he fantasy story of two lovers, *Mu Bai and Shu Lien, who cannot express their love because of cultural prohibitions, is vividly portrayed in Ang Lee's* Crouching Tiger, Hidden Dragon. *Although the film takes place in ancient China, it clearly illustrates the ever-present influence of culture on a wide variety of behaviors. In this chapter we look at culture and its influence on interpersonal communication, some of the ways in which cultures differ, and the nature of intercultural communication, especially ways you can increase your own intercultural communication effectiveness.*

CULTURE AND INTERPERSONAL COMMUNICATION

A walk through any large city and many small towns, through the schools and colleges, and into the business and manufacturing centers will convince you that the United States is largely a collection of many different cultures. These cultures coexist somewhat separately but also with each influencing each other. This coexistence has led some researchers to refer to these cultures as cocultures (Schuter, 1990; Samovar & Porter, 1991; Jandt, 2001). Consider these facts (*The New York Times Almanac,* 2002; *The World Almanac and Book of Facts*, 2002):

The foreign-born population of the United States is increasing dramatically. In 1980 the foreign-born population was 14 million (about 6.2 percent of the total population), in 1990 it was 19.8 million (7.9 percent), and in 2000 it was 28.4 million (10.4 percent). Increasingly frequent communication in a multicultural context is inevitable.

In your more immediate environment consider the number of foreign students who come to the United States to continue their education. For the years 2000-2001, China leads the list with 59,939 students. India is next with 54,664. Other countries with large numbers of students in the United States are Japan (46,497), South Korea (46,000), Taiwan (28,566), Canada (25,279), Indonesia (11,625), Thailand (11,187), Turkey (10,983), and Mexico (10,670) (*New York Times,* Education Life, Section 4A, January 13, 2002). Frequent intercultural communication is simply a part of college life today.

Also, corporations in the United States are becoming more and more intercultural. Large and small corporations commonly announce that future growth will depend on expansion into foreign countries. United States manufacturing, media, information technology, and farming interests depend on foreign purchase. Business opportunities, therefore, have an increasingly international dimension, making cultural awareness and intercultural communication competence essential skills for professional success.

The Nature of Culture

Culture refers to the relatively specialized lifestyle of a group of people—consisting of their values, beliefs, artifacts, ways of behaving, and ways of communicating. Included in culture would be all that members of a social group have produced and developed— their language, modes of thinking, art, laws, and religion.

Culture is not synonymous with race or nationality. However, members of a particular race or country are often taught similar beliefs, attitudes, and values. This similarity makes it possible to speak of "Hispanic culture" or "African American culture." But, lest we be guilty of stereotyping, recognize that within any large culture—especially a culture based on race or nationality—there will be enormous differences. The Kansas farmer and the Wall Street executive may both be, say, German American, but they may differ widely in their attitudes and beliefs and in their general lifestyles. In some ways the Kansas farmer may be closer in attitudes and values to the Chinese farmer than to the Philadelphia lawyer.

Gender—although transmitted genetically and not by communication—is considered a cultural variable largely because cultures teach boys and girls different attitudes, beliefs, values, and ways of communicating and relating to one another (Payne, 2001). So, you act like a man or a woman in part because of what your culture has taught you about how men and women should act. Further, you can view male–female communication as cross-cultural because of the numerous differences in the way men and women speak and listen (Eckstein & Goldman, 2001). This does not deny that biological differences also play a role in the differences between male and female behavior. In fact, recent research continues to uncover biological roots of behaviors we once thought were entirely learned, like happiness and shyness, for example (McCroskey, 1997).

Culture is passed on from one generation to the next through communication, not through genes. Thus, culture does not refer to color of skin or shape of eyes. Culture does refer to beliefs in a supreme being, to attitudes toward success and happiness, and to the values placed on friendship, love, family, or money, since these are transmitted through communication.

Culture is transmitted from one generation to another through **enculturation,** a process by which you learn the culture into which you're born (your native culture). Parents, peer groups, schools, religious institutions, and government agencies are the main teachers of culture. One relatively new instrument for spreading culture is the Internet. Because the Internet, although worldwide, is so dominated by the United States and by the English language and idiom, the culture of the Internet is dominated by the culture of the United States. "Some countries," notes one media watcher, "already unhappy with the encroachment of American culture—from jeans to Mickey Mouse to movies and TV programs—are worried that their cultures will be further eroded by an American dominance in cyberspace" (Pollack, 1995, D1).

Through enculturation you develop an ethnic identity, a commitment to the beliefs and philosophy of your culture (Chung & Ting-Toomey, 1999). The degree to which you identify with your cultural group can be measured by your responses to questions such as these (from Ting-Toomey, 1981).

Using a 5-point scale with "1" meaning strongly disagree and "5" meaning strongly agree, indicate how true of you the following statements are.

1. I am increasing my involvement in activities with my ethnic group.
2. I involve myself in causes that will help members of my ethnic group.
3. It feels natural being part of my ethnic group.
4. I have spent time trying to find out more about my own ethnic group.
5. I am happy to be a member of my ethnic group.
6. I have a strong sense of belonging to my ethnic group.
7. I often talk to other members of my group to learn more about my ethnic culture.

High scores (say 4s and 5s) indicate a strong commitment to your culture's values and beliefs; low numbers (1s and 2s) indicate a relatively weak commitment.

A different process of learning culture is **acculturation,** the process by which you learn the rules and norms of a culture different from your native culture. Through acculturation, your original or native culture is modified by direct contact with (or exposure to) a new and different culture. For example, when immigrants settle in the United States, the host country, their own culture becomes influenced by the host culture.

Gradually, the values, ways of behaving, and beliefs of the host culture become more and more a part of the immigrants' culture. At the same time, the host culture changes, too, as it interacts with the immigrants' culture. Generally, however, the culture of the immigrant changes more. The reasons for this are that the host country's members far outnumber the immigrant group, and the media are largely dominated by and reflect the values and customs of the host culture.

Before exploring further the role of culture in communication, consider your own cultural values and beliefs by taking the accompanying self-test. This test will suggest how your own cultural values and beliefs might influence the messages you send and the messages you listen to in your interpersonal communication.

TEST YOURSELF   *What Are Your Cultural Beliefs and Values?*

The extremes of 10 cultural differences are identified below. For each characteristic indicate your own values: If your values are *very* similar to the extremes, select 1 or 7. If your values are *quite* similar to the extremes, select 2 or 6. If your values are *fairly* similar to the extremes, select 3 or 5. If you're in the middle, select 4.

	Gender Equality 1 2 3 4 5 6 7	
Men and women are equal and are entitled to equality in all areas.		Men and women should stick to their specific and different cultural roles.
"Success" is measured by your contribution to the group.	**Group and Individual Orientation** 1 2 3 4 5 6 7	"Success" is measured by how far you outperform others.
You should enjoy yourself as much as possible.	**Pleasure Orientation/ Hedonism** 1 2 3 4 5 6 7	You should work as much as possible.
Religion is the final arbiter of what is right and wrong; your obligation is to abide by your religion's rules.	**Religion** 1 2 3 4 5 6 7	Religion is like any other social institution; it's not inherently moral or right just because it's a religion.
Your first obligation is to your family; each person is responsible for the welfare of her or his family.	**Family** 1 2 3 4 5 6 7	Your first obligation is to yourself; each person is responsible for her- or himself.
Work hard now for a better future.	**Time Orientation** 1 2 3 4 5 6 7	Live in the present; the future may never come.
Marriage, once made, is forever.	**Marriage** 1 2 3 4 5 6 7	Marriage should be maintained as long as it's rewarding and dissolved when it's not.
People should express their emotions openly and freely.	**Emotional Expression** 1 2 3 4 5 6 7	People should not reveal their emotions, especially negative ones.
Money should be a major consideration in just about any decision you make.	**Money** 1 2 3 4 5 6 7	Money should not enter into life's really important decisions such as what relationship to enter or what career to pursue.

The world is just; bad things happen to bad people and good things happen to good people.	**Belief in a Just World** 1 2 3 4 5 6 7	The world is random; bad and good things happen to people without reference to whether they're good or bad.

▶ **How did you do?** As demonstrated throughout this text and as research shows, your cultural values and beliefs influence your interpersonal communications as well as your decision making, assessments of coworkers, teamwork, trust in others, the importance you place on diversity in the workplace, and your attitudes toward the role of women in the workplace (Stephens & Greer, 1995; Bochner & Hesketh; 1994). For example, your beliefs and values about gender equality will influence the way in which you communicate with and about the opposite sex. Your group and individual orientation will influence how you perform in work teams and how you deal with your peers at school and at work. Your degree of hedonism will influence the kinds of interactions you engage in, the books you read, the television programs you watch.

▶ **What will you do?** So, there are no right or wrong answers to this test. What makes this particular test of value for our purposes is that it asks you to examine your own cultural values and beliefs and hopefully stimulates you to go the next step and ask yourself how these values and beliefs influence your interpersonal communication. As you review the 10 characteristics, try to identify at least one specific way in which your attitudes on each of these characteristics in the self-test influence your communication. ●

ETHICS in Interpersonal Communication

Culture and Ethics

One of the most shocking revelations to come to world attention from the events of September 11, 2001, was the way in which women were treated under Taliban rule in Afghanistan; they could not be educated or even go out in public without a male relative escort, and when in public had to wear garments that covered their entire body.

Throughout history, of course, there have been numerous cultural practices that today would be judged unethical and even illegal. Sacrificing virgins to the gods, burning people who held different religious beliefs, and sending children to fight wars are obvious examples. But, even today, there are practices woven deep into the fabric of different cultures that many people would find unethical, for example:

■ bronco riding, a practice where a bull's testicles are tied so that it experiences so much pain that it bucks and tries to throw off the rider

■ clitoridectomy, whereby part or all of a young girl's clitoris is surgically removed so that she can never experience sexual intercourse without extreme pain, a practice designed to keep her a virgin until marriage

■ the belief and practice that a woman must be subservient to her husband's will

■ the practice of wearing fur—in some cases necessitating the killing of wild animals and in others raising animals so they can be killed when their pelts are worth the most money

What would you do? *Imagine that you're on a television talk show on cultural diversity. During the discussion each of the above-mentioned practices is discussed with approval by different members of the panel who argue that each culture has a right to its own practices and beliefs and that no one has the right to object to these practices. Given your own beliefs about these issues and about cultural diversity in general, what ethical obligations do you have as a member of this panel?*

The Relevance of Culture

There are lots of reasons for the cultural emphasis you'll find in this book. Most obvious, perhaps, are the vast demographic changes taking place throughout the United States. Whereas at one time the United States was a country largely populated by Europeans, it's now a country greatly influenced by the enormous number of new citizens from Latin and South America, Africa, and Asia. Along with the aforementioned demographic shift so noticeable on college campuses, these changes have brought different interpersonal customs and the need to understand and adapt to new ways of looking at communication.

As a people we've become increasingly sensitive to cultural differences. American society has moved from an assimilationist perspective (people should leave their native culture behind and adapt to their new culture) to one that values cultural diversity (people should retain their native cultural ways). With some notable exceptions—hate speech, racism, sexism, homophobia, and classism come quickly to mind—we are more concerned with saying the right thing and ultimately with developing a society where all cultures can coexist and enrich each other. The ability to interact effectively with members of other cultures often translates into financial gain and increased employment opportunities and advancement prospects as well.

Today, most countries are economically dependent on each other. Our economic lives depend on our ability to communicate effectively across different cultures. Similarly, our political well-being depends in great part on that of other cultures. Political unrest in any part of the world—South Africa, Eastern Europe, Asia, and the Middle East, to take a few examples—affects our own security. Intercultural communication and understanding seem more crucial now than ever.

The rapid spread of technology has made intercultural communication as easy as it is inevitable. News from foreign countries is commonplace. You see nightly—in vivid detail—what is going on in remote countries just as you see what's happening in your own city and state. Of course, the Internet has made intercultural communication as easy as writing a note on your computer. You can now just as easily communicate by e-mail with someone in Asia or Europe, for example, as you can with someone in another U.S. city or state.

Still another reason culture is so important is that interpersonal competence is culture-specific; what proves effective in one culture may prove ineffective in another. For example, in the United States corporate executives get down to business during the first several minutes of a meeting. In Japan, business executives interact socially for an extended period and try to find out something about each other. Thus, the communication principle influenced by U.S. culture would advise participants to get down to the meeting's agenda during the first five minutes. The principle influenced by Japanese culture would advise participants to avoid dealing with business until everyone has socialized sufficiently and feels well enough acquainted to begin negotiations. Giving a birthday gift to a close friend would be appreciated by many, but among Jehovah's Witnesses, for example, this act would be frowned upon since they don't celebrate birthdays (Dresser, 1996). Neither principle is right, and neither is wrong. Each is effective within its own culture and ineffective outside its own culture.

The Aim of a Cultural Perspective

Because culture permeates all forms of communication, it's necessary to understand its influences if you're to understand how communication works and master its skills. As illustrated throughout this text, culture influences communications of all types

Cultural Imperialism

Cultural imperialism refers to a process whereby business and political practices, but especially media products, are exported to other cultures and come to extend the influence of the exporting culture over that of the importing culture. The theory argues that the media from developed countries such as the United States and Western Europe have come to dominate the cultures of countries importing such media and at the same time to denigrate the customs and values of the local, less technologically sophisticated cultures (Folkerts & Lacy, 2001).

Media products from the United States are likely to emphasize its dominant attitudes and values, for example, the preference for competition, the importance of individuality, and the advantages of capitalism and democracy. When these media products—movies, television programs, and music, for example—are consumed by other cultures, the values and attitudes embedded in these products can quickly become the values and attitudes of these other cultures.

Television programs, films, and music from the United States and Western Europe are so popular and so in demand in developing countries that they may actually inhibit the growth of the indigenous culture's own talent. To combat this trend, some countries (Canada, France, Taiwan, and South Korea among them) have imposed restrictions on the amount of United States television programming that can be imported (Rodman, 2001).

From another perspective, however, you might argue that much as people in the United States profit as new cultures exert their influence, developing cultures profit as United States media introduce new perspectives on government and politics, foods, educational technologies, and health, for example.

Follow Up   What do you think of the influence the media from the United States and Western Europe is having on cultures throughout the world? How do you evaluate it? Do you see advantages? Disadvantages?

(Moon, 1996). It influences what you say to yourself and how you talk with friends, lovers, and family in everyday conversation (for example, Shibazaki & Brennan, 1998). It influences how you interact in groups and how much importance you place on the group versus the individual. It influences the topics you talk about and the strategies you use in communicating information or in persuading. It influences how you use the media and the credibility you attribute to them.

A cultural emphasis helps distinguish what is universal (true for all people) from what is relative (true for people in one culture and not true for people in other cultures) (Matsumoto, 1994). The principles for communicating information and for changing listeners' attitudes, for example, will vary from one culture to another. If you're to understand communication, then you need to know how its principles vary and how the principles must be qualified and adjusted on the basis of cultural differences.

A good example is that of age. If you were raised in the United States, you probably grew up with a youth bias (young is good, old is not so good)—an attitude the media reinforces daily—and may well have assumed that this preference for youth is universal across all cultures. But it isn't and if you assume it is, you may be in for intercultural difficulties. A good example is the case of the American journalist in China who remarked that the government official he was talking with was probably too young to remember a particular event, a comment that would be taken as a compliment by most youth-oriented Americans. But to the Chinese it would be perceived as an insult, as a suggestion that the official was too young to deserve respect (Smith, 2002).

This cultural understanding is needed to communicate effectively in the wide variety of intercultural situations. Success in interpersonal communication—at your job and in

 Social Darwinism, or cultural evolution, holds that much as the human species evolved from lower life forms to Homo sapiens, cultures also evolve. Consequently, some cultures may be considered advanced and others primitive. Cultural relativism, on the other hand, holds that all cultures are different but that no culture is superior or inferior to any other (Berry, Poortinga, Segall, & Dasen, 1992). What argument can you advance in support of or against each position?

your social and personal life—will depend in great part on your understanding of and your ability to communicate effectively with persons who are culturally different from yourself. Daily the media bombard you with evidence of racial tensions, religious disagreements, sexual bias, and in general, the problems caused when intercultural communication fails.

This emphasis on culture does not imply that you should accept all cultural practices or that all cultural practices are equal (Hatfield & Rapson, 1996). Consider this case in point (*Time,* 2 December 1993, 61). Assume you're a judge and the following case is presented to you: A Chinese immigrant killed his wife in New York because he suspected her of cheating. A "cultural defense" was offered, essentially claiming that infidelity so shames a man that he is uncontrollable in his anger. Would this cultural defense have influenced your judgment? In the actual case, influenced by an anthropologist's testimony that infidelity is so serious in Chinese culture that it pushed the defendant to commit the crime, the judge sentenced the defendant to five years' probation.

Further, a cultural emphasis does not imply that you have to accept or follow all of the practices of your own culture. For example, even if the majority in your culture find cockfighting acceptable, you need not agree with or follow the practice. Nor need you consider this practice equal to a cultural practice in which animals are treated kindly. You can reject capitalism or communism or socialism regardless of the culture in which you were raised. Of course, going against your culture's traditions and values is often very difficult. But it's important to realize that culture influences, it does not determine, your values or behavior. Often personality factors (your degree of assertiveness, extroversion, or optimism, for example) will prove more influential than culture (Hatfield & Rapson, 1996).

As demonstrated throughout this text, cultural differences exist throughout the interpersonal communication spectrum—from the way you use eye contact to the way you develop or dissolve a relationship (Chang & Holt, 1996). But these should not blind you to the great number of similarities existing among even the most widely separated cultures. When discussing differences, remember that these are usually questions of degree rather than all-or-none. For example, most cultures value honesty, but some cultures give it greater emphasis than others. The advances in media and technology and the widespread use of the Internet, for example, are influencing cultures and cultural change and are perhaps homogenizing the different cultures, lessening the differences and increasing the similarities.

You'll see the cultural emphasis in this text in two ways. First, this chapter focuses on the role of culture in interpersonal communication, the ways cultures differ, and intercultural communication—especially the principles for increasing intercultural communication effectiveness. Second, cultural issues are integrated throughout the text as they relate to the topic being discussed. For example, when discussing self-disclosure or the meanings of nonverbal gestures, we also consider how different cultures view these forms of communication.

HOW CULTURES DIFFER

Cultures, of course, differ in a wide variety of ways and, for purposes of communication, the difference that probably comes to mind first is that of languages. And certainly, cultures do differ in the languages spoken and understood. In fact, one of the most popular theories in intercultural communication, the language relativity hypothesis, argued that the language you speak influences your thoughts and behaviors and since cultures differ so widely in their languages, they will also differ in their ways of thinking and behaving.

Subsequent research and theory, however, did not support the extreme claims made by linguistic relativity researchers (Pinker, 1994). A more modified hypothesis is currently supported: The language you speak helps to *highlight* what you see and how you talk about it. For example, if you speak a language that is rich in color terms (English is a good example), you would find it easier to highlight and talk about nuances of color than would someone from a culture that has fewer color terms (some cultures distinguish only two or three or four parts of the color spectrum). This does not mean, however, that people *see* the world differently; only that their language helps (or doesn't help) them to focus on certain variations in nature and makes it easier (or more difficult) to talk about them. Nor does it mean that people speaking widely differing languages are doomed to misunderstanding each other. Translation enables us to understand a great deal of the meaning in a foreign-language message. We also have a ready arsenal of communication skills, which you'll encounter throughout this course, that can help bridge the communication gap between members of different cultures.

Language differences are not the only differences between cultures that will influence intercultural communication. Let's take a look at five such differences: power distances, masculine and feminine orientation, collectivism and individualism, high and low context, and time orientations (Gudykunst, 1991; Hall & Hall, 1987; Hofstede, 1997). As you review these differences, recognize that they are matters of degree. Characteristics aren't necessarily present in one culture and absent in the other; rather they're present in both but to different degrees. And that's what this discussion focuses on: degrees of differences, not absolute differences.

Power Distances

In some cultures power is concentrated in the hands of a few, and there is a great difference in the power held by these people and that held by the ordinary citizen. These are called high-power-distance cultures; examples are Mexico, Brazil, India, and the Philippines (Hofstede, 1983, 1997). In low-power-distance cultures, power is more

WEB EXPLORATION
To learn more about power distances, go to
www.ablongman.com/
devito.

A S K the *Researcher*

Confronting Family Prejudice

My family, I'm embarrassed to say, is really prejudiced against other races and religions. They can't see any value in the contributions of other cultures or the wisdom in other religions. How can I insert a note of reason into their discussions and get them to be less prejudiced?

Deep-seated and strong prejudices are very resistant. They may be based on fear or dislike of any sort of difference—feelings the person may not even admit to himself or herself. Typically, these feelings have been supported by peer groups for a long time and so the prejudiced person sees these opinions as reasonable and natural.

The most realistic goal may be to get them to respect your own feelings. Tell them that you're upset by this type of talk and you don't wish to be around it. Be assertive and consistent. Make it clear that you're upset and that you're asking them to stop telling those types of jokes, using that kind of language, etc. It's your right. If they don't stop, leave the room.

Reducing their prejudice may take a very long time. You can try showing them that the same type of thinking can apply to their own group. You also can try to have them meet members of the group that disconfirm their stereotypes.

For further information see M. L. Hecht, ed. (1998). *Communicating prejudice.* Newbury Park, CA: Sage, and B. Lott and D. Maluso, eds. (1995). *The social psychology of interpersonal discrimination.* New York: Guilford.

Michael L. Hecht (Ph.D., University of Illinois) is professor and head of the Department of Communication Arts and Science at Penn State University where he teaches courses and conducts research in interethnic relationships, identity, culture and drug prevention, and interpersonal relationships. He's recently developed a successful culturally appropriate drug prevention program for middle school students and is involved in an international project to improve intergroup relationships. mhecht@psu.edu (Reprinted by permission of Dr. Michael L. Hecht.)

---

evenly distributed throughout the citizenry; examples include Denmark, New Zealand, Sweden, and to a lesser extent the United States. These differences affect interpersonal communication and relationships in a variety of ways.

Friendship and dating relationships will be influenced by the power distance between groups (Andersen, 1991). For example, in India (high power distance), friendships and romantic relationships are expected to take place within your cultural class; in Sweden (low power distance), a person is expected to select friends and romantic partners not on the basis of class or culture, but on individual factors such as personality, appearance, and the like.

In low-power-distance cultures there is a general feeling of equality that is consistent with acting assertively, and so you're expected to confront a friend, partner, or supervisor assertively (Borden, 1991). In high-power-distance cultures, direct confrontation and assertiveness may be viewed negatively, especially if directed at a superior.

In high-power-distance cultures you're taught to have great respect for authority; people in these cultures see authority as desirable and beneficial, and challenges to authority are generally not welcomed (Westwood, Tang, & Kirkbride, 1992; Bochner & Hesketh, 1994). In low-power-distance cultures, there's a certain distrust for authority; it's seen as a kind of necessary evil that should be limited as much as possible. This difference in attitudes toward authority can be seen right in the classroom. In high-power-distance cultures there's a great power distance between students and teachers; students are expected to be modest, polite, and totally respectful. In low-power-distance cultures students are expected to demonstrate their knowledge and command of the subject matter, participate in discussions with the teacher, and even challenge the teacher, something many high-power-distance culture members wouldn't even think of doing. The same differences can be seen in patient–doctor communication. Patients from high-power-distance cultures are less likely to challenge their doctors or admit that they don't understand the medical terminology than would patients in low-power-distance cultures.

High-power-distance cultures rely more on symbols of power. For example, titles (Dr., Professor, Chef, Inspector) are more important in high-power-distance cultures. Failure to include these in forms of address is a serious breach of etiquette. Low-power-distance cultures rely less on symbols of power, and less of a problem is created if you fail to use a respectful title (Victor, 1992). But even in low-power-distance cultures you may create problems if, for example, you call a medical doctor, police captain, military officer, or professor Ms. or Mr.

In the United States, two people quickly move from Title plus Last Name (Mr. or Ms. Smith) to First Name (Pat). In low-power-distance cultures less of a problem is created if you're too informal or if you presume to exchange first names before sufficient interaction has taken place. In high-power-distance cultures too great an informality—especially between those differing greatly in power—would be a serious breach of etiquette. Again, in even the lowest power distance culture, you may still create problems if you call your English professor Pat.

Masculine and Feminine Cultures

A popular classification of cultures is in terms of their masculinity and femininity (Hofstede, 1997, 1998). In a highly "masculine" culture men are viewed as assertive, oriented to material success, and strong; women on the other hand are viewed as modest, focused on the quality of life, and tender. In a highly "feminine" culture, both men and women are encouraged to be modest, oriented to maintaining the quality of life, and tender. The ten countries with the highest masculinity score (beginning with the highest) are Japan, Austria, Venezuela, Italy, Switzerland, Mexico, Ireland, Jamaica, Great Britain, and Germany. The ten countries with the highest femininity score (beginning with the highest) are Sweden, Norway, Netherlands, Denmark, Costa Rica, Yugoslavia, Finland, Chile, Portugal, and Thailand. Out of 53 countries ranked, the United States ranks 15th most masculine (Hofstede, 1997).

Masculine cultures emphasize success and socialize their people to be assertive, ambitious, and competitive. Members of masculine cultures are thus more likely to confront conflicts directly and to competitively fight out any differences; they're more likely to emphasize win–lose conflict strategies. **Feminine cultures** emphasize the quality of life and socialize their people to be modest and to emphasize close interpersonal relationships. Members of feminine cultures are thus more likely to emphasize compromise and negotiation in resolving conflicts; they're more likely to seek win–win solutions.

Organizations can also be viewed in terms of masculinity or femininity. Masculine organizations emphasize competitiveness and aggressiveness. They focus on the bottom line and reward their workers on the basis of their contribution to the organization. Feminine organizations are less competitive and less aggressive. They're more likely to emphasize worker satisfaction and reward their workers on the basis of need; those who have large families, for example, may get better raises than the single people, even if the singles have contributed more to the organization.

Individual and Collective Orientation

Cultures differ in the extent to which they promote individual values (for example, power, achievement, hedonism, and stimulation) versus collectivist values (for example, benevolence, tradition, and conformity). The countries with the highest individualist orientation (beginning with the highest) are the United States, Australia, Great

WEB EXPLORATION
To learn more about individual and collectivist orientation, go to www.ablongman.com/devito.

Britain, Canada, Netherlands, New Zealand, Italy, Belgium, Denmark, Sweden, France, and Ireland. Countries with the highest collectivist orientation (beginning with the highest) are Guatemala, Ecuador, Panama, Venezuela, Colombia, Indonesia, Pakistan, Costa Rica, Peru, Taiwan, and South Korea (Hofstede, 1983, 1997; Hatfield & Rapson, 1996; Kapoor, Wolfe, & Blue, 1995). With a few notable exceptions, the individualist countries are wealthy and the collectivist countries are poor. For example, Japan and Hong Kong—which score in the middle—are wealthier than many of the most individualist countries. The following self-test will help you examine your own orientation toward individualism or collectivism.

TEST YOURSELF *Are You an Individualist or a Collectivist?*

Respond to each of the following statements in terms of how true they are of your behavior and thinking: 1 = almost always true, 2 = more often true than false, 3 = true about half the time and false about half the time, 4 = more often false than true, and 5 = almost always false.

_____ 1. My own goals, rather than the goals of my group (for example, my extended family, my organization), are more important.

_____ 2. I feel responsible for myself and to my own conscience rather than for the entire group and to the group's values and rules.

_____ 3. Success to me depends on my contribution to the group effort and the group's success rather than to my own individual success or to surpassing others.

_____ 4. I make a clear distinction between who is the leader and who are the followers and similarly make a clear distinction between members of my own cultural group and outsiders.

_____ 5. In business transactions personal relationships are extremely important, so I would spend considerable time getting to know people with whom I do business.

_____ 6. In my communications I prefer a direct and explicit communication style; I believe in "telling it like it is," even if it hurts.

▶ **How did you do?** To compute your individualist–collectivist score, follow these steps:

1. Reverse the scores for items 3 and 5 (if your response was 1 reverse it to a 5, if your response was 2 reverse it to a 4, if your response was 3 keep it as 3, if your response was 4 reverse it to a 2, if your response was 5 reverse it to a 1).

2. Add your scores for all 6 items, being sure to use the reverse scores for items 3 and 5 in your calculations. Your score should be between 6 (indicating a highly individualist orientation) and 30 (indicating a highly collectivist orientation).

3. Position your score on the following scale:

6 _____ 15 _____ 30
highly individualist   about equally individualist   highly collectivist
                         and collectivist

▶ **What will you do?** Does this scale and score accurately measure the way in which you see yourself on this dimension? Is this orientation going to help you achieve your personal and professional goals? Might it hinder you?

One of the major differences between these two orientations is in the extent to which an individual's goals or the group's goals are given precedence. Individual and collective tendencies are, of course, not mutually exclusive; this is not an all-or-none orientation but rather one of emphasis. You probably have both tendencies. Thus, you may, for example, compete with other members of your basketball team for most baskets or most valuable player award (and thus emphasize individual goals). At the same time, however, you will—in a game—act in a way that will benefit the entire team (and thus emphasize group goals). In actual practice both individual and collective tendencies will help you and your team each achieve your goals. Yet most people and most cultures have a dominant orientation; they're more individually oriented (they see themselves as independent) or more collectively oriented (they see themselves as interdependent) in most situations, most of the time (cf., Singelis, 1994).

In some instances, however, these tendencies may come into conflict. For example, do you shoot for the basket and try to raise your own individual score or do you pass the ball to another player who is better positioned to score and thus benefit the team as a whole? You make this distinction in popular talk when you call someone a team player (collectivist orientation) or an individual player (individualist orientation).

In an **individualist culture** members are responsible for themselves and perhaps their immediate family. In a **collectivist culture** members are responsible for the entire group.

In an individualist culture success is measured by the extent to which you surpass other members of your group; you would take pride in standing out from the crowd.

In 1995, the Emma Lazarus poem inscribed on the Statute of Liberty was changed. The original last five lines of the poem, "The New Colossus," are as follows [the words in brackets were deleted]:

> Give me your tired, your poor,
> Your huddled masses yearning to breathe free,
> [the wretched refuse of your teeming shore]
> Send these, the homeless, tempest-tost to me
> I lift my lamp beside the golden door.

The late Harvard zoologist Stephen Jay Gould, commenting on this change, notes that it no longer represents what Lazarus wrote (Gould, 1995). "The language police triumph," Gould laments, "and integrity bleeds." On the other hand, it can be argued that calling immigrants "wretched refuse" is insulting and that if Lazarus were writing today, she wouldn't have used that phrase. Would you have supported deleting this line?

Your heroes—in the media, for example—are likely to be those who are unique and who stand apart. In a collectivist culture success is measured by your contribution to the achievements of the group as a whole; you would take pride in your similarity to other members of your group. Your heroes, in contrast, are more likely to be team players who do not stand out from the rest of the group's members. Not surprisingly, advertisements in individualist cultures emphasize individual preferences and benefits, independence, and personal success; advertisements in collectivist cultures emphasize group benefits, family integrity, and group harmony (Han & Shavitt, 1994).

In an individualist culture you're responsible to your own conscience, and responsibility is largely an individual matter; in a collectivistic culture you're responsible to the rules of the social group, and responsibility for an accomplishment or a failure is shared by all members. Competition is fostered in individualist cultures while cooperation is promoted in collectivist cultures.

In an individualist culture you might compete for leadership in a small group setting, and there would likely be a very clear distinction between leaders and members. In a collectivist culture leadership would be shared and rotated; there is likely to be little distinction between leader and members. These orientations will also influence the kinds of communication members consider appropriate in an organizational context. For example, individualist members will favor clarity and directness while collectivists will favor "face-saving" and the avoidance of hurting others or arousing negative evaluations (Kim & Sharkey, 1995).

Distinctions between in-group members and out-group members are extremely important in collectivist cultures. In individualist cultures, where the person's individuality is prized, the distinction is likely to be less important.

High- and Low-Context Cultures

Cultures also differ in the extent to which information is made explicit or is assumed to be in the context or in the persons communicating. A **high-context culture** is one in which much of the information in communication is in the context or in the person— for example, information that was shared through previous communications, through assumptions about each other, and through shared experiences. The information is thus known by all participants but isn't explicitly stated in the verbal messages. A **low-context culture** is one in which most of the information is explicitly stated in the verbal message. In formal transactions it would be stated in written (or contract) form.

To further appreciate the distinction between high and low context, consider giving directions ("Where's the voter registration center?") to someone who knows the neighborhood and to a newcomer to your city. With someone who knows the neighborhood (a high-context situation), you can assume that she or he knows the local landmarks. So you can give directions such as "next to the laundromat on Main Street" or "the corner of Albany and Elm." With the newcomer (a low-context situation), you can't assume that she or he shares any information with you. So you would have to use only those directions that a stranger would understand, for example, "make a left at the next stop sign" or "go two blocks and then turn right."

High-context cultures are also collectivist cultures (Gudykunst, Ting-Toomey, & Chua, 1988; Gudykunst & Kim, 1992). These cultures (Japanese, Arabic, Latin American, Thai, Korean, Apache, and Mexican are examples) place great emphasis on personal relationships and oral agreements (Victor, 1992). Low-context cultures are also individualist cultures. These cultures (German, Swedish, Norwegian, and American are examples) place less emphasis on personal relationships and more emphasis on verbalized, explicit explanation, and on written contracts in business transactions. The

Table 2.1

Differences in Individual (Low-Context) and Collective (High-Context) Cultures

In every culture there will be variations in each of these characteristics. View these, therefore, as general tendencies rather than absolutes. Further, increased mobility, changing immigration patterns, and exposure to media from different parts of the world will gradually decrease the differences between these two orientations. This table is based on the work of Hall (1983) and Hall & Hall (1987) and the interpretations by Gudykunst (1991) and Victor (1992).

Individual (Low-Context) Cultures	Collective (High-Context) Cultures
Your own goals are most important	The group's goals are most important
You're responsible for yourself and to your own conscience	You're responsible for the entire group and to the group's values and rules
Success depends on your surpassing others	Success depends on your contribution to the group
Competition is emphasized	Cooperation is emphasized
Clear distinction is made between leaders and members	Little distinction is made between leaders and members; leadership would normally be shared
In-group versus out-group distinctions are of little importance	In-group versus out-group distinctions are of great importance
Information is made explicit; little is left unsaid	Information is often left implicit and much goes unsaid
Personal relationships are less important; hence, little time is spent getting to know each other in meetings and conferences	Personal relationships are extremely important; hence, much time is spent getting to know each other in meetings and conferences
Directness is valued; face-saving is seldom thought of	Indirectness is valued and face-saving is a major consideration

characteristics of individual–collective and high- and low-context cultures discussed here are summarized in Table 2.1.

Members of high-context cultures spend lots of time getting to know each other interpersonally and socially before any important transactions take place. Because of this prior personal knowledge, a great deal of information is shared by the members and therefore does not have to be explicitly stated. Members of low-context cultures spend much less time getting to know each other and hence don't have that shared knowledge. As a result everything has to be stated explicitly.

This difference between high- and low-context orientation is partly responsible for the differences observed in Japanese and American business groups (alluded to in Chapter 1). The Japanese spend lots of time getting to know each other before conducting actual business, whereas Americans get down to business very quickly. The Japanese (and other high-context cultures) want to get to know each other because important information isn't made explicit. They have to know you so they can read your nonverbals, for example (Sanders, Wiseman, & Matz, 1991). Americans can get right down to business because all important information will be stated explicitly.

To high-context cultural members, what is omitted or assumed is a vital part of the communication transaction. Silence, for example, is highly valued (Basso, 1972). To low-context cultural members, what is omitted creates ambiguity, but this ambiguity is simply something that will be eliminated by explicit and direct communication. To high-context cultural members, ambiguity is something to be avoided; it's a sign that the interpersonal and social interactions have not proved sufficient to establish a shared base of information (Gudykunst, 1983).

When this simple difference isn't understood, intercultural misunderstandings can easily result. For example, the directness characteristic of the low-context culture may seem insulting, insensitive, or unnecessary to the high-context cultural member. Conversely, to the low-context member, the high-context cultural member may appear vague, underhanded, or dishonest in his or her reluctance to be explicit or engage in communication that a low-context member would consider open and direct.

Another frequent source of intercultural misunderstanding that can be traced to the differences in high and low context can be seen in face-saving (Hall & Hall, 1987). High-context cultures place much more emphasis on face-saving. For example, they're more likely to avoid argument for fear of causing others to lose face; on the other hand, low-context members (with their individualistic orientation) will use argument to win a point. Similarly, in high-context cultures criticism should only take place in private. Low-context cultures may not make this public–private distinction. Low-context managers who criticize high-context workers in public will find that their criticism causes interpersonal problems and does little to resolve the original difficulty (Victor, 1992).

Members of high-context cultures are reluctant to say no for fear of offending and causing the person to lose face. Thus, it's necessary to be able to read when the Japanese executive's "yes" means yes and when it means no. The difference isn't in the words used but in the way in which they're used.

Time Orientations

TRY IT!
Apply your insights on time orientations; go to **www.ablongman.com/devito**.

Cultures differ greatly in the way they view time. One important distinction is between displaced and diffused time orientations (Hall, 1959). In a **displaced time orientation,** time is viewed exactly. Persons with this orientation will be exactly on time. In a **diffused time orientation,** time is seen as approximate rather than exact. People with this orientation are usually late for appointments because they understand, for example, a scheduled time of 8:00 P.M. as meaning anywhere from 7:45 to 8:15 or 8:30.

Even the accuracy of clocks varies in different cultures and probably reflects each culture's time orientation. In one study, clocks in Japan were found to be the most accurate, while clocks in Indonesia were least accurate. Clocks in England, Italy, Taiwan, and the United States fell between these two extremes in accuracy. Not surprisingly, when the speed of pedestrians in these countries was measured, the Japanese were found to walk the fastest and the Indonesians the slowest. Such differences reflect the different ways in which cultures treat time and their general attitude toward the importance of time in everyday life (LeVine & Bartlett, 1984).

Another important distinction is that between monochronic and polychronic time orientations (Hall, 1959, 1976; Hall & Hall, 1987). Consider your own time behavior by asking yourself the following questions.

Do you

I SEE

1. (a) Do one thing at a time or (b) do several things at one time?
2. (a) Treat time schedules and plans very seriously and only break them for the most serious of reasons or (b) treat time schedules and plans as useful but not sacred and break them for any of a variety of reasons?

3. (a) Consider your job the most important part of your life, ahead of even family or (b) consider the family and interpersonal relationships more important than the job?

4. (a) Consider privacy extremely important, seldom borrow or lend to others, and work independently or (b) involve yourself actively with others and work in the presence of and with lots of people at the same time?

If you selected the (a) responses, you're more likely a monochronic person. If you selected the (b) responses, you're more likely a polychronic person. Monochronic people or cultures (the United States, Germany, Scandinavia, and Switzerland are good examples) schedule one thing at a time. Time is compartmentalized; there is a time for everything, and everything has its own time. Polychronic people or cultures (Latin Americans, Mediterranean people, and Arabs are good examples), on the other hand, schedule a number of things at the same time. Eating, conducting business with several different people, and taking care of family matters may all be conducted at the same time. No culture is entirely monochronic or polychronic; rather, these are general tendencies that are found across a large part of the culture. Some cultures combine both time orientations; Japanese culture and parts of American culture are examples where both orientations are found.

INTERCULTURAL COMMUNICATION

Understanding the role of culture in communication is an essential foundation for understanding intercultural communication as it occurs in an interpersonal context. As a preface to this discussion you may want to take the accompanying self-test to explore your own openness to intercultural communication.

TEST YOURSELF   *How Open Are You Interculturally?*

Select a specific culture (national, racial, or religious) different from your own, and substitute this culture for the phrase "interculturally different" in each question below. Indicate how open you would be to communicating in each of these situations, using the following scale: 5 = very open and willing, 4 = open and willing, 3 = neutral, 2 = closed and unwilling, and 1 = very closed and unwilling.

_____ 1. Talk with an interculturally different person while alone waiting for a bus.

_____ 2. Talk with an interculturally different person in the presence of those who are interculturally similar to you.

_____ 3. Have a close friendship with an interculturally different person.

_____ 4. Have a long-term romantic relationship with an interculturally different person.

_____ 5. Participate in a problem-solving group that is composed predominantly of interculturally different people.

_____ 6. Openly and fairly observe an information-sharing group consisting predominantly of interculturally different people.

_____ 7. Lead a group of interculturally different people through a problem-solving or information-sharing situation.

_____ 8. Participate in a consciousness-raising group that is composed of one half interculturally different people.

_____ 9. Listen openly and fairly to a conversation by an interculturally different person.

_____ 10. Ascribe a level of credibility for an interculturally different person identical to that ascribed to an interculturally similar person—all other things being equal.

▶ **How did you do?**   To calculate your total score, simply add your scores for all 10 questions. High scores (say, above 35) indicate considerable openness; low scores (say, below 20) indicate a lack of openness. Not surprisingly, research finds that people who are more willing to communicate interculturally have more friends from foreign countries than do those with less willingness (Kassing, 1997).

▶ **What will you do?**   Use these numbers for purposes of thinking critically about your intercultural openness rather than to indicate any absolute level of openness or closedness. For example, did you select the "interculturally different" group on the basis of how positively or negatively you felt about them? With what group would you be most open to interacting? Least open? Are there specific types of interpersonal communication you'd be less likely to be open to than others? For example, did you indicate a greater level of openness in Question 1 than Question 10? Why?

The Nature of Intercultural Communication

Intercultural communication refers to communication between persons who have different cultural beliefs, values, or ways of behaving. The model in Figure 2.1 illustrates this concept. The larger circles represent the culture of the individual communicator. The inner circles identify the communicators (the sources/receivers). In this model each communicator is a member of a different culture. In some instances the cultural differences are relatively slight—say, between persons from Toronto and New York. In other instances the cultural differences are great—say, between persons from Borneo and Germany, or between persons from rural Nigeria and industrialized England.

All messages originate from a specific and unique cultural context, and that context influences their content and form. You communicate as you do largely as a result of your culture. Culture (along with the processes of enculturation and acculturation) influences every aspect of your communication experience.

Principles for Improving Intercultural Communication

Murphy's Law ("Anything that can go wrong will go wrong") is especially applicable to intercultural communication. Intercultural communication is, of course, subject to all

Figure 2.1

A Model of Intercultural Communication
This model of intercultural communication illustrates that culture is a part of every communication act. More specifically, it illustrates that the messages you send and the messages you receive will be influenced by your cultural beliefs, values, and attitudes.

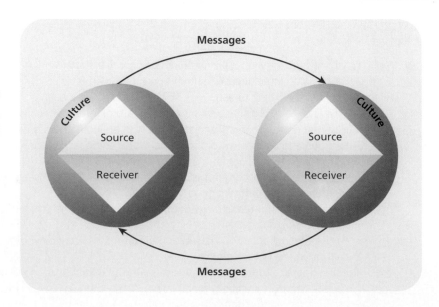

Increasing Interpersonal Effectiveness
Cultural Sensitivity

Cultural sensitivity is an attitude and way of behaving in which you're aware of and acknowledge cultural differences; it's crucial for global issues such as world peace and economic growth as well as for effective interpersonal communication and for general success (Franklin & Mizell, 1995). Without cultural sensitivity there can be no effective interpersonal communication between people who differ in gender, race, nationality, or affective orientation. So, be mindful of the cultural differences between yourself and the other person. Remember that the techniques of interpersonal communication that work well with European Americans may not work well with Asian Americans; what proves effective in Japan may not in Mexico. The close physical distance that is normal in Arab cultures may prove too familiar or too intrusive in much of the United States and Northern Europe. The empathy that most Americans welcome may be discomforting for the average Korean (Yun, 1976).

Increasing Cultural Sensitivity   In this chapter we identified several guidelines for more effective intercultural communication; these suggestions are the best advice to follow in achieving cultural sensitivity:

■ Prepare yourself. Read about and listen carefully for culturally influenced behaviors.
■ Recognize and face fears of acting inappropriately toward members of different cultures.
■ Recognize differences between yourself and people from other cultures.
■ Recognize that there are often enormous differences within cultural groups.
■ Recognize differences in meaning; words rarely mean the same thing to members of different cultures.
■ Become conscious of the cultural rules and customs of others.

the same barriers and problems as are the other forms of communication discussed throughout this text. Drawing on a number of intercultural researchers, we cover here the principles designed to counteract the barriers that are unique to intercultural communication (Barna, 1991; Ruben, 1985; Spitzberg, 1991).

Prepare Yourself   There's no better preparation for intercultural communication than learning about the other culture. Fortunately, there are numerous sources to draw on. View a documentary or movie that presents a realistic view of the culture. Read material about the culture by persons from that culture as well as by "outsiders." Scan magazines and websites from that culture. Talk with members of that culture. Chat on international IRC channels. Read materials addressed to people who need to communicate with those from other cultures. For example, recent titles include: *Do's and Taboos of Hosting International Visitors* (Axtell, 1990), *Mind Your Manners: Managing Business Cultures in Europe* (Mole, 1998), *Do's and Taboos around the World* (Axtell, 1994), *The Executive Guide to Asia-Pacific Communications* (James, 1995), *How to Negotiate Anything with Anyone Anywhere around the World* (Acuff, 1993), and *Internationally Yours: Writing and Communication Successfully in Today's Global Marketplace* (DeVries, 1994), *International Business Etiquette in Europe: What You Need to Know to Conduct Business Abroad with Charm and Savvy* (Sabath, 1999), and *Global Etiquette Guide to Mexico and Latin America* (Foster, 2002).

Another part of this preparation is to recognize and face your own fears that may stand in the way of effective intercultural communication (Gudykunst, 1994; Stephan & Stephan, 1985). For example, you may fear for your self-esteem. You may become anxious about your ability to control the intercultural situation or you may worry about your own level of discomfort. You may fear saying something that will be considered politically incorrect or culturally insensitive and thereby losing face.

You may fear that you'll be taken advantage of by the member of this other culture. Depending on your own stereotypes you may fear being lied to, financially duped, or made fun of. You may fear that members of this other group will react to you negatively. You may fear, for example, that they will not like you or may disapprove of your attitudes or beliefs or perhaps even reject you as a person. Conversely, you may fear negative reactions from members of your own group. They might, for example, disapprove of your socializing with the culturally different.

Some fears, of course, are reasonable. In many cases, however, they're groundless. Either way, they need to be assessed logically and their consequences weighed carefully. Then you'll be able to make informed choices about your communications.

Reduce Uncertainty   All communication interactions involve uncertainty and ambiguity. Not surprisingly, this uncertainty and ambiguity is greater when there are large cultural differences (Berger & Bradac, 1982; Gudykunst, 1989, 1993). Because of this greater uncertainty in intercultural communication, more time and effort are required to reduce it and thus to communicate meaningfully. Reducing your uncertainty about another person will not only make your communication more effective, but will also increase your liking for the person (Douglas, 1994). In situations of great uncertainty the techniques of effective communication (for example, active listening, perception checking, being specific, and seeking feedback) take on special importance.

View point In 1995, the United States Department of Education issued recommendations covering the types of religious communications public schools may permit (*New York Times,* August 26, 1995, pp. 1, 8). Among the permitted activities are: student prayer, student-initiated discussions of religion, saying grace, proselytizing that would not be considered harassment, and the wearing of religious symbols and clothing. Among the forbidden activities: prayer endorsed by teachers or administrators, invitations to prayer that could constitute harassment, teaching of a particular religion (rather than about religion), and encouraging either religious or antireligious activity. How do you feel about these recommendations and, more generally, about the appropriate role, if any, of religion in public schools?

Active listening (Chapter 5) and perception checking techniques (Chapter 4), for example, help you to verify the accuracy of your perceptions and allow you to revise and amend any incorrect perceptions. Being specific reduces ambiguity and the chances of misunderstandings. Misunderstanding is a lot more likely when talking about "neglect" (a highly abstract concept) than when talking about "forgetting your last birthday" (a specific event).

Seeking feedback helps you to correct any possible misconceptions almost immediately. Seek feedback on whether you're making yourself clear ("Does that make sense?" "Do you see where to put the widget?"). Similarly, seek feedback to make sure you understand what the other person is saying ("Do you mean that you'll never speak with them again? Do you mean that literally?").

Although you're always in danger of misperceiving and misevaluating another person, you're in special danger in intercultural situations. Therefore, try to resist your natural tendency to judge others quickly and permanently. A judgment made early is likely to be based on too little information. Because of this, flexibility and a willingness to revise opinions are essential intercultural skills.

Recognize Differences   To communicate interculturally you need to recognize the differences between yourself and people from other cultures, the differences within the other cultural group, and the numerous differences in meaning.

Differences between Yourself and the Culturally Different

A common barrier to intercultural communication occurs when you assume that similarities exist and that differences do not. This is especially true of values, attitudes, and beliefs. You might easily accept different hairstyles, clothing, and foods. In basic values and beliefs, however, you may assume that deep down everyone is really alike. They aren't. When you assume similarities and ignore differences, you'll fail to notice important distinctions and when communicating will convey to others that your ways are the right ways and that their ways are not important to you. Consider this example. An American invites a Filipino coworker to dinner. The Filipino politely refuses. The American is hurt and feels that the Filipino does not want to be friendly. The Filipino is hurt and concludes that the invitation was not extended sincerely. Here, it seems, both the American and the Filipino assume that their customs for inviting people to dinner are the same when, in fact, they aren't. A Filipino expects to be invited several times before accepting a dinner invitation. When an invitation is given only once it's viewed as insincere.

Here's another example. An American college student hears the news that her favorite uncle has died. She bites her lip, pulls herself up, and politely excuses herself from the group of foreign students with whom she is having dinner. The Russian thinks: "How unfriendly." The Italian thinks: "How insincere." The Brazilian thinks: "How unconcerned." To many Americans, it's a sign of bravery to endure pain (physical or emotional) in silence and without any outward show of emotion. To members of other groups, such silence is often interpreted negatively to mean that the individual does not consider them friends who can share such sorrow. In other cultures, people are expected to reveal to friends how they feel.

Differences within the Culturally Different Group

Within every cultural group there are vast and important differences. As all Americans are not alike, neither are all Indonesians, Greeks, Mexicans, and so on. When you ignore these differences, when you assume that all persons covered by the same label (in this case a national or racial label) are the same, you're guilty of stereotyping. A good example of this is seen in the use of the term "African American." The term stresses the unity of Africa and those who are of African descent and is analogous to "Asian American" or "European American." At the same time, it ignores the great diversity within the African continent when, for example, it's used as analogous to "German American" or "Japanese American." A more analogous comparison would be "Nigerian American" or "Ethiopian American." Within each culture there are smaller cultures that differ greatly from each other and from the larger culture.

Differences in Meaning   Meaning exists not in words but in people (a principle returned to in Chapter 6). Consider, for example, the differences in meaning for words such as *woman* to an American and a Muslim, *religion* to a born-again Christian and an atheist, and *lunch* to a Chinese rice farmer and a Madison Avenue advertising executive. Even though the same word is used, its meanings will vary greatly depending on the listeners' cultural definitions.

A left-handed American who eats with the left hand may be seen by a Muslim as obscene. To the Muslim, the left hand isn't used for eating or for shaking hands but to clean oneself after excretory functions. So, using the left hand to eat or to shake hands is considered insulting and obscene.

Adjust Your Communication   Intercultural communication (in fact, all interpersonal communication) takes place only to the extent that you and the person you're trying to communicate with share the same system of symbols. Your communication will be hindered to the extent that your language and nonverbal systems differ. This **adjustment** principle takes on particular relevance when you realize that no two persons share identical symbol systems. Parents and children, for example, not only have different vocabularies but also, even more important, have different meanings for some of the terms they have in common. People in close relationships—either as intimate friends or as romantic partners—realize that learning the other person's signals takes a long time and, often, great patience. If you want to understand what another person means—by smiling, by saying "I love you," by arguing about trivial matters, by self-deprecating comments—you have to learn their system of signals.

This principle is especially important in intercultural communication largely because people from different cultures use different signals and sometimes the same signals to signify quite different things. Focused eye contact means honesty and openness in much of the United States. But that same behavior may signify arrogance or disrespect in Japan and in many Hispanic cultures if it occurs between a youngster and someone significantly older.

Part of the art of intercultural communication is learning the other person's signals, how they're used, and what they mean. Furthermore, you have to share your own system of signals with others so that they can better understand you. Although some people may know what you mean by your silence or by your avoidance of eye contact, others may not. You cannot expect others to decode your behaviors accurately without help.

An interesting theory largely revolving around adjustment is communication accommodation theory. This theory holds that speakers will adjust to or accommodate the speaking style of their listeners to gain, for example, social approval and greater communication efficiency (Giles, Mulac, Bradac, & Johnson, 1987). For example, when two people have a similar speech rate, they're more attracted to each other than to those with dissimilar rates (Buller, LePoire, Aune, & Eloy, 1992). Also, the speaker who uses

A S K *the Researcher*

Accommodating for Effectiveness

I find your theory of communication accommodation really interesting, but I'm a really practical type of person and I'm taking this course to make myself a more effective communicator. So what I really want to know is how can I use this theory to make myself more effective socially and professionally, especially when talking with people who are culturally different from me?

Being seen to put effort after accommodating culturally dissimilar others is usually appreciated by them, leading to liking, respect, etc.,—but the trick is to get it just "right." Don't underaccommodate and be seen as uncaring or culturally insensitive, yet don't overdo it either (e.g., overaccommodating with an exaggerated accent to be "ethnically cool" or affiliative)—as that might be patronizing, invasive, or even ridiculing. Also, avoid accommodating to some stereotype of what you believe someone *should* sound like (given inferences about their ethnicity) but, rather, attune to how they actually do communicate. Finally, be wary of misattributing (and then getting upset at) their apparent divergence(s) from you as, necessarily, intended disrespect. Their nonaligning to your "language" and/or nonverbals may be more a statement of how they value and sustain their own distinctive heritage than any lack of interest in you as a person. Managing the converging–diverging balancing act is a critical element of communicative competence, be it between ethnicities, generations, genders, sexual orientations or whatever other cultural groupings.

For further information see Giles, H. & Noels, K. *Communication accommodation in intercultural encounters.* In J. Martin, T. Nakayama, & L. Flores (eds.), (2001). *Readings in cultural contexts* (2nd ed.) Mountain View: Mayfield, pp. 139–149.

Howard Giles (Ph.D., D.Sc., University of Bristol) is a professor of communication at the University of California, Santa Barbara, and teaches courses in intercultural, intergroup, and intergenerational communication. Giles is also a reserve sergeant with the Santa Barbara Police Department. HowieGiles@aol.com (Reprinted by permission of Dr. Howard Giles.)

language intensity similar to that of listeners is judged to have greater credibility than the speaker who uses intensity different from that of listeners (Aune & Kikuchi, 1993). Still another study found that roommates who were similar in communication competence and low in verbal aggressiveness were highest in roommate liking and satisfaction (Martin & Anderson, 1995).

As you adjust your communications, recognize that each culture has its own rules and customs for communicating (Barna, 1991; Ruben, 1985; Spitzberg, 1991). These rules identify what is appropriate and what is inappropriate. Thus, for example, in American culture you would call a person you wish to date three or four days in advance. In certain Asian cultures, you might call the person's parents weeks or even months in advance. In American culture you say, as a general friendly gesture and not as a specific invitation, "come over and pay us a visit." To members of other cultures, this comment is sufficient for the listeners to actually visit at their convenience. In some cultures, people show respect by avoiding direct eye contact with the person to whom they're speaking. In other cultures, this same eye avoidance would signal disinterest. If a young American girl is talking with an older Indonesian man, for example, she's expected to avoid direct eye contact. To an Indonesian, direct eye contact in this situation would be considered disrespectful. In some southern European cultures men walk arm in arm. In American culture this is considered inappropriate.

A good example of a series of rules for an extremely large and important culture appears in Table 2.2 on page 58, "Interpersonal Communication Tips between People with and without Disabilities."

Table 2.2 Interpersonal Communication Tips
Between people with and without disabilities

Other "Tips" tables focus on visual impairment (Chapter 1), hearing loss (Chapter 5), and speech and language disorders (Chapter 9); here we look at communication between those with general disabilities, for example, people in wheelchairs or with, say, cerebral palsy and those who have no such disability. The suggestions offered here are considered appropriate in the United States but not necessarily in other cultures. For example, although most people in the United States accept the phrase "person with mental retardation," it's considered offensive to many in the United Kingdom (Fernald, 1995).

If you're the one without such a disability:

1. Avoid negative terms and terms that define the person as disabled such as "the disabled" or "the handicapped." Instead say "person with a disability," always putting the person and not the disability first. Avoid terms that describe the person with a disability as abnormal; for example when you define the person without a disability as normal, you in effect say that the person with a disability isn't normal. Similarly, say "seizure" instead of "fit," "person with cerebral palsy," instead of "cerebral palsy victim," "wheelchair user" instead of "wheelchair bound."

2. Treat assistive devices such as wheelchairs, canes, walkers, or crutches as the personal property of the user; be careful not to move these out of your way since they're for the convenience of the person with the disability. Avoid leaning on a person's wheelchair, for example; it's similar to leaning on a person.

3. If you shake hands with others in a group, also shake hands with the person with the disability. Don't avoid shaking hands because the individual's hand is paralyzed, say.

4. Avoid talking about the person with a disability in the third person. For example, avoid saying, "Doesn't he get around beautifully with those new crutches." Always direct your comments directly to the individual.

5. Don't assume that people who have a disability (for example, if their speech is slurred as it may be with people who have cerebral palsy or cleft palate) are intellectually impaired; they definitely are not. So be especially careful not to talk down to such people, as research shows many people do (Unger, 2001). Similarly, use the same level of formality with people who have disabilities as you do with people who do not have such disabilities. Often, for example, people will be more informal and will, say, use a person's first name or even a diminutive ("Bobby" or "Katie") when addressing a person with disabilities when they will use a title plus last name to others.

6. If you're not sure how to act—for example, whether or not to offer walking assistance—ask: "Would you like me to help you into the dining room?" And, more important, accept the person's response. If he or she says "no," then that means no; don't insist.

7. If the person is in a wheelchair, it might be helpful for you to sit down or kneel down to get on the same eye level.

If you're the one with a disability:

1. Let the other person know if he or she can do anything to assist you in communicating. For example, if you want someone to speak in a louder voice, ask. If you want to relax and have someone push your wheelchair, say so.

2. Be patient and understanding with those who may not know how to act or what to say. Put them at ease as best you can.

3. If you detect discomfort in the other person, you might talk a bit about your disability to show that you're not uncomfortable and that you understand that others may not know how you feel. But, of course, you are under no obligation to educate the public so don't feel this is something you should or have to do. If it makes you more comfortable, then do it; otherwise, don't.

These suggestions are based on a number of sources, for example, http://www.empowermentzone.com/etiquet.txt (the website for the National Center for Access Unlimited), http://www.dol.gov/dol/odep/public/media/reports/fact/comucate.htm, http://www.dissvcs.uga.edu/com-peodis.html, and http://www.ucpa.org/ucp_generaldoc.cfm (all accessed 4/5/02).

Recognize Culture Shock   **Culture shock** refers to the psychological reaction you experience when you're in a culture very different from your own (Furnham & Bochner, 1986). Culture shock is normal; most people experience it when entering a new and different culture. Nevertheless, it can be unpleasant and frustrating. Part of this results from feelings of alienation, conspicuousness, and difference from everyone else. When you lack knowledge of the rules and customs of the new society, you cannot communicate effectively. You're apt to blunder frequently and seriously. In your culture shock you may not know basic things:

- how to ask someone for a favor or pay someone a compliment
- how to extend or accept an invitation for dinner
- how early or how late to arrive for an appointment
- how long you should stay when visiting someone
- how to distinguish seriousness from playfulness and politeness from indifference
- how to dress for an informal, formal, or business function
- how to order a meal in a restaurant or how to summon a waiter

TRY IT!
Apply your understanding of culture shock; go to **www.ablongman.com/devito**.

Anthropologist Kalervo Oberg (1960), who first used the term culture shock, notes that it occurs in stages. These stages are useful for examining many encounters with the new and the different. Going away to college, moving in together, or joining the military, for example, can also result in culture shock. In explaining culture shock, we use the example of moving away from home into your own apartment to illustrate its four stages.

Stage One: The Honeymoon   At first you experience fascination, even enchantment, with the new culture and its people. You finally have your own apartment. You're your own boss. Finally, on your own! When in groups of people who are culturally different, this stage is characterized by cordiality and friendship in these early and superficial relationships. Many tourists remain at this stage because their stay in foreign countries is so brief.

Stage Two: The Crisis   Here, the differences between your own culture and the new one create problems. No longer do you find dinner ready for you unless you do it yourself. Your clothes are not washed or ironed unless you do them yourself. Feelings of frustration and inadequacy come to the fore. This is the stage at which you experience the actual shock of the new culture. One study of foreign students coming from over 100 different countries and studying in 11 different countries found that 25 percent of the students experienced depression (Klineberg & Hull, 1979).

Stage Three: The Recovery   During this period you gain the skills necessary to function effectively. You learn how to shop, cook, and plan a meal. You find a local laundry and figure you'll learn how to iron later. You learn the language and ways of the new culture. Your feelings of inadequacy subside.

Stage Four: The Adjustment   At this final stage, you adjust to and come to enjoy the new culture and the new experiences. You may still experience periodic difficulties and strains, but on a whole, the experience is pleasant. Actually, you're now a pretty decent cook. You're even coming to enjoy it. You're making a good salary so why learn to iron?

People may also experience culture shock when they return to their original culture after living in a foreign culture, a kind of reverse culture shock (Jandt, 1999). Consider, for example, the Peace Corps volunteers who work in a rural and economically deprived area. Upon returning to Las Vegas or Beverly Hills, they too may experience culture shock. A sailor who serves long periods aboard ship and then returns to an isolated farming community might also experience culture shock. In these cases, however, the recovery period is shorter and the sense of inadequacy and frustration is less.

REVIEWING Key Terms and Concepts in Culture in Interpersonal Communication

This unit explored the nature of culture and identified some key concepts and principles that explain the role of culture in interpersonal communication.

Nature of Culture and Interpersonal Communication

What is culture and how is it transmitted?

■ **Culture:** The relatively specialized lifestyle of a group of people (values, beliefs, artifacts, ways of behaving) that are passed from one generation to the next by means of communication (not genes).

■ **Enculturation:** The process through which you learn the culture into which you're born.

■ **Acculturation:** The process by which you learn the rules and norms of a culture that is different from your native culture and that modifies your original or native culture.

How Cultures Differ

How do cultures differ from each other? How do these differences affect interpersonal communication?

■ In high-power-distance cultures, power is concentrated in the hands of a few and there is a great difference between those with and those without power. In low-power-distance cultures, the power is more equally shared throughout the citizenry.

■ In highly masculine cultures, men are viewed as strong, assertive, and focused on being successful, whereas women are viewed as modest, tender, and focused on the quality of life. In highly feminine cultures, men and women are viewed more similarly.

■ A collectivist culture emphasizes the group and subordinates the individual's goals to those of the group. An individualist culture emphasizes the individual and subordinates the group's goals to the individual's.

■ In high-context cultures, much of the information is in the context; in low-context cultures, information is explicitly stated in the verbal message.

■ Different cultures view time very differently.
  ■ Displaced and diffused time orientations identify how accurately and specifically time is viewed and defined.
  ■ Monochronic people do one thing at a time; polychronic people do several things at the same time.

Intercultural Communication

What is intercultural communication and what are its central principles?

■ Intercultural communication refers to communication between people who have different cultures, beliefs, values, and ways of behaving.

■ Some intercultural communication principles include: prepare yourself, reduce uncertainty, recognize differences (between yourself and others, within the culturally different group, and in meanings), adjust your communication, and recognize culture shock.

APPLYING Key Terms and Concepts in Culture in Interpersonal Communication

1. In this age of multiculturalism, how do you feel about Article II, Section 1 of the United States Constitution? The relevant section reads: "No person except a natural born citizen, or a citizen of the United States, at the time of the adoption of this Constitution, shall be eligible to the office of President."

2. It's been argued that in the United States women are more likely to view themselves as interdependents, having a more collectivist orientation, while men are more likely to view themselves as independents, having a more individualist orientation (Cross & Madson, 1997). Does your experience support this?

3. Visit one of the numerous travel websites (for example, **http://www.globalpassage.com/netstop, http://travel. epicurious.com/travel/g_cnt/home.html, http://www. travelchannel.com/, and http://www.lonelyplanet. com/**). What can you learn about intercultural communication from such sources?

4. Informal time terms (for example, soon, right away, early, in a while, as soon as possible) seem to create communication problems because they're ambiguous; different people will often give the terms different meanings. How might you go about reducing or eliminating the ambiguity created by these terms?

5. Visit one of the online news organizations (for example, **www.pbs.org/, www.npr.org, www.c/net.com, www. reu-tershealth.com,** or **www.cnnfn.com**) for a recent item on culture. Of what value might such information be to someone engaging in intercultural communication?

6. Has anyone ever assumed something about you because you were a member of a particular culture that was not true? Did you find this disturbing?

7. International students commonly experience culture shock. If you're an international student, describe your culture shock experiences. If you're not an international student, describe the culture shock you might experience if you were to study in another culture.

8. Do teachers and students or lawyers and witnesses or doctors and patients accommodate each other's communication style? In what direction is there likely to be greater accommodation? For example, is the teacher or the student more likely to accommodate the other?

9. Are the media and the Internet—because of their dominance by the United States—fostering an Americanization of different cultures? Do you see this as a loss of valuable

diversity? Or do you see it as the result of a democratic process whereby people select the values and customs they wish to adopt? Somewhere in between?

10. In a small group, with the class as a whole, or in a brief paper, discuss how your beliefs, attitudes, and values were influenced by the culture in which you were raised. Were you taught that penalties are incurred for going against these beliefs, attitudes, and values?

EXPERIENCING Key Terms and Concepts in Culture in Interpersonal Communication

Go to **www.ablongman.com/devito**.

These exercises enable you to explore a wide variety of cultural issues and their relationships to interpersonal communication.

(1) **Random Pairs** sets up specific intercultural dyads and asks you to consider how these dyads might influence communication. (2) **Cultural Beliefs** asks you to examine some of your own cultural beliefs. (3) **From Culture to Gender** explores the relationship of culture to gender beliefs. (4) **Cultural Identities** allows for the exploration of the strengths in the cultures represented by class members and others. (5) **The Sources of Your Cultural Beliefs** explores the origin of your own beliefs about a wide variety of issues. (6) **Confronting Intercultural Obstacles** presents situations that can cause intercultural conflict and asks you how you'd head off the potential conflict or resolve it.

RESEARCHING with Research Navigator Key Terms and Concepts in Culture in Interpersonal Communication

Go to **http://www.researchnavigator.com**.

Reading an article.

Read a popular or scholarly article on the nature of culture, cultural differences, or intercultural communication. On the basis of this article, what can you add to the discussion presented in this chapter?

Investigating key terms.

Investigate one of the key terms discussed in this chapter (for example, culture, power distances, masculine and feminine cultures, individual and collective orientation, high- and low-context cultures, language relativity, uncertainty reduction, culture

shock, intercultural communication, cultural imperialism, and cultural sensitivity). What additional insights can you provide?

Finding answers.

Try finding answers to one of the following questions or design a research study to answer it.

■ How does culture affect interpersonal communication?

■ How do cultures differ in their ways of communicating?

■ What are some of the culturally influenced communication differences between men and women?

■ Why is intercultural communication often more difficult than communicating with members of your own culture?

■ Are persons with greater education more likely to enter intercultural relationships than less educated persons?

3 The Self in Interpersonal Communication

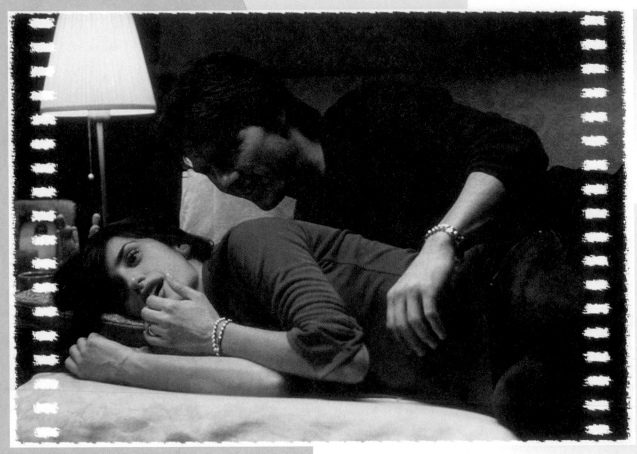

Vanilla Sky (2001)

In order to have a conversation with someone you must reveal yourself.

—James Baldwin

Dimensions of the Self
Self-Disclosure
Communication Apprehension

David Aames (Tom Cruise) *is a wealthy, attractive, and rich magazine owner who, through some mishap, becomes disfigured.* Vanilla Sky *illustrates how the person you think you are can influence what you think you can accomplish and what you actually do. And it influences your view of relationships, which is well illustrated in the film when a friend that David discarded is suddenly needed. This chapter addresses an important aspect of interpersonal communication: the self. Here we look at the nature of the self, self-disclosure (whereby you reveal yourself to others), and apprehension (the fear or anxiety that often accompanies communication).*

DIMENSIONS OF THE SELF

Of all aspects of the communication process, the self is the most important. Here we consider three dimensions of the self: self-concept (the way you see yourself), self-awareness (your insight into and knowledge about yourself), and self-esteem (the value you place on yourself). We will also look at how these dimensions influence and are influenced by the way you communicate.

Self-Concept

You no doubt have an image of who you are; this is your **self-concept.** It consists of your feelings and thoughts about your strengths and weaknesses, your abilities and limitations, and your aspirations and worldview (Black, 1999). Your self-concept develops from at least four sources: (1) the image of you that others have and that they reveal to you, (2) the comparisons you make between yourself and others, (3) the teachings of your culture, and (4) the way you interpret and evaluate your own thoughts and behaviors (see Figure 3.1 on page 64).

Others' Images of You   If you wished to see the way your hair looked, you would likely look in a mirror. But what would you do if you wanted to see how friendly or how assertive you are? According to Charles Horton Cooley's (1922) concept of the *looking-glass self,* you would look at the image of yourself that others reveal to you through the way they treat you and react to you (Hensley, 1996).

You'd look especially to those who are most significant in your life—to your *significant others.* As a child, you'd look to your parents and then to your teachers. As an adult, you might look to your friends, romantic partners, and colleagues at work. If these significant others think highly of you, you'll see this positive image of yourself reflected in their behaviors; if they think little of you, you'll see a more negative image. These reflections that you see in others help you define your self-concept.

Social Comparisons   Another way you develop your self-concept is by comparing yourself with others. When you want to gain insight into who you are and how effective or competent you are, you probably look to your peers. For example, after an examination you probably want to know how you performed relative to the other students in your class. If you play on a baseball team, it's important to know your batting average in comparison with others on the team. You gain an additional perspective when you see your score in comparison with the scores of your peers.

The Sources of Self-Concept

This diagram depicts the four sources of self-concept, the four contributors to how you see yourself: others' images of you, social comparisons, cultural teachings, and your own observations, interpretations, and evaluations. As you read about self-concept, consider the influence of each factor throughout your life. Which factor influenced you most as a pre-teen? Which influences you the most now? Which will influence you the most 25 or 30 years from now?

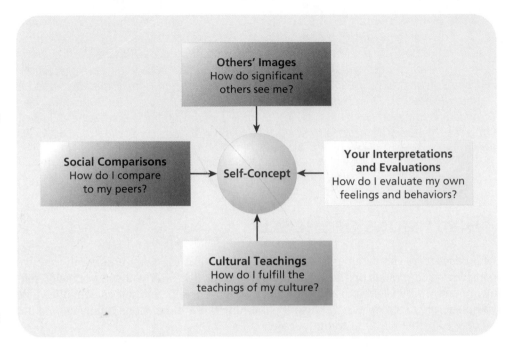

Cultural Teachings   Through your parents, teachers, and the media, your culture instills in you a variety of beliefs, values, and attitudes—about success (how you define it and how you should achieve it); about your religion, race, or nationality; about the ethical principles you should follow in business and in your personal life. These teachings provide benchmarks against which you can measure yourself. Your success in, for example, achieving what your culture defines as success will contribute to a positive self-concept. Your failure to achieve what your culture teaches (for example, not being married by the time you're 30) will contribute to a negative self-concept.

When you demonstrate the qualities that your culture (or your organization) teaches, you'll see yourself as a cultural success and will be rewarded by other members of the culture (or organization). Seeing yourself as culturally successful and getting rewarded by others will contribute positively to your self-concept. When you fail to demonstrate such qualities, you're more likely to see yourself as a cultural failure and to be punished by other members of the culture, contributing to a more negative self-concept.

You belong to a variety of cultures. Each of these cultures influences your attitudes and beliefs, and you may find that some of these influences contradict each other. For example, you may have been taught that it's important to be financially successful, but that money is the root of all evil. You may have been taught to be the best in your field, but also to be cooperative and helpful to others, perhaps even those you are competing against. Such contradictory beliefs may easily cause intrapersonal conflicts. In extreme cases, you may decide to reject the attitudes and beliefs of one culture—often "the old world" culture—in favor of those of the culture with which you feel more comfortable.

Your Own Interpretations and Evaluations   Much in the way others form images of you based on what you do, you also react to your own behavior; you interpret and evaluate it. These interpretations and evaluations help to form your self-concept. For example, let us say you believe that lying is wrong. If you lie, you will evaluate this behavior in terms of your internalized beliefs about lying. You'll thus react negatively to your own behavior. You may, for example, experience guilt if your behavior contradicts your beliefs. In contrast, let's say you tutored another student and helped him or her pass a course. You would probably evaluate this behavior positively; you would feel good about this behavior and, as a result, about yourself.

Self-Awareness

Your **self-awareness** represents the extent to which you know yourself. Understanding how your self-concept develops is one way to increase your self-awareness: The more you understand about why you view yourself as you do, the more you will understand who you are. Additional insight is gained by looking at self-awareness through the Johari model of the self, or your four selves (Luft, 1984).

Your Four Selves   Self-awareness is neatly explained by the model of the four selves, the **Johari window.** This model, presented in Figure 3.2, has four basic areas, or quadrants, each of which represents a somewhat different self. The Johari model emphasizes that the several aspects of the self are not separate pieces but are interactive parts of a whole. Each part is dependent on each other part. Like that of interpersonal communication, this model of the self is transactional.

The Open Self   The *open self* represents all the information, behaviors, attitudes, feelings, desires, motivations, and ideas that you and others know. The type of infor-

	Known to self	**Not known to self**
Known to others	**Open self** Information about yourself that you and others know	**Blind self** Information about yourself that you don't know but that others do know
Not known to others	**Hidden self** Information about yourself that you know but others don't know	**Unknown self** Information about yourself that neither you nor others know

The Johari Window

Visualize this model as representing your self. The entire model is of constant size, but each section can vary, from very small to very large. As one section becomes smaller, one or more of the others grows larger. Similarly, as one section grows, one or more of the others must get smaller. For example, if you reveal a secret and thereby enlarge your open self, this shrinks your hidden self. Further, this disclosure may in turn lead to a decrease in the size of your blind self (if your disclosure influences other people to reveal what they know about you but that you have not known). How would you draw your Johari window to show yourself when interacting with your parents? With your friends? With your college instructors? The name Johari, by the way, comes from the first names of the two people who developed the model, Joseph Luft and Harry Ingham.
(*Source:* From *Group Processes: An Introduction to Group Dynamics* by Joseph Luft, 1984, p. 60. Reprinted by permission of Mayfield Publishing Company, Mountain View, CA.)

mation included here might range from your name, skin color, and sex to your age, political and religious affiliations, and financial situation. Your open self will vary in size, depending on the situation you're in and the person with whom you're interacting. Some people, for example, make you feel comfortable and supported; to them, you open yourself wide, but to others you may prefer to leave most of yourself closed.

Communication depends on the degree to which you open yourself to others and to yourself (Luft, 1969). If you don't allow other people to know you (thus keeping your open self small), communication between you and others becomes difficult, if not impossible. You can communicate meaningfully only to the extent that you know others and yourself. To improve communication, work first on enlarging the open self.

The Blind Self   The *blind self* represents all the things about yourself that others know but of which you're ignorant. These may vary from the relatively insignificant habit of saying "You know," rubbing your nose when you get angry, or having a distinct body odor, to things as significant as defense mechanisms, fight strategies, or repressed experiences.

Some people have a very large blind self; they seem totally oblivious of their faults and sometimes (though not as often) their virtues. Others seem overly eager to have a small blind self. They seek therapy at every turn and join every self-help group. Some believe they know everything there is to know about themselves, that they have reduced the blind self to zero. Most of us lie between these extremes.

Communication and interpersonal relations are generally enhanced as the blind self becomes smaller. But be careful of trying to help someone else "discover" his or her blind self. This could cause serious problems. Such a revelation might trigger a breakdown in defenses; it might force people to admit their own jealousy or prejudice when they're not psychologically ready to deal with such information. Such revelations are best dealt with cautiously or under the guidance of trained professionals.

The Hidden Self   The *hidden self* contains all that you know of yourself and of others that you keep secret. In any interaction, this area includes everything you don't want to reveal, whether it's relevant or irrelevant to the conversation. At the extremes, we have the overdisclosers and the underdisclosers. The overdisclosers tell all. They tell you their marital difficulties, their children's problems, their financial status, and just about everything else. The underdisclosers tell nothing. They talk about you but not about themselves.

The problem with these extremes is that individuals don't distinguish between those who should and those who shouldn't be privy to such information. They also don't distinguish among the types of information they should or should not disclose. The vast majority of people, however, keep certain things hidden and disclose others; they make disclosures to some people and not to others. They're *selective* disclosers.

The Unknown Self   The *unknown self* represents truths about yourself that neither you nor others know. The existence of this self is inferred from a number of sources. Sometimes it's revealed through temporary changes brought about by special experimental conditions such as hypnosis or sensory deprivation. Sometimes this area is revealed by certain projective tests or dreams. Mostly, however, it's revealed by the fact that you're constantly learning things about yourself that you didn't know before (things that were previously in the unknown self)—for example, that you become defensive when someone asks you a question or voices disagreement, or that you compliment others in the hope of being complimented back.

Although you cannot easily manipulate this area, recognize that it does exist and that there are things about yourself and about others that you don't know and may never know.

Increasing Self-Awareness   You can increase your self-awareness in a number of ways: Ask yourself about yourself, listen to others, actively seek information about yourself, see your different selves, and increase your open self.

Ask Yourself about Yourself   One way to ask yourself about yourself is to take an informal "Who am I?" test (Bugental & Zelen, 1950). Title a piece of paper "Who Am I?" and write 10, 15, or 20 times "I am . . . ." Then complete each of the sentences. Try not to give only positive or socially acceptable responses; just respond with what comes to mind first. Take another piece of paper and divide it into two columns; label one column "Strengths" and the other column "Weaknesses." Fill in each column as quickly as possible. Using these first two tests as a base, take a third piece of paper, title it "Self-Improvement Goals," and complete the statement "I want to improve my . . ." as many times as you can in five minutes. Since you're constantly changing, these self-perceptions and goals also change and so must be updated frequently.

Your cultural background will significantly influence your responses to this simple "Who Am I?" test. In one study, for example, participants from Malaysia (a collectivist culture) and from Australia and Great Britain (individualist cultures) completed this test. Malaysians produced significantly more group self-descriptions and fewer idiocentric self-descriptions than did the Australian or British members (Bochner, 1994; also see Radford, Mann, Ohta, & Nakane, 1993). If you completed the "Who Am I?" test, can you identify responses that were influenced by your individualist or collectivist orientation? Did other cultural factors influence your statements?

Listen to Others   You can learn a lot about yourself by seeing yourself as others do. Conveniently, others are constantly giving you the very feedback you need to increase self-awareness. In every interpersonal interaction, people comment on you in some way—on what you do, what you say, how you look. Sometimes these comments are explicit; most often they're discoverable in the way in which others look at you, in what they talk about, in their interest in what you say. Pay close attention to this kind of information (verbal and nonverbal) and use it to increase your own self-awareness.

Actively Seek Information about Yourself   Actively seek out information to reduce your blind self. You need not be so obvious as to say, "Tell me about myself" or "What do you think of me?" Also, you don't want to seek such information from just anyone. People who are overly negative, who have personal agendas, or who know you only slightly are generally poor sources. But you can use everyday situations to gain self-information: "Do you think I was assertive enough when asking for the raise?" Or "Would I be thought too forward if I invited myself for dinner?" Do not, of course, seek this information constantly; your friends would quickly find others with whom to interact. But you can make use of some situations—perhaps those in which you're particularly unsure of what to do or how you appear—to reduce your blind self and increase self-awareness.

See Your Different Selves   Each of your friends and relatives views you differently; to each you're a somewhat different person. Yet you are really all of these selves. Practice seeing yourself as do the people with whom you interact. For starters, visualize how

WEB EXPLORATION
To learn more about actively seeking information about yourself, go to www.ablongman.com/devito.

Uses and Gratification Theory

In much the same way that you enter relationships to gain some kind of reward, you use the media to gain rewards. Rewards can be both immediate and delayed. You may watch a particular television program because it satisfies your immediate need for information or entertainment. Or you may read a book because it contributes to satisfying a delayed need you have to become a writer. Research claims you derive four general gratifications from media (Dominick, 2000):

■ learning something—finding out what the new tax laws will involve or how movie reviewers rate the film you want to see
■ diversion—stimulating you to release emotional energy while, say, watching a football game
■ affiliation—going to the movies together or talking about the developments on "Days of Our Lives"
■ withdrawal—escaping from responsibilities and other people

But different media require different amounts of effort. For example, there's less effort required—less expense, less time lost—in watching television than in going to a movie. There's less effort in buying a book from the Internet than in driving to a brick-and-mortar bookstore.

Media researchers propose that you're more likely to select those media that provide great rewards while requiring little effort and are less likely to select media that promise small rewards and require great effort. Internet service providers and online retailers seem to recognize the validity of this theory, called the uses and gratification theory, and are highly motivated to make online access and buying effortless and enjoyable (Ruggiero, 2000).

Follow Up   How do you use the media to get the rewards you want with the least possible effort?

you're seen by your mother, your father, your teachers, your best friend, the stranger you sat next to on the bus, your employer, your neighbor's child. Because you're a composite of all these views, it's important that you periodically see yourself through the eyes of others. The experience will give you new and valuable perspectives on yourself.

Increase Your Open Self   When you increase your open self and reveal yourself to others, you also reveal yourself to yourself. At the very least, you bring into clearer focus what you may have buried within. As you discuss yourself, you may see connections that you had previously missed, and with the aid of feedback from others you may gain still more insight. Also, by increasing the open self you increase the likelihood that a meaningful and intimate dialogue will develop; through such interactions you best get to know yourself. Do, however, consider the risks involved in such self-disclosures.

Self-Esteem

How much do you like yourself? How valuable a person do you think you are? How competent do you think you are? The answers to these questions reflect your **self-esteem,** the value you place on yourself. People who have high self-esteem, for example, are going to communicate this throughout their verbal and nonverbal messages. The ways they phrase their ideas and questions or the way they hold their head and maintain eye contact are likely to differ greatly from the way the person with low self-esteem would communicate. Similarly, people with different views of themselves will develop and maintain relationships with friends, lovers, and family differently. As you read this chapter, think about your own relationships and how the way you see yourself influences them.

View point Recently self-esteem has come under attack (for example, Bushman & Baumeister, 1998; Baumeister, Bushman, & Campbell, 2000; Bower, 2001; Coover & Murphy, 2000; Hewitt, 1998). Much current thinking holds that high self-esteem is not desirable: It does nothing to improve academic performance and it does not predict success, and, in fact, may lead to antisocial (especially aggressive) behavior. On the other hand, it's difficult to even imagine a person functioning successfully without positive self-feelings. How do you feel about the benefits or liabilities of self-esteem? Would you have included this topic in this text? Why?

Self-esteem is important, it is thought, because success breeds success (but see Viewpoint above). When you feel good about yourself—about who you are and what you're capable of doing—you will perform better. When you think like a success, you're more likely to act like a success. When you think you're a failure, you're more likely to act like a failure. Increasing self-esteem will, therefore, help you to function more effectively in school, in interpersonal relationships, and in careers. Here are a few suggestions for increasing self-esteem.

Attack Your Self-Destructive Beliefs   Being as honest with yourself as you can, ask yourself if you hold beliefs such as these

I SEE

1. I must be perfect.
2. I always have to be emotionally strong.
3. I need to please everyone always.
4. I need to hurry up, to get more done.
5. I must try hard in whatever I do.

As you can see, these beliefs are unrealistic (Butler, 1981). While it would be nice to be perfect, it is not a logical or realistic goal. Similarly, it would be nice to be emotionally strong or to please others, but it is not always possible. Because these kinds of beliefs set up unattainable and unrealistic goals, they inevitably lead you to fail and consequently can damage your self-esteem and prevent you from building meaningful and productive relationships.

Recognizing that you may have internalized self-destructive beliefs is a first step toward eliminating them. A second step involves recognizing that these beliefs are unrealistic and self-defeating. Psychotherapist Albert Ellis (1988; Ellis & Harper, 1975) and other cognitive therapists (for example, Beck, 1988) would argue that you can accomplish this by understanding why these beliefs are unrealistic and substituting more realistic ones. For example, following Ellis, you might try replacing an unrealistic desire to please everyone in everything you do with a more realistic belief that it would be nice if others were pleased with you but it certainly is not essential. A third step is giving yourself permission to fail, to be less than perfect, to be normal.

Do recognize that it's the unrealistic nature of these "drivers" that creates problems. Drivers are unrealistic beliefs that may motivate you to act in ways that are self-defeating (Butler, 1981). Certainly, trying hard and being strong are not unhealthy when they're realistic. It's only when they become absolute—when you try to be everything to everyone—that they become impossible to achieve and create problems.

Secure Affirmation

It is helpful to remind yourself of your successes, to focus on your good acts, good deeds, positive qualities, strengths and virtues, and your productive and meaningful relationships with friends, loved ones, and relatives (Aronson, Cohen, & Nail, 1998; Aronson, Wilson, & Akert, 1999). There are plenty of people who will remind you of your failures and weaknesses; your job is to engage in self-affirmation.

The idea behind this advice is that the way you talk to yourself will influence what you think of yourself. If you talk positively about yourself, you will come to feel more positive about yourself. If you tell yourself that you're a success, that others like you, that you will succeed on the next test, and that you will be welcomed when asking for a date, you will soon come to feel positive about yourself. Self-affirmations, such as the following, are often recommended:

- I'm a worthy person but there's room for improvement.
- I'm generally responsible and can be depended on.
- I'm capable of loving and being loved.
- I deserve good things to happen to me.
- I can forgive myself for mistakes and misjudgments.
- I deserve to be treated with respect.

However, not all researchers would agree with this advice. Some argue that such affirmations—although extremely popular in self-help books—may not be very helpful. If you have low self-esteem, you're not going to believe yourself because you don't have a very high opinion of yourself to begin with (Paul, 2001). The alternative to self-affirmation is to secure affirmation from others. You'd do this by, for example, becoming more interpersonally competent and by interacting with more positive people. In this way you'll get more positive feedback from others, which, it's argued, is more helpful than self-talk in raising self-esteem.

Seek Out Nourishing People

Psychologist Carl Rogers (1970) drew a distinction between *noxious* and *nourishing* people. Noxious people criticize and find fault with just about everything. Not surprisingly, these people are difficult to be around. More important, however, is that with time you may come to believe that their criticism and fault-finding are justified. When that happens, your self-esteem is likely to diminish.

Nourishing people, on the other hand, are positive. They're optimists. They reward you, they stroke you, they make you feel good about yourself. Here too, with time, you'll come to believe these compliments and positive statements and as a result are likely to raise your self-esteem.

Work on Projects That Will Result in Success

Some people want to fail, or so it seems. Often, they select projects that will result in failure. Perhaps the projects are too large or too difficult. In any event, they're impossible. Instead, select projects that will result in success. Each success helps build self-esteem. Each success makes the next success a little easier. This doesn't mean that you shouldn't dream big, only that in some cases you may be tempted to try the impossible and be hurt when you don't succeed.

When a project does fail, recognize that this doesn't mean that you're a failure. Everyone fails somewhere along the line. Failure is something that happens; it's not something inside you. Further, failing once does not mean that you will fail the next time. So put failure in perspective. Don't make it an excuse for not trying again.

SELF-DISCLOSURE

One of the most important forms of interpersonal communication that you could engage in is talking about yourself, or **self-disclosure.** Self-disclosure refers to your communicating information about yourself to another person. It may involve information about (1) your values, beliefs, and desires ("I believe in reincarnation"), (2) your behavior ("I committed grand larceny but was never caught"), or (3) your self-qualities or characteristics ("I'm dyslexic"). Overt and carefully planned statements about yourself as well as slips of the tongue would be classified as self-disclosing communications. Similarly, you could self-disclose nonverbally by, for example, wearing gang colors, a wedding ring, or a shirt with slogans that reveal your political or social concerns. Self-disclosure may also involve your reactions to the feelings of others: for example, when you tell your friend that you're sorry she was fired.

Self-disclosure occurs in all forms of communication, not just interpersonal. It frequently occurs in small group settings, in public speeches, and the increasingly common television talk show. As these examples make clear, self-disclosure can occur in face-to-face settings as well as through television and the Internet. In chat groups, for example, a great deal of self-disclosure goes on, as it does when people reveal themselves in personal e-mail and in newsgroup and listserv submissions. In fact, research finds that reciprocal self-disclosure occurs more quickly and at higher levels online than it does in face-to-face interactions (Levine, 2000; Joinson, 2001).

You probably self-disclose for a variety of reasons. Perhaps you feel the need for catharsis, to get rid of guilt feelings, or to confess some wrongdoing. Or you might wish to make yourself look good, so you might self-disclose your good qualities by giving examples of your bravery or compassion or determination. You might also disclose to help the listener, to show the listener, for example, how you dealt with an addiction or succeeded in getting a promotion. Of course, you may self-disclose to encourage relationship growth, or to maintain or repair a relationship, or even as a strategy for ending a relationship.

Although self-disclosure may occur as a single message—for example, you tell a stranger on a train that you're thinking about getting a divorce—it's best viewed as a *developing* process in which information is exchanged between people in a relationship over the period of their relationship (Spencer, 1993, 1994). If we view it as a developing process, we can then appreciate how self-disclosure changes as the relationship changes, for example, from initial contact through involvement to intimacy and then perhaps to deterioration or dissolution. We can also appreciate how self-disclosure will differ depending on the type of relationship you have with another person, for example, whether the other person is your friend, parent, child, or counselor.

Self-disclosure may involve information that you communicate to others freely or that you normally keep hidden. It may supply information ("I earn $46,000") or reveal feelings ("I'm feeling very depressed").

Self-disclosure involves at least one other individual; it cannot be an *intra*personal communication act. To qualify as self-disclosure, the information must be received and understood by another individual. As you can appreciate, self-disclosure can vary from the relatively insignificant ("I'm a Sagittarius") to the highly revealing and deeply personal ("I'm currently in an abusive relationship" or "I'm almost always depressed"). The remaining discussion of this important concept will be more meaningful if you first take the accompanying self-disclosure test.

TEST YOURSELF   *How Willing to Self-Disclose Are You?*

Respond to each of the following questions by indicating the likelihood that you would answer them (and thus disclose such items of information) to, say, other members of this class. Use the following scale: 1 = would definitely self-disclose, 2 = would probably self-disclose, 3 = don't know, 4 = would probably not self-disclose, and 5 = would definitely not self-disclose.

_____   1. What are your hobbies?
_____   2. What are your favorite foods?
_____   3. What is your educational background and how do you feel about it?
_____   4. What are some of your personal characteristics that you are proud of and that give satisfaction?
_____   5. What was the happiest moment of your life?
_____   6. What did your parents do in raising you that you would consider mistakes?
_____   7. Why do some people dislike you?
_____   8. What aspects of your personality do you dislike?
_____   9. With whom have you been sexually intimate?
_____   10. With whom would you most like to have a romantic affair?

▶ **How did you do?**   Obviously there are no right or wrong answers to these statements. The major purpose of this test is to stimulate you to think about what you would and would not disclose. These questions were drawn from Jourard's (1971a) list of self-disclosure topics and, according to Jourard, illustrate three levels of disclosure; questions 1–3 illustrate low levels of intimacy, questions 4–6 illustrate moderate levels, and questions 7–10 illustrate high levels. Does your own willingness to self-disclose depend on the intimacy of the topic? For example, would you be most willing to answer questions 1–3 and least willing to answer questions 7–10?

▶ **What will you do?**   This test, and ideally its discussion with others who also complete it, should get you started thinking about your own self-disclosing behavior, especially the factors that influence it. Can you identify what factors most influence your willingness or unwillingness to disclose each of these items of information? ●

WEB EXPLORATION
To learn more about influences on self-disclosure, go to
www.ablongman.com/devito.

Influences on Self-Disclosure

A number of factors influence whether or not you disclose, what you disclose, and to whom you disclose. Among the most important factors are who you are, your culture, your gender, who your listeners are, and what your topic is.

Who You Are   Highly sociable and extroverted people self-disclose more than those who are less sociable and more introverted. People who are apprehensive about talking in general also self-disclose less than do those who are more comfortable in communicating.

Competent people and those with high self-esteem engage in self-disclosure more than less competent people and those with low self-esteem. Perhaps competent people have greater self-confidence and more positive things to reveal. Similarly, their self-confidence may make them more willing to risk possible negative reactions (McCroskey & Wheeless, 1976; Dolgin, Meyer, & Schwartz, 1991).

Increasing Interpersonal Effectiveness
Flexibility

Flexibility is a quality of thinking and behaving in which you vary your messages based on the unique situation. One test of flexibility asks you to consider how true you believe certain statements are, for example, "People should be frank and spontaneous in conversation," or "When angry, a person should say nothing rather than say something he or she will be sorry for later." The "preferred" answer to all such questions is "sometimes true," underscoring the importance of flexibility in all interpersonal situations (Hart, Carlson, & Eadie, 1980). A more recent test appears on the website at www.ablongman.com/devito.

Increasing Flexibility   Here are a few ways to cultivate flexibility.

■ *Realize that no two situations or people are exactly alike.* Ask yourself what is different about this situation or person and take these differences into consideration as you construct your messages.

■ *Realize that communication always takes place in a context (Chapter 1).* Ask yourself what is unique about this specific context and how this uniqueness should influence your messages.

■ *Realize that everything is in a state of flux.* Just because the way you communicated last month was effective, doesn't mean it will be effective today or tomorrow. Realize, too, that sudden changes (the death of a lover or a fatal illness) will influence what messages are considered appropriate.

■ *Realize that every situation offers you different options for communicating.* Think about these options and try to predict the effects each option might have.

Your Culture   Different cultures view self-disclosure differently. People in the United States, for example, disclose more than do those in Great Britain, Germany, Japan, or Puerto Rico (Gudykunst, 1983). American students also disclose more than do students from nine different Middle East countries (Jourard, 1971a). Similarly, American students self-disclose more on a variety of controversial issues and also self-disclose more to different types of people than do Chinese students (Chen, 1992). Chinese students consider more topics to be taboo and inappropriate for self-disclosure than their British colleagues (Goodwin & Lee, 1994). Among the Kabre of Togo, secrecy is a major part of their everyday interactions (Piot, 1993).

Some cultures (especially those high in masculinity) view disclosing one's inner feelings as a weakness. Among some groups, for example, it would be considered out of place for a man to cry at a happy occasion like a wedding, but that same display of emotion would go unnoticed in some Latin cultures. Similarly, in Japan it's considered undesirable for colleagues to reveal personal information, whereas in much of the United States it's expected (Barnlund, 1989; Hall & Hall, 1987).

In some cultures—for example, Mexican—there is a strong emphasis on discussing all matters in a positive mode, and this undoubtedly influences the way Mexicans approach self-disclosure as well. Negative self-disclosures, in contrast, are usually made to close intimates and then only after considerable time has elapsed in a relationship. This pattern is consistent with evidence showing that self-disclosure and trust are positively related (Wheeless & Grotz, 1977). Additional research finds that the Hispanic reluctance to disclose negative issues such as one's positive HIV status is creating serious problems in preventing and treating HIV infection (Szapocznik, 1995).

These differences aside, there are also important similarities across cultures. For example, people from Great Britain, Germany, the United States, and Puerto Rico are all more apt to disclose personal information—hobbies, interests, attitudes, and opinions on politics and religion—than information on finances, sex, personality, and interpersonal relationships (Jourard, 1968, 1971a, 1971b). Similarly, one study showed self-

A S K *the Researcher*

Becoming More Flexible

I completed your flexibility scale and, unfortunately, I came out "much less flexible than average." Is there anything I can do to become more flexible in my communications and as a person?

Understanding the importance of being flexible and wanting to be more flexible are important first steps in becoming more flexible. Before you can increase your flexibility, you must (a) become aware that in any given situation there are options and alternative ways of communicating available, (b) be willing to adapt to different people and situations, and (c) have the confidence to adapt and possibly try new behaviors.

One suggestion for improving flexibility would include thinking beforehand of how you could communicate in different ways in a given situation. Flexibility requires that you be able to adapt to the demands of the specific situation; there is no one right or wrong way of communicating. Another suggestion would be to embrace rather than avoid different and new experiences. Talk to people you would normally not talk to, attend events that may not fall under your primary interests, try doing an activity you have not attempted before.

For further information see M. M. Martin and C. M. Anderson, "The Cognitive Flexibility Scale: Three Validity Studies," *Communication Reports* 11 (1998): 1–10 and M. M. Martin and R. B. Rubin, "A New Measure of Cognitive Flexibility," *Psychological Reports* 76 (1995): 623–626.

Matt Martin (Ph.D., Kent State University) is an associate professor of communication studies at West Virginia University and teaches courses in interpersonal and nonverbal communication and conducts research in communication traits, including flexibility and aggressiveness. mmartin@wvu.edu (Reprinted by permission of Dr. Matt Martin.)

---

disclosure patterns between American males to be virtually identical to those between Korean males (Won-Doornink, 1991).

Your Gender The popular stereotype of gender differences in self-disclosure emphasizes the male reluctance to speak about himself. For the most part, research supports this view and shows that women disclose more than men. This is especially true in same-sex dyads; women disclose more intimately (and with more emotion) when talking with other women than with men (Shaffer, Pegalis, & Bazzini, 1996). Men and women, however, make negative disclosures about equally (Naifeh & Smith, 1984).

More specifically, women disclose more than men about their previous romantic relationships, their feelings about their closest same-sex friends, their greatest fears, and what they don't like about their partners (Sprecher, 1987). Women also seem to increase the depth of their self-disclosures as the relationship becomes more intimate, whereas men seem not to change their self-disclosure levels. Men, for example, have more taboo topics that they will not disclose to their friends than do women (Goodwin & Lee, 1994). Finally, women even self-disclose more to members of the extended family than do men (Komarovsky, 1964; Argyle & Henderson, 1985; Moghaddam, Taylor, & Wright, 1993). One notable exception occurs in initial encounters. Here men will disclose more intimately than women, perhaps "in order to control the relationship's development" (Derlega, Winstead, Wong, & Hunter, 1985).

Men and women give different reasons for avoiding self-disclosure (Rosenfeld, 1979), but both genders share this reason: "If I disclose, I might project an image I don't want to project." In a society in which image is so important—in which one's image is often the basis for success or failure—this reason is not surprising. Other reasons for avoiding self-disclosure, however, are unique to men or women. Lawrence Rosenfeld (1979) sums up males' reasons for self-disclosure avoidance: "If I disclose to you, I might project an image I don't want to project, which could make me look bad and cause me to lose control over you. This might go so far as to affect relationships I have

 As might be expected, husbands and wives self-disclose to each other more than they do to any other person or group of persons. Marital status, at least for men, even affects self-disclosure to friends. Married men disclose significantly less to friends than do unmarried men. The marital status of women, however, does not affect the amount of their disclosure to friends. One explanation of this difference may be that women "place a higher value on personal relationships than men do, with the result that women continue friendships even when basic intimacy needs are being met by a spouse, while married men allow friendships to atrophy" (Tschann, 1988). What do you think of this explanation?

with people other than you." Men's principal objective in avoiding self-disclosure is to maintain control. The general reason women avoid self-disclosure, says Rosenfeld, is that "If I disclose to you, I might project an image I don't want to project, such as my being emotionally ill, which you might use against me and which might hurt our relationship." Women's principal objective for avoiding self-disclosure is "to avoid personal hurt and problems with the relationship."

Your Listeners   Self-disclosure occurs more readily in small groups than in large groups. Dyads or groups of two people are the most hospitable groups for self-disclosure. With one listener, you can attend to the responses carefully. You can monitor the disclosures, continuing if there is support from your listener and stopping if there isn't. With more than one listener, such monitoring becomes difficult since the listeners' responses are sure to vary.

Sometimes self-disclosure takes place in group and public speaking situations. In consciousness-raising groups and in meetings like those of Alcoholics Anonymous, members may disclose their most intimate problems to 10 or perhaps hundreds of people at one time. In these situations, group members are pledged to be totally supportive. These and similar groups are devoted specifically to encouraging self-disclosure and to giving each other support for the disclosures.

Because you disclose, generally at least, on the basis of support you receive, you probably disclose to people you like (Derlega, Winstead, Wong, & Greenspan, 1987; Collins & Miller, 1994) and to people you trust (Wheeless & Grotz, 1977). You probably also come to like those to whom you disclose (Berg & Archer, 1983; Collins & Miller, 1994). Not surprisingly, you're more likely to disclose to people who are close to you in age (Parker & Parrott, 1995).

At times self-disclosure occurs more in temporary than permanent relationships—for example, between strangers on a train or plane, a kind of "in-flight intimacy" (McGill, 1985). In this situation, two people set up an intimate self-disclosing relationship during a brief travel period, but they don't pursue it beyond that point. In a similar way, you might set up a relationship with one or several people on the Internet and engage in significant disclosure. Perhaps knowing you'll never see these other people and that they will never know where you live or work or what you look like makes it a bit easier.

You're more likely to disclose when the person you're with discloses. This dyadic effect (what one person does, the other person does likewise) probably leads you to feel more secure and reinforces your own self-disclosing behavior. Disclosures are also more intimate when they're made in response to the disclosures of others (Berg & Archer, 1983).

Your Topic   You're more likely to disclose about some topics than others. For example, you're probably more likely to self-disclose information about your job or hobbies than about your sex life or financial situation (Jourard, 1968, 1971a). You're also more likely to disclose favorable information than unfavorable information. Generally, the more personal and negative the topic, the less likely you would be to self-disclose.

Rewards of Self-Disclosure

Research shows that self-disclosure helps to increase self-knowledge, communication and relationship effectiveness, and physiological well-being.

Self-Knowledge   One reward of self-disclosure is that you gain a new perspective on yourself, a deeper understanding of your own behavior. Through self-disclosure you may bring to consciousness a great deal that you might otherwise keep from conscious analysis. For example, as Tony talks about the difficulties he had living with an alcoholic father, he may remember details of his early life or entertain new feelings.

Even self-acceptance is difficult without self-disclosure. You accept yourself largely through the eyes of others. Through self-disclosure and subsequent support, you may be in a better position to see the positive responses to you. Thus, you're more likely to respond by developing a more positive self-concept.

Communication and Relationship Effectiveness   You understand the messages of another person largely to the extent that you understand the person. For example, you can tell when a friend is serious and when joking, when someone is being sarcastic out of fear and when out of resentment. Self-disclosure is an essential condition for getting to know one another.

Couples who engaged in significant self-disclosure are found to remain together longer than couples who don't (Sprecher, 1987). Self-disclosure helps you achieve a closer relationship with the person to whom you self-disclose and increases relationship satisfaction (Schmidt & Cornelius, 1987; Meeks, Hendrick, & Hendrick, 1998). Within a sexual relationship, self-disclosure increases sexual rewards and general relationship satisfaction. These two benefits increase sexual satisfaction (Byers & Demmons, 1999). Without self-disclosure, meaningful relationships seem impossible to develop.

Interestingly enough, you also come to increase your affection for your partner when you self-disclose. Think about your own self-disclosures. Have you come to increase your liking for someone after you disclosed to this person? Do others seem to like you more after they disclose to you?

Physiological Health   People who self-disclose are less vulnerable to illnesses (Pennebacker, 1991). For example, bereavement over the death of someone very close is linked to physical illness for those who bear this alone and in silence. But it's unrelated to any physical problems for those who share their grief with others. Similarly, women who suffer sexual trauma normally experience a variety of illnesses (among them, headaches and stomach problems). Women who kept these experiences to themselves, however, suffered these illnesses to a much greater extent than did those who talked with others about these traumas. The physiological effort required to keep your burdens to yourself seems to interact with the effects of the trauma to create a combined stress that can lead to a variety of illnesses.

Dangers of Self-Disclosure: Risks Ahead

Realize that the more you reveal about yourself to others the more areas of your life you expose to possible attack. Especially in the competitive context of work (or even romance), the more that others know about you, the more they'll be able to use against you. This simple fact has prompted power watcher Michael Korda (1975, p. 302) to advise you to "never reveal all of yourself to other people; hold something back in reserve so that people are never quite sure if they really know you." This advice is not to suggest that you be secretive; rather, Korda is advocating "remaining slightly mysterious, as if [you] were always capable of doing something surprising and unexpected."

As you weigh your decision to self-disclose or not, keep Korda's advice in mind. Also, realize that there are considerable potential personal, relational, and professional risks to self-disclosure.

Personal Risks   If you self-disclose aspects of your life that vary greatly from the values of those to whom you disclose, you may be met by rejection from even the closest friends and family members. Men and women who disclose that they cheated on their relationship partner, stole, or suffer from extensive depression, for example, may find their friends and family no longer wanting to be quite as close as before.

Relational Risks   Even in close and long-lasting relationships, self-disclosure can cause problems. "Uncensored candor," notes interpersonal researcher Arthur Bochner (1984), "is a bad idea." Total self-disclosure may prove threatening to a relationship by causing a decrease in mutual attraction, trust, or any of the bonds holding the individuals together. Self-disclosures concerning infidelity, romantic fantasies, past indiscretions or crimes, lies, or hidden weaknesses and fears could easily have such negative effects.

Professional Risks   Revealing political views or attitudes toward different religious or racial groups may create problems on the job, as may disclosing any health problems, such as being HIV+ (Fesko, 2001). Teachers who disclose former or current drug use or cohabitation with students may find themselves denied tenure, teaching at undesirable hours, and eventually falling victim to "budget cuts." Teachers or students who, in the supportive atmosphere of their interpersonal communication course, disclose details about their sex lives or financial condition, or reveal self-doubts, anxieties, and fantasies may find some less-than-sympathetic listeners using that information against them. Openly gay and lesbian personnel in the military, as well as in education, fire protection, law enforcement, or health care agencies, to cite just a few examples, may find themselves confined to desk jobs, prevented from further advancement, or even charged with criminal behavior and fired.

In making your choice between disclosing and not disclosing, keep in mind—in addition to the advantages and dangers already noted—the irreversible nature of communication (discussed in Chapter 1). Regardless of how many times you may try to qualify something or take it back, once you have said something you cannot withdraw

A S K *the* **Researcher**

Retaining Privacy

"Why is it that every time I ask my girlfriend about her past relationships she changes the subject? I want to know who she dated and why these relationships broke up. But she just pretends that she didn't hear me and talks about something else. I really think she's trying to deceive me. What is she hiding? And, more important, what should I do?"

I'm sure your girlfriend heard what you said and she's probably not trying to deceive you. People in relationships often think that certain information, like personal histories, belong to both relational parties. It's clear that your girlfriend doesn't what to share this information with you. Instead of thinking she's deceiving you, consider that she might be defining her past relationships as private information. Your girlfriend may believe that information about whom she dated and why she broke up belongs to only her, and not see it as relevant to her relationship with you. I agree that when we're in relationships, we like to disclose things about ourselves. It helps to build the relationship. But, we also want to protect some things about ourselves so that we can retain a level of autonomy—we don't want to tell absolutely everything. It might be better not to judge your girlfriend's behavior as deception. Instead, respect her privacy and she may reward you with the information you want.

For further information see Sandra Petronio, *Boundaries of Privacy: Dialectics of Disclosure* (Albany, NY: SUNY Press, 2002), Sandra Petronio, "Communication Boundary Perspective: A Model of Managing the Disclosure of Private Information Between Marital Couples," *Communication Theory* 4 (1991), 311–332, and Sandra Petronio, "The Boundaries of Privacy: Praxis of Everyday Life," in *Balancing the Secrets of Private Disclosures*, ed. S. Petronio (Mahwah, NJ: LEA Publishers, 2000).

Sandra Petronio (Ph.D., University of Michigan) is a professor of communication at the School of Medicine at Wayne State University and teaches classes in interpersonal, family, and health communication. She conducts research in privacy, disclosure, health care, embarrassment, and divorce adjustment. (Reprinted by permission of Dr. Sandra Petronio, Wayne State University, Detroit, MI.)

it. You cannot erase the conclusions and inferences listeners have made on the basis of your disclosures.

Guidelines for Self-Disclosure

Because self-disclosure is so important and so delicate a matter, guidelines are offered here for (1) deciding whether and how to self-disclose, (2) responding to the disclosures of others, and (3) resisting pressures to self-disclosure.

Guidelines for Making Self-Disclosures   In addition to weighing the potential rewards and dangers of self-disclosure already discussed, consider the following guidelines; they will help raise the right questions before you make what must be *your* decision.

Consider the Motivation for the Self-Disclosure   Self-disclosure should be motivated by a concern for the relationship, for the others involved, and for oneself. Some people self-disclose out of a desire to hurt the listener. Persons who tell their parents that they never loved them or that the parents hindered rather than helped their emotional development may be disclosing out of a desire to hurt and perhaps punish rather than to improve the relationship. Neither should self-disclosure be used to punish oneself, perhaps because of some guilt feeling or unresolved conflict. Self-disclosure should serve a useful and productive function for all persons involved.

Consider the Appropriateness of the Self-Disclosure   Self-disclosure should be appropriate to the context and to the relationship between you and your listener. Before making any significant self-disclosure, ask whether this is the right time and place. Could a better time and place be arranged? Ask, too, whether this self-disclosure is appropriate to the relationship. Generally, the more intimate the disclosures, the closer the relationship should be. It's probably best to resist intimate disclosures (especially negative ones) with nonintimates or casual acquaintances, or in the early stages of a relationship.

Consider the Disclosures of the Other Person During your disclosures, give the other person a chance to reciprocate with his or her own disclosures. If reciprocal disclosures are not made, reassess your own self-disclosures. It may be a signal that for this person at this time and in this context, your disclosures are not welcome or appropriate. It's generally best to disclose gradually and in small increments. When you disclose too rapidly and all at once, you can't monitor your listener's responses and retreat if they're not positive enough. Further, you prevent the listener from responding with his or her own disclosures and thereby upset the natural balance that is so helpful in this kind of communication exchange.

Consider the Possible Burdens Self-Disclosure Might Entail Carefully weigh the potential problems that you may incur as a result of your disclosure. Can you afford to lose your job if you disclose your arrest record? Are you willing to risk relational difficulties if you disclose your infidelities? Also, ask yourself whether you're making unreasonable demands on the listener. For example, consider the person who swears his or her mother-in-law to secrecy and then self-discloses having an affair with a neighbor. This disclosure places an unfair burden on the mother-in-law, who is now torn between breaking her promise of secrecy or allowing her child to believe a lie. Parents often place unreasonable burdens on their children by self-disclosing relationship problems, financial difficulties, or self-doubts without realizing that the children may be too young or too emotionally involved to deal effectively with this information.

Guidelines for Responding to Self-Disclosures When someone discloses to you, it's usually a sign of trust and affection. In serving this most important receiver function, keep the following guidelines in mind. These guidelines will help you facilitate the disclosures of another person.

TRY IT!
Apply your insights into responding to self-disclosures; go to www.ablongman.com/devito.

Practice the Skills of Effective and Active Listening The skills of effective listening (Chapter 5) are especially important when listening to self-disclosures: listen actively, listen for different levels of meaning, listen with empathy, and listen with an open mind. Paraphrase the speaker so that you can be sure you understand both the thoughts and the feelings communicated. Express an understanding of the speaker's feelings to allow the speaker the opportunity to see them more objectively and through the eyes of another. Ask questions to ensure your own understanding and to signal your interest and attention.

Support and Reinforce the Discloser Express support for the person during and after the disclosures. Try refraining from evaluation. Concentrate on understanding and empathizing with the discloser. Allow the discloser to choose the pace; don't rush the discloser with the too-frequent "So how did it all end?" response. Make your supportiveness clear to the discloser through your verbal and nonverbal responses: maintain eye contact, lean toward the speaker, ask relevant questions, and echo the speaker's thoughts and feelings.

ETHICS in Interpersonal Communication

Keeping Secrets

In *Secrets* (1983), ethicist Sissela Bok identifies three types of situations in which she argues it would be unethical to reveal the secrets of another person. These conditions aren't always easy to identify, but they do provide excellent starting points for asking whether or not it's ethical to reveal what you know about another person.

■ It's unethical to reveal information that you have promised to keep secret. When you promise to keep information hidden, you take on an ethical responsibility.

■ It's unethical to talk about another person when you know the information to be false. When you try to deceive listeners by saying things about another person that you know to be false, your communications are unethical.

■ It's unethical to invade the privacy to which everyone has a right, to reveal information that no one else has a right to know. This is especially unethical when such disclosures can hurt the individual involved.

What would you do? *As Bok suggests, consider an 18-year-old student with whom you're fairly friendly who confides that he intends to commit suicide. Using these guidelines, how would you evaluate the ethics involved in revealing this secret? What ethical justification might be offered for revealing such a secret? If you were the confidant, what would you do in this situation?*

Keep the Disclosures Confidential   When a person discloses to you, it's because she or he wants you to know the feelings and thoughts that are communicated. If you reveal these disclosures to others, negative effects are inevitable. Revealing what was said will probably inhibit future disclosures by this individual in general and to you in particular, and it's likely that your relationship will suffer considerably. But most important, betraying a confidence is unfair; it debases what could and should be a meaningful interpersonal experience.

It's interesting to note that one of the netiquette rules of e-mail is that you shouldn't forward mail to third parties without the writer's permission. This rule is useful for self-disclosure generally: Maintain confidentiality; don't pass on disclosures made to you to others without the person's permission.

Don't Use the Disclosures against the Person   Many self-disclosures expose some kind of vulnerability or weakness. If you later turn around and use disclosures against the person who made them, you betray the confidence and trust invested in you. Regardless of how angry you might get, resist the temptation to use the disclosures of others as weapons—the relationship is sure to suffer and may never fully recover.

Guidelines for Resisting Self-Disclosure   You may, on occasion, find yourself in a position where a friend, colleague, or romantic partner pressures you to self-disclose. In such situations, you may wish to weigh the pros and cons of self-disclosure and then make your decision as to whether and what you'll disclose. If your decision is not to disclose and you're still being pressured, then you need to say something. Here are a few suggestions.

Don't Be Pushed   Although there may be certain legal or ethical reasons for disclosing, generally, if you don't want to disclose, you don't have to. Don't be pushed into disclosing because others are doing it or because you're asked to. Realize that you're in control of what you reveal to whom and when. Remember that self-disclosure has significant consequences. If you're not sure you want to reveal something, at least not until you've had additional time to think about it, then don't.

Be Assertive in Your Refusal to Disclose Say, very directly, "I'd rather not talk about that now" or "Now is not the time for this type of discussion." More specific guidelines for communicating assertiveness are offered in Chapter 6.

Be Indirect and Move to Another Topic Avoid the question and change the subject. This is a polite way of saying, "I'm not talking about it," and may be the preferred choice in certain situations. Most often people will get the hint and understand your refusal to disclose. If they don't, then you might have to use a more direct approach.

COMMUNICATION APPREHENSION

Communication apprehension is one of the most extensively researched variables in the field of interpersonal communication, so we know a great deal about this problem that many people experience. First, we look at the nature of communication apprehension, define it, and consider the factors that influence our level of apprehension. Second, we look at some of the theories of apprehension and how, on the basis of these theories, we can more effectively manage or control it. These discussions will prove more valuable if you first take the brief self-test on page 82, "How Apprehensive Are You?"

A S K *the* *Researcher*

Meeting New People

Unlike most people, I have very little fear of public speaking. But I do have a great deal of fear in meeting new people in joining a group when I don't know the people well. Is there anything I can do to reduce this type of interpersonal apprehension? I'm starting a new job in September and I want to make the right impression.

A certain amount of nervousness when meeting new people, going to an interview, or starting a new job is normal and may even be beneficial. You're not sure what you should do or say, and some nervousness is appropriate. It normally fades after you've interacted for a while. If it doesn't, or if you can't go to the interview, meet the new person, or move to the new job, that's another matter. Now your CA (communication apprehension) is interfering with your life. Self-help books and other "quick fixes" will not work. You need to seek professional help from someone who can administer therapy (either systematic desensitization or cognitive restructuring). Even then do not expect miracles. CA has a strong genetic base, so only limited change usually is possible. With professional help, however, most extreme CA conditions can be reduced to a level where the person can function acceptably in everyday life. If your problem is severe you might want to consult your physician; medication is available which many find helpful.

James C. McCroskey (Ed.D., Pennsylvania State University) is Professor of Communication, West Virginia University. His teaching and research concentrations are in interpersonal, organizational, nonverbal, and intercultural communication, communication avoidance, and communibiology. email@JamesCMcCroskey.com (Reprinted by permission of Dr. James C. McCroskey.)

TEST YOURSELF   *How Apprehensive Are You?*

This questionnaire is composed of six statements concerning your feelings about communicating in interpersonal conversations. Please indicate in the space provided the degree to which each statement applies to you. Use the following scale: 1 = strongly agree, 2 = agree, 3 = undecided, 4 = disagree, 5 = strongly disagree. There are no right or wrong answers. Many of the statements are similar to other statements; do not be concerned about this. Work quickly; record your first impression.

_____ 1. While participating in a conversation with a new acquaintance, I feel very nervous.

_____ 2. I have no fear of speaking up in conversations.

_____ 3. Ordinarily I am very tense and nervous in conversations.

_____ 4. Ordinarily I am very calm and relaxed in conversations.

_____ 5. While conversing with a new acquaintance, I feel very relaxed.

_____ 6. I'm afraid to speak up in conversations.

❱ **How did you do?**   Compute your score as follows:

1. Begin with the number 18; this is used as a base so that you won't wind up with negative numbers.
2. To 18, add your scores for items 2, 4, and 5.
3. Subtract your scores for items 1, 3, and 6 from your step 2 total.
4. The result (which should be somewhere between 6 and 30) is your apprehension score for interpersonal conversations. The higher the score, the greater your apprehension. A score above 18 indicates some degree of apprehension.

❱ **What will you do?**   First try to identify those interpersonal situations that create the greatest apprehension for you. What factors can you identify that contribute to heightening apprehension? What can you do to reduce the impact of those factors?

From James C. McCroskey. (1997). *Introduction to Rhetorical Communication,* 7th ed. (Englewood Cliffs, NJ: Prentice-Hall, 1997.)

The Nature of Communication Apprehension

Now that you have a general idea of your own communication apprehension, it might be of interest to note that "communication apprehension is probably the most common handicap . . . suffered by people in contemporary American society" (McCroskey & Wheeless, 1976). According to surveys of college students, between 10 percent and 20 percent suffer "severe, debilitating communication apprehension," while another 20 percent suffer from "communication apprehension to a degree substantial enough to interfere to some extent with their normal functioning."

The term **communication apprehension** (and **shyness,** unwillingness to communicate, stage fright, reticence) refers to a state of fear or anxiety about communication interaction. People develop negative feelings and predict negative results as a function of engaging in communication interactions. They may fear making mistakes and being humiliated (Bippus & Daly, 1999). They feel that whatever gain would accrue from engaging in communication would be outweighed by the fear. To those with high communication apprehension, the communication interaction just isn't worth the fear it engenders.

Trait apprehension refers to fear of communication generally, regardless of the specific situation. It appears in dyadic, small group, public speaking, and mass com-

 Shyness researchers have argued that the people we single out as heroes are those who call attention to themselves—the rock stars and media personalities, for example; "people who are most likely to be successful are those who are able to obtain attention and feel comfortable with it" (Carducci & Zimbardo, 1996, p. 66). Who are your heroes? Are they the people who call attention to themselves? Are any of your heroes high communication apprehensives or shy?

munication situations. **State apprehension,** in contrast, is specific to a given communication situation. For example, a speaker may fear public speaking but have no difficulty with dyadic communication, or a speaker may fear job interviews but have no fear of public speaking. State apprehension is extremely common; it's experienced by most people in some situations.

Communication apprehension exists on a continuum. People are not either apprehensive or unapprehensive. We all experience some degree of apprehension. Some people are extremely apprehensive and become incapacitated in a communication situation. They suffer a great deal in a society oriented, as ours is, around communication and in which one's success depends on the ability to communicate effectively. Others are so mildly apprehensive that they appear to experience no fear at all when confronted by communication situations; they actively seek out communication experiences and rarely feel any significant apprehension. Most of us fall between these two extremes.

Apprehensive Behaviors   Generally, apprehension leads to a decrease in the frequency, strength, and likelihood of engaging in communication transactions. High apprehensives avoid communication situations; when forced to participate, they do so as little as possible. This reluctance to communicate shows itself in a variety of forms. For example, those with high apprehension are found to be less willing to communicate, to volunteer, and to work with the terminally ill than were those who were low in apprehension (Ayres & Hopf, 1995). Your communication apprehension will even influence your satisfaction with dating (Powers & Love, 2000).

Consider the following statements about your own feelings about communicating with your dating partner. Are they basically true (yes) or basically false (no)?

1. I am comfortable in developing intimate conversations with my partner.
2. I feel I am an open communicator with my partner.
3. I am hesitant to develop a "deep" conversation with my partner.
4. Even in casual conversations with my partner, I feel I must guard what I say.

If you responded "yes" to statements 1 and 2 and "no" to statements 3 and 4, then, research shows, you're more likely to experience interpersonal communication satisfaction. If, on the other hand, you responded "no" to statements 1 and 2 and "yes" to statements 3 and 4, then you're likely to experience a lack of satisfaction. In small group situations, apprehensives not only talk less but also avoid the seats of influence—for example, those in the group leader's direct line of sight. High apprehensives are less likely to be seen as leaders in small group situations regardless of their actual behaviors. Even in classrooms, they avoid seats where they can be easily called on, and they maintain little direct eye contact with the instructor, especially when a question is likely to be asked. Related to this is that apprehensives have more negative attitudes toward school, earn poorer grades, and are more likely to drop out of college (McCroskey, Booth-Butterfield, & Payne, 1989).

Teachers and students consider apprehensives to be less desirable social choices. Apprehensives disclose little and avoid occupations with heavy communication demands (for example, teaching or public relations). Within their occupation, they're less desirous of advancement, largely because of the associated increase in communication. High apprehensives feel less satisfied with their jobs, probably because they're less successful in advancing and in developing interpersonal relationships. High apprehensives are even less likely to get job interviews. In the United States we value "rugged individualism and the conquering of new environments, whether in outer space or in overseas markets. Personal attributes held high in our social esteem are leadership, assertiveness, dominance, independence, and risk taking. Hence a stigma surrounding shyness" (Carducci & Zimbardo, 1996, p. 66).

All this does not mean that apprehensives are ineffective or unhappy people. Most apprehensives have learned or can learn to deal with their communication anxiety.

Influences on Communication Apprehension   Research has identified several factors that increase communication apprehension (McCroskey & Daly, 1987; Beatty, 1988; Richmond & McCroskey, 1999). A knowledge of these factors will help you to increase your understanding and control of your own apprehension.

■ *Degree of Evaluation.* The more you perceive the situation as one in which you will be evaluated, the greater your apprehension is likely to be. Employment interviews, for example, provoke anxiety largely because they're highly evaluative.

■ *Subordinate Status.* When you feel that others are better communicators than you are or that they know more than you do, your apprehension increases. For example, shy students report particular difficulty in speaking with authorities (Zimbardo, 1977).

■ *Degree of Conspicuousness.* The more conspicuous you are, the more likely you are to feel apprehensive. This is why delivering a speech to a large audience is more anxiety provoking than speaking in a small group; you're more conspicuous before the large group—you stand out, and all attention is on you.

■ *Degree of Unpredictability.* The more unpredictable the situation, the greater your apprehension is likely to be. Ambiguous and new situations are unpredictable; you cannot know beforehand what they will be like, hence you become anxious. A similar condition seems to increase your shyness when interacting with strangers; 70 percent of shy students surveyed said they were especially shy with strangers (Zimbardo, 1977).

■ *Degree of Dissimilarity.* When you feel you have little in common with your listeners, you're likely to feel anxious.

■ *Prior Successes and Failures.* Your experience in similar situations greatly influences the way you respond to new ones. Prior success generally (though not always) reduces apprehension, whereas prior failure generally (though not always) increases apprehension. There is no mystery here: Prior success says that you can succeed this time as well; prior failure warns that you may fail again.

■ *Lack of Communication Skills and Experience.* If you lack skills in typing, you can hardly expect to type very well. If you have never asked for a raise and have no idea how to go about doing it, for example, it's perfectly reasonable that you will feel apprehension.

Culture and Communication Apprehension   Apprehension, shyness, and the willingness to communicate generally vary from one culture to another (Breidenstein-Cutspec & Goering, 1989). For example, in one study of shyness, Israelis were found to be the least shy; only 24 percent reported they were currently experiencing shyness, compared to Mexicans (39 percent), Americans (42 percent), Germans (50 percent), Taiwanese (55 percent), and Japanese (60 percent) (Carducci & Zimbardo, 1995). In a study of the willingness to communicate, American college students indicated the highest willingness to communicate, whereas students from Micronesia indicated the lowest. Micronesian students also indicated the highest degree of shyness while, in this study, Puerto Ricans reported the lowest (McCroskey & Richmond, 1990).

When the interpersonal communication is intercultural communication, additional uncertainty, fear, and anxiety, all of which are intimately related to communication apprehension (Stephan & Stephan, 1985), may be experienced. When you're in an intercultural situation—say your coworkers are largely people of cultures very different from your own—you're more uncertain about the situation and about their possible responses and you're more likely to experience heightened communication apprehension. Not surprisingly, most people react negatively to high uncertainty and develop a decreased attraction for these other people (Gudykunst & Nishida, 1984; Gudykunst, Yang, & Nishida, 1985). When you're sure of the situation and can predict what will happen, you're more likely to feel comfortable and at ease. But when the situation is uncertain and you cannot predict what will happen, you become more apprehensive (Gudykunst & Kim, 1992).

Intercultural situations can engender fear. You might, for example, fear saying something that will prove offensive or reveal your own prejudices or ethnocentrism. The fear easily translates into apprehension. Intercultural situations can also create anxiety, a feeling very similar to apprehension. Anxiety may be felt for a number of reasons (Stephan & Stephan, 1985). For example, your *prior relationships* with members of a culturally different group will influence your apprehension. If your prior relationships were few or if they were unpleasant, then you're likely to experience greater apprehension when dealing with these members than if these prior experiences were numerous and positive.

Your *thoughts and feelings* about the group will also influence your apprehension. For example, if you have little knowledge of the other culture, hold stereotypes and prejudices, are high in ethnocentrism, or if you feel that you're very different from these others, then you're likely to experience more apprehension than if you saw these people as similar to you.

The *situation* you're in can also exert influence. If, for example, you feel that members of another group are competing with you or evaluating you, then you're likely to experience more apprehension than if the situation were more cooperative and equal. Similarly, unstructured and ambiguous situations create more anxiety because you aren't quite sure what is expected of you. Also, your status relative to the others in the group will influence your anxiety; if you're lower in status, you're likely to experience greater anxiety than if you were higher in status.

Theories of Communication Apprehension Management

Following communication researchers Virginia Richmond and James McCroskey (1999), we can distinguish three theoretical (and eminently practical) approaches to understanding communication apprehension and how it may be managed or controlled: cognitive restructuring, systematic desensitization, and skill acquisition.

Cognitive Restructuring   The cognitive restructuring theory, introduced earlier in this chapter, holds that your own unrealistic beliefs generate a fear of failure. Because you set unachievable goals ("Everyone must love me, I have to be thoroughly competent, I have to be the best in everything"), you logically fear failure. This fear of failure (and the irrational beliefs behind it) are at the foundation of your apprehension (for example, Markway, Carmin, Pollard, & Flynn, 1992). Cognitive restructuring, then, advises you to change your irrational beliefs and substitute more rational ones ("It would be nice if everyone loved me but I don't need that to survive. I can fail. Although it would be nice, I don't have to be the best in everything."). Your last step is to practice your new, more rational beliefs (Ellis & Harper, 1975; Ellis, 1988).

The process may go something like this: Unrealistic beliefs give rise to anxiety because you know you can never achieve these unrealistically high goals and that you'll fail at some point. There's not a speaker in the world who wouldn't fail given these unrealistic beliefs. You then focus on the inevitable failure; you can almost see yourself failing. This image leads to a loss of confidence and further visions of failure.

A special type of cognitive restructuring is *performance visualization,* designed specifically to reduce the outward manifestations of communication apprehension and also to reduce negative thinking (Ayres & Hopf, 1993; Ayres, Ayres, Grudzinskas, Hopf, et al., 1995). This technique, not surprisingly, has been shown to be significantly more effective with those who can create vivid mental images (Ayres, Hopf, & Ayres, 1994). The first part of performance visualization is to develop a positive attitude and a positive self-perception. This involves visualizing yourself in the role of, say, the effective employment interviewee. Visualize yourself walking into the interview—fully and totally confident. You scan the room and sit down. Throughout the interview you're fully in control of the situation. The interviewer is in rapt attention as you ask and respond to questions and, at the end, begs you to take the job. Throughout this visualization, avoid all negative thoughts. As you visualize yourself interviewing effectively, take special note of how you walk, look at the interviewer, respond to questions, and especially how you feel about the whole experience.

The second part of performance visualization is designed to help you model your performance on that of an especially effective communicator. Here you would view a particularly competent interviewee on video and make a mental movie of it. As you review the actual and the mental movie, you begin to shift yourself into the role of the interviewee. You, in effect, become this effective individual.

Systematic Desensitization   Systematic desensitization is a technique for dealing with a variety of fears including communication apprehension (Wolpe, 1958) and has even been found to reduce dating anxiety (Allen, Bourhis, Emmers-Sommer, & Sahlstein, 1998). The general assumption of systematic desensitization is that apprehension was learned, and because it was learned, it can be unlearned. The procedure involves creating a hierarchy of behaviors leading up to the desired but feared behavior (say, asking for a date). One specific hierarchy might look like this:

- Asking for the date
- Making small talk
- Introducing yourself to your prospective date
- Dialing the phone

You would begin at the bottom of this hierarchy and rehearse this behavior mentally until you can clearly visualize dialing the phone without any uncomfortable anxiety. Once you can accomplish this, you can move to the second level. Here you would visualize the somewhat more threatening, introducing yourself to your prospective date. Once you can do this, you can move to the third level, and so on until you get to the desired behavior.

Skill Acquisition   The third general approach to communication apprehension holds that you develop apprehension largely because you see yourself as having inadequate skills. So you logically fear failing. The strategy for managing apprehension, therefore, is to acquire the specific skills involved in any given behavior. For example, the skills for business communication would involve a number of more specific skills. These more specific skills would be mastered individually and then put together into the process of, say, talking with subordinates and supervisors. For example, some such skills would include presenting a positive self-image, complimenting the work of others, and criticizing tactfully another's performance. Other types of skills might be using deep breathing to relax yourself, creative visualization to help you see yourself as successful, or self-affirmation to help you feel better about yourself.

With mastery, the task—in this case business communication, but it could just as logically be any task—becomes less forbidding and hence less anxiety provoking. With mastery also comes successful experiences. These successes help build your confidence and further lessen anxiety. It's probably impossible to eliminate communication apprehension. However, we can manage apprehension effectively so that it does not debilitate us or prevent us from achieving goals that require us to communicate in a variety of situations. Here are some additional suggestions for building skills:

Prepare and Practice   The more preparation and practice you put into something, the more comfortable you feel with it and, consequently, the less apprehension you feel. If you're apprehensive telling jokes, then practice the joke you wish to tell. Rehearse it mentally and perhaps aloud until you're comfortable with it. In this way, you'll acquire the very communication skills and experiences you'll need to help you master the tasks at which you want to be effective.

Focus on Success   Think positively. Concentrate your energies on doing the very best job you can in whatever situation you are in. Visualize yourself succeeding, and you stand a good chance of doing just that. Remember that having failed in the past does not mean that you must fail again in the future. You now have new skills and new experiences, and they increase your chances for success. But even if you do have a setback, put the setback and the apprehension in perspective; the world will not cave in if you don't succeed in any given communication situation.

TRY IT!
Apply your understanding of communication apprehension management; go to **www.ablongman.com/devito**.

Familiarize Yourself with the Situation   The more familiar you are with the situation, the better. The reason is simple: When you're familiar with the situation and with what will be expected of you, you're better able to predict what will happen. This will reduce ambiguity and make you feel more comfortable.

Try to Relax   Apprehension is reduced when you're physically and mentally relaxed. For example, knowing that you have acquired new communication skills and that you have prepared yourself for the task of asking for a raise should help alleviate your normal anxiety.

REVIEWING   Key Terms and Concepts of the Self in Interpersonal Communication

This chapter looked at the self in interpersonal communication and focused on three basic topics: dimensions of the self (self-concept, self-awareness, and self-esteem), self-disclosure, and communication apprehension.

Dimensions of the Self

What are self-concept, self-awareness, and self-esteem and how do they influence interpersonal communication?

■ Self-Concept
  ■ Self-concept is the image you have of who you are.
  ■ Sources of self-concept include others' images of you, social comparisons, cultural teachings, and your own interpretations and evaluations.
■ Self-Awareness
  ■ Self-awareness is your knowledge of yourself; the extent to which you know who you are.
  ■ A useful way of looking at self-awareness is with the Johari window, which consists of four parts. The open self: information known to self and others; the blind self: information known only to others; the hidden self: information known only to self; and the unknown self: information known to neither self nor others.
  ■ To increase self-awareness, ask yourself about yourself, listen to others, actively seek information about yourself, see your different selves, and increase your open self.
■ Self-Esteem
  ■ Self-esteem is the value you place on yourself; your perceived self-worth.
  ■ To increase self-esteem, try attacking your self-destructive beliefs, seeking affirmation, seeking out nourishing people, and working on projects that will result in success.

Self-Disclosure

What is self-disclosure? What influences self-disclosure? What are its potential rewards and dangers? What guidelines are useful in making decisions to self-disclose and in listening to the disclosures of others?

■ Self-disclosure is revealing information about yourself to others, information that is normally hidden.
■ Self-disclosure is influenced by a variety of factors: who you are, your culture, your gender, your listeners, and your topic.
■ Among the rewards of self-disclosure are self-knowledge, ability to cope, communication effectiveness, meaningfulness of relationships, and physiological health. Among the dangers are personal risks, relational risks, professional risks, and the fact that communication is irreversible; once something is said, you can't take it back.
■ In self-disclosing consider your motivation, the appropriateness of the disclosure to the person and context, the disclo-

sures of others (the dyadic effect), and the possible burdens that the self-disclosure might impose on others and on yourself.
■ In responding to the disclosures of others, listen effectively, support and reinforce the discloser, keep disclosures confidential, and don't use disclosures as weapons.
■ In some situations you'll want to resist self-disclosing by being determined not to be pushed into it, being assertive and direct, or being indirect.

Communication Apprehension

What is communication apprehension? How can you effectively manage your own apprehension? How can you help empower those who are apprehensive?

■ Communication apprehension is a state of fear or anxiety about communication situations. Trait apprehension is a fear of communication generally. State apprehension is a fear of communication that is specific to a situation (for example, an interview or public speaking situation).
■ Theories and management of communication apprehension include cognitive restructuring, systematic desensitization, and skill acquisition.
  ■ Cognitive restructuring focuses on unrealistic beliefs and seeks to substitute more realistic ones.
  ■ Systematic desensitization attempts to train you to respond without apprehension to increasingly more anxiety-provoking situations.
  ■ Skill acquisition focuses on training you to master the skills involved in situations that normally provoke apprehension. To build skills: Prepare and practice, focus on success, familiarize yourself with the situation, and try to relax.

APPLYING   Key Terms and Concepts of the Self in Interpersonal Communication

1. How satisfied are you with your self-concept? How satisfied are you with your current level of self-esteem? If you're unsatisfied, what are you going to do about it?
2. Do you engage in downward social comparison (comparing yourself to those you know are inferior to you in some way) or upward social comparison (comparing yourself to those who you think are better than you) (Aspinwall & Taylor, 1993)? What are the purposes of these comparisons?
3. Research finds that members of middle-class, two-parent families are reluctant to share financial problems with their children, preferring to shelter them from some of life's harsher realities (McLoyd & Wilson, 1992). Low-income, single mothers, however, believe that sharing this with their children will protect them because they will know how difficult life is. What would your general advice be to parents about disclosing such matters?

4. Joseph Luft (1969), one of the developers of the Johari window, argued that "the smaller the first quadrant [the open self], the poorer the communication." Do you agree with this? Can you provide a personal example that supports or contradicts Luft's observation?

5. One research study suggests that gender differences in self-disclosure may be changing. In a study of men and women discussing how their family relationships had changed since they entered college, for example, men disclosed more than women (Leaper, Carson, Baker, Holliday, et al., 1995). What changes in gender differences in self-disclosure do you observe?

6. One response that is seldom mentioned in discussions of disclosure is to say that you simply don't want to hear the disclosure. What kinds of disclosures are you most apt to *not* want to hear? How might you communicate this refusal to listen? Under what conditions would such refusals be appropriate?

7. How would you characterize your own communication apprehension? In what communication situations are you most apprehensive? Why?

8. Research finds that in the classroom, increased instructor clarity and immediacy (language that creates a connection between sender and receiver) helps to reduce receiver apprehension (the fear people have that they won't be able to understand the message they're listening to). What might health care professionals do to help reduce receiver apprehension among patients (Chesebro & McCroskey, 1998)?

9. Are you more likely to become apprehensive in an intercultural situation than in a situation in which everyone is culturally similar to you? Why do you think you experience intercultural apprehension?

10. Try creating a hierarchy (as described in the discussion of systematic desensitization) for a communication behavior for which you have apprehension. What insights does creating this hierarchy give you into the causes of your specific apprehension?

11. How will apprehension affect your professional life? Your relational life?

12. Persons high in communication apprehension are found to engage in more steady dating than those who are low in apprehension. Why do you think this is so?

EXPERIENCING   Key Terms and Concepts of the Self in Interpersonal Communication

Go to www.ablongman.com/devito.

These exercises enable you to further explore the concepts of the self, especially self-disclosure and communication apprehension, discussed in this chapter.

(1) **How Can You Attack Self-Defeating Drivers?** asks you to consider your own drivers and how you deal with them. (2) **What Do You Have a Right to Know?** explores a different perspective on self-disclosure, namely the obligation to reveal parts of yourself. (3) **Disclosing Your Hidden Self** presents an exciting class experience on the types of behaviors people keep hidden and the potential reactions to their disclosures. (4) **Weighing the Rewards and Dangers of Self-Disclosure** presents a variety of scenarios of impending self-disclosure and asks you to consider the advantages and disadvantages of disclosing. (5) **Time for Self-Disclosure** explores the appropriateness of time in revealing certain information. (6) **Using Performance Visualization to Reduce Apprehension** and (7) **Reducing Apprehension with Systematic Desensitization** provide guided experience in using these techniques to reduce communication apprehension. (8) **How Flexible Is Your Communication?** provides an interesting self-test on your own flexibility.

RESEARCHING with Research Navigator   Key Terms and Concepts of the Self in Interpersonal Communication

Go to http://www.researchnavigator.com.

Reading an article.

Read a popular or scholarly article on the self (for example, self-concept, self-awareness), self-disclosure, or communication apprehension. On the basis of this article what can you add to the discussion presented in this chapter?

Investigating key terms.

Investigate one of the key terms discussed in this chapter (for example, self-concept, self-awareness, social comparisons, self-awareness, self-disclosure, communication apprehension, se-

cret, flexibility, uses and gratifications theory). What additional insights can you provide?

Finding answers.

Try finding answers to one of the following questions or design a research study to answer it.

■ Do people change their self-concept as they age?

■ Do men and women differ in the topics they self-disclose to their best friends? Do they differ in disclosures to romantic partners?

■ Are more intelligent people more self-aware than less intelligent people? Does one group have higher self-esteem?

■ Are shyness and communication apprehension hereditary? Learned?

4 Perception in Interpersonal Communication

Harry Potter and the Sorcerer's Stone (2001)

We must always tell what we see. Above all, and this is more difficult, we must always see what we see.

—Charles Peguy

Stages of Perception
Perceptual Processes
Increasing Accuracy in Interpersonal
    Perception

One of the many lessons we learn from Harry Potter and the Sorcerer's Stone *is that first impressions can be wrong. Forming a quick first impression and then filtering later information through this first impression is extremely common and is just one of the ways we misperceive people. In this chapter we look at perception, how it works, and how you can increase your own perceptual accuracy.*

STAGES OF PERCEPTION

Perception is the process by which you become aware of objects, events, and especially people through your senses: sight, smell, taste, touch, and hearing. Perception is an active, not a passive process. Your perceptions result from what exists in the outside world and from your own experiences, desires, needs and wants, loves and hatreds. Among the reasons perception is so important in interpersonal communication is that it influences your communication choices. The messages you send and listen to will depend on how you see the world, on how you size up specific situations, on what you think of the people with whom you interact.

Interpersonal perception is a continuous series of processes that blend into one another. For convenience of discussion we can separate them into five stages: (1) you sense, you pick up some kind of stimulation, (2) you organize the stimuli in some way, (3) you interpret and evaluate what you perceive, (4) you store it in memory, and (5) you retrieve it when needed.

Stage One: Stimulation

At this first stage, your sense organs are stimulated—you hear a new CD, see a friend, smell someone's perfume, taste an orange, feel another's sweaty palm. Naturally, you don't perceive everything; rather, you engage in *selective perception,* a general term that includes selective attention and selective exposure. In selective attention, you attend to those things that you anticipate will fulfill your needs or will prove enjoyable. For example, when daydreaming in class, you don't hear what the instructor is saying until your name is called. Your selective attention mechanism focuses your senses on your name.

Through **selective exposure** you expose yourself to people or messages that will confirm your existing beliefs, contribute to your objectives, or prove satisfying in some way. For example, after you buy a car, you're more apt to read and listen to advertisements for the car you just bought because these messages tell you that you made the right decision. At the same time, you would avoid advertisements for the cars that you considered but eventually rejected because these messages would tell you that you made the wrong decision.

You're also more likely to perceive stimuli that are greater in intensity than surrounding stimuli and those that have novelty value. For example, television commercials normally play at a greater intensity than regular programming to ensure that you take special notice. You're also more likely to notice the coworker who dresses in a novel way than you are to notice the one who dresses like everyone else. You will quickly perceive someone who shows up in class wearing a tuxedo or at a formal party in shorts.

WEB EXPLORATION
To learn more about stage two: organization, go to www.ablongman.com/devito.

Stage Two: Organization

At the second stage, you organize the information your senses pick up. Three interesting ways in which people organize their perceptions are by rules, by schemata, and by scripts. Let's look at each briefly.

Organization by Rules One frequently used **rule of perception** is that of *proximity* or physical closeness: Things that are physically close together constitute a unit. Thus, using this rule, you would perceive people who are often together, or messages spoken one immediately after the other, as units, as belonging together. You also assume that the verbal and nonverbal signals sent at about the same time are related and constitute a unified whole; you assume they follow a *temporal* rule: Things occurring together in time belong together.

Another rule is *similarity:* Things that are physically similar, things that look alike, belong together and form a unit. This principle of similarity would lead you to see people who dress alike as belonging together. Similarly, you might assume that people who work at the same jobs, who are of the same religion, who live in the same building, or who talk with the same accent belong together.

The rule of *contrast* is the opposite of similarity: When items (people or messages, for example) are very different from each other, you conclude that they don't belong together; they're too different from each other to be part of the same unit. If you're the only one who shows up at an informal gathering in a tuxedo, you'd be seen as not belonging to the group because you contrast too much with other members.

Organization by Schemata Another way you organize material is by creating **schemata,** mental templates or structures that help you organize the millions of items of information you come into contact with every day as well as those you already have in memory. (*Schemata* is the plural of *schema.*) Schemata may thus be viewed as general ideas about people (for Pat and Chris, for Japanese, for Baptists, for New Yorkers), yourself (your qualities, abilities, and even liabilities), or social roles (police officer, professor, or multibillionaire CEO).

You develop schemata from your own experience—actual as well as from television, reading, and hearsay. You might have a schema for college athletes, for example, and this might include that they're strong, ambitious, academically weak, and egocentric. You've probably developed schemata for different religious, racial, and national groups, for men and women, and for people of different affectional orientations. Each group that you have some familiarity with will be represented in your mind in some kind of schema. Schemata help you organize your perceptions by allowing you to classify millions of people into a manageable number of categories or classes. As we'll see below, however, schemata can also create problems and influence you to see what is not there or to miss seeing what is there.

Organization by Scripts A **script** is really a type of schema, but because it's a different type, it's given a different name. Like a schema, a script is an organized body of information about some action, event, or procedure. It's a general idea of how some event should play out or unfold; it's the rules governing events and their sequence. For example, you probably have a script for eating in a restaurant, with the actions organized into a pattern something like this: enter, take a seat, review the menu, order from the menu, eat your food, ask for the bill, leave a tip, pay the bill, exit the restaurant. Similarly, you probably have scripts for how you do laundry, how an interview is to be conducted, the stages you go through in introducing someone to someone else, and the way you ask for a date.

Stage Three: Interpretation–Evaluation

The interpretation–evaluation (hyphenated because the two processes cannot be separated) step is inevitably subjective and is greatly influenced by your experiences, needs, wants, values, beliefs about the way things are or should be, expectations, physical and emotional state, and so on. Your interpretation–evaluation will be influenced by your rules, schemata, and scripts as well as by your gender; for example, women have been found to view others more positively than men (Winquist, Mohr, & Kenny, 1998).

For example, upon meeting a new person who is introduced to you as a college football player, you would apply your schema to this person and view him as strong, ambitious, academically weak, and egocentric. You would, in other words, see this person through the filter of your schema and evaluate him according to your schema for college athletes. Similarly, when viewing someone performing some series of actions (say, eating in a restaurant), you apply your script to this event and view the event through the script. You would interpret the actions of the diner as appropriate or inappropriate depending on the script you had for this behavior and the ways in which the diner performed the sequence of actions.

Stage Four: Memory

Your perceptions and their interpretations–evaluations are put into memory; they're stored so that you may ultimately retrieve them at some later time. So, for example, you have in memory your schema for college athletes and that Ben Williams is a football player. Ben Williams is then stored in memory with "cognitive tags" that tell you that he's strong, ambitious, academically weak, and egocentric. Despite the fact that you've not witnessed Ben's strength or ambitions and have no idea of his academic record or his psychological profile, you still may store your memory of Ben along with the qualities that make up your script for "college athletes."

Let's say that at different times you hear that Ben failed Spanish I, normally an A or B course at your school, that Ben got an A in Chemistry (normally a tough course), and that Ben is transferring to Harvard as a theoretical physics major. Schemas act as filters or gatekeepers; they allow certain information to get stored in relatively objective form, much as you heard or read it, and may distort or prevent other information from getting

View point In making evaluations of events or people, it would seem logical that you first think about the event or person and then make the evaluation. Some research claims, however, that you really don't think before assigning any perception a positive or negative value. This research argues that all perceptions have a positive or negative value attached to them and that these evaluations are most often automatic and involve no conscious thought. Immediately upon perceiving a person, idea, or thing a positive or negative value is attached (*New York Times*, August 8, 1995, C1, C10). What do you think of this? One bit of evidence against this position would be the ability to identify three, four, or five things, ideas, or people about which you feel *completely* neutral. Can you do it?

stored. As a result, these three items of information about Ben may get stored very differently in your memory along with your schema for college athletes.

For example, you might readily store the information that Ben failed Spanish because it's consistent with your schema; it fits neatly into the template you have of college athletes. Information that's consistent with your schema—such as in this example—will strengthen your schema and make it more resistant to change (Aronson, Wilson, & Akert, 1999). Depending on the strength of your schema, you might also store in memory (even though you didn't hear it) that Ben did poorly in other courses as well. The information that Ben got an A in chemistry, because it contradicts your schema (it just doesn't seem right), might easily be distorted or lost. The information that Ben is transferring to Harvard, however, is a bit different. This information is also inconsistent with your schema, but it is so drastically inconsistent that you begin to look at this mindfully and may even begin to question your schema or perhaps view Ben as an exception to the general rule. In either case, you're going to etch Ben's transferring to Harvard very clearly in your mind.

Stage Five: Recall

At some later date, you may want to recall or access the information you have stored in memory. Let's say you want to retrieve your information about Ben because he's the topic of discussion among you and a few friends. As we'll see in our discussion of listening in the next chapter, memory isn't reproductive; you don't simply reproduce what you've heard or seen. Rather, you reconstruct what you've heard or seen into a whole that is meaningful to you—depending in great part on your schemata and scripts—and it's this reconstruction that you store in memory. When you want to retrieve this information, you may recall it with a variety of inaccuracies. You're likely to:

- recall information that is consistent with your schema; in fact, you may not even be recalling the specific information (say, about Ben) but may actually just be recalling your schema (which contains the information about college athletes and, because of this, also about Ben)
- fail to recall information that is inconsistent with your schema; you have no place to put that information, so you easily lose it or forget it
- recall information that drastically contradicts your schema because it forces you to think (and perhaps rethink) about your schema and its accuracy; it may even force you to revise your schema for college athletes in general

Before moving on to the more specific processes involved in interpersonal perception, let's spell out some of the implications of this five-stage model.

1. Everyone relies on shortcuts—rules, schemata, and scripts, for example, are all useful shortcuts to simplify your understanding, remembering, and recalling information about people and events. They also enable you to generalize, make connections, and otherwise profit from previously acquired knowledge. If you didn't have these shortcuts, you'd have to treat every person, role, or action differently from each other person, role, or action. This would make every experience a new one, totally unrelated to anything you already know.
2. Shortcuts, however, may mislead you; they may contribute to your remembering things that are consistent with your schemata (even if they didn't occur) and distorting or forgetting information that is inconsistent.
3. What you remember about a person or an event isn't an objective recollection but is more likely heavily influenced by your preconceptions or your schemata about what belongs and what doesn't belong, what fits neatly into the templates in your

ETHICS in Interpersonal Communication

Perspectives on Ethics

In thinking about the ethics of interpersonal communication, you can take the position that ethics is objective or that it's subjective.

■ An *objective* view argues that morality is absolute and exists apart from the values or beliefs of any individual or culture. This view holds that standards apply to all people in all situations at all times. If lying, false advertising, using illegally obtained evidence, or revealing secrets are considered unethical, then they would be considered unethical regardless of the circumstances surrounding them or the context in which they occur. In a strict objective view the end doesn't justify the means; you cannot justify an unethical act regardless of how good or beneficial its results (or ends) might be.

■ A *subjective* view argues that absolute statements of morality are too rigid and that the ethics of a message depend on the culture's values and beliefs as well as the particular circumstances. Thus, a subjective position would claim that lying may be wrong to win votes or sell cigarettes, but that it may be quite ethical if done to make someone feel better by telling them that they'll get well soon.

What would you do? *After an examination, the instructor accuses a student of cheating and asks you if you witnessed it. Although you believe that both cheating and lying are unethical and you did witness the cheating, you don't want to make trouble for the student or for yourself. Besides, the examination wasn't announced in advance and it only counted a few points toward the final grade. What would you do in this situation?*

brain and what doesn't. Your reconstruction of an event or person contains a lot of information that was not in the original sensory experience and may omit a lot that was in this experience.

4. Judgments about members of other cultures are often ethnocentric; because your schemata and scripts are created on the basis of your own cultural beliefs and experiences, you can easily (but inappropriately) apply these to members of other cultures. And so, it's easy to infer that when members of other cultures do things that conform to your scripts, they're right, and when they do things that contradict your scripts, they're wrong—a classic example of ethnocentric thinking. This tendency can easily contribute to intercultural misunderstandings.

5. A similar problem arises when you base your scripts for different cultural groups on stereotypes that you may have derived from television or movies. For example, you may have scripts for religious Muslims that you derived from the stereotypes presented in the media that you then apply to all Muslims, seeing what conforms to your script and failing to see or distorting what does not conform to your script.

6. Memory is especially unreliable when the information can be interpreted in different ways, when it's ambiguous. Thus, for example, consider the statement that "Ben didn't do as well in his other courses as he would have liked." If your schema of Ben was "brilliant" then you might "remember" that Ben got Bs. But if, as in our example, your schema was of the academically weak athlete, you might "remember" that Ben got Ds. Conveniently, but unreliably, schemata reduce ambiguity.

PERCEPTUAL PROCESSES

Before reading about the specific processes that you use in perceiving other people, examine your own perception strategies by taking the self-test "How Accurate Are You at People Perception?" on page 96.

TEST YOURSELF   *How Accurate Are You at People Perception?*

Respond to each of the following statements with T if the statement is usually or generally accurate in describing your behavior or F if the statement is usually or generally inaccurate in describing your behavior.

_____ 1. When I know some things about a person, I can easily fill in what I don't know.

_____ 2. I make predictions about people's behaviors that generally prove to be true.

_____ 3. My expectations are usually borne out by what I actually see; that is, my initial expectations usually match my eventual perceptions.

_____ 4. I base most of my impressions of people on the first few minutes of our meeting.

_____ 5. I generally find that people I like possess positive characteristics and people I don't like possess negative characteristics.

_____ 6. I have clear ideas of what people of different national, racial, and religious groups are really like.

_____ 7. I generally attribute people's attitudes and behaviors to their most obvious physical or psychological characteristic.

_____ 8. I believe that the world is basically just, that good things happen to good people and bad things happen to bad people.

▶ **How did you do?**   This brief perception test was designed to raise questions to be considered in this chapter and not to provide you with a specific perception score. All statements refer to perceptual processes that many of us use, but that often get us into trouble, leading us to form inaccurate impressions. The questions refer to the processes to be discussed in this chapter: implicit personality theory (statement 1), self-fulfilling prophecy (2), perceptual accentuation (3), primary–recency (4), consistency (5), and stereotyping (6). Statements 7 and 8 refer to two common problems made when we attempt to attribute motives to other people's and even our own behaviors: overattribution (7), and the self-serving bias that often involves a belief that the world is fundamentally just (8). Ideally, you would have responded with "false" to all of these statements, indicating that you regularly avoid falling into these potential traps.

▶ **What will you do?**   As you read this chapter, think about these principles and consider how you might use them to form more accurate and reasonable perceptions of people. Recognize that situations vary widely and that these suggestions will prove useful most of the time, but not all of the time. In fact, you may want to identify situations in which you shouldn't follow these suggestions. ●

WEB EXPLORATION
To learn more about implicit personality theory, go to **www.ablongman. com/devito**.

Implicit Personality Theory

Each person has a subconscious or implicit theory that says which characteristics of an individual go with other characteristics. Consider, for example, the following brief statements.

Note the word in parentheses that you think best completes each sentence.

1. Carlo is energetic, eager, and (intelligent, stupid).
2. Kim is bold, defiant, and (extroverted, introverted).
3. Joe is bright, lively, and (thin, heavy).
4. Eve is attractive, intelligent, and (likable, unlikable).
5. Susan is cheerful, positive, and (outgoing, shy).
6. Angel is handsome, tall, and (friendly, unfriendly).

What makes some of these choices seem right and others wrong is your **implicit personality theory,** the system of rules that tells you which characteristics go with which other characteristics. Your theory may, for example, have told you that a person who is energetic and eager is also intelligent, not stupid, although there is no logical reason why a stupid person could not be energetic and eager.

The widely documented **halo effect** is a function of the implicit personality theory (Dion, Berscheid, & Walster, 1972; Riggio, 1987). If you believe a person has some positive qualities, you're likely to infer that she or he also possesses other positive qualities. There is also a *reverse halo effect*: If you know a person possesses several negative qualities, you're more likely to infer that the person also has other negative qualities.

In using implicit personality theories, apply them carefully and critically so as to avoid perceiving qualities in an individual that your theory tells you should be present when they actually are not. For example, you see "goodwill" in a friend's "charitable" acts when a tax deduction may have been the real motive. Similarly, be careful of ignoring or distorting qualities that don't conform to your theory but that are actually present in the individual. For example, you may ignore negative qualities in your friends that you would easily perceive in your enemies.

As might be expected, the implicit personality theories that people hold differ from culture to culture, group to group, and even person to person. For example, the Chinese have the concept *shi gu,* which refers to "someone who is worldly, devoted to his or her family, socially skillful, and somewhat reserved" (Aronson, Wilson, & Akert, 1999, p. 117). In English, on the other hand, we have a concept of the "artistic type," a generalization that seems absent in Chinese. Thus, although it is easy for speakers of English or Chinese to refer to specific concepts—such as "socially skilled" or "creative"—each language creates its own generalized categories. Thus, in Chinese the qualities that make up *shi gu* are more easily seen as going together than they might be for an English speaker; they're part of the implicit personality theory of more Chinese speakers than English speakers.

Self-Fulfilling Prophecy

A **self-fulfilling prophecy** occurs when you make a prediction that comes true because you act on it as if it were true (Merton, 1957). Put differently, a self-fulfilling prophecy occurs when you act on your schema as if it were true and in doing so make it true. There are four basic steps in the self-fulfilling prophecy:

TRY IT!
Apply your knowledge of self-fulfilling prophecies; go to **www.ablongman. com/devito**.

1. You make a prediction or formulate a belief about a person or a situation. For example, you predict that Pat is friendly in interpersonal encounters.
2. You act toward that person or situation as if that prediction or belief were true. For example, you act as if Pat were a friendly person.
3. Because you act as if the belief were true, it becomes true. For example, because of the way you act toward Pat, Pat becomes comfortable and friendly.
4. You observe your effect on the person or the resulting situation, and what you see strengthens your beliefs. For example, you observe Pat's friendliness, and this reinforces your belief that Pat is in fact friendly.

The self-fulfilling prophecy can also be seen when you make predictions about yourself and fulfill them. For example, you might enter a group situation convinced that the other members will dislike you. Almost invariably you'll be proved right; the other members will appear to you to dislike you. What you may be doing is acting in a way that encourages the group to respond to you negatively. In this way, you fulfill your prophecies about yourself.

A widely known example of the self-fulfilling prophecy is the **Pygmalion effect.** In one study, teachers were told that certain pupils were expected to do exceptionally well,

Racial profiling (the practice whereby the police focus on members of specific races as possible crime suspects) has been widely reported and widely condemned as racist. In the aftermath of the attacks on the World Trade Center and the Pentagon on September 11, 2001, many people came to view racial profiling—specifically of Muslims and those who looked "Arab"—as acceptable, as helpful in preventing further acts of terrorism. How did you feel about racial profiling prior to September 11? How did you feel about it in the weeks following September 11th? How do you feel about it now?

that they were late bloomers. The names of these students were actually selected at random by the experimenters. The results, however, were not random. The students whose names were given to the teachers actually performed at a higher level than the others. In fact, these students' IQ scores even improved more than did the other students'. The teachers' expectations probably prompted them to give extra attention to the selected students, thereby positively affecting their performance (Rosenthal & Jacobson, 1968; Insel & Jacobson, 1975). The same general effect is found in military training and business settings where trainees and workers performed better when their supervisors were given positive information about them (McNatt, 2001). The Pygmalion effect is also seen in such areas as leadership, athletic coaching, and effective stepfamilies (Eden, 1992; Solomon et al., 1996; Einstein, 1995). Findings such as these have led one researcher to suggest applying the Pygmalion effect to improve worker productivity. By creating positive attitudes about employees in supervisors and by helping employees to feel that their supervisors and the organizations as a whole value them highly productivity would increase (McNatt, 2001).

Self-fulfilling prophecies can short-circuit critical thinking and influence another's behavior (or your own) so that it conforms to your prophecy. As a result, you may see what you predicted rather than what is really there (for example, to perceive yourself as a failure because you have predicted it rather than because of any actual failures).

Perceptual Accentuation

When poor and rich children were shown pictures of coins and later asked to estimate their size, the poor children's size estimates were much greater than the rich children's. Similarly, hungry people need fewer visual cues to perceive food objects and food terms than do people who are not hungry. This process, called **perceptual accentuation,** leads you to see what you expect or want to see. You see people you like as better looking and smarter than those you don't like. You magnify or accentuate what will satisfy your needs and desires: The thirsty person sees a mirage of water, the sexually deprived person sees a mirage of sexual satisfaction.

Perceptual accentuation can lead you to perceive what you need or want to perceive rather than what is really there, and to fail to perceive what you don't want to perceive. For example, you may not perceive signs of impending problems because you focus on what you want to perceive.

Perceptual accentuation can also lead you to perceive and remember positive qualities more than negative ones (a phenomenon referred to as the *Pollyanna effect*) and thus distort your perceptions of others.

Another interesting distortion created by perceptual accentuation is that you may perceive certain behaviors as indicative that someone likes you simply because you want to be liked. For example, general politeness and friendly behavior used as a persuasive strategy (say, by a salesperson) are frequently seen as indicating a genuine personal liking.

Primacy–Recency

Assume for a moment that you're enrolled in a course in which half the classes are extremely dull and half extremely exciting. At the end of the semester, you evaluate the course and the instructor. Would your evaluation be more favorable if the dull classes occurred in the first half of the semester and the exciting classes in the second? Or would it be more favorable if the order were reversed? If what comes first exerts the most influence, you have a *primacy effect*. If what comes last (or most recently) exerts the most influence, you have a *recency effect*.

In the classic study on the effects of **primacy–recency** in interpersonal perception, college students perceived a person who was described as "intelligent, industrious, impulsive, critical, stubborn, and envious" more positively than a person described as "envious, stubborn, critical, impulsive, industrious, and intelligent" (Asch, 1946). Clearly, there's a tendency to use early information to get a general idea about a person and to use later information to make this impression more specific. The initial information helps you form a schema for the person. Once that schema is formed, you're likely to resist information that contradicts it.

One interesting practical implication of primacy–recency is that the first impression you make is likely to be the most important. The reason for this is that the schema that others form of you functions as a filter to admit or block additional information about you. If the initial impression or schema is positive, others are likely to readily remember additional positive information because it confirms this original positive image or schema and to easily forget or distort negative information because it contradicts this original positive schema, and they are also more likely to interpret ambiguous information as positive. You win in all three ways—if the initial impression is positive.

The tendency to give greater weight to early information and to interpret later information in light of early impressions can lead you to formulate a total picture of an individual on the basis of initial impressions that may not be typical or accurate. For example, if you judge a job applicant as generally nervous when he or she may simply be showing normal nervousness at being interviewed for a much needed job, you will have misperceived this individual.

Similarly, this tendency can lead you to discount or distort subsequent perceptions so as not to disrupt your initial impression or upset your original schema. For example, you may fail to see signs of deceit in someone you like because of your early impressions that this person is a good and honest individual.

Consistency

The tendency to maintain balance among perceptions or attitudes is called **consistency** (McBroom & Reed, 1992). You expect certain things to go together and other things not to go together.

On a purely intuitive basis, for example, respond to the following sentences by noting your expected response.

1. I expect a person I like to (like, dislike) me.
2. I expect a person I dislike to (like, dislike) me.
3. I expect my friend to (like, dislike) my friend.
4. I expect my friend to (like, dislike) my enemy.
5. I expect my enemy to (like, dislike) my friend.
6. I expect my enemy to (like, dislike) my enemy.

According to most consistency theories, your expectations would be as follows: You would expect a person you liked to like you (1) and one you disliked to dislike you (2). You would expect a friend to like a friend (3) and to dislike an enemy (4). You would expect your enemy to dislike your friend (5) and to like your other enemy (6). All these expectations are intuitively satisfying.

Further, you would expect someone you liked to possess characteristics you like or admire and would expect your enemies not to possess characteristics you like or admire. Conversely, you would expect people you liked to lack unpleasant characteristics and those you disliked to possess unpleasant characteristics.

Uncritically assuming that an individual is consistent can lead you to ignore or distort your perceptions of behaviors that are inconsistent with your picture of the whole person. For example, you may misinterpret Karla's unhappiness because your image of Karla is "happy, controlled, and contented." Consistency can also lead you to see certain behaviors as positive if you interpreted other behaviors positively (the halo effect) or as negative if you interpreted other behaviors negatively (the reverse halo effect).

Stereotyping

One of the most common shortcuts in interpersonal perception is stereotyping. A sociological or psychological **stereotype** is a fixed impression of a group of people; it's a schema. We all have attitudinal stereotypes—of national, religious, sexual, or racial groups, or perhaps of criminals, prostitutes, teachers, or plumbers. If you have these fixed impressions, you will, upon meeting a member of a particular group, often see that person primarily as a member of that group and apply to him or her all the characteristics you assign to that group. If you meet someone who is a prostitute, for example, there is a host of characteristics for prostitutes that you may apply to this one person. To complicate matters further, you will often "see" in this person's behavior the manifestation of characteristics that you would not "see" if you didn't know that this person was a prostitute. In online communication there are few visual and auditory cues, so it's not surprising to find that people form impressions of their online communication partner with a heavy reliance on stereotypes (Jacobson, 1999). Stereotypes can easily distort accurate perception and prevent you from seeing an individual as an individual rather than as a member of a group.

The tendency to group people and to respond to individuals primarily as members of groups can lead you to perceive an individual as possessing those qualities (usually negative) that you believe characterize his or her group (for example, all Mexicans are . . . or all Baptists are . . .) and, therefore, fail to appreciate the multifaceted nature of all

Increasing Interpersonal Effectiveness
Other-Orientation

Other-orientation refers to the ability to adapt your messages to the other person. It involves communicating attentiveness and interest in the other person and in what the person says.

Communicating Other-Orientation You'll recognize the following behaviors in those with whom you enjoy talking.

■ *Show consideration and respect.* For example, asking if it's all right to dump your troubles on someone before doing so, or asking if your phone call comes at a good time before launching into your conversation.

■ *Acknowledge the other person's feelings as correct and legitimate.* Comments like "You're right" or "That's interesting" or "I can understand why you're so angry; I would be, too" help focus the interaction on the other person and assure the person that you're listening.

■ *Acknowledge the presence and the importance of the other person.* Ask the other person for suggestions and opinions. Similarly, ask for clarification as appropriate. This will ensure that you understand what the other person is saying from that person's point of view.

■ *Focus your messages on the other person.* Verbally, use open-ended questions to involve the other person in the interaction (as opposed to questions that merely ask for a yes or no answer) and statements that directly address the person. Nonverbally, use focused eye contact, appropriate facial expressions, smiling, nodding, and leaning toward the other person.

■ *Grant the other person permission to express (or to not express) her or his feelings.* A simple statement such as "I know how difficult it is to talk about feelings" opens up the topic of feelings and gives permission to pursue such a discussion or to say nothing.

---

individuals and groups. Stereotyping can also lead you to ignore each person's unique characteristics and, therefore, fail to benefit from the special contributions each individual can bring to an encounter.

Attribution

Think about each of the following situations:

1. A woman is begging in the street.
2. A store owner kills a thief.
3. A father leaves his children.

To what do you attribute the causes of these situations? Did the begging, killing, and abandonment result from something within the person or from within the situation? The way you would answer these questions is neatly explained in **attribution** theory. Attribution theory explains the process you go through in trying to understand others' behaviors as well as your own (in **self-attribution**), particularly the reasons or motivations for these behaviors. Attribution helps you to impose order and logic and to better understand the possible causes of the behaviors you observe.

Attribution also helps you to make predictions about what will happen, what others are likely or unlikely to do. If you can be reasonably sure that Pat gave money out of a desire to help the poor (that is, you can attribute the behavior to a desire to help), then you can make predictions about Pat's future behaviors that are more likely to be correct than predictions made without this initial attribution to guide you.

Attribution Processes In trying to discover the causes of another's behavior, your first step is to determine whether the individual or some outside factor is responsible. That is, you must first determine whether the cause is *internal* (for example, due to some personality trait) or *external* (for example, due to some situational factor). Your assessment of someone's behavior as internally or externally motivated will greatly influence your evaluation of that person. If you judge people's cooperative behavior as internally caused (that is, as motivated by their personality), you're more apt to form a positive evaluation of them and, eventually, to like them. In contrast, if you judge that very same behavior to be externally caused (the watchful eye of the boss is forcing someone to behave cooperatively, for example), you're more apt to form a negative evaluation and, eventually, to dislike the person (because he or she isn't "really" cooperative).

Consider another example. You look at an instructor's grade book and observe that 10 Fs were assigned in cultural anthropology. In an attempt to discover what this reveals about the instructor, you first have to discover whether the instructor was in fact responsible for the assignment of the 10 Fs or whether the grading could be attributed to external factors. Let's say you discover that the examinations on which the grades were based had been made up by a faculty committee, which also set the standards for passing or failing. In this case, you could not attribute any particular motives to this individual instructor because the behavior was not internally caused.

On the other hand, let's assume the following: This instructor made up the examination without any assistance, no departmental or university standards were used, and the instructor created a personal set of standards for passing and failing. Now you would be more apt (though perhaps not fully justified) to attribute the 10 Fs to internal causes. You would be strengthened in your beliefs that there was something within this instructor, some personality characteristic, for example, that led to this behavior if you discovered that (1) no other instructor in anthropology gave nearly as many Fs, (2) this particular instructor frequently gives Fs in cultural anthropology, (3) this instructor frequently gives Fs in other courses as well, and (4) this instructor is the only one responsible for assigning grades and could have assigned grades other than F. These four bits of added information would lead you to conclude that there was something within this instructor that motivated the behavior. In forming such causal judgments, which you make every day, you use four principles: (1) consensus, (2) consistency, (3) distinctiveness, and (4) controllability.

Consensus: Similarity with Others

When you use the principle of consensus, you ask, "Do other people behave in the same way as the person on whom I'm focusing?" That is, is the person acting in accordance with the consensus, the majority? If the answer is no, you're more likely to attribute the behavior to some internal cause and conclude: "This person is different." In the instructor example, you would be strengthened in your belief that something internal caused the Fs to be given if you learned that other instructors didn't do this; that is, there was low consensus. When only one person acts contrary to the norm, you're more likely to attribute that person's behavior to internal motivation. If all instructors gave many Fs (that is, if there was high consensus), you'd be more likely to look for causality outside the individual instructor; you might conclude that the anthropology department uses a particular curve in determining grades or that the students were not very bright—or any other reason external to the specific instructor.

Consistency: Similarity over Time

When you use the principle of consistency, you ask if this person repeatedly (consistently) behaves in the same way in similar situations. If the answer is yes, there's high consistency, and you're likely to attribute the behavior to internal motivation. If you knew that this instructor frequently gives Fs in cultural anthropology, it would lead you to attribute the cause to the instructor rather than to outside sources. If, on the other hand, there was low consistency—that is, if this instructor rarely gives Fs—you'd be more likely to look for external reasons. Again, you might conclude, for example, that this specific class was not very bright or that the department required the instructor to start giving out Fs.

Distinctiveness: Similarity in Different Situations

When you use the principle of distinctiveness, you ask if this person reacts in similar ways in different situations. If the answer is yes, there is low distinctiveness, and you're likely to conclude that the behavior has an internal cause. If the instructor reacted the same way (gave lots of Fs) in different situations (other courses), it would lead you to conclude that this particular class was not distinctive and that the motivation for the behavior could not be found in the unique situation. You'd further conclude that this behavior is likely due to the instructor's inner motivation. Consider the alternative: If this instructor gave all high grades and no Fs in other courses (that is, if the cultural anthropology class situation was highly distinctive), you'd conclude that the motivation for the failures was to be found in sources outside the instructor and for reasons unique to this class.

Controllability: Behavior Control

Let's say your friend is an hour late for a dinner appointment (cf., Weiner, Amirkhan, Folkes, & Verette, 1987). How would you feel about the following two possible excuses?

Excuse 1: I was reading this book, and I just couldn't put it down. I had to find out who the killer was.

Excuse 2: I was stuck on the subway for two hours; a water main broke, killing all the electricity.

It's likely you'd resent the first and accept the second excuse. The first excuse says that the reason for the lateness was controllable: Your friend chose to be late by completing the novel. You'd therefore hold your friend responsible for wasting your time and for a lack of consideration. The second excuse says that the reason was uncontrollable: Your friend couldn't help being late. Here you'd not hold your friend responsible. This, by the way, is why excuses involving uncontrollable factors are more effective than those involving controllable factors.

Think about your own tendency to make similar judgments based on controllability. For example, how you would respond to situations such as the following:

■ Doris fails her midterm history exam.
■ Sidney's car is repossessed because he failed to make the payments.
■ Thomas's wife has just filed for divorce and he is feeling depressed.

Very probably you'd be sympathetic to each of these people if you felt they were not in control of what happened—for example, if the examination was unfair, if Sidney lost his job because of employee discrimination, and if Thomas's wife is leaving him for a billionaire. On the other hand, you might blame these people for their problems if you felt that they were in control of the situation—for example, if Doris partied instead of studied, if Sidney gambled his payments away, and if Thomas had been repeatedly unfaithful and his wife finally gave up trying to change him.

In perceiving other people and especially in evaluating their behavior, you frequently ask if the person was in control of the behavior. Generally, research shows that if you feel people are in control of negative behaviors, you'll come to dislike them. But you'll feel sorry for someone you feel isn't in control of negative behaviors, and you won't blame the person for his or her negative circumstances.

Table 4.1 **A Summary of Causal Attribution**

Situation: John was fired from a job he began a few months ago. On what basis will you decide whether this behavior is internally caused (John is responsible) or externally caused (John isn't responsible)?

Internal If	External If
No one else was fired (low consensus).	Lots of others were fired (high consensus).
John was fired from lots of other jobs (high consistency).	John was never fired from any other job (low consistency).
John has failed at many other things (low distinctiveness).	John has always been successful (high distinctiveness).
John could have been retained if he agreed to move to another shop (high controllability).	John was not given any alternatives (low controllability).

Low consensus, high consistency, low distinctiveness, and high controllability lead to an attribution of internal causes. As a result, you praise or blame the person for his or her behaviors. High consensus, low consistency, high distinctiveness, and low controllability lead to an attribution of external causes. Table 4.1 summarizes these four principles of attribution.

Attribution Errors   Attribution of causality can lead to several major barriers. Here are three such barriers: the self-serving bias, overattribution, and the fundamental attribution error.

The Self-Serving Bias   The **self-serving bias** is a mechanism designed to preserve self-esteem. You commit the self-serving bias when you take credit for the positive and deny responsibility for the negative. For example, you're more likely to attribute your positive behaviors (say, you get an A on an exam) to internal and controllable factors, to your personality, intelligence, or hard work (Bernstein, Stephan, & Davis, 1979). You're more likely to attribute your negative behaviors (say, you get a D) to external and uncontrollable factors, to the exam being exceptionally difficult or unfair.

Similarly, the self-serving bias influences the way you view conflict (Schutz, 1999). For example, you're more likely to describe your partner's negative behavior as internally motivated and your negative behavior as externally caused ("I couldn't help it" or "They made me do it"). Similarly, you're more likely to make excuses and justify your own behavior rather than your partner's.

There is some evidence (though it's not overwhelming) that we explain the behaviors of ingroup and outgroup members differently (Taylor & Jaggi, 1974; Berry, Poortinga, Segall, & Dasen, 1992). For example, you're more likely to explain members' positive behavior as internally motivated and nonmembers' positive behaviors as externally motivated. Thus, you would be more apt to explain, say, a high record of charitable contributions for members of your own culture with something like "We're a charitable people; we believe in helping others." If this is shown to be true for members of another culture, you'd be more apt to say something like "They're rich; they need tax deductions."

Alternatively, you're likely to explain the negative behavior of members of your own culture as externally or situationally caused but to explain the very same behavior of members of other cultures as internally motivated. Thus, for example, you would be more apt to attribute a high college dropout rate (a negatively evaluated behavior) to external sources (instructors who were not motivating or irrelevant educational programs) if this was shown to be true of your own cultural group. If, on the other hand, it were shown to be true of another culture, then you'd be more apt to attribute it to internal sources (the people aren't interested in education; they lack motivation).

At times you might construct defensive attributions by which you try to explain behavior in ways that make you seem less vulnerable. One way you might do this is with unrealistic optimism, maintaining the belief that good things are more likely to happen to you than to others. For example, most people think that they will ultimately experience more good things and less bad things than their peers (Aronson, Wilson, & Akert, 1999). A similar belief is the *just world* hypothesis, the belief that bad things will happen only to bad people. Since you are a good person, good things will happen to you. Of course, in your mindful state, you know that good things often happen to bad people and that bad things often happen to good people.

Overattribution   Overattribution is the tendency to single out one or two obvious characteristics of a person and attribute everything that person does to these characteristics. For example, if the person had alcoholic parents or is blind or was born into great wealth, there's often a tendency to attribute everything that person does to such factors. So you might say Sally has difficulty forming meaningful relationships because she grew up in a home of alcoholics, Alex overeats because he's blind, and Lillian is irresponsible because she never had to work for her money. To prevent overattribution, recognize that most behaviors and personality characteristics result from lots of factors. You almost always make a mistake when you select one factor and attribute everything to it. When you make a judgment, ask yourself if other factors might be operating here: Are there other factors that might be creating difficulties for Sally to form relationships, for Alex to control his eating habits, and for Lillian to behave irresponsibly?

The Third-Person Effect

How effective are the media in influencing you as compared to, say, the influence media exert on a group of your peers? Are you influenced less than your peers, about the same as your peers, or more than your peers? In a variety of studies conducted on college students, research finds that students believe that they were influenced less by the media than were their peers (Davison, 1983). Whether the topic was political advertising, rap music, or pornography, students felt they were less susceptible to media influence than were their peers (Hoffner et al., 2001). This belief, called the third-person effect, is especially strong when the media message is a negative or socially unacceptable one; for example, people think that messages of violence, racism, or sexism influence them much less than they influence their peers. The effect is weakened but still present when the message is a more acceptable one (for example, public service announcements).

Follow Up   Try testing out this theory. For example, survey 10 or 20 people and ask them how influenced they feel they are by, say, media violence or racism. Then ask them if their friends and relatives are more influenced than they are. Perform another survey based on a more socially acceptable issue such as media campaigns on the value of education or the importance of proper diet. Follow this up by questions about how influenced they feel their friends and relatives are by these same messages. Do you find a third-person effect?

The Fundamental Attribution Error   The fundamental attribution error occurs when you overvalue the contribution of internal factors and undervalue the influence of external factors. It's the tendency to conclude that people do what they do because that's the kind of people they are not because of the situation they're in. When Pat is late for an appointment, you're more likely to conclude that Pat is inconsiderate or irresponsible rather than attribute the lateness to the bus breaking down or to a traffic accident.

When you explain your own behavior, you also favor internal explanations although not to as great an extent as when explaining the behaviors of others. One reason for giving greater weight to external factors in explaining your own behavior than you do in explaining the behavior of others is that you know the situation surrounding your own behavior. You know, for example, what's going on in your love life and you know your financial condition, so you naturally see the influence of these factors. But you rarely know as much about others and, thus, are more likely to give less weight to the external factors in their cases.

This fundamental attribution error is at least in part culturally influenced. For example, in the United States people are more likely to explain behavior by saying that people did what they did because of who they are. But when Hindus in India were asked to explain why their friends behaved as they did, they gave greater weight to external factors than did Americans in the United States (Miller, 1984; Aronson, Wilson, & Akert, 1999). Further, Americans have little hesitation in offering causal explanations of a person's behavior ("Pat did this because . . ."). Hindus, on the other hand, are generally reluctant to explain a person's behavior in causal terms (Matsumoto, 1994).

Let's return to the three examples with which we opened this discussion of attribution as a way of summarizing the principles of consensus, consistency, distinctiveness, and controllability. Generally, you would consider the three actions—begging, killing, and abandonment—to result from something inherent in the begging woman, the store owner, and the father if other people behaved differently in situations similar to these (low consensus), if these people had engaged in these behaviors in the past (high consistency), if these people behaved similarly in other situations (low distinctiveness), and if these people were in control of their own behaviors (high controllability). Under these conditions, you'd probably conclude that the persons bear the responsibility for their behaviors.

Alternatively, you would consider these actions to have resulted from something external to the persons if many other people reacted the same way in similar situations (high consensus), if these people had never behaved in this way before (low consistency), if these people never engaged in these behaviors in different situations (high distinctiveness), and if these people were not in control of their own behavior (low controllability). Under these conditions, you'd probably conclude that these actions resulted from external factors, that these people had little or no control, and that, therefore, they're not personally responsible.

INCREASING ACCURACY IN INTERPERSONAL PERCEPTION

Successful interpersonal communication depends largely on the accuracy of your interpersonal perception. We've already identified the potential barriers that can arise with each of the perceptual processes, for example, the self-serving bias, overattribution, and the fundamental attribution error in attribution. There are, however, additional ways to increase your accuracy in interpersonal perception.

Analyze Your Perceptions

When you become aware of your perceptions, you'll be able to subject them to logical analysis, to critical thinking. Here are two suggestions.

- *Recognize your own role in perception.* Your emotional and physiological state will influence the meaning you give to your perceptions. A movie may seem hysterically funny when you're in a good mood but just plain stupid when you're in a bad mood or when you're preoccupied with family problems. Beware of your own biases. Know when your perceptual evaluations are unduly influenced by your own biases. For example, perceiving only the positive in people you like and only the negative in people you don't like. Even your gender will influence your perceptions. Women consistently evaluate other people more positively than do men on factors such as agreeableness, conscientiousness, and emotional stability (Winquist, Mohr, & Kenny, 1998).

- *Avoid early conclusions.* On the basis of your observations of behaviors, formulate hypotheses to test against additional information and evidence rather than drawing conclusions you then look to confirm. Delay formulating conclusions until you have had a chance to process a wide variety of cues. Similarly, avoid the one-cue conclusion. Look for a variety of cues pointing in the same direction. The more cues pointing to the same conclusion, the more likely your conclusion will be correct. Be especially alert to contradictory cues, ones that refute your initial hypotheses. It's relatively easy to perceive cues that confirm your hypotheses but more difficult to acknowledge contradictory evidence. At the same time, seek

Cultivation Theory

According to cultivation theory, the media, especially television, are the primary means by which you learn about your society and your culture: What you watch and how often you watch it will influence your perception of the world and of people (Gerbner, Gross, Morgan, & Signorielli, 1980; Signorielli & Lears, 1992; Morgan & Shanahan, 1991; Vergeer, Lubbers, & Scheepers, 2000).

Cultivation theory argues that heavy television viewers form an image of reality that is inconsistent with the facts (Potter, 1986; Potter & Chang, 1990). For example:

- Heavy viewers see their chances of being a victim of a crime to be 1 in 10. In reality the ratio is 1 in 50.
- Heavy viewers think that 20 percent of the world's population lives in the United States. In reality it's only

6 percent. (As of the 2000 Census, it's actually 4.6 percent.)

- Heavy viewers believe that the percentage of workers in managerial or professional jobs is 25 percent. In reality it's 5 percent.
- Heavy sports program viewers are more likely to believe in the values of hard work and good conduct.
- Heavy soap opera viewers are more likely to believe that "luck is important" and that "the strong survive" than are light viewers.

Follow Up   How might you go about counteracting the false sense of reality given by a great number of media messages? For example, what specific changes in your reading, television viewing, or Internet surfing might help you see reality more accurately?

validation from others. Do others see things in the same way you do? If not, ask yourself if your perceptions may be distorted in some way.

Check Your Perceptions

TRY IT!
Apply your understanding of perception checking; go to <u>www.ablongman.com/devito</u>.

Perception checking is another way to reduce uncertainty and to make your perceptions more accurate. The goal of perception checking is to further explore the thoughts and feelings of the other person, not to prove that your initial perception is correct. With this simple technique, you lessen your chances of misinterpreting another's feelings. At the same time, you give the other person an opportunity to elaborate on his or her thoughts and feelings. In its most basic form, perception checking consists of two steps.

■ Describe what you see or hear, recognizing that descriptions are not really objective but are heavily influenced by who you are, your emotional state, and so on. At the same time, you may wish to describe what you think is happening. Try to do this as descriptively (not evaluatively) as you can. Sometimes you may wish to offer several possibilities.

- You've called me from work a lot this week. You seem concerned that everything is all right at home.
- You've not wanted to talk with me all week. You say that my work is fine but you don't seem to want to give me the same responsibilities that other editorial assistants have.

■ Avoid mind reading. Don't try to read the thoughts and feelings of another person just from observing their behaviors. Regardless of how many behaviors you observe and how carefully you examine them, you can only *guess* what is going on in someone's mind. A person's motives are not open to outside inspection; you can only make assumptions based on overt behaviors. So, seek confirmation. Ask the other person if your description is accurate. Be careful that your request for confirmation does not sound as though you already know the answer. Avoid phrasing your questions defensively as in, for example, "You really don't want to go out, do you? I knew you didn't when you turned on that lousy television." Instead, ask for confirmation in as supportive a way as possible.

- Would you rather watch TV?
- Are you worried about me or the kids?
- Are you displeased with my work? Is there anything I can do to improve my job performance?

Reduce Your Uncertainty

Reducing uncertainty enables you to achieve greater accuracy in perception. In large part you learned about uncertainty and how to deal with it from your culture. In some cultures people do little to avoid uncertainty and have little anxiety about not knowing what will happen next; uncertainty to them is a normal part of life and is accepted as it comes. Members of these cultures don't feel threatened by unknown situations. Examples of such low-anxiety cultures include Singapore, Jamaica, Denmark, Sweden, Hong Kong, Ireland, Great Britain, Malaysia, India, the Philippines, and the United States. Other cultures do much to avoid uncertainty and have a great deal of anxiety about not knowing what will happen next; uncertainty is seen as threatening and something that must be counteracted. Examples of such high-anxiety cultures include Greece, Portugal, Guatemala, Uruguay, Belgium, El Salvador, Japan, Yugoslavia, Peru, France, Chile, Spain, and Costa Rica (Hofstede, 1997).

The potential for communication problems can be great when people come from cultures with different attitudes toward uncertainty. For example, managers from cul-

A S K *the Researcher*

Learning about Your Workplace

I'm starting a new job this month and want to learn as much as I can about the organization as fast as I can. In academic terms, how can I reduce my uncertainty about my new workplace—its dos and don'ts, its culture, its reward system? I'm planning on going as high as I can as fast as I can.

I think the best way to address your question is simply to provide a list of things you might do:

■ Observe carefully. Watch individuals' actions, especially those who have recently achieved success. Don't rely so much on verbal reports and "stories" about success. These "stories" may be more myth than reality.

■ Talk to as many people as possible at all levels of the organization. Don't rely on a few individuals' opinions/observations.

■ Try to determine what behavior is rewarded by the organization. Most organizations are constantly evolving, so it is vital that information acquisition be an ongoing activity rather than something you do only at the beginning of a career.

■ Identify sub-goals that will lead to your primary goals and develop plans to reach these goals. However, when the environment is highly dynamic, be prepared to alter goals and plans as the environment changes. Here again, goal setting and planning are ongoing activities, not just one-time events.

For more information, see C. R. Berger, *Planning Strategic Interaction: Attaining Goals through Communicative Action* (Mahwah, NJ: Erlbaum, 1997).

Charles R. Berger (Ph.D., Michigan State University) is a professor in the Department of Communication, University of California, Davis. His teaching concentrations include communication and cognition, interpersonal communication, nonverbal communication, risk communication, and mass media effects. His research focuses on message planning and communication effectiveness and the cognitive processing of risk communication. (Reprinted by permission of Dr. Charles R. Berger.)

tures with weak uncertainty avoidance will accept workers who work only when they have to and will not get too upset when workers are late. Managers from cultures with strong uncertainty avoidance will expect workers to be busy at all times and will have little tolerance for lateness.

Because weak uncertainty avoidance cultures have great tolerance for ambiguity and uncertainty, they minimize the importance of rules governing communication and relationships (Hofstede, 1997; Lustig & Koester, 1999). People who don't follow the same rules as the cultural majority are readily tolerated. Different approaches and perspectives may even be encouraged in cultures with weak uncertainty avoidance. Strong uncertainty avoidance cultures create very clear-cut rules for communication that must not be broken.

Students from weak uncertainty avoidance cultures appreciate freedom in education and prefer vague assignments without specific timetables. These students will want to be rewarded for creativity and will easily accept an instructor's lack of knowledge in some areas. Students from strong uncertainty avoidance cultures prefer highly structured experiences where there is little ambiguity; they prefer specific objectives, detailed instructions, and definite timetables. These students expect to be judged on the basis of the right answers and expect the instructor to have all the answers all the time (Hofstede, 1997).

A variety of strategies can help reduce uncertainty (Berger & Bradac, 1982; Gudykunst, 1993).

■ Observing another person while he or she is engaged in an active task, preferably interacting with others in an informal social situation, will often reveal a great deal about the person since people are less apt to monitor their behaviors and more likely to reveal their true selves in informal situations.

View point As your relationship with another person becomes closer and more intimate, you generally reduce your uncertainty about each other; you become more predictable to each other. Do you think high predictability makes a relationship more stable or less stable? More enjoyable or less enjoyable?

■ You can manipulate the situation in such a way that you observe the person in more specific and revealing contexts. Employment interviews, theatrical auditions, and student teaching are some of the ways situations can be created to observe how the person might act and react, and will help you reduce your uncertainty about the person.

■ When you log on to an Internet chat group for the first time and lurk, reading the exchanges between the other group members before saying anything yourself, you're learning about the people in the group and about the group itself; thus reducing uncertainty. When uncertainty is reduced, you're more likely to make contributions that will be appropriate to the group and less likely to violate the group's norms; in short, you're more likely to communicate effectively.

■ Another way to reduce uncertainty is to collect information about the person through asking others. You might inquire of a colleague if a third person finds you interesting and might like to have dinner with you.

■ Interact with the individual. For example, you can ask questions: "Do you enjoy sports?" "What did you think of that computer science course?" "What would you do if you got fired?" You also gain knowledge of another by disclosing information about yourself. Your disclosures will help to create an environment that encourages disclosures from the person about whom you wish to learn more.

Increase Your Cultural Sensitivity

Recognizing and being sensitive to cultural differences will help increase your accuracy in perception. For example, Russian or Chinese artists such as ballet dancers will often applaud their audience by clapping. Americans seeing this may easily interpret this as egotistical. Similarly, a German man will enter a restaurant before the woman in order to see if the place is respectable enough for the woman to enter. This simple custom can easily be interpreted as rude when viewed by people from cultures in which it's considered courteous for the woman to enter first (Axtell, 1994).

Within every cultural group there are wide and important differences. As all Americans are not alike, neither are all Indonesians, Greeks, or Mexicans. When you make assumptions that all people of a certain culture are alike, you're thinking in stereotypes. Recognizing differences between another culture and your own, and among members of the same culture, will help you perceive the situation more accurately.

Cultural sensitivity will help counteract the difficulty most people have in understanding the nonverbal messages of people from other cultures. For example, it's easier to interpret the facial expressions of members of your own culture than those of members of other cultures (Weathers, Frank, & Spell, 2002). This "in-group advantage" will assist your perceptional accuracy for members of your own culture but will often hinder your accuracy for members of other cultures (Elfenbein & Ambady, 2002).

The suggestions for improving intercultural communication offered in Chapter 2 are applicable to increasing your cultural sensitivity; they are listed here to refresh your memory.

- Prepare yourself.
- Reduce uncertainty.
- Recognize differences (between yourself and people from other cultures, among members of other cultures, and between your meanings and the meanings that people from other cultures might have).
- Adjust your communication.
- Recognize the likelihood and the impact of culture shock.

REVIEWING   Key Terms and Concepts in Interpersonal Perception

This chapter examined perception, a fundamental process in all interpersonal communication encounters, and looked at the stages you go through in perceiving people, the processes that influence your perceptions, and some of the ways in which you can make your perceptions more accurate.

Stages of Perception
What is perception and how does it work?
- Perception is the process by which you become aware of objects and events in the external world.
- Perception occurs in five stages: (1) stimulation, (2) organization, (3) interpretation–evaluation, (4) memory, and (5) recall.

Perceptual Processes
What influences your interpersonal perceptions?
- Your implicit personality theory allows you to conclude that certain characteristics go with certain other characteristics.
- Your self-fulfilling prophecy may influence the behaviors of others.
- Perceptual accentuation may lead you to perceive what you expect to perceive instead of what is really there.
- Perceptions may be affected by primacy–recency. Your tendency to give extra importance to what occurs first (a primacy effect) may lead you to see what conforms to this judgment and to distort or otherwise misperceive what contradicts it. First impressions often serve as filters, as schemata, for more recent information. In some cases,

you may give extra weight to what occurs last (a recency effect).
- The tendency to seek and expect consistency may influence you to see what is consistent and to not see what is inconsistent.
- A stereotype, a fixed impression about a group, may influence your perceptions of individual members; you may see individuals only as members of the group instead of as unique individuals.
- Judgments of attribution, the process through which you try to understand the behaviors of others (and your own behaviors, in self-attribution), particularly the reasons or motivations for these behaviors, are made on the basis of consensus, consistency, distinctiveness, and controllability. Errors of attribution include the self-serving bias, overattribution, and the fundamental attribution error.

Increasing Accuracy in Interpersonal Perception
How might you increase your accuracy in perception?
- Perceive critically: For example, recognize your role in perception, avoid early conclusions, and avoid mind reading.
- Check your perceptions; describe what you see or hear and ask for confirmation.
- Reduce uncertainty: For example, by lurking before actively participating in an Internet chat group, collecting information about the person or situation, interacting and observing the situation.
- Be culturally sensitive; recognize the differences between you and others and also the differences among people from another culture.

APPLYING   Key Terms and Concepts in Interpersonal Perception

1. What role do first impressions play in your perception of other people? Have you ever been wrong? What might you do to make your first impressions more accurate?
2. Although most of the research on the self-fulfilling prophecy illustrates its distorting effect on behavior, consider how you might go about using the self-fulfilling prophecy to encourage behaviors you want to increase in strength and frequency. For example, what might you do to encourage persons who are high in communication apprehension to speak up with greater confidence? What might you do to encourage people who are reluctant to self-disclose to reveal more of their inner selves?
3. What stereotypes do you think men entertain about women? What stereotypes do you think women entertain about men? How might these stereotypes influence their interpersonal communication?
4. View a few episodes of *Ally McBeal* and analyze the portrayal of women. What positive portrayals of women can you identify? What negative portrayals of women can you identify? In your analysis you may wish to take a look at Patton (2001).
5. Geert Hofstede (1997, p. 119), who conducted much of the cultural research reported in this chapter, claims that those cultures that have strong uncertainty avoidance believe "What is different, is dangerous." Weak uncertainty avoidance cultures believe "What is different, is curious." Is there anything in your experience that supports this distinction?
6. Do you engage in selective perception when listening to people talk about you? For example, are you more likely to attend to the positives than the negatives?
7. Has anyone's self-fulfilling prophecy about you ever influenced your behavior? What happened?
8. Using the concepts of attribution—especially controllability—how would you explain the attitudes that many people have about homeless people? About drug addicts or alcoholics? About successful politicians, scientists, or millionaires?
9. Writers to advice columnists generally attribute their problems to external sources, whereas the columnists' responses often focus on internal sources, and their advice is therefore directed at the writer (you shouldn't have done that; apologize; get out of the relationship) (Schoeneman & Rubanowitz, 1985). Do you find this true when people discuss their problems face-to-face, in letters, in e-mail to you? Do you generally respond as would the columnist?
10. What one suggestion for increasing accuracy do you wish others would use more often when they make judgments about you?

EXPERIENCING   Key Terms and Concepts in Interpersonal Perception

Go to **www.ablongman.com/devito**.

These exercises focus on sensitizing you to the influences on your perceptions and how you can make your perceptions more accurate.

(1) **Perceiving My Selves** invites you to consider how you see yourself and how you think others see you. This exercise is also an excellent icebreaker. (2) **How Might You Perceive Others' Perceptions?** presents a variety of situations in which people are likely to see things very differently and sensitizes you to the variety of perceptions possible from the "same" event. (3) **How Do You Make Attributions?** looks at a few specific situations and asks how you might make attributions in explaining the reasons for the behaviors. (4) **Barriers to Accurate Perception** presents a dialogue containing a variety of perceptional errors and asks you to identify them. (5) **Perspective Taking** asks you to take positive and negative perspectives on the same situations to help you explore the different conclusions people may draw from the same incident.

RESEARCHING with Research Navigator   Key Terms and Concepts in Interpersonal Perception

Go to **http://www.researchnavigator.com**.

Reading an article.
Read a popular or academic article on perception, how it works or how it can be made more effective. On the basis of this article what can you add to the discussion presented here?

Investigating key terms.
Investigate one of the key terms discussed in this chapter (for example, perception, memory, self-fulfilling prophecy, primacy–recency, consistency, stereotype, attribution, other-orientation, the third-person effect, and cultivation theory). What additional insights can you provide?

Finding answers.
Try finding answers to one of the following questions or design a research study to answer it.
- In what ways are people who think largely in stereotypes different from people who think with few stereotypes?
- Are people who attribute controllability to the homeless more negative in their evaluation of homelessness than those who attribute a lack of controllability?
- Do different cultures hold different implicit personality theories? Do men and women hold different theories?
- Does training in perception actually improve perceptual accuracy?

5 Listening in Interpersonal Communication

What Women Want (2000)

Listening, not imitation, may be the sincerest form of flattery.

—Joyce Brothers

*T*he importance of listening in communication *is shown imaginatively in* What Women Want. *Nick Marshall (Mel Gibson), a chauvinist advertising executive, hasn't a clue as to what women are thinking and want. But, after electrocuting himself and acquiring the ability to listen in on what women are thinking, he becomes not only a more creative advertiser but much more popular with women, eventually finding true love with his competitor, Darcy (Helen Hunt).*

Before reading about this area of interpersonal communication, examine your own listening habits and tendencies by taking the accompanying self-test "How Well Do You Listen?"

TEST YOURSELF *How Well Do You Listen?*

Respond to each question with the following scale: 1 = always, 2 = frequently, 3 = sometimes, 4 = seldom, and 5 = never.

_____ 1. I listen to what the speaker is saying and feeling; I try to feel what the speaker feels.

_____ 2. I listen objectively; I focus on the logic of the ideas rather than on the emotional meaning of the message.

_____ 3. I listen without judging the speaker.

_____ 4. I listen critically, evaluating the speaker and what the speaker is saying.

_____ 5. I listen to the literal meanings that a speaker communicates; I don't look too deeply into hidden meanings.

_____ 6. I look for the hidden meanings; the meanings that are revealed by subtle verbal or nonverbal cues.

_____ 7. I listen actively, communicate acceptance of the speaker, and prompt the speaker to further explore his or her thoughts.

_____ 8. I listen without active involvement; I generally remain silent and take in what the other person is saying.

▶ **How did you do?** These statements focus on the ways of listening discussed in this chapter, all of which are appropriate at some times but not at others. The only responses that are inappropriate are "always" and "never." Effective listening is listening that is tailored to the specific communication situation.

▶ **What will you do?** Consider how you might use these statements to begin to improve your listening effectiveness. A good way to begin doing this is to review these statements and try to identify situations in which each statement would be appropriate and situations in which each statement would be inappropriate.

If you measured importance by the time you spend on an activity, then—according to the research studies available—listening would be your most important communication activity. Studies conducted from 1929 to 1980 show that listening is the most often used form of communication, followed by speaking, reading, and writing (Rankin, 1929; Werner, 1975; Barker, Edwards, Gaines, Gladney, & Holley, 1980; Steil, Barker, & Watson, 1983; Wolvin & Coakley, 1996). This was true of high school and college students as well as of adults from a wide variety of fields. But with the widespread use of the In-

Table 5.1 **Effective Listening: Purposes and Payoffs**

This table identifies the major purposes and payoffs of effective listening. Can you identify other purposes and payoffs?

Purposes and Payoffs	Examples
Learn: to acquire knowledge of others, the world, and yourself, so as to avoid problems and make more reasonable decisions	Listening to Peter about his travels to Cuba will help you understand more about Peter as well as about life in a communist country; listening to the difficulties your sales staff has may help you improve sales training
Relate: form and maintain friendships and love relationships on the basis of social acceptance and popularity because people come to like those who are attentive and supportive	Others will increase their liking for you once they feel you have genuine concern for them
Influence: have an effect on the attitudes and behaviors of others because people are more likely to respect and follow those who they feel have listened to and understood them	Workers are more likely to follow your advice once they feel you have truly listened to and heard their points of view, concerns and insights
Play: know when to suspend critical and evaluative thinking and when to simply engage in passive and accepting listening	Listening to the stories and anecdotes of coworkers will allow you to gain a more comfortable balance between the world of work and the world of play and perhaps to see humor in a world of seriousness
Help: be able to assist other people because you hear more, empathize more, and come to understand others more deeply	Listening to your child's complaints about her teacher (instead of responding "What did you do wrong?") will put you in a better position to help your child cope with school and with her teacher

ternet these studies are dated and their findings of limited value. Your communication patterns are very different from someone raised and educated before widespread use of home computers. However, anecdotal evidence (certainly not conclusive in any way) suggests that listening is probably still the most used communication activity. Just think of how you spend your day; listening probably occupies a considerable amount of time.

Another way to look at the importance of listening is to consider the numerous benefits or payoffs that accrue to the effective listener. For example, the effective listener is more likely to emerge as group leader and is a more effective adaptive seller and salesperson in general (Johnson & Bechler, 1998; Kramer, 1997; Castleberry & Shepherd, 1993). Additional benefits are identified in Table 5.1 where the varied payoffs are illustrated along with the purposes of listening—which, not surprisingly, are the same as those identified for interpersonal communication in Chapter 1: to learn, relate, influence, play, and help.

STAGES OF LISTENING

Listening is not the same as hearing. Hearing is a physiological process that occurs when you're in the vicinity of vibrations in the air and these vibrations impinge on your eardrum. Hearing is basically a passive process that occurs without any attention or effort on your part. Listening is different.

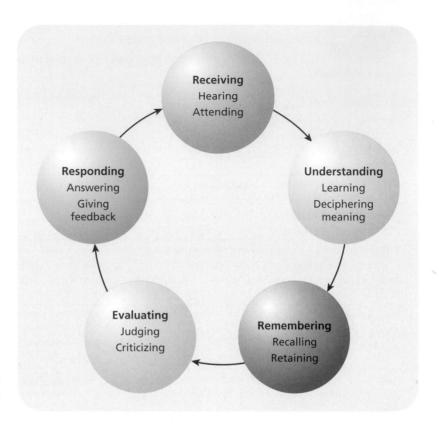

A Five-Stage Model of Listening
Recognize that at each stage there will be lapses. Thus, for example, at the receiving stage a listener receives part of the message and because of noise and perhaps other reasons fails to receive other parts. Similarly, at the stage of understanding, a listener understands part of the message and, because of one's inability to share another's meanings exactly, fails to understand other parts. The same is true for remembering, evaluating, and responding. This model draws on a variety of previous models that listening researchers have developed (for example, Alessandra, 1986; Barker, 1990; Brownell, 1987; Steil, Barker, & Watson, 1983).

Listening involves a series of five steps: receiving, understanding, remembering, evaluating, and responding (Figure 5.1). Note that the listening process is circular. The responses of one person serve as the stimuli for the other person, whose responses in turn serve as the stimuli for the first person, and so on.

Stage One: Receiving

Listening begins with receiving the messages the speaker sends. The messages are both verbal and nonverbal; they consist of words as well as gestures, facial expressions, and variations in volume and rate.

At this stage, you note not only what is said (verbally and nonverbally) but also what is omitted. You receive, for example, your boss's summary of your accomplishments as well as the omission of your shortcomings.

Analyze your own receiving. Do you

1. Focus your attention on the speaker's verbal and nonverbal messages, on what is said and on what isn't said?
2. Avoid distractions in the environment?
3. Focus your attention on the speaker rather than on what you'll say next?
4. Maintain your role as listener and avoid interrupting?

In this brief discussion of receiving and, in fact, in this entire chapter on listening, the unstated assumption is that both individuals can receive auditory signals without difficulty. But, for a large part of the population who have hearing impairments listening presents a variety of problems. Table 5.2 provides tips for communicating between deaf and hearing people.

Table 5.2 *Interpersonal Communication Tips*
Between deaf and hearing people

People differ greatly in their hearing ability; some are totally deaf and can hear nothing, others have some hearing loss and can hear some sounds, and still others have impaired hearing but can hear most speech. Although people with profound hearing loss can speak, their speech may appear labored and not as clear as the speech of those with unimpaired hearing. Here are some suggestions for more effective communication between deaf and hearing people.

If you have unimpaired hearing:

1. Reduce the distance between yourself and the person with a hearing impairment.
2. Reduce the background noise; turn off the television, the air conditioner, and other noisy appliances.
3. Face the person and avoid any interference with your visual cues. For example, avoid smoking, chewing gum, or holding your hand over your mouth. Make sure the lighting is adequate for ease in seeing your face and mouth; sunlight shining on your face or too little light, for example, can interfere with the visual cues that a hearing-impaired person can use.
4. Speak with an adequate volume, but don't shout. Shouting can distort your speech and may insult the person with a hearing loss. Be especially careful to avoid the tendency to reduce your volume at the ends of sentences.
5. Because some words are easier to lip-read than others, it often helps if you could rephrase your ideas in different ways.
6. When in a group situation, be especially careful that only one person speaks at a time. Similarly, make sure you direct your comments to the hearing impaired as you would to others. Elementary school teachers, for example, have been found to direct fewer comments to deaf children than to hearing students (Cawthon, 2001).
7. Ask the person if there is anything you can do to make it easier for him or her to understand you.
8. Don't avoid terms like "hear," "listen," "music," or "deaf" when they're relevant to the conversation. Trying to avoid these common terms will make your speech sound artificial.
9. Don't talk to the person with a hearing loss through a third party; direct your comments to the hearing-impaired person.
10. Use nonverbal cues that can help you communicate your meaning. For example, gestures indicating size or location and facial expressions indicating emotions and feelings are often helpful to the person with a hearing loss. Similarly, along with the verbal cues, use visual conversational turn-taking cues to indicate that you're passing the speaker's role to the person who's hearing impaired.

If you have impaired hearing:

1. Do your best to eliminate background noise.
2. Move closer to the speaker if this helps you hear better. Alert the other person that this closer distance will help you hear better.
3. If you feel the speaker can make adjustments that will make it easier for you to understand, ask. For example, ask the speaker to repeat a message, to speak more slowly or more distinctly, or to increase his or her volume.
4. If you hear better in one ear than the other, position yourself accordingly and, if necessary, clue the other person in to this fact.
5. If necessary, ask the person to write down certain information, for example, phone numbers or website addresses. Carrying a pad and pencil will prove helpful in the event that you wish to write something down for others.

These suggestions were drawn from a variety of sources: *Tips for Communicating with Deaf People* (Rochester Institute of Technology, National Technical Institute for the Deaf, Division of Public Affairs), http://www.his.com/~lola/deaf.html, http://www.zak.co.il/deaf-info/old/comm_strategies.html, http://www.agbell.org/information/brochures_communication.cfm (all websites accessed 4/5/02).

Stage Two: Understanding

Understanding is the stage at which you learn what the speaker means—the thoughts and emotional tone.

In understanding, do you

1. Avoid assuming you understand what the speaker is going to say before he or she actually says it?
2. Relate the new information the speaker is giving to what you already know?
3. See the speaker's messages from the speaker's point of view; avoid judging the message until you fully understand it as the speaker intended it?
4. Ask questions for clarification, if necessary; ask for additional details or examples if they're needed?
5. Rephrase (paraphrase) the speaker's ideas in your own words?

Stage Three: Remembering

For listening to take place, you need to remember the messages. In some small group and public speaking situations, you can augment your memory by taking notes or by taping the messages. In most interpersonal communication situations, however, note taking is inappropriate, although you often do write down a telephone number, an appointment, or directions. And, in many work situations, taking notes is common and may even be expected.

For example, when Susan says she is planning to buy a new car, the effective listener remembers this and at later meetings asks about the car. When Joe says his mother is ill, the effective listener remembers this and inquires about her health later in the week.

What you remember is actually not what was said but what you think (or remember) was said. Memory for speech isn't reproductive; you don't simply reproduce in your memory what the speaker said. Rather, memory is reconstructive; you actually reconstruct the messages you hear into a system that makes sense to you.

View point In the famous McMartin trial—the photo here is a scene from the HBO movie based on that trial—children accused the McMartins (who ran a children's school) of sexual molestation. The jury, however, found that the children's recollections were false. Often false memories are implanted by therapists and interviewers whose persistent questioning over a period of time creates such a realistic scenario that the individual comes to believe these things actually occurred (Porter, Brit, Yuille, & Lehman, 2000). In what other, less dramatic ways, can false memory syndrome occur?

Increasing Interpersonal Effectiveness
Openness

Openness refers to your willingness to self-disclose—to reveal information about yourself that might normally be kept hidden—provided that such disclosure is appropriate (as discussed in Chapter 3). Openness also refers to your willingness to listen openly to and react honestly to the messages of others.

Communicating Openness   Consider these ideas.

■ *Self-disclose when appropriate.* Be mindful about your self-disclosures, remembering that there are benefits and dangers to this form of intimate communication.

■ *Respond to those with whom you're interacting with spontaneity and appropriate honesty* However, be aware of what you're saying and what the possible outcomes of your messages might be.

■ *Own your feelings and thoughts.* Take responsibility for what you say. Use **I-messages** instead of **you-messages.** Instead of saying, "You make me feel stupid when you don't ask my opinion," own your feelings and say, for example, "I feel stupid when you ask everyone else what they think but don't ask me." When you own your feelings and thoughts—when you use I-messages—you say, in effect, "This is how *I* feel," "This is how *I* see the situation," and "This is what *I* think." When you use I-messages, you make it explicit that your feelings result from the interaction between what is going on outside your skin (what others say, for example) and what is going on inside your skin (your preconceptions, attitudes, and prejudices, for example).

To illustrate this important concept, try to memorize the list of 12 words presented below (Glucksberg & Danks, 1975). Don't worry about the order of the words. Only the number remembered counts. Take about 20 seconds to memorize as many words as possible. Don't read any further until you have tried to memorize the list of words.

BED	DREAM	COMFORT
REST	AWAKE	SOUND
WAKE	NIGHT	SLUMBER
TIRED	EAT	SNORE

Now close the book and write down as many of the words from this list as you can remember. Don't read any further until you have tested your own memory.

If you're like my own students, you not only remembered a good number of the words on the list, but you also "remembered" at least one word that was not on the list: "sleep." You didn't simply reproduce the list; you reconstructed it. In this case, you gave the list meaning, and part of that meaning included the word "sleep." You frequently reconstruct messages so they make sense to you. In the process, however, the messages often get distorted.

In remembering, do you

1. Identify the central ideas and the major support advanced?
2. Summarize the message in a more easily retained form, but be careful not to ignore crucial details or qualifications?
3. Repeat names and key concepts to yourself or, if appropriate, aloud?

I SEE

Stage Four: Evaluating

Evaluating consists of judging the messages in some way. At times, you may try to evaluate the speaker's underlying intentions or motives. Often this evaluation process goes on without much conscious awareness. For example, Elaine tells you that she is up for a promotion and is really excited about it. You may then try to judge her intention: She wants you to use your influence with the company president, or she's preoccupied with the promotion and so tells everyone, or she's looking for a compliment.

In other situations, your evaluation is more in the nature of critical analysis. For example, in listening to proposals advanced in a business meeting, you might ask: Are they practical? Will they increase productivity? What's the evidence? Is there contradictory evidence?

In evaluating, do you

1. Resist evaluation until you fully understand the speaker's point of view?
2. Assume that the speaker is a person of goodwill, and give the speaker the benefit of any doubt by asking for clarification on positions to which you feel you might object?
3. Distinguish facts from inferences (see Chapter 7), opinions, and personal interpretations by the speaker?
4. Identify any biases, self-interests, or prejudices that may lead the speaker to slant unfairly what is presented?

Stage Five: Responding

Responding occurs in two phases: responses you make while the speaker is talking and responses you make after the speaker has stopped talking. These responses are feedback—information that you send back to the speaker; this information tells the speaker how you feel and what you think about his or her messages. Responses made while the speaker is talking should be supportive and should acknowledge that you're listening to the speaker. These responses include what nonverbal researchers call **back-channeling cues,** such as "I see," "yes," "uh-huh," and similar signals that let the speaker know you're listening.

Responses made after the speaker has stopped talking are generally more elaborate and might include expressing empathy ("I know how you must feel"), asking for clarification ("Do you mean that this new health plan is to replace the old one?"), challenging ("I think your evidence is weak here"), and agreeing ("You're absolutely right on this; I'll support your proposal").

In responding, do you

1. Support the speaker throughout the speaker's talk by using and varying your back-channeling cues?
2. Express support for the speaker in your final responses?
3. Act honestly? The speaker has a right to expect honest responses, even if they express disagreement.
4. Own your responses? State your thoughts and feelings as your own, and use I-messages.
5. Resist (as men are often accused of doing) "responding to another's feelings" with "solving the person's problems" (Tannen, 1990)? It's usually more productive to view your task in more limited terms: to encourage the person to express and perhaps to clarify his or her feelings and to provide a supportive atmosphere.

Table 5.3 identifies some types of difficult listeners and their problem-causing ways of responding. Review this table and see if it includes some of your own listening behaviors.

Table 5.3   **Problem-Causing Listening Responses**

Listener Type	Listening (Responding) Behavior	(Mis)interpreting Thoughts
The static listener	gives no feedback, remains relatively motionless, reveals no expression	Why isn't she reacting: Am I not producing sound?
The monotonous feedback giver	seems responsive but the responses never vary; regardless of what you say, the response is the same	Am I making sense? Why is he still smiling? I'm being dead serious.
The overly expressive listener	reacts to just about everything with extreme responses	Why is she so expressive? I didn't say anything that provocative. She'll have a heart attack when I get to the punchline.
The reader/writer	reads or writes about matters having nothing to do with what the speaker is saying, while "listening" and only occasionally glances up	Am I that boring? Is last week's student newspaper more interesting than me?
The eye avoider	looks all around the room and at others but never you	Why isn't he looking at me? Do I have spinach on my teeth?
The preoccupied listener	listens to other things at the same time, often with headphones with the sound so loud that it interferes with your own thinking	When is she going to shut that music off and really listen? Am I so boring that my talk needs background music?
The waiting listener	listens for a cue to take over the speaking turn	Is he listening to me or rehearsing his next interruption?
The thought-completing listener	listens a little and then finishes your thought	Am I that predictable? Why do I bother saying anything? He already knows what I'm going to say.

STYLES OF LISTENING

Because you listen for different reasons, the way to listen effectively should vary from one situation to another. Below are four dimensions of listening and suggestions for adjusting them depending on the specifics of the communication situation.

Empathic and Objective Listening

If you're to understand what a person means and what a person is feeling, you need to listen with some degree of empathy (Rogers, 1970; Rogers & Farson, 1981). To empathize with others is to feel with them, to see the world as they see it, to feel what they feel. Only when you achieve this can you fully understand another person's meaning. Empathic listening will also help you enhance your relationships (Barrett & Godfrey, 1988; Snyder, 1992).

Although for most communication situations empathic listening is the preferred mode of responding, there are times when you need to go beyond it to measure the meanings and feelings against some objective reality. It's important to listen to Peter tell you how the entire world hates him and to understand how Peter feels and why he feels this way. But then you need to look a bit more objectively at Peter and perhaps see the

WEB EXPLORATION
To learn more about styles of listening, go to **www.ablongman.com/devito**.

A S K *the Researcher*

Becoming More Listenable

Although I think of myself as an interesting person, I do notice that others don't listen to me as carefully or as intently as they do my colleagues at work. Is there anything I can do to make people listen to me with greater interest and attention?

Your question is one that many of us face in our professional and personal lives. What we know about listening suggests that speakers need to present "listenable" messages—messages that are easily comprehended and remembered by their listeners. This requires that we engage listeners through our verbal and nonverbal messages alike, and the best way to do that is to be a storyteller. Think of your communication as a story; your task is to present your point so that the listener will cut through all the competing stimuli and focus on your message. Since we're bombarded with so much information, the soundbite that captures your point quickly and succinctly is probably what will stick with your listener in his or her memory. It's not easy to be "listenable," but it's our only hope in connecting with listeners in today's cluttered, rapid-fire information age.

For further information see Andrew D. Wolvin and Carolyn G. Coakley, *Listening* (New York: McGraw-Hill, 1996), and Andrew D. Wolvin, Roy M. Berko, and Darlyn R. Wolvin, *The Public Speaker/The Public Listener* (Los Angeles: Roxbury, 1999).

Andrew D. Wolvin (Ph.D., Purdue University) is a professor of communication at the University of Maryland, where he teaches courses in listening, communication management, and speechwriting. He also hosts a cable news show on researchers and their research. awolvin@umd.edu (Reprinted by permission of Dr. Andrew D. Wolvin.)

paranoia or the self-hatred. Sometimes you have to put your empathic responses aside and listen with objectivity and detachment.

In adjusting your empathic and objective listening, keep the following recommendations in mind:

- Punctuate from the speaker's point of view (Chapter 1). If you want to understand the speaker's perspective, see the sequence of events as the speaker does and try to figure out how this can influence what the speaker says and does.
- Engage in equal, two-way conversation. Try to eliminate any physical or psychological barriers to equality to encourage openness and empathy (for example, step from behind the large desk separating you from your employees). Avoid interrupting the speaker—a sign that what you have to say is more important.
- Seek to understand both thoughts and feelings. Don't consider your listening task finished until you've understood what the speaker is feeling as well as thinking.
- Avoid "offensive listening," the tendency to listen to bits and pieces of information that will enable you to attack the speaker or find fault with something the speaker has said (Floyd, 1985).
- Strive to be objective when listening to friends and foes alike. Your attitudes may lead you to distort messages—to block out positive messages about a foe and negative messages about a friend. Guard against "expectancy hearing," when you fail to hear what the speaker is really saying and hear what you expect to hear instead.

Nonjudgmental and Critical Listening

TRY IT!
Apply your understanding of nonjudgmental and critical listening; go to www.ablongman.com/devito.

Effective listening includes both nonjudgmental and critical responses. You need to listen nonjudgmentally—with an open mind with a view toward understanding. You need to listen critically—with a view toward making some kind of evaluation or judgment. Clearly listen first for understanding while suspending judgment. Only after you've fully understood the relevant messages should you evaluate or judge.

 Although empathy is almost universally considered a positive feeling, there is some evidence to show that it also has a negative side. For example, people are most empathic with those who they closely resemble—racially and ethnically as well as in appearance and social status. The more empathy you feel toward your own group, the less empathy you feel toward other groups. The same empathy that increases your understanding of your own group decreases your understanding of other groups and may even promote hostility. So while empathy may encourage group cohesiveness and identification, it can also create dividing lines between your group and "them" (Angier, 1995b). Can you describe a situation in which negative empathy played a role?

Supplement open-minded listening with critical listening. Listening with an open mind will help you understand the messages better; listening with a critical mind will help you analyze and evaluate the messages. In adjusting your nonjudgmental and critical listening, focus on the following guidelines:

■ Keep an open mind. Avoid prejudging. Delay your judgments until you fully understand the intention and the content the speaker is communicating. Avoid both positive and negative evaluation until you have a reasonably complete understanding.

■ Avoid filtering out or oversimplifying complex messages. Similarly, avoid filtering out undesirable messages. You don't want to hear that something you believe in is untrue, that people you care for are unkind, or that ideals you hold are self-destructive. Yet, it's important that you reexamine your beliefs by listening to these messages.

■ Recognize your own biases. These may interfere with accurate listening and cause you to distort message reception through the process of assimilation—the tendency to integrate and interpret what you hear or think you hear with your own biases, prejudices, and expectations. For example, are your ethnic, national, or religious biases preventing you from appreciating a speaker's point of view?

■ Be sure to listen critically to the entire message when you need to make evaluations and judgments. Recognize and combat the normal tendency to sharpen—a process in which one or two aspects of the message become highlighted, emphasized, and perhaps embellished. Often the concepts that are sharpened are incidental remarks that somehow stand out from the rest of the message.

■ Recognize some of the popular but fallacious forms of reasoning such as the following (Lee & Lee, 1972, 1995; Pratkanis & Aronson, 1991):
  ■ *Name-calling* involves giving an idea, a group of people, or a political philosophy a bad name ("atheist," "Neo-Nazi," "cult"). In the opposite of name-calling, the speaker tries to make you accept some idea by associating it with things you value highly ("democracy," "free speech," "academic freedom"). Remember that labels are useful most of the time but can often obscure the actual person

WEB EXPLORATION
To learn more about fallacious forms of reasoning, go to **www.ablongman.com/ devito**.

or idea. Listen first to evidence and argument; never take labels as evidence or reasons for judgment.

- *Testimonial* involves using the image associated with some person to gain your approval (if you respect the person) or your rejection (if you don't respect the person). This technique is used by advertisers who use people dressed up to look like doctors or plumbers or chefs to sell their products. Listen carefully to the person's credentials; be suspicious when you hear such phrases as "experts agree," "scientists say," "good cooks know," or "dentists advise." Ask yourself exactly who these experts are and what the source of their expertise is.

- *Bandwagon* is a technique that tries to persuade you to accept or reject an idea or proposal because "everybody is doing it," so "jump on the bandwagon." You'll hear this technique used frequently during election time where results of polls are used to get you to join the group and vote for one person or another. Again, listen to the evidence; 50,000 Frenchmen—as the saying goes—can be wrong.

- *Agenda-setting* involves claiming that a particular issue is crucial and all others are unimportant and insignificant. This technique is used frequently in interpersonal conflict situations where each person may claim that her or his viewpoint is the accurate and important one and that the other person's is less accurate and less important. In almost all situations, and especially in interpersonal conflict situations, there are many issues and many sides to each issue.

- *Attack* involves accusing another person (usually an opponent) of some serious wrongdoing so that the issue under discussion never gets examined as in the argument, "How can I ever believe you after you lied." Although a person's reputation and past behavior are often relevant, listen most carefully to the issue at hand. When personal attack draws attention away from other issues, then it becomes fallacious.

Gatekeeping

When you were growing up, your parents gave you certain information and withheld other information. Depending on the culture in which you were raised, you may have been told about Santa Claus and the tooth fairy, but not about cancer or mutual funds. Your parents were serving as gatekeepers, regulating the information to which you were exposed. When you went to school, your teachers served a similar function. They taught you about certain historical events, for example, but not others. The term *gatekeeping,* introduced by Kurt Lewin in his *Human Relations* (1947), as the above examples illustrate, refers to the process by which a message passes through various gates, as well as to the people or groups that allow the message to pass (gatekeepers).

The media, because they are the largest disseminators of information, are also the most important gatekeepers. Newspaper editors, publishing houses, television networks, search engines, and Internet service providers are examples of media gatekeepers (Lewis, 1995; Bodon, Powell, & Hickson, 1999). What you see and hear in the media has been filtered through various gatekeepers and only certain parts get through.

Follow Up   How do the media compare to your friends, romantic partners, family members, and work colleagues as gatekeepers in your ability to acquire information? In your ability to participate in new experiences?

Surface and Depth Listening

In Shakespeare's *Julius Caesar*, Marc Antony, in giving the funeral oration for Caesar, says: "I come to bury Caesar, not to praise him. / The evil that men do lives after them; / The good is oft interred with their bones." And later: "For Brutus is an honourable man; / So are they all, all honourable men." But Antony, as we know, did come to praise Caesar and to convince the crowd that Brutus was not an honorable man.

In most messages there's an obvious meaning that you can derive from a literal reading of the words and sentences. But there's often another level of meaning, sometimes, as in *Julius Caesar*, it's the opposite of the literal meaning. At other times it seems totally unrelated. In reality, most messages have more than one level of meaning. Consider some frequently heard messages: Carol asks you how you like her new haircut. On one level, the meaning is clear: Do you like the haircut? But there's also another, perhaps more important, level: Carol is asking you to say something positive about her appearance. In the same way, the parent who complains about working hard at the office or in the home may, on a deeper level, be asking for an expression of appreciation. The child who talks about the unfairness of the other children in the playground may be asking for comfort and love. To appreciate these other meanings you need to engage in depth listening.

If you respond only to the surface-level communication (the literal meaning), you miss the opportunity to make meaningful contact with the other person's feelings and needs. If you say to the parent, "You're always complaining. I bet you really love working so hard," you fail to respond to this call for understanding and appreciation. In regulating your surface and depth listening, consider the following guidelines:

- ■ *Focus on both verbal and nonverbal messages.* Recognize both consistent and inconsistent "packages" of messages and use these as guides for drawing inferences about the speaker's meaning. Ask questions when in doubt. Listen also to what is omitted. Remember that speakers communicate by what they leave out as well as by what they include.
- ■ *Listen for both content and relational messages.* The student who constantly challenges the teacher is, on one level, communicating disagreement over content. However, on another level—the relationship level—the student may be voicing objections to the instructor's authority or authoritarianism. The instructor needs to listen and respond to both types of messages.
- ■ *Make special note of statements that refer back to the speaker.* Remember that people inevitably talk about themselves. Whatever a person says is, in part, a function of who that person is. Attend carefully to those personal, self-reference messages.
- ■ *Don't disregard the literal meaning of interpersonal messages in trying to uncover the hidden meaning.* Balance your listening between the surface and the underlying meaning. Respond to the different levels of meaning in the messages of others, as you would like others to respond to yours—be sensitive but not obsessive. Be attentive but not too eager to uncover hidden messages.

Active and Inactive Listening

One of the most important communication skills you can learn is that of **active listening** (Gordon, 1975). Consider the following interaction; you're disappointed that you have to redo your entire report and you say: "I can't believe I have to redo this entire budget report. I really worked hard on this project and now I have to do it all over again." To this, you get three different responses.

TRY IT!
Apply your insights into the techniques of active listening; go to **www. ablongman.com/devito**.

Apollo: That's not so bad; most people find they have to redo their first reports. That's the norm here.

Athena: You should be pleased that all you have to do is a simple rewrite. Peggy and Michael both had to completely redo their entire projects.

Diana: You have to rewrite that report you've worked on for the last three weeks? You sound really angry and frustrated.

All three listeners are probably trying to make you feel better. But they go about it in very different ways and, we can be sure, with very different results. Apollo tries to lessen the significance of the rewrite. This well-intended response is extremely common but does little to promote meaningful communication and understanding. Athena tries to give the situation a positive spin. With these responses, however, both these listeners are also suggesting that you should not be feeling the way you do. They're also saying that your feelings are not legitimate and should be replaced with more logical feelings.

Diana's response, however, is different from the others. Diana uses active listening. Active listening, which owes its development to Thomas Gordon (1975) who made it a cornerstone of his P-E-T (Parent-Effectiveness-Training) technique, is a process of sending back to the speaker what you as a listener think the speaker meant—both in content and in feelings. Active listening, then, is not merely repeating the speaker's exact words, but rather putting together your understanding of the speaker's total message into a meaningful whole.

Active listening serves several important functions. First, it helps you as a listener check your understanding of what the speaker said and, more important, what he or she meant. Reflecting back perceived meanings to the speaker gives the speaker an opportunity to offer clarification and correct any misunderstandings.

Second, through active listening you let the speaker know that you acknowledge and accept his or her feelings. In the sample responses given, the first two listeners challenged the speaker's feelings. Diana, the active listener, accepted what you were feeling. In addition, she also explicitly identified your feelings: "You sound angry and frustrated," allowing you an opportunity to correct her interpretation if necessary.

Third, active listening stimulates the speaker to explore feelings and thoughts. Diana's response encourages you to elaborate on your feelings, and helps you deal with them by talking them through.

Three simple techniques may prove useful in learning the process of active listening: paraphrase the speaker's meaning, express understanding, and ask questions.

- *Paraphrase the speaker's meaning.* Stating in your own words what you think the speaker means and feels helps ensure understanding and also shows interest in the speaker. Paraphrasing gives the speaker a chance to extend what was originally said. Thus, when Diana echoes your thoughts, you're given the opportunity to elaborate on why rewriting the budget report meant so much to you. In paraphrasing, be objective; be especially careful not to lead the speaker in the direction you think he or she should go.

  Also, be careful that you don't overdo paraphrase; only a very small percentage of statements need paraphrasing. Paraphrase when you feel there's a chance for misunderstanding or when you want to express support for the other person and keep the conversation going.

- *Express understanding of the speaker's feelings.* Echo the feelings the speaker expressed or implied ("You must have felt horrible"). This expression of feelings will help you further check your perception of the speaker's feelings. This will also allow the speaker to see his or her feelings more objectively (especially helpful when they're feelings of anger, hurt, or depression) and the opportunity to elaborate on them.

■ *Ask questions.* Asking questions ensures your own understanding of the speaker's thoughts and feelings and secures additional information ("How did you feel when you read your job appraisal report?"). Ask questions to provide just enough stimulation and support for the speaker to feel he or she can elaborate on these thoughts and feelings. These questions should further confirm your interest and concern for the speaker but not pry into unrelated areas or challenge the speaker in any way.

Consider this dialogue and note the active listening techniques used throughout:

Pat: That jerk demoted me. He told me I wasn't an effective manager. I can't believe he did that, after all I've done for this place.

Chris: I'm with you. You've been manager for three or four months now, haven't you?

Pat: A little over three months. I know it was probationary, but I thought I was doing a good job.

Chris: Can you get another chance?

Pat: Yes, he said I could try again in a few months. But I feel like a failure.

Chris: I know what you mean. It sucks. What else did he say?

Pat: He said I had trouble getting the paperwork done on time.

Chris: You've been late filing the reports?

Pat: A few times.

Chris: Is there a way to delegate the paperwork?

Pat: No, but I think I know now what needs to be done.

Chris: You sound as though you're ready to give that manager's position another try.

Pat: Yes, I think I am, and I'm going to let him know that I intend to apply in the next few months.

Even in this brief interaction, Pat has moved from unproductive anger with the supervisor as well as a feeling of failure to a determination to correct an unpleasant situation. Note, too, that Chris didn't offer solutions but "simply" listened actively.

As stressed throughout this discussion, listening is situational; the type of listening that is appropriate varies with the situation. You can visualize a listening situation as one in which you have to make choices among the four dimensions of listening just discussed (Figure 5.2). Each listening situation should call for a somewhat different configuration of listening responses; the art of effective listening is largely one of making appropriate choices along these four dimensions.

Empathic ___:___:___:___:___:___ Objective

Nonjudgmental ___:___:___:___:___:___ Critical

Surface ___:___:___:___:___:___ Deep

Active ___:___:___:___:___:___ Inactive

Figure 5.2

Listening Choices
Effective listening is largely a matter of adjusting your behavior along dimensions such as these. Can you identify an interpersonal situation that would call for listening that is highly empathic, nonjudgmental, surface, and active and another situation that would call for listening that is objective, critical, in depth, and inactive?

CULTURE, GENDER, AND LISTENING

Listening is difficult, in part, because of the inevitable differences in the communication systems between speaker and listener. Because each person has had a unique set of experiences, each person's meaning system is going to be different from every other person's. When speaker and listener come from different cultures or are of different genders, the differences and their effects are naturally much greater. Consider culture first.

Culture and Listening

Among the cultural differences we may consider are those concerning language, nonverbal communication, style, story versus evidence, credibility, and feedback. These will give you an idea of some of the many cultural factors that can influence listening.

Even when speaker and listener speak the same language, they speak it with different meanings and different accents. Every speaker speaks an idiolect—a unique variation of the language. Speakers of the same language will, at the very least, have different meanings for the same terms because they have had different experiences.

Speakers and listeners who have different native languages and who may have learned English as a second language will have even greater differences in meaning. Translations are never precise and never fully capture the meaning in the other language. Your meaning for "house" if learned in a culture in which everyone lived in their own house with lots of land around it is going to be very different from someone who learned the word living in a neighborhood of high-rise tenements. Although you will each hear the same word, the meanings you'll each create will be drastically different. In adjusting your listening—especially when in an intercultural setting—understand that the speaker's meanings may be very different from yours even though you're each speaking the same language.

Another cultural factor that affects speaking and listening is accents. In many classrooms throughout the country, there will be a wide range of accents. Those whose

ETHICS in Interpersonal Communication

Ethical Listening

As a listener you have at least two ethical obligations.

■ You owe the speaker an *honest hearing,* without prejudgment, putting aside prejudices and preconceptions as best you can. At the same time, you owe the speaker your best attempt at understanding emotionally as well as intellectually what he or she means. You owe the speaker the right to have his or her ideas accepted or rejected on the basis

of the information offered, and not on the basis of bias or misunderstanding.
■ Second, you owe the speaker *honest responses.* This means

giving open and honest feedback and also reflecting honestly on the questions that the speaker raises.

What would you do? *Your friend seems to have the need to reveal her innermost secrets—problems at home, a lack of money, no friends, and so on. You really don't want to hear all this; in fact, it depresses you. So you want to ignore these disclosures by making excuses to cut the conversation short or change the subject. At the same time, however, you wonder about your ethical obligations to your friend and if you should listen openly and respond honestly. What would you do in this situation?*

native language is a tonal one such as Chinese (where differences in pitch signal important meaning differences) may speak English with variations in pitch that may seem puzzling to others. Those whose native language is Japanese may have trouble distinguishing "l" from "r" since Japanese does not include this distinction. The native language acts as a filter and influences the accent given to the second language.

Speakers from different cultures have different display rules, cultural rules that govern what nonverbal behaviors are appropriate and which are inappropriate in a public setting. As you listen to another person, you also "listen" to their nonverbals (Chapters 6 and 8). If these are drastically different from what you expect on the basis of the verbal message, you may see them as a kind of interference or perhaps as contradictory messages. Also, different cultures may give very different meanings to the same nonverbal gesture.

Some cultures—Western Europe and the United States, for example—favor **direct speech** in communication; they advise us to "say what you mean and mean what you say." Many Asian cultures, on the other hand, favor **indirect speech;** they emphasize politeness and maintaining a positive public image rather than absolute truth. Listen carefully to persons with different styles of directness. Consider the possibility that the meanings the speaker wishes to communicate with indirectness may be very different from the meanings you would communicate with indirectness.

Variations in directness are often especially clear in giving feedback. Members of some cultures give very direct and very honest feedback. Speakers from these cultures—the United States is a good example—expect the feedback to be an honest reflection of what their listeners are feeling. In other cultures—Japan and Korea are good examples—it's more important to be positive, so speakers from these cultures may respond with compliments (say, in commenting on a business colleague's proposal) even though they don't feel it. Listen to feedback, as you would all messages, with the recognition that cultures view feedback differently.

Gender and Listening

Men and women learn different styles of listening just as they learn different styles for using verbal and nonverbal messages. Not surprisingly, these different styles can create

View point The popular belief is that men listen in the way they do to prove themselves superior and that women listen as they do to ingratiate themselves. Although there is no evidence to show this is true, it persists in the assumptions that people make about the opposite sex. What do you believe accounts for the differences in the way men and women listen?

major difficulties in opposite-sex interpersonal communication. According to Deborah Tannen (1990) in her best-selling *You Just Don't Understand: Women and Men in Conversation,* women seek to build rapport and establish a closer relationship and use listening to achieve these ends. Men, on the other hand, will play up their expertise, emphasize it, and use it in dominating the interaction. Women play down their expertise and are more interested in communicating supportiveness. Tannen argues that the goal of a man in conversation is to be given respect, so he seeks to show his knowledge and expertise. A woman, on the other hand, seeks to be liked, so she expresses agreement.

Men and women also show that they're listening in different ways. In conversation, a woman is more apt to give lots of listening cues such as interjecting "Yeah" or "Uh-uh," nodding in agreement, and smiling. Women also make more eye contact when listening than do men, who are more apt to look around and often away from the speaker (Brownell, 2002). A man is more likely to listen quietly, without giving lots of listening cues as feedback. Subsequent research seems to confirm Tannen's position. For example, an analysis of calls to a crisis center in Finland revealed that calls received by a female counselor were significantly longer for both men and women callers (Salminen & Glad, 1992). It's likely that the greater number of listening cues given by the women encouraged the callers to keep talking. This same study also found that male callers were helped by "just listening," whereas women callers were helped by "empathic understanding."

Tannen argues, however, that men listen less to women than women listen to men. The reason, says Tannen, is that listening places the person in an inferior position, whereas speaking places the person in a superior position. Men may seem to assume a more argumentative posture while listening, as if getting ready to argue. They may also appear to ask questions that are more argumentative or that seek to puncture holes in your position as a way to play up their own expertise. Women are more likely to ask supportive questions and perhaps offer criticism that is more positive than men. Women let the speaker see that they're listening. Men, on the other hand, use fewer listening cues in conversation. Men and women act this way to both men and women; their customary ways of talking don't seem to change depending on whether the listener is male or female.

There is no evidence to show that these differences represent any negative motives on the part of men to prove themselves superior or of women to ingratiate themselves. Rather, these differences in listening seem largely the result of the way in which men and women have been socialized.

REVIEWING Key Terms and Concepts in Interpersonal Listening

This chapter focused on the nature of listening, the influence of culture and gender on listening, and the dimensions of listening that you need to consider for effective listening.

Stages of Listening

What is listening? What purposes does listening serve?

■ Listening is an active process of receiving, understanding, remembering, evaluating, and responding to communications.

■ Listening enables you (1) to learn, to acquire information; (2) to relate, to help form and maintain relationships; (3) to influence, to have an effect on the attitudes and behaviors of others; (4) to play, to enjoy oneself; and (5) to help, to assist others.

Styles of Listening

What are your listening options?

■ Empathic–objective listening refers to the extent to which you focus on feeling what the speaker is feeling.

■ Nonjudgmental–critical listening refers to the extent to which you accept and support the speaker.

■ Surface–depth listening refers to the extent to which you focus on the obvious surface meanings.

■ Active–inactive listening refers to the extent to which you reflect back on what you think the speaker means in content and feeling.

Culture, Gender, and Listening

How is listening influenced by culture and gender?

■ Members of different cultures vary on a number of communication dimensions that influence listening: speech and language, nonverbal behavioral differences, and preferences for direct and indirect styles of communication.

■ Men and women may listen differently; generally, women give more specific listening cues to show they're listening than do men.

APPLYING Key Terms and Concepts in Interpersonal Listening

1. Think of someone whose level of listening does not meet your expectations. How might you go about increasing this person's level of active and empathic listening?

2. Are some people more deserving of empathy than others? What makes a person deserving of your empathic listening? For example, would you find it more difficult to empathize with someone who is overjoyed because of winning the lottery for $7 million or with someone who is overcome with sadness because of the death of a loved one? How easy would it be for you to empathize with someone who was depressed because the expected bonus of $60,000 turned out to be only $35,000?

3. Rob, a server at the Dinner Diner, is efficient in most areas but frequently makes mistakes in taking the customers' orders. This often results in customer dissatisfaction and ruined meals, and it irritates the temperamental cook. Rob's supervisor says that he doesn't listen effectively. What specific advice might the supervisor give Rob to improve his listening effectiveness?

4. How much of your listening is active? Do your close friends practice active listening when they listen to you? Can you give a specific example of active listening that you were recently involved in?

5. How would you describe your own culture's teachings and rules as they might influence listening in the classroom or in the workplace?

6. Describe a situation where you "heard" what you hoped or expected to hear, only to find out later that what you heard was different from what was said.

7. Is your classroom listening ever characterized by your filtering out unpleasant or difficult messages or messages that contradict your own deeply held beliefs? What effects might this have?

8. How might sharpening (the process of message distortion in which the details of messages, when repeated, are crystallized and heightened) work in workplace gossip? In campus gossip?

9. What types of listening would you use (and which types would you definitely not use) in each of the following situations: (a) Your steady dating partner for the last five years tells you that spells of depression are becoming more frequent and more long lasting. (b) An instructor lectures on the contributions of Ancient China to modern civilization. (c) A physician discusses your recent physical tests and makes recommendations. (d) A salesperson tells you the benefits of the new computer. (e) A gossip columnist details the secret life of your favorite movie star.

EXPERIENCING Key Terms and Concepts in Interpersonal Listening

Go to www.ablongman.com/devito.

This group of listening experiences will help you gain new insights into listening and will help to sharpen your listening skills.

(1) **Listening to Other Perspectives** and (2) **How Might You Listen to New Ideas?** present two creative thinking tools to sharpen a variety of skills, especially listening. (3) **Regulating Your Listening Perspective** presents different scenarios that call for different types of listening to heighten your awareness of potential listening choices. (4) **Experiencing Active Listening** asks you how you'd listen in a variety of situations calling for active listening. (5) **Sequential Communication,** which you might recognize as the game of telephone, will help you identify some of the major errors made in listening. (6) **Reducing Barriers to Listening** asks how you'd listen effectively in difficult situations. (7) **Typical Man, Typical Woman** explores some of the differences in the way you think of men and women as listeners. (8) **Paraphrasing to Ensure Understanding** and (9) **How Can You Express Empathy?** provide practice in essential listening skills.

RESEARCHING with Research Navigator Key Terms and Concepts in Interpersonal Listening

Go to http://www.researchnavigator.com.

Reading an article.

Read an academic or popular article on listening, styles or types of listening, or culture or gender differences in listening. On the basis of this article what can you add to the discussion presented here?

Investigating key terms.

Investigate one of the key terms discussed in this chapter (for example, listening, direct and indirect styles, credibility, feedback, empathy, active listening, or gatekeeping). What additional insights can you provide?

Finding answers.

Try finding answers to one of the following questions or design a research study to answer it.

■ Are women and men equally effective as listeners? Why or why not?

■ What kinds of listening make health professional–patient communication more effective? More personally satisfying?

■ What attitudes do business executives have toward listening and its importance in the workplace?

■ How do men or women differ in their empathic abilities? In their empathic behaviors?

■ Would some cultures respond negatively to active listening? Why?

6 Universals of Verbal and Nonverbal Messages

The Miracle Worker (1962)

There is nothing more beautiful, I think, than the evanescent fleeting images and sentiments presented by a language one is just becoming familiar with— ideas that flit across the mental sky, shaped and tinted by capricious fancy.

—Helen Keller

Messages and Meanings

Message Characteristics

*T*he story of how *Annie Sullivan* (Anne Bancroft) *teaches the young deaf and blind Helen Keller (Patty Duke) how to make her thoughts known to others by signing is told in* The Miracle Worker. *The dramatic change this brings to Helen Keller shows us the crucial role that communication plays in making us truly functional members of society. This chapter introduces verbal and nonverbal message systems and explains how they work together to enable you to communicate your thoughts and feelings.*

In face-to-face communication, you blend verbal and nonverbal messages to best convey your meanings. There is also evidence to show that you blend verbal and nonverbal messages to help you think and remember (Iverson & Goldin-Meadow, 1999). Identifying the six major ways in which nonverbal messages interact with verbal messages will help to highlight this important verbal–nonverbal connection and will serve as a useful introduction to the various characteristics of meanings and messages.

Nonverbal communication is often used to *accent,* to emphasize some part of the verbal message. You might, for example, raise your voice to underscore a particular word or phrase, bang your fist on the desk to stress your commitment, or look longingly into someone's eyes when saying "I love you."

Nonverbal communication may be used to *complement,* to add nuances of meaning not communicated by your verbal message. Thus, you might smile when telling a story (to suggest that you find it humorous) or frown and shake your head when recounting someone's deceit (to suggest your disapproval).

You may deliberately *contradict* your verbal messages with nonverbal movements, for example, by crossing your fingers or winking to indicate that you're lying.

Nonverbal movements may be used to *control,* or to indicate your desire to control, the flow of verbal messages, as when you purse your lips, lean forward, or make hand movements to indicate that you want to speak. You might also put up your hand or vocalize your pauses (for example, with "um") to indicate that you have not finished and aren't ready to relinquish the floor to the next speaker.

You can *repeat* or restate the verbal message nonverbally. You can, for example, follow your verbal "Is that all right?" with raised eyebrows and a questioning look, or you can motion with your head or hand to repeat your verbal "Let's go."

You may also use nonverbal communication to *substitute* for verbal messages. You can, for example, signal "OK" with a hand gesture. You can nod your head to indicate yes or shake your head to indicate no.

When you communicate electronically, of course, your message is communicated by means of typed letters without facial expressions or gestures that normally accompany face-to-face communication and without the changes in rate and volume that are a part of normal telephone communication. To compensate for this lack of nonverbal behavior, the emoticon was created. Sometimes called a "smiley" after the ever-present :), the emoticon is a typed symbol that communicates through a keyboard the nuances of the message normally conveyed by nonverbal expression and changes in vocal expression. The absence of the nonverbal channel where you can clarify your message—for example, smiling or winking to communicate sarcasm or humor—make such typed symbols extremely helpful. Research is just beginning to look into the factors influencing the use of emoticons and the effects they have (Rezabeck & Cochenour, 1995). Here are some of the more popular emoticons used in computer talk.

: -)	= smile; I'm only kidding
: - (	= frown; I'm feeling sad; this saddens me
*	= kiss
:-	= male
>-	= female
{ }	= hug
{{{***}}}	= hugs and kisses
; -)	= sly smile
this is important	= underlining, adds emphasis
this is important	= asterisks, adds emphasis
ALL CAPS	= shouting, emphasizing
<G> or <grin>	= grin

Not surprisingly, these symbols aren't used universally (Pollack, 1996). For example, because it's considered impolite for a Japanese woman to show her teeth when she smiles, the Japanese emoticon for a woman's smile is (^ . ^) where the dot signifies a closed mouth. A man's smile is written (^ _ ^). Other emoticons popular in Japan but not used in Europe or the United States are (^ ^ ;) for "cold sweat," (^ o ^ ; Ò) for "excuse me," and (^ o ^) for "happy."

MESSAGES AND MEANINGS

Meaning is an active process created in cooperation between source and receiver, speaker and listener, writer and reader. Understanding what meanings are and how they're passed from one person to another will help maximize your own verbal and nonverbal message potential.

Increasing Interpersonal Effectiveness
Metacommunication

Metacommunication is communication that refers to other communications; it's communication about communication. Both verbal and nonverbal messages can be metacommunicational. Verbally, you can say, for example, "Do you understand what I'm trying to say?" or nonverbally you can hug someone you're consoling.

Interpersonal effectiveness often hinges on the ability to metacommunicate. For example, in conflict situations it's often helpful to talk about the way you fight. In romantic relationships, it's often helpful to talk about what each of you means by "steady" or "really care." On the job, it's often necessary to talk about the way tasks are delegated or the way criticism should be expressed.

Metacommunicating   Here are a few suggestions for increasing your metacommunicational effectiveness.

■ *Explain the feelings that go with the thoughts.* Often people communicate only the thinking part of their message, with the result that listeners aren't able to appreciate the other parts of the meaning.

■ *Give clear feedforward.* Help the other person get a general picture of the messages that will follow.

■ *Paraphrase your own complex messages so as to make your meaning extra clear.* Similarly, check your understanding of another's message by paraphrasing what you think the other person means. Then ask if that's what the person meant.

■ *If you have doubts about another's meaning, ask for clarification.*

■ *Use metacommunication when you want to clarify the communication patterns of yourself and another person.* Say, for example, "I'd like to talk about the way you talk about me to our friends" or "I think we should talk about the way we talk about sex."

Meanings Are in People

Meaning depends not only on messages (whether verbal, nonverbal, or both) but also on the interaction of these messages and the receiver's own thoughts and feelings. You don't "receive" meaning; you create meaning. You construct meaning out of the messages you receive combined with your own social and cultural perspectives (beliefs, attitudes, and values, for example) (Berger & Luckmann, 1980; Delia, 1977; and Delia, O'Keefe, & O'Keefe, 1982). Words don't mean; people mean. Consequently, to discover meaning, you need to look into people and not merely into words.

To illustrate the implications of the principle that meanings are in people, record your meanings for the terms listed below on the 7-point scales. Write each term's first letter in the appropriate space for the various dimensions of meaning provided, depending on how close you feel the term's meaning is to the adjectives in the scale. Thus, if you feel that a concept is extremely good or extremely bad, then place the term's first letter on the space closest to good or bad. If you feel that the concept is quite good or quite bad, then place the term's first letter in the second or the seventh position. If you feel that the concept is fairly good or fairly bad, then place the letter in the third or the fifth position. If you feel that the concept is neither good nor bad, then place the letter in the middle position. Do likewise for all six scales and for all five terms.

Terms: (a) abortion, (b) biological warfare, (c) college, (d) death penalty, (e) euthanasia

good ___:___:___:___:___:___:___ bad

ugly ___:___:___:___:___:___:___ beautiful

weak ___:___:___:___:___:___:___ strong

active ___:___:___:___:___:___:___ passive

large ___:___:___:___:___:___:___ small

hot ___:___:___:___:___:___:___ cold

ETHICS in Interpersonal Communication

Lying

Lying occurs when "one person intends to mislead another, doing so deliberately, without prior notification of this purpose, and without having been explicitly asked to do so by the target [the person the liar intends to mislead]" (Ekman, 1985, p. 28). As this definition makes clear, lying may be committed by omission as well as commission. When you omit something relevant, thereby misleading others, you've lied just as surely as if you had made a false statement (Bok, 1978).

Similarly, although most lies are verbal, some are nonverbal and most seem to involve at least some nonverbal elements. The innocent facial expression and the focused eye contact despite the commission of some unethical act, and the knowing nod instead of the honest expression of ignorance are common examples of nonverbal lying.

What would you do? *On the basis of your own ethical beliefs about lying, what would you do in the following situations?*

■ Would you lie in an employment interview in answer to a question that is too personal (and irrelevant) or illegal?
■ Would you lie to make another person feel good? For example, would you tell someone that he or she looks great or has a great sense of humor even if you think the opposite is true?
■ Would you lie to get out of jury duty? To the IRS so as to pay less taxes in April?
■ Would you lie to get yourself out of an unpleasant situation, for example, to get out of a date, an extra office chore, or a boring conversation?

If you have the opportunity, compare your meanings with those of others in small groups or in the class as a whole. Are there large differences between your meanings and those of others? How would you describe these differences in terms of connotation and denotation? What accounts for the differences in meanings? That is, what factors contribute to your meanings for these terms? Put differently, how did you acquire the meanings you indicated on these scales? What does this experience illustrate about the principle that meanings are in people?

Meanings Are More Than Words and Gestures

When you want to communicate a thought or feeling to another person, you do so with relatively few symbols. These symbols represent just a small part of what you're thinking or feeling, much of which remains unspoken. If you were to try to describe every feeling in detail, you would never get on with the job of living. The meanings you seek to communicate are much more than the sum of the words and nonverbal behaviors you use to represent them.

Because of this, you can never fully know what another person is thinking or feeling. You can only approximate it on the basis of the meanings you receive, which, as already noted, are greatly influenced by who you are and what you are feeling. Conversely, others can never fully know you; they, too, can only approximate what you're feeling. Failure to understand another person or to be understood is not an abnormal occurrence.

Meanings Are Unique

Because meanings are derived from both the messages communicated and the receiver's own thoughts and feelings, no two people ever derive the same meanings. Similarly, because people change constantly, no one person can derive the same meanings on two separate occasions. Who you are can never be separated from the meanings you create. As a result, check your perceptions of another's meanings by asking questions, echoing what you perceive to be the other person's feelings or thoughts, seeking elaboration and clarification, and in general practicing the skills identified in the discussion on effective interpersonal perception and listening.

Also recognize that as you change, you also change the meanings you create out of past messages. Thus, although the message sent may not have changed, the meanings you created from it yesterday and the meanings you create today may be quite different. Yesterday, when a special someone said, "I love you," you created certain meanings. But today, when you learn that the same "I love you" was said to three other people or when you fall in love with someone else, you drastically change the meanings you perceive from these words.

Meanings Are Context-Based

Verbal and nonverbal communications exist in a context that, to a large extent, determines the meaning of any verbal or nonverbal behavior. The same words or behaviors may have totally different meanings when they occur in different contexts. For example, the greeting, "How are you?" means "Hello" to someone you pass regularly on the street but means "Is your health improving?" when said to a friend in the hospital. A wink to an attractive person on a bus means something completely different from a wink that signifies a put-on or a lie. Similarly, the meaning of a given signal depends on the other behavior it accompanies or is close to in time. Pounding a fist on the table during a speech in support of a politician means something quite different from that same gesture in response to news of a friend's death. Divorced from the context, it's impossible to tell what meaning was intended from just examining the signals. Of course, even if you know the context in detail, you still might not be able to decipher the meaning of the message.

Especially important is the cultural context, which is emphasized throughout this text. The cultural context will influence not only the meaning assigned to speech and gesture but whether your meaning is friendly, offensive, lacking in respect, condescending, sensitive, and so on.

MESSAGE CHARACTERISTICS

You'll be in a better position to control the message process once you understand how interpersonal messages work and the principles they follow. Here we consider seven basic characteristics of messages; interpersonal messages occur in packages, are governed by rules, and vary in abstraction, politeness, inclusion, directness, and assertiveness.

Messages Are Packaged

The sounds you make with your mouth or the gestures you make with your hands or eyes usually occur in "packages" where the verbal and nonverbal behaviors reinforce one another. Usually, all parts of the message system work together to communicate a unified meaning. When you speak words of anger, your body and face also communicate anger by tensing, scowling, and perhaps assuming a fighting posture. You often fail to notice this because it seems so natural. But when the nonverbal messages of someone's posture or face contradict what is said verbally, you take special notice. For ex-

---

A S K *the Researcher*

Becoming Less Interpersonally Awkward

My roommate is an interpersonal clod. I'm embarrassed in social situations because conversations are awkward and others have to work pretty hard to keep the conversation going. What to do?

Your roommate needs to work on some basic interpersonal skills. For instance, if your roommate is apprehensive about interacting with others, relaxation should be enhanced to allow him/her to feel more comfortable and secure. If there is trouble with interaction management, perhaps the two of you could practice shifting topics smoothly, negotiating which topic gets discussed next, and being perceptive about meanings. If your roommate has difficulty focusing on the other person, perhaps you could practice some techniques to show support, to be more attentive, and to be more responsive. Some people don't understand that both communicators in a dyad are responsible for carrying on the conversation and that sometimes this requires flexibility and adaptability. You can't just tell someone to be more flexible, but you can enlarge the number of strategies that people have by increasing successful experiences. Your roommate may just need more experience, and you can help by offering additional conversation opportunities, even though they may be painful at the beginning.

For more information see R. B. Rubin, "Development of a Measure of Interpersonal Communication Competence," *Communication Research Reports* 11 (1994): 33–44, and R. B. Rubin and R. A. Nevins, *The Road Trip: An Interpersonal Adventure* (Prospect Heights, IL: Waveland, 1988).

Rebecca B. Rubin (Ph.D., University of Illinois) is a professor of communication studies at Kent State University and teaches courses in interpersonal communication, research methods, and communication competence. She has developed various scales, indexes, and tests of communication skills and has worked with the National Communication Association and U.S. Department of Education on identifying essential skills for college students. rrubin@kent.edu (Reprinted by permission of Dr. Rebecca B. Rubin.)

ample, the person who says, "I'm so glad to see you," but avoids direct eye contact and looks around to see who else is present is sending contradictory messages. You also see contradictory or mixed messages when couples say they love each other but seem to go out of their way to hurt each other nonverbally—for example, being late for important dates, flirting with others, or avoiding touching each other.

In the packaged nature of communication, then, is a warning against the too easy interpretation of another's meaning, especially as revealed in nonverbal behaviors. Before you identify or guess the meaning of any bit of behavior, look at the entire package or cluster of which it's a part, the way in which the cluster is a response to its context, and the role of the specific nonverbal behavior within that cluster. That attractive person winking in your direction may be giving you the come-on; however, don't rule out the possibility of ill-fitting contact lenses.

Messages Are Rule-Governed

The rule-governed nature of verbal communication is well known. These are the rules of a language (the rules of grammar) that native speakers follow in producing and understanding sentences, although they may be unable to state such rules explicitly. You learned these rules from observing the behaviors of the adult community. For example, you learned how to express sympathy along with the rules that your culture has established for expressing it appropriately. You learned that touch is permissible under certain circumstances but not others. You learned which types of touching are permissible and which aren't. You learned that women may touch each other in public; for example, they may hold hands, walk arm in arm, engage in prolonged hugging, and even dance together. You also learned that men may not do these things, at least not without inviting social criticism. Further, perhaps most obvious, you learned that certain parts of the body may not be touched and others may. As a relationship changes, so do the rules for touching. As you become more intimate, the rules for touching become less restrictive.

Nonverbal communication is also regulated by a system of rules or norms that state what is and what is not appropriate, expected, and permissible in specific social situations. Of course, these rules vary greatly from one culture to another. Rules are cultural (and relative) institutions; they're not universal laws. In the United States, for example, direct eye contact usually signals openness and honesty. Among some Latin Americans and Native Americans, however, direct eye contact between, say, a teacher and a student is considered inappropriate, perhaps aggressive; appropriate student behavior is to avoid eye contact with the teacher. From this simple example it's easy to see how miscommunication can take place. To a teacher in the United States, avoidance of eye contact by a Latin American or Native American could signify guilt, lack of interest, or disrespect when in fact the student was following her or his own culturally established rules. Table 6.1 on page 140, drawn from Axtell (1993) and Sabath (1999), gives you an idea of the problems that can arise when you assume that the rules governing message behavior in one culture are the same rules used in other cultures.

Messages Vary in Abstraction

Consider the following list of terms:

    entertainment
    film
    American film
    recent American film
    Red Dragon

TRY IT!
Apply your understanding of rule-governed messages; go to www.ablongman.com/devito.

Table 6.1   **Some Nonverbal Taboos**

These are only a small number of the nonverbal taboos that exist throughout the world. Can you add any nonverbal taboos to this list?

Nonverbal Behavior	Taboo
Blinking your eyes	Considered impolite in Taiwan
Folding your arms over your chest	Considered disrespectful in Fiji
Putting your hands in your pockets	Considered impolite in Malaysia
Waving your hand	Insulting in Nigeria and Greece
Gesturing with the thumb up	Considered rude in Australia
Tapping your two index fingers together	In Egypt this means that a couple is sleeping together or represents a request to sleep together
Pointing with the index finger	Considered impolite in many Middle-Eastern countries, China, and Indonesia
Bowing to a lesser degree than your host	Implies that you're superior in Japan
With a clenched fist, inserting your thumb between your index and middle finger (called the *fig*)	Considered obscene in some southern European countries
Using your left hand to eat or shake hands	Considered impolite in a wide variety of cultures, for example, Malaysia, Indonesia, and Arab countries
Pointing at someone with your index and third fingers	Means you're wishing evil on the person in some African countries
Resting your feet on a table or chair	Insulting in some Middle-Eastern countries

At the top is the general or abstract category of entertainment. Note that entertainment includes all the items on the list plus various others—television, novels, drama, comics, and so on. Film is more specific and concrete. It includes all of the items below it as well as various other items such as Indian film or Russian film. It excludes, however, all entertainment that is not film. "American film" is again more specific than film and excludes all films that aren't American. "Recent American film" further limits American film to a time period. *Red Dragon* specifies concretely the one item to which reference is made.

The more general term—in this case, entertainment—conjures up a number of different images. One person in the audience may focus on television, another on music, another on comic books, and still another on radio. To some, "film" may bring to mind the early silent films. To others, it brings to mind high-tech special effects. To still others, it recalls Disney's animated cartoons. *Red Dragon* guides the listener still further—in this case to one film. But note that even though *Red Dragon* identifies one film, different listeners are likely to focus on different aspects of the film, perhaps its special effects, perhaps its love story, perhaps its historical accuracy, perhaps its financial success.

Effective verbal messages include words from a wide range of abstractions. At times a general term may suit your needs best; at other times a more specific term may serve

INTER MEDIA

Hate Speech

Hate speech is speech that is hostile, offensive, degrading, or intimidating to a particular group of people. Hate speech occurs in all forms of communication and is certainly not restricted to the media. But, because the media are so influential, the issue of hate speech in the media takes on special importance. Hate speech occurs when:

■ People utter insults to someone passing by
■ Posters and fliers degrade specific groups
■ Radio talk shows denigrate members of certain groups
■ Websites insult, demean, and encourage hostility toward certain groups
■ Movies foster negative stereotypes of certain groups and, indirectly, encourage verbal and even physical hostility

One of the difficulties in eliminating hate speech is that it's hard to draw a clear line between speech that should

be protected by the first amendment but is simply at odds with the majority viewpoint and speech that's designed to denigrate members of certain cultural groups and encourage hostility against them.

Some colleges are instituting hate speech codes, written statements of what constitutes hate speech as well as the penalties for hate speech. Proponents of such codes argue that they teach students that hate speech is unacceptable and may be curtailed in the same way as other undesirable acts (for example, child pornography or rape). Opponents argue that such codes do not address the underlying prejudices and biases that give rise to hate speech and may stifle free expression, especially minority opinion and dissent.

Follow Up   What kinds of hate speech do you witness on your campus? Does your college have a code governing hate speech?

View point   On your college campus, which would most likely be considered hate speech: sexist, racist, or heterosexist language? Which would least likely be? How do you respond when you hear other students using racist language? Using sexist language? Using heterosexist language?

better. Generally, however, the specific term will prove the better choice. As you get more specific—less abstract—you more effectively guide the images that will come into your listeners' minds.

Messages Vary in Politeness

Politeness is a universally desirable trait across most cultures (Brown & Levinson, 1988). Cultures differ, however, in how they define politeness and in how important it is compared with, say, openness or honesty. Cultures also differ in the rules for expressing politeness or impoliteness and in the punishments for violating the accepted rules (Mao, 1994; Strecker, 1993). Asian cultures, especially Chinese and Japanese, are often singled out because they emphasize politeness and mete out harsher social punishments for violations than would people in the United States or Western Europe, for example (Fraser, 1990).

There are large gender differences in the expression of politeness (Holmes, 1995). Generally, studies from a number of different cultures show that women's speech is more polite than men's speech, even on the telephone (Brown, 1980; Wetzel, 1988; Holmes, 1995; Smoreda & Licoppe, 2000). Women more often seek areas of agreement in conversation and conflict situations than do men. Similarly, young girls are more apt to try to modify disagreements while young boys are more apt to express "bald disagreements" (Holmes, 1995). Women also use more polite speech when seeking to gain another person's compliance than men do (Baxter, 1984).

There are also similarities. For example, both men and women in the United States and New Zealand seem to pay compliments in similar ways (Manes & Wolfson, 1981; Holmes, 1986, 1995) and men and women use politeness strategies when communicating bad news in an organization (Lee, 1993). Politeness also seems to vary with the type of relationship. One researcher, for example, has proposed that politeness varies among strangers, friends, and intimates as depicted in Figure 6.1.

WEB EXPLORATION
To learn more about "netiquette," go to www.ablongman.com/devito.

Netiquette   The Internet has very specific rules for politeness, called *netiquette*. Much as the rules of etiquette provide guidance in communicating in social situations, the rules of netiquette provide guidance in communicating over the Net. These rules are helpful for making Internet communication more pleasant and easier and also for

Wolfson's Bulge Model of Politeness
This figure depicts a proposed relationship between the levels of politeness and intimacy. Politeness, according to this model, is greatest with friends and significantly less with strangers and intimates. Can you build a case for an inverted u theory: Politeness is especially high for both strangers and intimates and low for friends?

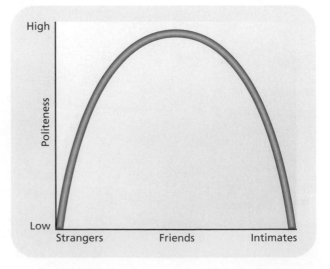

View point Politeness varies with the type of relationship. One researcher, for example, has proposed that politeness is greatest with friends and considerably less with strangers and intimates (see Figure 6.1, Wolfson, 1988; Holmes, 1995). Do you treat your family less politely than you treat friends? Do family members treat you less politely than they treat their friends? What role does politeness play in your family interactions?

achieving greater personal efficiency. They also help to lessen the strain on the system and on other users. Here are several netiquette guidelines:

- *Read the FAQs.* Before asking questions about the system, read the Frequently Asked Questions. Your question has probably been asked before, and you'll put less strain on the system.
- *Don't shout.* WRITING IN CAPS IS PERCEIVED AS SHOUTING. It's okay to use caps occasionally to achieve emphasis. If you wish to give emphasis, highlight _like this_ or *like this*.
- *Lurk before speaking.* Lurking refers to reading posted notices and conversations without contributing anything. In computer communication, lurking is good, not bad. Lurking will help you learn the rules of the particular group and will help you avoid saying things you'd like to take back.
- *Don't contribute to traffic jams.* Try connecting during off hours whenever possible. If you're unable to connect, try later. In securing information, try local information sources before trying more distant sources; it requires fewer connections and less time. Be economical in using files (for example, photographs) that may tie up lines for long periods of time.
- *Be brief.* Follow the maxim of quantity by communicating only the information that is needed; follow the maxim of manner by communicating clearly, briefly, and in an organized way.
- *Treat newbies kindly.* Remember you were once a newbie yourself.
- *Don't send commercial messages to those who didn't request them.* Junk mail is junk; but on the Internet, the receiver often has to pay for the time it takes to read and delete these unwanted messages.
- *Don't spam.* Spamming occurs when you send someone unsolicited mail, repeatedly sending the same mail, or posting the same message to lots of newsgroups, even when the message is irrelevant to the focus of the group. Spamming may cost you money to maintain the Internet connection needed to download the e-mail you didn't want in the first place and it costs you time. Also, it clogs the system, slowing it down for everyone.

ETHICS in *Interpersonal Communication*

Communicating in Cyberspace

Because of the explosion in computer communication, nethics (ethics of Internet communication) has become an important part of ethical communication. Of course, the same principles that govern ethical face-to-face interaction should also prevail when you communicate on the Internet. Here, however, are a few ethical principles with special relevance to computer communication. It is unethical to:

1. *Invade the privacy of others.* Reading the files of another person or breaking into files that you're not authorized to read is unethical.
2. *Harm others or their property.* Creating computer viruses, pub-

lishing instructions for making bombs, or creating websites that promote sexism, racism, or heterosexism are some ways the computer can be used to harm others.

3. *Spread falsehoods.* Lying on the Internet—about other people, the powers of medical or herbal treatment, or yourself—is just as unethical as it is in other forms of communication.

4. *Plagiarize.* Appropriating the work of another as your own—whether the original work appeared on the Internet or in a book or journal—is unethical.
5. *Steal the passwords, pin, or authorization codes that belong to others.*
6. *Copy software programs that you haven't paid for.*

What would you do? *As an experiment you develop a computer virus that can destroy websites. Recently, you've come across a variety of websites that you feel promote child pornography. You wonder if you can ethically destroy these websites. And, further, you wonder if not destroying them is actually more unethical than using your newly developed virus.*

■ *Don't flame.* Flaming refers to making personal attacks on another user. As in face-to-face conflict, personal attacks are best avoided on the Internet. So avoid flaming and participating in flame wars.

The internet also has specific rules for what is and is not ethical, an issue that is tackled in the ethics box, Communicating in Cyberspace.

Messages Vary in Inclusion

Some messages are inclusive; they include all people present and they acknowledge the relevance of others. Other messages exclude specific people and in some cases entire cultural groups.

You see messages of exclusion in the use of in-group language in the presence of an out-group member. When doctors get together and discuss medicine, there is no problem. But when they get together with someone who isn't a doctor, they often fail to adjust to this new person. Instead, they simply continue with discussions of prescriptions, symptoms, medication, and all the talk that excludes others present.

Excluding talk also occurs when people of the same nationality get together within a larger, more heterogeneous group and use the language of their nationality, sometimes just isolated words, sometimes sentences, and sometimes even entire conversations. Similarly, the use of experiences not shared by all (common topics include having children, exotic vacations, and people we know) can serve to include some and exclude others. The use of these terms and experiences in the presence of nonmembers emphasizes their status as outsiders and excludes these people from full participation in the communication act.

Another form of excluding talk is the use of the terms of one's own cultural group as universal, as applying to everyone. In using such terms, you exclude others. For example, *church* refers to the place of worship for specific religions, not all religions. Similarly, *Bible* refers to the Christian religious scriptures and is not a general term for *religious scriptures.* Nor does *Judeo-Christian tradition* include the religious traditions of everyone. Similarly, the terms *marriage, husband,* and *wife* refer to some heterosexual relationships and exclude others; they also exclude gay and lesbian relationships.

Instead of trying to emphasize the exclusion of one or more members, consider the principle of **inclusion.** Regardless of the type of communication situation we are in, everyone needs to be included in the interaction. Even if job-related issues have to be discussed in the presence of a nonmember, that person can be included in a variety of ways, for example, by seeking the nonmember's perspective or drawing an analogy from his or her field.

Another way to practice inclusion is to fill in relevant details discussed by the group for those who may be unaware. For example, when people, places, or events are mentioned in a group discussion, briefly identify them for those to whom they may be unfamiliar. Brief parenthetical identifying phrases are usually sufficient: "Margo—she's Jeff's daughter—loved San Francisco State."

When someone asks a question or makes a comment requiring a response, be sure to respond in some way, even if you're talking, attending to someone else, or otherwise engaged. Acknowledge the comment—verbally, if possible, or nonverbally with a nod or smile, for example. Practicing inclusion is so easy that it's surprising that it's violated so blatantly and so often. When inclusion is practiced, everyone gains a great deal more satisfaction from the interaction.

Also, consider the vast array of alternative terms that are inclusive rather than exclusive. For example, the Association of American University Presses (Schwartz et al., 1995) recommends using *place of worship* instead of *church* when you wish to include the religious houses of worship of all people. Similarly, *committed relationship* is more inclusive than *marriage, couple's therapy* is more inclusive than *marriage counseling,* and *life partner* is more inclusive than *husband* or *wife. Religious scriptures* is more inclusive than *Bible.* Of course, if you're referring to, say, a specific Baptist church or married heterosexual couples. then the terms *church* and *marriage* are perfectly appropriate.

Messages Vary in Directness

Consider your own tendency to be direct or indirect. Imagine you're talking with a friend.

Would you be more likely to use the sentences from Column A or from Column B to communicate essentially the same information?

I SEE

Column A	*Column B*
Would you like to watch *The West Wing*?	I'd like to watch *The West Wing.*
I'd really like some ice cream.	Would you get me a bowl of ice cream?
Isn't it chilly in here?	Jenny, please close the window.
It must have been expensive.	How much did you pay?
I really need to find someone to watch the dog for the weekend.	Would you mind watching my dog next weekend?
Are you doing anything this weekend?	I'd like to go to the movies this weekend; want to come?
The phone's ringing.	Would you please answer the phone?

The statements in Column A are relatively indirect; they're attempts to get the listener to say or do something without committing the speaker. The statements in Column B,

WEB EXPLORATION
To learn more about indirect messages, go to **www.ablongman.com/ devito.**

on the other hand, are direct; they state more clearly the speaker's preferences and then ask the listener to do or say something. Direct and indirect messages can also be nonverbal. For example, you may use an indirect message by glancing at your watch to communicate that it's late or you may use a more direct message such as getting up and putting on your jacket. Indirect messages have both advantages and disadvantages.

Advantages of Indirect Messages   Indirect messages allow you to express a desire without insulting or offending anyone; they allow you to observe the rules of polite interaction. So instead of saying, "I'm bored with this group," you say, "It's getting late and I have to get up early tomorrow," or you look at your watch and pretend to be surprised by the time. Instead of saying, "This food tastes like cardboard," you say, "I just started my diet" or "I just ate." In each instance you're stating a preference but are saying it indirectly so as to avoid offending someone.

Sometimes indirect messages allow you to ask for compliments in a socially acceptable manner, such as saying, "I was thinking of getting my eyes done." You hope to get the desired compliment: "Your eyes? They're perfect as they are."

Disadvantages of Indirect Messages   Indirect messages can create problems. Consider the following dialogue in which an indirect request is made:

Pat: You wouldn't like to have my parents over for dinner this weekend, would you?
Chris: I really wanted to go to the beach and just relax.
Pat: Well, if you feel you have to go to the beach, I'll make the dinner myself. You go to the beach. I really hate having them over and doing all the work myself. It's such a drag shopping, cooking, and cleaning all by myself.

Given this situation, Chris has two basic alternatives. One is to stick with the plans to go to the beach and relax. In this case Pat is going to be upset and Chris is going to be made to feel guilty for not helping with the dinner. A second alternative is to give in to Pat, help with the dinner, and not go to the beach. In this case Chris is going to have to give up a much desired plan and is likely to resent Pat's "manipulative" tactics. Regardless of which decision is made, one person wins and one person loses. This win–lose situation creates resentment, competition, and often an "I'll get even" attitude. With direct requests, this type of situation is much less likely to develop. Consider:

Pat: I'd like to have my parents over for dinner this weekend. What do you think?
Chris: Well, I really wanted to go to the beach and just relax.

Regardless of what develops next, both individuals are starting out on relatively equal footing. Each has clearly and directly stated a preference. Although at first these preferences seem mutually exclusive, it might be possible to meet both persons' needs. For example, Chris might say, "How about going to the beach this weekend and having your parents over next weekend? I'm really exhausted; I could use the rest." Here is a direct response to a direct request. Unless there is some pressing need to have Pat's parents over for dinner this weekend, this response may enable each to meet the other's needs.

Gender and Cultural Differences in Directness   The popular stereotype in much of the United States holds that women are indirect in making requests and in giving orders. This indirectness communicates powerlessness, discomfort with their own authority. Men, the stereotype continues, are direct, sometimes to the point of being blunt or rude. This directness communicates power and comfort with one's own authority.

In the classic film, *The Graduate,* there's a particularly good example of direct and indirect messages. Benjamin, the graduate (played by Dustin Hoffman), and Mrs. Robinson (Anne Bancroft) are having an affair. Because of the age difference and the fact that Benjamin is actually in love with Mrs. Robinson's daughter, their affair is uncomfortable and awkward. Mrs. Robinson, contrary to the research evidence that shows that women are indirect, is very direct in expressing what she wants and what she doesn't want. Benjamin, also contrary to the research, is very indirect, often failing to even voice his feelings. Under what other type of circumstances would you think this direct and indirect pattern would be reversed with men being the more indirect and women being more direct?

Deborah Tannen (1994b) provides an interesting perspective on these stereotypes. Women are, it seems, more indirect in giving orders and are more likely to say, for example, "It would be great if these letters could go out today" than "Have these letters out by three." But Tannen (1994b, p. 84) argues that "issuing orders indirectly can be the prerogative of those in power" and does in no way show powerlessness. Power, to Tannen, is the ability to chose your own style of communication.

Men, however, are also indirect but in different situations (Rundquist, 1992). According to Tannen, men are more likely to use indirectness when they express weakness, reveal a problem, or admit an error. Men are more likely to speak indirectly in expressing emotions other than anger. Men are also more indirect when they refuse expressions of increased romantic intimacy. Men are thus indirect, the theory goes, when they're saying something that goes against the masculine stereotype.

Many Asian and Latin American cultures stress the value of indirectness largely because it enables people to save face by avoiding criticism and contradictions. A somewhat different kind of indirectness is seen in the greater use of intermediaries to resolve conflict among the Chinese than among North Americans, for example (Ma, 1992). In most of the United States, however, directness is preferred. "Be up front" and "tell it like it is" are commonly heard communication guidelines. Contrast these with the following two principles of indirectness found in the Japanese language (Tannen, 1994b):

omoiyari, close to empathy, says that listeners need to understand the speaker without the speaker being specific or direct. This style obviously places a much greater demand on the listener than would a direct speaking style.

sassuru advises listeners to anticipate a speaker's meanings and use subtle cues from the speaker to infer his or her total meaning.

But, in one study, American males were found to be less direct than a similar group of Egyptian males (Nelson, Al Batal, & El Bakary, 2002). Comparisons like these between Americans, Japanese, and Egyptians are especially helpful in illustrating how difficult it is to draw generalizations concerning the communication tendencies of any one culture.

In thinking about direct and indirect messages, it's important to realize how easily misunderstandings can occur. For example, a person who uses an indirect style of speech may be doing so to be polite and may have been taught this style by his or her culture. If you assume, instead, that the person is using indirectness to be manipulative, because your culture regards it so, then miscommunication is inevitable.

Messages Vary in Assertiveness

If you disagree with other people in a group, do you speak your mind? Do you allow others to take advantage of you because you're reluctant to say what you want? Do you feel uncomfortable when you have to state your opinion in a group? Questions such as these speak to your degree of **assertiveness.** Before reading further about this type of communication, take the self-test "How Assertive Is Your Communication?"

TEST YOURSELF *How Assertive Is Your Communication?*

Indicate how true each of the following statements is about your own communication. Respond instinctively rather than in the way you feel you should respond. Use the following scale: 5 = always or almost always true, 4 = usually true, 3 = sometimes true, sometimes false, 2 = usually false, 1 = always or almost always false.

_____ 1. I would express my opinion in a group even if it contradicts the opinions of others.

_____ 2. When asked to do something that I really don't want to do, I can say "No" without feeling guilty.

_____ 3. I can express my opinion to my superiors on the job.

_____ 4. I can start up a conversation with a stranger on a bus or at a business gathering without fear.

_____ 5. I voice objection to people's behavior if I feel it infringes on my rights.

_____ 6. I express my feelings directly, using I-messages ("I need you to be more accurate in recording appointments"), rather than you-messages ("Your work is sloppy and inaccurate") or third-person messages ("Everyone says your work isn't up to par").

_____ 7. I use factual and descriptive terms when stating what I object to ("The last three letters you typed contained too many errors"; "You complained about the service in the last seven restaurants we ate at") rather than allness or extreme terms ("You never do the right thing"; "You always complain").

_____ 8. I try to understand and accept the behaviors of others rather than criticize them and label them with such expressions as "That's silly" or "That's insane."

_____ 9. I believe that in most interactions, both people should gain something—rather than one win and one lose.

_____ 10. I believe that my desires are as important as those of others—not more important, but not less important either.

▶ **How did you do?** All 10 items in this test identified characteristics of assertive communication. So, high scores (40 and above) would indicate a high level of assertiveness. Low scores (20 and below) would indicate a low level of assertiveness.

▶ **What will you do?** The remaining discussion in this chapter clarifies the nature of assertive communication and offers guidelines for increasing your own assertiveness. Try following these suggestions to increase your own assertiveness and at the same time to reduce your aggressiveness tendencies. ●

In addition to identifying some specific assertive behaviors (as in the self-test), the nature of assertive communication can be further explained by distinguishing it from nonassertiveness and aggressiveness (Alberti, 1977).

Nonassertiveness, Aggressiveness, and Assertiveness   *Nonassertiveness* refers to a lack of assertiveness in certain types of or in all communication situations. People who are nonassertive fail to assert their rights. In many instances, these people do what others tell them to do—parents, employers, and the like—without questioning and without concern for what is best for them. They operate with a "You win, I lose" philosophy; they give others what they want without concern for themselves (Lloyd, 2001). Nonassertive people often ask permission from others to do what is their perfect right. Social situations create anxiety for these individuals, and their self-esteem is generally low.

Aggressiveness is the other extreme. Aggressive people operate with an "I win, you lose" philosophy; they care little for what the other person wants and focus only on their own needs. Some people communicate aggressively only under certain conditions or in certain situations (for example, after being taken advantage of over a long period of time) while others communicate aggressively in all or at least most situations. Aggressive communicators think little of the opinions, values, or beliefs of others and yet are extremely sensitive to others' criticisms of their own behavior. Consequently, they frequently get into arguments with others.

Assertive behavior—behavior that enables you to act in your own best interests without denying or infringing upon the rights of others—is the generally desired alternative to nonassertiveness or aggressiveness (Alberti, 1977; Alberti & Emmons, 2001). Assertive communication enables you to act in your own best interests without denying or infringing upon the rights of others and is especially useful in making interpersonal contact and in interpersonal conflict (Fodor & Collier, 2001). Assertive people operate with an "I win, you win" philosophy; they assume that both people can gain something from an interpersonal interaction, even from a confrontation. Assertive people are more positive and score lower on measures of hopelessness than do nonassertive people (Velting, 1999). Assertive people are willing to assert their own rights. Unlike their aggressive counterparts, however, they don't hurt others in the process. Assertive people speak their minds and welcome others' doing likewise.

People who are assertive in interpersonal communication display four major characteristics (Norton & Warnick, 1976). To what extent do these characteristics apply to you?

I SEE

- Do you engage in frank and open expression of your feelings to people in general as well as to those for whom you may have a romantic interest?
- Do you readily volunteer opinions and beliefs, deal directly with interpersonal communication situations that may be stressful, and question others without fear?
- Do you stand up and argue for your rights, even if this might entail a certain degree of disagreement or conflict with relatives or close friends?
- Do you make up your mind based on evidence and argument instead of just accepting what others say?

Research shows that people who are assertive would answer "yes" to these questions. Assertive people are more open, less anxious, more contentious, and less likely to be intimidated or easy to persuade. People who are unassertive would answer "no."

Unassertive people are less open, more anxious, less contentious, and are more likely to be intimidated and easily persuaded.

Do realize that as with communication apprehension, there will be wide cultural differences when it comes to assertiveness. For example, the values of assertiveness are more likely to be extolled in individualistic cultures rather than in collectivist cultures. Assertiveness will be valued more by those cultures that stress competition, individual success, and independence. It will be valued much less by those cultures that stress cooperation, group success, and interdependence of all members on each other. American students, for example, are found to be significantly more assertive than Japanese or Korean students (Thompson, Klopf, & Ishii, 1991; Thompson & Klopf, 1991). Thus, for some situations assertiveness may be an effective strategy in one culture, but in another culture may create problems. Assertiveness with an elder in many Asian and Hispanic cultures may be seen as insulting and disrespectful.

TRY IT!
Apply your understanding of the principles for increasing assertive communication; go to **www.ablongman.com/ devito**.

Principles for Increasing Assertive Communication   Most people are non-assertive in certain situations. If you're one of these people and if you wish to modify your behavior, there are steps you can take to increase your assertiveness. (If you are always nonassertive and are unhappy about this, then you may need training with a therapist to change your behavior.)

Analyze Assertive Communications   The first step in increasing your assertiveness skills is to understand the nature of these communications. Observe and analyze the messages of others. Learn to distinguish the differences among assertive, aggressive, and nonassertive messages. Focus on what makes one behavior assertive and another behavior nonassertive or aggressive. Table 6.2 reviews some of the verbal and nonverbal messages that distinguish assertive from nonassertive or aggressive communication.

After you've gained some skills in observing the behaviors of others, turn your analysis to yourself. Analyze situations in which you're normally assertive and situations in which you're more likely to act nonassertively or aggressively. What characterizes these situations? What do the situations in which you're normally assertive have in common? How do you speak? How do you communicate nonverbally?

Table 6.2   **Assertive and Aggressive Messages**

As you read this table, consider your customary ways of interacting. How often do you use assertive messages? How often do you use aggressive messages?

Assertive Messages	Aggressive Messages
I-messages, accept responsibility for your own feelings (I feel angry when you . . .)	You-messages, attribute your feelings to others (You make me angry when you . . .)
Descriptive and realistic expressions	Allness and extreme expressions
Equality messages (recognizes the essential equality of oneself and others)	Inequality (overly submissive, polite, subservient or overly aggressive, insulting, condescending)
Relaxed and erect body posture	Tense, overly rigid, overly relaxed
Focused but not threatening eye contact	Intense eye contact or excessive eye contact avoidance
Expressive and genuine facial expressions	Unexpressive or overly expressive (and often insincere) facial expressions
Normal vocal volume and rhythm pattern	Overly soft or overly loud and accusatory

Rehearse Assertive Communications   Select a situation in which you're normally nonassertive. Build a hierarchy that begins with a relatively nonthreatening message and ends with the desired communication. For example, let's say that you have difficulty voicing your opinion to your supervisor at work. The desired behavior, then, is to tell your supervisor your opinions. You would construct a hierarchy of situations leading up to this desired behavior. Such a hierarchy might begin with visualizing yourself talking with your boss. Visualize this scenario until you can do it without any anxiety or discomfort. Once you have mastered this visualization, visualize a step closer to your goal, such as walking into your boss's office. Again, do this until your visualization creates no discomfort. Continue with these successive visualizations until you can visualize yourself telling your boss your opinion. As with the other visualizations, do this until you can do it while totally relaxed. This is the mental rehearsal.

You might add a vocal dimension to this by actually acting out (with voice and gesture) your telling your boss your opinion. Again, do this until you experience no difficulty or discomfort. Next, try doing this in front of a trusted and supportive friend or group of friends. Ideally this interaction will provide you with useful feedback. After this rehearsal, you're probably ready for the next step.

Communicate Assertively   This step is naturally the most difficult but obviously the most important. Here's a generally effective pattern to follow in communicating assertively:

- Describe the problem; don't evaluate or judge it. *We're all working on this advertising project together. You're missing half our meetings and you still haven't produced your first report.* Be sure to use I-messages and to avoid messages that accuse or blame the other person.
- State how this problem affects you. *My job depends on the success of this project and I don't think it's fair that I have to do extra work to make up for what you're not doing.*
- Propose solutions that are workable and that allow the person to save face. *If you can get your report to the group by Tuesday, we'll still be able to meet our deadline. I could give you a call on Monday to remind you.*
- Confirm understanding. *It's clear that we can't produce this project if you're not going to pull your own weight. Will you have the report to us by Tuesday?*
- Reflect on your own assertiveness. Think about what you did. How did you express yourself verbally and nonverbally? What would you do differently next time?

Keep in mind that assertiveness is not always the most desirable response. Assertive people are assertive when they want to be, but they can be nonassertive if the situation calls for it. For example, you might wish to be nonassertive in a situation in which assertiveness might emotionally hurt the other person. Let's say that an older relative wishes you to do something for her or him. You could assert your rights and say no, but in doing so you would probably hurt this person; it might be better simply to do as asked. Of course, there are limits that should be observed. You should be careful, in such a situation, that you're not hurt instead. For example, if your parents want you to continue to live at home until marriage, they may be hurt by your assertive behavior in refusing. Yet the alternative is to hurt yourself by living with your parents when you're ready to be on your own.

After communicating, get feedback from others. Start with people who are generally supportive. They should provide you with the social reinforcement so helpful in learning new behavioral patterns. This feedback is particularly important because your intention and the perception of your behavior by an observer may be totally different. For example, you may behave in certain ways with the intention of communicating confidence, but the observer may perceive arrogance. Thus, another person's perception of your behavior can often help you to see yourself as others do.

In all behaviors, but especially with new behaviors, recognize that you may at first fail. You might, for example, try to answer the teacher's question and find that not only do you have the wrong answer but that you don't even understand the question. You might raise your hand and find yourself at a loss for words when you're recognized. Such incidents should not discourage you; realize that in all attempts to change behaviors, you will experience both failure and success.

A note of caution should be added to this discussion. It's easy to visualize a situation in which, for example, people are talking behind you in a movie, and with your new-found enthusiasm for assertiveness, you tell them to be quiet. It's also easy to see yourself getting smashed in the teeth as a result. In applying the principles of assertive communication, be careful that you don't go beyond what you can handle effectively.

REVIEWING   Key Terms and Concepts in Verbal and Nonverbal Messages

This chapter introduced the message system and examined some of the similarities and differences in verbal and nonverbal messages.

Messages and Meanings

What is meaning and what principles regulate the communication of meaning from one person to another?

■ Meanings are in people, in their thoughts and feelings, not just in their words.

■ Meaning is more than words and gestures; meaning includes what speaker and listener bring to interpersonal interaction.

■ Meaning is unique; no two people experience exactly the same meaning.

■ Meanings are context-based; the context heavily influences the meanings that words and gestures are given.

Message Characteristics

What are the major characteristics of verbal and nonverbal messages?

■ Messages are packaged; they occur in clusters and usually reinforce each other but may also contradict each other.

■ Messages are rule-governed; they follow the rules of the culture.

■ Messages vary in abstraction; they vary from very specific to highly abstract and general.

■ Messages vary in politeness from rude to extremely polite.

■ Messages vary in inclusion and may include or exclude other people.

■ Messages vary in assertiveness, a quality that may be increased by analyzing the communications around you, rehearsing assertive communication, and communicating with assertive messages.

APPLYING   Key Terms and Concepts in Verbal and Nonverbal Messages

1. Describe a situation where others have misinterpreted the meaning you wanted to communicate because they failed to look for meaning in you.

2. A weasel is a slippery rodent; just when you're going to catch it, it slips away. Weasel words are words whose meanings are difficult to pin down. For example, the medicine that claims to work better than Brand X doesn't specify how much better or in what respect it performs better. It's possible that it performs better in one respect and less effective on the other nine measures. "Better" is a weasel word. "Like" is another word often used for weaseling, as when a claim is made that "Brand X will make you feel like a new man." Other weasel words are "helped," "virtually," "as much as," and "more economical." How many weasel words can you identify in a half-hour television show's commercials?

3. Most lies are told to benefit the liar, generally to gain a reward (for example, to increase desirable relationships, to protect one's self-esteem, or to obtain money) or to avoid punishment. In an analysis of 322 lies researchers found that 75.8 percent benefited the liar, 21.7 percent benefited the person who was told the lie, and 2.5 percent benefited a third party (Camden, Motley, & Wilson, 1984). Are lies told to benefit others less unethical than lies told to benefit yourself?

4. How would you state the rules for the appropriateness of such common nonverbal messages as (a) smiling, (b) winking, and (c) shaking hands?

5. Consider the differences in meaning for such words as *woman* to an American and an Iranian, *religion* to a born-again Christian and an atheist, and *lunch* to a Chinese rice farmer and a Wall Street executive. What principles might

help such diverse groups understand the different meanings?

6. Using a good search engine such as Google (www.google.com), Dogpile (www.dogpile.com), or AskJeeves (www.aj.com) look up "hate speech," especially college codes on hate speech. After reading about hate speech and the codes that have been developed, formulate your own position on college codes regarding hate speech. Are you in favor of such codes? Against such codes? What reasons can you give to support your position? If you're in favor of such codes, how would you write such a code of conduct?

7. How polite is your communication with those in positions of authority—say, professors, supervisors, or police officers—compared with your communication with those who are in positions similar to your own—say, other students, colleagues, and neighbors? Can you phrase these differences in the form of a communication rule?

8. Many people who practice direct communication see those who communicate indirectly as being manipulative. According to Tannen (1994b, p. 92), however, "'manipulative' is often just a way of blaming others for our discomfort with their styles." Do you agree with Tannen? Or do you think that indirectness is often intentionally manipulative?

EXPERIENCING Key Terms and Concepts in Verbal and Nonverbal Messages

Go to www.ablongman.com/devito.

This group of experiences will help clarify the nature of verbal and nonverbal messages and some of their major characteristics.

(1) **Integrating Verbal and Nonverbal Messages** explores some of the connections between verbal and nonverbal messages. (2) **Climbing the Abstraction Ladder** and (3) **Using the Abstraction Ladder as a Creative Thinking Tool** will clarify the nature of the abstraction process and explain a useful creative thinking technique. (4) **How Can You Vary Directness for Greatest Effectiveness?** provides practice in varying directness. (5) **How Can You Rephrase Clichés?** identifies some of the many clichés and provides an opportunity to replace these with more creative and meaningful expressions. (6) **Who?** is a class game-experience that asks you to identify characteristics of other people on the basis of their various verbal and nonverbal messages. This exercise can be used as an introduction to the messages section or as a conclusion. (7) **Analyzing Assertiveness** provides practice scenarios calling for assertiveness.

RESEARCHING with Research Navigator Key Terms and Concepts in Verbal and Nonverbal Messages

Go to http://www.researchnavigator.com.

Reading an article.

Read an academic or popular article on meaning or messages, for example, message directness or assertiveness. On the basis of this article what can you add to the discussion presented here?

Investigating key terms.

Investigate one of the key terms discussed in this chapter (for example, meaning, message, abstraction, denotation and connotation, abstraction, directness, lying, assertiveness, or hate speech).What additional insights can you provide?

Finding answers.

Try finding answers to one of the following questions or design a research study to answer it.

■ Are men or women more effective liars? More effective lie detectors?

■ Are close relationship partners better at detecting their partners' lies than are casual acquaintances? For an interesting investigation of this question see Metts (1989).

■ Do men and women follow different rules for politeness in, say, conversation? In business? If yes, describe the differences.

■ Under what circumstances would politeness prove an ineffective interpersonal communication strategy?

■ Are men and women equally assertive? Equally aggressive?

7 Verbal Messages

Philadelphia (1993)

"When I use a word," Humpty Dumpty said in rather a scornful tone, "it means just what I choose it to mean; neither more nor less."

—Lewis Carroll

Language Symbolizes Reality
Language Expresses Both Facts and Inferences
Language Expresses Both Denotation and Connotation
Language Can Criticize and Praise
Language Can Obscure Distinctions
Language Can Confirm and Disconfirm

Jonathan Demme's Philadelphia *tells the story of a lawyer (Tom Hanks) stricken with AIDS who is fired from his prestigious law position because of the firm's homophobia. Another lawyer (Denzel Washington) signs on to handle the case to sue the law firm, but he does so reluctantly because of his own homophobia. This film illustrates how interpersonal interactions are influenced by homophobia as well as sexism and racism, which we look at as parts of the process of disconfirmation. In addition, we examine the general principles underlying verbal messages, namely that language symbolizes reality, expresses both facts and inferences, communicates both denotative and connotative meaning, praises and criticizes, and may obscure important distinctions.*

LANGUAGE SYMBOLIZES REALITY

Language symbolizes reality; of course, it's not the reality itself. Consider: Have you ever reacted to the way something was labeled or described rather than to the actual item? Have you ever bought something because of its name rather than because of the actual object? If so, you were probably responding as if language was the reality, a distortion called intensional orientation.

Intensional Orientation

Intensional orientation refers to the tendency to view people, objects, and events in terms of how they're talked about or labeled rather than in terms of how they actually exist. **Extensional orientation** is the opposite, the tendency to look first at the actual people, objects, and events and then at the labels. It's the tendency to be guided by what you see happening rather than by the way something or someone is talked about or labeled.

Intensional orientation occurs when you act as if the words and labels are more important than the things they represent—as if the map is more important than the territory. In its extreme form, intensional orientation is seen in the person who is afraid of dogs and who begins to sweat when shown a picture of a dog or when hearing people talk about dogs. Here the person is responding to a label as if it were the actual thing. In its more common form it occurs when you see people through your schemata instead of on the basis of their specific behaviors. It occurs when you think of a professor as an unworldly egghead before getting to know the specific professor.

The corrective to intensional orientation is to focus first on the object, person, or event and then on the way in which the object, person, or event is talked about. Labels are certainly helpful guides, but don't allow them to obscure what they're meant to symbolize.

Cultural Identifiers   Having said that the word is not the thing does not mean that words may be chosen at random or that all words are equal. This is seen most clearly in the preferences people have for identifying their cultural origins. As always, when in doubt, find out. The preferences and many of the specific examples identified here are drawn largely from the findings of the Task Force on Bias-Free Language of the Association of American University Presses. Do realize that not everyone would agree with these recommendations; they're presented here—in the words of the Task Force—"to encourage sensitivity to usages that may be imprecise, misleading, and needlessly offensive" (Schwartz et al., 1995, p. ix).

WEB EXPLORATION
To learn more about cultural identifiers, go to www.ablongman.com/devito.

Many people feel that it's permissible for members of a culture to refer to themselves with terms that, if said by outsiders, would be considered racist, sexist, or heterosexist. One possible problem with this is that these terms may actually reinforce the negative stereotypes that society has already assigned to this group. By using these terms, members may come to accept these labels with their negative connotations and thus contribute to their own stereotyping and their own deprecation. Others would argue that by using such terms they're making them less negative. Do you refer to yourself with terms that would be considered offensive or politically incorrect if said by "outsiders"? What effects, if any, do you think such self-talk has?

Generally, the term *girl* should only be used to refer to very young females and is equivalent to *boy.* Neither term should be used for people older than, say, 13 or 14, though some popular uses extend the terms through high school age. *Girl* is never used to refer to a grown woman, nor is *boy* used to refer to persons in blue-collar positions, as it once was. *Lady* is negatively evaluated by many because it connotes the stereotype of the prim and proper woman. *Woman* or *young woman* is preferred. *Older person* is preferred to *elder, elderly, senior,* or *senior citizen* (which technically refers to someone older than 65).

Generally, *gay* is the preferred term to refer to a man who has an affectional preference for another man and *lesbian* is the preferred term for a woman who has an affectional preference for another woman. (*Lesbian* means "homosexual woman" so the phrase *lesbian woman* is redundant.) This preference for the term *lesbian* is not universal among homosexual women; in one survey, for example, 58 percent preferred *lesbian;* 34 percent preferred *gay* (Lever, 1995). *Homosexual* refers to both gay men and lesbians but more often to a sexual orientation to members of one's own sex. *Gay* and *lesbian* refer to a lifestyle and not just to sexual orientation. *Gay* as a noun, although widely used, may prove offensive in some contexts, for example, "We have two gays on the team." Although used within the gay community in an effort to remove the negative stigma through frequent usage, the term *queer*—as in *queer power*—is often resented when used by outsiders. Because most scientific thinking holds that one's sexuality is genetically determined rather than being a matter of choice, the term *sexual orientation* rather than *sexual preference* or *sexual status* (which is also vague) is preferred.

Generally, most African Americans prefer *African American* to *black* (Hecht, Collier, & Ribeau, 1993) though *black* is often used with *white* and is used in a variety of other contexts (for example, Department of Black and Puerto Rican Studies, the *Journal of Black History,* and Black History Month). The American Psychological Association recommends that both terms be capitalized, but *The Chicago Manual of Style* (the manual used by most publishing houses) recommends using lowercase. The terms *Negro* and *colored,* although used in the names of some organizations (for example, the United Negro College Fund and the National Association for the Advancement of Colored People) aren't used outside of these contexts.

White is generally used to refer to those whose roots are in European cultures and usually does not include Hispanics. Similar to *African American* is the phrase *European American.* Few European Americans, however, would want to be called that; most prefer their national origins be emphasized, for example, *German American* or *Greek American.* This preference may well change as Europe moves into a more cohesive and united entity. *People of color*—a more literary-sounding term appropriate perhaps to public speaking but awkward in most conversations—is preferred to *nonwhite,* which implies that whiteness is the norm and nonwhiteness is a deviation from that norm. The same is true of the term *non-Christian.*

Generally, *Hispanic* is used to refer to anyone who identifies himself or herself as belonging to a Spanish-speaking culture. *Latina* (female) and *Latino* (male) refer to those whose roots are in one of the Latin American countries, for example, Dominican Republic, Nicaragua, or Guatemala. *Hispanic American* refers to those United States residents whose ancestry is a Spanish culture and includes Mexican, Caribbean, and Central and South Americans. In emphasizing a Spanish heritage, the term is really inadequate in referring to those large numbers in the Caribbean and in South America whose origins are French or Portuguese. *Chicana* (female) and *Chicano* (male) refer to those with roots in Mexico, though it often connotes a nationalist attitude (Jandt, 1995) and is considered offensive by many Mexican Americans. *Mexican American* is preferred.

Inuk (pl. *Inuit*) was officially adopted at the Inuit Circumpolar Conference to refer to the group of indigenous people of Alaska, Northern Canada, Greenland, and Eastern Siberia. This term is preferred to *Eskimo* (a term the United States Census Bureau uses), which was applied to the indigenous peoples of Alaska by Europeans and derives from a term that means "raw meat eaters" (Maggio, 1997).

Indian refers only to someone from India and is incorrectly used when applied to members of other Asian countries or to the indigenous peoples of North America. In the United States *American Indian* or *Native American* are preferred, even though many Native Americans refer to themselves as *Indians* and *Indian people* and the Bureau of Indian Affairs is still so named. In Canada "First People" is the preferred designation for indigenous people. The term *native American* (with a lowercase *n*) is most often used to refer to persons born in the United States. Although the term technically could refer to anyone born in North or South America, people outside the United States generally prefer more specific designations such as *Argentinean, Cuban,* or *Canadian.* The term *native* means an indigenous inhabitant; it's not used to mean "someone having a less developed culture."

Muslim is the preferred form (rather than the older *Moslem*) to refer to a person who adheres to the religious teachings of Islam. *Quran* (rather than *Koran*) is the preferred term for the scriptures of Islam. The terms *Mohammedan* or *Mohammedanism* aren't considered appropriate since they imply worship of Muhammad, the prophet, "considered by Muslims to be a blasphemy against the absolute oneness of God" (Maggio, 1997, p. 277).

Although there is no universal agreement, generally *Jewish people* is preferred to *Jews,* and *Jewess* (a Jewish female) is considered derogatory. *Jew* should only be used as a noun and is never correctly used as a verb or an adjective (Maggio, 1997).

When in the United States history was being written from a European perspective, it was taken as the focal point and the rest of the world was defined in terms of its location from Europe. Thus, Asia became the *east* or the *orient* and Asians became *Orientals*—a term that is today considered inappropriate or Eurocentric. Thus, people from Asia are *Asians* just as people from Africa are *Africans* and people from Europe are *Europeans.*

Allness

Another way in which your messages fail to recognize that language only partially symbolizes reality is with **allness.** The world is infinitely complex, and because of this you can never say all there is to say about anything—at least not logically. This is particularly true in dealing with people. You may think you know all there is to know about certain individuals or about why they did what they did, yet clearly you don't know all. You can never know all the reasons you yourself do something, so there is no way you can know all the reasons your parents, friends, or enemies did something.

You may, for example, be assigned to read a textbook, and because previous texts have been dull and perhaps the first chapter of this one is dull, you might infer that the rest of the book will likewise be dull. Of course, the rest of a book is often even worse than its beginning. Yet it could be that the rest of the book would prove exciting were it read with an open mind. The problem here is that you run the risk of judging an entire

Increasing Interpersonal Effectiveness
Confidence

Confidence refers to your belief that you're an effective and competent communicator and to the belief that you project this when interacting with others. Researchers find that a relaxed posture communicates a sense of control, superior status, and power (Spitzberg & Cupach, 1984, 1989). Tenseness, rigidity, and discomfort, on the other hand, signal a lack of self-control, which in turn signals an inability to control your own environment or perhaps to manage and lead other people.

Communicating Confidence   Here are a few suggestions for communicating confidence in interpersonal interactions.

■ *Take the initiative in introducing yourself to others and in introducing topics of conversation.* This will help you communicate confidence and control over the situation.

■ *Demonstrate the nonverbal behavior of a confident communicator.* Appear relaxed (not rigid), flexible (not locked into one or two vocal ranges or body movements), and controlled (not shaky or awkward).

■ *Control your emotions.* Once your emotions get the best of you, you'll appear to have lost confidence. A confident person approaches situations and makes decisions on the basis of logic and evidence, not on the basis of emotions. Of course, not all cultures think this way; in some Latin cultures, for example, strong emotions like anger may make a person appear powerful.

■ *Admit your mistakes.* Only a confident person can openly admit mistakes and not worry about what others will think.

■ *Avoid turning declarative sentences into questions by a rising intonation.* For example, "I'll arrive at nine?" Asking for agreement generally communicates a lack of confidence.

text in such a way as to preclude any other possibilities. If you tell yourself that the book is dull, it will probably seem dull; if you say a required course will be useless, it will be extremely difficult for the instructor to make the course anything but what you have defined it to be. Only occasionally do people allow themselves to be proven wrong.

The parable of the six blind men and the elephant is an excellent example of an "allness orientation"—the tendency to judge the whole on the basis of experience with part of the whole—and its attendant problems. You may recall from elementary school the poem by John Saxe that concerns six blind men of Indostan who came to examine an elephant, an animal they had only heard about. The first blind man touched the elephant's side and concluded that the elephant was like a wall. The second felt the tusk and said the elephant must be like a spear. The third held the trunk and concluded that the elephant was much like a snake. The fourth touched the knee and knew the elephant was like a tree. The fifth felt the ear and said the elephant was like a fan. The sixth grabbed the tail and concluded that the elephant was like a rope. Each of these learned men reached his own conclusion regarding what the elephant was really like. Each argued that he was correct and that the others were wrong.

Each, of course, was correct; at the same time, however, all were wrong. The point this parable illustrates is that you can never see all of anything; you can never experience anything fully. You see part of an object, event, or person—and on that limited basis, you conclude what the whole is like. This procedure is universal, and you follow it because you cannot possibly observe everything. Yet recognize that when making judgments of the whole based on only a part, you're actually making inferences that can later be proved wrong. If you assume that you know everything there is to know about something or someone, you fall into the pattern of misevaluation called allness.

Famed British prime minister Disraeli once said that "to be conscious that you are ignorant is a great step toward knowledge." This observation is an excellent example of a **nonallness** attitude. If you recognize that there is more to learn, more to see, more to hear, you leave yourself open to this additional information, and you're better prepared to assimilate it.

A useful device to avoid allness is to end each statement, sometimes verbally but always mentally, with an **"etc."** (et cetera), a reminder that there is more to learn, know, and say—a reminder that every statement is inevitably incomplete. Some people, however, overuse the et cetera. They use it as a substitute for being specific, which defeats its purpose. Instead, it should be used to mentally remind yourself that there is more to know and more to say.

LANGUAGE EXPRESSES BOTH FACTS AND INFERENCES

Language enables you to form statements of facts and inferences without making any linguistic distinction between the two. Similarly, when you speak or listen to such statements you often don't make a clear distinction between statements of facts and statements of inference. Yet there are great differences between the two. Barriers to clear thinking can be created when inferences are treated as facts, a tendency called **fact–inference confusion.**

For example, you can make statements about things that you observe, and you can make statements about things that you have not observed. In form or structure, these statements are similar and cannot be distinguished from each other by any grammatical analysis. For example, you can say, "She is wearing a blue jacket" as well as "She is harboring an illogical hatred." If you diagrammed these sentences, they would yield identical structures, and yet you know that they're different types of statements. In the first one, you can observe the jacket and the blue color. But how do you observe "illogical hatred"? Obviously, this is not a descriptive statement but an **inferential statement,** a statement that you make not solely on the basis of what you observe but on the basis of what you observe plus your own conclusions.

There's no problem with making inferential statements; you must make them if you're to talk about much that is meaningful. The problem arises when you act as though those inferential statements are factual statements. Consider, for example, the following anecdote (Maynard, 1963):

> A woman went for a walk one day and met her friend, whom she had not seen, heard from, or heard of in ten years. After an exchange of greetings, the woman said, "Is this your little boy?" and her friend replied, "Yes. I got married about six years ago." The woman then asked the child, "What is your name?" and the little boy replied, "Same as my father's." "Oh," said the woman, "then it must be Peter."

The question, of course, is how did the woman know the boy's father's name? The answer is obvious, but only after you recognize that in reading this short passage you have, quite unconsciously, made an inference that is preventing you from arriving at the answer. You have inferred that the woman's friend is a woman. Actually, the friend is a man named Peter.

Perhaps the classic example of this type of fact–inference confusion concerns the case of the "empty" gun that unfortunately proves to be loaded. With amazing frequency, we find in the newspapers examples of people being so sure that the guns are empty that they point them at someone else and fire. Often, of course, they're empty. But unfortunately, often they're not. Here one draws the inference that the gun is empty but acts as if it were a fact and fires the gun.

You may wish to test your ability to distinguish facts from inferences by taking the self-test "Can You Distinguish Facts from Inferences?"

TEST YOURSELF *Can You Distinguish Facts from Inferences?*

Carefully read the following report, modeled on that developed by William Haney (1973), and the observations based on it. Indicate whether you think the observations are true, false, or doubtful on the basis of the information presented in the report. Circle T if the observation is definitely true, F if the observation is definitely false, and ? if the observation may be either true or false. Judge each observation in order. Don't reread the observations after you have indicated your judgment, and don't change any of your answers.

A well-liked college teacher had just completed making up the final examinations and had turned off the lights in the office. Just then a tall, broad figure appeared and demanded the examination. The professor opened the drawer. Everything in the drawer was picked up and the individual ran down the corridor. The dean was notified immediately.

T F ?   1. The thief was tall and broad.
T F ?   2. The professor turned off the lights.
T F ?   3. A tall figure demanded the examination.
T F ?   4. The examination was picked up by someone.
T F ?   5. The examination was picked up by the professor.
T F ?   6. A tall figure appeared after the professor turned off the lights in the office.

T   F   ?   7. The man who opened the drawer was the professor.
T   F   ?   8. The professor ran down the corridor.
T   F   ?   9. The drawer was never actually opened.
T   F   ?   10. Three persons are referred to in this report.

▌ **How did you do?**   After you answer all 10 questions, form small groups of five or six and discuss the answers. Look at each statement from each member's point of view. For each statement, ask yourself "How can you be absolutely certain that the statement is true or false?" You should find that only one statement can be clearly identified as true and only one as false; eight should be marked "?".

▌ **What will you do?**   As you read this chapter try to formulate specific guidelines that will help you distinguish facts from inferences as a speaker and as a listener.

This test is designed to trap you into making inferences and treating them as facts. Statement 3 is true (it's in the report), statement 9 is false (the drawer was opened), but all other statements are inferences and should have been marked "?". Review the remaining eight statements to see why you cannot be certain that any of them are either true or false.   ⬤

A related communication barrier is created by the tendency to draw **pragmatic implications.** Consider the following: The sales manager has been replaced. You know that this manager was not doing a particularly good job and that many sales representatives complained about poor leadership. On the basis of this knowledge, you draw a pragmatic implication, an inference that is probably but not necessarily true that the sales manager was fired. This type of situation occurs every day. You see your supervisor in a romantic restaurant with the new sales manager. You draw the pragmatic conclusion that they're having an affair. You might even further infer that the reason the old sales manager was fired was because of the supervisor's affair with the new manager.

Some of the essential differences between factual and inferential statements are summarized in Table 7.1. Distinguishing between these two types of statements does not imply that one type is better than the other. Both types of statements are useful;

Table 7.1   **Differences between Factual and Inferential Statements**

These differences highlight the important distinctions between factual and inferential statements and are based on the discussions of Haney (1973) and Weinberg (1959). As you go through this table, consider how you would classify such statements as: "God exists," "Democracy is the best form of government," "This paper is white," "The Internet will grow in size and importance over the next 10 years," and "This table is based on Haney and Weinberg."

Factual Statements	Inferential Statements
May be made only after observation	May be made at any time
Are limited to what has been observed	Go beyond what has been observed
May be made only by the observer	May be made by anyone
May be about only the past or the present	May be about any time—past, present, or future
Approach certainty	Involve varying degrees of probability
Are subject to verifiable standards	Are not subject to verifiable standards

both are important. The problem arises when you treat an inferential statement as if it were fact. Phrase your inferential statements as tentative. Recognize that such statements may be wrong. Leave open the possibility of other alternatives.

LANGUAGE EXPRESSES BOTH DENOTATION AND CONNOTATION

WEB EXPLORATION
To learn more about denotation and connotation, go to **www.ablongman.com/ devito**.

Consider a word such as "death." To a doctor this word might mean the point at which the heart stops beating. This is denotative meaning, a rather objective description of an event. To a mother whose son has just died, however, the word means much more. It recalls the son's youth, his ambitions, his family, his illness, and so on. To her, the word is emotional, subjective, and highly personal. These emotional, subjective, and personal associations are the word's connotative meaning. The **denotation** of a word is its objective definition; the **connotation** is its subjective or emotional meaning.

Now consider a simple nod of the head in answer to the question, "Do you agree?" This gesture is largely denotative and simply says yes. What about a wink, a smile, or an overly rapid speech rate? These nonverbal expressions are more connotative; they express your feelings rather than objective information.

The denotative meaning of a message is general or universal; most people would agree with the denotative meanings and would give similar definitions. Connotative meanings, however, are extremely personal, and few people would agree on the precise connotative meaning of a word or nonverbal behavior.

"Snarl words" and "purr words" may further clarify the distinction between denotative and connotative meaning (Hayakawa & Hayakawa, 1989). Snarl words are highly negative ("She's an idiot," "He's a pig," "They're a bunch of losers"). Sexist, racist, and heterosexist language and hate speech provide lots of other examples. Purr words are highly positive ("She's a real sweetheart," "He's a dream," "They're the greatest"). Although they may sometimes seem to have denotative meaning and refer to the "real world," snarl and purr words are actually connotative in meaning. They don't describe people or events, but rather, they reveal the speaker's feelings about these people or events.

LANGUAGE CAN CRITICIZE AND PRAISE

Throughout your communication experiences, you're expected to criticize, to evaluate, and otherwise to render judgment on some person or on something someone did or created. Especially in helping professions, such as teaching, nursing, or counseling, criticism is an important and frequently used skill. The problem arises when criticism is used outside of its helping function, when it's inappropriate or excessive. An important interpersonal skill is to develop a facility for detecting when a person is asking for criticism and when that person is simply asking for a compliment. For example, when a friend asks how you like the new apartment, he or she may be searching for a compliment rather than wanting you to itemize all the things wrong with it. Similarly, the person who says, "Do I look okay?" may be asking for a compliment.

Sometimes the desire to be liked (or perhaps the need to be appreciated) is so strong that we go to the other extreme and paint everything with praise. The most ordinary jacket, the most common thought, the most average meal are given extraordinary praise, way beyond their merits. The overly critical and the overly complimentary soon find that their comments are no longer met with concern or interest.

As an alternative to excessive criticism or praise, consider the principle of honest appraisal. Tell the truth, but note that there is an art to truth telling, just as there is an art to all other forms of effective communication. First, distinguish between instances in which an honest appraisal is sought and those in which the individual needs a compliment. Respond to the appropriate level of meaning. Second, if an honest appraisal is desired and if yours is a negative one, give some consideration to how you should phrase your criticism.

In giving criticism focus on the event or the behavior rather than on personality; for example, say "This paper has four errors and has to be redone" rather than "You're a lousy typist; do this over." In offering criticism, be specific. Instead of saying "This paper is weak," as some English teachers might, say "I think the introduction wasn't clear enough. Perhaps a more specific statement of purpose would have worked better."

Try to state criticism positively, if at all possible. Rather than saying "You look terrible in black," it might be more helpful to say "You look much better in bright colors." In this way, you're also being constructive; you're explaining what could be done to make the situation better. If you do express criticism that seems to prove destructive, it may be helpful to offer a direct apology or to disclaim any harmful intentions (Baron, 1990). In your positive statement of criticism, try to state your concern for the other person along with your criticism, if appropriate. Instead of saying "The introduction to your report is boring," say "I really want your report to be great; I'd open with some humor to get the group's attention." Say "I want you to make a good impression. I think the dark suit would work better."

Own your thoughts and feelings. Instead of saying "Your report was unintelligible," say "I had difficulty following your ideas." At the same time, avoid mind reading. Instead of saying "Don't you care about the impression you make? This report is terrible," say "I think I would use a stronger introduction and a friendlier writing style."

ETHICS in *Interpersonal Communication*

Libel, Slander, and More

The First Amendment to the United States Constitution states:

> Congress shall make no law . . . abridging the freedom of speech, or of the press; or the right of the people peaceably to assemble and to petition the Government for a redress of grievances.

But speech is not always free and, in fact, it becomes unlawful and unethical in a variety of ways. For example, it's considered unethical (and it's illegal as well) to defame another person, to falsely attack his or her reputation and thereby cause damage to it. When this attack is done in print or in pictures, it's *libel*; when done through speech or gesture, it's *slander*.

Whereas just decades ago using racial, sexist, or homophobic terms in conversation or telling jokes at the expense of various cultural groups, would have gone unnoticed by many, today it would be considered inappropriate and unethical. It would also be considered unethical to demean another person because of that person's sex, age, race, nationality, affectional orientation, physical condition, or religion or to speak in cultural stereotypes.

What would you do? *At the water cooler in the office, you join two of your colleagues only to discover that they're exchanging racist jokes. You don't want to criticize them for fear that you'll become unpopular, with the likelihood that these colleagues will make it harder for you to get ahead. At the same time, however, you don't want to remain silent for fear it would imply that you accept this type of talk. What would you do in this situation?*

Be clear. Many prefer to phrase their criticism ambiguously thinking that this will hurt less. Research suggests that ambiguous criticism will appear more polite but it will also appear less honest, less competent, and not necessarily more positive (Edwards & Bello, 2001).

Avoid ordering or directing the other person to change; try identifying possible alternatives. Instead of saying "Don't be so forward when you're first introduced to someone," consider saying "I think they might respond better to a less forward approach."

Consider the context of the criticism. Generally, it's best to express criticism in situations where you can interact with the person and express your attitudes in dialogue rather than monologue. By this principle, then, your first choice would be to express criticism face-to-face, your second choice would be by telephone, and a distant third choice by letter, memo, or e-mail. Also, try to express your criticism in private. This is especially important when dealing with members from cultures where public criticism could result in a serious loss of face.

In expressing praise, keep the following in mind:

- *Use I-messages.* Instead of saying "That report was good," say "I thought that report was good" or "I liked your report."
- *Make sure your affect (facial movement) communicates your positive feelings.* Often when people praise others simply because it's the socially correct response, they may betray their lack of conviction with too little or inappropriate affect.
- *Name the behavior you're praising.* Instead of saying "That was good," say "I enjoyed your speech" or "I thought your introduction was great."
- *Take culture into consideration.* Many Asians, for example, feel uncomfortable when praised because it's often taken as a sign of veiled criticism (Dresser, 1996).

LANGUAGE CAN OBSCURE DISTINCTIONS

Language can obscure distinctions among people or events that are covered by the same label but are really quite different (indiscrimination) by making it easy to focus on extremes rather than on the vast middle ground between opposites (polarization) and by ignoring the inevitable process of change (static evaluation).

Indiscrimination

Nature seems to abhor sameness at least as much as vacuums, for nowhere in the universe can you find identical entities. Everything is unique. Language, however, provides common nouns, such as *teacher, student, friend, enemy, war, politician, liberal,* and the like, which may lead you to focus on similarities. Such nouns can lead you to group together all teachers, all students, and all friends and perhaps divert attention from the uniqueness of each individual, object, and event.

The misevaluation of **indiscrimination,** then, occurs when you focus on classes of individuals, objects, or events and fail to see that each is unique and needs to be looked at individually. Indiscrimination can be seen in such statements as these:

- He's just like the rest of them: lazy, stupid, a real slob.
- I really don't want another ethnic on the board of directors. One is enough for me.
- Read a romance novel? I read one when I was 16. That was enough to convince me.

A useful antidote to indiscrimination is the **index,** a verbal or mental subscript that identifies each individual in a group as an individual even though all members of the group may be covered by the same label: Politician₁ is not politician₂; teacher₁ is not teacher₂.

Ethnocentrism   An interesting perspective can be gained on indiscrimination by looking briefly at **ethnocentrism.** Before reading about this important concept, examine your own ethnocentrism by taking the accompanying self-test.

TEST YOURSELF   *How Ethnocentric Are You?*

Here are 18 statements representing your beliefs about your culture. For each statement indicate how much you agree or disagree, using the following scale: 5 = strongly agree, 4 = agree, 3 = neither agree nor disagree, 2 = disagree, 1 = strongly disagree.

_____   1. Most cultures are backward compared to my culture.
_____   2. My culture should be the role model for other cultures.
_____   3. Lifestyles in other cultures are just as valid as those in my culture.
_____   4. Other cultures should try to be like my culture.
_____   5. I'm not interested in the values and customs of other cultures.
_____   6. People in my culture could learn a lot from people in other cultures.
_____   7. Most people from other cultures just don't know what's good for them.
_____   8. I have little respect for the values and customs of other cultures.
_____   9. Most people would be happier if they lived like people in my culture.
_____ 10. People in my culture have just about the best lifestyles of anywhere.
_____ 11. Lifestyles in other cultures are not as valid as those in my culture.
_____ 12. I'm very interested in the values and customs of other cultures.
_____ 13. I respect the values and customs of other cultures.
_____ 14. I do not cooperate with people who are different.
_____ 15. I do not trust people who are different.
_____ 16. I dislike interacting with people from different cultures.
_____ 17. Other cultures are smart to look up to my culture.
_____ 18. People from other cultures act strange and unusual when they come into my culture.

❱ **How did you do?**   This test was presented to give you the opportunity to examine some of your own cultural beliefs, particularly those cultural beliefs that contribute to ethnocentrism. The person low in ethnocentrism would have high scores (4s and 5s) for items 3, 6, 12, and 13 and low scores (1s and 2s) for all the others. The person high in ethnocentrism would have low scores for items 3, 6, 12, and 13 and high scores for all the others.

❱ **What will you do?**   Use this test to bring to consciousness your own cultural beliefs so you can examine them logically and objectively. Ask yourself if your beliefs are productive beliefs that will help you achieve your professional and social goals or if they're counterproductive beliefs that will actually hinder your progress.

This test is taken from James W. Neuliep, Michelle Chaudoir, and James C. McCroskey (2001). A cross-cultural comparison of ethnocentrism among Japanese and United States college students. *Communication Research Reports* 18 (Spring):137–146. Used by permission of Eastern Communication Association.

As you've probably gathered from taking this test, ethnocentrism is the tendency to evaluate the values, beliefs, and behaviors of your own culture as being more positive, logical, and natural than those of other cultures. Although normally thought of negatively, there are positive aspects to ethnocentrism. For example, if a group is under at-

A S K *the Researcher*

Becoming Less Ethnocentric

Intellectually I understand that ethnocentrism often has negative effects and is limiting. Emotionally, however, I'm highly ethnocentric and down deep I wonder why members of other cultures don't see the superiority of my culture. Is there anything I can do to become less ethnocentric and more open to other cultures?

Recognize that seeing your culture as "the best" is quite normal in all cultures; that feeling is not necessarily harmful. For example, the "black pride" movement is aimed specifically at promoting feelings of being "the best" within black culture. What is harmful in ethnocentrism is when we treat emotional statements as though they were logical statements. If the University of Miami is playing Florida State in football, fans from both teams engage in yelling and "chest pounding" behaviors fully believing that "we" are "the best." The problem occurs when the emotional attitude "We're the best" is translated into the cognitive belief "We're the best" and treated as a logical statement. Logically, if I am the best, you must be less than I am. But emotionally and psychologically, we can both be the best at the same time. Be proud of your culture. But be open to and proud of other cultures at the same time.

For further information see Everett M. Rogers and Thomas M. Steinfatt, *Intercultural Communication* (Prospect Heights, IL: Waveland, 1999).

Thomas M. Steinfatt (Ph.D., Michigan State University) is a professor of communication, University of Miami, where he teaches courses in intercultural communication, organizational communication, and persuasion and propaganda. Dr. Steinfatt also works as a consultant in diversity training and executive communication, and as an expert witness in persuasion/propaganda and organizational communication. tms@miami.edu (Reprinted by permission of Dr. Thomas M. Steinfatt, University of Miami.)

tack, ethnocentrism will help create cohesiveness. It has also been argued that it forms the basis of patriotism and a willingness to sacrifice for the benefit of the group (Neuliep & McCroskey, 1997).

But ethnocentrism can also create considerable problems. Although the research is not conclusive, it appears that it may create obstacles to communication with those who are culturally different from you. It can also lead to hostility toward outside groups and may blind you to seeing other perspectives, other values, other ways of doing things (Neuliep & McCroskey, 1997; Cashdan, 2001).

Ethnocentrism exists on a continuum (see Table 7.2). People aren't either ethnocentric or not ethnocentric; rather, most are somewhere between these polar opposites. Of course, your degree of ethnocentrism varies, depending on the group on which you focus. For example, if you're Greek American, you may have a low degree of ethnocentrism when dealing with Italian Americans but a high degree when dealing with Turkish Americans or Japanese Americans. Most important for our purposes is that your degree of ethnocentrism (and we are all ethnocentric to at least some degree) will influence your interpersonal interactions.

Ethnocentric thinking is at the heart of the common practice of stereotyping national, sexual, racial, and religious groups. A **stereotype** is a relatively fixed mental picture of some group that is applied to each individual of the group without regard to his or her unique qualities. It's important to note that although stereotypes are usually thought of as negative, they may also be positive. You can, for example, consider certain national groups as lazy, superstitious, mercenary, or criminal, but you can also consider them as intelligent, progressive, honest, or hardworking. Regardless of whether such stereotypes are positive or negative, however, the problems they create are the same. They

Table 7.2   The Ethnocentrism Continuum

This table summarizes some of the interconnections between ethnocentrism and communication. In this table, five degrees of ethnocentrism are identified; in reality, there are as many degrees as there are people. The "communication distances" are general terms that highlight the attitude that dominates that level of ethnocentrism. Under "communications" are some of the major ways people might interact given their particular degree of ethnocentrism. Can you identify your own ethnocentrism on this table? For example, are there groups to which you have low ethnocentrism? Middle? High? What accounts for these differences? This table draws on the work of a number of intercultural researchers (Lukens, 1978; Gudykunst & Kim, 1992; Gudykunst, 1991).

Degree of Ethnocentrism	Communication Distance	Communications
Low	Equality	Treats others as equals; views different customs and ways of behaving as equal to one's own
	Sensitivity	Wants to decrease distance between self and others
	Indifference	Lacks concern for others; prefers to interact in a world of similar others
	Avoidance	Avoids and limits communications, especially intimate ones with interculturally different others
High	Disparagement	Engages in hostile behavior; belittles others; views different cultures and ways of behaving as inferior to one's own

provide shortcuts that are usually inappropriate. For example, when you see someone through a stereotype, you invariably fail to devote sufficient attention to his or her unique characteristics.

There is nothing wrong with classifying. In fact, it's an extremely useful method of dealing with any complex matter; it puts order into thinking. The problem arises not from classification itself but from applying an evaluative label to a class and using that label as an "adequate" map for each and every individual in the group.

Polarization

Polarization, often referred to as the fallacy of "either-or," is the tendency to look at the world and to describe it in terms of extremes—good or bad, positive or negative, healthy or sick, brilliant or stupid, rich or poor, and so on. Polarized statements come in many forms, for example:

- After listening to the evidence, I'm still not clear who the good guys are and who the bad guys are.
- Well, are you for us or against us?
- College had better get me a good job. Otherwise, this has been a big waste of time.

Most people exist somewhere between the extremes of good and bad, healthy and sick, brilliant and stupid, rich and poor. Yet there seems to be a strong tendency to view only the extremes and to categorize people, objects, and events in terms of these polar opposites.

 Ethnocentrism gives people pride in their culture and its achievements and contributes to a willingness to sacrifice for the culture. At the same time, however, it may lead people to see other cultures and members of other cultures as inferior and to an unwillingness to profit from the insights and contributions of other cultures. How would you describe the influence of ethnocentrism on the events of September 11, 2001, and those that followed over the next several months? For example, did you become more ethnocentric after these events? Less ethnocentric? Why?

 You can easily demonstrate this tendency by filling in the opposites for each of the following words:

	Opposite
tall ___:___:___:___:___:___	_____
heavy ___:___:___:___:___:___	_____
strong ___:___:___:___:___:___	_____
happy ___:___:___:___:___:___	_____
legal ___:___:___:___:___:___	_____

Filling in the opposites should have been relatively easy and quick. The words should also have been fairly short. Further, if a number of people supplied opposites, there would be a high degree of agreement among them.

Now try to fill in the middle positions with words meaning, for example, "midway between tall and short," "midway between heavy and light," and so on. Do this before reading any further.

These midway responses (compared to the opposites) were probably more difficult to think of and took you more time. The responses should also have been long words or phrases of several words. Further, you would probably find less agreement among different people filling in these midway responses than the opposites.

This exercise clearly illustrates the ease with which you can think and talk in opposites and the difficulty you have in thinking and talking about the middle. Recognize that the vast majority of cases exist between extremes. Don't allow the ready availability of extreme terms to obscure the reality of what lies in between.

In some cases, of course, it's legitimate to talk in terms of two values. For example, this thing you're holding is either a book or it isn't. Clearly, the classes "book" and "not-book" include all possibilities. There is no problem with this kind of statement. Similarly, you may say that a student will either pass this course or will not, as these two categories include all the possibilities.

You create problems when you use this either-or form in situations where it's inappropriate: for example, "The supervisor is either for us or against us." Note that these two choices don't include all possibilities; the supervisor may be for us in some things and against us in others, or he or she may be neutral. During the Vietnam War, there was a tendency to categorize people as either "hawk" or "dove," but clearly many people were neither and many were probably both—hawks on certain issues and doves on others. More recently, you see examples of polarization in the war in the Middle East with some people entirely and totally supportive of one side and others entirely and totally supportive of the other side.

Static Evaluation

Another distinction language often obscures is that of change. Language changes very slowly, especially when compared to the rapid pace at which people and things change.

Thinking Critically about the Media

Watching a televised news show, reading a post on the Internet, or reading a newspaper or newsmagazine has to involve serious critical thinking. The ways to use verbal messages effectively discussed in this chapter offer useful critical thinking guidelines that you can easily apply to the media:

■ *Beware of intensional orientation.* Distinguish between the way the media present and talk about something with what exists in reality.

■ *Beware of allness.* Recall that the media cannot say all about anything; always assume there is more to be said, more to learn.

■ *Beware of fact–inference confusion.* Distinguish between facts and inferences and treat them differently.

■ *Beware of static evaluation.* Remember that the world and people are constantly changing; what was true in a news broadcast six months ago, may no longer be true today. Update your evaluations frequently.

■ *Beware of indiscrimination.* No two things, no two people, no two cultures are the same. In the media's effort to simplify, they frequently oversimplify, often treating different things as if they were the same, often validating popular stereotypes.

■ *Beware of polarization.* The media, in a need to grab attention, often present people and events in their extremes (Gamson, 1998). But, extremes don't represent the majority of people.

Follow Up   Over a few evenings, watch several different kinds of television programs and record as many examples as you can find of each of the aforementioned critical thinking errors. What critical thinking principle do you find most often violated?

TRY IT!
Apply your knowledge about static language; go to www.ablongman. com/devito.

When you retain an evaluation, despite the changes in the person or thing, you're engaging in **static evaluation.**

Alfred Korzybski (1933) used an interesting illustration in this connection: In a tank there is a large fish and many small fish that are its natural food source. Given freedom in the tank, the large fish will eat the small fish. After some time, the tank is partitioned, with the large fish on one side and the small fish on the other, divided only by glass. For a time, the large fish will try to eat the small fish but will fail; each time it tries, it will knock into the glass partition. After some time, it will "learn" that trying to eat the small fish means difficulty, and it will no longer go after them. Now, however, the partition is removed and the small fish swim all around the big fish. But the big fish does not eat them and in fact will die of starvation while its natural food swims all around. The large fish has learned a pattern of behavior, and even though the actual territory has changed, the map remains static.

While you would probably agree that everything is in a constant state of flux, the relevant question is whether you act as if you know this. Do you act in accordance with the notion of change, instead of just accepting it intellectually? Do you treat your little sister as if she were 10 years old, or do you treat her like the 20-year-old woman she has become? Your evaluations of yourself and others must keep pace with the rapidly changing real world. Otherwise you'll be left with attitudes and beliefs—static evaluations— about a world that no longer exists.

To guard against static evaluation, date your statements and especially your evaluations. Remember that Gerry Smith$_{1994}$ is not Gerry Smith$_{2001}$; academic abilities$_{1995}$ are not academic abilities$_{2001}$. T. S. Eliot, in *The Cocktail Party,* said that "what we know of other people is only our memory of the moments during which we knew them. And they have changed since then . . . at every meeting we are meeting a stranger."

LANGUAGE CAN CONFIRM AND DISCONFIRM

Before reading about these important concepts, take the self-test "How Confirming Are You?" to examine your own message behavior.

TEST YOURSELF   *How Confirming Are You?*

In your typical communications, how likely are you to display the following behaviors? Use the accompanying scale in responding to each statement: 5 = always, 4 = often, 3 = sometimes, 2 = rarely, l = never.

_____ 1. I acknowledge the presence of another person both verbally and nonverbally.

_____ 2. I acknowledge the contributions of the other person—for example, by supporting or taking issue with what the person says.

_____ 3. During the conversation, I make nonverbal contact by maintaining direct eye contact, touching, hugging, kissing, and otherwise demonstrating acknowledgment of the other person.

_____ 4. I communicate as both speaker and listener with involvement, and with a concern and respect for the other person.

_____ 5. I signal my understanding of the other person both verbally and nonverbally.

_____ 6. I reflect the other person's feelings as a way of showing that I understand these feelings.

_____ 7. I ask questions when appropriate concerning the other person's thoughts and feelings.

_____ 8. I respond to the other person's requests, for example, by returning phone calls and answering letters within a reasonable time.

_____ 9. I encourage the other person to express his or her thoughts and feelings.

_____ 10. I respond directly and exclusively to what the other person says.

▶ **How did you do?** All 10 statements express confirming behaviors. Therefore, high scores (say, above 35) reflect a strong tendency to be confirming. Low scores (say, below 25) reflect a strong tendency to be disconfirming. Don't assume, however, that all situations call for confirmation and that only insensitive people express disconfirming messages. You may find it interesting to consider situations from your own recent experiences in which disconfirmation would have been, if not an effective response, at least a legitimate one.

▶ **What will you do?** Because most people want to become more confirming, suggestions are offered in the text for increasing your own tendencies to become more confirming. Treating the statements in the self-test as suggestions for increasing confirmation is a good way to start increasing your own confirming behavior. ●

Confirmation and disconfirmation—as illustrated in the self-test—refer to the extent to which you acknowledge another person. Consider this situation. You've been living with someone for the last six months and you arrive home late one night. Your partner, let's say Pat, is angry and complains about your being so late. Of the following responses which are you most likely to give?

I SEE

1. Stop screaming. I'm not interested in what you're babbling about. I'll do what I want, when I want. I'm going to bed.

2. What are you so angry about? Didn't you get in three hours late last Thursday when you went to that office party? So knock it off.

3. You have a right to be angry. I should have called to tell you I was going to be late, but I got involved in an argument at work, and I couldn't leave until it was resolved.

In response 1, you dismiss Pat's anger and even indicate dismissal of Pat as a person. In response 2, you reject the validity of Pat's reasons for being angry but do not dismiss either Pat's feelings of anger or of Pat as a person. In response 3, you acknowledge Pat's anger and the reasons for being angry. In addition, you provide some kind of explanation and, in doing so, show that both Pat's feelings and Pat as a person are important and that Pat has the right to know what happened. The first response is an example of disconfirmation, the second of rejection, and the third of confirmation.

Psychologist William James once observed that "no more fiendish punishment could be devised, even were such a thing physically possible, than that one should be turned loose in society and remain absolutely unnoticed by all the members thereof." In this often-quoted observation, James identifies the essence of disconfirmation (Watzlawick, Beavin, & Jackson, 1967; Veenendall & Feinstein, 1995).

Disconfirmation is a communication pattern in which you ignore a person's presence as well as that person's communications. You say, in effect, that the person and what she or he has to say aren't worth serious attention. Disconfirming responses often lead to loss of self-esteem (Sommer, Williams, Ciarocco, & Baumeister, 2001).

Note that disconfirmation is not the same as **rejection.** In rejection, you disagree with the person; you indicate your unwillingness to accept something the other person says or does. In disconfirming someone, however, you deny that person's significance; you claim that what this person says or does simply does not count.

Table 7.3   Confirmation and Disconfirmation

This table parallels the self-test presented earlier in this chapter so that you can see clearly not only the confirming but also the opposite, disconfirming behaviors. As you review this table, try to imagine a specific illustration for each of the ways of communicating disconfirmation and confirmation (Pearson, 1993; Galvin & Brommel, 2000).

Confirmation	Disconfirmation
1. Acknowledge the presence of the other verbally or nonverbally	1. Ignore the presence of the other person
2. Acknowledge the contributions of the other by either supporting or taking issue with what the other says	2. Ignore what the other says; express (nonverbally and verbally) indifference to anything the other says
3. Make nonverbal contact by maintaining direct eye contact, and, when appropriate, touching, hugging, kissing, and otherwise demonstrating acknowledgment of the other	3. Make no nonverbal contact; avoid direct eye contact; avoid touching other person
4. Engage in dialogue—communication in which both persons are speakers and listeners, both are involved, and both are concerned with and have respect for each other	4. Engage in monologue—communication in which one person speaks and one person listens, there is no real interaction, and there is no real concern or respect for each other
5. Demonstrate understanding of what the other says and means	5. Jump to interpretation or evaluation rather than working at understanding what the other means
6. Reflect the other's feelings to demonstrate your understanding of these feelings	6. Express your own feelings, ignore feelings of the other, or give abstract intellectualized responses
7. Ask questions of the other concerning both his or her thoughts and feelings	7. Make statements about yourself; ignore any lack of clarity in the other's remarks
8. Acknowledge the other's requests; answer the other's questions, return phone calls, and answer letters	8. Ignore the other's requests; fail to answer questions, return phone calls, and answer letters
9. Encourage the other to express thoughts and feelings	9. Interrupt or otherwise make it difficult for the other to express himself or herself
10. Respond directly and exclusively to what the other says	10. Respond tangentially by acknowledging the other's comment but then shifting the focus of the message in another direction

Confirmation is the opposite communication pattern. In confirmation, you not only acknowledge the presence of the other person but also indicate your acceptance of this person, of this person's definition of self, and of your relationship as defined or viewed by this other person. Confirming responses often lead to gains in self-esteem. You can communicate confirmation (and disconfirmation) in a wide variety of ways; Table 7.3 shows just a few.

Talking with the Grief Stricken

TRY IT!
Apply your insights about talking with the grief stricken; go to www. ablongman.com/devito.

Talking with the grief stricken provides an interesting perspective on confirmation. Grief is something everyone experiences at some time. It may be experienced because of illness or death, the loss of a highly valued relationship (for example, a romantic breakup), the loss of certain physical or mental abilities, or the loss of material possessions (your house burning down or stock market losses). Consider the following example of one attempt to talk with a grief stricken individual.

I just heard that Harry died—I mean—passed away. I'm so sorry. I know exactly how you feel. But you know, it's for the best. I mean the man was suffering. I remember seeing him last month; he was so weak he could hardly stand. And he looked so sad. He must have been in constant pain. It's better this way. He's at peace. You'll get over it. You'll see. Time heals all wounds. It was the same way with me, and you know how close we were. I mean we were devoted to each other. Everyone said we were the closest pair they had ever seen. And I got over it. So how about we go to dinner tonight? We'll talk about old times. Come on. Come on. Don't be a spoilsport. I really need to get out. I've been in the house all week. Come on, do it for me. After all, you have to forget; you have to get on with your own life. I won't take no for an answer. I'll pick you up at seven.

To avoid the kind of communication illustrated above and to make this often difficult form of communication easier, confirm the other person and the person's feelings. "You must miss him a great deal" confirms the person's feelings, for example. Avoid expressions that are disconfirming: "You'll see, things will be better tomorrow." At the same time, give the grieving person permission to grieve. Let the person know that it's acceptable for him or her to grieve in the ways that feel most comfortable—for example, crying or talking about old times.

Encourage the grieving person to express feelings and talk about the loss. Most people who experience grief welcome the opportunity to talk about it. However, don't try to force the person to talk about experiences or feelings she or he may not be ready to share. At the same time, avoid trying to force the grief-stricken individual to focus on the bright side; she or he may not be ready. Avoid expressions such as "You're so lucky you still have some vision left" or "It's better this way; Pat was suffering so much."

Empathize with the grief-stricken person and communicate this empathic understanding. Let the person know that you can understand what he or she is feeling. Don't assume, though, that your feelings (however empathic) are the same in depth or in kind. If, having never experienced this tragedy, you say to a parent who has lost a child, "I know exactly what you're feeling," you risk arousing resentment.

Be especially sensitive to **leave-taking cues.** Don't try to force your presence on someone who is grief stricken or press the person to stay with you or a group of people. When in doubt, ask.

These concepts of confirmation and disconfirmation also give unique insight into a wide variety of offensive language practices, language that alienates and separates, language that disconfirms. The three obvious practices are racism, sexism, and heterosexism.

Racism

According to Andrea Rich (1974), "any language that, through a conscious or unconscious attempt by the user, places a particular racial or ethnic group in an inferior position is racist." **Racist language** expresses racist attitudes. It also contributes to the development of racist attitudes in those who use or hear such language. Even when racism is subtle, unintentional, and unconscious, its effects are systematically damaging (Dovidio, Gaertner, Kawakami, & Hodson, 2002).

Racist terms are used by members of one culture to disparage members of other cultures—their customs or their accomplishments. Racist language emphasizes differences rather than similarities and separates rather than unites members of different cultures. Traditionally, racist language has been used by the dominant group to establish and maintain power over other groups. Today, however, it is used by racists (or the racist-talking) in all groups. The social consequences of racist language in terms of employment, education, housing opportunities, and general community acceptance are well known.

It's interesting to note that the terms denoting some of the major movements in art—for example, "impressionism" and "cubism"—were originally applied negatively. The terms were adopted by the artists themselves and eventually became positive. A parallel can be seen in the use of the word "queer" by some lesbian and gay organizations. Their purpose in using the term is to cause it to lose its negative connotation.

It has often been pointed out (Davis, 1973; Bosmajian, 1974; Purnell, 1982) that some aspects of language may be inherently racist. For example, Davis's examination of English found 134 synonyms for "white." Of these, 44 have positive connotations (for example, "clean," "chaste," and "unblemished") and only 10 have negative connotations (for example, "whitewash" and "pale"); the remaining synonyms are relatively neutral. Of the 120 synonyms for "black," 60 were found to have unfavorable connotations ("unclean," "foreboding," and "deadly") and none to have positive connotations.

Consider such phrases as the following:

the Korean doctor
the Latino prodigy
the African American mathematician
the white nurse
the Indian physicist

Often, such identifiers are used to emphasize that the combination of race and occupation (or talent or accomplishment) is rare and unexpected, that this member of the race is an exception. It also implies that racial factors are somehow important in the context. In some cases, of course, you may want to include the racial identifier because it's relevant to the conversation. For example, in commenting on the changes in Hollywood you might say, "This is the first year that both best acting awards were won by African Americans."

Sexism

The National Council of Teachers of English (NCTE) has proposed guidelines for nonsexist (gender-free, gender-neutral, or sex-fair) language. These concern the use of generic *man,* the use of generic *he* and *his,* and sex-role stereotyping (Penfield, 1987).

Generic Man   The word *man* refers most clearly to an adult male. To use the term to refer to both men and women emphasizes "maleness" at the expense of "femaleness." Similarly the terms *mankind* or *the common man* or even *cavemen* imply a primary focus on adult males. Gender-neutral terms can easily be substituted. Instead of *mankind,* you can say *humanity, people,* or *human beings.* Instead of *the common man,* you can say *the average person* or *ordinary people.* Instead of *cavemen,* you can say *prehistoric people* or *cave dwellers.*

Similarly, the use of such terms as *policeman* or *fireman* and other terms that presume maleness as the norm and femaleness as a deviation from this norm are clear and common examples of **sexist language.** Consider using nonsexist alternatives for these and similar terms; make these alternatives (for example, *police officer* and *firefighter*) a part of your active vocabulary. What alternatives can you offer for each of these terms: chairman, the common man, countryman, doorman, man, mankind, manmade, mailman, manpower, repairman, fireman, freshman, salesman, stewardess, waitress, web master, and womanizer?

 What do you feel is the current status of sexism and sexist language in your area of the world? Can you identify specific types of sexism that you've observed? In what types of situations is sexism seen most clearly (for example, on the job, in schools, in the military, in the ministry)?

Generic He and His   The use of the masculine pronoun to refer to any individual regardless of sex is certainly declining. But it was only as far back as 1975 that all college textbooks, for example, used the masculine pronoun as generic. There seems to be no legitimate reason the feminine pronoun could not alternate with the masculine pronoun in referring to hypothetical individuals, or why such terms as he and she or her and him could not be used instead of just he or him. Alternatively, you can restructure your sentences to eliminate any reference to gender. For example, the NCTE Guidelines (Penfield, 1987) suggest that instead of saying, "The average student is worried about his grades," say, "The average student is worried about grades." Instead of saying, "Ask the student to hand in his work as soon as he is finished," say, "Ask students to hand in their work as soon as they're finished."

Sex-Role Stereotyping   The words you use often reflect a sex-role bias, the assumption that certain roles or professions belong to men and others belong to women. In eliminating sex-role stereotyping, avoid, for example, making the hypothetical elementary school teacher female and the college professor male. Avoid referring to doctors as male and nurses as female. Avoid noting the sex of a professional with terms such as "female doctor" or "male nurse." When you're referring to a specific doctor or nurse, the person's sex will become clear when you use the appropriate pronoun: "Dr. Smith wrote the prescription for her new patient" or "The nurse recorded the patient's temperature himself." Here are a few additional examples.

How would you rephrase these?

1. You really should get a second doctor's opinion. Just see what he says.
2. Johnny went to school today and met his kindergarten teacher. I wonder who she is?
3. Everyone needs to examine his own conscience.
4. The effective communicator is a selective self-discloser; he discloses to some people about some things some of the time.
5. The effective waitress knows when her customers need her.
6. The history of man is largely one of technology replacing his manual labor.

Heterosexism

A close relative of sexism is heterosexism. The term is a relatively new addition to our list of linguistic prejudices. **Heterosexist language** refers to language used to disparage lesbians and gay men (Rothblum & Bond, 1996). As in the case of racist and sexist language, we see heterosexism in the derogatory terms used for lesbians and gay men and in more subtle forms. For example, when we qualify a description of a profession—as in "gay athlete" or "lesbian doctor"—we are in effect stating that athletes and doctors are not normally gay or lesbian. Further, we are highlighting the affectional orientation of the athlete and the doctor in a context in which it may have no relevance. This practice is, of course, the same as qualifying by race or gender, as already noted.

Still another instance of heterosexism is the presumption of heterosexuality. Usually, people assume that the person they're talking to or about is heterosexual. Usually, they're correct, because the majority of the population is heterosexual. At the same time, however, note that heterosexism denies lesbians and gay males their true identity. The practice of assuming that a person is heterosexual is very similar to the presumption of whiteness and maleness that we have made significant progress toward eliminating.

Perhaps the most important step in eliminating heterosexism is to avoid any offensive nonverbal mannerisms that parody stereotypes when talking about gays and lesbians. At the same time, avoid "complimenting" gay men and lesbians by saying they "don't look it." To gays and lesbians, that is not a compliment. Similarly, expressing disappointment that a person is gay—for example, saying "What a waste!" and meaning it as a compliment is not really a compliment.

A S K *the* **Researcher**

Confronting Homophobia

A lot of homophobic language is used around the office and I'd like to know what I can do to respond effectively to such homophobic statements. I don't want to be a language cop, ready to pounce on every politically incorrect word, yet I don't want to remain silent and thereby imply agreement with what is being said. Any suggestions?

Homophobic language is wrong because it perpetuates cruel images of inadequacy and marginality which rob all sexual minorities of human dignity. Moreover, employing homophobic language "erases" gay and lesbian people by presuming, contrary to fact, that nearly everyone is heterosexual. Choosing what to say in this situation depends, of course, on your relationship with the other individual, the organizational culture in which you work, and the motive which you perceive behind the remark. Generally, your response can be either distant or personal. A distant response would stress the effects of antigay language, perhaps equating hostile words with gay bashing. Depending on the context, you might also stress that the effect of antigay remarks on organizational morale and image is equivalent to racist and sexist language. The use of a personal voice could include objections on grounds of a commitment to inclusiveness and equal treatment, genuine concern for the self-esteem of gay people and, if you are a gay or lesbian person, disclosure of your own identity.

For further information, see Amy J. Zuckerman and George F. Simons, *Sexual Orientation in the Workplace.* Thousand Oaks: Sage, 1996; Dan Woog, *Gay Men, Straight Jobs.* Los Angeles: Alyson, 2001.

Ralph Smith (Ph.D., University of Southern California) is a professor of communication at Southwest Missouri State University, where he teaches courses in public relations and the rhetoric of social movements. rrs953f@smsu.edu Russel Windes (Ph.D., Northwestern University) is a professor emeritus of the City University of New York, where he taught courses in argumentation, persuasion, and political communication. windesmith@aol.com (Reprinted by permission of Dr. Ralph R. Smith and Dr. Russell Windes.)

Avoid, too, the assumption that every gay man or lesbian knows what every other gay man or lesbian is thinking. To do so is very similar to asking someone from Japan why Sony is investing heavily in the United States, or as one comic put it, asking an African American, "What do you think Jesse Jackson meant by that last speech?" Similarly, saying things like "Lesbians are so loyal" or "Gay men are so open with their feelings"—statements that ignore the wide differences within any group—are potentially insulting to all groups and deny the vast individual differences within any large group.

Avoid *overattribution,* the tendency to attribute just about everything a person does, says, and believes to being gay or lesbian. As already discussed in Chapter 4 overattribution distorts perception and helps to recall and perpetuate stereotypes.

Remember that relationship milestones are important to all people. Ignoring the anniversary of your uncle and his same-sex partner or that partner's birthday while remembering and celebrating similar milestones of another uncle and his opposite-sex partner is unfair and will be resented.

Racist, Sexist, and Heterosexist Listening

Just as racist, sexist, and heterosexist attitudes influence your language, they also influence your listening. In this type of listening you only hear what the speaker is saying through your stereotypes. You assume that what the speaker is saying is unfairly influenced by the speaker's sex, race, or affectional orientation.

Sexist, racist, and heterosexist listening occurs in a wide variety of situations. For example, when you dismiss a valid argument or give weight to an invalid argument, when you refuse to give someone a fair hearing, or when you give less credibility (or more credibility) to a speaker because the speaker is of a particular sex, race, or affectional orientation, you're practicing sexist, racist, or heterosexist listening. Put differently, sexist, racist, or heterosexist listening occurs when you listen differently to a person because of his or her sex, race, or affectional orientation when these characteristics are irrelevant to the message.

But in many instances these characteristics are relevant and pertinent to your evaluation of the message. For example, the sex of the speaker talking on pregnancy, fathering a child, birth control, or surrogate motherhood or fatherhood is, most would agree, probably relevant to the message. It's not sexist listening to take the sex of the speaker into account when listening to such messages. However, it is sexist listening to assume that only one sex has anything to say that's worth hearing or that what one sex says can be discounted without a fair hearing. The same is true when your listening is filtered through your schemata or stereotypes of race, gender, or affectional orientation.

REVIEWING   Key Terms and Concepts in Verbal Messages

This chapter covered some of the barriers to effective interpersonal communication.

Language Symbolizes Reality
What is intensional orientation and how can you combat it? What is allness and how can you correct it?
- Intensional orientation is the tendency to view the world in the way it's talked about or labeled. To combat intensional orientation, respond to things first; look for the labels second.

- Allness is the tendency to describe the world in extreme terms that imply one knows all or is saying all there is to say. To combat allness, remind yourself that you can never know all or say all about anything; use a mental and sometimes verbal "etc."

Language Expresses Both Facts and Inferences
How do facts and inferences differ? How can you distinguish them more clearly?
- Fact–inference confusion is the tendency to confuse factual and inferential statements and to respond to inferences as if they were facts.

■ To combat such confusions, distinguish facts from inferences and respond to inferences as inferences, not as facts.

Language Expresses Both Denotation and Connotation

What is the difference between denotation and connotation?
■ Denotative meaning is the dictionary-like, objective meaning of a word or sentence.
■ Connotation is the subjective and personal meaning of a
word or sentence.

Language Can Criticize and Praise

How can you more effectively communicate both criticism and
praise?
■ Excessive criticism or praise is talk that is basically dishonest
and in many instances manipulative.
■ The principle of honest appraisal calls for saying what you
feel, but gently and kindly.

Language Can Obscure Distinctions

What are indiscrimination and ethnocentrism, and how can
you reduce them? What is polarization and what can you do to
eliminate it? What is static evaluation and how can you eliminate it?
■ Indiscrimination is the tendency to group unique individuals
or items because they're covered by the same term or label.
To combat indiscrimination, recognize uniqueness, and index
each individual in a group (teacher$_1$, teacher$_2$).
■ Polarization is the tendency to describe the world in terms
of extremes or polar opposites. To combat polarization use
middle terms and qualifiers.
■ Static evaluation is the tendency to describe the world in
static terms, denying constant change. To combat static
evaluation, recognize the inevitability of change; date statements and evaluations, realizing, for example, that Gerry
Smith$_{1991}$ is not Gerry Smith$_{2001}$.

Language Can Confirm and Disconfirm

What is disconfirmation and confirmation (and the related sexist, racist, and heterosexist communications)?
■ Disconfirmation is communication that ignores another,
that denies the other person's definition of self.
■ Confirmation expresses acknowledgment and acceptance
of others and avoids racist, sexist, and heterosexist expressions that are disconfirming.

APPLYING   Key Terms and Concepts in Verbal Messages

1. Do you accept the assumptions about language that are
discussed throughout this chapter? Can you think of reasons to reject any of these assumptions?
2. Do the media give greater attention to ideas phrased in
the extreme than to ideas phrased more logically as somewhere between the extremes?
3. Visualize yourself seated with a packet of photographs of
strangers before you. You're asked to scratch out the eyes

in each photograph. As you go through the photos, scratching out the eyes, you come upon a photograph of your
mother. Are you able to scratch out the eyes as you have
done with the pictures of the strangers? Are you responding intensionally or extensionally?
4. What cultural identifiers do you prefer? How can you let
other people know the cultural descriptions that you want
to be used to refer to you?
5. Watch a few television situation comedies. How many
plots revolving around fact–inference confusion can you
identify?
6. Do you ever commit the fallacy of allness? Do you, for example, group all teachers together? All gay people? All
politicians? All born-again Christians? All atheists? All
African Americans? All European Americans? All Jews? All
Hispanics? How might you avoid allness?
7. In light of the events of September 11, 2001, new terms
and new meanings for old terms came into being. How
would you describe your own denotation and connotation
of the following terms: *crusade, war, terrorist, cowardly,*
and *hero*? Now, select someone from a totally different
culture and ask how he or she would describe the deno-
tations and connotations of these terms.
8. Would it be possible to have ethnocentric thinking without indiscrimination? Why or why not? Does prejudice depend on indiscrimination? Why or why not?
9. Look up your own city and the cities you've visited or
hope to visit and examine their cultural makeup (try
http://tiger.census.gov/cgi-bin/gazetteer). Are the labels used for cultural groups consistent with those cultural
identifiers suggested in this chapter?
10. Describe a situation in which someone committed indiscrimination against you or someone you know by assuming that you (or a person you know) believed something
or behaved in a particular way because of sex, race, nationality, religion, or affectional orientation.

EXPERIENCING   Key Terms and Concepts in Verbal Messages

Go to **www.ablongman.com/devito**.

*This group of experiences deals with verbal messages and ways
to use such messages more critically.*

(1) **Identifying the Barriers to Communication** provides a
dialogue containing the various barriers discussed in this chapter. (2) **How Do You Talk? As a Woman? As a Man?** and (3)
Recognizing Gender Differences look at gender differences
in language and at our perceptions of the speech of others. (4)
Thinking with E-Prime focuses on the difficulties that can be
created when you use and think with the verbal "to be." (5)
How Do You Talk about the Middle? illustrates the ways in
which our language makes it easy to polarize. (6) **Confirming,
Rejecting, and Disconfirming** looks at specific examples of
these varied messages. (7) **"Must Lie" Situations** examines
scenarios in which many people would consider it ethical, even
necessary, to lie.

RESEARCHING with Research Navigator   Key Terms and Concepts
in Verbal Messages

Go to http://www.researchnavigator.com.

Reading an article.

Read a popular or scholarly article on language, confirmation or disconfirmation, or the relationship of language and culture. On the basis of this article what can you add to the discussion presented here?

Investigating key terms.

Investigate one of the key terms discussed in this chapter (for example, intensional orientation, allness, denotation and connotation, ethnocentrism, polarization, language, symbol, hate speech, disconfirmation, racism, sexism, or heterosexism. What additional insights can you provide?

Finding answers.

Try finding answers to one of the following questions or design a research study to answer it.

■ How is politically incorrect language dealt with in the workplace?

■ How does using derogatory language about your own group influence your self-esteem?

■ How is disconfirmation used in Internet communication?

■ What unique qualities do ethnocentric individuals possess? That is, do people high in ethnocentrism differ from people who are low in ethnocentrism?

■ What are the effects of using racist, sexist, and heterosexist language on campus?

■ Which, if any, of the principles discussed in this chapter relate to a person's interpersonal popularity?

8 Nonverbal Messages

Erin Brockovich (2000)

The body says what words cannot.

—Martha Graham

Body Communication
Facial Communication
Eye Communication
Touch Communication
Paralanguage and Silence
Spatial Messages
Artifactual Communication
Temporal Communication

The story of a woman's fight for the rights of victims of corporate miscon-
duct is told in Erin Brockovich. *Throughout the film you see how people base
their initial impressions of Erin Brockovich (Julia Roberts) on how she looks and
dresses—on her nonverbal communication messages. Although she is incredibly
competent and resourceful, many persist in dismissing the validity of her arguments
because of her flamboyant appearance. This tendency is actually not uncommon;
much research has shown that when verbal and nonverbal messages contradict each
other, it is the nonverbal message that people believe. In this chapter we explore nonverbal messages, those communicated by the body as well as those communicated
through touch, sound, space, and time.*

BODY COMMUNICATION

Generally, we can consider body communication in two parts—the gestures you make
with your body and your body's appearance.

Body Gestures

An especially useful classification of body movement (sometimes called **kinesics**)
identifies five types: emblems, illustrators, affect displays, regulators, and adaptors
(Ekman & Friesen, 1969). Table 8.1 summarizes and provides examples of these five
movements.

Emblems   **Emblems** are substitutes for words; they're body movements that have
rather specific verbal translations: for example, the nonverbal signs for "OK," "peace,"

Table 8.1   The Five Body Movements

Can you identify similar gestures that mean different things in different
cultures and that might create interpersonal misunderstandings?

	Name and Function	*Examples*
	Emblems directly translate words or phrases.	"OK" sign, "come here" wave, hitchhiker's sign
	Illustrators accompany and literally "illustrate" verbal messages.	Circular hand movements when talking of a circle, hands far apart when talking of something large
	Affect displays communicate emotional meaning.	Expressions of happiness, surprise, fear, anger, sadness, disgust/contempt
	Regulators monitor, maintain, or control the speaking of another.	Facial expressions and hand gestures indicating "keep going," "slow down," or "what else happened?"
	Adaptors satisfy some need.	Scratching one's head

WEB EXPLORATION
To learn more about emblems, go to
www.ablongman.com/ devito.

"come here," "go away," "who me?" "be quiet," "I'm warning you," "I'm tired," and "it's cold." Emblems are as arbitrary as any words in any language. Consequently, your present culture's emblems are not necessarily the same as your culture's emblems of 300 years ago or the same as the emblems of other cultures. For example, the sign made by forming a circle with the thumb and index finger may mean "nothing" or "zero" in France, "money" in Japan, and something sexual in certain southern European cultures. But just as the English language is spreading throughout the world, so, too, is the English nonverbal language. The American use of this emblem to mean "OK" is spreading just as fast, for example, as English technical and scientific terms.

Illustrators   **Illustrators** accompany and literally illustrate the verbal messages. Illustrators make your communications more vivid and help to maintain your listener's attention. They also help to clarify and intensify your verbal messages. In saying, "Let's go up," for example, you probably move your head and perhaps your finger in an upward direction. In describing a circle or a square, you more than likely make circular or square movements with your hands. Recent research points to another advantage of illustrators: that they increase your ability to remember. People who illustrated their verbal messages with gestures remembered some 20 percent more than those who didn't gesture (Goldin-Meadow, Nusbaum, Kelly, & Wagner, 2001).

We are aware of illustrators only part of the time; at times, they may have to be brought to our attention. Illustrators are more universal than emblems; illustrators will be recognized and understood by members of more different cultures than will emblems.

Affect Displays   **Affect displays** are the movements of the face that convey emotional meaning—the expressions that show anger and fear, happiness and surprise, eagerness and fatigue. They're the facial expressions that give you away when you try to present a false image and that lead people to say, "You look angry. What's wrong?" We can, however, consciously control affect displays, as actors do when they play a role. Affect displays may be unintentional (as when they give you away) or intentional (as when you want to show anger, love, or surprise).

Regulators   **Regulators** monitor, maintain, or control the speaking of another individual. When you listen to another, you're not passive; you nod your head, purse your lips, adjust your eye focus, and make various paralinguistic sounds such as "mm-mm" or "tsk." Regulators are culture-bound: Each culture develops its own rules for the regulation of conversation. Regulators also include such broad movements as shaking your head to show disbelief or leaning forward in your chair to show that you want to hear more.

Regulators communicate what you expect or want speakers to do as they're talking: for example, "Keep going," "Tell me what else happened," "I don't believe that. Are you sure?" "Speed up," and "Slow down." Speakers often receive these nonverbal signals without being consciously aware of them. Depending on their degree of sensitivity, they modify their speaking behavior in accordance with these regulators.

Adaptors   **Adaptors** satisfy some need and usually occur without conscious awareness; they're unintentional movements that usually go unnoticed. Nonverbal researchers identify three types of adaptors based on their focus, direction, or target: self-adaptors, alter-adaptors, and object-adaptors (Burgoon, Buller, & Woodall, 1996).

Self-adaptors usually satisfy a physical need, especially to make you more comfortable, for example, scratching your head to relieve an itch, moistening your lips because they feel dry, or pushing your hair out of your eyes. When these adaptors occur in private, they occur in their entirety: You scratch until the itch is gone. But in public, these adaptors usually occur in abbreviated form. When people are watching you, for example, you might put your fingers to your head and move them around a bit but probably not scratch with the same vigor as when in private.

Alter-adaptors are the body movements you make in response to your current interactions. Examples would include crossing your arms over your chest when someone unpleasant approaches or moving closer to someone you like.

Object-adaptors are those movements that involve your manipulation of some object. Frequently observed examples include punching holes in or drawing on a styrofoam coffee cup, clicking a ball point pen, or chewing on a pencil. Object-adaptors are usually signs of negative feelings; for example, you emit more adaptors when feeling hostile than when feeling friendly. Further, as anxiety and uneasiness increase, so does the frequency of adaptors (Burgoon, Buller, & Woodall, 1996).

Body Appearance

Of course, the body communicates even without movement. For example, others may form impressions of you from your general body build, from your height and weight, and from your skin, eye, and hair color. Assessments of your power, your attractiveness, and your suitability as a friend or romantic partner are often made on the basis of your body appearance (Sheppard & Strathman, 1989).

Height, for example, is significant in a wide variety of situations. Tall presidential candidates have a much better record of winning elections than do their shorter opponents. Tall people seem to be paid more and are favored by interviewers over shorter applicants (Keyes, 1980; Guerrero, DeVito, & Hecht, 1999; Knapp & Hall, 2002; Jackson & Ervin, 1992).

View point On a 10-point scale, with 1 indicating "not at all important" and 10 indicating "extremely important," how important is body appearance to your own romantic interest in another person? Do the men and women you know conform to the stereotypes of the male being more concerned with the physical and the female being more concerned with personality?

ETHICS in *Interpersonal Communication*

Interpersonal Silence

In the U.S. legal system, you have the right to remain silent and to refuse to incriminate yourself. But you don't have the right to refuse to reveal information about the criminal activities of others that you may have witnessed, for example. Rightly or wrongly (and this in itself is an ethical issue) psychiatrists and lawyers are often exempt from this general rule. Similarly, a wife can't be forced to testify against her husband nor a husband against his wife.

In interpersonal situations, however, there aren't any written rules and so it's not always clear if or when silence is ethical or unethical. For example, most people (but not all) would agree that you have the right to withhold information that has no bearing on the matter at hand. Your previous relationship history, affectional orientation, or religion is usually irrelevant to your ability to function as a doctor or police officer and may thus be kept private in most job-related situations.

What would you do? *While at the supermarket, you witness a mother verbally abusing her three-year-old child. You worry that the mother might psychologically harm the child, and your first impulse is to speak up and tell this woman that verbal abuse can have lasting effects on the child and often leads to physical abuse. At the same time, you don't want to interfere with a mother's right to say what she wants to her child. Nor do you want to aggravate a mother who may later take out her frustration on the child. What is your ethical obligation in this case? What would you do in this situation?*

Your body also reveals your race through skin color and tone and may also give clues as to your more specific nationality. Your weight in proportion to your height will also communicate messages to others, as will the length, color, and style of your hair.

Your general attractiveness is also a part of body communication. Attractive people have the advantage in just about every activity you can name. They get better grades in school, are more valued as friends and lovers, and are preferred as coworkers (Burgoon, Buller, & Woodall, 1996). Although we normally think that attractiveness is culturally determined—and to some degree it is—recent research seems to be showing that definitions of attractiveness are becoming universal (Brody, 1994). A person rated as attractive in one culture is likely to be rated as attractive in other cultures—even cultures that are widely different in appearance.

FACIAL COMMUNICATION

Throughout your interpersonal interactions, your face communicates, especially your emotions. In fact, facial movements alone seem to communicate the degree of pleasantness, agreement, and sympathy felt; the rest of the body doesn't provide any additional information. For other aspects, however—for example, the intensity with which an emotion is felt—both facial and bodily cues are used (Graham, Bitti, & Argyle, 1975; Graham & Argyle, 1975).

Some nonverbal communication researchers claim that facial movements may communicate at least the following eight emotions: happiness, surprise, fear, anger, sadness, disgust, contempt, and interest (Ekman, Friesen, & Ellsworth, 1972). Others propose that, in addition, facial movements may communicate bewilderment and determination (Leathers, 1997).

Try to communicate surprise using only facial movements. Do this in front of a mirror, and try to describe in as much detail as possible the specific movements of the face that make up surprise. If you signal surprise as most people do, you probably exhibit raised and curved eyebrows, long horizontal forehead wrinkles, wide-open eyes, dropped-open mouth, and lips parted with no tension. Even if there were differences—and clearly there would be from one person to another—you could probably recognize the movements listed here as indicative of surprise.

Of course, some emotions are easier to communicate and to decode than others. For example, in one study, happiness was judged with an accuracy ranging from 55 percent to 100 percent, surprise from 38 percent to 86 percent, and sadness from 19 percent to 88 percent (Ekman, Friesen, & Ellsworth, 1972). Research finds that women and girls are more accurate judges of facial emotional expression than men and boys (Hall, 1984; Argyle, 1988).

As you've probably experienced, you may interpret the same facial expression differently depending on the context in which it occurs. For example, in a classic study, when a smiling face was presented looking at a glum face, the smiling face was judged to be vicious and taunting. But, when the same smiling face was presented looking at a frowning face, it was judged peaceful and friendly (Cline, 1956).

Another factor influencing facial expression is culture. Members of different cultures use facial expressions very differently largely because cultures have different rules for the way in which emotional expression is to be displayed. For example, in one study Japanese and American students watched a film of an operation (Ekman, 1985). The students were videotaped in two situations: alone while watching the film and in an interview situation about the film. When alone, the students showed very similar reactions, but in the interview, the American students displayed facial expressions indicating displeasure, whereas the Japanese students didn't show any great emotion. Similarly, Japanese women aren't supposed to reveal broad smiles and so will hide their smiles, sometimes with their hands (cf., Ma, 1996). Women in the United States, on the other hand, have no such restrictions and so are more likely to smile openly. Thus, the differences in facial expressions and in the meanings attributed to such expressions seem to depend on the culture's rules for what is and what is not appropriate emotional display and not on the way different cultures express emotions (cf., Matsumoto, 1991).

Similarly, cultural differences exist in decoding the meaning of a facial expression. For example, American and Japanese students judged the meaning of a smiling and a neutral facial expression. The Americans rated the smiling face as more attractive, more intelligent, and as displaying greater sociability than the neutral face. The Japanese, however, rated the smiling face as more sociable but not as more attractive and they rated the neutral face as the more intelligent (Matsumoto & Kudoh, 1993).

Facial Management

As you learned the nonverbal system of communication, you also learned certain facial management techniques that enable you to communicate your feelings to achieve the effect you want, for example, to hide certain emotions and to emphasize others. Consider your own use of such facial management techniques. As you do so, think about the types of interpersonal situations in which you would use each of these facial management techniques (Malandro, Barker, & Barker, 1989).

Would you

1. Intensify? For example, would you exaggerate surprise when friends throw you a party to make your friends feel better?
2. Deintensify? For example, would you cover up your own joy in the presence of a friend who didn't receive such good news?

3. Neutralize? For example, would you cover up your sadness so as not to depress others?
4. Mask? For example, would you express happiness in order to cover up your disappointment at not receiving the gift you expected?

These facial management techniques help you display emotions in a socially acceptable way. For example, when someone gets bad news in which you may secretly take pleasure, the display rule dictates that you frown and otherwise nonverbally signal your displeasure. If you place first in a race and your best friend barely finishes, the display rule requires that you minimize your expression of pleasure in winning and avoid any signs of gloating. If you violate these display rules, you'll be judged insensitive. So, although these techniques may be deceptive, they're also expected and, in fact, required by the rules for polite interaction.

Facial Feedback

In one interesting study, participants held a pen in their teeth to simulate a sad expression. They then rated photographs. Results showed that mimicking sad expressions actually increased the degree of sadness the subjects reported feeling when viewing the photographs (Larsen, Kasimatis, & Frey, 1992). This finding is an example of the facial feedback hypothesis that holds that your facial expression influences physiological arousal (Lanzetta, Cartwright-Smith, & Kleck, 1976; Zuckerman, Klorman, Larrance, & Spiegel, 1981).

Further support for this hypothesis comes from a study that compared participants who feel emotions such as happiness and anger with those who both feel and express these emotions. In support of the **facial feedback hypothesis,** subjects who felt and expressed the emotions became emotionally aroused faster than did those who only felt the emotion (Hess, Kappas, McHugo, & Lanzetta, 1992). So not only does your facial expression influence the judgments and impressions that others have of you; it also influences your level of emotional arousal (Cappella, 1993).

EYE COMMUNICATION

The messages communicated by the eyes vary depending on the duration, direction, and quality of the eye behavior. For example, in every culture there are rather strict, though unstated, rules for the proper duration for eye contact. In much of England and the United States, for example, the average length of gaze is 2.95 seconds. The average length of mutual gaze (two persons gazing at each other) is 1.18 seconds (Argyle, 1988; Argyle & Ingham, 1972). When the duration of eye contact is shorter than 1.18 seconds, you may think the person is uninterested, shy, or preoccupied. When the appropriate amount of time is exceeded, you may perceive this as showing high interest.

In much of the United States direct eye contact is considered an expression of honesty and forthrightness. But the Japanese often view this as a lack of respect. The Japanese will glance at the other person's face rarely and then only for very short periods (Axtell, 1993). In many Hispanic cultures, direct eye contact signifies a certain equality and so should be avoided by, say, children when speaking to a person in authority. Try visualizing the potential misunderstandings that eye communication alone could create when people from Tokyo, San Francisco, and San Juan try to communicate.

The direction of the eye also communicates. Generally, in communicating with another person, you would glance alternatively at the other person's face, then away, then again at the face, and so on. When these directional rules are broken, different meanings are communicated—abnormally high or low interest, self-consciousness, nervousness over the interaction, and so on. The quality—how wide or how narrow your eyes get during interaction—also communicates meaning, especially interest level and such emotions as surprise, fear, and disgust.

Eye Contact

You use eye contact to serve several important functions (Knapp & Hall, 1992; Malandro, Barker, & Barker, 1989; Marshall, 1983; Marsh, 1988). You can use eye contact to *monitor feedback.* For example, when you talk with someone, you look at the person intently, as if to say, "Well, what do you think?" or "React to what I've just said." You also look at speakers to let them know that you're listening. Studies show that listeners gaze at speakers more than speakers gaze at listeners (Knapp & Hall, 1992). The percentage of interaction time spent gazing while listening, for example, ranges from 62 percent to 75 percent; the percentage of time spent gazing while talking, however, ranges from 38 percent to 41 percent. When these percentages are reversed—when a speaker gazes at the listener for longer than "normal" periods or when a listener gazes at the speaker for shorter than "normal" periods—the conversational interaction becomes awkward. You may wish to try this with a friend. Even with mutual awareness, you'll notice the discomfort caused by this seemingly minor communication change.

When you speak with two or three other people, you maintain eye contact to *secure the attention and interest* of your listeners. When someone fails to pay the attention you want, you probably increase your eye contact, hoping your focus on this person will increase attention. When making an especially important point, you would look intently at your listeners—assuming what nonverbal researchers call "visual dominance behavior"—almost as a way of preventing them from devoting attention to anything but what you're saying.

Eye communication can also *regulate or control the conversation.* For example, with eye movements you can inform the other person that the channel of communication is open and that she or he should now speak. A clear example of this occurs in the college classroom, where the instructor asks a question and then locks eyes with a student. Without any verbal message, it's assumed that the student should answer the question. Similarly, when you're nearing the end of what you want to say, you'll probably focus eye contact on the person you think wants to speak next and then turn over the conversation to that person.

Eye communication also helps *signal the nature of the relationship* between two people—for example, one of positive or negative regard. In the United States when you like someone, you increase your eye contact. When eye contact exceeds 60 percent in an interaction, the people are probably more interested in each other than in the verbal messages being exchanged (Argyle, 1988).

Eye contact in the higher primates is often used to signal status and aggression. Among many younger people, prolonged eye contact from a stranger is taken to signify aggressiveness and has frequently prompted physical violence, just because one person looked perhaps a little longer than is considered normal in that specific culture (Matsumoto, 1996). A less extreme way to assert one's position is with **visual dominance** behavior (Exline, Ellyson, & Long, 1975). The average person maintains a higher level of eye contact while listening and a lower level while speaking. When people want to signal dominance, they may reverse this pattern and maintain a high level of eye contact while talking but a much lower level while listening. If you visualize a manager criticizing a subordinate you'll probably picture the manager maintaining direct eye contact with the subordinate while criticizing and maintaining little eye contact when listening to excuses he or she considers inadequate. Another way people try to signal dominance is to lower their eyebrows. Research does support this general interpretation of the behavior. For example, faces with lowered eyebrows, in both cartoons and photographs, were judged to communicate greater dominance than raised eyebrows (Keating, Mazur, & Segall, 1977). Eye movements may also signal whether the relationship between two people is amorous, hostile, or indifferent.

Eye movements are often used to *compensate for increased physical distance.* By making eye contact, we overcome psychologically the physical distance between us. When we catch someone's eye at a party, for example, we become psychologically close even though we may be separated by considerable physical distance. Eye contact and other expressions of psychological closeness, such as self-disclosure and intimacy, have been found to vary in proportion to each other.

Eye Avoidance

The eyes, sociologist Erving Goffman observed in *Interaction Ritual* (1967), are "great intruders." When you avoid eye contact or avert your glance, you allow others to maintain their privacy. You probably do this when you see a couple arguing in the street or on a bus. You turn your eyes away as if to say, "I don't mean to intrude; I respect your privacy." Goffman refers to this behavior as **civil inattention.**

Eye avoidance can also signal lack of interest—in a person, a conversation, or some visual stimulus. At times, like the ostrich, we hide our eyes to try to cut off unpleasant stimuli. Notice, for example, how quickly people close their eyes in the face of some extreme unpleasantness. Interestingly enough, even if the unpleasantness is auditory, we tend to shut it out by closing our eyes. At other times, we close our eyes to block out visual stimuli and thus heighten our other senses; for example, we often listen to music

Increasing Interpersonal Effectiveness
Immediacy

Immediacy refers to the joining of speaker and listener; it's the creation of a sense of togetherness, of oneness. When you communicate immediacy you convey a sense of interest and attention, a liking for and an attraction to the other person. People respond to communication that is immediate more favorably than to communication that is not. For example, students of instructors who communicated immediacy felt that the instruction was better and the course more valuable than students of instructors who did not communicate immediacy (Moore, Masterson, Christophel, & Shea, 1996; Witt & Wheeless, 2001). Students and teachers liked each other largely on the basis of immediacy (Wilson & Taylor, 2001; Baringer & McCroskey, 2000).

Communicating Immediacy   Here are a few suggestions for communicating immediacy.

■ *Express psychological closeness and openness* by, for example, maintaining physical closeness and

arranging your body to exclude third parties. Maintain appropriate eye contact and limit looking around at others.

■ *Smile and express your interest in the other person.*
■ *Use the other person's name.* For example, say, "Joe, what do you think?" instead of "What do you think?"
■ *Focus on the other person's remarks.* Make the speaker know that you heard and understood what was said, and give the speaker appropriate verbal and nonverbal feedback.
■ *Express immediacy with cultural sensitivity.* In the United States immediacy behaviors are generally seen as friendly and appropriate. In other cultures, however, the same immediacy behaviors may be viewed as overly familiar, as presuming that a close relationship exists when it's only one of acquaintanceship (Axtell, 1993).

with our eyes closed. Lovers often close their eyes while kissing, and many prefer to make love in a dark or dimly lit room.

Pupil Dilation

In the fifteenth and sixteenth centuries, Italian women used to put drops of belladonna (which literally means "beautiful woman") into their eyes to enlarge the pupils so that they would look more attractive. Contemporary research supports the intuitive logic of these women: Dilated pupils are in fact judged more attractive than constricted ones (Hess, 1975; Marshall, 1983).

In one study, photographs of women were retouched (Hess, 1975). In one set of photographs, the pupils were enlarged, and in the other they were made smaller. Men were then asked to judge the women's personalities from the photographs. The photos of women with small pupils drew responses such as cold, hard, and selfish; those with dilated pupils drew responses such as feminine and soft. However, the male observers could not verbalize the reasons for the different perceptions. **Pupil dilation** and reactions to changes in the pupil size of others both seem to function below the level of conscious awareness.

Pupil size also reveals your interest and level of emotional arousal. Your pupils enlarge when you're interested in something or when you're emotionally aroused. When homosexuals and heterosexuals were shown pictures of nude bodies, the homosexuals' pupils dilated more when viewing same-sex bodies, whereas the heterosexuals' pupils dilated more when viewing opposite-sex bodies (Hess, Seltzer, & Schlien, 1965). These pupillary responses are unconscious and are even observed in persons with profound mental retardation (Chaney, Givens, Aoki, & Gombiner, 1989). Perhaps we judge dilated pupils more attractive because we judge them as indicative of a person's interest in us. That may be why models, Beanie Babies, and Teletubbies have exceptionally large pupils.

Although belladonna is no longer used, the cosmetics industry has made millions selling eye enhancers—eye shadow, eyeliner, false eyelashes, and tinted contact lenses that change eye color. These items function (ideally, at least) to draw attention to these most powerful communicators.

TOUCH COMMUNICATION

Touch communication, also referred to as **haptics,** is perhaps the most primitive form of communication. Developmentally, touch is probably the first sense to be used; even in the womb, the child is stimulated by touch. Soon after birth, the child is fondled, caressed, patted, and stroked. In turn, the child explores its world through touch. In a very short time, the child learns to communicate a wide variety of meanings through touch.

The Meanings of Touch

Touch may communicate five major meanings (Jones & Yarbrough, 1985). *Positive emotions* may be communicated by touch, mainly between intimates or others who have a relatively close relationship. Among the most important of these positive emotions are support, appreciation, inclusion, sexual interest or intent, and affection. It's interesting to note that people in relationships touch each other more during the intermediate stage than in either the beginning or firmly established relationship stages (Guerrero & Andersen, 1991). Additional research found that touch communicated such positive feelings as composure, immediacy, affection, trust, similarity and quality, and informality (Burgoon, 1991). Touch has also been found to facilitate self-disclosure (Rabinowitz, 1991).

Touch often communicates *playfulness,* either affectionately or aggressively. When touch is used in this manner, the playfulness deemphasizes the emotion and tells the other person that it's not to be taken seriously. Playful touches lighten an interaction.

Touch may also *control* the behaviors, attitudes, or feelings of the other person. Such control may communicate a number of messages. To ask for compliance, for example, we touch the other person to communicate "Move over," "Hurry," "Stay here," or "Do it." Touching to control may also communicate dominance (Henley, 1977). The higher-status and dominant person, for example, initiates touch. In fact, it would be a breach of etiquette for the lower-status person to touch the person of higher status.

Ritualistic touching centers on greetings and departures. Shaking hands to say hello or goodbye is perhaps the clearest example of ritualistic touching, but we might also hug, kiss, or put an arm around another's shoulder.

Task-related touching is associated with the performance of a function, such as removing a speck of dust from another person's face, helping someone out of a car, or checking someone's forehead for fever. Task-related touching seems generally to be regarded positively. For example, book borrowers had a more positive attitude toward the library and the librarian when touched lightly, and customers gave larger tips when lightly touched by the waitress (Marsh, 1988). Similarly, diners who were touched on the shoulder or hand when being given their change in a restaurant tipped more than diners who were not touched (Crusco & Wetzel, 1984).

Touch Avoidance

Much as we have a need and desire to touch and be touched by others, we also have a tendency to avoid touch from certain people or in certain circumstances (Andersen & Leibowitz, 1978). Before reading about the research findings on **touch avoidance,** you may wish to take the accompanying touch avoidance self-test.

Consider, as Nancy Henley suggests in her *Body Politics* (1977), who would touch whom—say, by putting an arm on the other person's shoulder or by putting a hand on the other person's back—in the following dyads: teacher and student, doctor and patient, manager and worker, minister and parishioner, business executive and assistant. Most people would say that the first person in each dyad would be more likely to touch the second person than the other way around. It's the higher status person who is permitted to touch the lower status person. How do gender differences figure into touching and being touched?

> **TEST YOURSELF**   *Do You Avoid Touch?*

This instrument is composed of 18 statements concerning how you feel about touching other people and being touched. Please indicate the degree to which each statement applies to you by indicating whether you: 1 = strongly agree, 2 = agree, 3 = are undecided, 4 = disagree, 5 = strongly disagree.

_____ 1. A hug from a same sex friend is a true sign of friendship.
_____ 2. Opposite-sex friends enjoy it when I touch them.
_____ 3. I often put my arm around friends of the same sex.
_____ 4. When I see two friends of the same sex hugging, it revolts me.
_____ 5. I like it when members of the opposite sex touch me.
_____ 6. People shouldn't be so uptight about touching persons of the same sex.
_____ 7. I think it is vulgar when members of the opposite sex touch me.
_____ 8. When a member of the opposite sex touches me, I find it unpleasant.
_____ 9. I wish I were free to show emotions by touching members of the same sex.
_____ 10. I'd enjoy giving a massage to an opposite-sex friend.
_____ 11. I enjoy kissing a person of the same sex.
_____ 12. I like to touch friends that are the same sex as I am.
_____ 13. Touching a friend of the same sex does not make me uncomfortable.
_____ 14. I find it enjoyable when my date and I embrace.
_____ 15. I enjoy getting a back rub from a member of the opposite sex.
_____ 16. I dislike kissing relatives of the same sex.
_____ 17. Intimate touching with members of the opposite sex is pleasurable.
_____ 18. I find it difficult to be touched by a member of my own sex.

▶ **How did you do?**   To score your touch avoidance questionnaire:

1. Reverse your scores for items 4, 7, 8, 16, and 18. Use these reversed scores in all future calculations.
2. To obtain your same-sex touch avoidance score (the extent to which you avoid touching members of your sex), total the scores for items 1, 3, 4, 6, 9, 11, 12, 13, 16, and 18.
3. To obtain your opposite-sex touch avoidance score (the extent to which you avoid touching members of the opposite sex), total the scores for items 2, 5, 7, 8, 10, 14, 15, and 17.
4. To obtain your total touch avoidance score, add the subtotals from steps 2 and 3.

The higher the score, the higher the touch avoidance—that is, the greater your tendency to avoid touch. In studies by Andersen and Leibowitz (1978), who constructed this test, average opposite-sex touch avoidance scores for males was 12.9 and for females 14.85. Average same-sex touch avoidance scores were 26.43 for males and 21.70 for females. How do your scores compare with the college students in Andersen and Leibowitz's study? Is your touch avoidance likely to be higher when interacting with persons who are culturally different from you? Can you identify types of people and types of situations in which your touch avoidance would be especially high? Especially low?

▶ **What will you do?**   Are you satisfied with your score? Would you like to change your touch avoidance tendencies? What might you do about them?

Adapted from Peter Andersen and Ken Liebowitz, "The Development and Nature of the Construct Touch Avoidance," *Environmental Psychology and Nonverbal Behavior* 3 (1978): 89–106. Used by permission of Plenum Publishers.

Among the important findings is that touch avoidance is positively related to communication apprehension. Those who fear oral communication also score high on touch avoidance. (You may wish to compare your scores on this touch avoidance test with your scores on the communication apprehension test presented in Chapter 3.) Touch avoidance is also high among those who self-disclose little; touch and self-disclosure are intimate forms of communication, and people who are reluctant to get close to another person by self-disclosure also seem reluctant to get close through touch.

Older people have higher touch avoidance scores for opposite-sex persons than do younger people. Apparently, as we get older we are touched less by members of the opposite sex, and this decreased frequency of touching may lead us to avoid touching. Males score higher than females on same-sex touch avoidance. This accords well with our stereotypes: men avoid touching other men, but women may and do touch other women. Women, it is found, have higher touch avoidance scores for opposite-sex touching than do men.

Gender and Cultural Differences

A great deal of research has been directed at the question of who touches whom where. Most of it addresses two basic questions: (1) Are there gender differences? Do men and women communicate through touch in the same way? (2) Are there cultural differences? Do people in different cultures communicate through touch in the same way?

Gender Differences and Touch   Early research reported that touching and being touched differ little between men and women (Jourard, 1968). Men touch and are touched as often and in the same places as women. The major exception to this finding is the touching behavior of mothers and fathers. Mothers touch children of both sexes and of all ages more than do fathers. In fact, many fathers go no further than touching the hands of their children. More recent research has found differences.

Contrary to popular stereotype, research shows that females initiate more opposite-sex touching (especially more opposite-sex touching designed to control) than do men (Jones, 1986). In another study, women were found to initiate touch more in married relationships and less in casual romantic relationships than did men (Guerrero & Andersen, 1994).

Opposite-sex friends report more touching than do same-sex friends. Male and female college students report that they touch and are touched more by their opposite-sex friends than by their same-sex friends. No doubt the strong societal bias against same-sex touching accounts for these generalizations.

Cultural Differences and Touch   The several functions and examples of touching discussed here have been based on studies in North America; in other cultures these functions might not be served in the same way. In some cultures, for example, some task-related touching is viewed negatively and is to be avoided. Among Koreans, it's considered disrespectful for a store owner to touch a customer in, say, handing back change; it's considered too intimate a gesture. Members of other cultures, expecting such touching, may consider the Korean's behavior cold and insulting. Muslim children are not supposed to touch members of the opposite sex, which can easily be interpreted as unfriendly by American children who are used to touching each other (Dresser, 1996).

In one study students from the United States reported being touched twice as much as did the Japanese students (Barnlund, 1975). In Japan, there is a strong taboo against strangers touching, and the Japanese are therefore especially careful to maintain sufficient distance.

Some cultures are contact cultures and others are noncontact cultures. Members of contact cultures (for example, southern European) maintain close distances, touch each other in conversation, face each other more directly, and maintain longer and more focused eye contact. Members of noncontact cultures (for example, northern European or Japanese) maintain greater distance in their interactions, touch each other only rarely, if at all, avoid facing each other directly, and maintain much less direct eye contact. As a result, northern Europeans and Japanese may be perceived as cold, distant, and uninvolved by southern Europeans, who may in turn be perceived as pushy, aggressive, and inappropriately intimate.

PARALANGUAGE AND SILENCE

Two aspects of nonverbal communication, often considered together because they involve manipulating sound, are paralanguage and silence. Let's consider paralanguage first.

Paralanguage

Paralanguage is the vocal (but nonverbal) dimension of speech. It refers to the manner in which you say something rather than to what you say. An old exercise used to increase a student's ability to express different emotions, feelings, and attitudes was to have the student say the following sentence while accenting or stressing different words: "Is this the face that launched a thousand ships?" Significant differences in

The Spiral of Silence

The spiral of silence theory argues that you're more likely to voice agreement than disagreement (Noelle-Neumann, 1973, 1980, 1991; Severin & Tankard, 2001; Scheufele & Moy, 2000). The theory claims that when a controversial issue arises, you estimate public opinion and figure out which views are popular and which are not, largely by attending to the media (Gonzenbach, King, & Jablonski, 1999). You also estimate the punishments you're likely to get for expressing minority opinions. You then use these estimates to regulate your expression of opinions.

Generally, you're more likely to voice your opinions when you agree with the majority than when you disagree. You may do this to avoid being isolated from the majority or being proven wrong. Or, you may simply assume that the majority—because they're a majority—must be right.

As people with minority views remain silent, the media position gets stronger (because those who agree with it are

the only ones speaking). As the media's position grows stronger, the silence of the opposition also grows and the situation becomes an ever-widening spiral. So, when you hear opinions from the media, you're likely to assume that nearly everyone is in agreement—after all, those who do disagree aren't voicing their opinions.

Follow Up   The Internet may in some ways act as a counteragent to the spiral of silence since it provides so many free ways for you to express minority viewpoints (anonymously if you wish) and to quickly find like-minded others. Do you find the Internet a hospitable place for minority views? What types of media are the least hospitable to minority views?

meaning are easily communicated, depending on where the stress is placed. Consider, for example, the following variations:

1. *Is* this the face that launched a thousand ships?
2. Is *this* the face that launched a thousand ships?
3. Is this the *face* that launched a thousand ships?
4. Is this the face that *launched* a thousand ships?
5. Is this the face that launched a *thousand ships?*

Each of these five sentences communicates something different. Each, in fact, asks a totally different question, even though the words used are identical. All that distinguishes the sentences is stress, one of the aspects of paralanguage.

In addition to stress, paralanguage includes such vocal characteristics as **rate** and **volume.** Paralanguage also includes the vocalizations we make when laughing, yelling, moaning, whining, and belching; vocal segregates—sound combinations that aren't words—such as "uh-uh" and "shh"; and **pitch,** the highness or lowness of vocal tone (Argyle, 1988; Trager 1958, 1961).

A good way to appreciate the workings of paralanguage is to examine your own vocal behavior when communicating different meanings. Try reading each of the sentences below first to communicate praise and then to communicate criticism. What changes in your vocal expression communicate the differences in meaning?

1. Now that looks good on you.
2. That was some meal.
3. You're an expert.
4. You're so sensitive.
5. Are you ready?

People Perception and Paralanguage   It does seem that certain voices are symptomatic of certain personality types or problems and, specifically, that the personality orientation gives rise to the vocal qualities. When listening to people—regardless of what they're saying—we form impressions based on their paralanguage as to what kind of people they are. Our impressions from paralanguage cues span a broad range and consist of physical impressions (perhaps about body type and certainly about sex and age), personality impressions (they sound shy, they appear aggressive), and evaluative impressions (they sound like good people, they sound evil and menacing, they have vicious laughs).

One of the most interesting findings on voice and personal characteristics is that listeners can accurately judge the socioeconomic status (high, middle, or low) of speakers after hearing a 60-second voice sample. In fact, many listeners reported that they made their judgments in less than 15 seconds. It has also been found that the speakers judged to be of high status were rated as being of higher credibility than those rated of middle or low status.

It's interesting to note that listeners agree with each other about the personality of the speaker even when their judgments are in error. Listeners seem to have stereotyped ideas about the way vocal characteristics and personality characteristics are related, and they use these stereotypes in their judgments.

Persuasion and Paralanguage   The rate of speech is the aspect of paralanguage that has received the most attention. It's of interest to the advertiser, the politician, and, in fact, anyone who tries to convey information or to influence others orally, especially when time is limited or expensive. The research on rate of speech shows that in one-way communication situations, persons who talk fast are more persuasive and are evaluated more highly than those who talk at or below normal speeds (MacLachlan, 1979). This greater persuasiveness and higher regard holds true whether the person talks fast naturally or the speech is sped up electronically (as in time-compressed speech).

In one experiment, subjects were asked to listen to taped messages and then to indicate both the degree to which they agreed with the message and their opinions as to how intelligent and objective they thought the speaker was (MacLachlan, 1979). Rates of 111, 140, and 191 words per minute were used. (The average speaking rate is about 130 to 150 words per minute.) Subjects agreed most with the fastest speech and least with the slowest speech. Further, they rated the fastest speaker as the most intelligent and objective and the slowest speaker as the least intelligent and objective. Even in experiments in which the speaker was known to have something to gain personally from persuasion (as would, say, a salesperson), the speaker who spoke at the fastest rate was the most persuasive. Research also finds that faster speech rates increase listeners' perceptions of speaker competence and dominance (Buller, LePoire, Aune, & Eloy, 1992).

These general findings need to be qualified in two ways. First, there are cultural differences. For example, among Koreans the opposite effect was found. Male speakers who spoke rapidly were given unfavorable credibility ratings (Lee & Boster, 1992). Researchers have suggested that in individualistic societies a rapid-rate speaker is seen as more competent than a slow-rate speaker, whereas in collectivist cultures a speaker who uses a slower rate is judged to be more competent.

Second, whether or not rapid speech rate is more persuasive depends on whether the speaker is speaking for or against your existing position (Smith & Shaffer, 1991, 1995). The rapid speaker who speaks *against* your existing attitudes is generally more effective than the speaker who speaks at a normal rate. But, the rapid speaker who speaks *in favor of* your existing attitudes (say, in an attempt to strengthen them) is actually less effective than the speaker who speaks at a normal rate. The reason for this is quite logical. In the case of the speaker speaking against your attitudes, the rapidity of speech doesn't give you the time you need to think of counterarguments to rebut the speaker's position. And so you're more likely to be persuaded by the speaker's position since you don't have the time to consider why the speaker may be incorrect. In the case of the speaker speaking in favor of your attitudes, the rapidity of speech doesn't give you the time you need to mentally elaborate on the speaker's arguments. Therefore, they don't carry as much persuasive force as they would if spoken more slowly, giving you the time to think of reasons to agree with the speaker.

Rapid speech also has the advantage in comprehension. Subjects who listened to speeches at 201 words per minute (about 140 is average) comprehended 95 percent of the message, and those who listened to speeches at 282 words per minute (that is, double the normal rate) comprehended 90 percent. Even though the rates increased dramatically, the comprehension rates fell only slightly. These 5 percent and 10 percent losses are more than offset by the increased speed and thus make the faster rates much more efficient in communicating information. If the speech speeds are increased more than 100 percent, however, comprehension falls dramatically.

Exercise caution in applying this research to your own interpersonal interactions (MacLachlan, 1979). Realize that while the speaker is speaking, the listener is generating and framing a reply. If the speaker talks too rapidly, there may not be enough time to compose this reply, and resentment may be generated. Furthermore, the increased rate may seem so unnatural that the listener may come to focus on the speed of speech rather than the thought expressed.

TRY IT!
Apply your knowledge of cultural differences and silence; go to www. ablongman.com/devito.

Silence

"Speech," wrote Thomas Mann, "is civilization itself. The word, even the most contradictory word, preserves contact; it's silence which isolates." Philosopher Karl Jaspers, on the other hand, observed that "the ultimate in thinking as in communication is silence," and philosopher Max Picard noted that "silence is nothing merely negative; it's not the mere absence of speech. It's a positive, a complete world in itself." The one thing on which these contradictory observations agree is that silence communicates. Your silence communicates just as intensely as anything you verbalize (see Jaworski, 1993).

Functions of Silence   Like words and gestures, **silence,** too, serves important communication functions. Silence allows the speaker *time to think,* time to formulate and organize his or her verbal communications. Before messages of intense conflict, as well as those confessing undying love, there is often silence. Again, silence seems to prepare the receiver for the importance of these future messages.

Some people use silence as a weapon *to hurt* others. We often speak of giving someone "the silent treatment." After a conflict, for example, one or both individuals might remain silent as a kind of punishment. Silence used to hurt others may also take the form of refusing to acknowledge the presence of another person, as in disconfirmation (see Chapter 7); here silence is a dramatic demonstration of the total indifference one person feels toward the other.

Sometimes silence is used as a *response to personal anxiety,* shyness, or threats. You may feel anxious or shy among new people and prefer to remain silent. By remaining silent you preclude the chance of rejection. Only when the silence is broken and an attempt to communicate with another person is made do you risk rejection.

Silence may be used to *prevent communication* of certain messages. In conflict situations, silence is sometimes used to prevent certain topics from surfacing and to prevent one or both parties from saying things they may later regret. In such situations, silence often allows us time to cool off before expressing hatred, severe criticism, or personal attacks that we know are irreversible.

Like the eyes, face, or hands, silence can also be used to *communicate emotional responses* (Ehrenhaus, 1988). Sometimes silence communicates a determination to be uncooperative or defiant; by refusing to engage in verbal communication, you defy the authority or the legitimacy of the other person's position. Silence is often used to communicate annoyance, usually accompanied by a pouting expression, arms crossed in front of the chest, and nostrils flared. Silence may express affection or love, especially when coupled with long and longing stares into each other's eyes.

Silence may also be used strategically, to *achieve specific effects.* The pause before what you feel is an important comment or after hearing about some mishap may be strategically positioned to communicate a desired impression—to make your idea stand out among others or perhaps to give others the impression that you care a lot more than you really do. In some cases a prolonged silence after someone voices disagreement may give the appearance of control and superiority. It's a way of saying, "I can respond in my own time." Generally, research finds that people use silence strategically more with strangers than they do with close friends (Hasegawa & Gudykunst, 1998).

Of course, you may also use silence when you simply have *nothing to say,* when nothing occurs to you, or when you don't want to say anything. James Russell Lowell expressed this well: "Blessed are they who have nothing to say, and who cannot be persuaded to say it."

Cultural Differences and Silence   The communicative functions of silence in the situations just cited are not universal; each culture seems to view silence very differently (cf., Kivlk, 1998; Jaworski, 1993). In the United States, for example, silence is often taken as negative. At a business meeting or even in informal social groups, silence may often be interpreted negatively—perhaps the silent member wasn't listening, has nothing interesting to add, doesn't understand the issues, is insensitive, is too self-absorbed to focus on the messages of others, or isn't interested in and isn't paying attention to the conversation. Other cultures, however, view silence more positively. In many situations in Japan, for example, silence is preferred to speech (Haga, 1988). Among first-generation Japanese women, silence is used as a means of maintaining power, though in the process it often alienates their daughters, who feel they know little of their mothers (Von Hassell, 1993).

The traditional Apache regard silence very differently (Basso, 1972). Among the Apache, mutual friends don't feel the need to introduce strangers who may be working in the same area or on the same project. The strangers may remain silent for several days. During this time they're looking each other over, trying to determine if the other person is all right. Only after this period do the individuals talk. When courting, especially during the initial stages, the Apache remain silent for hours; if they do talk, they generally talk very little. Only after a couple has been dating for several months will they have lengthy conversations. These periods of silence are generally attributed to shyness or self-consciousness. The use of silence is explicitly taught to Apache women, who are discouraged from engaging in long discussions with their dates. Silence during courtship is a sign of modesty to many Apache.

SPATIAL MESSAGES

WEB EXPLORATION
To learn more about spatial messages, go to
www.ablongman.com/ devito.

Space is an especially important factor in interpersonal communication, although we seldom think about it. Edward T. Hall (1959, 1963, 1966), who pioneered the study of spatial communication, called this area **proxemics.** We can examine this broad area by looking at proxemic distances, the theories about space, and territoriality.

Proxemic Distances

Four proxemic distances correspond closely to the major types of relationships. They are intimate, personal, social, and public distances (see Table 8.2 on page 198).

Intimate Distance   Within **intimate distance,** ranging from the close phase of actual touching to the far phase of 6 to 18 inches, the presence of the other person is unmistakable. You experience the sound, smell, and feel of the other's breath. The close phase is used for lovemaking and wrestling, for comforting and protecting. In the close phase, the muscles and the skin communicate, while actual words play a minor role. The far phase allows people to touch each other by extending their hands. The individuals are so close that this distance is not considered proper for strangers in public. Because of the feeling of inappropriateness and discomfort (at least for some Americans) if strangers are this close (say, on a crowded bus), their eyes seldom meet but remain fixed on some remote object.

Personal Distance   You carry a protective bubble defining your **personal distance,** which allows you to stay protected and untouched by others, and ranges from 18 inches

Table 8.2 **Relationships and Proxemic Distances**

Note that these four distances can be further divided into close and far phases and that the far phase of one level (say, personal) blends into the close phase of the next level (social). Do your relationships also blend into one another? Or are, say, your personal relationships totally separate from your social relationships?

Relationship	Distance
Intimate relationship	Intimate distance 0 ——————————— 18 inches close phase — far phase
Personal relationship	Personal distance 1½ ——————————— 4 feet close phase — far phase
Social relationship	Social distance 4 ——————————— 12 feet close phase — far phase
Public relationship	Public distance 12 ——————————— 25+ feet close phase — far phase

to about 4 feet. In the close phase, people can still hold or grasp each other but only by extending their arms. You can then take into your protective bubble certain individuals—for example, loved ones. In the far phase, you can touch another person only if you both extend your arms. This far phase is the extent to which you can physically get your hands on things; hence, it defines, in one sense, the limits of your physical control over others. At times, you may detect breath odor, but generally at this distance etiquette demands that you direct your breath to some neutral area.

Social Distance   At the **social distance,** ranging from 4 to 12 feet, you lose the visual detail you had at the personal distance. The close phase is the distance at which you conduct impersonal business or interact at a social gathering. The far phase is the distance at which you stand when someone says, "Stand away so I can look at you." At this distance, business transactions have a more formal tone than they do when conducted in the close phase. In the offices of high officials, the desks are often positioned so that clients are kept at least this distance away. Unlike the intimate distance, where eye contact is awkward, the far phase of the social distance makes eye contact essential—otherwise, communication is lost. The voice is generally louder than normal at this level. This distance frees you from constant interaction with those with whom you work without seeming rude.

Public Distance   **Public distance** ranges from 12 to more than 25 feet. In the close phase, a person seems protected by space. At this distance, you're able to take defensive action should you feel threatened. On a public bus or train, for example, you might keep at least this distance from a drunkard. Although you lose the fine details of the face and eyes, you're still close enough to see what is happening.

At the far phase, you see others not as separate individuals but as part of the whole setting. People automatically establish a space of approximately 30 feet around important public figures, and they seem to do this whether or not there are guards preventing their coming closer. The far phase is the distance by which actors on stage are separated from their audience; consequently, their actions and voices have to be somewhat exaggerated.

The specific distances that you'd maintain between yourself and another person depend on a wide variety of factors (Burgoon, Buller, & Woodall, 1996). Among the most significant are *gender* (women sit and stand closer to each other than do men in same-sex dyads; people approach women more closely than they approach men), *age* (people maintain closer distances with similarly aged others than they do with those much older or much younger), *personality* (introverts and highly anxious people maintain greater distances than do extroverts). Not surprisingly, you'd maintain shorter distances with people you're familiar with (than with strangers) and with people you like (than with those you don't like).

Theories about Space

A number of nonverbal communication researchers have offered explanations as to why people maintain the distances they do. Prominent among these explanations are

A S K *the* **Researcher**

Building for Interaction

I'm an urban planning and design student, and for my senior project I have to design a suburban community for 2,000 people. Since I'm also taking a course in interpersonal communication, I'm wondering what I can do to incorporate the interpersonal communication needs of the residents into my design. Any suggestions?

Designing such a community begins with the creation of mixed use zones that encourage individuals to leave their homes for nearby activities, such as shopping and work. Mixed use zones incorporating local shopping within easy walking distance to residential areas provide reason for people to leave their home, thereby creating opportunities for unplanned interaction with neighbors along the way. Residential streets would be placed in a pattern leading to nodes of activity every few blocks in which parks, benches, shops, or cafes/pubs would be located.

The infrastructure of the city is changing. The technical support system upon which cities are dependent including wires, broadband, and other connections are central to the changing relationship of individual to city. The cell phone and handheld communication devices are commonplace. Communication options meet needs for contact and control. The important thing to remember is that mediated and face-to-face interaction are different from each other. The challenge is to balance communication options in meeting interpersonal communication needs.

For further information see S. Drucker and G. Gumpert, "Public Space and Communication: The Zoning of Public Interaction," *Communication Theory* 1 (4) (1991): 296–310 and G. Gumpert and S. Drucker, "Public Boundaries: Privacy and Surveillance in a Technological World," *Communication Quarterly* 49 (2) (2001): 115–129.

Gary Gumpert (Ph D., Wayne State University) is Professor Emeritus, Queens College, CUNY. listra@optonline. net Susan Drucker (J.D., St. John's University School of Law) is Associate Professor, Hofstra University School of Communication. sphsjd@hofstra.edu Their current research focuses on the relationship of new communication technologies and the use of public spaces, social cohesion, and planning and architecture. They are cofounders of Communication Landscapers, a communication consulting firm specializing in designing for the human factor in a technological environment. (Reprinted by permission of Dr. Gary Gumpert and Dr. Susan Drucker.)

protection theory, equilibrium theory, and expectancy violation theory—rather complex names for simple and interesting concepts.

Protection Theory

Protection theory holds that you establish a body buffer zone around yourself as protection against unwanted touching or attack (Dosey & Meisels, 1976). When you feel that you may be attacked, your body buffer zone increases; you want more space around you. For example, if you found yourself in a dangerous neighborhood at night, your body buffer zone would probably expand well beyond what it would be if you were in familiar and safe surroundings. If someone entered this buffer zone, you would probably feel threatened and seek to expand the distance by walking faster or crossing the street.

In contrast, when you're feeling secure and protected, your buffer zone becomes much smaller. For example, if you're with a group of close friends and feel secure, your buffer zone shrinks, and you may welcome the close proximity and mutual touching.

Equilibrium Theory

Equilibrium theory holds that intimacy and distance vary together: the greater the intimacy, the closer the distance; the lower the intimacy, the greater the distance. This theory says that you maintain close distances with those with whom you have close interpersonal relationships and that you maintain greater distances with those with whom you do not have close relationships (Argyle & Dean, 1965).

At times, of course, your interpersonal distance does not accurately reflect your level of intimacy. When this happens, you make adjustments. For example, let's say that you have an intimate relationship with someone, but for some reason you're separated—perhaps because you could not get concert seats next to each other or you're at a party and have each been led to different parts of a large banquet hall. When this happens, you probably try to preserve your psychological closeness by maintaining frequent eye contact or perhaps by facing each other.

At other times, however, you're forced into close distances with someone with whom you're not intimate (or may even dislike)—for example, on a crowded bus or in the dentist's chair. In these situations, you also compensate, but in such cases you seek to make the psychological distance greater. Consequently, you might avoid eye contact and turn in an opposite direction. In the dentist's chair, you probably close your eyes to decrease this normally intimate distance. If seated to the right of a stranger, you might cross your legs and turn your torso to the left.

Expectancy Violations Theory

Expectancy violations theory explains what happens when you increase or decrease the distance between yourself and another in an interpersonal interaction (Burgoon & Hale, 1988; Burgoon, Buller, & Woodall, 1995). Each culture has certain expectancies for the distance people are to maintain in their conversations. Of course, each person has certain idiosyncrasies. Together, these determine "expected distance." What happens when these expectations are violated?

If you violate the expected distance to a great extent—small violations most often go unnoticed—then the relationship itself comes into focus. The other person begins to turn attention away from the topic of conversation and toward you and your relationship with him or her. It's also interesting to note that those who violate normal expected spatial relationships are judged to be less truthful than those who didn't commit such violations (Feeley & deTurck, 1995).

If this other person perceives you positively—for example, you're a high-status person or you're particularly attractive—then you'll be perceived even more positively if you violate the norm. If, however, you're perceived negatively and you violate the norm, you'll be perceived even more negatively. Thus, the positively evaluated person will be perceived more positively if he or she violates the norm, whereas the negatively evaluated person will be more positively perceived if the distance norm is not violated.

Territoriality

Another type of communication having to do with space is **territoriality,** the possessive reaction to an area or to particular objects. You interact basically in three types of territories (Altman, 1975):

TRY IT!
Apply your knowledge of territoriality; go to **www.ablongman.com/ devito**.

- ■ **Primary territories** are areas that you might call your own; these areas are your exclusive preserve and might include your room, your desk, or your office.
- ■ **Secondary territories** are areas that don't belong to you, but you have occupied them and you're associated with them. Secondary territories might include the table in the cafeteria that you regularly eat at, your classroom seat, or your neighborhood turf.
- ■ **Public territories** are areas that are open to all people; they may be owned by some person or organization, but they are used by everyone and might include a movie house, a restaurant, or a shopping mall.

When you operate in your own primary territory, you have an interpersonal advantage, often called the **home field advantage.** In their own home or office, people take on a kind of leadership role: They initiate conversations, fill in silences, assume relaxed and comfortable postures, and maintain their positions with greater conviction. Because the territorial owner is dominant, you stand a better chance of getting your raise, your point accepted, and the contract resolved in your favor if you're in your own territory (your office, your home) rather than in someone else's (your supervisor's office, for example) (Marsh, 1988).

Like animals, humans mark both their primary and secondary territories to signal ownership and use three types of markers: central, boundary, and ear markers (Goffman, 1971). **Central markers** are items you place in a territory to reserve it for you—for example, a drink at the bar, books on your desk, or a sweater over a library chair.

Boundary markers set boundaries that divide your territory from that of others. In the supermarket checkout line, the bar that is placed between your groceries and those of the person behind you is a boundary marker, as are a fence, the armrests separating chairs, and the contours of the molded plastic seats on a bus.

Ear markers—a term taken from the practice of branding animals on their ears—are identifying marks that indicate your possession of a territory or object. Trademarks, nameplates, and initials on a shirt or attaché case are all examples of ear markers.

Markers are important in giving you a feeling of belonging. For example, students in college dormitories who marked their rooms by displaying personal items stayed in school longer than did those who didn't personalize their spaces (Marsh, 1988).

Again, like animals, humans use territory to signal their status. For example, the size and location of your territory (your home or office, say) indicates something about your status. Status is also signaled by the unwritten law granting the right of invasion. Higher status individuals have a "right" to invade the territory of lower status persons, but the reverse is not true. The boss of a large company, for example, can barge into the office of a junior executive, but the reverse would be unthinkable. Similarly, a teacher may invade a student's personal space by looking over her or his shoulder as the student writes, but the student cannot do the same to the teacher.

ARTIFACTUAL COMMUNICATION

Artifactual communication concerns the messages conveyed by objects that are made by human hands. Thus, aesthetics, color, clothing, jewelry, hairstyle, or scents such as perfume, cologne, or incense are considered artifactual. We look at each of these briefly.

Space Decoration

That the decoration or surroundings of a place exert influence on perceptions should be obvious to anyone who has ever entered a hospital, with its sterile walls and furniture, or a museum, with its imposing columns, glass-encased exhibits, and brass plaques. Even the way a room is furnished exerts influence on us. In a classic study, researchers attempted to determine if the aesthetic conditions of a room would influence the judgments people made in it (Maslow & Mintz, 1956; Mintz, 1956). Three rooms were used: one was beautiful, one average, and one ugly. The beautiful room had large windows, beige walls, indirect lighting, and attractive, comfortable furnishings. The average room was a professor's office with mahogany desks and chairs, metal bookcases and filing cabinets, and window shades. The ugly room was painted battleship gray; lighting was provided by an overhead bulb with a dirty, torn shade. The room was furnished to give the impression of a janitor's storeroom in horrible condition. The ashtrays were filled and the window shades torn.

In the three different rooms, students rated art prints in terms of the fatigue/energy and displeasure/well-being depicted in them. As predicted, the students in the beautiful room rated the prints as more energetic and as displaying well-being; the prints judged in the ugly room were rated as displaying fatigue and displeasure, while those judged in the average room were perceived as somewhere between these two extremes.

The way you decorate your private spaces communicates something about who you are. The office with a mahogany desk, bookcases, and oriental rugs communicates importance and status within the organization, just as the metal desk and bare floors communicate a status much further down in the hierarchy. At home, the cost of the furnishings may communicate your status and wealth, and their coordination may communicate your sense of style. The magazines may communicate your interests. The arrangement of chairs around a television set may reveal how important watching television is. Bookcases lining the walls reveal the importance of reading. In fact, there is probably little in your home that would not send messages to others and that others would not use for making inferences about you. Computers, wide-screen televisions, well-equipped kitchens, and oil paintings of great grandparents, for example, all say something about the people who own them. Likewise, the lack of certain items will communicate something about you. Consider, for example, what messages you would get from a home in which there was no television, telephone, or books.

Color Communication

When you're in debt, you speak of being "in the red"; when you make a profit, you're "in the black." When you're sad, you're "blue"; when you're healthy, you're "in the pink"; when you're jealous, you're "green with envy." To be a coward is to be "yellow" and to be inexperienced is to be "green." When you talk a great deal, you talk "a blue streak"; when you're angry, you "see red." As revealed through these timeworn clichés, language abounds in color symbolism.

Colors vary greatly in their meanings from one culture to another. Some of these cultural differences are illustrated in Table 8.3, but before looking at the table, think about

Table 8.3 Some Cultural Meanings of Color

This table, constructed from the research reported by Henry Dreyfuss (1971), Nancy Hoft (1995), and Norine Dresser (1996), illustrates only some of the different meanings that colors may communicate and especially how they're viewed in different cultures. As you read this table, consider the meanings you give to these colors and where your meanings came from.

Color	Cultural Meanings and Comments
Red	In China red signifies prosperity and rebirth and is used for festive and joyous occasions, in France and the United Kingdom masculinity, in many African countries blasphemy or death, and in Japan anger and danger. Red ink, especially among Korean Buddhists, is used only to write a person's name at the time of death or on the anniversary of the person's death and creates lots of problems when American teachers use red ink to mark homework.
Green	In the United States green signifies capitalism, go ahead, and envy; in Ireland patriotism; among some Native Americans femininity; to the Egyptians fertility and strength; and to the Japanese youth and energy.
Black	In Thailand black signifies old age, in parts of Malaysia courage, and in much of Europe death.
White	In Thailand white signifies purity, in many Muslim and Hindu cultures purity and peace, and in Japan and other Asian countries death and mourning.
Blue	In Iran blue signifies something negative, in Ghana joy; among the Cherokee it signifies defeat and for the Egyptian virtue and truth.
Yellow	In China yellow signifies wealth and authority, in the United States caution and cowardice, in Egypt happiness and prosperity, and in many countries throughout the world femininity.
Purple	In Latin America purple signifies death, in Europe royalty, in Egypt virtue and faith, in Japan grace and nobility, and in China barbarism.

the meanings your own culture gives to such colors as red, green, black, white, blue, yellow, and purple.

There is some evidence that colors affect us physiologically. For example, respiratory movements increase in the presence of red light and decrease in the presence of blue light. Similarly, eye blinks increase in frequency when eyes are exposed to red light and decrease when exposed to blue. This seems consistent with our intuitive feelings that blue is more soothing and red more provocative. After changing a school's walls from orange and white to blue, the students' blood pressure decreased and their academic performance improved.

Colors surely influence our perceptions and behaviors (Kanner, 1989). People's acceptance of a product, for example, is largely determined by its package. For example, the very same coffee taken from a yellow can was described as weak, from a dark brown can as too strong, from a red can as rich, and from a blue can as mild. Even our acceptance of a person may depend on the colors worn. Consider, for example, the comments of one color expert (Kanner, 1989): "If you have to pick the wardrobe for your defense lawyer heading into court and choose anything but blue, you deserve to lose the case." Black is so powerful that it can work against the lawyer with the jury. Brown lacks sufficient authority. Green will probably elicit a negative response.

Clothing and Body Adornment

Clothing serves a variety of functions. It protects you from the weather and, in sports like football, from injury. It helps you conceal parts of your body and so serves a modesty function. Clothing also serves as a cultural display (Morris, 1977). It communicates your cultural and subcultural affiliations. In the United States, where there are so many different ethnic groups, you regularly see examples of dress that indicate what country the wearers are from.

The very poor and the very rich don't dress in the same way, nor do white- and blue-collar workers or the young and the old (Lurie, 1983). People dress, in part at least, to identify with the groups of which they are or want to be members.

Similarly, college students will perceive an instructor dressed informally as friendly, fair, enthusiastic, and flexible, and the same instructor dressed formally as prepared, knowledgeable, and organized (Malandro, Barker, & Barker, 1989).

Your jewelry likewise communicates messages about you. Wedding and engagement rings are obvious examples of jewelry that communicates very specific messages. College rings and political buttons also communicate specific messages. If you wear a Rolex watch or large precious stones, others are likely to infer that you're rich. Men with earrings will be judged differently from men without earrings.

Today body piercings have become increasingly popular, especially among the young. Nose and nipple rings and tongue and belly button jewelry send a variety of messages. Although people wearing such jewelry may wish to communicate a variety of meanings, those interpreting these messages seem to infer that the wearer is communicating an unwillingness to conform to social norms and a willingness to take greater risks than those without such piercings (Forbes, 2001). It's worth noting that in a study of employers' perceptions, applicants with eyebrow piercings were rated and ranked significantly lower than those without such piercings (Acor, 2001).

Tattoos—temporary or permanent ones—likewise communicate a variety of messages, often the name of a loved one or some symbol of allegiance or affiliation. Tattoos also communicate to the wearer's themselves. For example, tattooed students see themselves (and perhaps others do as well) as more adventurous, creative, individualistic, and risky than those without tattoos (Drews, Allison, & Probst, 2000).

The way you wear your hair communicates who you are. Your hair may communicate a concern for being up-to-date, a desire to shock, or perhaps a lack of concern for appearances. Men with long hair will generally be judged as less conservative than men with shorter hair.

In a study on interpersonal attraction, slides of male and female models were shown with and without glasses and were evaluated by men and women. Results indicated that persons with glasses were rated more negatively than the very same persons without glasses (Hasart & Hutchinson, 1993).

Clothing also seems to influence your own behavior and the behavior of groups. For example, it has been argued that people who dress casually act more informally (Morand, cited in *Psychology Today*, March/April 1995, p. 16). Therefore, meetings with such casually dressed people are more likely to involve a freer exchange of thoughts and ideas that stimulates creativity. This casual attire seems to work well in companies that must rely heavily on creative developments, such as a computer software company. IBM, for example, relaxed its conservative dress code and allowed some measure of informal dress among its workers (*New York Times*, 7 February 1995, p. B1). But banks and insurance companies, which traditionally have resisted change, may prefer a more formal attire that creates distance between workers as well as between employees and customers.

Scent

Smell is a peculiar aspect of nonverbal communication and is discussed in widely different ways by different writers. Here, because the emphasis is on using scents (for example, perfume or cologne), it's grouped with artifactual communication. But recognize that body odor also communicates, and perhaps that part of smell is best thought of as a form of body communication. You also use smells to make yourself feel better. When the smells are pleasant, you feel better about yourself; when the smells are unpleasant, you feel less good about yourself. In fact, research finds that smells can influence your body's chemistry, which, in turn, influences your emotional state. For example, the smell of chocolate results in the reduction of theta brain waves, which produces a sense of relaxation and a reduced level of attention (Martin, 1998).

Olfactory communication, or olfactics, is extremely important in a wide variety of situations. Scientists estimate that you can smell some 10,000 different odors (Angier, 1995a). Smell is now big business (Kleinfield, 1992). There is some, though not conclusive, evidence showing that the smell of lemon contributes to a perception of health, the smell of lavender and eucalyptus seems to increase alertness, and the smell of rose oil seems to reduce blood pressure. Findings such as these have contributed to the growth of aromatherapy and to a new profession of aromatherapist (Furlow, 1996). Because humans possess "denser skin concentrations of scent glands than almost any other mammal," it has been argued that it only remains for us to discover how we use scent to communicate a wide variety of messages (Furlow, 1996, p. 41). Some of the most important messages scent seems to communicate are attraction, taste, memory, and identification.

In many animal species the female gives off a scent that *draws* males, often from far distances, and thus ensures the continuation of the species. Humans, too, emit sexual *attractants,* called sex pheromones, body secretions that arouse sexual desire. Humans, of course, supplement that with perfumes, colognes, after-shave lotions, powders, and the like to further enhance attractiveness and sexuality. Not surprisingly, biotechnology companies are busily at work with the aim of bottling human sex pheromones (Bishop, 1993). Women, recent research finds, prefer the scent of men who bear a close genetic similarity to themselves, a finding that may account in part, for our attraction to people much like ourselves (Ober, Weitkamp, Cox, Dytch, Kostyu, & Elias, 1997; Wade, 2002).

Without smell, *taste* would be severely impaired. For example, it would be extremely difficult to taste the difference between a raw potato and an apple without the sense of smell. Street vendors selling hot dogs, sausages, and similar foods are aided greatly by the smells that stimulate the appetites of passersby.

Smell is a powerful *memory* aid; you can often recall situations from months and even years ago when you happen upon a similar smell. One reason smell can so effectively recall a previous situation is that it's often associated with significant emotional experiences (Rubin, Groth, & Goldsmith, 1984; Malandro, Barker, & Barker, 1989).

Smell is often used to create an image or an *identity* for a product. Advertisers and manufacturers spend millions of dollars each year creating scents for cleaning products and toothpastes, for example, which have nothing to do with their cleaning power. Instead, they function solely to help create an image for the product. There is also evidence that we can identify specific significant others by smell. For example, infants find their mothers' breasts through smell, mothers can identify their newborns solely through smell, and young children were able to identify the T-shirts of their brothers and sisters solely on the basis of smell (Porter & Moore, 1981; Angier, 1995a). One researcher goes so far as to advise: "If your man's odor reminds you of Dad or your brother, you may want genetic tests before trying to conceive a child" (Furlow, 1996, p. 41).

TEMPORAL COMMUNICATION

We've already discussed the cultural dimension of time differences (Chapter 2). Here we look at another dimension of time, psychological time.

Psychological time refers to the importance placed on the past, present, or future. In a *past orientation,* you give particular reverence to the past; you might relive old times and regard the old methods as the best. Events are seen as circular and recurring, so that the wisdom of yesterday is applicable also to today and tomorrow. In a *present orientation,* you live in the present for the present. Present activities command your attention; you engage in them not for their future rewards or their past significance but because they're happening now. In its extreme form, this orientation is hedonistic. In a *future orientation,* you give primary attention to the future. You save today, work hard in college, and deny yourself certain enjoyments and luxuries, all because you're preparing for the future.

Researchers have provided some interesting correlations to these different time orientations (Gonzalez & Zimbardo, 1985; Rappaport, Enrich, & Wilson, 1985). Before reading their conclusions, you may wish to take the self-test "What Time Do You Have?"

View point An especially interesting aspect of cultural time is your "social clock," your culture's schedule for the right time to do important things, for example, the right time to start dating, to finish college, to buy your own home, to have a child (Neugarten, 1979). On the basis of this social clock, which you probably internalized as you were growing up, you then evaluate your own social and professional development. If you're on time with the rest of your peers, then you'll feel well adjusted, competent, and a part of the group. If you're late, you'll probably experience feelings of dissatisfaction. What does your social clock look like? How is it influenced by your gender?

> **TEST YOURSELF**   *What Time Do You Have?*

For each statement, indicate whether the statement is true (T) of your general attitude and behavior, or untrue (F) of your general attitude and behavior. (A few statements are purposely repeated to facilitate scoring and analyzing your responses.)

_____   1. Meeting tomorrow's deadlines and doing other necessary work comes before tonight's partying.

_____   2. I meet my obligations to friends and authorities on time.

_____   3. I complete projects on time by making steady progress.

_____   4. I am able to resist temptations when I know there is work to be done.

_____   5. I keep working at a difficult, uninteresting task if it will help me get ahead.

_____   6. If things don't get done on time, I don't worry about it.

_____   7. I think that it's useless to plan too far ahead because things hardly ever come out the way you planned anyway.

_____   8. I try to live one day at a time.

_____   9. I live to make better what is rather than to be concerned about what will be.

_____ 10. It seems to me that it doesn't make sense to worry about the future, since fate determines that whatever will be, will be.

_____ 11. I believe that getting together with friends to party is one of life's important pleasures.

_____ 12. I do things impulsively, making decisions on the spur of the moment.

_____ 13. I take risks to put excitement in my life.

_____ 14. I get drunk at parties.

_____ 15. It's fun to gamble.

_____ 16. Thinking about the future is pleasant to me.

_____ 17. When I want to achieve something, I set subgoals and consider specific means for reaching these goals.

_____ 18. It seems to me that my career path is pretty well laid out.

_____ 19. It upsets me to be late for appointments.

_____ 20. I meet my obligations to friends and authorities on time.

_____ 21. I get irritated at people who keep me waiting when we've agreed to meet at a given time.

_____ 22. It makes sense to invest a substantial part of my income in insurance premiums.

_____ 23. I believe that "a stitch in time saves nine."

_____ 24. I believe that "a bird in the hand is worth two in the bush."

_____ 25. I believe it is important to save for a rainy day.

_____ 26. I believe a person's day should be planned each morning.

_____ 27. I make lists of things I must do.

_____ 28. When I want to achieve something, I set subgoals and consider specific means for reaching those goals.

_____ 29. I believe that "a stitch in time saves nine."

> ▶ **How did you do?**   This time test measures seven different factors. If you selected true (T) for all or most of the questions within any given factor, you're high on that factor. If you selected untrue (F) for all or most of the questions within any given factor, you're low on that factor.

The first factor, measured by questions 1–5, is a future, work motivation, perseverance orientation. These people have a strong work ethic and are committed to completing a task despite difficulties. The second factor (questions 6–10) is a present, fatalistic, worry-free orientation.

High scorers on this factor live one day at a time, not necessarily to enjoy the day but to avoid planning for the next day.

The third factor (questions 11–15) is a present, pleasure-seeking, partying orientation. These people enjoy the present, take risks, and engage in a variety of impulsive actions. The fourth factor (questions 16–18) is a future, goal-seeking, and planning orientation. These people derive pleasure from planning and achieving a variety of goals.

The fifth factor (questions 19–21) is a time-sensitivity orientation. People who score high are especially sensitive to time and its role in social obligations. The sixth factor (questions 22–25) is a future, practical action orientation. These people do what they have to do—take practical actions—to achieve the future they want.

The seventh factor (questions 26–29) is a future, somewhat obsessive daily planning orientation. High scorers make daily "to do" lists and devote great attention to detail.

▶ **What will you do?**   Now that you have some idea of how you treat time, consider how these attitudes and behaviors work for you. For example, will your time orientations help you achieve your social and professional goals? If not, what might you do about changing these attitudes and behaviors?

From A. Gonzalez and P. Zimbardo, "Time in Perspective," *Psychology Today,* March 1985. Copyright 1985 by Sussex Publishers, Inc. Reprinted by permission of *Psychology Today.*

One of the findings of this time study is that future income is positively related to future orientation. The more future oriented a person is, the greater that person's income is likely to be. Present orientation is strongest among lowest-income males.

The time orientation that people develop depends a great deal on their socio-economic class and personal experiences. Gonzalez & Zimbardo (1985) observe: "A child with parents in unskilled and semi-skilled occupations is usually socialized in a way that promotes a present-oriented fatalism and hedonism. A child of parents who are managers, teachers, or other professionals learns future-oriented values and strategies designed to promote achievement."

Different time perspectives also account for much intercultural misunderstanding, because different cultures often teach their members drastically different time orientations. The future-oriented person who works for tomorrow's goals will frequently look down on the present-oriented person who focuses on enjoying today as being lazy and poorly motivated. In turn, the present-oriented person may see those with strong future orientations as obsessed with accumulating wealth or rising in status.

REVIEWING   Key Terms and Concepts in Nonverbal Messages

In this chapter we introduced nonverbal communication: body movements, facial communication, eye communication, touch, paralanguage and silence, spatial messages, artifactual messages, and temporal communication.

Body Communication

What meanings are communicated with body movements? What meanings can your general body appearance communicate?

■ Among the body gestures identified are emblems, which translate words and phrases rather directly; illustrators, which accompany and literally illustrate the verbal messages; affect displays, which convey emotional meaning; regulators, which monitor or control the speaking of the other person; and adaptors, which serve some need and are usually performed only partially in public.

■ General body appearance (height, weight, level of attractiveness, and skin color, for example) can communicate your power, attractiveness, and suitability as a friend or romantic partner.

Facial Communication

What meanings do facial movements communicate?

■ Facial movements express emotions, such as happiness, surprise, fear, anger, sadness, disgust/contempt, interest, bewilderment, and determination.

■ Some facial movements manage the meanings being communicated using these techniques: intensifying, deintensifying, neutralizing, and masking.

Eye Communication

What messages do eye contact, eye avoidance, and pupil dilation communicate?

■ *Eye contact:* monitor feedback, maintain interest/attention, signal conversational turns, signal nature of relationship, compensate for physical distance

■ *Eye avoidance:* give others privacy, signal disinterest, cut off unpleasant stimuli, heighten other senses

■ *Pupil dilation:* indicate interest/arousal, increase attractiveness

Touch Communication

What meanings can you communicate by touching?

■ Among the meanings touch can communicate are positive affect, playfulness, control, ritual, and task-relatedness.

■ Significant gender and cultural differences are found in touching behavior and in the tendencies to avoid touch.

Paralanguage and Silence

What meanings do variations in paralanguage and silence communicate?

■ Paralanguage cues are used for forming impressions, for identifying emotional states, and for making judgments of credibility, intelligence, and objectivity.

■ Silence is used in widely different ways in different cultures: to provide thinking time, to inflict hurt, to hide anxiety, to prevent communication, to communicate feelings, or to communicate "nothing."

Spatial Messages

How do you communicate using space?

■ The major types of distance that correspond to types of relationships are intimate distance (touching to 18 inches), personal distance (18 inches to 4 feet), social distance (4 to 12 feet), and public distance (12 or more feet).

■ Theories about space include protection theory, which claims you maintain spatial distance to protect yourself; equilibrium theory, which claims that you regulate distance according to the intimacy level of your relationship; and expectancy violations theory, which explains what happens when you increase or decrease the distance between yourself and another in an interpersonal interaction.

■ Your territories may be identified as primary (areas you own), secondary (areas that you occupy regularly), and public (areas open to everyone). Like animals, humans often mark their territories with central, boundary, and ear markers as proof of ownership. Your territory (its appearance and the way it's used) also communicates status.

Artifactual Communication

How do you communicate with artifacts, for example, with space decoration, color, clothing and body adornment, and scents?

■ Space decoration influences perceptions of energy, time, status, and personal characteristics.

■ Colors communicate different meanings depending on the culture.

■ Clothing and body adornment serve especially as cultural display and communicate messages about status and social thinking.

■ Scents can communicate messages of attraction, taste, memory, and identification.

Temporal Communication

What are the different time orientations and how do these influence behavior?

■ Three main time orientations can be distinguished: past, present, and future.

■ These orientations influence a wide variety of behaviors, such as your willingness to plan for the future, your tendency to party, and even your potential income.

APPLYING Key Terms and Concepts in Nonverbal Communication

1. What messages are communicated by your general physical appearance? Check your theories with those who know you.

2. Research shows that women are perceived to be and are in reality more skilled at both encoding and decoding nonverbal messages (Briton & Hall, 1995). Do you notice this in your own interactions? Do these differences give women an advantage in conversation? In negotiation? In conflict resolution?

3. A popular defense tactic in sex crimes against women, gay men, and lesbians is to blame the victim by referring to the way the victim was dressed and to imply that the victim's clothing provoked the attack. What do you think of this tactic?

4. What nonverbal cues do you look for in judging whether someone likes you? Do men and women indicate liking with the same cues?

5. Describe an instance when "reading" nonverbal messages through your own cultural and gender rules prevented you from accurately assessing another person or another's meaning.

6. Why do you suppose people who are angry or tense need greater space around them?

7. Can you recall a situation in which your territory was violated? Invaded? Contaminated? How did you respond to these encroachments?

8. What messages does your clothing (including your jewelry, hairstyle, makeup, and the colors you're wearing) communicate? Does it communicate different messages to different people?

9. The "Pygmalion gift" is one that is designed to change the person into what the donor wants that person to become. For example, the parent who gives a child books or science equipment may be asking the child to be a scholar or a scientist. What messages have you recently communicated in your gift-giving behavior? What messages do you think others communicated to you by the gifts they gave you?

10. Another type of time is biological time, which refers to your body clock, the ways your body functions differently at different times. Your intellectual, physical, and emotional lives, according to theories of biorhythms, are lived in cycles that influence your effectiveness. Detailed explanations and instructions for calculating your own intellectual, physical, and emotional cycles can be found in

DeVito (1989), or even better, you can visit a website that will compute your biorhythms (**www.kfu.com/~nsayer/compat.html**).

EXPERIENCING   Key Terms and Concepts in Nonverbal Communication

Go to **www.ablongman.com/devito**.

This group of experiences deals with nonverbal messages and provides opportunities to work with these various channels of communication.

(1) **Facial Expressions** and (2) **Eye Contact** focus on the various meanings the face and the eyes communicate. (3) **Interpersonal Interactions and Space** and (4) **Sitting at the Company Meeting** look at the meanings communicated by the way you use space. (5) **The Meanings of Color** helps sensitize you to the various meanings that different colors communicate. (6) **Communicating Emotions Nonverbally** and (7) **Praising and Criticizing** look at how a variety of meanings can be communicated without words. (8) **Artifacts and Culture: The Case of Gifts** illustrates the vast cultural differences in what is considered appropriate gift-giving.

RESEARCHING with Research Navigator   Key Terms and Concepts in Nonverbal Communication

Go to **http://www.researchnavigator.com**.

Reading an article.

Read a popular or scholarly article on one of the types of nonverbal communication discussed in this chapter. On the basis of this article what can you add to the discussion presented here?

Investigating key terms.

Investigate one of the key terms discussed in this chapter (for example, body gestures, facial management, facial feedback, eye contact, touch, paralanguage, silence, space, distance, territoriality, artifactual communication, scent, time communication, immediacy, or spiral of silence). What additional insights can you provide?

Finding answers.

Try finding answers to one of the following questions or design a research study to answer it.

■ Do high status people touch each other more than lower status people?
■ Do children born blind express emotions with the same facial expressions that sighted children use?
■ How do men and women in different cultures express romantic interest?
■ Are concepts of body attractiveness universal across all cultures?
■ What is the ideal outfit for a college teacher to wear on the first day of class?
■ What types of uniforms command the greatest respect? Have the highest credibility?
■ Do family photographs on an executive's desk contribute to credibility? Do sports trophies?

As Good as It Gets (1997)

Conversation is the socializing instrument par excellence, and in its style one can see reflected the capacities of a race.

—José Ortega y Gasset

The Conversation Process
Conversational Management
Conversational Problems: Prevention and Repair

*I*n James L. Brooks's As Good as It Gets, *Jack Nicholson plays a most inef-fective communicator—at least at the beginning—and becomes involved in the lives of a waitress (Helen Hunt) and a neighbor (Greg Kinnear). As these relation-ships develop and as Nicholson's character begins to care for and help these two people, he learns to communicate and in the process becomes more human.*

Conversation can be defined as "relatively informal social interaction in which the roles of speaker and hearer are exchanged in a nonautomatic fashion under the col-laborative management of all parties" (McLaughlin, 1984). Examining conversation pro-vides an excellent opportunity to look at verbal and nonverbal messages as they're used in day-to-day communications and thus serves as a useful culmination for this second part of the text.

Before reading about the process of conversation, think of your own conversations, the ones that were satisfactory and the ones that were unsatisfactory. Think of a spe-cific recent conversation as you respond to the self-test "How Satisfying Is Your Con-versation?" Taking this test now will help highlight the characteristics of conversational behavior and what makes some conversations satisfying and others unsatisfying.

TEST YOURSELF *How Satisfying Is Your Conversation?*

Respond to each of the following statements by recording the number best representing your feelings, using this scale: 1 = strongly agree, 2 = moderately agree, 3 = slightly agree, 4 = neu-tral, 5 = slightly disagree, 6 = moderately disagree, 7 = strongly disagree.

_____ 1. The other person let me know that I was communicating effectively.
_____ 2. Nothing was accomplished.
_____ 3. I would like to have another conversation like this one.
_____ 4. The other person genuinely wanted to get to know me.
_____ 5. I was very dissatisfied with the conversation.
_____ 6. I felt that during the conversation I was able to present myself as I wanted the other person to view me.
_____ 7. I was very satisfied with the conversation.
_____ 8. The other person expressed a lot of interest in what I had to say.
_____ 9. I did *not* enjoy the conversation.
_____ 10. The other person did *not* provide support for what he or she was saying.
_____ 11. I felt I could talk about anything with the other person.
_____ 12. We each got to say what we wanted.
_____ 13. I felt that we could laugh easily together.
_____ 14. The conversation flowed smoothly.
_____ 15. The other person frequently said things which added little to the conversation.
_____ 16. We talked about something I was *not* interested in.

▶ **How did you do?** To compute your score, follow these steps:

1. Add the scores for items 1, 3, 4, 6, 7, 8, 11, 12, 13, and 14.
2. Reverse the scores for items 2, 5, 9, 10, 15, and 16 such that 7 becomes 1, 6 becomes 2, 5 becomes 3, 4 remains 4, 3 becomes 5, 2 becomes 6, and 1 becomes 7.
3. Add the reversed scores for items 2, 5, 9, 10, 15, and 16.
4. Add the totals from steps 1 and 3 to yield your communication satisfaction score.

You may interpret your score along the following scale:

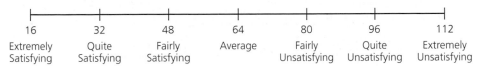

16	32	48	64	80	96	112
Extremely Satisfying	Quite Satisfying	Fairly Satisfying	Average	Fairly Unsatisfying	Quite Unsatisfying	Extremely Unsatisfying

▶ **What will you do?**   Before reading the remainder of this chapter, try to identify those qualities that make a conversation satisfying for you. What interpersonal qualities are most important to making a person a satisfying conversational partner? How might you cultivate these qualities? Table 9.1 identifies some unsatisfying conversational partners that you'll likely want to avoid in our own conversations.

This test was developed by Michael Hecht, "The Conceptualization and Measurement of Interpersonal Communication Satisfaction," *Human Communication Research* 4 (1978): 253–264 and is reprinted by permission of the author.

Table 9.1   **Unsatisfying Conversational Partners and How Not to Become One of Them**

As you read this table, consider your own conversations. Have you met any of these people? Have you ever been one of these people?

Unsatisfying Conversational Partners	*How Not to Become One of Them*
The **Detour Taker** begins to talk about the topic and then goes off pursuing a totally different one.	Follow a logical pattern in conversation and avoid frequent and long detours.
The **Complainer** complains and rarely tires of listing each of them.	Be positive; emphasize what's good before what's bad.
The **Moralist** evaluates and judges everyone and everything.	Avoid evaluation and judgment; see the world through the eyes of the other person.
The **Inactive Responder** gives no reaction regardless of what you say.	Respond overtly with verbal and nonverbal messages.
The **Story Teller** tells stories, too often substituting them for two-way conversation.	Talk about yourself in moderation; be other oriented.
The **Interrogator** asks questions about everything, even about matters that are obvious or irrelevant.	Ask questions in moderation—to secure needed information and not to get every imaginable detail.
The **Egotist** talks only about topics that are self-related.	Be other oriented; focus on the other person; listen as much as you speak.
The **Doomsayer** is the ultimate negative thinker; everything is a problem.	Be positive.
The **Arguer** listens only to find something to take issue with.	Be supportive but argue and disagree when it's appropriate.
The **Thought Completer** "knows" exactly what you're going to say and so says it for you.	Don't interrupt; assume that the speaker wants to finish her or his own thoughts.
The **Self-Discloser** discloses more than you need or want to hear.	Disclose selectively, in ways appropriate to your relationship with the listener.
The **Advisor** regularly and consistently gives advice, whether you want it or not.	Don't assume that the expression of a problem is a request for a solution.
The **Psychiatrist** analyzes everything you say and mindreads your motives.	Avoid playing the therapist as a regular role; be a friend, lover, or parent.

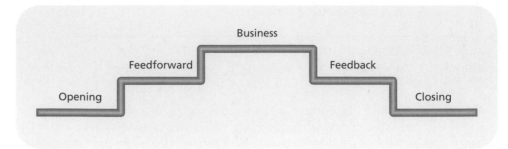

A Five-Stage Model of Conversation
This model of the stages of conversation is best seen as a way of talking about conversation and not as the unvarying stages all conversations follow. As you review the model, consider how accurately it depicts conversation as you experience it. Can you develop a more accurate and more revealing model?

THE CONVERSATION PROCESS

WEB EXPLORATION
To learn more about opening a conversation, go to www.ablongman.com/devito.

It's convenient to divide up **conversation** into chunks or stages and view each stage as requiring a choice as to what you'll say and how you'll say it. Here we divided the sequence into five steps: opening, feedforward, business, feedback, and closing (see Figure 9.1). These stages and the way people follow them will vary depending on the personalities of the communicators, their culture, the context in which the conversation occurs, the purpose of the conversation, and the entire host of factors considered throughout this text.

When reading about the process of conversation, keep in mind that not everyone speaks with the fluency and ease that many textbooks often assume. Speech and language disorders, for example, can seriously disrupt the conversation process when some elementary guidelines aren't followed. Table 9.2 offers suggestions for making such conversations run more smoothly.

Opening

The first step is to open the conversation, usually with some kind of greeting: "Hi. How are you?" "Hello, this is Joe." The greeting is a good example of **phatic communion.** It's a message that establishes a connection between two people and opens up the channels for more meaningful interaction. Openings, of course, may be nonverbal as well as verbal. A smile, kiss, or handshake may be as clear an opening as "Hello." Greetings are so common that they often go unnoticed. But when they're omitted—as when the doctor begins the conversation by saying, "What's wrong?"—you may feel uncomfortable and thrown off guard.

In normal conversation, the greeting is reciprocated with a greeting similar in degree of formality and intensity. When it isn't—when the other person turns away or responds coldly to your friendly "Good morning"—you know that something is wrong.

Openings are also generally consistent in tone with the main part of the conversation; a cheery "How ya doing today, bud?" is not normally followed by news of a family death, and a friendly conversation is not begun with insensitive openers: "Wow, you've gained a few pounds haven't you?"

Table 9.2 *Interpersonal Communication Tips*
Between people with and without speech and language disorders

Speech and language disorders vary widely—from fluency problems in stuttering, to indistinct articulation, to difficulty in finding the right word in aphasia. Communication between people with and without speech and language disorders can be facilitated by following a few simple guidelines.

If you're the person without a speech or language disorder:	If you're the person with a speech or language disorder:
1. Avoid finishing sentences for someone who stutters or has word-finding difficulty. First, you may be wrong as to what the speaker wants to say. This will make it even more difficult for the person to tell you that that's not what he or she wanted to say, and then he or she will have to start over. Second, finishing sentences may convey the idea that you're impatient and don't want to spend the extra time necessary to communicate effectively. 2. Avoid giving directions to the person with a speech disorder. Saying "slow down" or "relax" will generally prove insulting and will only make subsequent communication more difficult. 3. Maintain eye contact and avoid showing any signs of impatience or embarrassment. 4. If you don't understand what the person said, ask him or her to repeat it. Don't pretend that you understand when you don't; it will only make subsequent communication more difficult and more uncomfortable. 5. Don't treat people who have language problems like children. A person with aphasia, say, who has difficulty with names or nouns generally, is in no way childlike, so be careful to avoid talking down to such people.	1. Let the other person know what your special needs are. For example, if you stutter, you might tell others that you have difficulty with certain sounds and so they need to be patient. 2. Demonstrate your comfort with and positive attitude toward the interpersonal situation. If you appear comfortable and positive, others will also.

These suggestions were drawn from a variety of sources: http://wwww.nsastutter.org/documents/listenrs.html, http://www.aphasia.org/NAAcommun.html, and http://www.conniedugan.com/tips.html (all accessed 4/5/02).

Feedforward

At the second step, you usually provide some kind of feedforward (see Chapter 1), which gives the other person a general idea of the conversation's focus: "I've got to tell you about Jack," "Did you hear what happened in class yesterday?" or "We need to talk about our vacation plans." Feedforward may also identify the tone of the conversation ("I'm really depressed and need to talk with you") or the time required ("This will just take a minute") (Frentz, 1976; Reardon, 1987).

Conversational awkwardness often occurs when feedforwards are used inappropriately. For example, using overly long feedforwards may make the listener wonder whether you'll ever get to the business at hand and may make you seem disorganized and lacking in focus. Omitting feedforward before a truly shocking message (for example, the death or illness of a friend or relative) can make you seem insensitive or uncaring.

Often the feedforward is combined with the opening, as when you see someone on campus, for example, and say, "Hey, listen to this" or when, in a work situation, someone says, "Well, folks, let's get the meeting going."

Business

At the third step, you talk "business," the substance or focus of the conversation. The term "business" is used to emphasize that most conversations are goal directed; you converse to fulfill one or several of the general purposes of interpersonal communication: to learn, relate, influence, play, or help (see Chapter 1). The term is also sufficiently general to incorporate all kinds of interactions. The business is conducted through an exchange of speaker and listener roles. Brief, rather than long, speaking turns characterize most satisfying conversations.

In the business stage, you talk about Jack, what happened in class, or your vacation plans. This is obviously the longest part of the conversation and the reason for the opening and the feedforward.

Feedback

The fourth step is feedback (see Chapter 1), the reverse of the second step. Here you reflect back on the conversation to signal that, as far as you're concerned, the business is completed: "So you want to send Jack a get-well card," "Wasn't that the craziest class you ever heard of?" or "I'll call for reservations, and you'll shop for what we need."

Of course, the other person may not agree that the business has been completed and may therefore counter with, for example, "But what hospital is he in?" When this happens, you normally go back a step and complete the business.

Closing

The fifth and last step, the opposite of the first step, is the closing, the goodbye, which often reveals how satisfied the persons were with the conversation: "I hope you'll call

The Diffusion of Innovations

The diffusion of innovations theory illustrates the diversity in media audiences by focusing on the way media influence people to adopt something new or different. *Diffusion* refers to the passage of an innovation through society. The *innovation* may be anything new, for example, soft contact lenses, laptop computers, personal data assistants, or PowerPoint presentations. Obviously, not all people adopt or reject the innovation at the same time. Research distinguishes five types of adopters (see the figure below).

■ The *innovators* (approximately 3 percent of the population) are not necessarily the originators of the new idea, but they're the ones who first introduce it on a reasonably broad scale.

■ The *early adopters* (approximately 14 percent) legitimize the idea and make it acceptable to people in general.

■ The *early majority* (approximately 34 percent) follows the early adopters and further legitimates the innovation.

■ The *late majority* (approximately 34 percent) adopts the innovation after about half the population has adopted it.

■ The *laggards* (approximately 14 percent) are the last group to adopt the innovation.

One last group, the *diehards,* never adopt the innovation. These include the accountants who continue to do tax returns without the aid of computer software or the lawyers and doctors who never use computerized databases.

Follow Up   What is the role of the media in influencing your adoptions? What is the role of interpersonal conversation in influencing your adoptions? How do the media and interpersonal messages interact to influence your adoption of innovation decisions?

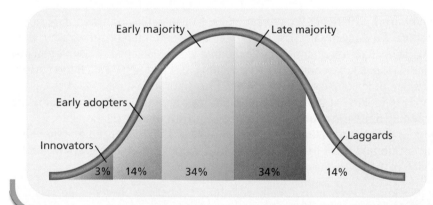

The Five Types of Adopters
The five types of adopters as represented in the population according to the diffusion of innovations theory.
Source: Reprinted with the permission of The Free Press, an imprint of Simon & Schuster Adult Publishing Group, from *The Diffusion of Innovations,* Fourth Edition, by Everett M. Rogers. Copyright © 1995 by Everett M. Rogers. Copyright © 1962, 1971, 1983 by The Free Press.

soon" or "Don't call us, we'll call you." The closing may also be used to schedule future conversations: "Give me a call tomorrow night" or "Let's meet for lunch at twelve." When closings are indefinite or vague, conversation often becomes awkward; you're not quite sure if you should say goodbye or if you should wait for something else to be said.

In a way similar to the opening and the feedforward being combined, the closing and the feedback might be combined, as when you say: "Look, I've got to think more about this commitment, okay?"

CONVERSATIONAL MANAGEMENT

Speakers and listeners have to work together to make conversation an effective and satisfying experience. **Conversational management** includes initiating, maintaining, and closing conversations.

Initiating Conversations

Several approaches to opening a conversation can be derived from the elements of the interpersonal communication process discussed in Chapter 1:

- *Self-references* say something about yourself. Such references may be of the "name, rank, and serial number" type—for example: "My name is Joe. I'm from Omaha." On the first day of class, students might say, "I'm worried about this class" or "I took this instructor last semester; she was excellent."
- *Other-references* say something about the other person or ask a question: "I like that sweater." "Didn't we meet at Charlie's?" Of course, there are pitfalls here. Generally, it's best not to comment on the person's race ("My uncle married a Korean"), the person's affectional orientation ("Nice to meet you; I have a gay brother"), or physical disability ("It must be awful to be confined to a wheelchair").
- *Relational references* say something about the two of you: for example, "May I buy you a drink?" "Would you like to dance?" or simply "May I join you?"
- *Context references* say something about the physical, social–psychological, cultural, or temporal context. The familiar "Do you have the time?" is a reference of this type. But you can be more creative and say, for example, "This restaurant seems very friendly" or "This Dali is fantastic."

As you know from experience, conversations are most satisfying when they're upbeat and positive. So it's generally best to lead off with something positive rather than something negative. Say, for example, "I like the music here" instead of "Don't you just hate this place?" Also, it's best not to be too revealing, disclosing too much too early in an interaction. It can make the other person feel uncomfortable.

Another way of looking at the process of initiating conversations is to examine the infamous "opening line," the opener designed to begin a romantic relationship.

Consider your own opening lines (or the opening lines that were used on you). Let's say you're at a club and want to strike up a conversation—and perhaps spark a relationship. Which of the following are you most likely to use (Kleinke, 1986)?

1. A *cute-flippant* opener? "Is that really your hair?" "I bet the cherry jubilee isn't as sweet as you are."
2. An *innocuous (highly ambiguous) opener*? "What do you think of the band?" "Could you show me how to work this machine?"
3. A *direct opener*? "I feel a little embarrassed about this, but I'd like to meet you," "Would you like to have a drink with me?" "May I join you?"

The *cute-flippant* openers are humorous, indirect, and ambiguous as to whether the person opening the conversation actually wants an extended encounter. One advantage of these opening lines is that they're indirect enough to cushion any rejection. These are also, however, the lines least preferred by men and women.

The *innocuous* openers are highly ambiguous as to whether they're simple comments that might be made to just anyone or whether they're in fact openers designed

A S K the *Researcher*

Seeking Library Assistance

I'm a returning student, and today's college library is frightening to me; on top of this I have great difficulty in asking for assistance. Can you give me any advice for approaching a librarian and learning what I have to learn?

Today's libraries can be intimidating, especially in light of the fact that electronic resources are changing so rapidly. In approaching librarians, demonstrate a positive attitude and warm nonverbal behaviors like direct eye contact and a smile. Librarians are professionals, with master's degrees, and want to help you. They do, however, expect you to be prepared. Take time to think about your assignment. Don't procrastinate, for although many resources (but not all!) are available in full text (in paper, on the Internet, or on electronic databases), it will take more time than you think to locate needed information. Be open to the librarian's advice as to whether paper or electronic sources are best suited to your purposes. By cultivating positive relationships with librarians, you'll find the library will become much less intimidating. If you're too shy to approach a librarian in person, many universities now have e-mail and/or "Ask a Librarian" chat services that you can access through your library's home page.

For further information see M. L. Radford, *The Reference Encounter: Interpersonal Communication in the Academic Library* (Chicago: Association of College and Research Libraries, American Library Association, 1999).

Marie L. Radford (Ph.D., Rutgers University) is Acting Dean at the Pratt Institute, School of Information and Library Science. She teaches courses in interpersonal communication, reference, and electronic information retrieval and conducts research on interpersonal communication, especially in library settings, and in media images of librarians. mradford@pratt.edu (Reprinted by permission of Dr. Marie L. Radford.)

to initiate an extended encounter. Men and women generally like these openers; they're indirect enough to allow for an easy out if the other person doesn't want to talk.

The *direct* openers clearly demonstrate the speaker's interest in meeting the other person. Men like direct openers that are very clear in meaning, possibly because men are not used to having another person initiate a meeting. Women prefer openers that aren't too strong and that are relatively modest.

In e-mail conversations, the situation is a bit different. Even before your message is opened, the receiver knows who the sender is, when the message was composed, and, from the title or subject line, something about the nature of your message. In addition to this general hint at the nature of the message, most e-mail users begin their e-mail with a kind of orientation or preface to what will follow, for example, "I'm writing to ask the name of your acupuncturist" or "I want to fill you in as to what happened at the party." Generally, such openers are direct and relate closely to what is to follow.

Maintaining Conversations

In maintaining conversations you follow a variety of principles and rules. Here we discuss, first, the principles and maxims you follow in conversation and, second, the ways in which the speaker and listener exchange turns in conversation.

The Principle of Cooperation   During conversation you probably follow the principle of cooperation, implicitly agreeing with the other person to cooperate in trying to understand what each is saying (Grice, 1975; Lindblom, 2001). You cooperate largely by using four **conversational maxims**—principles that speakers and listeners in the United States and in many other cultures follow in conversation. Although the names for these maxims may be new, the principles themselves will be easily recognized from your own experiences.

TRY IT!
Apply your knowledge about maintaining conversations; go to **www.ablongman.com/devito**.

The Maxim of Quantity   Be as informative as necessary to communicate the intended meaning. Thus, you include information that makes the meaning clear but omit what does not. In following this principle, you give neither too little nor too much information. You see people violate this maxim when they try to relate an incident and digress to give unnecessary information. You find yourself thinking or saying, "Get to the point; so what happened?" This maxim is also violated when necessary information is omitted. In this situation, you find yourself constantly interrupting to ask questions: "Where were they?" "When did this happen?" "Who else was there?"

This simple maxim is frequently violated in e-mail communication. Here, for example, are three ways in which e-mail often violates the maxim of quantity and some suggestions on how to avoid these violations.

WEB EXPLORATION
To learn more about quantity and e-mail messages, go to www.ablongman.com/devito.

- Chain e-mails often violate the maxim of quantity by sending people information they don't really need or want. Some people maintain lists of e-mail addresses and send all these people the same information. It's highly unlikely that everyone on these lists needs or wants to read the long list of jokes you find so funny. *Suggestion:* Avoid chain e-mail (at least most of the time). When something comes along that you think someone you know would like to read, send it on to the specific one, two, or three people you know would like to receive it.
- When chain e-mails are used, they often contain the e-mail addresses of everyone on the chain. These extensive headers clog the system and also reveal e-mail addresses that some people may want to keep private or made known to others at their own discretion. *Suggestion:* When you do send chain e-mails (and in some situations, they serve useful purposes) conceal the e-mail addresses of your recipients by using some general description, for example, "undisclosed recipients."
- Lengthy attachments take time to download and often create problems for people who do not have the latest technology. Not everyone wants to see the two hundred photos of your last vacation. *Suggestion:* Use attachments in moderation; find out first who would like to receive photos and who would not.

The Maxim of Quality   Say what you know or assume to be true, and do not say what you know to be false. When you're in conversation, you assume that the other person's information is true—at least as far as he or she knows. When you speak with people who frequently violate this principle by lying, exaggerating, or minimizing major problems, you come to distrust what the person is saying and wonder what is true and what is fabricated.

The Maxim of Relation   Talk about what is relevant to the conversation. Thus, if you're talking about Pat and Chris and say, for example, "Money causes all sorts of relationship problems," it's assumed by others that your comment is somehow related to Pat and Chris. This principle is frequently violated by speakers who digress widely or frequently interject irrelevant comments and you wonder how these comments are related to what you're discussing.

The Maxim of Manner   Be clear, avoid ambiguities, be relatively brief, and organize your thoughts into a meaningful sequence. Thus, you use terms that the listener understands and clarify terms that you suspect the listener will not understand. When talking with a child, for example, you would simplify your vocabulary. Similarly, you adjust your manner of speaking on the basis of the information you and the listener share.

When talking to a close friend, for example, you can refer to mutual acquaintances and to experiences you've had together. When talking to a stranger, however, you'd either omit such references or explain them.

The four maxims just discussed aptly describe most conversations as they take place in much of the United States. Recognize, however, that maxims will vary from one culture to another. Here are two maxims appropriate in cultures other than that of the United States, but also appropriate to some degree throughout the United States.

In Japanese conversations and group discussions, a maxim of *preserving peaceful relationships* with others may be observed (Midooka, 1990). Thus, for example, it would be considered inappropriate to argue and to directly demonstrate that another person is wrong. It would be inappropriate to contribute to another person's embarrassment or, worse, loss of face.

The maxim of *self-denigration,* observed in the conversations of Chinese speakers, may require that you avoid taking credit for some accomplishment or make less of some ability or talent you have (Gu, 1990). To put yourself down in this way is a form of politeness that seeks to elevate the person to whom you're speaking.

The Principle of Dialogue   Think about your own communication tendencies. Which of the following paired statements *generally* characterizes your interpersonal interactions?

1. You frequently use negative criticism ("I didn't like that explanation") and negative personal judgments ("You're not a very good listener, are you?").

1. You avoid negative criticism and negative personal judgments; you practice using positive criticism ("I like those first two explanations best; they were really well reasoned").

2. You frequently use dysfunctional communication, such as expressing unwillingness to talk, or use messages that are unrelated to the topic of discussion ("There's no sense discussing this; I can see you're not rational").

2. You keep the channels of communication open ("I really don't know what I did that offended you, but tell me. I don't want to hurt you again.").

3. You rarely demonstrate through paraphrase or summary that you understand the other person's meaning.

3. You frequently paraphrase or summarize what the other person has said to ensure accurate understanding.

4. You rarely request clarification of the other person's perspectives or ideas.

4. You request clarification as necessary and ask for the other person's point of view because of a genuine interest in the other person's perspective.

5. You frequently request personal positive statements or statements of self-approval ("How did you like the way I told that guy off? Clever, no?").

5. You avoid requesting self-approval statements.

View point   In dialogic interaction between, say, a fluent speaker and one who has a severe physical or psychological communication problem, the more fluent speaker tries to help the speaker with the problem communicate more effectively. In fact, some researchers have argued that the more competent communicator has an ethical responsibility to equalize the interaction by helping the other person to better convey his or her meaning (von Tetzchner & Jensen, 1999). Do you consider this an ethical responsibility?

The statements in the left column are examples of monologue. The statements on the right are examples of dialogue. **Monologue** is communication in which one person speaks and the other listens; there's no real interaction among participants. The term *monologic communication* is an extension of this basic definition and refers to communication in which there is no genuine interaction, in which you speak without any real concern for the other person's feelings or attitudes. The monologic communicator is concerned only with his or her own goals and is interested in the other person only insofar as that person can be used to achieve those goals. In monologic interaction, you communicate what will advance your own goals, prove most persuasive, and benefit you.

Not surprisingly, effective communication is based not on monologue but on its opposite, *dialogue* (Buber, 1958; Brown & Keller, 1979; Thomlison, 1982; Yau-fair Ho, Chan, Peng, & Ng, 2001; McNamee & Gergen, 1999). In **dialogue,** there is two-way interaction. Each person is both speaker and listener, sender and receiver. In *dialogic communication* there is deep concern for the other person and for the relationship between the two people. The objective of dialogue is mutual understanding and empathy. There is respect for the other person, not because of what this person can do or give, but simply because this person is a human being and therefore deserves to be treated honestly and sincerely.

In a dialogic interaction, you respect the other person enough to allow that person the right to make his or her own choices without coercion, without the threat of punishment, without fear or social pressure. A dialogic communicator respects other people enough to believe that they can make their own decisions and implicitly or explicitly lets them know that whatever choices they make, they will still be respected as people.

The Principle of Turn Taking   The defining feature of conversation is that the speaker and listener exchange roles throughout the interaction. You accomplish this through a wide variety of verbal and nonverbal cues that signal **conversational turns**—the changing (or maintaining) of the speaker or listener role during the conversation. Combining the insights of a variety of communication researchers (Duncan,

1972; Burgoon, Buller, & Woodall, 1995; Pearson & Spitzberg, 1990), we can look at conversational turns in terms of cues that speakers use and cues that listeners use.

Speaker Cues   As a speaker, you regulate conversation through two major types of cues: turn-maintaining and turn-yielding. *Turn-maintaining cues* are designed to help you maintain the speaker's role. You can do this with a variety of cues, for example, audibly inhaling to show that you have more to say, continuing a gesture or gestures to show that you have not completed the thought, avoiding eye contact with the listener so there's no indication that you're passing the speaking turn to him or her, sustaining your intonation pattern to indicate that you intend to say more, or vocalizing pauses ("er," "um") to prevent the listener from speaking and to show that you're still talking (Duncan, 1972; Burgoon, Buller, & Woodall, 1996). In most cases, speakers are expected to maintain relatively brief speaking turns and to turn over the speaking role willingly to the listener (when so signaled by the listener).

With *turn-yielding cues* you tell the listener that you're finished and wish to exchange the role of speaker for that of listener. These cues tell the listener (sometimes a specific listener) to take over the role of speaker. For example, at the end of a statement you might add some paralinguistic cue such as "eh?" that asks one of the listeners to assume the role of speaker. You can also indicate that you've finished speaking by dropping your intonation, by prolonged silence, by making direct eye contact with a listener, by asking some general question, or by nodding in the direction of a particular listener.

In much the same way that you expect a speaker to yield the role of speaker, you also expect the listener to willingly assume the speaking role. Those who don't may be regarded as reticent or unwilling to involve themselves and take equal responsibility for the conversation. For example, in an analysis of turn-taking violations in the conversations of marrieds, the most common violation found was that of no response. Forty-five percent of the 540 violations identified involved a lack of response to an invitation to assume the speaker role. Of these "no response" violations, 68 percent were committed by men and 32 percent by women. Other turn-taking violations include interruptions, delayed responses, and inappropriately brief responses. From this it's been argued that with these violations, all of which are committed more frequently by men, men silence women in marital interactions (DeFrancisco, 1991).

Listener Cues   As a listener, you can regulate the conversation by using a variety of cues. *Turn-requesting cues* let the speaker know that you'd like to take a turn as speaker. Sometimes you can do this by simply saying, "I'd like to say something," but often you do it more subtly through some vocalized "er" or "um" that tells the mindful speaker that you'd now like to speak. This request to speak is also often made with facial and mouth gestures. You can, for example, indicate a desire to speak by opening your eyes and mouth widely as if to say something, by beginning to gesture with your hand, or by leaning forward.

You can also indicate your reluctance to assume the role of speaker by using *turn-denying cues*. For example, intoning a slurred "I don't know" or a brief grunt signals you have nothing to say. Turn denying is often accomplished by avoiding eye contact with the speaker who wishes you to take on the role of speaker or by engaging in some behavior that is incompatible with speaking—for example, coughing or blowing your nose.

Back-channeling cues are used to communicate various types of information back to the speaker without your assuming the role of speaker. Some researchers call these "acknowledgment tokens"—brief utterances such as "mm-hm," "uh-huh," and "yeah," the

Table 9.3 **Functions of Back-Channeling Cues**

Although you're probably seldom mindful of using back-channeling cues, you would miss them sorely if your listeners didn't use them. As you read through this table, consider how you communicate these various functions and how responsive you are to the back-channeling cues of others. This table is based on the excellent research summaries of Burgoon, Buller, and Woodall (1996) and Pearson and Spitzberg (1990).

Functions	Examples
To indicate agreement or disagreement	Smiles, nods of approval, brief comments such as "Right" and "Of course," or a vocalization like "uh-huh" signal agreement. Frowning, shaking your head, or making comments such as "No" or "Never" signal disagreement.
To indicate degree of involvement	An attentive posture, forward leaning, and focused eye contact tell the speaker that you're involved in the conversation. An inattentive posture, backward leaning, and avoidance of eye contact communicate a lack of involvement.
To pace the speaker	Ask the speaker to slow down by raising your hand near your ear and leaning forward or to speed up by continued nodding of your head. Cue the speaker verbally by simply asking the speaker to slow down or to speed up.
To ask for clarification	Puzzled facial expressions, perhaps coupled with a forward lean, signal your need for clarification. Directly interjecting "Who?," "When?," or "Where?"

three most often used such tokens—that tell the speaker you're listening (Schegloff, 1982; Drummond & Hopper, 1993). You can communicate a variety of messages with these back-channeling cues; four such types are included in Table 9.3.

Some back-channeling cues are actually *interruptions.* These interruptions, however, are generally confirming rather than disconfirming. They tell the speaker that you're listening and are involved (Kennedy & Camden, 1988). Other interruptions are not as confirming and simply take the speaking turn away from the speaker, either temporarily or permanently. Sometimes the interrupter may apologize for breaking in and at other times may not even seem aware of interrupting.

Interruptions can serve a variety of specific functions. For example, interruptions may be used to change the topic ("I gotta tell you this story before I bust"), to correct the speaker ("You mean four months, not years, don't you?"), to seek information and perhaps interject a question of clarification ("Do you mean Jeff's cousin?"), or to introduce essential information ("Your car's on fire"). Of course, you can interrupt to end the conversation ("I hate to interrupt, but I really have to get back to the office").

Not surprisingly, research finds that superiors (bosses, supervisors) and those in positions of authority (police officers, interviewers) interrupt those in inferior positions more than the other way around (Carroll, 1994; Ashcraft, 1998). In fact, it would probably strike you as strange to see a worker repeatedly interrupting a supervisor or a student repeatedly interrupting a professor.

Another and even more often studied aspect of interruption is that of gender difference. Do men or women interrupt more? Research here is conflicting. These few re-

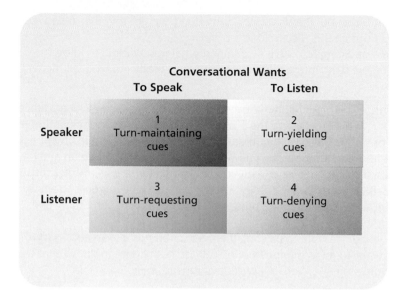

Turn Taking and Conversational Wants
Quadrant 1 represents the speaker who wishes to speak (continue to speak) and uses turn-maintaining cues; Quadrant 2 the speaker who wishes to listen and uses turn-yielding cues; Quadrant 3 the listener who wishes to speak and uses turn-requesting cues; and Quadrant 4 the listener who wishes to listen (continue listening) and uses turn-denying cues. Back-channeling cues would appear in Quadrant 4, since they're cues that listeners use while they continue to listen. Interruptions would appear in Quadrant 3, though they're not so much cues that request a turn but are actual takeovers of the speaker's position. Does this system allow for the representation of all conversational cues? Are there other types of cues that are not represented here?

search findings will give you an idea of the differing results (Pearson, West, & Turner, 1995).

- The more malelike the person's gender identity—regardless of the person's biological sex—the more likely it is that the person will interrupt (Drass, 1986).
- There are no significant differences between boys and girls (ages 2–5) in interrupting behavior (Greif, 1980).
- Fathers interrupt their children more than mothers do (Greif, 1980).
- Women more so than men judge "simultaneous talk" as being interruptions (Bresnahan & Cai, 1996).
- Men interrupt more than women do (Zimmerman & West, 1975; West & Zimmerman, 1977).
- Men and women do not differ in their interrupting behavior (Roger & Nesshoever, 1987).
- No single linguistic feature has been found that definitely identifies a message as an interruption (Coon & Schwanenflugel, 1996).

The various turn-taking cues and how they correspond to the conversational wants of speaker and listener are summarized in Figure 9.2.

Closing Conversations

Closing a conversation is often a difficult task. It can be an awkward and uncomfortable part of interpersonal interaction. Here are a few suggestions you might consider:

- Reflect back on the conversation and briefly summarize it so as to bring it to a close. For example: "I'm glad I ran into you and found out what happened at that union meeting. I'll probably be seeing you at the meetings next week."
- Directly state the desire to end the conversation and to get on with other things. For example: "I'd like to continue talking, but I really have to run. I'll see you around."

- Refer to future interaction. For example: "Why don't we get together next week sometime and continue this discussion?"
- Ask for closure. For example: "Have I explained what you wanted to know?"
- State that you enjoyed the interaction. For example: "I really enjoyed talking with you."

Closing a conversation in e-mail follows the same principles as closing a face-to-face conversation. But, exactly when you end the e-mail exchange is often not clear due in part to the absence of nonverbal cues that creates ambiguity. For example, if you ask someone a question and the other person answers, do you then e-mail again and say "thanks"? If so, should the other person e-mail you back and say "It was my pleasure"? And, if so, should you then e-mail back and say "I appreciate your willingness to answer my questions"? And, if so, should the other person then respond with something like "It was no problem"?

On the one hand, you don't want to prolong the interaction more than necessary, on the other, you don't want to appear impolite. So, how do you signal (politely) that the e-mail exchange should stop? Here are a few suggestions (Cohen, 2002).

- Include in your e-mail the notation NRN (No Reply Necessary).
- If you're replying with information the other person requested, end your message with something like "I hope this helps."
- Title or head your message FYI (For Your Information), indicating that your message is just to keep someone in the loop.
- When you make a request for information, end your message with "thank you in advance."

With any of these closings, it should be clear to the other person that you're attempting to end the conversation. Obviously, you will have to use more direct methods with those who don't take these subtle hints or don't realize that both persons are responsible for the interpersonal interaction and for bringing it to a satisfactory close.

Increasing Interpersonal Effectiveness
Expressiveness

Expressiveness refers to the skill of communicating genuine involvement, for example, taking responsibility for your thoughts and feelings, encouraging expressiveness or openness in others, and providing appropriate feedback.

Communicating Expressiveness   Here are a few suggestions for communicating expressiveness.

- *Use appropriate variations in vocal rate, pitch, volume, and rhythm to convey involvement and interest.* Use appropriate variations in verbal language, avoiding clichés and trite expressions that signal a lack of originality and personal involvement.
- *Use appropriate gestures,* especially those that focus on the other person rather than yourself. For example, maintain eye contact and lean toward the person, at the same time, avoid self-touching gestures or directing your eyes to others in the room.
- *Communicate expressiveness with cultural awareness.* Some cultures (Italian, for example) encourage expressiveness and teach children to be expressive. Other cultures (Japanese and Thai, for example) encourage a more reserved response style (Matsumoto, 1996). Some cultures (Arab and many Asian cultures, for example) consider expressiveness by women in business settings to be generally inappropriate (Lustig & Koester, 1999; Axtell, 1993; Hall & Hall, 1987).
- *Give verbal and nonverbal feedback to show that you're listening.* Such feedback—called "conversational pitchback" by one researcher—promotes relationship satisfaction (Ross, 1995).

CONVERSATIONAL PROBLEMS: PREVENTION AND REPAIR

In conversation, you may anticipate a problem and seek to prevent it. Or you may discover that you said or did something that will lead to disapproval, and you may seek to excuse yourself. Here we give just one example of a device to prevent potential conversational problems (the disclaimer) and one example of a device to repair conversational problems (the excuse). Our purpose is simply to illustrate the complexity of these processes, not to present you with an exhaustive list of the ways conversational problems may be prevented or repaired.

Preventing Conversational Problems: The Disclaimer

Let's say, for example, that you fear your listeners will at first think a comment you're about to make is inappropriate, that they may rush to judge you without hearing your full account, or will think that you're not in full possession of your faculties. In these cases, you may use some form of disclaimer. A **disclaimer** is a statement that aims to ensure that your message will be understood and will not reflect negatively on you (Hewitt & Stokes, 1975; McLaughlin, 1984). There are several types of disclaimer.

Hedging helps you to separate yourself from the message, so that if your listeners reject your message, they need not reject you (for example, "I may be wrong here, but . . ."). If the hedges are seen as indicating a lack of certainty or conviction because of some inadequacy, they decrease the attractiveness of both women and men (Wright & Hosman, 1983). However, they'll be more positively received if they're seen as indicating a lack of belief in allness (as indicating that no one can know all about any sub-

ETHICS in Interpersonal Communication

The Ethics of Pathos

Emotional appeals (called *pathos* by the classical Greek rhetoricians) are all around us. Persons who want to censor the Internet may appeal to the fear of children accessing pornographic materials; those who want to restrict the media's portrayal of violence may appeal to the fear of increased violence in your community. The real estate broker who wants to sell the overpriced condo appeals to your desire for status while the friend who wants a favor appeals to your desire for social approval. The advertiser appeals to your vanity and desire for increased sexual attractiveness and tries to sell you cosmetics and expensive clothing.

What would you do? *You want to dissuade your teenage children from engaging in sexual relationships. Would it be ethical for you to use emotional appeals to scare them so that they'll avoid sexual relationships? Would it be ethical to use the same appeals if your goal was to get them to avoid associating with teens of other races?*

You're working for an advertising agency that wants to use fear appeals to sell SUVs. Would it be ethical for you to participate in this work? Would it be ethical to use the same appeals if your motive was to discourage smoking among teenagers?

You've been hired by a religious organization that wants you to write speeches using fear appeals to get people to live their lives as this religion holds. For example, they want you to vividly depict the horrors of hell that will befall anyone who does not follow their beliefs. Would it be ethical for you to use such appeals?

ject), as well as a belief that tentative statements are all one can reasonably make (Hosman, 1989; Pearson, Turner, & Todd-Mancillas, 1991).

Credentialing helps you establish your special qualifications for saying what you're about to say ("Don't get me wrong, I'm not homophobic" or "As someone who telecommutes, I . . ."). *Sin licenses* ask listeners for permission to deviate in some way from some normally accepted convention ("I know this may not be the place to discuss business, but . . ."). *Cognitive disclaimers* help you make the case that you're in full possession of your faculties ("I know you'll think I'm crazy, but let me explain the logic of the case"). *Appeals for the suspension of judgment* ask listeners to hear you out before making a judgment ("Don't hang up on me until you hear my side of the story").

Generally, disclaimers are effective when you think you might offend listeners in telling a joke ("I don't usually like these types of jokes, but . . ."). In one study, for example, 11-year-old children were read a story about someone whose actions created negative effects. Some children heard the story with a disclaimer, and others heard the same story without the disclaimer. When the children were asked to indicate how the person should be punished, those who heard the story with the disclaimer recommended significantly lower punishments (Bennett, 1990).

Disclaimers, however, can also get you into trouble. For example, to preface remarks with "I'm no liar" may well lead listeners to think that perhaps you are lying. Also,

View point Not surprisingly, each culture has its own conversational taboos, topics that should be avoided, especially by visitors from other cultures. A few examples: In Norway avoid talk of salaries and social status; in Spain avoid the topics of family, religion, jobs, and negative comments on bullfighting; in Egypt avoid talk of Middle-Eastern politics; in Iraq avoid talk of religion and Middle-Eastern politics; in Japan avoid talking about World War II; in the Philippines avoid talk of politics, religion, corruption, and foreign aid; in Mexico avoid talking about the Mexican-American war and illegal aliens; in the Caribbean avoid discussing race, local politics, and religion (Axtell, 1993). Do you consider some topics taboo such that you do not want members of other cultures to talk about them? Why?

if you use too many disclaimers, you may be perceived as someone who doesn't have any strong convictions or as one who wants to avoid responsibility for just about everything. This seems especially true of hedges.

In responding to statements containing disclaimers, it's often necessary to respond to both the disclaimer and to the statement. By doing so, you let the speaker know that you heard the disclaimer and that you aren't going to view this communication negatively. Appropriate responses might be: "I know you're no sexist, but I don't agree that . . ." or "Well, perhaps we should discuss the money now even if it doesn't seem right."

Repairing Conversational Problems: The Excuse

At times you may say the wrong thing, but because you can't erase the message (communication really is irreversible), you may try to account for it. Perhaps the most common method for doing so is the excuse. You learn early in life that when you do something that others will view negatively, an excuse is in order to justify your performance. **Excuses,** central to all forms of communication and interaction, are "explanations or actions that lessen the negative implications of an actor's performance, thereby maintaining a positive image for oneself and others" (Snyder, 1984; Snyder, Higgins, & Stucky, 1983).

Excuses seem especially in order when you say or are accused of saying something that runs counter to what is expected, sanctioned, or considered "right" by the people with whom you're talking. Ideally, the excuse lessens the negative impact of the message.

TRY IT!
Apply your insights into excuses; go to www. ablongman.com/devito.

Some Motives for Excuse Making   The major motive for excuse making seems to be to maintain your self-esteem, to project a positive image to yourself and to others. Excuses are also offered to reduce the stress that may be created by a bad performance. You may feel that if you can offer an excuse—especially a good one that is accepted by those around you—it will reduce the negative reaction and the subsequent stress that accompanies a poor performance.

Excuses also enable you to maintain effective interpersonal relationships even after some negative behavior. For example, after criticizing a friend's behavior and observing the negative reaction to your criticism, you might offer an excuse such as, "Please forgive me; I'm really exhausted. I'm just not thinking straight." Excuses enable you to place your messages—even your possible failures—in a more favorable light.

Types of Excuses   Think of the recent excuses you have used or heard. Did they fall into any of these three classes (Snyder, 1984)?

1. **I didn't do it?** Here you deny that you have done what you're being accused of. You might then bring up an alibi to prove you couldn't have done it or perhaps you might accuse another person for doing what you're being blamed for. ("I never said that" or "I wasn't even near the place when it happened").

2. **It wasn't so bad?** Here you admit to doing it, but claim the offense was not really so bad or perhaps that there was justification for the behavior. ("I only padded the expense account and even then only modestly" or "Sure, I hit him but he was asking for it").

3. **Yes, but?** Here you claim that extenuating circumstances accounted for the behavior, for example, you weren't in control of yourself at the time or you didn't in-

tend to do what you did. ("It was the liquor talking" or "I never intended to hurt him; I was actually trying to help").

Good and Bad Excuses   The most important question for most people is what makes a good excuse and what makes a bad excuse (Snyder, 1984; Slade, 1995). How can you make good excuses and thus get out of problems, and how can you avoid bad excuses and thus only make matters worse? Good excuse makers use excuses in moderation; bad excuse makers rely on excuses too often. Good excuse makers avoid blaming others, especially those they work with; bad excuse makers blame even their work colleagues. In a similar way, good excuse makers don't attribute their failure to others or to the company; bad excuse makers do. Good excuse makers acknowledge their own responsibility for the failure by noting that they did something wrong (not that they lack competence); bad excuse makers refuse to accept any responsibility for their failures.

The best excuses contain five elements (Slade, 1995; Coleman, 2002).

1. You demonstrate that you really understand the problem and that your partner's feelings are legitimate and justified. Avoid minimizing the issue or your partner's feelings ("It was only $100; you're overreacting," "I was only two hours late").
2. You acknowledge your responsibility. Avoid qualifying your responsibility ("I'm sorry *if* I did anything wrong") or expressing a lack of sincerity ("Okay, I'm sorry; it's obviously my fault—*again*").
3. You acknowledge your own displeasure at what you did; make it clear that you're not happy with yourself for having done what you did.
4. You request forgiveness for what you did; be specific.
5. You make it clear that this will never happen again.

Table 9.4 provides examples of excuses you might use in romantic and business situations.

Table 9.4   **Excuses in Romantic and Workplace Relationships**
Here are the five intended messages along with some specific examples. As you read this table visualize a specific situation in which you recently made an excuse. Can what you said (or should have said) be organized into this five-step plan?

Intended Message	In Romantic Relationships	At Work
1. I see.	I should have asked you first; you have a right to be angry.	I understand that we lost the client because of this.
2. I did it.	I was totally responsible.	I should have acted differently.
3. I'm sorry.	I'm sorry that I didn't ask you first.	I'm sorry I didn't familiarize myself with the client's objections to our last offer.
4. Forgive me.	Forgive me?	I'd really like another chance.
5. I'll do better.	I'll never loan anyone money without first discussing it with you.	This will never happen again.

REVIEWING Key Terms and Concepts in Conversation

This chapter reviewed the process of conversation and focused on its stages, rules and principles for effective management, and conversational problems.

The Conversation Process

What are the major stages in conversation?

- The *opening* initiates and begins the conversation.
- The *feedforward* previews or prefaces the major part of the conversation that is to follow.
- The *business* is the major part of the conversation; it's the reason for the conversation.
- The *feedback* summarizes or reflects back on the conversation.
- The *closing* brings the conversation to an end.

Conversational Management

How do you go about initiating, maintaining, and closing conversations so that they're effective and satisfying?

- Initiating conversations is often accomplished with self-references, other-references, relational references, and context references.
- Maintaining conversations depends on the principle of cooperation; the maxims of quantity, quality, relation, and manner; the principle of dialogue; and the principle of turn taking.
- Closing conversations is often accomplished by reflecting back on the conversation, directly stating the desire to end the conversation, referring to future interactions, asking for closure, and expressing pleasure with interaction.

Conversational Problems: Prevention and Repair

How might conversational problems be prevented and repaired?

- Preventing conversational problems may be aided by the disclaimer, a statement that helps to ensure that your message will be understood and will not reflect negatively on the speaker. Disclaimer types include hedging, credentialing, sin licenses, cognitive disclaimers, and appeals for the suspension of judgment.
- Conversational repair is often accomplished with the excuse, an explanation designed to lessen the negative impact of a speaker's messages. Excuses generally come in three types: *I didn't do it, It wasn't so bad,* and *Yes, but.*

APPLYING Key Terms and Concepts in Conversation

1. How would conversational openers for friendships differ from those for romantic relationships?
2. Does your experience agree with or disagree with Chris Kleinke's conclusions about how men and women use and respond to opening lines?
3. Can you give examples to illustrate the importance of the general skills of mindfulness, flexibility, cultural sensitivity,

and metacommunication from your own conversation experiences?

4. Visit a chat room and lurk for 5 to 10 minutes. What characterizes the conversation in the chat room you observed? What is the topic of conversation? What is the most obvious purpose of the group?
5. After the World Trade Center and Pentagon attacks comedian Bill Maher criticized the use of "cowardly" to define those who committed these acts. "We have been the cowards lobbing cruise missiles from 2,000 miles away. . . . Staying in the airplane when it hits the building, say what you want about it, that's not cowardly." As a result Sears and FedEx cancelled their ads and various ABC affiliates suspended the program. Actually, as *BusinessWeek Online* (September 26, 2001) notes, Maher was not making a case for the terrorists. On Jay Leno's *Tonight Show,* Maher excused his comments, saying that he was not implying that the U.S. military was cowardly but that he was simply angry at policymakers for not letting our military personnel do their jobs. What do you think of this excuse? If you were Maher and on the *Tonight Show,* what would you have said?
6. If you were compiling excuses for a book called *The World's Worst Excuses,* which ones would you include? Which would you include in *The World's Best Excuses?*
7. How sensitive are you to the back-channeling cues of others? How sensitive are others to your own back-channeling cues? Explain.
8. Blind and sighted people make use of the same vocal and verbal cues in managing a conversation, but the blind make little use of touch cues, postural shifts, and gestures (Sharkey & Stafford, 1990). What implications can you draw from this finding for improving communication between blind and sighted persons? In this connection, you may wish to revisit Table 1.2 on communication between blind and sighted persons.

EXPERIENCING Key Terms and Concepts in Conversation

Go to www.ablongman.com/devito.

This group of experiences deals with the conversation process and with a special type of conversational situation, namely communicating emotions.

(1) **How Do You Open a Conversation?** and (2) **How Do You Close a Conversation?** provide practice in beginning and ending conversations effectively. (3) **Conversational Analysis: A Chance Meeting** provides a dialogue that you can analyze for the elements and principles of conversation covered in this chapter. (4) **Giving and Taking Directions** is a game-like experience that will illustrate the difficulties in giving and taking directions and how these difficult communication situations can be made more effective. (5) **Communicating Your Emotions,** (6) **Expressing Negative Feelings,** (7) **Communicating Emotions Effectively,** and (8) **Emotional Advice** provide experience in communicating your emotions to others. (9)

Gender and the Topics of Conversation looks at gender differences in conversation. (10) **Responding Effectively in Conversation** and (11) **The Qualities of Effectiveness** are summary-type exercises that provide the opportunity to apply the qualities of effectiveness that you've already encountered to conversation. (12) **Formulating Excuses** provides practice in developing and expressing excuses.

RESEARCHING with Research Navigator   Key Terms and Concepts in Conversation

Go to http://www.researchnavigator.com.

Reading an article.

Read a popular or scholarly article on the conversation process, conversational problems, or conversational effectiveness. On the basis of this article what can you add to the discussion presented here?

Investigating key terms.

Investigate one of the key terms discussed in this chapter (for example, conversation, disclaimer, excuse, conversational turns, opening lines, conversational maxims, or diffusion of innovations). What additional insights can you provide?

Finding answers.

Try finding answers to one of the following questions or design a research study to answer it.

■ How are people who violate conversational maxims perceived?

■ Are people who give lots of back-channeling cues perceived in the same way as people who give few or no back-channeling cues?

■ How might disclaimers increase the perception of the user's credibility?

■ Do men and women use the same kinds of excuses?

■ Do happy and unhappy couples use the same kinds of disclaimers and excuses?

10 Universals of Interpersonal Relationships

Monster's Ball (2001)

Communication is to a relationship what breathing is to maintaining life.

—Virginia Satir

Characteristics of Interpersonal Relationships
Stages in Interpersonal Relationships
Relationships in a Context of Culture and Technology

The close interconnection between culture and interpersonal relationships, especially the role of racism, is seen in Monster's Ball, *as it explores the relationship between Hank (Billy Bob Thornton) and Leticia (Halle Berry). In addition to culture, interpersonal relationships are influenced by a wide variety of other factors, many of which we explore in this chapter. In addition, we consider the way in which interpersonal relationships develop and change.*

Contact with other human beings is so important that when you're deprived of it for long periods, depression sets in, self-doubt surfaces, and you may find it difficult to manage even the basics of daily life. Research shows clearly that the most important contributor to happiness—outranking money, job, and sex—is a close relationship with one other person (Freedman, 1978; Laroche & deGrace, 1997; Lu & Shih, 1997). The desire for relationships is universal; they're important to men and to women, to homosexuals and to heterosexuals, to young and to old (Huston & Schwartz, 1995).

CHARACTERISTICS OF INTERPERSONAL RELATIONSHIPS

Relationships may be viewed on a continuum, from the impersonal at one end to highly personal (that is, interpersonal) at the other end. Interpersonal relationships are those that exist between people who are interdependent, where one person's behavior has a significant impact on the other person. We can distinguish interpersonal relationships from impersonal relationships on the basis of three main factors: psychological data, explanatory knowledge, and personally established rules.

Psychological Data

In impersonal relationships, people respond to each other chiefly as members of the class or group to which each belongs. For example, initially you respond to a particular college professor as you respond to college professors in general. Similarly, the college professor responds to you as he or she responds to students generally. As your relationship becomes more personal, however, both of you begin to respond to each other not as members of groups but as unique individuals. Put differently, in impersonal relationships, the social or cultural role of the person governs your interaction, while in personal or interpersonal relationships, the psychological uniqueness of the person tells you how to interact.

This progression from social to psychological data happens in the United States and in most European cultures. In many Asian and African cultures, however, the individual's group membership is always important; it never recedes into the background. Thus, in these cultures, one's group membership (one's social data)—even in the closest intimate relationships—is always important, often more important than one's individual or psychological characteristics (Moghaddam, Taylor, & Wright, 1993).

Explanatory Knowledge

In impersonal relationships, you can do little more than *describe* a person or a person's way of communicating. As you get to know someone a bit better, you can *predict* his or her behavior. If you get to know the person even better, you'll become able to *explain* the behavior. The college professor, in an impersonal relationship, may be able to describe, say, your lateness and perhaps also predict that you'll be five minutes late to class each Friday. In an interpersonal situation, however, the professor can go beyond these levels to explain the behavior—in this case, give reasons why you're late.

Personally Established Rules

In impersonal relationships, the rules of interaction are set down by social norms. Students and professors behave toward one another—in impersonal situations—according to the social norms established by their culture and society. However, as the relationship between student and professor becomes interpersonal, the social rules no longer totally regulate the interaction. Student and professor begin to establish rules of their own largely because they begin to see each other as unique individuals rather than merely as members of the social groups "student" and "professor."

A good way to begin the study of interpersonal relationships is to examine your own relationships (past, present, or those you look forward to) by taking the self-test "What Do Your Relationships Do for You?" It highlights the advantages and the disadvantages that relationships serve.

TEST YOURSELF   *What Do Your Relationships Do for You?*

Focus on your own relationships in general (friendship, romantic, family, and work) or focus on one particular relationship (say, your life partner, your child, or your best friend) or focus on one type of relationship (say, friendships) and respond to the following by indicating the extent to which your relationship(s) serve each of these functions. Use a 10-point scale with "1" indicating that your relationship(s) never serves this function, "10" indicating that your relationship(s) always serves this function, and the numbers in between indicating levels between these extremes.

_____ 1. My relationships help to lessen my loneliness.
_____ 2. My relationships put uncomfortable pressure on me to expose my vulnerabilities.
_____ 3. My relationships help me to secure stimulation (intellectual, physical, and emotional).
_____ 4. My relationships increase my obligations.
_____ 5. My relationships help me gain in self-knowledge and in self-esteem.
_____ 6. My relationships prevent me from developing other relationships.
_____ 7. My relationships help enhance my physical and emotional health.
_____ 8. My relationships scare me because they may be difficult to dissolve.
_____ 9. My relationships maximize my pleasures and minimize my pains.
_____ 10. My relationships hurt me.

▶ **How did you do?**   The numbers from 1–10 that you used to respond to each statement should give you some idea of how strongly your relationships serve these advantages. The odd-numbered statements (1, 3, 5, 7, and 9) express what most people would consider advantages of interpersonal relationships.

(1) One of the major benefits of relationships is that they help to lessen loneliness (Rokach, 1998; Rokach & Brock, 1995). They make you feel that someone cares, that someone likes you, that someone will protect you, that someone ultimately will love you.

(3) As plants are *heliotropic* and orient themselves to light, humans are *stimulotropic* and orient themselves to sources of stimulation (Davis, 1973). Human contact is one of the best ways to secure this stimulation—intellectual, physical, and emotional.

(5) Through contact with others you learn about yourself and see yourself from different perspectives and in different roles, as a child or parent, as a coworker, as a manager, as a best friend. Healthy interpersonal relationships help enhance self-esteem and self-worth. Simply having a friend or romantic partner (at least most of the time) makes you feel desirable and worthy.

(7) Research consistently shows that interpersonal relationships contribute significantly to physical and emotional health (Rosen, 1998; Goleman, 1995a; Rosengren et al., 1993; Pennebacker, 1991) and to personal happiness (Berscheid & Reis, 1998). Without close interpersonal relationships you're more likely to become depressed and this depression, in turn, contributes significantly to physical illness. Isolation, in fact, contributes as much to mortality as high blood pressure, high cholesterol, obesity, smoking, or lack of physical exercise (Goleman, 1995a).

(9) The most general function served by interpersonal relationships, and one that encompasses all the others, is that of maximizing pleasure and minimizing pain. Your good friends, for example, will make you feel even better about your good fortune and less hurt when you're confronted with hardships.

The even-numbered statements (2, 4, 6, 8, and 10) express what most people consider disadvantages of interpersonal relationships:

(2) Close relationships put pressure on you to reveal yourself and to expose your vulnerabilities. While this is generally worthwhile in the context of a supporting and caring relationship, it may backfire if the relationship deteriorates and these weaknesses are used against you.

(4) Close relationships increase your obligations to these other people, sometimes to great extents. Your time is no longer entirely your own. And although you enter relationships to spend more time with these special people, you also incur time (and perhaps financial) obligations with which you may not be happy.

(6) Close relationships can result in abandoning other relationships. Sometimes, it involves someone you like but your partner can't stand. More often, however, it's simply a matter of time and energy; relationships take a lot of both and you have less to give to these other and less intimate relationships.

(8) The closer your relationship, the more emotionally difficult it is to dissolve, a feeling that may be uncomfortable for some people. If the relationship is deteriorating, you might feel distress or depression. In some cultures, for example, religious pressures may prevent married couples from separating. And, if lots of money is involved, dissolving a relationship can often mean giving up the fortune you've spent your life accumulating.

(10) And, of course, your partner may break your heart. Your partner may leave you—against all your pleading and promises. Your hurt will be in proportion to how much you care and need your partner. If you care a great deal, you're likely to experience great hurt; if you care less, the hurt will be less—it's one of life's little ironies.

WEB EXPLORATION
To learn more about advantages and disadvantages of interpersonal relationships, go to www.ablongman.com/devito.

▶ **What will you do?** One way to use this self-test is to consider how you might lessen the disadvantages of your interpersonal relationships, at least those disadvantages that you indicate are always or almost always present in your relationships. Consider, for example, if your own behaviors are contributing to the disadvantages. For example, do you bury yourself in one or two relationships and discourage the development of others? At the same time, consider how you can maximize the advantages that your relationships currently serve. ●

STAGES IN INTERPERSONAL RELATIONSHIPS

You and another person don't become intimate friends immediately upon meeting. Rather, you build an intimate relationship gradually, through a series of steps or stages.

The same is true of most relationships. The "love at first sight" phenomenon creates a problem for a stage model of relationships. So rather than argue that such love cannot occur (my own feeling is that it can and frequently does), it seems wiser to claim that the stage model characterizes most relationships for most people most of the time.

Within each relationship and within each relationship stage, there are dynamic tensions between several opposites. The assumption made by this theory—called **relationship dialectics theory**—is that all relationships can be defined by a series of opposites. For example, some research has found three such opposites (Baxter, 1988, 1990; Baxter & Simon, 1993). The tension between *autonomy and connection* expresses your desire to remain an individual but also to intimately connect to another person and to a relationship. This theme appears in women's magazines and seems to teach readers to want both autonomy and connection (Prusank, Duran, & DeLillo, 1993). The tension between *novelty and predictability* centers on the dual desires for newness and adventure on the one hand and sameness and comfortableness on the other. The tension between *closedness and openness* relates to the desires to be in an exclusive relationship and one that is open to different people. The closedness–openness tension is more in evidence during the early stages of relationship development. Autonomy–connection and novelty–predictability are more a factor as the relationship progresses.

The six-stage model in Figure 10.1 describes the main stages in most relationships. For a particular relationship, you might wish to modify the basic model. But as a general

TRY IT!
Apply your insights into interpersonal relationships; go to **www.ablongman.com/devito**.

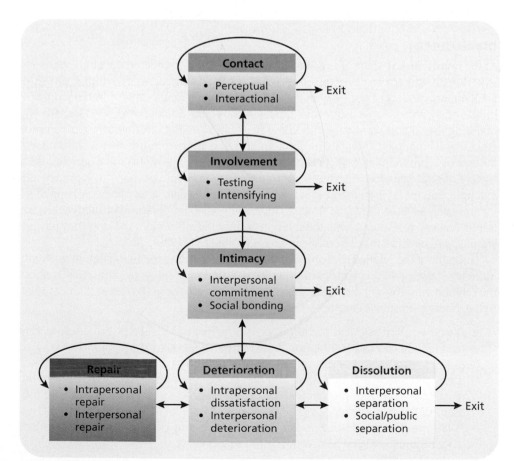

Figure
10.1

A Six-Stage Model of Relationships
Because relationships differ so widely, it's best to think of any relationship model as a tool for talking about relationships rather than as a specific map that indicates how you move from one relationship position to another. Can you identify other steps or stages that would further explain what goes on in relationship development? What happens when the two people in a relationship experience the stages differently? Can you provide an example from literature or from your own experience?

description of relationship development, the stages seem fairly standard. Do realize, of course, that both partners may not perceive their relationship in the same way; one person, for example, may see the relationship as an intimate one but the other may not.

The six stages of relationships are contact, involvement, intimacy, deterioration, repair, and dissolution. Each stage has an early and a late phase. These stages describe relationships as they are; they don't evaluate or prescribe how relationships should be.

Contact

At the initial phase of the **contact** stage, there is some kind of *perceptual contact*—you see, hear, and perhaps smell the person. From this you get a physical picture—sex, approximate age, height, and so on. After this perception, there is usually *interactional contact.* Here the contact is superficial and relatively impersonal. This is the stage at which you exchange basic information that is preliminary to any more intense involvement ("Hello, my name is Joe"). Here you initiate interaction ("May I join you?") and engage in invitational communication ("May I buy you a drink?"). According to some researchers, it's at this stage—within the first four minutes of initial interaction—that you decide whether you want to pursue the relationship (Zunin & Zunin, 1972).

At the contact stage, physical appearance is especially important because it's the most readily seen. Yet through verbal and nonverbal behaviors, qualities such as friendliness, warmth, openness, and dynamism are also revealed.

Involvement

At the **involvement** stage, a sense of mutuality, of being connected develops. Here you experiment and try to learn more about the other person. At the initial phase of involvement, a kind of *testing* goes on. You want to see whether your initial judgment proves reasonable. So you may ask questions: "Where do you work?" "What are you majoring in?" If you want to get to know the person even better, you might continue your involvement by intensifying your interaction by beginning to reveal yourself, though in a preliminary way. In a dating relationship, you might, for example, use a variety of strategies to help you move to the next stage and perhaps to intimacy. For example, you might increase contact with your partner; give your partner tokens of affection such as gifts, cards, or flowers; increase your own personal attractiveness; do things that suggest intensifying the relationship, such as flirting or making your partner jealous; and become more sexually intimate (Tolhuizen, 1989).

Throughout the relationship process, but especially during the involvement and early intimacy stages, you test your partner; you try to find out how your partner feels about the relationship. Among the strategies you might use are these (Baxter & Wilmot, 1984; Bell & Buerkel-Rothfuss, 1990):

- *Directness.* You ask your partner directly how he or she feels, or you disclose your own feelings on the assumption that your partner will also self-disclose.
- *Indirect suggestion.* For example, you joke about a shared future together, touch more intimately, or hint that you're serious about the relationship. Similar responses from your partner will mean that he or she wishes to increase the intimacy of the relationship.
- *Public presentation.* For example, you introduce your partner as your "boyfriend" or "girlfriend" and see how your partner responds.

- *Separation.* You separate yourself physically to see how the other person responds. If your partner calls, then you know he or she is interested in the relationship.
- *Third party.* You ask mutual friends about your partner's feelings and intentions.

Intimacy

At the **intimacy** stage, you commit yourself still further to the other person and establish a relationship in which this individual becomes your best or closest friend, lover, or companion. You also come to share each other's social networks, a practice followed by members of widely different cultures (Gao & Gudykunst, 1995). Not surprisingly, your relationship satisfaction also increases with the move to this stage (Siavelis & Lamke, 1992). One research study defined intimacy as the feeling that you could be honest and open when talking about yourself, your thoughts, and your feelings that you don't reveal in other relationships (Mackey, Diemer, & O'Brien, 2000).

The intimacy stage usually divides itself into two phases. In the *interpersonal commitment* phase the two people commit themselves to each other in a private way. In the *social bonding* phase the commitment is made public—perhaps to family and friends, perhaps to the public at large. Here you and your partner become a unit, an identifiable pair.

When the intimacy stage involves a lifetime partnership, you face three main anxieties (Zimmer, 1986). A *security anxiety* leads you to worry that your partner may leave you for someone else or that he or she will be sexually unfaithful. A *fulfillment anxiety* leads to concerns that you may not be able to achieve a close, warm, and special rapport or that you won't be able to have an equal relationship. An *excitement anxiety* makes you worry that boredom and routine may set in or that you'll lose your freedom and become trapped.

Of course, not everyone strives for intimacy (Bartholomew, 1990; Thelen, Sherman, & Borst, 1998; Bumby & Hansen, 1997). Some are so fearful of the consequences of intimacy that they actively avoid it. Others dismiss intimacy and defensively deny their need for more and deeper interpersonal contact. And still others, of course, are happy without an intimate relationship.

 Some cultures consider sexual relationships to be undesirable outside of marriage; others consider it a normal part of intimacy and chastity as undesirable. Intercultural researchers (Hatfield & Rapson, 1996, p. 36) recall a meeting where colleagues from Sweden and the United States were discussing ways of preventing AIDS. When members from the United States suggested teaching abstinence, Swedish members asked, "How will teenagers ever learn to become loving, considerate sexual partners if they don't practice?" "The silence that greeted the question," note the researchers, "was the sound of two cultures clashing." How have your cultural beliefs and values influenced what you consider appropriate relationship behavior?

Intimacy and Risk   To some people, relational intimacy is extremely risky. To others, it involves only low risk.

Consider your own view of relationship risk by responding to the following questions.

1. Is it dangerous to get really close to people?
2. Are you afraid to get really close to someone because you might get hurt?
3. Do you find it difficult to trust other people?
4. Do you believe that the most important thing to consider in a relationship is whether you might get hurt?

People who answer "yes" to these and similar questions see intimacy as involving considerable risk (Pilkington & Richardson, 1988). Such people have fewer close friends, are less likely to have a romantic relationship, have less trust in others, have a low level of dating assertiveness, have lower self-esteem, are more possessive and jealous in their love, and are generally less sociable and extroverted than those who see intimacy as involving little risk (Pilkington & Woods, 1999). And, not surprisingly, comfort with risk taking has been found to be common to those people who made mid-life career changes (Ingram, 1998).

Intimacy and Social Penetration   As you progress from contact through involvement to intimacy, you can see that the number of topics you talk about (***breadth***) and the degree of "personalness" with which you pursue them (***depth***) increase (Altman & Taylor, 1973; Hensley, 1996). Such increases are influenced greatly by attitude similarity; when you perceive attitude similarity between yourself and another person, you're more likely to increase social penetration than if you didn't see this similarity (Hammer, 1986). Visualize an individual as a circle divided into various parts (to represent the topics of interpersonal communication or the breadth of the relationship) and into layers (to represent the degree of personalness with which you talk or the depth of the relationship). For illustration, see Figure 10.2. Each circle in the figure contains eight topic areas to depict breadth (identified A through H) and five levels of intimacy to depict depth (represented by the concentric circles). Note that in circle 1, only three topic areas are penetrated. Of these, two are penetrated only to the first level and one to the second. In this type of interaction, three topic areas are discussed, and only at rather superficial levels. This is the type of relationship you might have with an ac-

Figure 10.2

Models of Social Penetration
How accurately do the concepts of breadth and depth express your communication in relationships of different intensities? Can you identify other aspects of messages that change as you go from talking to an acquaintance, to a friend, or to an intimate?

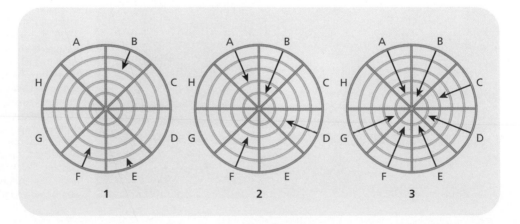

quaintance. Circle 2 represents a more intense relationship, one that has greater breadth and depth, more topics are discussed and to deeper levels of penetration. This is the type of relationship you might have with a friend. Circle 3 represents a still more intense relationship. Here there is considerable breadth (seven of the eight areas are penetrated) and depth (most of the areas are penetrated to the deepest levels). This is the type of relationship you might have with a lover or a parent.

All relationships—friendships, loves, families—may be described in terms of breadth and depth, concepts that are central to the **social penetration theory** (Altman & Taylor, 1973). In its initial stage, a relationship is normally characterized by narrow breadth (few topics are discussed) and shallow depth (the topics are discussed only superficially). As the relationship grows in intensity and intimacy, breadth and depth increase. Equally important, these increases are seen as comfortable, normal, and natural progressions. At the same time, your communication becomes more personalized, more synchronized, and easier (Gudykunst, Nishida, & Chua, 1987).

Deterioration

The **relationship deterioration** stage is characterized by a weakening of the bonds between the friends or lovers. The first phase of deterioration is usually *intrapersonal dissatisfaction:* You begin to experience personal dissatisfaction with everyday interactions and begin to view the future with your partner more negatively. If this dissatisfaction grows, you pass to the second phase, *interpersonal deterioration.* You withdraw and grow further and further apart. You share less of your free time. When you're together,

ETHICS in Interpersonal Communication

Your Obligation to Reveal Yourself

At some point in a relationship, an ethical issue arises as to your obligation to reveal information about yourself. After all, if you're in a close relationship your influence on each other is considerable and so you may have an obligation to reveal certain things about yourself. And, conversely you may feel that the other person—because he or she is so close to you—has an ethical obligation to reveal certain information to you.

What would you do? *At what point—if any—do you feel you have an ethical obligation to reveal each of the 10 items of information listed here? Use numbers from 1 to 10 to indicate at what point you would feel your romantic partner or friend has a right to know this information about you by visualizing a relationship as existing on a continuum from initial contact at 1 to extreme intimacy at 10. If you feel you would never have the obligation to reveal this information use 0. As you respond to these items, consider what gives one person the right to know personal information about another person.*

Romantic Partner	Friend	At what point do you have an ethical obligation to reveal:
_____	_____	1. Age
_____	_____	2. History of family genetic disorders
_____	_____	3. HIV status
_____	_____	4. Past sexual experiences
_____	_____	5. Marital history
_____	_____	6. Annual salary, net financial worth
_____	_____	7. Affectional orientation
_____	_____	8. Attitudes toward other races and nationalities
_____	_____	9. Religious beliefs
_____	_____	10. Past criminal activity or incarceration

there are awkward silences, fewer disclosures, less physical contact, and a lack of psychological closeness. Conflicts become more common and their resolution more difficult.

When a relationship begins to deteriorate, the breadth and depth (which increase as the relationship becomes more intimate) will often reverse themselves—a process of **depenetration,** sometimes referred to as the *reversal hypothesis*. For example, in the process of terminating a relationship, you might eliminate certain topics from your interpersonal interactions and at the same time discuss acceptable topics in less depth. You might reduce the level of your disclosure, revealing less and less of your inner feelings. This reversal does not always occur (Baxter, 1983). There is some evidence to show, for example, that, among friends, although depth decreases in the early stages of deterioration, it may later increase (Tolhuizen, 1986).

Relationship deterioration involves special communication patterns. These patterns are in part a response to the deterioration; you communicate the way you do because you feel that your relationship is in trouble. However, these patterns are also causative: The communication patterns you use largely determine the fate of your relationship. Here are a few communication patterns that are seen during relationship deterioration.

- *Withdrawal.* Nonverbally, withdrawal is seen in the greater space you need and the speed with which tempers and other signs of disturbance arise when that space is invaded. Other nonverbal signs of withdrawal include a decrease in eye contact, and touching, less similarity in clothing, and fewer displays of items associated with the other person, for example, bracelets, photographs, and rings (Miller & Parks, 1982; Knapp & Vangelisti, 2000). Verbally, withdrawal is marked by a decreased desire to talk and especially to listen. At times, small talk is used not as a preliminary to serious conversation but as an alternative, perhaps to avoid confronting the serious issues.

- *Decline in self-disclosure.* Self-disclosing communications decline significantly. If the relationship is dying, you may think it not worth the effort. Or you might limit your self-disclosures because you feel that the other person may not accept them or can no longer be trusted to be supportive and empathic.

- *Deception.* Deception increases as relationships break down. Sometimes this takes the form of clear-cut lies that may be used to avoid arguments over such things as staying out all night, not calling, or being seen in the wrong place with the wrong person. At other times, lies may be used because of a feeling of shame; you might not want the other person to think less of you. One of the problems with deception is that it has a way of escalating, eventually creating a climate of distrust and disbelief.

- *Positive and negative messages.* During deterioration, there's an increase in negative and a decrease in positive messages. Where once you praised the other's behaviors, you now criticize them. Often the behaviors have not changed significantly; what has changed is your way of looking at them. What was once a cute habit now becomes annoying; what was once "different" now becomes inconsiderate. When a relationship is deteriorating, requests for pleasurable behaviors decrease ("Will you fix me my favorite dessert?") while requests to stop unpleasant or negative behaviors increase ("Will you stop monopolizing the phone?") (Lederer, 1984). Even the social niceties that accompany requests get lost as they deteriorate from "Would you please make me a cup of coffee, honey?" to "Get me some coffee, will you?" to "Where's my coffee?"

Repair

The **relationship repair** stage is optional; some relational partners may pause during deterioration and try to repair their relationship. Others, however, may progress—without stopping, without thinking—to dissolution.

At the first repair phase, *intrapersonal repair,* you analyze what went wrong and consider ways of solving your relational difficulties. You might at this stage consider changing your behaviors or perhaps changing your expectations of your partner. You might also evaluate the rewards of your relationship as it is now and the rewards to be gained if your relationship ended.

Should you decide that you want to repair your relationship, you might discuss this with your partner at the *interpersonal repair* phase—the problems in the relationship, the changes you want to see, and perhaps what you'd be willing to do and what you'd want your partner to do. This is the stage of negotiating new agreements and new behaviors. You and your partner might try to repair your relationship by yourselves, by seeking the advice of friends or family, or perhaps going for professional counseling.

Dissolution

At the **relationship dissolution** stage, the bonds between the individuals are broken. In the beginning, it usually takes the form of *interpersonal separation,* in which you might move into separate apartments and begin to lead lives apart from each other. If this separation proves acceptable and if the original relationship isn't repaired, you enter the phase of *social or public separation.* If the relationship is a marriage, this phase corresponds to divorce. In some cases, the former partners change the definition of their relationship, and, for example, the "ex-lovers" become "friends" or "business partners." Avoidance of each other and a return to being "single" are among the primary characteristics of dissolution.

Increasing Interpersonal Effectiveness
Positiveness

Positiveness in interpersonal communication refers to the use of positive rather than negative messages. For example, instead of the negative "I wish you wouldn't ignore my opinions," consider the value of the positive alternative: "I feel good when you ask my opinions." Instead of the negative "You look horrible in stripes" consider the value of the positive: "I think you look great in solid colors."

Communicating Positiveness   Here are just a few suggestions for communicating positiveness. This may be a bit easier for women than for men because women generally are more apt to express positiveness in their evaluations in both face-to-face and computer-mediated communication (Adrianson, 2001).

Look for the positive in the person or in the person's work and compliment it. Compliment specifics;

overly general compliments ("Your project was interesting") are rarely as effective as those that are specific and concrete ("Your proposal will be a great financial saving").

■ Express satisfaction when communicating with others by, for example, using facial expressions, maintaining a reasonably but appropriate close distance, and focusing eye contact and avoiding glancing away from the other person for long periods of time.

■ Express positiveness with a recognition of cultural differences (Dresser, 1996; Chen, 1992). For example, in the United States it's considered appropriate for a supervisor to compliment a worker for doing an exceptional job. But in other cultures (collectivist cultures, for example) this would be considered inappropriate because it singles out one individual and separates that person from the group.

Dissolution is also the stage during which the ex-partners begin to look upon themselves as individuals rather than halves of a pair. They try to establish a new and different life, either alone or with another person. Some people, it's true, continue to live psychologically with a relationship that has already been dissolved; they frequent old meeting places, reread old love letters, daydream about all the good times, and fail to extricate themselves from a relationship that has died in every way except in their memory.

In cultures that emphasize continuity from one generation to the next and where being "old-fashioned" is evaluated positively—as in, say, China—interpersonal relationships are likely to be long lasting and permanent. Those who maintain long-term relationships will be rewarded and those who break relationships will be punished. But in cultures where change is seen as positive and being old-fashioned as negative—as in, say, the United States—interpersonal relationships are likely to be more temporary (Moghaddam, Taylor, & Wright, 1993). Here the rewards for long-term relationships and the punishments for broken relationships will be significantly less.

Movement among the Stages

Notice that Figure 10.1 contains three different types of arrows. The exit arrows indicate that each stage offers the opportunity to exit the relationship. After saying hello, you can say good-bye and exit. The vertical or movement arrows between stages represent the fact that you can move to another stage, either a more intense one (say, from involvement to intimacy) or a less intense one (say, from intimacy to deterioration). You can also go back to a previously established stage. For example, you may have established an intimate relationship with someone but don't want to maintain it at that level. You want it to be less intense. So you may go back to the involvement stage and reestablish the relationship at that more comfortable level (Masheter & Harris, 1986). The self-reflexive arrows—the arrows that loop back to the beginning of the same level or stage—signify that any relationship may become stabilized at any point. You may, for example, maintain a relationship at the intimate level without its deteriorating or returning to the less intense stage of involvement. Or you might remain at the "Hello, how are you?" stage—the contact stage—without ever getting any further involved.

WEB EXPLORATION
To learn more about relationships and culture, go to **www.ablongman. com/devito**.

A S K *the Researcher*

Arguing Productively

My life partner and I seem to argue about the littlest things, and all these little arguments are causing major dissatisfaction, at least on my part. What can I do to put an end to these petty arguments?

Sometimes people in a relationship don't know how to discuss things that upset them or they're afraid to raise those issues because they fear doing so would end their relationship. Often people who can't or won't express these feelings openly express them indirectly in what is called a passive-aggressive communication style. Petty arguments can then arise over spending, driving skills, anything but the real feelings.

If this is your situation, first assure your partner of your commitment to the relationship and then model constructive conflict resolution behaviors by sharing your emotions and asking to discuss relationship issues. Consider saying, "I value our relationship. When you criticize my driving I really worry that our relationship is in jeopardy. Even though it's hard to do, I want to work on any relationship issues that we might have because I love you. Is there anything on your mind about us that's worrying you?"

Fred E. Jandt (Ph.D., Bowling Green State University) is a professor of communication at California State University, San Bernardino, where he teaches courses in mediation and conflict and in intercultural communication. He is the author of *Win-Win Negotiating: Turning Conflict into Agreement*. fjandt@csusb.edu (Reprinted by permission of Dr Fred E. Jandt.)

View point   Throughout the life of a relationship, there exist "turning points," those jumps or leaps that project you from one relationship level to another. Do men and women see turning points in the same way? For example, which turning points are most important to women? Which are most important to men?

Movement through the various stages is usually a gradual process; you don't jump from contact to involvement to intimacy. Rather, you progress gradually, a few degrees at a time. Yet there are leaps that must and do take place. For example, during the involvement stage of a romantic relationship, the first kiss or the first sexual encounter requires a leap. It requires a change in the kind of communication and in the kind of intimacy experienced by the two people. Before you take these leaps, you probably first test the waters. Before the first kiss, for example, you may hold each other, look longingly into each other's eyes, and perhaps caress each other's face. You might do this (in part) to discover if the leap—the kiss, for example—will be met with a favorable response. No one wants rejection—especially of romantic advances. These major jumps or turning points provide an interesting perspective on how relationships develop. Table 10.1 presents the five most frequently reported turning points in romantic relationships among college students (Baxter & Bullis, 1986).

Table 10.1   Turning Points in Romantic Relationships

Can you identify similar turning points in your own relationships? What turning points were most important to you? If you're in a close relationship now, ask your partner to identify the five most important turning points as he or she sees them and see if these match your own. This table is based on research by Baxter and Bullis (1986).

Turning Point	Examples
Getting-to-know time	The first meeting, the time spent together studying, the first date
Quality time	Meeting the family or getting away together
Physical separation	Separations due to vacations or trips (not to breakups)
External competition	The presence of a new or old rival and demands that compete for relationship time
Reunion	Getting back together after physical separation

RELATIONSHIPS IN A CONTEXT OF CULTURE AND TECHNOLOGY

The research and theory discussed here and in the next two chapters derive in great part from research conducted in the United States and on heterosexual couples. This research and the corresponding theory reflect the way most heterosexual relationships are viewed in the United States. Although we paused periodically to note cultural differences, it's helpful to bring the influence of culture together now that we've covered a major part of our relationship discussion.

Relationships and Culture

For example, it's assumed in the model and in the discussion of relationship development that you voluntarily choose your relationship partners. You consciously choose to pursue certain relationships and not others. In some cultures, however, your romantic partner is chosen for you by your parents. In some cases, your husband or wife is chosen to solidify two families or to bring some financial advantage to your family or village. An arrangement such as this may have been entered into by your parents when you were an infant or even before you were born. In most cultures, of course, there's pressure to marry "the right" person and to be friends with certain people and not others.

In the United States, researchers study and textbook authors write about dissolving relationships and how to survive relationship breakups. It's assumed that you have the right to exit an undesirable relationship. But in some cultures, you simply cannot dissolve a relationship once it's formed or once there are children. In the practice of Roman Catholicism, once people are validly married, they're always married and can-

A S K the Researcher

Interacting with Media Personalities

I have a friend who watches a lot of television and seems to develop almost real relationships with the characters from a variety of shows. Is this typical behavior? Is it dangerous for interpersonal relationships?

We often experience a sense of friendship, or parasocial interaction, with TV characters. Parasocial interaction is a normal response to media exposure, providing we realize these are one-sided relationships that don't replace interpersonal interaction. It's an emotional tie with media personalities, which reminds us of face-to-face interaction. It's based on feelings of similarity, attraction, and empathy. We may seek guidance from what that TV personality says, see her as a friend, imagine being part of his social world, and feel that we want to meet or be like that person. Media performers even use informal gestures and a conversational style that mirrors interpersonal communication to invite this interaction. Similar to reducing uncertainty in interpersonal communication, we may attribute motives to the behavior of the characters, predict their attitudes, and develop expectations about their behavior. By involving the audience in the news, the program, or the story, TV producers are able to retain audience members as continuing viewers.

For further information see D. Horton and R. R. Wohl, "Mass Communication and Parasocial Interaction: Observations on Intimacy at a Distance," *Psychiatry* 19 (1956): 215–229, and A. M. Rubin, E. M. Perse, and R. A. Powell, "Loneliness, Parasocial Interaction, and Local Television News Viewing," *Human Communication Research* 12 (1985): 155–180.

Alan M. Rubin (Ph.D., University of Illinois) is a professor of communication studies at Kent State University. He teaches courses in and conducts research about the uses and effects of the media and the links between personal and mediated communication. (Reprinted by permission of Dr. Alan Rubin.)

not dissolve that relationship. More important to such cultures may be such issues as "How do you maintain a relationship that has problems?" "What can you do to survive in this unpleasant relationship?" "How can you repair a troubled relationship?" (Moghaddam, Taylor, & Wright, 1993).

Further, the culture will influence the difficulty that you go through when relationships break up. For example, married persons whose religion forbids divorce and remarriage will experience religious disapproval and condemnation as well as the same economic and social difficulties everyone else goes through. In the United States, child custody almost invariably goes to the woman, and this presents an added emotional burden for the man. In Iran, child custody goes to the man, which presents added emotional burdens for the woman. In India, women experience greater difficulty than men in divorce because of their economic dependence on men, the cultural beliefs about women, and the patriarchal order of the family (Amato, 1994). And, it was only recently that the first wife in Jordan was granted a divorce. Prior to this, only men had been granted divorces (*New York Times,* May 15, 2002, A6).

In most of the United States, interpersonal friendships are drawn from a relatively large pool. Out of all the people you come into regular contact with, you choose relatively few of these as friends. With computer chat groups, the number of friends you can have has increased enormously as has the range from which these friends can be chosen. In rural areas and in small villages throughout the world, however, you would have very few choices. The two or three other children your age become your friends; there's no real choice because these are the only possible friends you could make.

Most cultures assume that relationships should be permanent or at least long lasting. Consequently, it's assumed that people want to keep relationships together and will expend considerable energy to maintain relationships. Because of this bias, there is little research that has studied how to move effortlessly from one intimate relationship to another or that advises you how to do this more effectively and efficiently.

Culture influences heterosexual relationships by assigning different roles to men and women. In the United States, men and women are supposed to be equal—at least that is the stated ideal. As a result, both men and women can initiate relationships and both can dissolve them. Both men and women are expected to derive satisfaction from their interpersonal relationships and when that satisfaction isn't present, either may

View point What do you think of a person who maintains extensive and intimate friendship and romantic relationships online but very few face-to-face relationships? Are your attitudes basically positive or negative? Why?

seek to exit the relationship. In Iran, on the other hand, only the man has the right to dissolve a marriage without giving reasons.

Gay and lesbian relationships are accepted in some cultures and condemned in others. In some areas of the United States "domestic partnerships" may be registered and these grant gay men, lesbians, and (in some cases) unmarried heterosexuals rights that were formerly reserved only for married couples, such as health insurance benefits and the right to make decisions when one member is incapacitated. In Norway, Sweden, and Denmark, on the other hand, same-sex relationship partners have the same rights as married partners.

TRY IT!
Apply your knowledge of online relationships; go to **www.ablongman.com/ devito**.

Relationships and Technology

Perhaps even more obvious than culture is the influence of technology on interpersonal relationships. Clearly, online interpersonal relationships are on the increase. The number of Internet users is rapidly increasing, and commercial websites devoted to meeting other people are proliferating, making it especially easy to develop online relationships. Books such as Phyllis Phlegar's (1995) *Love Online: A Practical Guide to Digital Dating* and Linda K. Fuller's (1996) *Media-Mediated Relationships: Straight and Gay, Mainstream and Alternative Perspectives* attest to the growing importance of online relationships. The afternoon television talk shows frequently focus on computer relationships, especially getting people together who have established a relationship online but who have never met. Clearly, many are turning to the Internet to find a friend or romantic partner. In MOOs (online role-playing games), 93.6 percent of the users formed ongoing friendship and romantic relationships (Parks & Roberts, 1998). Some are using the Internet as their only means of interaction; others are using it as a way of beginning a relationship and

INTER MEDIA

Parasocial Relationships

Parasocial relationships are relationships that media users perceive themselves to have with media personalities (Rubin & McHugh, 1987). At times viewers develop these relationships with real people—Rosie O'Donnell, Regis Philbin, or Oprah Winfrey, for example. As a result they may watch these people faithfully and communicate with the individual in their own imaginations. At other times, the relationship is with the fictional character—a crime scene investigator from *CSI* or a CIA operative on *The Agency*. In fact, television doctors frequently get mail asking for medical advice. And about-to-be-killed soap opera characters often get warnings from their parasocial relationship fans. Obviously, most people don't go quite this far.

Celebrity chat sessions on the Internet further support the illusion of a real interpersonal relationship. And the screensavers of television performers make it difficult not to think of them in relationship terms.

Parasocial relationships develop from an initial attraction with the character's social and task roles, to a perceived relationship, and finally to a sense that this relationship is an important one (Rubin & McHugh, 1987). The more you can predict the behavior of a character, the more likely you are to develop a parasocial relationship (Perse & Rubin, 1989). Parasocial relationships are most important to those who spend a great deal of time with the media and who have few interpersonal relationships (Rubin, Perse, & Powell, 1985; Cole & Leets, 1999).

Follow Up   Some research indicates that parasocial relationships actually facilitate interpersonal interaction (May, 1999). How might (or do) parasocial relationships facilitate interpersonal interactions? Can you think of how parasocial relationships might hinder interpersonal interactions?

intend to later supplement computer talk with photographs, phone calls, and face-to-face meetings.

Almost two-thirds of newsgroup users had formed new acquaintances, friendships, or other personal relationships with someone they met on the Internet. Almost one-third said that they communicated with their partner at least three or four times a week; more than half communicated on a weekly basis (Parks & Floyd, 1996).

Women, it seems, are more likely to form relationships on the Internet than men. About 72 percent of women and 55 percent of men had formed personal relationships online (Parks & Floyd, 1996). Not surprisingly, those who communicated more frequently formed more relationships.

As relationships develop on the Internet, network convergence occurs; that is, as a relationship between two people develops, they begin to share their network of other communicators with each other (Parks, 1995; Parks & Floyd, 1996). This, of course, is similar to relationships formed through face-to-face contact. Online work groups are also on the increase and have been found to be more task oriented and more efficient than face-to-face groups (Lantz, 2001). Online groups also provide a sense of belonging that may once have been thought possible only through face-to-face interactions (Silverman, 2001).

There are lots of advantages to establishing relationships online. For example, online relationships are safe in terms of avoiding the potential for physical violence or sexually transmitted diseases. Unlike relationships established in face-to-face encounters where physical appearance tends to outweigh personality, on the Internet your inner qualities are communicated first. Rapport and mutual self-disclosure become more important than physical attractiveness in promoting intimacy (Cooper & Sportolari, 1997). And contrary to some popular opinions, online relationships rely just as heavily on the ideals of trust, honesty, and commitment as do face-to-face relationships (Whitty & Gavin, 2001). Friendship and romantic interaction on the Internet are a natural boon to shut-ins and the extremely shy for whom traditional ways of meeting someone are often difficult. Computer talk is more empowering for those with "physical disabilities or disfigurements" where face-to-face interactions are often superficial and often end with withdrawal (Lea & Spears, 1995; Bull & Rumsey, 1988). By eliminating the physical cues, computer talk equalizes the interaction and doesn't put the disfigured person, for example, at an immediate disadvantage in a society where physical attractiveness is so highly valued. You're then free to reveal as much or as little about your physical self as you wish, when you wish.

Another obvious advantage is that the number of people you can reach is so vast that it's relatively easy to find someone who matches what you're looking for. The situation is like finding a book that covers just what you need from a library of millions of volumes rather than from one of only several thousand. Still another advantage for many is that the socioeconomic and educational status of people on the Net is significantly higher than you're likely to find in a bar or singles group.

Of course, there are also disadvantages. For one thing, you can't see the person. Unless you exchange photos or meet face-to-face, you won't know what the person looks like. Even if photos are exchanged, how certain can you be that the photos are of the person or that they were taken recently? In addition, you can't hear the person's voice, and this too hinders you in formulating a total picture of the other person. Of course, you can always add an occasional phone call to give you this added information.

Online, people can present a false self with little chance of detection. For example, minors may present themselves as adults, and adults may present themselves as children for illicit and illegal sexual communications and, perhaps, meetings. Similarly, people can present themselves as poor when they're rich, as mature when they're immature, as serious and committed when they're just enjoying the experience. Although you can also misrepresent yourself in face-to-face relationships, the fact that it's easier to do online probably accounts for greater misrepresentation in computer relationships (Cornwell & Lundgren, 2001).

Another potential disadvantage—though some might argue it is actually an advantage—is that computer interactions may become all consuming and may substitute for face-to-face interpersonal relationships.

REVIEWING   Key Terms and Concepts in Interpersonal Relationships

This chapter introduced interpersonal relationships and focused on three areas: the advantages and disadvantages of relationships, the stages you go through in developing and perhaps dissolving relationships, and the influence of culture on interpersonal relationships.

Characteristics of Interpersonal Relationships

How do interpersonal relationships differ from impersonal relationships?

■ Among the differences are that interpersonal relationships are those in which the people base their predictions on psychological (rather than sociological) data, explanatory (rather than descriptive) knowledge, and personally established (rather than socially established) rules.

■ Interpersonal relationships have both advantages and disadvantages. Some advantages are that interpersonal relationships help alleviate loneliness, enable you to secure stimulation, help you to gain self-knowledge and enhance your self-esteem, and enable you to maximize pleasure and minimize pain. Some of the disadvantages are that interpersonal relationships put pressure on you to reveal yourself to others; impose significant financial, emotional, and temporal obligations; may lead to increased isolation from former friends; and may present difficulties in dissolving.

Stages in Interpersonal Relationships

What are the stages that a relationship goes through?

■ At the *contact stage* you make perceptual contact and later interact with the person.

■ At the *involvement stage* you test your potential partner, and if this proves satisfactory, you move on to intensifying your relationship.

■ At the *intimacy stage* you may make an interpersonal commitment and later enter the stage of social bonding, where you publicly reveal your relationship status.

■ At the *deterioration stage* the bonds holding you together begin to weaken. Intrapersonal dissatisfaction is experienced and later becomes interpersonal when you discuss it with your partner and perhaps others.

■ At the *repair stage* you first engage in intrapersonal repair, analyzing what went wrong and perhaps what you can do to set things right; later you may engage in interpersonal re-

pair, where you and your partner consider ways to mend your deteriorating relationships.

■ At the *dissolution stage* you separate yourself from your partner and later perhaps separate socially and publicly.

Relationships in a Context of Culture and Technology

In what ways does culture influence interpersonal relationships?

■ Culture influences the beliefs you have about relationships, the purposes and values you feel they should serve, the choices involved in developing and in dissolving relationships, the rules that relationships should follow, and the roles that are considered appropriate in relationships.

■ Technology has now assumed a major role in all interpersonal relationships, especially their development and maintenance.

APPLYING   Key Terms and Concepts in Interpersonal Relationships

1. What reasons motivated you to develop the relationships you did? What maintains them?

2. What advantages and disadvantages do you see in the relationships existing among the characters in any specific television situation comedy or drama?

3. How do your interpersonal relationships help to lessen loneliness? Do they ever increase loneliness?

4. Do any of your relationships involve tension between such opposites as autonomy–connection, novelty–predictability, or closedness–openness? How do you deal with them?

5. Can you supply personal examples that illustrate the three types of movement among the relationship stages—one that moved from one stage to another, one that remained at one stage for a long period, and one that ended?

6. What strategies have you used in testing your friendships or romantic relationships? Can you identify strategies that others have used on you?

7. How do you know when you have reached "relational intimacy"?

8. Have you ever experienced anxieties concerning security, fulfillment, and excitement as you considered entering a relationship (Zimmer, 1986)? What happened?

9. Is the six-stage model presented here an adequate way to describe most interpersonal relationships as you under-

stand them? How would you describe the stages of interpersonal relationships?

10. In one research study the author predicted that people who develop parasocial relationships are more shy and lonelier than those who do not develop such relationships (Ashe & McCutcheon, 2001). But the prediction was not borne out by the research findings. Do you think that this is because the prediction is simply not true or because this particular research study didn't find the relationship between shyness and loneliness on the one hand and the tendency to develop parasocial relationships on the other? How might you study these predicted relationships?

11. Oddly enough, chat room conversation that is negative seems to increase the amount of conversation that takes place (Rollman, Krug, & Parente, 2000). Why do you think this is so?

EXPERIENCING   Key Terms and Concepts in Interpersonal Relationships

Go to www.ablongman.com/devito.

The following exercises focus on interpersonal relationships and the communication that takes place at each stage.

(1) **Analyzing Stage Talk** and (2) **Learning to Hear Stage Talk** provide opportunities to look at the various cues to the different relationship stages. (3) **Giving Repair Advice** looks at relationship difficulties and encourages you to offer relationship repair advice based on the discussions in this chapter (4) **'Til This Do Us Part** is an exercise that looks at some of the relationship issues that can break up the relationship.

Research
Navigator.c⊕m

RESEARCHING with Research Navigator   Key Terms and Concepts in Interpersonal Relationships

Go to http://www.researchnavigator.com.

Reading an article.

Read a popular or scholarly article on interpersonal relationships, the stages that relationships go through, or the influence of culture or technology on relationships. On the basis of this article what can you add to the discussion presented here?

Investigating key terms.

Investigate one of the key terms discussed in this chapter (for example, interpersonal relationship, parasocial relationship, online relationship, relationship development, relationship maintenance, relationship deterioration, relationship repair, or intimacy). What additional insights can you provide?

Finding answers.

Try finding answers to one of the following questions or design a research study to answer it.

■ How do the advantages and disadvantages of relationships change with age?

■ Do men and women see relationship advantages and disadvantages in the same way?

■ Do the tensions in interpersonal relationships (for example, autonomy versus connection) vary from one culture to another?

■ How can relationship communication be improved?

■ What are the common consequences of relationship dissolution?

Interpersonal Relationships: Growth and Deterioration

The Wedding Planner (2001)

After all, my erstwhile dear,
My no longer cherished.
Need we say it was not love,
Just because it perished?

—Edna St. Vincent Millay

Relationship Development
Relationship Maintenance
Relationship Deterioration
Relationship Repair
Relationship Dissolution

Mary Fiore (Jennifer Lopez) *plans great weddings for others but can't seem to find a love of her own, until handsome Dr. Steve Edison (Matthew Mc-Conaughey) comes into her life in* The Wedding Planner. *The only problem is that it's his wedding that she's currently planning. As Mary and Steve interact more, eventually realizing that they should be marrying each other, we see the various stages that relationships pass through, the subject of this chapter, where we look at relationship development, maintenance, deterioration, repair, and dissolution.*

Now that we have a general idea of the functions that relationships serve and the various stages relationships go through, we can explore relationship development and relationship deterioration in greater detail.

RELATIONSHIP DEVELOPMENT

A number of theories offer insight into why you develop your relationships. Several theories bearing directly on relationship development have already been discussed.

Uncertainty reduction theory (Chapter 4) describes relationship development as a process of reducing uncertainty about one another (Berger & Calabrese, 1975). For example, the theory predicts that high uncertainty prevents intimacy, whereas low uncertainty creates intimacy. Similarly, high uncertainty decreases liking for another person, whereas low uncertainty increases liking.

Social penetration theory (Chapter 10) describes the progression of a relationship along the communication dimensions of breadth and depth. As a relationship moves to greater intimacy, relationship depth and breadth increase; as a relationship moves away from intimacy, relationship depth and breadth decrease (usually).

Relationship dialectics theory (Chapter 10) describes relationships along a series of opposites representing competing desires or motivations, such as the desire for autonomy and the desire to belong to someone, for novelty and predictability, and for closedness and openness.

Rules theory (discussed more fully on pages 262–263) describes relationships as interactions governed by a series of rules that a couple agrees to follow. When the rules are followed, the relationship is maintained; when they're broken, the relationship experiences difficulty and perhaps deteriorates or even dissolves.

In this chapter, three additional theories are singled out: attraction theory, social exchange theory, and equity theory. The theories offer interesting perspectives on relationships. They help explain what happens in interpersonal relationships (and in interpersonal communication generally) during the stages of development, maintenance, deterioration, and repair. They shed light on important interpersonal processes—for example, power and conflict—and on significant interpersonal relationships, such as friendship, love, and family.

Attraction Theory

You're no doubt attracted to some people and not attracted to others. In a similar way, some people are attracted to you and some aren't. If you were to examine the people to whom you're attracted and those to whom you're not attracted, you would probably see patterns in your judgments, even though many of them seem unconsciously motivated. **Attraction theory** holds that you develop relationships with others on the basis of three major factors: attractiveness (physical appearance and personality), proximity, and similarity.

Physical Appearance and Personality   When you say, "I find that person attractive," you probably mean either that you find that person physically attractive or that you find that person's personality or behavior attractive. For the most part, you probably like physically attractive rather than physically unattractive people, and you probably like people who possess a pleasant rather than an unpleasant personality. Generally, you attribute positive characteristics to people you find attractive and negative characteristics to people you find unattractive.

Supporting the popular belief, research—in Bulgaria, Nigeria, Indonesia, Germany, and the United States—finds that men consider physical attractiveness in their partner more important than do women (Buss & Schmitt, 1993). Similarly, in a study of gay male dating behavior, the physical attractiveness of the partner was the most important factor in influencing how much the person enjoyed his date and how much he wished to date that person again (Sergios & Cody, 1985). The more attractive you find someone, the more you are apt to exaggerate your good qualities in order to get a date with that person (Rowatt, Cunningham, & Druen, 1999). Apparently, such exaggeration is seen as more acceptable when the goal is a date with an exceptionally attractive person but less acceptable when the prospective date is less attractive.

Note that the importance of physical attractiveness enters the face-to-face relationship immediately, whereas it's only revealed after considerable communication via computer. Information conveyed by computer or mail often comes gradually: First some general verbal descriptions ("I'm 6 feet tall, brown hair, brown eyes"), then perhaps a photo, and then perhaps a face-to-face meeting. It seems reasonable to assume that physical attractiveness will prove most important when it's immediate and less important when it's revealed after a period of acquaintanceship.

Those who are perceived as attractive are also seen as competent, and conversely, those who are perceived as competent—say, as a team member working on a project or in social situations—are also seen as more attractive (Duran & Kelly, 1988).

Proximity   If you look around at people you find attractive, you'll probably notice that they're the ones who live or work close to you. For example, in a study of friendships in a student housing development, researchers found that the closer the students' rooms were to each other, the better the chances that the occupants would become friends (Festinger, Schachter, & Back, 1950). The people who became friends were those who had the greatest opportunity to interact. One reason proximity influences attraction is that it allows you to get to know the other person. You come to like people you know because you can better predict their behavior, and perhaps because of this they seem less frightening than complete strangers do (Berger & Bradac, 1982).

Another approach argues that "mere exposure" to others leads you to develop positive feelings for them (Zajonc, 1968). In one study a female stranger attended some classes 5 times, some classes 10 times, some classes 15 times, and some classes not at all (Moreland & Beach, 1992). At the end of the semester the students in the classes rated this woman (who never spoke but just sat where people could see her) in terms of how attractive they felt she was and how much they liked her. Consistent with the mere exposure hypothesis, the woman was least liked and considered least attractive in the class in which she never appeared, more liked and more attractive in the class in which she appeared 5 times, still more in the class in which she appeared 10 times, and most in the class in which she appeared 15 times. How can you account for these results except by "mere exposure"? Exposure increases attraction when the initial inter-

action is favorable or neutral. When the initial interaction is negative, repeated exposure may actually decrease attraction.

Similarity   If you could construct your mate, he or she would probably look, act, and think very much like you. By being attracted to people like yourself, you validate yourself; you tell yourself that you're worthy of being liked. Although there are exceptions, you probably are attracted to your own mirror image, to people who are similar to you in nationality, race, ability, physical characteristics, intelligence, attitudes, and so on.

If you were to ask a group of friends, "To whom are you attracted?" they would probably name very attractive people; in fact, they would probably name the most attractive people they know. But if you were to observe these friends, you would find that they go out with and establish relationships with people who are similar in physical attractiveness. This tendency, known as the **matching hypothesis,** predicts that although you may be attracted to the most physically attractive people, you will date and mate with people who are similar to yourself in physical attractiveness (Walster, Walster, & Berscheid, 1978). Intuitively, this seems satisfying. In some cases, however, you notice discrepancies: for example, an attractive person dating someone much less attractive. In cases such as these, you would probably look for compensating factors, for qualities that compensate for the lack of physical attractiveness. Prestige, money, power, intelligence, youth, and various personality characteristics are obvious factors that compensate for a lack of attractiveness.

In addition to physical similarity, you're likely attracted to people who have attitudes similar to your own, who like what you like, and who dislike what you dislike. The more significant the attitude, the more important the similarity. Marriages between people with great dissimilarities are more likely to end in divorce than marriages between people whose attitudes are similar (Blumstein & Schwartz, 1983).

Attitude similarity as an essential element in attraction has been found in such diverse cultures as the United States, India, Japan, and Mexico, and is especially significant in initial attraction (Hatfield & Rapson, 1992). It also seems to predict relationship success. People who are similar in attitude become more attracted to each other over time, whereas people who are dissimilar in attitude become less attracted to each other over time (Neimeyer & Mitchell, 1988; Honeycutt, 1986). Also, the more intellectually

WEB EXPLORATION
To learn more about similarity in relationship development, go to **www.ablongman.com/ devito**.

It's been argued that you don't actually develop an attraction for those who are similar to you but rather develop a repulsion for those who are dissimilar (Rosenbaum, 1986). For example, you may be repulsed by those who disagree with you and therefore exclude them from those with whom you might develop a relationship. You're therefore left with a pool of possible partners who are similar to you. What do you think of this "repulsion hypothesis"? Do you and your relationship history more closely follow the predictions of repulsion theory or of attraction theory? Or might both be operating?

similar people are and the more they see the world similarly, the greater their attraction to each other (Neimeyer & Neimeyer, 1983).

Although most people would argue that "birds of a feather flock together" (the similarity position), others argue that "opposites attract." This concept, called **complementarity,** argues that people are attracted to dissimilar others (at least in certain situations). For example, the submissive student may get along especially well with an assertive teacher but may not get along with an assertive romantic partner. Theodore Reik (1944), in his classic *A Psychologist Looks at Love,* takes a complementarity position when he argues that you fall in love with people who possess characteristics that you do not possess and actually envy. The introvert, for example, if displeased with being shy, might be attracted to an extrovert. Most research, however, clearly supports the greater importance of similarity over difference.

Affinity-Seeking Strategies   Attractiveness, proximity, and similarity are factors that influence interpersonal attraction apart from anything you may do or say. In addition, however, you can increase your attractiveness by using **affinity-seeking strategies.** These strategies are derived from studies in which some people were asked to list the things that people can say or do to get others to like them and others were asked to list the things that lead others to dislike them. Thus, the strategies represent what people *think* makes them attractive to others, what people *think* makes people like them, and what people *think* makes others feel positive toward them. Here are the major strategies found in this study (Bell & Daly, 1984).

Be of help to Other (the other person).

Appear "in control," as a leader, as one who takes charge.

Present yourself as socially equal to Other.

Present yourself as comfortable and relaxed when with Other.

Allow Other to assume control over relational activities.

Follow the cultural rules for polite, cooperative conversation with Other.

Appear active, enthusiastic, and dynamic.

Stimulate and encourage Other to talk about himself or herself; reinforce disclosures and contributions of Other.

Ensure that activities with Other are enjoyable and positive.

Include Other in your social activities and groupings.

Show that your relationship with Other is closer than it really is.

Listen to Other attentively and actively.

Communicate interest in Other.

Engage in self-disclosure with Other.

Appear optimistic and positive rather than pessimistic and negative.

Appear to Other as an independent and freethinking individual.

Appear to Other as physically attractive as possible.

Appear to Other as an interesting person to get to know.

Appear as one who is able to administer rewards to Other for associating with you.

Show respect for Other, and help Other to feel positively about himself or herself.

Arrange circumstances so that you and Other come into frequent contact.

Communicate warmth and empathy to Other.

Demonstrate that you share significant attitudes and values with Other.

Communicate supportiveness in Other's interpersonal interactions.

Appear to Other as honest and reliable.

Social Exchange Theory

Social exchange theory, based on an economic model of profits and losses, claims that you develop relationships that enable you to maximize your profits (Chadwick-Jones, 1976; Gergen, Greenberg, & Willis, 1980; Thibaut & Kelley, 1959).

Profits, Rewards, and Costs   The theory begins with the following equation·

$$\text{Profits} = \text{Rewards} - \text{Costs}$$

Rewards are anything that you want, that you enjoy, and that you'd be willing to incur costs to obtain. For example, to acquire the reward of financial gain, you might have to work rather than play. To earn an A in an interpersonal communication course, you might have to write a term paper or study more than you want to. To gain a promotion, you might have to do unpleasant tasks or work overtime. Love, affection, status, money, gifts, security, social acceptance, companionship, friendship, and intimacy are just a few examples of rewards for which you would be willing to work (that is, incur costs).

Costs are those things that you normally try to avoid—things you consider unpleasant or difficult. Working overtime, washing dishes and ironing clothes, watching a television show that your partner enjoys but you find boring, dressing in ways that are physically uncomfortable, and doing favors for people you dislike might all be considered costs.

Using this basic economic model, social exchange theory claims that you seek to develop relationships (friendship and romantic) that will give you the greatest profit, relationships in which the rewards are greater than the costs. The preferred relationships, according to this theory, are those that are most profitable and thus give you the greatest rewards with the least costs.

Comparison Levels   You enter a relationship with a general idea of the kinds of profit you ought to get out of it. This is your *comparison level,* your realistic expectations of what you feel you deserve from a relationship. For example, in a study of couples, it was found that most people expect reasonably high levels of trust, mutual respect, love, and commitment. Their expectations are significantly lower for time spent together, privacy, sexual activity, and communication (Sabatelli & Pearce, 1986). When the rewards you get equal or surpass this comparison level, you feel satisfied with your relationship.

You also have a *comparison level for alternatives.* That is, you probably compare the profits you get from your current relationships with the ones you think you can get from alternative relationships. For example, if you believe you'll not be able to find another suitable partner, you're more likely to stay in your relationship, even if it's an abusive one (Berscheid, 1985). If you see that the profits from your present relationship are less than the profits you could get from an alternative relationship, you might decide to leave your current relationship and enter this new and potentially more profitable one.

Equity Theory

Equity theory uses the concepts of social exchange but goes a step further. It claims that you develop and maintain relationships in which your ratio of rewards to costs is approximately equal to your partner's (Walster, Walster, & Berscheid, 1978; Messick & Cook, 1983). An equitable relationship, then, is one in which participants derive rewards that are proportional to their costs. If you work harder for the relationship than your partner does, then equity demands that you should get greater rewards than your partner. If you work equally hard, then equity demands that each of you should get ap-

TRY IT!
Apply your insights into profits, rewards, and costs; go to www. ablongman.com/devito.

proximately equal rewards. Much research finds that people want equity and feel that relationships should be characterized by equity (Ueleke et al., 1983). The idea behind this is that if you're underbenefited (you get less than you put in), you'll be angry. If, on the other hand, you're overbenefited (you get more than you put in), you'll feel guilty (Walster, Walster, & Traupman, 1978). However, some research has questioned this rather neat but intuitively unsatisfying assumption and finds that the overbenefited person is often quite happy and contented; guilt deriving from getting more than you deserve seems easily forgotten (Noller & Fitzpatrick, 1993; Sprecher & Schwartz, 1994).

Relationship Satisfaction and Equity   Equity theory puts into clear focus the sources of relational dissatisfaction you see every day. For example, in a traditional marriage, husband and wife may have full-time jobs, but the wife may also do the major share of the household chores. Thus, although both may be deriving equal rewards—they have equally good cars, they live in the same three-bedroom house, and so on—the wife is paying more of the costs. According to equity theory, she will be dissatisfied because of this lack of equity. In a work situation, you see the same dynamic with two management trainees: Each does an equal amount of work but one gets a bonus of $2,000 and the other a bonus of $5,000. Clearly, there is inequity, and there will be dissatisfaction.

Equity, Culture, and Gender   Equity is consistent with the capitalistic orientation of Western culture, where each person is paid, for example, according to his or her contributions. The more you contribute to the organization or the relationship, the more rewards you should get out of it. In other cultures, a principle of equality or need might operate. According to the principle of equality, each person would get equal rewards, regardless of their individual contribution. According to the principle of need, each person would get rewards according to individual need (Moghaddam, Taylor, & Wright, 1993). People from India are, for example, more likely to distribute rewards on the basis of need than are Americans, who would distribute rewards on the basis of equity, on the basis of the costs paid into the relationship (Berman, Murphy-Berman, & Singh, 1985;

View point   How would you feel if you were in a relationship in which you and your partner contributed an equal share of the costs (that is, you each worked equally hard) but your partner derived significantly greater rewards? How would you feel if you and your partner contributed an equal share of the costs but you derived significantly greater rewards?

Moghaddam, Taylor, & Wright, 1993). It's not surprising to find that in the United States equity is highly correlated with relationship satisfaction and with relationship endurance (Schafer & Keith, 1980). In much of Europe, on the other hand, equity seems to be unrelated to satisfaction or endurance (Lujansky & Mikula, 1983).

Women are more likely to engage in extramarital affairs when they perceive their relationship as inequitable (Prins, Buunk, & Van Yperen, 1994). Perceptions of inequity by men, however, did not influence their likelihood of engaging in extramarital affairs. Further, women are more likely than men to break up a relationship as a result of their own extrarelational affair (Janus & Janus, 1993).

RELATIONSHIP MAINTENANCE

Relationship maintenance concerns what you do to continue (maintain, retain) your relationship. Of course, maintenance behaviors can serve a variety of functions, for example:

- To keep the relationship intact, to retain the semblance of a relationship, to prevent dissolution of the relationship
- To keep the relationship at its present stage, to prevent it from moving too far toward either less or greater intimacy
- To keep the relationship satisfying, to maintain an appropriate balance between rewards and penalties

Some people, after entering a relationship, assume that it will continue unless something catastrophic happens. Consequently, while they may seek to prevent any major mishaps, they're unlikely to engage in much maintenance behavior. Others will be ever on the lookout for something wrong and will seek to patch it up as quickly and as effectively as possible. In between lie most people, who will engage in maintenance behaviors when things are going wrong and when there is the possibility that the relationship can be improved. Not surprisingly a great deal of relationship maintenance is taking place through e-mail (Stafford, Kline, & Dimmick, 1999; Howard, Rainie, & Jones, 2001). Because an increasing number of relationships are developed online and because online contact is so easy to maintain even when partners are widely separated geographically, the use of e-mail is likely to increase in frequency and importance. The use of e-mail to maintain relationships is more common among women than men; women also find such e-mail contact more gratifying than do men (Boneva, Kraut, & Frohlich, 2001). Behaviors directed at improving badly damaged or even broken relationships are considered under the topic of repair (pp. 271–276).

Reasons for Maintaining Relationships

The reasons for maintaining relationships are as numerous and varied as the reasons for beginning them. Before looking at the specific reasons, let's look at what the theories predict. Attraction theory holds that relationships are maintained when there is significant attraction, generally of the kind that led to the development of the relationship. Although both individuals, as well as their definitions of what constitutes attractiveness, may have changed, the importance of attraction—however defined—is likely to continue throughout the life of the relationship.

Social exchange theory holds that relationships will be maintained as long as the relationship is profitable, as long as the rewards exceed the costs. Note, of course, that

A S K *the Researcher*

Keeping Relationships Exciting

I've been dating this woman for two years now, and we're planning to get married in about a year. But I'm worried be-cause our relation-ship has become routine and stale; it's comfortable but there's little excite-ment—it's all very predictable. Is there anything I can do to make our relation-ship more exciting, less predictable?

It's probably not possible to keep any relationship exciting all the time. Indeed, one of the major goals of developing relationships is to make them more stable and predictable. It appears that you've achieved that goal. However, you can add variety to the predictability of a close relationship. Look at the activities that make your relationship predictable. Do you watch TV every night? Do you eat the same meal a lot? Do you stay at home over the weekends? Of course, these are common patterns that can be easily detected and changed. Instead of watching a video, try going to a live performance of a play. Instead of cooking the same meals, buy a cookbook and learn some new recipes. If you stay home all weekend, try getting out of the house (if only for a couple of hours). On the other hand, if you've been on the go for a long period of time, then relaxing at home might be the most exciting thing you want to do!

Dan Canary (Ph.D., University of Southern California) is a professor at the Hugh Downs School of Human Communication, Arizona State University, where he teaches courses in interpersonal communication at the undergraduate and graduate levels and writes books and articles about interpersonal communication, conflict management, and sex differences and similarities. http://www.asu.edu (Reprinted by permission of Dr. Dan Canary.)

what constitutes a reward and how significant that reward is can only be defined by the individual. More specifically, you're likely to maintain a relationship when it's more re-warding than what you expected (your comparison level) or better than what you feel you could get elsewhere (your comparison level for alternatives). You're also likely to maintain your present relationship even when it falls short of your comparison level as long as it's still higher than what you could get elsewhere (your comparison level for al-ternatives). So even though you may think you deserve more, if you can't get more, then you're likely to stay put.

Equity theory holds that you maintain a relationship when you perceive relative eq-uity. If you feel that you're getting rewards from the relationship proportional to the costs you're paying, then you're likely to maintain the relationship. If either person—but especially the person who is being shortchanged—perceives a lack of equity, the rela-tionship may experience difficulty.

In addition to these theoretical predictions, let's look at some of the more popular and frequently cited reasons for relationship maintenance.

- *Emotional attachment.* Often you maintain a relationship because you love each other and want to preserve your relationship and you don't find alternative cou-plings as inviting or as potentially enjoyable.
- *Convenience.* The difficulties involved in finding another person to live with, an-other business partner, or another social escort may make it more convenient to stay together than to break up.
- *Children.* A couple may stay together because they feel, rightly or wrongly, that it's in the best interests of the children, or the children may provide a socially ac-

ceptable excuse to mask the real reason—convenience, financial advantage, fear of being alone, and so on.

■ *Fear.* People may fear the outside world, being alone, facing others as "single," or even of making it on one paycheck and so may elect to preserve their current relationship as the better alternative.

■ *Inertia.* Some relationships are maintained because of inertia, the tendency for a body at rest to remain at rest and a body in motion to remain in motion; change seems too much trouble.

■ *Commitment.* People may have a strong commitment to each other or to the relationship (Yela, 2000). In fact, recent research finds that women's commitment is more closely related to relationship maintenance and stability than any other factor (Sprecher, 2001).

You may find the self-test "How Committed Are You?" interesting at this point (Knapp & Taylor, 1994; Kurdek, 1995).

TEST YOURSELF   *How Committed Are You?*

Think about a current romantic relationship—long-term and serious or short-term and casual—and respond to each of the following questions according to the following scale: 1 = the statement is "absolutely" true, 7 = the statement is "absolutely not" true, and numbers 2–6 for statements that are sometimes true and sometimes not true.

_____ 1. I am likely to pursue another relationship or a single lifestyle.
_____ 2. I believe there will be a lot of future rewards associated with the relationship.
_____ 3. I feel a strong sense of "we" when thinking of my partner and me.
_____ 4. I am willing to exert a great deal of effort on behalf of this relationship.
_____ 5. I have a lot invested in this relationship.
_____ 6. I can imagine having an affair with another person and not having it affect my relationship with _____.
_____ 7. I expect to be with _____ for the rest of my life.
_____ 8. There is nothing holding me in this relationship except my own free choice.

▶ **How did you do?**   To compute your score follow these steps:

1. Add your scores from questions 2, 3, 4, 5, 7, and 8.
2. Add your scores from items 1 and 6 and subtract this sum from 16 (the number 16 is chosen simply to eliminate negative numbers).
3. Add the totals from steps 1 and 2.

Your score should range somewhere between 8 and 56. Low scores indicate great commitment and high scores indicate less commitment.

▶ **What will you do?**   This self-test encourages you to look at your own commitment in very specific terms; it stimulates you to ask yourself the reasons for your own relationship commitment. On the basis of this experience, are there any changes that you'd like to make in your own tendencies toward commitment in friendship or romantic relationships? Are there any changes that you'd like to make in your responses to the commitment of others?

From "Commitment and Its Communication in Romantic Relationships" by Mark L. Knapp and Eric H. Taylor. In Ann L. Weber and John H. Harvey, eds. *Perspectives on Close Relationships.* Boston: Allyn & Bacon, pp. 153–175. Reprinted by permission of Mark L. Knapp.

Rules for Maintaining Relationships

You gain an interesting perspective by looking at interpersonal relationships in terms of the rules that govern them. The general assumption of this perspective is that relationships (in a wide variety of cultures)—friendship and love in particular—are held together by mutual adherence to certain rules (Argyle, 1986; Argyle, Henderson, Bond, Iizuka, et al., 1986). When those rules are broken, the relationships may deteriorate and eventually dissolve.

Relationship rules help distinguish successful from destructive relationship behavior. They help pinpoint why relationships break up and how they may be repaired. Further, if you know what the rules are, you'll be better able to learn (and teach) the social skills involved in relationship development and maintenance. As you'll see below, rules of loyalty, openness, honesty, and respect are especially important and regulate both friendship and romantic relationships (Baxter, Dun, & Sahlstein, 2001).

Friendship Rules   The left half of Table 11.1 presents some of the most important rules of friendship (Argyle & Henderson, 1984). When these rules are followed, the friendship is strong and mutually satisfying. When these rules are broken, interpersonal conflict is likely to occur (Samter & Cupach, 1998). Sometimes rule breaking creates problems that cannot be fixed, and so the friendship dies. The right half of Table 11.1 presents the abuses that are most significant in breaking up a friendship (Argyle & Henderson, 1984). Note that some of the rules for maintaining a friendship directly correspond to the abuses that break up friendships. For example, it's important to "demonstrate emotional support" to maintain a friendship; when emotional support is not shown, the friendship will prove less satisfying and may well break up. The general assumption here is that friendships break down when a significant friendship rule is violated. The maintenance strategy depends on your knowing the rules and having the ability to apply the appropriate skills (Trower, 1981; Blieszner & Adams, 1992).

TRY IT!
Apply your knowledge about romantic rules; go to **www.ablongman.com/devito**.

Romantic Rules   Other research has identified the rules that couples in romantic relationships establish and follow. Here, for example, are rules that both keep the relationship together and, when broken, lead to deterioration and eventually to dissolution (Baxter, 1986). If you have had a serious romantic relationship think about it as you examine the rules below; if you have not had such a relationship, think about the relationship you want. Try arranging the following rules in order of importance to you. Which of the following rules is true of your past, present, or future relationship?

Do you each

1. Acknowledge one another's individual identities and lives beyond the relationship?
2. Express similar attitudes, beliefs, values, and interests?
3. Enhance one another's self-worth and self-esteem?
4. Try to be open, genuine, and authentic with one another?
5. Remain loyal and faithful to one another?
6. Have substantial shared time together?
7. Reap rewards commensurate with their investments relative to the other party?
8. Experience a mysterious and inexplicable "magic" in one another's presence?

Communication for Maintaining Relationships

One reason relationships last is that you try to make them work. Interestingly enough, among married couples, the wives' use of maintenance strategies have a more signifi-

Table 11.1   **Maintaining and Breaking Up a Friendship**

Have you seen these rules in operation in your own friendships? Are there other important rules that you would add to the list presented here?

Maintaining a Friendship	Breaking Up a Friendship
Stand up for the friend in his or her absence.	Be intolerant of the friend's friends.
Share information and feelings about successes.	Criticize the friend in public.
Demonstrate emotional support.	Discuss confidences between yourself and the friend with others.
Trust each other; confide in each other.	Don't display any positive regard for the friend.
Offer to help the friend in time of need.	Don't demonstrate any positive support for the friend.
Try to make the friend happy when the two of you are together.	Nag the friend.
Don't criticize in public.	Don't trust or confide in the friend.
Keep confidences.	Don't volunteer to help the friend in time of need.
Don't be jealous or negative about other relationships.	Be jealous or critical of the friend's other relationships.
Respect the friend's privacy.	Feel free to take up as much of the friend's time as you want.

cant effect on the satisfaction, love, and commitment the couple experiences than do the husband's use of such strategies (Weigel & Ballard-Reisch, 1999). This is not to say that the man's maintenance strategies are ineffective, just that in heterosexual married relationships the couple is more influenced by the wives' maintenance behaviors.

There is conflicting research evidence on the value of electronic communication in maintaining relationships. In one study, for example, the researchers found that 55 percent of Internet users claimed that e-mail has strengthened their family ties and 66 percent claimed that it improved their connections with close friends. Related to this is the finding that Internet users seem to experience significantly less social isolation than those who don't use the Internet. Only 8 percent of Internet users noted that they felt socially isolated, while 18 percent of nonusers reported feelings of social isolation (Raney, 2000). Another study reports contrary findings, claiming that the more people use the Internet the less they communicate with family members in their home, the smaller their social circle, and the more they experience loneliness and depression (Kraut et al., 1999). The only reasonable conclusion now seems to be that for some using the Internet strengthens social connections with friends and family and for others it substitutes for face-to-face social interactions and connections.

A number of researchers have focused on the maintenance strategies people use in their various relationships (Ayres, 1983; Dindia & Baxter, 1987; Dainton & Stafford, 1993; Guerrero, Eloy, & Wabnik, 1993; Canary, Stafford, Hause, & Wallace, 1993; Canary & Stafford, 1994). Here are some examples of how people maintain their relationships, presented in the form of suggestions for maintaining relationships.

■ *Be nice.* Researchers call this *prosocial behavior.* You're polite, cheerful, and friendly; you avoid criticism; and you compromise even when it involves self-sacrifice. Prosocial behaviors also include talking about a shared future, for example, talking about a future vacation or buying a house together. It also includes acting affectionately and romantically.

ETHICS in Interpersonal Communication

Preserving Relationships

In our culture, it's generally thought worthwhile to preserve relationships, especially romantic ones, of long standing. People who have long-term relationships are admired whereas those who have numerous short-term relationships are looked down on. If the relationship is a marriage or a domestic partnership or if it involves children, for example, then it seems that most people would advise you to do what you have to do to preserve the relationship. In fact, the legal systems of many states may require you to go through all sorts of hurdles to dissolve such relationships. Whereas you don't need to provide any evidence of relationship competence to *establish* a relationship, you do need evidence to *dissolve* certain relationships such as a marriage. But at what point does "doing what you have to do" to preserve a relationship become unethical?

What would you do? *You've recently met a wonderful person, the kind of person you can easily see as a life partner. The only obstacle that you foresee is that this person would have serious reservations about the relationship if it were known that you've had several long-term (six months or more) romantic relationships and several short-term sexual adventures, behaviors with which you see nothing wrong. Given these differences, you wonder if you can omit talk of past relationships—or lie about them if necessary—to preserve and maintain what you see as a truly great relationship.*

- *Communicate.* You call just to say, "How are you?" or send cards or letters. Sometimes it's just "small talk" that is in itself insignificant but is engaged in because it preserves contact. Also included would be talking about the honesty and openness in the relationship and talking about shared feelings. Responding constructively in a conflict (even when your partner may act in ways harmful to the relationship) is another type of communicative maintenance strategy (Rusbult & Buunk, 1993).
- *Be open.* You engage in direct discussion and listen to the other—for example, you self-disclose, talk about what you want from the relationship, give advice, and express empathy.
- *Give assurances.* You assure the other person of the significance of the relationship—for example, you comfort the other, put your partner first, and express love.
- *Share joint activities.* You spend time with the other—for example, playing ball, visiting mutual friends, doing specific things as a couple (even cleaning the house), and sometimes just being together and talking with no concern for what is done. Controlling (eliminating or reducing) extrarelational activities would be another type of togetherness behavior (Rusbult & Buunk, 1993). Also included here would be ceremonial behaviors, for example, celebrating birthdays and anniversaries, discussing past pleasurable times, and eating at a favorite restaurant.
- *Be positive.* You try to make interactions pleasant and upbeat—for example, holding hands, giving in to make your partner happy, and doing favors. At the same time, you would avoid certain issues that might cause arguments.
- *Focus on improving yourself,* for example, making yourself look especially good and attractive to the other person.

RELATIONSHIP DETERIORATION

Relationship deterioration refers to the weakening of the bonds that hold people together. The process of deterioration may be gradual or sudden. Gradual deterioration might occur in a situation in which one of the parties in a relationship develops close ties with a new intimate, and this new relationship gradually pushes out the old. Sudden deterioration might occur when a rule that was essential to the relationship (for example, the rule of complete fidelity) is broken and both realize that the relationship cannot be sustained.

In terms of the theories introduced earlier, relationship deterioration would occur when you no longer find your partner attractive physically and in personality, when you no longer experience closeness, or when the differences become more important than the similarities. When relationships break up, it's the more attractive person who leaves (Blumstein & Schwartz, 1983). There is no denying the power of attractiveness in the development of relationships and the influence of its loss to the deterioration of relationships. According to social exchange, deterioration would set in when the costs begin to exceed the rewards. Similarly, a relationship may deteriorate when you feel that you could do better with someone else. Even if your relationship is less than you expected it to be, you would probably not dissolve it unless you perceived that another relationship (or being alone) will provide a greater profit. In terms of equity, deterioration would occur when you feel that you're putting more into the relationship than you're getting out of it or that your partner is benefiting from the relationship disproportionately.

When relationships deteriorate or break up, a number of things happen. Although we're conditioned to view relationship breakup as something negative, it's certainly not always negative and, in fact, may bring a variety of positive benefits as well. On the negative side, perhaps the most obvious is a loss of all the positives you enjoyed as a result of the relationship. Regardless of how unsatisfying the relationship might ultimately have been, it probably also had many good aspects. These are now lost.

There is also, generally, a loss of self-esteem. You may feel unworthy or perhaps guilty. You may blame yourself for doing the wrong things, not doing the right things, or being responsible for the losses you now confront. Of course, there are likely to be friends and family members who will give you a hard time, often implying that you're to blame.

There are also practical issues. Most relationship breakups have financial implications, and you may now encounter money problems. Paying the rent, tuition, or outstanding loans by yourself may prove difficult. If the relationship is a marriage, then there are legal and perhaps religious implications of the breakup. If there are children, the situation becomes even more complicated.

Nevertheless, not all relationships should be sustained. Not all breakups are bad, and few, if any, bad breakups are entirely bad. In the midst of a breakup, this may be difficult to appreciate. In retrospect, it's almost always true.

Some relationships are unproductive for one or both parties, and a breakup is often the best alternative. A breakup may provide an opportunity for the individuals to regain their independence and to become self-reliant again. Some relationships are so absorbing that there is little time for reflection on oneself, on others, and on the relationship. Sometimes distance helps. A breakup may also allow you to develop new associations and to explore different types of relationships with different types of people. Relational deterioration need not have only negative consequences; it's up to you to take away the positive lessons from a decaying relationship.

The Stages of Relationship Deterioration

One research study, based on responses from 1,480 men and women, found that you go through 16 steps (several of which repeat) in breaking up a romantic relationship (Battaglia, Richard, Datteri, & Lord, 1998).

1. You lose interest
2. You notice other people
3. You act distant
4. You try to work things out
5. You put distance between yourself and your partner
6. You lose interest
7. You consider breaking up
8. You talk about your feelings
9. You try to work things out
10. You notice other people
11. You act distant
12. You date other people
13. You get back together
14. You consider breaking up
15. You move on and recover
16. You break up

Another approach argues that relationship breakups can be explained in four phases, identified in the Ask the Researcher box below.

Causes of Relationship Deterioration

There are as many reasons for relationship deterioration as there are people in relationships. It is, therefore, extremely difficult to identify specific causes for any specific relationship deterioration. Still, some general causes—applicable to a wide variety of relationship breakups—may be identified.

A S K *the Researcher*

Breaking Up

I've been really unlucky in my romantic relationships; all of them have broken up, leaving me in severe depression for long periods. Since I seem doomed to relationships that will break up, I'm wondering if there's a way of avoiding relationships that cause me so many problems or at least a strategy for breaking up in less stressful ways. Any suggestions?

Most romantic relationships do break up—especially during college years and ages 16–26, when it is important for you to find "what works for you." Remember, you learn from these relationships. Breakups may be stressful and depressing, but changing attitudes is a good first step! Relationships break up for many reasons, some of them not anyone's "fault," for example because of processes between partners (mismatched personalities, different interests, inability to handle conflicts) or just plain chance (relocation, different career needs).

Breakups involve phases: Intrapsychic (thinking/reflection), Dyadic (discussion with partner), Social (talking to other people), and Grave Dressing (constructing accounts). To break up more easily/less hurtfully, recognize that process rather than blaming yourself. To prevent breakup in the first place you need different communication strategies for the different stages—Intrapsychic: reflect on partner's good qualities; Dyadic: talk the difficulties out with partner; Social: enlist help from your network of friends; Grave Dressing: create a relational account that stresses the positives and goodwill of both people.

For further information see S. W. Duck, "A Topography of Relationship Disengagement and Dissolution," in *Personal Relationships 4: Dissolving Personal Relationships,* ed. S. W. Duck (London: Academic Press, 1982), pp. 1–30.

Steve Duck (Ph.D , University of Sheffield, UK) is Daniel and Amy Starch Distinguished Research Chair, University of Iowa, Departments of Communication Studies and Psychology (adjunct). His main research and teaching interests are in various aspects of personal relationships, especially the management of "good" and "bad" aspects of relating as this concerns everyday life communication. He is the editor or author of 34 books, the founding editor of the *Journal of Social and Personal Relationships,* and a former president of the International Network on Personal Relationships. steve-duck@uiowa.edu (Reprinted by permission of Dr. Steve Duck.)

All these "causes" can also be effects of relationship deterioration. For example, when things start to go sour, you may remove yourself physically from your partner. This physical separation in turn causes further deterioration by driving you farther apart emotionally and psychologically. Similarly, the degree of mutual commitment between you may lessen as other signs of deterioration appear.

As a preface, recall that the factors that are important in establishing relationships (discussed in Chapter 10) may, when no longer present, contribute to deterioration. For example, when loneliness is no longer reduced by the relationship (when one or both individuals feel lonely frequently or for prolonged periods), the relationship may well be on the road to decay because it's not serving a function it was entered into to serve. Similarly, when relationships no longer provide stimulation, gains in knowledge and esteem, enhancement of physical and emotional health, and maximizing of pleasures and minimizing of pain, they are likely to be in trouble.

Beliefs about Relationships   The beliefs you have about relationships will greatly influence the course of your relationships. For example, if you and your partner have similar beliefs and these beliefs are realistic, then your relationship is likely to be strengthened by your similar belief systems. If, on the other hand, you and your partner hold widely different beliefs about, say, gender or financial expectations, then your relationship is more likely to experience instability and interpersonal distancing than if you both held similar beliefs (Pasley, Kerpelman, & Guilbert, 2001). Similarly, if you or your partner hold unrealistic beliefs, then your relationship is likely to experience difficulties. This role of unrealistic beliefs is well illustrated in the self-test "What Do You Believe about Relationships?"

TEST YOURSELF   *What Do You Believe about Relationships?*

On the line next to each statement, enter the number that best fits how much you agree or disagree. Use the following scale: agree completely = 7, agree a good deal = 6, agree somewhat = 5, neither agree nor disagree = 4, disagree somewhat = 3, disagree a good deal = 2, disagree completely = 1.

_____   1. If a person has any questions about the relationship, then it means there is something wrong with it.

_____   2. If my partner truly loved me, we would not have any quarrels.

_____   3. If my partner really cared, he or she would always feel affection for me.

_____   4. If my partner gets angry at me or is critical in public, this indicates he or she doesn't really love me.

_____   5. My partner should know what is important to me without my having to tell him or her.

_____   6. If I have to ask for something that I really want, it spoils it.

_____   7. If my partner really cared, he or she would do what I ask.

_____   8. A good relationship should not have any problems.

_____   9. If people really love each other, they should not have to work on their relationship.

_____ 10. If my partner does something that upsets me, I think it is because he or she deliberately wants to hurt me.

_____ 11. When my partner disagrees with me in public, I think it is a sign that he or she doesn't care for me very much.

_____ 12. If my partner contradicts me, I think that he or she doesn't have much respect for me.

_____ 13. If my partner hurts my feelings, I think that it is because he or she is mean.

_____ 14. My partner always tries to get his or her own way.

_____ 15. My partner doesn't listen to what I have to say.

▶ **How did you do?**   Aaron Beck, one of the leading theorists in cognitive therapy and the author of the popular _Love Is Never Enough_, claims that all of these beliefs are unrealistic and may create problems in your interpersonal relationships. The test was developed to help people identify potential sources of difficulty for relationship development and maintenance. The more statements that you indicated you believe in, the more unrealistic your expectations are.

▶ **What will you do?**   If you hold these beliefs and you agree that they are counterproductive, what can you do about them? You may want to begin this analysis by reviewing the list—individually or in small groups—and identifying with hypothetical or real examples why each belief is unrealistic (or realistic).

This test was taken from Aaron Beck, _Love Is Never Enough_, pp. 67–68. Copyright © 1988 by Aaron T. Beck, M.D. Reprinted by permission of Harper Collins Publishers Inc. and Arthur Pine Associates, Inc. Beck notes that this test was adapted in part from the Relationship Belief Inventory of N. Epstein, J. L. Pretzer, and B. Fleming, "The Role of Cognitive Appraisal in Self-Reports of Marital Communication," _Behavior Therapy_ 18 (1987): 51–69.

Excessive Intimacy Claims   In most relationships—especially intense ones—the members make intimacy claims on each other (Blood, 1973). Such claims may include expectations that the partner will sympathize and empathize, attend to self-disclosures with total absorption, or share the other's preferences with equal intensity. These intimacy claims often restrict personal freedom and may take the form of possessiveness. To be always responsive, always sympathetic, always loving, always attentive is more than many can manage. In some relationships, the intimacy claims and demands are so great that the partners' individual identities may be in danger of being absorbed or destroyed.

Third-Party Relationships   You establish and maintain relationships to maximize your pleasure and minimize your pain. When this ceases to be the case, the relationship stands little chance of survival. These needs are so great that when they're not met within the existing relationship, their fulfillment will be sought elsewhere. When a new relationship serves these needs better, the old relationship may deteriorate. At times, this may be a romantic interest; at other times, the new relationship may be with a parent or, frequently, a child. When your need for affection or attention, once supplied by the other person, is now supplied by a friend or a child, the primary relationship may be in trouble.

Relationship Changes   The development of incompatible attitudes, vastly different intellectual interests and abilities, and major goal changes may contribute to relationship deterioration. Similarly, changes in behavior may create difficulties. For example, if you once devoted lots of time to your partner and to the relationship and now are totally absorbed with business or school, your relationship is going to face significant repercussions. The person who develops an addiction (to drugs, alcohol, or even stamp collecting) will likewise present the relationship with a serious problem.

Undefined Expectations   Unresolved expectations over who is in charge are a frequent cause of relationship difficulties (Lederer, 1984). Often, conflicts over such trivial issues as who does the dishes or who walks the dog mask resentment and hostility concerning some more significant unresolved expectation.

At times, the expectations each person has of the other may be unrealistic, and when reality enters the relationship, difficulties arise. This type of situation often occurs early in a relationship when, for example, the individuals think they will want to spend all their time together. When it's discovered that neither one does, each resents this "lessening" of feeling in the other. The resolution of such problems lies in demonstrating that the original expectations are unrealistic and that realistic and satisfying ones can be substituted.

Another kind of undefined expectation may involve sex-role stereotypes. One person, for example, might hold very traditional views about the role of the man and the role of the woman, whereas the other person may hold very liberal views, rejecting the more conservative sex-role assignments. With this type of difference, conflicts over who puts the children to bed or who works a second job are easy to imagine.

Sex-Related Problems   Few relationships are free of sexual differences and problems. In fact, sexual problems rank among the top three problems in almost all studies of newlyweds (Blumstein & Schwartz, 1983). When these same couples are surveyed later in their relationship, the sexual problems have not gone away; they're just discussed less. Apparently, people resign themselves to living with the problems. In one survey, for example, 80 percent of the respondents identified their marriages as either "very happy" or "happy," but some 90 percent said they had sexual problems (Freedman, 1978).

Although sexual frequency isn't related to relationship breakdown, sexual satisfaction is. It's the quality of the sexual relationship, not the quantity of sexual encounters, that is crucial (Blumstein & Schwartz, 1983). When the quality is poor, outside affairs may be sought, and these contribute significantly to breakups for all couples, whether married or cohabiting (Blumstein & Schwartz, 1983).

View point Even though women are now firmly in the workplace, they are still the primary caregivers and perform the bulk of household duties. In fact, Switzerland has initiated a campaign to get men to take on more of the household chores with a "fair play at home" campaign (Olson, 2002). If you were in charge of such a campaign in the Untied States, what would you say to men? What would you say to women?

Work-Related Problems   Problems associated with either partner's job often lead to difficulties within the relationship. This is true for all types of couples. With heterosexual couples (both marrieds and cohabitants), if the man is disturbed about the woman's job—for example, if she earns a great deal more than he does or devotes a great deal of time to the job—the relationship is in considerable trouble. This is true whether the relationship is in its early stages or is well established (Blumstein & Schwartz, 1983). One research study found that husbands whose wives worked were less satisfied with their own jobs and lives than were men whose wives didn't work (Staines, Pottick, & Fudge, 1986). This personal dissatisfaction will naturally have negative effects on the relationship. Another study found that men and women who retire while their spouses continue to work experience considerable marital conflict, regardless of gender (Moen, Jim, & Hofmeister, 2001).

With homosexual relationships the situation is a bit different. Gay men, like heterosexual men, are career oriented. Because of this, work-related problems may be magnified, since both devote considerable time to work with less time available for the more relational concerns. Lesbians, on the other hand, are less career oriented than gay men and are more relationship oriented. This may be one reason lesbian relationships seem to last longer than gay male relationships (Blumstein & Schwartz, 1983; Huston & Schwartz, 1995).

Financial Difficulties   In surveys of problems among couples, financial difficulties loom large. Money is a major taboo topic for couples beginning a relationship, yet it proves to be the cause of major problems as people settle into their relationship. One-fourth to one-third of all couples rank money as their primary problem; almost all rank it as one of their major problems (Blumstein & Schwartz, 1983).

Increasing Interpersonal Effectiveness
Empathy

Empathy is an ability to feel what another person feels from that person's point of view without losing your own identity, to feel as the person feels, to walk in the same shoes, to feel the feelings in a somewhat similar way. Empathy enables you to understand emotionally what another person is experiencing. (To sympathize, in contrast, is to feel *for* the person—to feel sorry or happy for the person, for example.)

Communicating Empathy   Here are a few suggestions to help you communicate empathy effectively (Authier & Gustafson, 1982).

■ *Avoid evaluating, judging, or criticizing the other person's behaviors.* Make it clear that you're not evaluating or judging but trying to understand.
■ *Focus your concentration.* Maintain eye contact, an attentive posture, and physical closeness. Express your involvement through appropriate facial expressions and gestures.

■ *Reflect back to the speaker the feelings that you think are being expressed to help you check the accuracy of your perceptions and to show your commitment to understanding the speaker.* In doing so, you may find it helpful to make tentative statements about what you think the person is feeling. For example, "You seem really angry with your father" or "I hear some doubt in your voice."
■ *When appropriate use your own self-disclosures to communicate your understanding.* Be careful, however, that you don't get so caught up in your own disclosures that you refocus the discussion on yourself.
■ *Address mixed messages to help foster more open and honest communication.* When your friend verbally expresses contentment but shows nonverbal signs of depression it may be prudent to question the possible discrepancy.

Money is so important in relationships because of its close connection with power. Money brings power in relationships, as it does in business. The person bringing in the most money wields the most power. This person has the final say, for example, on the purchase of expensive items as well as on decisions having nothing to do with money. The power that money brings quickly spreads to nonfinancial issues as well.

Money also creates problems because men and women view it differently (Blumstein & Schwartz, 1983). To many men, money is power. To many women, it's security and independence. To men, money is accumulated to exert power and influence. To women, money is accumulated to achieve security and reduce dependence on others. Conflicts over the way the couple's money is to be spent or invested can easily result from such different views. Further, when the wife earns a high income, marital conflict increases and the husband's satisfaction with the relationship decreases (Harrell, 1990).

Dissatisfaction with money creates relationship problems for married and cohabiting couples and gay male couples but not for lesbian couples, who seem to care a great deal less about financial matters (Blumstein & Schwartz, 1983). This difference has led some researchers to postulate (though without conclusive evidence) that the concern over money and its equation with power and relational satisfaction are largely male attitudes.

Figure 11.1 on page 272 summarizes the changes in communication (discussed in this chapter and the previous one) that take place as you move toward or away from intimacy. The general and most important point this figure makes is that communication effectiveness and satisfaction increase as you move toward intimacy and decrease as you move away from intimacy.

RELATIONSHIP REPAIR

If you wish to save a relationship, you may try to do so by changing your communication patterns and, in effect, putting into practice the insights and skills learned in this course. First, let's look at some general ways to repair a relationship, and second we can examine ways to deal with repair when you're the only one who wants to change the relationship.

Interpersonal Repair

We can look at the strategies for repairing a relationship in terms of the following six suggestions, which conveniently spell out the word repair, a useful reminder that repair is not a one-step but a multistep process (see Figure 11.2 on page 273).

Recognize the Problem   Your first step is to identify the problem and to recognize it both intellectually and emotionally. Specify what is wrong with your present relationship (in concrete terms) and what changes would be needed to make it better (again, in specific terms). Create a picture of your relationship as you would want it to be, and compare that picture to the way the relationship looks now. Specify the changes that would have to take place if the ideal picture were to replace the present picture.

Try also to see the problem from your partner's point of view and to have your partner see the problem from yours. Exchange these perspectives, empathically and with open minds. Try, too, to be descriptive when discussing grievances, taking special care to avoid such troublesome terms as "always" and "never." Own your feelings and thoughts; use I-messages and take responsibility for your feelings instead of blaming your partner.

WEB EXPLORATION
To learn more about relationship repair, go to www.ablongman.com/devito.

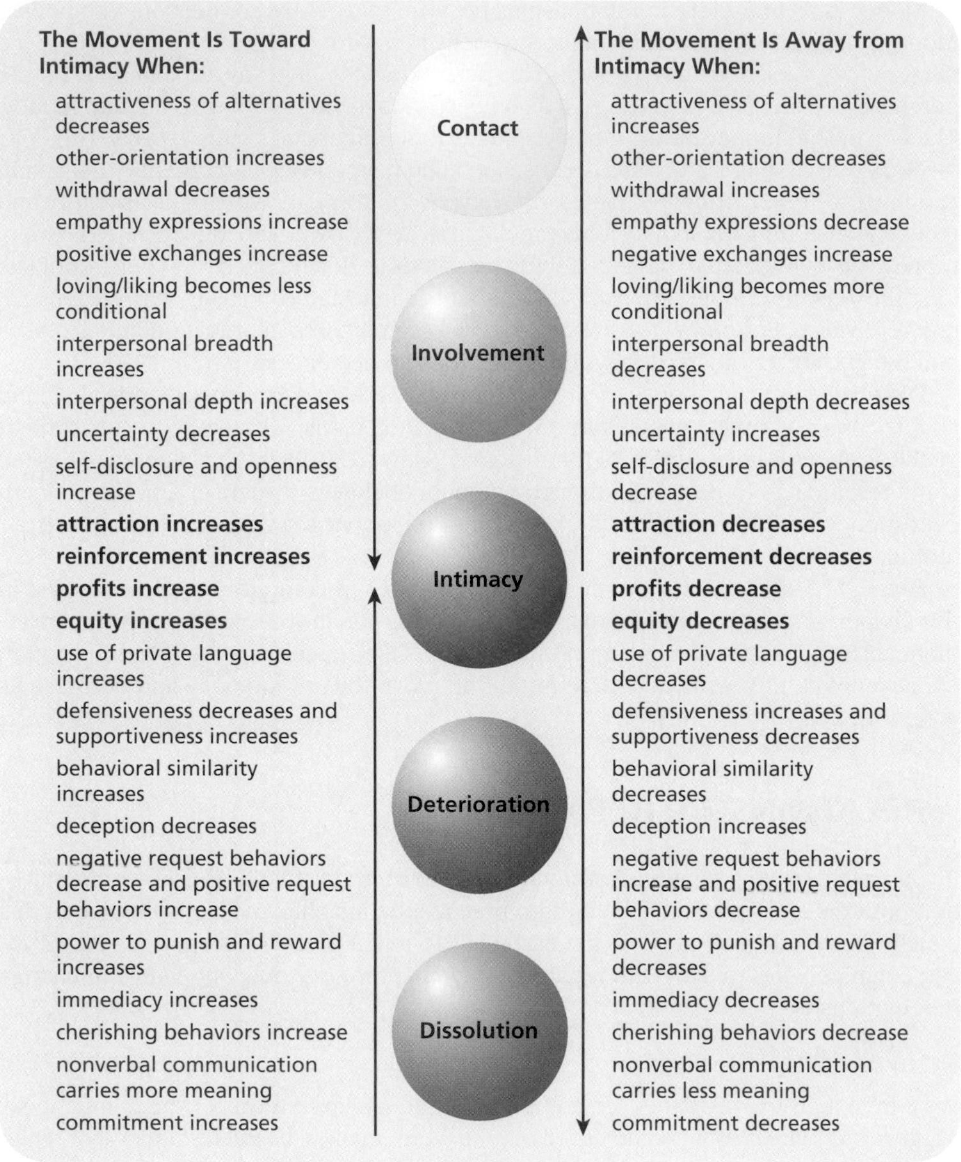

The Movement Is Toward Intimacy When:

- attractiveness of alternatives decreases
- other-orientation increases
- withdrawal decreases
- empathy expressions increase
- positive exchanges increase
- loving/liking becomes less conditional
- interpersonal breadth increases
- interpersonal depth increases
- uncertainty decreases
- self-disclosure and openness increase
- **attraction increases**
- **reinforcement increases**
- **profits increase**
- **equity increases**
- use of private language increases
- defensiveness decreases and supportiveness increases
- behavioral similarity increases
- deception decreases
- negative request behaviors decrease and positive request behaviors increase
- power to punish and reward increases
- immediacy increases
- cherishing behaviors increase
- nonverbal communication carries more meaning
- commitment increases

The Movement Is Away from Intimacy When:

- attractiveness of alternatives increases
- other-orientation decreases
- withdrawal increases
- empathy expressions decrease
- negative exchanges increase
- loving/liking becomes more conditional
- interpersonal breadth decreases
- interpersonal depth decreases
- uncertainty increases
- self-disclosure and openness decrease
- **attraction decreases**
- **reinforcement decreases**
- **profits decrease**
- **equity decreases**
- use of private language decreases
- defensiveness increases and supportiveness decreases
- behavioral similarity decreases
- deception increases
- negative request behaviors increase and positive request behaviors decrease
- power to punish and reward decreases
- immediacy decreases
- cherishing behaviors decrease
- nonverbal communication carries less meaning
- commitment decreases

Stages: Contact, Involvement, Intimacy, Deterioration, Dissolution

Figure 11.1

Communication in Relationships

This summary of some of the changes that accompany increased intimacy and some that accompany decreased intimacy contains many of the findings discussed here and in Chapter 10. The major theories discussed in this chapter are noted here in boldface. As you read down the list, try to identify examples that influenced your own relationships. Did any factors listed here produce effects on your relationships different from those predicted here? For example, did one of the factors listed here as leading to greater intimacy actually result in decreased intimacy? What else happens as a relationship moves toward intimacy? Toward deterioration? How would you go about testing the validity of these movement predictions?

Engage in Productive Communication and Conflict Resolution   Interpersonal communication skills such as those considered throughout the text (for example, other orientation, openness, confidence, immediacy, expressiveness, and empathy, considered in the Increasing Effectiveness boxes throughout the text) are especially important during repair and are an essential part of any repair strategy. Here are several suggestions to refresh your memory.

Do you generally follow these productive conflict strategies?

1. Look closely for relational messages that will help clarify motivations and needs. Respond to these messages as well as to the content messages.
2. Exchange perspectives and see the situation as your partner does.
3. Practice empathic and positive responses, even in conflict situations.

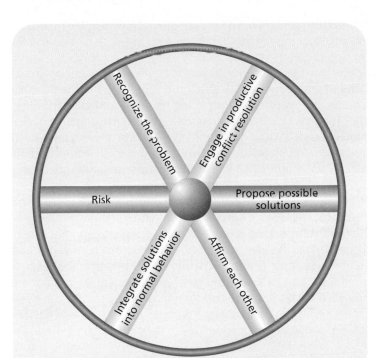

Figure
11.2

The Relationship Repair Wheel
The wheel seems an apt metaphor for the repair process; the specific repair strategies—the spokes—all work together in constant process. The wheel is difficult to get moving, but once in motion it becomes easier to turn. Also, it's easier to start when two people are pushing but not impossible for one to move it in the right direction. What metaphor do you find helpful in thinking about relationship repair?

4. Own your feelings and thoughts. Use I-messages and take responsibility for these feelings.
5. Use active-listening techniques to help your partner explore and express relevant thoughts and feelings.
6. Remember the principle of irreversibility; think carefully before saying things you may later regret.
7. Keep the channels of communication open. Be available to discuss problems, to negotiate solutions, and to practice new and more productive communication patterns.

Similarly, the skills of effective interpersonal conflict resolution are crucial in any attempt at relationship repair. If relationship problems are confronted with productive conflict resolution strategies, the difficulties may be resolved, and the relationship may actually emerge stronger and healthier. If, however, unproductive and destructive strategies are used, then the relationship may well deteriorate further. The nature and skills of conflict resolution are considered in depth in Chapter 13.

Pose Possible Solutions   After the problem is identified, you discuss solutions, the ways to lessen or eliminate the difficulty. Look for solutions that will enable both of you to win. Try to avoid "solutions" in which one person wins and the other loses. With such win–lose solutions, resentment and hostility are likely to fester.

Affirm Each Other   Any strategy of relationship repair should incorporate supportiveness and positive evaluations. For example, happy couples engage in greater positive behavior exchange; they communicate more agreement, approval, and positive affect than do unhappy couples (Dindia & Fitzpatrick, 1985). Clearly, these behaviors result from the positive feelings the partners have for each other. However, it can also be argued that these expressions help to increase the positive regard each person has for the other.

One way to affirm another is to talk positively. Reverse negative communication patterns. For example, instead of withdrawing, talk about the causes of and the possible cures for your disagreements and problems. Reverse the tendency to hide your inner self. Disclose your feelings. Increase positive evaluations and decrease negative evaluations. Positive expressions and behaviors help to increase the positive regard each person has for his or her partner. Compliments, positive stroking, and all the nonverbals that say "I care" are especially important when you wish to reverse negative communication patterns.

Cherishing behaviors are an especially insightful way to affirm another person and to increase favor exchange (Lederer, 1984). **Cherishing behaviors** are those small gestures you enjoy receiving from your partner (a smile, a wink, a squeeze, a kiss). Cherishing behaviors should be (1) specific and positive, (2) focused on the present and future rather than related to issues about which the partners have argued in the past, (3) capable of being performed daily, and (4) easily executed. People can make a list of the cherishing behaviors they each wish to receive and then exchange lists. Each person then performs the cherishing behaviors desired by the partner. At first, these behaviors may seem self-conscious and awkward. In time, however, they will become a normal part of interaction.

Integrate Solutions into Normal Behavior   Often solutions that are reached after an argument are followed for only a very short time; then the couple goes back to their previous, unproductive behavior patterns. Instead, integrate the solutions into your normal behavior; make them an integral part of your everyday relationship behavior. Make the exchange of favors, compliments, and cherishing behaviors a part of your normal relationship behavior.

Interpersonal Relationships and the Media

The media are currently teaching millions of people about interpersonal relationships.

Whether for good or ill, millions of people tune in to the ubiquitous television talk show to learn about friendship, romantic, family, and workplace relationships. Talk shows often present themselves as educational, as therapy, and as arbiters of how you, your parents, and your friends should develop and maintain relationships. Especially in the monologue that closes many of the shows, talk show hosts with little to no professional training dispense interpersonal advice. For instance, they regularly give communication advice with no basis in scientific research and foster myths about communication—perhaps the most prevalent being that the more communication a couple has the better the relationship will be.

Newspaper and magazine columnists offer advice without knowing even a modicum of information about who you are, what difficulties you may be experiencing, and what you really want and need. And astrology columns and psychic hotlines give you advice that has no basis in research.

Follow Up   What forms of media exert the most influence on your views about relationships and on your relational behavior itself? What role do talk shows, advice columns, and psychic hotlines play in your relational life and in the lives of your peers? Look at your answers in light of the research evidence supporting the third-person effect discussed in the Intermedia box in Chapter 4.

A Stimulus–Response View of Relationship Problems
This view of the relationship process implies that one behavior is the stimulus and one behavior is the response. It implies that a pattern of behavior can only be modified if you change the stimulus, which will produce a different (more desirable) response.

Risk   Take risks in trying to improve your relationship. Risk giving favors without any certainty of reciprocity. Risk rejection by making the first move to make up or by saying you're sorry. Be willing to change, to adapt, to take on new tasks and responsibilities.

Risk the possibility that a significant part of the problem is you, that you're being unreasonable or controlling or stingy and that this is causing problems and needs to be changed.

Intrapersonal Repair

One of the most important implications for repair comes from the principle of punctuation (see Chapter 1) and the idea that communication is circular rather than linear (see Chapter 1; Duncan & Rock, 1991). Let's consider an example involving Pat and Chris: Pat is highly critical of Chris; Chris is defensive and attacks Pat for being insensitive, overly negative, and unsupportive. If you view the communication process as beginning with Pat's being critical (that is, the stimulus) and with Chris's attacks being the response, you have a pattern such as occurs in Figure 11.3.

With this view, the only way to stop the unproductive communication pattern is for Pat to stop criticizing. But what if you are Chris and can't get Pat to stop being critical? What if Pat doesn't want to stop being critical?

You get a different view of the problem when you see communication as circular and apply the principle of punctuation. The result is a pattern such as appears in Figure 11.4.

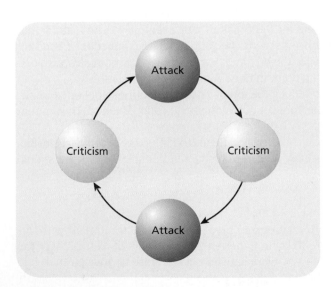

A Circular View of Relationship Problems
Note that in this view of relationships, as distinguished from that depicted in Figure 11.3, relationship behaviors are seen in a circular pattern where no specific behavior is singled out as a stimulus and none as a response. The pattern can thus be broken by interference anywhere along the circle.

Note that no assumptions are made about causes. Instead, the only assumption is that each response triggers another response; each response depends in part on the previous response. Therefore, the pattern can be broken at any point: Pat's criticism, for example, may be stopped by Chris not responding with attacks. Similarly, Pat can stop Chris's attacks by not responding with criticism.

In this view, either person can break an unproductive circle. Clearly, relationship communication can be most effectively improved when both parties change their unproductive patterns. Nevertheless, communication can be improved even if only one person changes and begins to use a more productive pattern. This is true to the extent that Pat's criticism depends on Chris's attacks and to the extent that Chris's attacks depend on Pat's criticism.

RELATIONSHIP DISSOLUTION

Some relationships, of course, do end. Sometimes there is simply not enough to hold the couple together. Sometimes there are problems that cannot be resolved. Sometimes the costs are too high and the rewards too few, or the relationship is recognized as destructive and escape is the only alternative. As a relationship ends, you're confronted with two general issues: how to end the relationship, and how to deal with the inevitable problems that relationship endings cause.

Strategies of Disengagement

When you wish to exit a relationship, you need some way of explaining this—to yourself as well as to your partner. You need a strategy for getting out of a relationship that you no longer find satisfying or profitable. Five such strategies are presented below (Cody, 1982). As you read down the list, note that the strategies depend on your goal. For example, you're more likely to remain friends if you use de-escalation than if you use justification or avoidance (Banks, Altendorf, Greene, & Cody, 1987).

Have you heard these or used any of these yourself?

I SEE

1. The use of a positive tone to preserve the relationship and to express positive feelings for the other person. For example, "I really care for you a great deal, but I'm not ready for such an intense relationship."
2. Negative identity management to blame the other person for the breakup and to absolve yourself of the blame for the breakup. For example, "I can't stand your jealousy, your constant suspicions, your checking up on me. I need my freedom."
3. Justification to give reasons for the breakup. For example, "I'm going away to college for four years; there's no point in not dating others."
4. Behavioral de-escalation to reduce the intensity of the relationship. For example, you might avoid the other person, cut down on phone calls, or reduce the amount of time you spend together.
5. De-escalation to reduce the exclusivity and hence the intensity of the relationship. For example, "I'm just not ready for an exclusive relationship. I think we should see other people."

Dealing with a Breakup

Regardless of the specific reason, relationship breakups are difficult to deal with; invariably they cause stress. You're likely to experience high levels of distress over the breakup of a relationship in which you were satisfied, were close to your partner, had dated your partner for a long time, and felt it would not be easy to replace the relationship with another one (Simpson, 1987; Frazier & Cook, 1993).

Given both the inevitability that some relationships will break up and the importance of such breakups, here are some suggestions to ease the difficulty that is sure to be experienced. These suggestions apply to the termination of any type of relationship—between friends or lovers, through death, separation, or breakup.

Break the Loneliness–Depression Cycle   The two most common feelings following the end of a relationship are loneliness and depression. These feelings are significant; treat them seriously. Realize that depression often leads to serious illness. In most cases, fortunately, loneliness and depression are temporary. Depression, for example, usually does not last longer than three or four days. Similarly, the loneliness that follows a breakup is generally linked to this specific situation and will fade when the situation changes. When depression does last, is especially deep, or disturbs your normal functioning, it's time for professional help.

Take Time Out   Resist the temptation to jump into a new relationship while the old one is still warm or before a new one can be assessed with some objectivity. At the same time, resist swearing off all relationships. Neither extreme works well.

Take time out for yourself. Renew your relationship with yourself. If you were in a long-term relationship, you probably saw yourself as part of a team, as part of a couple. Now get to know yourself as a unique individual, standing alone at present but fully capable of entering a meaningful relationship in the near future.

Bolster Self-Esteem   When relationships fail, self-esteem often declines. This seems especially true for those who did not initiate the breakup (Collins & Clark, 1989). You may feel guilty for having caused the breakup or inadequate for not holding on to the relationship. You may feel unwanted and unloved. Your task is to regain the positive self-image needed to function effectively.

Recognize, too, that having been in a relationship that failed—even if you view yourself as the main cause of the breakup—does not mean that you are a failure. Neither does it mean that you cannot succeed in a new and different relationship. It does mean that something went wrong with this one relationship. Ideally, it was a failure from which you have learned something important about yourself and about your relationship behavior.

Remove or Avoid Uncomfortable Symbols   After any breakup, there are a variety of reminders—photographs, gifts, and letters, for example. Resist the temptation to throw these out. Instead, remove them. Give them to a friend to hold or put them in a closet where you'll not see them. If possible, avoid places you frequented together. These symbols will bring back uncomfortable memories. After you have achieved some emotional distance, you can go back and enjoy these as reminders of a once pleasant relationship. Support for this suggestion comes from research showing that the more vivid your memory of a broken love affair—a memory greatly aided by these relationship symbols—the greater your depression is likely to be (Harvey, Flanary, & Morgan, 1986).

Seek Support   Many people feel they should bear their burdens alone. Men, in particular, have been taught that this is the only "manly" way to handle things. But seeking the support of others is one of the best antidotes to the unhappiness caused when a relationship ends. Tell your friends and family of your situation—in only general terms, if you prefer—and make it clear that you want support. Seek out people who are positive and nurturing. Avoid negative individuals who will paint the world in even darker tones. Make the distinction between seeking support and seeking advice. If you feel you need advice, seek out a professional.

Avoid Repeating Negative Patterns   Many people repeat their mistakes. They enter second and third relationships with the same blinders, faulty preconceptions, and unrealistic expectations with which they entered earlier ones. Instead, use the knowledge gained from your failed relationships to prevent repeating the same patterns.

At the same time, don't become a prophet of doom. Don't see in every relationship vestiges of the old. Don't jump at the first conflict and say, "Here it goes all over again." Treat the new relationship as the unique relationship it is. Don't evaluate it through past experiences. Use past relationships and experiences as guides, not filters.

REVIEWING   Key Terms and Concepts in Interpersonal Relationships: Growth and Deterioration

Relationship Development

What are some of the major theories that explain why you develop the relationships you do?
■ Attraction theory holds that you develop relationships with those you consider attractive (physically and in personality), who are physically close to you, and who are similar to you.
■ Social exchange theory holds that you develop relationships that enable you to maximize profits, relationships from which you derive more rewards than costs.
■ Equity theory holds that you develop and maintain relationships in which the ratio of rewards compared to costs is approximately equal to your partner's.

Relationship Maintenance

What are the reasons for relationship maintenance? What behaviors do people use to maintain their relationships?
■ Reasons for maintaining a relationship include emotional attachment, convenience, children, fear, inertia, and commitment.
■ Maintenance behaviors include being nice, communicating, being open, giving assurances, sharing joint activities, being positive, and improving yourself.
■ Relationship maintenance can be achieved by following the rules for keeping the relationship, whether friendship or romance, together.

Relationship Deterioration

What is relationship deterioration? Why do relationships deteriorate?
■ Relationship deterioration refers to the weakening of the bonds holding people together. It occurs when one or both parties are unhappy with the current state of the relationship.
■ Among the causes of relationship deterioration are maintaining unrealistic beliefs about relationships, excessive intimacy claims, third-party relationships, relationship changes, undefined expectations, sex-related problems, work-related problems, and financial difficulties.

Relationship Repair

What is relationship repair? What strategies can you use to repair a relationship?
■ Relationship repair refers to the process of correcting the problems that beset a relationship and bringing the relationship to a more intimate, more positive state.
■ General repair strategies include: recognizing the problem, engaging in productive communication and conflict resolution, posing possible solutions, affirming each other, integrating solutions into normal behavior, and risking.
■ Repair isn't necessarily a two-person process; one person can break unproductive and destructive cycles.

Relationship Dissolution

What is relationship dissolution? What strategies are used to dissolve relationships?
■ Dissolution refers to the breaking or dissolving of the bonds that hold the relationship together.
■ Among the strategies are positive tone, negative identity management, justification, behavioral de-escalation, and de-escalation.

APPLYING   Key Terms and Concepts in Interpersonal Relationships: Growth and Deterioration

1. What has to be going on in a relationship for you to say that it's "developing" or that it's "deteriorating"?
2. Research shows that teachers' affinity-seeking strategies influence classroom climate. For example, if the teacher is supportive, the students are more likely to view the classroom environment as supportive (Cabello & Terrell, 1994; Myers, 1995). Given this finding, what suggestions would you offer a new instructor about affinity seeking?
3. Do you "comparison shop" (compare your own relationship against potential alternative relationships) regardless

of the type of relationship you're in, or do you stop "shopping" when the relationship reaches a certain level of commitment?

4. Do a cost-benefit analysis of any one of your current relationships. In one column, identify all the costs, and in the other column identify all the benefits you get from the relationship. Next, altercast, playing the role of the person you just did an analysis of, do a cost-benefit analysis of yourself (as you think you might be seen by this person). What can you learn from this type of analysis?

5. How would you feel if you were in a relationship in which you and your partner contributed an equal share of the costs (that is, you each worked equally hard) but your partner derived significantly greater rewards?

6. How do your communication patterns change during relationship deterioration? What effects do these changed patterns have?

7. What practical suggestions for dealing with relationship deterioration, repair, or dissolution do the theories of attraction, social exchange, and equity offer?

8. How would you explain the finding that when relationships break up, it's the more attractive person who leaves first? What other factors might account for who leaves first?

9. What factors help to maintain and preserve your own friendship or romantic relationships?

10. What maintenance strategies would you feel comfortable using? What strategies would make you uncomfortable?

11. How would you describe a current or past friendship or romantic relationship in terms of the rules discussed in this chapter?

12. How have your own cultural beliefs and values influenced your evaluation of the maintenance and repair processes?

EXPERIENCING Key Terms and Concepts in Interpersonal Relationships: Growth and Deterioration

Go to www.ablongman.com/devito.

This group of experiences deals with interpersonal relationships, their development, maintenance, deterioration, repair, and dissolution.

(1) **Interpersonal Relationships in Songs and Greeting Cards** explores the way cards and songs talk about relationships. (2) **Applying Theories to Problems** provides an opportunity to apply the theories discussed in this chapter to common relationship problems. (3) **Male and Female** looks at gender differences in relationships. (4) **Changing the Distance between You** illustrates how relationship changes can be made. (5) **Relational Repair from Advice Columnists** encourages you to critically examine the advice given by relationship columnists. (6) **How Can You Get Someone to Like You?** looks at affinity-seeking strategies and how they're used to change people's perceptions. (7) **How Might You Repair Relationships?** presents a variety of relationship problems and asks you to apply the insights gained here and from your own experience in suggesting repair strategies.

RESEARCHING with Research Navigator Key Terms and Concepts in Interpersonal Relationships: Growth and Deterioration

Go to http://www.researchnavigator.com.

Reading an article.

Read a popular or scholarly article on relationship development, maintenance, deterioration, repair, or dissolution. On the basis of this article what can you add to the discussion presented here?

Investigating key terms.

Investigate one of the key terms discussed in this chapter (for example, attraction theory, proximity, similarity, affinity-seeking strategies, social exchange theory, equity theory, relationship deterioration, relationship rules, relationship repair, or empathy). What additional insights can you provide?

Finding answers.

Try finding answers to one of the following questions or design a research study to answer it.

■ Which personality characteristics are especially attractive to men and which are especially attractive to women?
■ How equitable are the relationships of those in this class?
■ When a relationship isn't equitable, which person is more likely to leave first—the one who is getting more profit than deserved or the one getting less?
■ Are certain repair strategies more effective than others?
■ Do men and women see relationship commitment in the same way?
■ How do romantic and friendship rules vary between two cultures?
■ Do people talk about different things with their acquaintances, friends, and intimates?

12 Interpersonal Relationships: Friendship, Love, Family, and Workplace

Waiting to Exhale (1995)

*Love is a gross exaggeration of
the difference between one
person and everybody else.*

—George Bernard Shaw

Friendship
Love
Family
Workplace Relationships

Four women in Arizona (Whitney Houston, Angela Bassett, Loretta Devine, and Lela Rochon) struggle with the difficulties of finding suitable relationship partners in Waiting to Exhale. *In addition to depicting the difficulties in finding romantic love, the film illustrates how friendships and families are developed, maintained, and strengthened. In this chapter we look at some of the types of friendship, love, and family you may encounter and some of the ways in which you may nurture such relationships.*

FRIENDSHIP

Friendship has engaged the attention and imagination of poets, novelists, and artists of all kinds. In television, our most influential mass medium, friendships have become almost as important as romantic pairings. Friendship now engages the attention of a range of interpersonal communication researchers. Throughout your life you'll meet many people, but out of this wide array you'll develop few relationships you would call friendships. Yet despite the low number of friendships you may form, their importance is great.

Friendship is a relationship between two persons that is *mutually productive* and *characterized by mutual positive regard.* Friendship is an interpersonal relationship; communication interactions must have taken place between the people. Further, the relationship involves a "personalistic focus" (Wright, 1978, 1984); friends react to each other as complete persons, as unique, genuine, and irreplaceable individuals.

Friendships must be mutually productive—they cannot be destructive either to oneself or to the other person. Once destructiveness enters into a relationship, it can no longer be characterized as friendship. Lover relationships, marriage relationships, parent–child relationships, and just about any other possible relationship can be either destructive or productive, but friendship must enhance the potential of each person and can only be productive.

Friendships are characterized by mutual positive regard. Liking people is essential if we are to call them friends. Three major characteristics of friends—trust, emotional support, and sharing of interests (Blieszner & Adams, 1992)—facilitate mutual positive regard.

When friends are especially close, the actions of one will impact more significantly on the other than they would if the friends were just casual acquaintances. The closer friends are the more interdependent they become. At the same time, however, the closer friends are the more independent they are of, for example, the attitudes and behaviors of others. Also, they're less influenced by the societal rules that govern more casual relationships. Close friends are likely to make up their own rules for interacting with each other; they decide what they will talk about and when, what they can say to each other without offending and what they can't, when and for what reasons they can call each other, and so on.

In North America, friendships clearly are a matter of choice; you choose —within limits—who your friends will be. The density of the cities and the ease of communication and relocation makes friendships voluntary. But in many parts of the world—for example, small villages miles away from urban centers, where people are born, live, and die without venturing much beyond their village—relationships aren't voluntary. In these cases, you simply form relationships with those in your village. You don't have the luxury of selecting certain people to interact with and others to ignore. You must inter-

TRY IT!
Apply your knowledge about friendship types; go to **www.ablongman. com/devito**.

act with and form relationships with members of the community simply because these people are the only ones you come into contact with on a regular basis (Moghaddam, Taylor, & Wright, 1993).

Friendship Types

Not all friendships are the same. But how do they differ? One way of answering this question is by distinguishing among the three major types of friendship: reciprocity, receptivity, and association (Reisman, 1979, 1981).

The friendship of *reciprocity* is the ideal type, characterized by loyalty, self-sacrifice, mutual affection, and generosity. A friendship of reciprocity is based on equality: Each individual shares equally in giving and receiving the benefits and rewards of the relationship.

In the friendship of *receptivity,* in contrast, there is an imbalance in giving and receiving; one person is the primary giver and one the primary receiver. This imbalance, however, is a positive one because each person gains something from the relationship. The different needs of both the person who receives and the person who gives affection are satisfied. This is the friendship that may develop between a teacher and a student or between a doctor and a patient. In fact, a difference in status is essential for the friendship of receptivity to develop.

The friendship of *association* is a transitory one. It might be described as a friendly relationship rather than a true friendship. Associative friendships are the kind we often have with classmates, neighbors, or coworkers. There is no great loyalty, no great trust, no great giving or receiving. The association is cordial but not intense.

Another answer to the question of how friendships differ can be seen by examining the needs that friends serve. On the basis of your experiences or your predictions, you select as friends those who will help to satisfy your basic growth needs. Selecting friends on the basis of need satisfaction is similar to choosing a marriage partner, an employee, or any person who may be in a position to satisfy your needs. Thus, for example, if you need to be the center of attention or to be popular, you might select friends who allow you, and even encourage you, to be the center of attention or who tell you, verbally and nonverbally, that you're popular.

As your needs change, the qualities you look for in friendships also change. In many instances, old friends are dropped from your close circle to be replaced by new friends who better serve these new needs. One way to look at the needs that friendships serve is to look at the values or rewards that you seek to gain through your friendships (Wright 1978, 1984).

Consider the values you look for in a friend. Do you look for values such as these?

1. *Utility* (someone who may have special talents, skills, or resources that prove useful to you in achieving your specific goals and needs). For example, might you become friends with someone who is particularly bright because such a person might assist you in getting better grades, in solving problems, or in getting a better job?
2. *Affirmation* (someone who would affirm your personal value and help you to recognize your attributes). For example, might you develop a friendship with someone to help you see more clearly your leadership abilities, your athletic prowess, or sense of humor?
3. *Ego support* (someone who behaves in a supportive, encouraging, and helpful manner). For example, would you seek friendships to help you view yourself as worthy and competent?

4. *Stimulation* (someone who introduces you to new ideas and new ways of seeing the world and helps you to expand your worldview). For example, would you form friendships with those who might bring you into contact with previously unfamiliar people, issues, religions, cultures, and experiences?
5. *Security* (someone who does nothing to hurt you or to emphasize or call attention to your inadequacies or weaknesses). For example, would you select friends because you'd not have to worry about them betraying you or making negative comments about you?

Friendship and Communication

Friendships develop over time in stages. At one end of the friendship continuum are strangers, or two persons who have just met, and at the other end are intimate friends. What happens between these two extremes?

As you progress from the initial contact stage to intimate friendship, the depth and breadth of communications increase (see Chapter 10). You talk about issues that are closer and closer to your inner core. Similarly, the number of communication topics increases as your friendship becomes closer. As depth and breadth increase, so does the satisfaction you derive from the friendship. This increase in depth and breadth can and does occur in all forms of communication—face-to-face as well as online. It's interesting to note that research has found that friendship was the primary goal for Internet communication among college students. Over 60 percent of online users established successful online friends and about 50 percent felt more comfortable meeting someone online than in person (Knox, Daniels, Sturdivant, & Zusman, 2001). In another study 36 percent indicated that they established an online friendship compared to 22 percent who established an online romance (Nice & Katzev, 1998).

Earlier (Chapter 10) the concept of dynamic tension in relationships was discussed. It was pointed out that there is a tension between, for example, autonomy and connection—the desire to be an individual but also to be connected to another person. Friendships are also defined by dynamic tensions (Rawlins, 1983). One tension is between the impulse to be open and to reveal personal thoughts and feelings on the one hand, and the impulse to protect yourself by not revealing personal information on the other. Also, there is the tension between being open and candid with your friend and being discreet. These contradictory impulses make it clear that friendships don't always follow a straight path of increasing openness and candor. This is not to say that openness and candor don't increase as you progress from initial to casual to close friendships; they do. But the pattern does not follow a straight line; throughout the friendship development process, there are tensions that periodically restrict openness and candor.

There are regressions that may temporarily pull the friendship back to a less intimate stage. Friendships stabilize at a level that is comfortable to both persons; some friendships will remain casual and others will remain close. Again, although friendship is presented in stages, the progression is not always a straight line to ever increasing intimacy.

With these qualifications in mind, we can discuss three stages of friendship development and integrate 10 of the characteristics of effective interpersonal communication identified in the Increasing Effectiveness boxes. The assumption made here is that as the friendship progresses from initial contact and acquaintanceship through casual friendship to close and intimate friendship, the qualities of effective interpersonal communication increase. However, there is no assumption made that close relationships are necessarily the preferred type or that they're better than casual or temporary relationships. We need all types.

Initial Contact and Acquaintanceship   The first stage of friendship development is an initial meeting of some kind. This does not mean that what happened prior to the encounter is unimportant—quite the contrary. In fact, your prior history of friendships, your personal needs, and your readiness for friendship development are extremely important in determining whether the relationship will develop.

At the initial stage, the characteristics of effective interpersonal communication are usually present to only a small degree. You're guarded rather than open or expressive, lest you reveal aspects of yourself that might be viewed negatively. Because you don't yet know the other person, your ability to empathize with or to orient yourself significantly to the other is limited, and the relationship—at this stage, at least—is probably viewed as too temporary to be worth the effort. Because the other person is not well known to you, supportiveness, positiveness, and equality would all be difficult to manifest in any meaningful sense. The characteristics demonstrated are probably more the result of politeness than any genuine expression of positive regard.

At this stage, there is little genuine immediacy; the people see themselves as separate and distinct rather than as a unit. The confidence that is demonstrated is probably more a function of the individual personalities than of the relationship. Because the relationship is so new and because the people don't know each other very well, the interaction is often characterized by awkwardness—for example, overlong pauses, uncertainty over the topics to be discussed, and ineffective exchanges of speaker and listener roles.

Casual Friendship   In this second stage, there is a dyadic consciousness, a clear sense of "we-ness," of togetherness; communication demonstrates a sense of immediacy. At this stage, you participate in activities as a unit rather than as separate individuals. A casual friend is one we would go with to the movies, sit with in the cafeteria or in class, or ride home with from school.

At this casual friendship stage, the qualities of effective interpersonal interaction begin to be seen more clearly. You start to express yourself openly and become interested in the other person's disclosures. You begin to own your feelings and thoughts and respond openly to his or her communications. Because you're beginning to understand this person, you empathize and demonstrate significant other-orientation. You also demonstrate supportiveness and develop a genuinely positive attitude toward both the other person and mutual communication situations. As you learn this person's needs and wants, you can stroke more effectively.

There is an ease at this stage, a coordination in the interaction between the two persons. You communicate with confidence, maintain appropriate eye contact and flexibility in body posture and gesturing, and use few adaptors that signal discomfort.

Close and Intimate Friendship   At the stage of close and intimate friendship, there is an intensification of the casual friendship; you and your friend see yourselves more as an exclusive unit, and each of you derives greater benefits (for example, emotional support) from intimate friendship than from casual friendship (Hays, 1989).

Because you know each other well (for example, you know one another's values, opinions, attitudes), your uncertainty about each other has been significantly reduced—you're able to predict each other's behaviors with considerable accuracy. This knowledge makes significant interaction management possible. Similarly, you can read the other's nonverbal signals more accurately and can use these signals as guides to your interactions—avoiding certain topics at certain times or offering consolation on the basis of facial expressions. At this stage, you exchange significant messages of affection, messages that express fondness, liking, loving, and caring for the other person. Openness and expressiveness are more clearly in evidence.

You become more other-oriented and willing to make significant sacrifices for the other person. You'll go far out of your way for the benefit of this friend, and the friend does the same for you. You empathize and exchange perspectives a great deal more, and you expect in return that your friend will also empathize with you. With a genuinely positive feeling for this individual, your supportiveness and positive stroking become spontaneous. Because you see yourselves as an exclusive unit, equality and immediacy are in clear evidence. You view this friend as one who is important in your life; as a result, conflicts—inevitable in all close relationships—are important to resolve through compromise and understanding rather than through, for example, refusal to negotiate or a show of force.

You're willing to respond openly, confidently, and expressively to this person and to own your feelings and thoughts. Your supportiveness and positiveness are genuine expressions of the closeness you feel for this person. Each person in an intimate friendship is truly equal; each can initiate and each can respond; each can be active and each can be passive; each speaks and each listens.

Friendship, Culture, and Gender

Your friendships and the way you look at friendships will be influenced by your culture and your gender. Let's look first at culture. In the United States you can be friends with someone yet never really be expected to go much out of your way for this person. Many Middle Easterners, Asians, and Latin Americans would consider going significantly out of their way an absolutely essential ingredient in friendship; if you're not willing to sacrifice for your friend, then this person is not really your friend (Dresser, 1996).

Generally friendships are closer in collectivist cultures than in individualist cultures (see Chapter 2). In their emphasis on the group and on cooperating, collectivist cultures foster the development of close friendship bonds. Members of a collectivist culture are expected to help others in the group. When you help or do things for someone else, you increase your own attractiveness to this person and this is certainly a good start for a friendship. Of course, the culture continues to reward these close associations.

Members of individualist cultures, on the other hand, are expected to look out for Number One, themselves. Consequently, they're more likely to compete and to try to do better than each other—conditions that don't support, generally at least, the development of friendships.

As noted earlier (Chapter 2), these characteristics are extremes; most people have both collectivist and individualist values but have them in different degrees, and that is what we are talking about here—differences in degree of collectivist and individualist orientation.

Gender also influences your friendships—who becomes your friend and the way you look at friendships. Perhaps the best-documented finding—already noted in our discussion of self-disclosure—is that women self-disclose more than men (e.g., Dolgin, Meyer, & Schwartz, 1991). This difference holds throughout male and female friendships. Male friends self-disclose less often and with less intimate details than female friends do. Men generally don't view intimacy as a necessary quality of their friendships (Hart, 1990).

Women engage in significantly more affectional behaviors with their friends than do males; this difference may account for the greater difficulty men experience in beginning and maintaining close friendships (Hays, 1989). Women engage in more casual communication; they also share greater intimacy and more confidences with their

WEB EXPLORATION
To learn more about friendship and culture, go to **www.ablongman. com/devito**.

friends than do men. Communication, in all its forms and functions, seems a much more important dimension of women's friendships.

When women and men were asked to evaluate their friendships, women rated their same-sex friendships higher in general quality, intimacy, enjoyment, and nurturance than did men (Sapadin, 1988). Men, in contrast, rated their opposite-sex friendships higher in quality, enjoyment, and nurturance than did women. Both men and women rated their opposite-sex friendships similarly in intimacy. These differences may be due, in part, to our society's suspicion of male friendships; as a result, a man may be reluctant to admit to having close relationship bonds with another man.

Men's friendships are often built around shared activities—attending a ball game, playing cards, working on a project at the office. Women's friendships, on the other hand, are built more around a sharing of feelings, support, and "personalism." Similarity in status, in willingness to protect one's friend in uncomfortable situations, in academic major, and even in proficiency in playing the game Password were significantly related to the relationship closeness of male–male friends but not of female–female or female–male friends (Griffin & Sparks, 1990). Perhaps similarity is a criterion for male friendships but not for female or mixed-sex friendships.

The ways in which men and women develop and maintain their friendships will undoubtedly change considerably—as will all sex-related variables—in the next several years. Perhaps there will be a further differentiation or perhaps an increase in similarities. In the meantime, given the present state of research in gender differences, we need to be careful not to exaggerate and to treat small differences as if they were highly significant. We need to avoid stereotypes and the stress on opposites to the neglect of the huge number of similarities in men and women (Wright, 1988; Deaux & LaFrance, 1998).

Increasing Interpersonal Effectiveness
Supportiveness

Supportiveness in communication is behavior that is descriptive rather than evaluative and provisional rather than certain (cf., Gibb, 1961). *Descriptive messages* state in relatively objective terms what you see or what you feel and are opposed to evaluative messages that express your opinions and judgments. Descriptive messages lead to supportiveness; judgmental or evaluative messages, on the other hand, often lead to defensiveness. This doesn't mean that all evaluative communications elicit a defensive response. The would-be actor who wants to improve technique often welcomes both positive and negative evaluations.

Provisional messages likewise contribute to supportiveness. Provisional messages express an open-minded attitude and a willingness to hear opposing viewpoints. With such people you're likely to feel supported and are more apt to communicate openly. Certainty messages, on the other hand, tolerate no differences of opinion. With such people, you're more likely to

become defensive, to hold back your thoughts and feelings rather than subject them to attack.

Communicating Supportiveness   Here are a few suggestions for communicating supportiveness through being descriptive and provisional.

- *Avoid accusations or blame* ("I should have stayed with my old job and not listened to your brother's advice.").
- *Avoid negative evaluative terms* ("Didn't your sister look horrible in that red dress?").
- *Avoid "preaching"* ("You need to learn word-processing and spreadsheet skills.").
- *Express your willingness to listen with an open mind* and without prejudice and that you're willing to change your own way of thinking and doing things.
  - *Ask for the opinions of others* and show that these are important to you. Resist the temptation to focus too much on your own way of seeing things.

Further, friendship researchers warn that even when we find differences, the reasons for them aren't always clear (Blieszner & Adams, 1992). An interesting example is the finding that middle-aged men have more friends than middle-aged women and that women have more intimate friendships (Fischer & Oliker, 1983). But why is this so? Do men have more friends because they're friendlier than women or because they have more opportunities to develop such friendships? Do women have more intimate friends because they have more opportunities to pursue such friendships or because they have a greater psychological capacity for intimacy?

LOVE

Of all the qualities of interpersonal relationships, none seems as important as love. "We are all born for love," noted famed British Prime Minister Disraeli; "It is the principle of existence and its only end." It's also an interpersonal relationship developed, maintained, and sometimes destroyed through communication.

Love Types

Although there are many theories about love, the one that has captured the attention of interpersonal researchers was one proposing that there is not one but six types of love (Lee, 1976). View the descriptions of each type as broad characterizations that are generally but not always true. As a preface to this discussion of the types of love, you may wish to respond to the self-test "What Kind of Lover Are You?"

TEST YOURSELF   *What Kind of Lover Are You?*

Respond to each of the following statements with T for true (if you believe the statement to be a generally accurate representation of your attitudes about love) or F for false (if you believe the statement does not adequately represent your attitudes about love).

_____   1. My lover and I have the right physical "chemistry" between us.

_____   2. I feel that my lover and I were meant for each other.

_____   3. My lover and I really understand each other.

_____   4. I believe that what my lover doesn't know about me won't hurt him or her.

_____   5. My lover would get upset if he or she knew of some of the things I've done with other people.

_____   6. When my lover gets too dependent on me, I want to back off a little.

_____   7. I expect to always be friends with my lover.

_____   8. Our love is really a deep friendship, not a mysterious, mystical emotion.

_____   9. Our love relationship is the most satisfying because it developed from a good friendship.

_____   10. In choosing my lover, I believed it was best to love someone with a similar background.

_____   11. An important factor in choosing a partner is whether or not he or she would be a good parent.

_____   12. One consideration in choosing my lover was how he or she would reflect on my career.

_____   13. Sometimes I get so excited about being in love with my lover that I can't sleep.

_____   14. When my lover doesn't pay attention to me, I feel sick all over.

_____   15. I cannot relax if I suspect that my lover is with someone else.

_____   16. I would rather suffer myself than let my lover suffer.

_____   17. When my lover gets angry with me, I still love him or her fully and unconditionally.

_____   18. I would endure all things for the sake of my lover.

▶ **How did you do?**   This scale, from Hendrick and Hendrick (1990), is based on the work of Lee (1976) as is the discussion of the six types of love that follows. The statements refer to the six types of love that we discuss below: eros, ludus, storge, pragma, mania, and agape. True answers represent your agreement and false answers represent your disagreement with the type of love to which the statements refer. Statements 1–3 are characteristic of the eros lover. If you answered true to these statements, you have a strong eros component to your love style. If you answered false, you have a weak eros component. Statements 4–6 refer to ludus love, 7–9 refer to storge love, 10–12 to pragma love, 13–15 to manic love, and 16–18 to agapic love.

▶ **What will you do?**   What things might you do to become more aware of the different love styles and to become a more well-rounded lover? How might you go about incorporating the qualities of effective interpersonal communication, for example, being more flexible, more polite, and more other-oriented to make you a more responsive, more exciting, more playful love partner?

From "A Relationship Specific Version of the Love Attitude Scale" by C. Hendrick and S. Hendrick, *Journal of Social Behavior and Personality 5,* 1990. Reprinted by permission of Select Press.

Eros: Beauty and Sexuality   Like Narcissus, who fell in love with the beauty of his own image, the erotic lover focuses on beauty and physical attractiveness, sometimes to the exclusion of qualities you might consider more important and more lasting. Also like Narcissus, the erotic lover has an idealized image of beauty that is unattainable in reality. Consequently, the erotic lover often feels unfulfilled. Not surprisingly, erotic lovers are particularly sensitive to physical imperfections in the ones they love.

Ludus: Entertainment and Excitement   Ludus love is experienced as a game, as fun. The better you can play the game, the greater the enjoyment. Love is not to be taken too seriously; emotions are to be held in check lest they get out of hand and make trouble; passions never rise to the point where they get out of control. A ludic lover is self-controlled, always aware of the need to manage love rather than allow it to be in control. Perhaps because of this need to control love, some researchers have proposed that ludic love tendencies may reveal tendencies to sexual aggression (Sarwer, Kalichman, Johnson, Early, et al., 1993). Not surprisingly, the ludic lover retains a partner only as long as the partner is interesting and amusing. When interest fades, it's time to change partners. Perhaps because love is a game, sexual fidelity is of little importance. In fact, recent research shows that people who score high on ludic love are more likely to engage in "extradyadic" dating and sex than those who score low on ludus (Wiederman & Hurd, 1999).

Storge: Peaceful and Slow   Storge love lacks passion and intensity. Storgic lovers don't set out to find lovers but to establish a companionable relationship with someone they know and with whom they can share interests and activities. Storgic love is a gradual process of unfolding thoughts and feelings; the changes seem to come so slowly and so gradually that it's often difficult to define exactly where the relationship is at any point in time. Sex in storgic relationships comes late, and when it comes, it assumes no great importance.

Pragma: Practical and Traditional   The pragma lover is practical and seeks a relationship that will work. Pragma lovers want compatibility and a relationship in which their important needs and desires will be satisfied. They're concerned with the social qualifications of a potential mate even more than with personal qualities; family and background are extremely important to the pragma lover, who relies not so much on feelings as on logic. The pragma lover views love as a useful relationship, one that makes the rest of life easier. So the pragma lover asks such questions about a potential mate as "Will this person earn a good living?" "Can this person cook?" "Will this person help me advance in my career?" Pragma lovers' relationships rarely deteriorate. This is partly because pragma lovers choose their mates carefully and emphasize similarities. Another reason is that they have realistic romantic expectations.

Mania: Elation and Depression   Mania is characterized by extreme highs and extreme lows. The manic lover loves intensely and at the same time intensely worries about the loss of the love. This fear often prevents the manic lover from deriving as much pleasure as possible from the relationship. With little provocation, the manic lover may experience extreme jealousy. Manic love is obsessive; the manic lover must possess the beloved completely. In return, the manic lover wishes to be possessed, to be loved intensely. The manic lover's poor self-image seems capable of being improved only by love; self-worth comes from being loved rather than from any sense of inner satisfaction. Because love is so important, danger signs in a relationship are often ignored; the manic lover believes that if there is love, then nothing else matters.

Agape: Compassionate and Selfless   Agape is a compassionate, egoless, self-giving love. The agapic lover loves even people with whom he or she has no close ties. This lover loves the stranger on the road even though they will probably never meet again. Agape is a spiritual love, offered without concern for personal reward or gain. This lover loves without expecting that the love will be reciprocated. Jesus, Buddha, and Gandhi preached this unqualified love, agape (Lee, 1976). In one sense, agape is more a philosophical kind of love than a love that most people have the strength to achieve.

View point   One researcher defines love as a combination of intimacy, passion, and commitment (Sternberg, 1986, 1988; Lemieux & Hale, 1999, 2001). *Intimacy,* the emotional aspect of love, includes sharing, communicating, and mutual support. *Passion,* the motivational aspect, consists of physical attraction and romantic passion. *Commitment,* the cognitive aspect, consists of the decisions you make concerning your lover. A relationship characterized by intimacy only is one of "liking." One with only passion is "infatuation." One with only commitment is "empty" love. When you have all three to about equal degrees, you have complete or consummate love. How does this definition match the meaning that you have for "love"?

Not surprisingly people who believe in *yuan,* a Chinese concept that comes from the Buddhist belief in predestiny, are more likely to favor agapic (and pragmatic) love and less likely to favor erotic love (Goodwin & Findlay, 1997).

Each of these varieties of love can combine with others to form new and different patterns (for example, manic and ludic or storge and pragma). These six, however, identify the major types of love and illustrate the complexity of any love relationship. The six styles should also make it clear that different people want different things, that each person seeks satisfaction in a unique way. The love that may seem lifeless or crazy or boring to you may be ideal for someone else. At the same time, another person may see these very same negative qualities in the love you're seeking.

Love changes. A relationship that began as pragma may develop into ludus or eros. A relationship that began as erotic may develop into mania or storge. One approach sees this as a developmental process having three major stages (Duck, 1986):

- First stage: Eros, mania, and ludus (initial attraction)
- Second stage: Storge (as the relationship develops)
- Third stage: Pragma (as relationship bonds develop)

In reading about the love styles, you may have felt that certain personality types are likely to favor one type of love over another. Here are personality traits that research finds people assign to each love style (Taraban & Hendrick, 1995).

Which personality characteristics go with which love style (eros, ludus, storge, pragma, mania, and agape)?

1. inconsiderate, secretive, dishonest, selfish, dangerous
2. honest, loyal, mature, caring, loving, understanding
3. jealous, possessive, obsessed, emotional, dependent
4. sexual, exciting, loving, happy, optimistic
5. committed, giving, caring, self-sacrificing, loving
6. family-oriented, planning, careful, hard-working, concerned

Very likely you perceived these personality factors in the same way as did the participants in research from which these traits were drawn: 1 = ludus, 2 = storge, 3 = mania, 4 = eros, 5 = agape, and 6 = pragma. Do note, of course, that these results do not imply that ludus lovers *are* inconsiderate, secretive, and dishonest; they merely mean that people in general (and perhaps you in particular) *think* of ludus lovers as inconsiderate, secretive, and dishonest.

Love and Communication

How do you communicate when you're in love? What do you say? What do you do nonverbally? According to research, you exaggerate your beloved's virtues and minimize his or her faults. You share emotions and experiences and speak tenderly, with an extra degree of courtesy, to each other; "please," "thank you," and similar polite expressions abound. You frequently use "personalized communication." This type of communication includes secrets you keep from other people and messages that have meaning only within your specific relationship (Knapp, Ellis, & Williams, 1980). You also create and use personal idioms (and pet names), those words, phrases, and gestures that carry meaning only for the particular relationship and that say you have a special language that signifies your special bond (Hopper, Knapp, & Scott, 1981). When outsiders try to use personal idioms—as they sometimes do—the expressions seem inappropriate, at times even an invasion of privacy.

You engage in significant self-disclosure. There is more confirmation and less disconfirmation among lovers than among either nonlovers or those who are going through romantic breakups. You're also highly aware of what is and is not appropriate to the one you love. You know how to reward, but also how to punish, each other. In short, you know what to do to obtain the reaction you want.

Among your most often used means for communicating love are telling the person face-to-face or by telephone (in one survey 79 percent indicated they did it this way), expressing supportiveness, and talking things out and cooperating (Marston, Hecht, & Robers, 1987).

Nonverbally, you also communicate your love. Prolonged and focused eye contact is perhaps the clearest nonverbal indicator of love. So important is eye contact that its avoidance almost always triggers a "what's wrong?" response. You also have longer periods of silence than you do with friends (Guerrero, 1997).

You grow more aware not only of your loved one but also of your own physical self. Your muscle tone is heightened, for example. When you're in love you engage in preening gestures, especially immediately prior to meeting your lover, and you position your body attractively—stomach pulled in, shoulders square, legs arranged in appropriate masculine or feminine positions. Your speech may even have a somewhat different vocal quality. There is some evidence to show that sexual excitement enlarges the nasal membranes, which introduces a certain nasal quality into the voice (M. Davis, 1973).

You eliminate socially taboo adaptors, at least in the presence of the loved one. You would curtail, for example, scratching your head, picking your teeth, cleaning your ears, and passing wind. Interestingly enough, these adaptors often return after the lovers have achieved a permanent relationship.

You touch more frequently and more intimately (Guerrero, 1997). You also use more "tie signs," nonverbal gestures that show that you're together, such as holding hands, walking with arms entwined, kissing, and the like. You may even dress alike. The styles of clothes and even the colors selected by lovers are more similar than those worn by nonlovers.

Love, Culture, and Gender

Like friendship, love is heavily influenced by culture and gender (Dion & Dion, 1996). Let's consider first some of the cultural influences on the way you look at love and perhaps on the love you're seeking or maintaining. Although most of the research on these love styles has been done in the United States, some research has been conducted in other cultures (Bierhoff & Klein, 1991). Here is just a sampling of the research findings— just enough to illustrate that culture is an important factor in love. Asians have been found to be more friendship oriented in their love style than are Europeans (Dion & Dion, 1993b). Members of individualist cultures (for example, Europeans) are likely to place greater emphasis on romantic love and on individual fulfillment. Members of collectivist cultures are likely to spread their love over a large network of relatives (Dion & Dion, 1993a).

One study finds a love style among Mexicans characterized as calm, compassionate, and deliberate (Leon, Philbrick, Parra, Escobedo, et al., 1994). In comparisons between love styles in the United States and France, it was found that subjects from the United States scored higher on storge and mania than the French; in contrast, the French scored higher on agape (Murstein, Merighi, & Vyse, 1991). Caucasian women, compared to African American women, scored higher on mania, whereas African American women scored higher on agape. Caucasian and African American men, however, scored very similarly; no statistically significant differences have been found (Morrow, Clark, & Brock, 1995).

Gender also influences love. In the United States, the differences between men and women in love are considered great. In poetry, novels, and the mass media, women and men are depicted as acting very differently when falling in love, being in love, and ending a love relationship. As Lord Byron put it in *Don Juan*, "Man's love is of man's life a thing apart, / 'Tis woman's whole existence." Women are portrayed as emotional, men as logical. Women are supposed to love intensely; men are supposed to love with detachment.

Women and men seem to experience love to a similar degree and recent research continues to find great similairites between men's and women's conceptions of love (Rubin, 1973; Fehr & Broughton, 2001). However, women indicate greater love than men do for their same-sex friends. This may reflect a real difference between the sexes, or it may be a function of the greater social restrictions on men. A man is not supposed to admit his love for another man. Women are permitted greater freedom to communicate their love for other women.

Men and women also differ in the types of love they prefer (Hendrick, Hendrick, Foote, & Slapion-Foote, 1984). For example, on one version of the love self-test presented earlier, men scored higher on erotic and ludic love, whereas women scored higher on manic, pragmatic, and storgic love. No difference was found for agapic love.

Another gender difference frequently noted is that of romanticism. Before reading about this topic, you may wish to take the self-test "How Romantic Are You?"

TEST YOURSELF *How Romantic Are You?*

Indicate the extent to which you agree or disagree with each of the following beliefs. Use the following scale: 7 = agree strongly, 6 = agree a good deal, 5 = agree somewhat, 4 = neither agree nor disagree, 3 = disagree somewhat, 2 = disagree a good deal, and 1 = disagree strongly.

_____ 1. I don't need to know someone for a period of time before I fall in love with him or her.

_____ 2. If I were in love with someone, I would commit myself to him or her even if my parents and friends disapproved of the relationship.

_____ 3. Once I experience "true love," I could never experience it again, to the same degree, with another person.

_____ 4. I believe that to be truly in love is to be in love forever.

_____ 5. If I love someone, I know I can make the relationship work, despite any obstacles.

_____ 6. When I find my "true love," I will probably know it soon after we meet.

_____ 7. I'm sure that every new thing I learn about the person I choose for a long-term commitment will please me.

_____ 8. The relationship I will have with my "true love" will be nearly perfect.

_____ 9. If I love someone, I will find a way for us to be together regardless of the opposition to the relationship, physical distance between us, or any other barrier.

_____ 10. There will be only one real love for me.

_____ 11. If a relationship I have was meant to be, any obstacles (for example, lack of money, physical distance, career conflicts) can be overcome.

_____ 12. I am likely to fall in love almost immediately if I meet the right person.

_____ 13. I expect that in my relationship, romantic love will really last; it won't fade with time.

_____ 14. The person I love will make a perfect romantic partner; for example, he or she will be completely accepting, loving, and understanding.

_____   15. I believe if another person and I love each other, we can overcome any differences
and problems that may arise.

▶ **How did you do?**   To compute your romanticism score, add your scores for all 15
items; it should range between 15 and 105. The higher your score, the stronger your romantic
beliefs are. In research by Sprecher and Metts (1989), the mean score for this test was 60.45 for
males and females taken together. The mean score for males was 62.55 and for females 59.10.
Are you more romantic than the average person in this study?

▶ **What will you do?**   Consider how your present beliefs might be creating obstacles for
you, perhaps setting up unrealistic ideals. If you do feel your romantic beliefs are unrealistic,
consider how you might substitute more realistic beliefs.

From Susan Sprecher and Sandra Metts, "Development of the 'Romantic Beliefs Scale' and Examination of the Effects of Gender and Gender-Role Orientation," _Journal of Social and Personal Relationships_ 6 (1989): 387–411.
Copyright 1989 Sage Publications Ltd. Reprinted by permission of Sage Publications Ltd.

Women have their first romantic experiences earlier than men. The median age of
first infatuation for women is 13 and for men 13.6; the median age for first time in love
for women is 17.1 and for men 17.6 (Kirkpatrick & Caplow, 1945; Hendrick, Hendrick,
Foote, & Slapion-Foote, 1984).

In much research, men are found to place more emphasis on romance than women.
For example, when college students were asked the question "If a man (woman) has
all the other qualities you desired, would you marry this person if you were not in love
with him (her)?" Approximately two-thirds of the men responded no, which seems to
indicate that a high percentage were concerned with love and romance. However, less
than one-third of the women responded no (LeVine, Sato, Hashimoto, & Verma, 1994).
Further, when men and women were surveyed concerning their view on love—
whether it's basically realistic or basically romantic—it was found that married women
had a more realistic (less romantic) conception of love than did married men (Knapp
& Vangelisti, 1992).

View point   Men and women from different cultures were
asked the following question: "If a man
(woman) has all the other qualities you de-
sired, would you marry this person if you were not in love with
him (her)?" Results varied from one culture to another (LeVine,
Sato, Hashimoto, & Verma, 1994). For example, 50 percent of
the respondents from Pakistan said "yes," 49 percent of those
from India said "yes," and 19 percent from Thailand said
"yes." At the other extreme were those from Japan (only 2
percent said "yes"), the United States (only 3.5 percent said
"yes"), and Brazil (only 4 percent said "yes"). How would you
answer this question? How is your answer influenced by your
culture?

Additional research (based on the romanticism questionnaire presented here) also supports the view that men are more romantic. For example, "Men are more likely than women to believe in love at first sight, in love as the basis for marriage and for overcoming obstacles, and to believe that their partner and relationship will be perfect" (Sprecher & Metts, 1989). This difference seems to increase as the romantic relationship develops: Men become more romantic and women less romantic (Fengler, 1974).

One further gender difference may be noted, and that is the difference between men and women in breaking up a relationship (Blumstein & Schwartz, 1983; cf., Janus & Janus, 1993). Popular myth would have us believe that love affairs break up as a result of the man's outside affair. But the research does not support this. When surveyed as to the reason for breaking up, only 15 percent of the men indicated that it was their interest in another partner, whereas 32 percent of the women noted this as a cause of the breakup. These findings are consistent with their partners' perceptions as well: 30 percent of the men (but only 15 percent of the women) noted that their partner's interest in another person was the reason for the breakup.

In their reactions to broken romantic affairs, women and men exhibit similarities and differences. For example, the tendency for women and men to recall only pleasant memories and to revisit places with past associations was about equal. However, men engaged in more dreaming about the lost partner and in more daydreaming generally as a reaction to the breakup than did women.

FAMILY

If you had to define **family,** you might reply that a family consists of a husband, a wife, and one or more children. When pressed, you might add that some of these families also consist of other relatives-in-law, brothers and sisters, grandparents, aunts and uncles, and so on. But other types of relationships are, to their own members, "families." Table 12.1 provides a few statistics on the family as constituted in 1970 and in 2000.

One obvious example is the family with one parent. There are now almost 12 million single-family households in the United States. About 28 percent of children under 18 lived with just one parent in 1998 (about 23 percent with their mother and about 4 percent with their father), according to the *World Almanac and Book of Facts,* 2002.

Another obvious example is people living together in an exclusive relationship who are not married. For the most part, these cohabitants live as if they were married: There is an exclusive sexual commitment; there may be children; there are shared financial responsibilities, shared time, and shared space. These relationships mirror traditional marriages, except that in marriage the union is recognized by a religious body, the state, or both, whereas in a relationship of cohabitants it generally is not. In the most comprehensive study to date, *American Couples* (Blumstein & Schwartz, 1983), the authors report that although cohabiting couples represent only about 2 percent to 3.8 percent of all couples, their number is increasing. One bit of supporting evidence for increase is that among couples in which the male is under age 25, the percentage of cohabiting couples is 7.4 percent. In Sweden, a country that often leads in sexual trends, 12 percent of all couples are cohabitants.

Another example is the gay or lesbian couple who live together as "domestic partners"—a relatively new term for people living in a committed relationship—and have all the characteristics of a "family." Many of these couples have children from previous heterosexual unions, through artificial insemination, or by adoption. Although accurate statistics are difficult to secure, primary relationships among gays and lesbians seem

Table 12.1   **The Changing Face of the American Family**

Here are a few statistics on the nature of the American family for 1970 and 2000, as reported by the *New York Times Almanac* (2002) and some possible trends theses figures indicate. Do you view these trends as positive developments? Negative? What other trends do you see occurring in the family?

Family Characteristic	1970	2000	Trends
Number of members in average family	3.58	3.17	Reflects the tendency toward smaller families
Families without children	44.1%	52.9%	Reflects the growing number of families opting not to have children
Families headed by married couples	86.9%	76.8%	Reflects the growing trend for heterosexual couples to live as a family without marriage, for singles to have children, and for gay men and lesbians to form families
Females as heads of households	10.7%	17.6%	Reflects the growing trend of women having children without marriage and of the increase in divorce and separation
Unmarried couples living together	523,000	4.7 million	Reflects the growing trend to form families without being married
Unmarried couples living together with children under 15	196,000	1.675 million	Reflects the growing trend to form families and have children without marriage

more common than the popular media lead us to believe. Research estimates the number of gay and lesbian couples to be 70 percent to more than 80 percent of the gay population (itself estimated variously at between 4 percent and 16 percent of the total population, depending on the definitions used and the studies cited). In summarizing these previous studies and their own research, Blumstein and Schwartz (1983) conclude, "'Couplehood,' either as a reality or as an aspiration, is as strong among gay people as it is among heterosexuals."

The communication principles that apply to the traditional nuclear family (the mother–father–child family) also apply to these relationships. In the following discussion, the term *primary relationship* denotes the relationship between the two principal parties—the husband and wife, the lovers, the domestic partners, for example—and the term family denotes the broader constellation that includes children, relatives, and assorted significant others.

Characteristics of Families

All primary relationships and families have several qualities that further characterize this relationship type: defined roles, recognition of responsibilities, shared history and future, shared living space, and established rules.

Defined Roles   Primary relationship partners have a relatively clear perception of the roles each person is expected to play in relation to the other and to the relationship as a whole. Each acquired the rules of the culture and social group; each knows approximately what his or her obligations, duties, privileges, and responsibilities are. The partners' roles might include wage earner, cook, house cleaner, child care giver, social secretary, home decorator, plumber, carpenter, food shopper, money manager, and so on. At times, the roles may be shared, but even then it's generally assumed that one person has primary responsibility for certain tasks and the other person for others.

Most heterosexual couples divide the roles rather traditionally, with the man as primary wage earner and maintenance person and the woman as primary cook, child rearer, and housekeeper. This is less true among the more highly educated and those in the higher socioeconomic classes, where changes in traditional role assignments are first seen. However, among gay and lesbian couples, clear-cut, stereotypical male and female roles are not found. One research review, for example, noted that scientific studies "have consistently debunked this myth. Most contemporary gay relationships do not conform to traditional 'masculine' and 'feminine' roles; instead, role flexibility and turn taking are more common patterns. . . . In this sense, traditional heterosexual marriage is not the predominant model or script for current homosexual couples" (Peplau, 1988).

Recognition of Responsibilities

Family members see themselves as having certain obligations and responsibilities to each other. A single person does not have the same kinds of obligations to another as someone in a primary relationship. For example, individuals have an obligation to help each other financially. There are also emotional responsibilities: to offer comfort when our family members are distressed, to take pleasure in their pleasures, to feel their pain, to raise their spirits. Each person also has a temporal obligation to reserve some large block of time for the other. Time sharing seems important to all relationships, although each couple will define it differently.

Shared History and Future

Primary relationships have a shared history and the prospect of a shared future. For a relationship to become a primary one, there must be some history, some significant past interaction. This interaction enables the members to get to know each other, to understand each other a little better, and ideally to like and even love each other. Similarly, the individuals view the relationship as having a potential future. Despite researchers' prediction that 50 percent of those couples now entering first marriages will divorce (the rate is higher for second marriages) and that 41 percent of all persons of marriageable age will experience divorce, most couples entering a relationship such as marriage view it—ideally, at least—as permanent.

Shared Living Space

In general American culture, persons in primary interpersonal relationships usually share the same living space. When living space is not shared, the situation is generally seen as an "abnormal" or temporary one both by the culture as a whole and by the individuals involved in the relationship. Even those who live apart for significant periods probably perceive a shared space as the ideal and, in fact, usually do share some special space at least part of the time. In some cultures, men and women don't share the same living space; the women may live with the children while the men live together in a communal arrangement (Harris, 1993).

Although shared living space is generally a goal of most primary relationships, the number of long-distance relationships is increasing. Further, although living together is a goal, this does not mean that long-distance relationships are necessarily less satisfying. After a thorough review of the research, one researcher concludes that "there is little, if any, decrease in relationship satisfaction, intimacy, and commitment as long as lovers are able to reunite with some frequency (approximately once a month)" (Rohlfing, 1995, pp. 182–183).

Not surprisingly, research finds that lovers employ a variety of strategies to maintain long-distance relationships, acknowledging in their use of strategies that something extra has to be done to keep the relationships satisfying and together. Among these strategies are recognizing that long-distance relationships are common, establishing support systems while apart, and communicating in creative ways, for example, sending cards or videos (Westefeld & Liddell, 1982).

Established Rules   Family communication research points to the importance of rules in defining the family (Galvin & Brommel, 2000). You can view rules as concerning three main interpersonal communication issues (Satir, 1983): (1) What can you talk about? Can you talk about the family finances? Grandpa's drinking? Your sister's lifestyle? (2) How can you talk about something? Can you joke about your brother's disability? Can you directly address questions of family history or family skeletons? (3) To whom can you talk? Can you talk openly to extended family members such as cousins and aunts and uncles? Can you talk to close neighbors about family health issues?

All families teach rules for communication. Some of these are explicit, such as "Never contradict the family in front of outsiders" or "Never talk finances with outsiders." Other rules are unspoken; you deduce them as you learn the communication style of your family. For example, if financial issues are always discussed in secret and in hushed tones, then you can infer that you shouldn't tell others about family finances.

These rules tell you which behaviors will be rewarded (and therefore what you should do) and which will be punished (and therefore what you should not do). Rules tell you what moves are permissible and what moves are not permissible. Rules also provide a kind of structure that defines the family as a cohesive unit and that distinguishes it from other similar families.

Not surprisingly, the rules a family develops are greatly influenced by the culture. Although there are many similarities among families throughout the world, there are

Agenda-Setting Theory

Agenda-setting theory argues that the media establish your agenda by telling you—by virtue of what they cover—who is important and what events are significant (McCombs & Shaw, 1972, 1993). Agenda-setting theory emphasizes the media's influence, not in telling you what to think, but in telling you what to think about (Edelstein, 1993; McCombs, Lopez-Escobar, & Llamas, 2000).

Both salience and obtrusiveness influence the media's ability to establish your agenda (Folkerts & Lacy, 2001).

■ *Salience* refers to the importance of an issue to you. For example, if you live in a high crime city, then news of crime, crime deterrents, and crime statistics are probably important to you. If the media cover such salient issues, then its ability to establish your agenda is enhanced. If it fails to cover such issues, then you're less likely to set your agenda on the basis of what the media says.

■ *Obtrusiveness* refers to your experience with an issue. If you have direct experience with an issue then it's obtrusive; if you don't have direct experience, then it's unobtrusive. If tuition costs go up then the issue is obtrusive since you (presumably) have direct experience with it. But, if a volcano erupts on some unknown island, it's unobtrusive. The media's agenda-setting influence is greater for unobtrusive issues since you have no direct experience with them and hence have to rely on what the media tell you is or isn't important.

Follow Up   What relationship issues have high salience for you? What relationship issues are obtrusive? How do the media help set your friendship, love, family, and workplace relationship agenda?

also differences (Georgas et al., 2001). For example, members of collectivist cultures are more likely to restrict family information from outsiders as a way of protecting the family than are members of individualist cultures. As already noted, this tendency to protect the family can create serious problems in cases of wife abuse. Many women will not report spousal abuse due to this desire to protect the family image and not let others know that things aren't perfect at home (Dresser, 1996).

Family communication theorists argue that rules should be flexible so that special circumstances can be accommodated; there are situations that necessitate changing the family dinner time, vacation plans, or savings goals (Noller & Fitzpatrick, 1993). Rules should be negotiable so that all members can participate in their modification and feel a part of family government.

Family Types

Based on responses from more than 1,000 couples to questions concerning their degree of sharing, their space needs, their conflicts, and the time they spend together, researchers have identified three basic types of primary relationships: traditionals, independents, and separates (Fitzpatrick, 1983, 1988, 1991; Noller & Fitzpatrick, 1993). At this point, you may wish to examine your own relational attitudes and style by taking the self-test "What Type of Relationship Do You Prefer?" If you have a relational partner, you might wish to have him or her also complete the test and then compare your results.

TEST YOURSELF　*What Type of Relationship Do You Prefer?*

Respond to each of the following 16 statements by indicating the degree to which you agree with each. Circle High if you agree strongly, Med (medium) if you agree moderately, and Low if you feel little agreement. For now, don't be concerned with the fact that these terms appear in different positions in the columns to the right. Note that in some cases there are only two alternatives. When you agree with an alternative that appears twice, circle it both times. These statements are from Mary Anne Fitzpatrick's Relational Dimensions Instrument and are reprinted by permission of Mary Anne Fitzpatrick.

Ideology of Traditionalism (the extent to which you believe in the traditional sex roles for couples)

1. A woman should take her husband's last name when she marries.　High　Low　Med
2. Our wedding ceremony was (will be) very important to us.　High　Low　Med

Ideology of Uncertainty and Change (the extent to which you tolerate and welcome unpredictability and change)

3. In marriage or close relationships, there should be no constraints or restrictions on individual freedom.　Low　High　Med
4. The ideal relationship is one marked by novelty, humor, and spontaneity.　Low　High　Med

Sharing (the extent to which you share your feelings for each other and engage in significant self-disclosure)

5. We tell each other how much we love or care about each other.　High　Med　Low
6. My spouse/mate reassures and comforts me when I am feeling low.　High　Med　Low

Undifferentiated Space (the extent to which you each have your own space and privacy)

7. I have my own private work space (study, workshop, utility room, etc.).	Low	High	High
8. My spouse has his/her own private work space (workshop, utility, etc.).	Low	High	High

Autonomy (the extent to which you each retain your own identity and autonomy)

9. I feel free to interrupt my spouse/mate when he/she is concentrating on something if he/she is in my presence.	High	High	Low
10. I open my spouse/mate's personal mail without asking permission.	High	Med	Low

Temporal Regularity (the extent to which you spend time together)

11. We eat our meals (i.e., the ones at home) at the same time every day.	High	Low	High
12. In our house, we keep a fairly regular daily time schedule.	High	Low	High

Conflict Avoidance (the extent to which you seek to avoid conflict and confrontation)

13. If I can avoid arguing about some problems, they will disappear.	Med	Low	High
14. It is better to hide one's true feelings in order to avoid hurting your spouse/mate.	Med	Low	High

Assertiveness (the extent to which you assert your own rights)

15. We are likely to argue in front of friends or in public places.	Low	Med	Med
16. My spouse/mate tries to persuade me to do things I do not want to do.	Low	Med	Med

▶ **How did you do?**   The responses noted in column 1 are characteristic of traditionals. The number of circled items in this column, then, indicates your agreement with and similarity to those considered traditionals. Responses noted in column 2 are characteristic of independents; those noted in column 3 are characteristic of separates.

▶ **What will you do?**   Consider how you might use these insights in your own relationships. For example, does this self-test enable you to better understand your own needs or the needs of your partner? How might you go about helping your partner better satisfy his or her needs while also enabling you to satisfy your needs?   ●

Traditional couples share a basic belief system and philosophy of life. They see themselves as a blending of two persons into a single couple rather than as two separate individuals. They're interdependent and believe that an individual's independence must be sacrificed for the good of the relationship. Traditionals believe in mutual sharing and do little separately. This couple holds to the traditional sex roles, and there are seldom any role conflicts. There are few power struggles and few conflicts because each person knows and adheres to a specified role within the relationship. In their communications, traditionals are highly responsive to each other. Traditionals lean toward each other, smile, talk a lot, interrupt each other, and finish each other's sentences.

A S K the Researcher

Resolving Relationship Difficulties

I'm planning on getting married at the end of this semester. My fiancé and I are at opposite ends of the patterns you describe. He very clearly falls into what you describe as the traditional pattern, whereas I score very high on the independent pattern. Will this create problems in our marriage?

Every relationship experiences difficulties. How you resolve those difficulties is the key. The particular mixed couple type you're part of is an interesting one that we've studied in our work. This Traditional husband/Independent wife pairing demonstrates a commitment to a strong relationship although each sees companionship and sharing in different ways. The Independent wife is willing to argue and discuss a variety of issues, is not afraid of expressing feelings, and is less bound to conventional gender roles than other wives. Her more Traditional spouse is able to express his concerns but believes they should only fight about major issues. This husband wants a close relationship although he's more conventional than she about gender roles. Clearly, both sides have to understand the way the other approaches relationship differences. She may need to moderate her need for total expressivity, and he may need to engage in more bargaining and negotiation. Being sensitive to one another's preferences for conflict management should go a long way toward helping this marriage succeed.

Mary Anne Fitzpatrick (Ph.D., Temple University) is currently Deputy Dean of the College of Letters and Science at the University of Wisconsin, Madison, where she also conducts research and teaches in the area of interpersonal communication in social and personal relationships. (Reprinted by permission of Dr. Mary Anne Fitzpatrick.)

Independent couples stress their individuality. The relationship is important but never more important than each person's individual identity. Although independents spend a great deal of time together, they don't ritualize it, for example, with schedules. Each individual spends time with outside friends. Independents see themselves as relatively androgynous, as individuals who combine the traditionally feminine and the traditionally masculine roles and qualities. The communication between independents is responsive. They engage in conflict openly and without fear. Their disclosures are quite extensive and include high-risk and negative disclosures that are typically absent among traditionals.

Separate couples live together but view their relationship more as a matter of convenience than a result of their mutual love or closeness. They seem to have little desire to be together and, in fact, usually are together only at ritual functions, such as mealtime or holiday get-togethers. It's important to these separates that each has his or her own physical as well as psychological space. Separates share little; each seems to prefer to go his or her own way. Separates hold relatively traditional values and beliefs about sex roles, and each person tries to follow the behaviors normally assigned to each role. What best characterizes this type, however, is that each person sees himself or herself as a separate individual and not as a part of a "we."

In addition to these three pure types, there are also combinations. For example, in the separate–traditional couple one individual is a separate and one a traditional. Another common pattern is the traditional–independent, in which one individual believes in the traditional view of relationships and one in autonomy and independence.

Family and Communication

One helpful way to understand families and primary relationships is in terms of the communication patterns that dominate the relationship. Four general communication

 If you looked at the family from an evolutionary, Darwinian point of view, one research-watcher notes, you'd have to conclude that families are "inherently unstable" and that it's necessity, not choice, that keeps them together. If they had better opportunities elsewhere, they would leave immediately (Goleman, 1995b). What do you think of this position? What do you see as the greatest advantages of family? What do you see as the greatest disadvantages?

patterns are identified here; each interpersonal relationship may then be viewed as a variation on one of these basic patterns.

The Equality Pattern   The equality pattern probably exists more in theory than in practice, but it's a good starting point for looking at communication in primary relationships. It exists more among same-sex couples than opposite-sex couples (Huston & Schwartz, 1995). In the equality pattern, each person shares equally in the communication transactions; the roles played by each are equal. Thus, each person is accorded a similar degree of credibility; each is equally open to the ideas, opinions, and beliefs of the other; each engages in self-disclosure on a more or less equal basis. The communication is open, honest, direct, and free of the power plays that characterize so many other interpersonal relationships. There is no leader or follower, no opinion giver or opinion seeker; rather, both parties play these roles equally. Because of this basic equality, the communication exchanges themselves, over a substantial period, are equal. For example, the number of questions asked, the depth and frequency of self-disclosures, and the nonverbal behaviors of touching and eye gaze would all be about the same for both people.

Both parties share equally in the decision-making processes—the insignificant ones, such as which movie to attend, as well as the significant ones, such as where to send the child to school, whether to attend religious services, and what house to buy. Conflicts in equality relationships may occur with some frequency, but they're not seen as threatening to the individuals or to the relationship. They're viewed, rather, as exchanges of ideas, opinions, and values. These conflicts are content rather than relational in nature (Chapter 13), and the couple has few power struggles within the relationship domain.

Equal relationships are also equitable. According to equity theory, family or relationship satisfaction will be highest when there is equity, when the rewards are distributed in proportion to the costs one pays into the relationship (Chapter 11). Dissatisfaction

A S K the Researcher

Improving Family Communication

My family rarely communicates, except to argue. Now that I am taking a course in interpersonal communication, I want to put some of this knowledge to work. Can you give me some suggestions for encouraging better family communication?

Not all arguments are bad! It's not that you disagree; it's how you disagree that causes trouble. If arguments lead to fairer, more equitable outcomes that enhance the quality of life within the family, they have value. However, if they demean members, unfairly dominate those with good ideas, or are used to reinforce the family "pecking order" of who is really in charge, changes should be sought.

Talk with your family members about how they argue and ask if there are other ways to resolve differences. Tell one another how you feel when through arguments you are "put down" unfairly. Ask those that argue unfairly to consider your right to be heard. Maybe your family needs to create some new rules to govern how you argue. For example: only one person speaks at a time; no interruptions until a person finishes his or her comment; everyone will get a chance to speak on an issue; no shouting or "hogging" the time available; etc.

For more information see K. M. Galvin and B. J. Brommel, *Family Communication: Cohesion and Change* (New York: Allyn & Bacon, 2000), and V. Escuerdo, L. E. Rogers, and E. Gutierrez, "Patterns of Relational Controls and Nonverbal Affect in Clinic and Nonclinic Couples," *Journal of Social and Personal Relationships* 14 (1997): 5–29.

Bernard J. Brommel (Ph.D., Indiana University) is Professor Emeritus of Communication, Northeastern Illinois University, Chicago, where he taught courses in interpersonal and family communication. With K. M. Galvin, he wrote the first textbook in the field of family communication. For 19 years he was a member of the Board of the Lakeview Mental Health Center in Chicago and has a private practice in individual and marital counseling. BmBrommel@aol.com (Reprinted by permission of Dr. Bernard J. Brommel.)

over inequities can lead to a "balancing of the scales" reaction. For example, an under-benefited partner may seek an outside affair as a way to get more relationship benefits—more love, more consideration, more support (Walster, Walster, & Traupmann, 1978; Noller & Fitzpatrick, 1993).

The Balanced Split Pattern   In the balanced split pattern, an equality relationship is maintained, but each person has authority over different domains. Each person is seen as an expert or a decision maker in different areas. For example, in the traditional nuclear family, the husband maintains high credibility in business matters and perhaps in politics. The wife maintains high credibility in such matters as child care and cooking. These sex roles are, in many cultures, breaking down although they still define many families throughout the world (Hatfield & Rapson, 1996).

Conflict is generally viewed as nonthreatening by these individuals because each has specified areas of expertise. Consequently, the outcome of the conflict is almost predetermined.

The Unbalanced Split Pattern   In the unbalanced split relationship, one person dominates; one person is seen as an expert in more than half the areas of mutual communication. In many unions, this expertise takes the form of control. Thus, in the unbalanced split, one person is more or less regularly in control of the relationship. In some cases, this person is the more intelligent or more knowledgeable, but in many cases he or she is the more physically attractive or the higher wage earner. The less attractive or lower income partner compensates by giving in to the other person, allowing the other to win arguments or to have his or her way in decision making.

The person in control makes more assertions, tells the other person what should or will be done, gives opinions freely, plays power games to maintain control, and seldom asks for opinions in return. The noncontrolling person, conversely, asks questions, seeks opinions, and looks to the other for decision-making leadership.

The Monopoly Pattern   In a monopoly relationship, one person is seen as the authority. This person lectures rather than communicates. Rarely does this person seek others' advice, and he or she always reserves the right to have the final say. In this type of couple, the arguments are few because both individuals already know who is boss and who will win the argument should one arise. When the authority is challenged, there are arguments and bitter conflicts. One reason the conflicts are so bitter is that these individuals have had no rehearsal for adequate conflict resolution. They don't know how to argue or how to disagree agreeably, so their arguments frequently take the form of hurting the other person.

The controlling person tells the partner what is and what is not to be. The controlling person talks more frequently and goes off the topic of conversation more than does the noncontrolling partner (Palmer, 1989). The noncontrolling person looks to the other to give permission, to voice opinion leadership, and to make decisions, almost as a child looks to an all-knowing, all-powerful parent.

WORKPLACE RELATIONSHIPS

The workplace is a context in which all forms of communication take place and, not surprisingly, all kinds of relationships may be seen. Here we discuss three kinds of relationships that are especially important in the workplace: romantic, mentoring, and network relationships.

ETHICS in Interpersonal Communication

Workplace Ethics

The ethical issues and guidelines already offered in the Ethics boxes are similar to those that would operate within a workplace environment (Johannesen, 1996). These guides can be reviewed with the acronym ETHICS—empathy (Cheney & Tompkins, 1987), talk, honesty (Krebs, 1989), interaction management, confidentiality, and supportiveness.

- *Empathy.* Workers in an organization have an ethical obligation to understand what others are feeling as well as thinking from their points of view.
- *Talk.* Organizational conflicts should be resolved by talk rather than force, by persuasion rather than coercion.

- *Honesty.* Organizational communication—whether from the highest levels of management or from the trainees in the mail room—should be honest and truthful.
- *Interaction management.* Organizational communication and relationships should be satisfying and comfortable.

- *Confidentiality.* Members have a right to expect that what they say in confidence will not be made public.
- *Supportiveness.* A supportive and cooperative climate should characterize the interpersonal interactions throughout the organization.

What would you do? *You're managing a team of colleagues charged with redesigning the company office space. The problem is that Jack doesn't do any work. You spoke with Jack about it, and he confided that he's going through a divorce and child custody battles and really can't concentrate on the project. You feel sorry for Jack but you realize that you'll never be able to bring the project in on time if you don't get someone to replace Jack. In addition, you really don't want to get a negative appraisal because of Jack; in fact, you were counting on the raise that this project was going to get you. What would you do in this situation?*

TRY IT!
Apply your insights into romantic relationships in the workplace; go to **www.ablongman.com/ devito**.

Romantic Relationships

Unlike television depictions where workers are always best friends who would do anything for each other and where the characters move in and out of interoffice romances with little difficulty—at least with no difficulty that can't be resolved in 24 minutes—real life is quite different. Opinions vary widely concerning workplace romances. Some organizations, on the assumption that romantic relationships are basically detrimental to the success of the workplace, have explicit rules prohibiting such relationships. In some organizations (including the military), members can be fired for such relationships. In other organizations, the prohibitions are unwritten and informal but nevertheless clearly in opposition to office romances.

On the positive side, the work environment seems a perfect place to meet a potential romantic partner. After all, by virtue of the fact that you're working in the same office, you're probably both interested in the same field, have similar training and ambitions, and will spend considerable time together—all factors that foster the development of a successful interpersonal relationship. Also, since people are marrying later in life, they are less likely to meet their perspective partners in school and so work seems the logical alternative. One study found that some 80 percent of workers in the United States have experienced some sort of office romance (Pierce & Aguinis, 2001). And another study of 31,000 workers, conducted by MSNBC and *Elle* magazine (**www. elle.com/Contests/sex%20survey/statistics.asp**, accessed May 20, 2002), found that the majority were willing to engage in office romance. Sixty-two percent of these had at least one office romance. And, of course, even Bill Gates met his wife at work.

Similarly, office romances can lead to greater work satisfaction. For example, if you're romantically attracted to another worker, it can make going to work, working together, and even working added hours more enjoyable and more satisfying. If the relationship is a good one and one that is mutually satisfying, the individuals are likely to develop empathy for each other and act in ways that are supportive, cooperative, and friendly; in short, the workers are more likely to act with all the characteristics of effective communication noted throughout this book.

However, even when the relationship is a good one for the two individuals, it may not be good for other workers. Seeing the loving couple together every day may generate office gossip that may prove destructive. Others may think the lovers are a team that has to be confronted as a pair, and that you can't criticize one without incurring the wrath of the other.

Workplace romantic relationships may cause problems for management when, for example, a promotion is to be made or relocation decisions are necessary. Can you legitimately ask one lover to move to Boston and the other to move to San Francisco? Will it prove difficult for management to promote one lover who then becomes the supervisor of the other?

The workplace also puts pressure on the individuals. Most organizations, at least in the United States, are highly competitive; one person's success often means another's failure. In this environment, the normal self-disclosures (which often reveal weaknesses, doubts, and misgivings) that regularly accompany increased intimacy may actually prove a liability in this kind of competitive context.

When the romance goes bad or when it's one-sided, there are even more disadvantages. One obvious problem is that it can be stressful for the former partners to see each other regularly and perhaps to work together. Other workers may feel they have to take sides, being supportive of one partner and critical of the other. This can easily cause friction throughout the organization. Another and perhaps more serious issue is the potential for charges of sexual harassment, especially if the romance is between a supervisor and a worker. Whether the charges are legitimate, or the result of an unhappy love affair and unrelated to the organization, management will find itself in the middle, facing lawsuits and time and money lost from investigating and ultimately acting on the charges.

The generally negative attitude of management toward such relationships and the problems in dealing with the normal stress of both work and romance seem to present significant obstacles to such relationships and to the workplace, so workers are generally advised (by management) not to romance their colleagues. Friendships, on the other hand, which seem the much safer course, are often encouraged by company sports teams, dinners, and lounge and exercise areas.

Mentoring Relationships

A **mentoring relationship** is one in which an experienced individual helps to train one who is less experienced. An accomplished teacher, for example, might mentor one who is newly arrived or who has never taught before. The mentor guides the new person through the organization maze, teaches the strategies and techniques for success, and otherwise communicates his or her accumulated knowledge and experience to this "mentee."

The mentoring relationship provides an ideal learning environment. It's usually a one-on-one relationship between expert and novice, a relationship that is supportive and trusting. There's a mutual and open sharing of information and thoughts about the job. The relationship enables the novice to try out new skills under the guidance of an expert, to ask questions, and to obtain the feedback so necessary in learning complex skills. It's a relationship that is perhaps best characterized as one in which the experienced and powerful mentor empowers the novice, giving the novice the tools and techniques for gaining the same power the mentor holds.

The mentoring relationship has been found to be one of the three primary paths for career achievement among African American men and women (Bridges, 1996). In another study (of middle-level managers), those who had mentors and participated in mentoring relationships were found to get more promotions and higher salaries than those who didn't have mentors (Scandura, 1992).

At the same time, the mentor benefits from clarifying his or her thoughts, seeing the job from the perspective of a newcomer, and considering and formulating answers to a variety of questions. Much as a teacher learns from teaching, a mentor learns from mentoring.

Networking Relationships

In the popular mind, **networking** is often viewed simply as a technique for securing a job. But it's actually a much broader process that can be viewed as one of using other people to help you solve your problems, or at least offer insights that bear on your problem—for example, how to publish your manuscript, where to look for low-cost auto insurance, how to find an affordable apartment, or how to empty your cache.

Networking comes in at least two forms: informal and formal. Informal networking is what we do every day when we find ourselves in a new situation or unable to answer questions. Thus, for example, if you're new at a school, you might ask someone in your class where to eat or shop for new clothes or who's the best teacher for interpersonal communication. In the same way, when you enter a new work environment, you might ask more experienced workers how to perform certain tasks or whom you should avoid or approach when you have questions.

WEB EXPLORATION
To learn more about networking, go to **www.ablongman.com/ devito**.

Formal networking is the same thing except that it's much more systematic and strategic. It's the establishment of connections with people who can help you—answer your questions, get you a job, help you get promoted, help you relocate or accomplish any task you want to accomplish.

At the most obvious level, you can network with people you already know. If you review the list of people in your acquaintance, you'll probably discover that you know a great number of people with very specialized knowledge who can be of assistance to you in a wide variety of ways. In some cultures, Brazil is one example, friendships are established in part because of potential networking connections (Rector & Neiva, 1996). You can also network with people who know people you know. Thus, you may contact a friend's friend to find out if the firm he or she works for is hiring. Or you may contact people you have no connection with. Perhaps you've read something the person wrote or you've heard the person's name raised in connection with an area in which you're interested and you want to get more information. With e-mail addresses so readily available, it's now quite common to e-mail individuals who have particular expertise and ask them questions you might have.

The great value of networking, of course, is that it provides you with access to a wealth of specialized information. At the same time, it often makes accessing that information a lot easier than if you had to find it all by yourself.

In networking, it's often recommended that you try to establish relationships that are mutually beneficial. After all, much as others are useful sources of information for you, you're likely to be a useful source of information for others. If you can provide others with helpful information, it's more likely that they will provide helpful information for you. In this way, a mutually satisfying and productive network is established.

Some networking experts advise you to develop files and directories of potentially useful sources that you can contact for needed information. For example, if you're a freelance artist, you might develop a list of people who might be in positions to offer you work or who might lead you to others who might offer such work. Authors, editors, art directors, administrative assistants, people in advertising, and a host of others might eventually provide useful leads for such work. Creating a directory of such people and keeping in contact with them on a fairly regular basis can often simplify your obtaining freelance work.

Formal networking requires that you take an active part in locating and establishing these connections. Be proactive; initiate contacts rather than wait for them to come to you. Of course, this can be overdone; you don't want to rely on people to do the work you can easily do yourself. Yet if you're also willing to help others, there is nothing wrong in asking these same people to help you. If you're respectful of their time and expertise, it's likely that your networking attempts will be responded to favorably. Following up your requests with thank-you notes will help you establish networks that can be ongoing, productive relationships rather than one-shot affairs.

REVIEWING Key Terms and Concepts in Friendship, Love, Family, and Workplace Relationships

This chapter explored some major kinds of interpersonal relationships, specifically friendship, love, family, and workplace relationships.

Friendship

What is friendship? What are the types of friendship? What purposes does it serve? How does friendship differ in different cultures and between men and women?

■ Friendship is an interpersonal relationship between two persons that is mutually productive and characterized by mutual positive regard.

- The types of friendships are:
  - *Reciprocity,* characterized by loyalty, self-sacrifice, mutual affection, and generosity.
  - *Receptivity,* characterized by a comfortable and positive imbalance in the giving and receiving of rewards; each person's needs are satisfied by the exchange.
  - *Association,* a transitory relationship, more like a friendly relationship than a true friendship.
- Friendships serve a variety of needs and give us a variety of values, among which are the values of utility, affirmation, ego-support, stimulation, and security.
- Friendship demands vary between collectivist and individualist cultures.
- Women share more and are more intimate with same-sex friends than are men. Men's friendships are often built around shared activities rather than shared intimacies.

Love

What is love? What are the major kinds of love? What is the effect of love on communication? How does love vary in different cultures and between men and women?

- Love is a feeling that may be characterized by passion and caring and by intimacy, passion, and commitment.
- Types of love:
  - *Eros love* focuses on beauty and sexuality, sometimes to the exclusion of other qualities.
  - *Ludus love* is seen as a game and focuses on entertainment and excitement.
  - *Storge love* is a kind of companionship, peaceful and slow.
  - *Pragma love* is practical and traditional.
  - *Mania love* is obsessive and possessive, characterized by elation and depression.
  - *Agape love* is compassionate and selfless, characterized as self-giving and altruistic.
- Verbal and nonverbal messages echo the intimacy of a love relationship. With increased intimacy, you share more, speak in a more personalized style, engage in prolonged eye contact, and touch each other more often.
- Members of individualist cultures are likely to place greater emphasis on romantic love than are members of collectivist cultures.
- Men generally score higher on erotic and ludic love, whereas women score higher on manic, pragmatic, and storgic love. Men generally score higher on romanticism than women.

Family

What is a family? What are the types of families? How do families communicate?

- Characteristics of Families
  - *Defined roles.* Members understand the roles each of them serves.
  - *Recognition of responsibilities.* Members realize that each person has certain responsibilities to the relationship.
  - *Shared history and future.* Members have an interactional past and an anticipated future together.
  - *Shared living space.* Generally, members live together.
  - *Established rules.* The relationship is rule governed, rather than random or unpredictable.
- Family Types
  - *Traditionals* see themselves as a blending of two people into a single couple.
  - *Independents* see themselves as primarily separate individuals, an individuality that is more important than the relationship or the connection between the individuals.
  - *Separates* see their relationship as a matter of convenience rather than of mutual love or connection.
- Communication in Families
  - *Equality.* Each person shares equally in the communication transactions and decision making.
  - *Balanced split.* Each person has authority over different but relatively equal domains.
  - *Unbalanced split.* One person maintains authority and decision-making power over a wider range of issues than the other.
  - *Monopoly.* One person dominates and controls the relationship and the decisions made.

Communicating in Workplace Relationships

What types of relationships occur in the workplace, and what influence does the workplace have on such relationships?

- Romantic relationships in the workplace, although having a variety of benefits, are often frowned upon and often entail a variety of problems that would not arise in other contexts.
- Mentoring relationships help you learn the ropes of the organization through the experience and knowledge of someone who has gone through the processes you'll be going through.
- Networking enables you to expand your area of expertise and enables you to secure information bearing on a wide variety of problems you want to solve and questions you want to answer.

APPLYING   Key Terms and Concepts in Friendship, Love, Family, and Workplace Relationships

1. Have you witnessed one type of friendship changing into another type? For example, can a friendship of receptivity or association change into one of reciprocity?
2. After meeting someone for the first time, how long (on average) does it take you to decide whether this person will become a friend? What specific qualities do you look for?
3. In what ways do you find men and women different in their friendship behaviors? In what ways are they the same?
4. When college students were asked to identify the features that characterize romantic love, the five most frequently noted qualities were trust, sexual attraction, acceptance and tolerance, spending time together, and sharing thoughts and secrets (Regan, Kocan, & Whitlock, 1998). How would you characterize love? Would men and women characterize love similarly? Would heterosexuals and homosexuals characterize love similarly?

5. Psychotherapist Albert Ellis (1988) has argued that love and infatuation are actually the same emotion; he claims that we use the term "infatuation" to describe relationships that didn't work out and "love" to describe our current romantic relationships. How would you compare infatuation and love?

6. How would you describe your own family in terms of (1) the characteristics of primary relationships and families discussed in this chapter (defined roles, recognition of responsibilities, shared history and future, shared living space, and established rules), (2) the most often used communication pattern (equality, balanced split, unbalanced split, or monopoly), and (3) the rules that are most important to them?

7. Although studies show there is no disadvantage in a child's growing up in a gay home (Goleman, 1992), the major argument made against granting adoption rights to gay men and lesbians is that the child will suffer. How do you account for this?

8. What are your feelings about romantic relationships in the workplace? Altercast—put yourself into both the position of the worker who sees great opportunities for relationships and the manager who focuses on making sure the company makes money.

9. In what ways might you serve as a mentor? What values might you gain from mentoring those less experienced than you?

10. How do you feel about an employer's monitoring the e-mail, listservs, and websites an employee uses (Miller & Weckert, 2000)? How do you feel about employer surveillance in general?

EXPERIENCING   Key Terms and Concepts in Friendship, Love, Family, and Workplace Relationships

Go to **www.ablongman.com/devito**.

These experiences look at a variety of interpersonal relationships and the communication that takes place within these interactions.

(1) **Friendship Behaviors** stimulates you to look at friendship in terms of the responses friends are expected to have to a variety of situations. (2) **How Can You Talk Cherishing?** examines a simple but powerful technique for increasing relationship satisfaction. (3) **Mate Preferences: I Prefer Someone Who . . .** stimulates you to look at the kinds of qualities you look for in a mate. (4) The **Television Relationship** provides a structured opportunity to look at relationships as presented in television sitcoms and dramas.

RESEARCHING with Research Navigator   Key Terms and Concepts in Friendship, Love, Family, and Workplace Relationships

Go to **http://www.researchnavigator.com**.

Reading an article.
Read a popular or scholarly article on friendship, love, family, or workplace relationships. On the basis of this article what can you add to the discussion presented here?

Investigating key terms.
Investigate one of the key terms discussed in this chapter (for example, friendship, love, family, primary relationship, or agenda-setting theory).What additional insights can you provide?

Finding answers.
Try finding answers to one of the following questions or design a research study to answer it.

■ How do men's friendships differ from women's friendships?

■ What love types (eros, ludus, storge, pragma, mania, and agape) apply to the great lovers from history and literature?

■ What are the major ways in which men differ from women in the way they communicate when in love?

■ Do men and women differ in the satisfaction they derive from their current romantic, friendship, or workplace relationships?

■ Do persons who are high in self-disclosure make better primary relationship partners than those who are low in self-disclosure?

■ Are couples with children happier than couples without children?

■ Do couples who live together stay together longer than couples who live separately? Is one group significantly happier than the other?

■ In what ways are primary relationships among heterosexuals and homosexuals different? In what ways are they the same?

13 Conflict in Interpersonal Relationships

John Q (2001)

Beware of allowing a tactless word, a rebuttal, a rejection to obliterate the whole sky.

—Anaïs Nin

Nature of Conflict
Conflict Resolution Stages
Conflict Management Strategies

*T*he story of a man who takes hostages when his son is denied a heart transplant because of the family's inability to pay is told in John Q. Throughout the film you see conflict in a wide variety of forms, between people who love each other (John and Denise, Denzel Washington and Kimberly Elise) as well as between people who distrust and fear each other (John and the negotiator and the chief of police). You also see a variety of conflict management strategies, some of which are constructive and advance a reasonable solution and some of which are destructive, criminal, and immoral. In this chapter we examine conflict; we explore the nature of conflict, the stages of conflict resolution, and the strategies you can use to manage conflict.

Interpersonal conflict refers to a disagreement between or among connected individuals: close friends, lovers, or family members. The word "connected" emphasizes the fact that each person's position and each person's actions affect the other person.

Conflict is a part of every interpersonal relationship, between parents and children, brothers and sisters, friends, lovers, coworkers. As Louis Nizer put it, "Where there is no difference, there is only indifference."

NATURE OF CONFLICT

Do you think the following statements are true or false?

1. If two people engage in relationship conflict, it means their relationship is in trouble.
2. Conflict hurts an interpersonal relationship.
3. Conflict is bad because it reveals our negative selves—for example, our pettiness, our need to be in control, our unreasonable expectations.

As with most things, simple answers are usually wrong. The three statements may all be true or may all be false; it depends. (1) Conflict is inevitable, so the fact that a relationship experiences it merely means the relationship is typical. (2) If the conflict is approached properly, the relationship may not only not be hurt but may be improved as a result of the conflict's resolution. (3) Similarly, it's not the conflict that reveals your negative side but the fight strategies you use. Thus, if you attack the other person personally or use force, you do reveal a negative side. But you can also reveal a positive self, as when you show your willingness to listen to opposing points of view, to change unpleasant behaviors, and to accept imperfection in others.

Negative and Positive Effects of Conflict

Because people are different and will necessarily see things differently, interpersonal conflict is inevitable. The way you deal with conflict, however, can have both negative and positive effects.

Negative Effects   Among the disadvantages of conflict is that it often leads to increased negative feelings. Many conflicts involve unfair fighting methods and focus largely on hurting the other person. If this happens, negative feelings are sure to increase. Conflict may also deplete energy better spent on other areas, especially when unproductive conflict strategies are used.

At times, conflict may lead you to close yourself off from the other individual. When you hide your feelings from your partner, you prevent meaningful communication and interaction; this, in turn, creates barriers to intimacy. Because the need for intimacy is so strong, one possible outcome is that one or both parties may seek intimacy elsewhere. This often leads to further conflict, mutual hurt, and resentment—qualities that add heavily to the costs carried by the relationship. As these costs increase, the rewards may become more difficult to exchange. Here, then, is a situation in which costs increase and rewards decrease, one that often results in relationship deterioration and eventual dissolution.

Positive Effects   Among the advantages of conflict is that it forces you to examine a problem and work toward a potential solution. If you use productive conflict strategies, your relationship is likely to become stronger, healthier, and more satisfying than it was before.

Conflict often prevents hostilities and resentments from festering. Say you're annoyed at your partner, who comes home from work and then talks on the phone with colleagues for two hours instead of giving that time to you. If you say nothing, your annoyance is likely to grow. Further, by saying nothing you implicitly approve of such behavior, so it's likely that such phone calls will continue. Through your conflict and its resolution, you each let your needs be known: your partner needs to review the day's work to gain assurance that it's been properly completed, and you have a need for your partner's attention. If you both can appreciate the legitimacy of these needs, then you stand a good chance of finding workable solutions. Perhaps your partner can make the phone call after your attention needs are met. Perhaps you can delay your need for attention until your partner gets closure about work. Perhaps you can learn to provide for your partner's closure needs and in doing so get your own attention needs met. Again, you have win–win solutions; each of your needs are met.

Conflict also enables you to state what you each want and perhaps to get it. For example, let's say that you want to spend your money on a new car because your old one is unreliable. Your partner, on the other hand, wants to spend it on a vacation, feeling the need for a change of pace. Through your conflict and its resolution, you learn what each wants; from this you may then be able to figure how each of you can get what you want. You might accept a used car and your partner might accept a shorter vacation. Or you might buy a used car and take an inexpensive motor trip. Each of these solutions may prove satisfying. They're win–win solutions—each of you wins, each of you gets what you want.

Consider, too, that when you try to resolve conflict within an interpersonal relationship, you're saying that the relationship is worth the effort; otherwise, you'd walk away. Although there may be exceptions—as when you confront conflict to save face or to gratify some ego need—confronting a conflict often indicates concern, commitment, and a desire to protect and preserve the relationship.

Content and Relationship Conflicts

Using concepts developed earlier (Chapter 1), you can distinguish between content and relationship conflicts. *Content conflict* centers on objects, events, and persons in the world that are usually external to the people involved in the conflict. These include the millions of issues that you argue and fight about every day—the value of a particular movie, what to watch on television, the fairness of the last examination, who should get promoted, and the way to spend your savings.

Relationship conflicts are equally numerous and include conflicts concerned with the relationships between the individuals, with such issues as who's in charge, the equality or lack of it in the relationship, and who has the right to establish rules of behavior. Relationship conflicts include such examples as a younger brother who does not obey his older brother, two partners who each want an equal say in making vacation plans, and the mother and daughter who each want to have the final word concerning the daughter's lifestyle.

Relationship conflicts are often hidden and disguised as content conflicts. Thus, a conflict over where you should vacation may, on the content level, center on the advantages and disadvantages of Mexico versus Hawaii. On a relationship level, however, it may center on who has the greater right to select the place to vacation, who should win the argument, or who is the decision maker in the relationship.

Interpersonal conflicts involve a variety of issues. For example, in a study on the issues argued about by gay, lesbian, and heterosexual couples, six major issues were identified and were virtually identical for all couples (Kurdek, 1994).

Consider your own conflict behavior by determining which, if any, of these issues you argue about. (They're arranged in order, with 1 being the most often mentioned.)

1. Intimacy issues such as affection and sex.
2. Power issues such as excessive demands or possessiveness, lack of equality in the relationship, friends, and leisure time.
3. Personal flaws such as drinking or smoking, grooming, and driving style.
4. Personal distance issues such as frequently being absent and school or job commitments.
5. Social issues such as politics, parents, and personal values.
6. Distrust issues such as romantic affairs and lying.

Another study found that four conditions led up to a couple's "first big fight": uncertainty over commitment, jealousy, violation of expectations, and personality differences (Siegert & Stamp, 1994).

Among top managers, the major source of conflict revolved around the issue of executive responsibility and coordination. Other conflicts focused on differences in organizational objectives, in how resources are to be allocated, and in what constitutes an appropriate management style (Morrill, 1992).

In a study of same-sex and opposite-sex friends, the four issues most often argued about were: sharing living space or possessions, violating friendship rules, sharing activities, and disagreement about ideas (Samter & Cupach, 1998).

Culture and Conflict

WEB EXPLORATION
To learn more about culture and conflict, go to **www.ablongman. com/devito**.

Culture influences the topics people fight about as well as what are considered appropriate and inappropriate ways of dealing with conflict. For example, cohabitating 18-year-olds are more likely to have conflict with their parents over their living style if they live in the United States than if they live in Sweden, where cohabitation is much more accepted. Similarly, male infidelity is more likely to cause conflict among American couples than among Southern European couples. Students from the United States are more likely to pursue a conflict with another United States student than with someone from another culture. Chinese students, on the other hand, are more likely to pursue a conflict with a non-Chinese than with another Chinese student (Leung, 1988).

The topics of conflicts will also depend on whether the culture is high or low context. In high-context cultures, conflicts are more likely to center on violating collective or group norms and values. Conversely, in low-context cultures, conflicts are more likely to come up when individual norms are violated (Ting-Toomey, 1985).

Cultures also differ in how they define what constitutes conflict. For example, in some cultures it's quite common for women to be referred to negatively and as less than equal. To most people in the United States, this would constitute a clear basis for conflict. To some Japanese women, however, this isn't uncommon and isn't perceived as abusive (*New York Times*, 11 February 1996, pp. 1, 12). Further, Americans and Japanese differ in their view of the aim or purpose of conflict. The Japanese see conflicts and their resolution in terms of compromise; Americans, on the other hand, see conflict in terms of winning (Gelfand, Nishii, Holcombe, Dyer, Ohbuchi, & Fukuno, 2001).

Cultures vary widely in their responses to physical and verbal abuse. In some Asian and Hispanic cultures, for example, the fear of losing face or embarrassing the family is so great that people prefer not to report or reveal abuses. When looking over statistics, it may at first appear that little violence occurs in the families of certain cultures. Yet we know from research that wife beating is quite common in India, Taiwan, and Iran, for example (Counts, Brown, & Campbell, 1992; Hatfield & Rapson, 1996). In much of the United States, and in many other cultures as well, such abuse would not be tolerated no matter who was embarrassed or insulted.

African Americans and European Americans engage in conflict in very different ways (Kochman, 1981; Hecht, Collier, & Ribeau, 1993). The issues that cause and aggravate conflict, the conflict strategies that are expected and accepted, and the attitude toward conflict vary from one group to the other.

Each culture seems to teach its members different views of conflict strategies (Tardiff, 2001). In one study, African American females were found to use more direct controlling strategies (for example, assuming control over the conflict and arguing persistently for their point of view) than did white females. White females, on the other hand, used more solution-oriented conflict styles than did African American females. African American and white men were similar in their conflict strategies; both avoided or withdrew from relationship conflict, preferring to keep quiet about their differences or make them seem insignificant (Ting-Toomey, 1986). Another example of this cultural influence on conflict is seen in the tendency of collectivist cultures to avoid conflict more than members of individualist cultures (Dsilva & Whyte, 1998; Haar & Krabe, 1999; Cai & Fink, 2002).

The following brief dialogue (modeled on an idea by Crohn, 1995) is designed to illustrate the issue of cultural differences in conflict and some of the problems these may create. As you read it, try to explain what is possibly going on interculturally.

Pat: Why did you tell her I was home? I told you an hour ago that I didn't want to speak with her. You just don't listen.

Chris: I'm sorry. I completely forgot. But you seemed to have a nice talk. So no harm done—right?

Pat: Wrong. You just don't understand. I didn't want to talk with her.

Chris: Okay. Sorry.

Chris withdraws to the next room and remains silent, saying nothing to Pat's repeated comments and criticisms. After about two hours:

Pat: I can't stand your silent treatment. You're making me the villain. You're the one who screwed up.

Chris: I'm sorry. [Walks away]

Communication continues in this way for the rest of the evening—with Pat ranting and raving every several minutes and with Chris saying hardly anything and always trying to walk away. Pat comes from a culture where anger is regularly and expectedly expressed. Yelling and screaming are customary ways of dealing with conflict. Chris comes from a culture where anger is expressed by silence. The extent to which Chris remains silent is a measure of how great the anger is.

Their different cultural beliefs about conflict can lead each to draw incorrect conclusions about the other. For example, from Chris's silence it's easy for Pat to conclude that Chris doesn't care about what happened and is indifferent to Pat's anger. From Pat's outburst Chris may easily conclude that Pat is unhappy in their relationship.

Even if Pat and Chris came from the same culture—with the same rules for expressing anger—or if they had sufficient intercultural awareness, their argument would have been no less real. Don't let us fool ourselves into thinking that cultural awareness will resolve all conflicts or that culture is the only factor that can cause such differences; it won't and it isn't. However, even a modicum of cultural awareness would have prevented a large part of the conflict—for example, the anger over the way the other person expressed anger—and would have prevented each from making inaccurate assumptions about the other.

The cultural norms of an organization will also influence the types of conflicts that occur and the ways in which they may be dealt with. In some work environments, for example, the expression of conflict with high-level management would not be tolerated; in others it might be welcomed. In individualist cultures, there is greater tolerance for conflict even when it might involve different levels of the hierarchy. In collectivist cultures, there is less tolerance. And, not surprisingly, culture influences how conflicts will be re-

Increasing Interpersonal Effectiveness
Equality

Equality refers to that characteristic of interpersonal communication in which each person is seen as an important and vital contributor to the interaction. In any situation, there will be some inequality. One person will be higher in the organizational hierarchy, more knowledgeable, or more interpersonally effective. But, despite this inequality, interpersonal communication is generally more effective when the atmosphere is one of equality. In an equal relationship, for example, disagreement and conflict are seen as attempts to understand differences rather than as opportunities to put down the other person; there's an explicitly stated desire to work together to address a specific problem.

Communicating Equality   Here are a few suggestions for communicating an equality in all interactions but especially in those involving conflict.

■ *Avoid "should" and "ought" statements* (for example, "You really should call your mother more often" or "You should learn to speak up").

These statements put the listener in a one-down position.
■ *Make requests (especially courteous ones) and avoid demands (especially discourteous ones).*
■ *Avoid interrupting.* This signals an unequal relationship and says, in effect, that what you have to say is more important than what the other person is saying.
■ *Acknowledge the other person's contributions before expressing your own.* Saying "I see," "I understand," or "That's right" lets the other person know you're listening and understanding.
■ *Recognize that different cultures treat equality very differently.* In the United States and in low-power-distance cultures generally there is great equality. In high-power-distance cultures, Japan, for example, where status differences greatly influence interpersonal interactions, this presumption of equality would not hold. Similarly, in many Muslim cultures women are not considered equal to men in communicating about a variety of topics.

solved. For example, American managers (members of an individualistic culture) deal with workplace conflict by seeking to integrate the demands of the different sides while Chinese managers (members of a collectivist culture) are more likely to call on higher management to make decisions or to leave the conflict unresolved (Tinsley & Brett, 2001).

Another factor that influences conflict is your own position on the organizational hierarchy. For example, if you're a temporary worker in a large organization, you're not likely to have conflict with the CEO because you'll probably never meet. But workplace conflicts with those at your own level or with those a level above and a level below are much more likely to occur. When you experience conflict with, say, supervisors it's more likely to be job related and focus on, for example, job satisfaction or organizational commitment. When you experience conflict with coworkers, it's more likely to be related to personal issues such as self-esteem and depression (Frone, 2000).

Gender and Conflict

One of the few stereotypes that is supported by research is that of the withdrawing and sometime aggressive male. Men are more apt to withdraw from a conflict situation, often coupled with a denial that anything is wrong, than are women (Haferkamp, 1991/1992). Women, on the other hand, want to get closer to the conflict; they want to talk about it and resolve it. One theory accounting for this tendency to withdraw is that men experience *flooding* (a sense of being out of control, of extreme negative feelings of anger or rage, for example) more easily and with less provocation than women (Gottman, 1993, 1994; Goleman, 1995a; Gottman & Carrere, 1994; Canary, Cupach, & Messman, 1995). Physiologically, flooding occurs at 10 heartbeats per minute more than normal; when the heart rate increases to about 100, the distress level—because of the extra adrenaline pumped in—will remain high for some time, even after the conflict is "settled." The tendency to withdraw from an argument or to say nothing in response to a woman's desire to discuss the conflict may be due to a desire to avoid or reduce the effects of flooding.

Even adolescents reveal differences in avoidance. In a study of boys and girls ages 11 to 17, boys withdrew more than girls but were more aggressive when they didn't withdraw (Lindeman, Harakka, & Keltikangas-Jarvinen, 1997). Similarly, in a study of offensive language, girls were found to be more easily offended by language than were boys, but boys were more apt to fight when they were offended by the words used (Heasley, Babbitt, & Burbach, 1995).

One study found that African American men preferred clear arguments and a focus on problem-solving, whereas African American women preferred assertiveness and respect (Collier, 1991). Other research has found that women are more emotional and men are more logical when they argue (Schaap, Buunk, & Kerkstra, 1988; Canary, Cupach, & Messman, 1995). Women have been defined as conflict "feelers" and men as conflict "thinkers" (Sorenson, Hawkins, & Sorenson, 1995). Another difference found is that women are more apt to reveal their negative feelings than are men (Schaap, Buunk, & Kerkstra, 1988; Canary, Cupach, & Messman, 1995).

Of course, many cultures have different rules for men and women. These rules don't seem to vary on the basis of affectional orientation; gay and lesbian couples use essentially the same conflict resolution strategies as do heterosexual couples (Metz, Rosser, & Strapko, 1994). For example, one study found that in the United States when men argue with other men, they both use assertiveness and reason throughout. When women argue with women, they begin with assertiveness, then reasoning, and then move to bargaining. When women and men argue, they both use reason and bargaining throughout the discussion (Papa & Natalle, 1989).

Asian cultures are more strongly prohibitive of women's conflict strategies. Asian women are expected to be exceptionally polite; this is even more important when women are in conflict with men and when the conflict is public (Tannen, 1994b). In the United States, there is a verbalized equality; men and women have equal rights when it comes to permissible conflict strategies. In reality, many expect women to be more polite and to pursue conflict in a nonargumentative way, whereas men are expected to argue forcefully and logically.

Despite these gender differences, there are also great similarities in the ways men and women approach and deal with conflict. Much research fails to find the gender differences that cartoons, situation comedies, novels, and films portray so readily and so clearly. For example, in a number of studies, dealing with college students and men and women in business, no significant differences were found in the way men and women engage in conflict (Wilkins & Andersen, 1991; Canary & Hause, 1993; Canary, Cupach, & Messman, 1995).

Online Conflicts

Just as you experience conflicts in face-to-face communication, you can experience the same conflicts online. A few conflict situations that are unique to online communication are noted here.

Sending commercial messages to those who didn't request them often creates conflict. Junk mail is junk mail; but on the Internet, the receiver often has to pay for the time it takes to read and delete these unwanted messages. Even if there is no financial cost, there is still a loss of time.

Sending messages to an entire listserv when they're only relevant to one member may annoy members who expect to receive only messages relevant to the entire group and not personal exchanges between two people. This often occurs when someone sends a message seeking specific information, and then individual members reply, not just to the person seeking the information, but to the entire listserv. Sometimes the reply is simply, "I can't help you with that question," a message relevant only to the person asking the question and not to the entire listserv.

Spamming often causes conflict. Spamming is sending someone unsolicited mail, repeatedly sending the same mail, or posting the same message in lots of newsgroups, even when the message is irrelevant to the focus of the group. Like commercial messages, these unwanted messages absorb your valuable time and energy. Another reason, of course, is that spamming clogs the system, slowing it down for everyone.

Flaming, especially common in newsgroups, refers to sending messages that personally attack another user. Frequently, flaming leads to flame wars where everyone in the group gets into the act and attacks each other. Generally, flaming and flame wars prevent you from achieving your goals and are counterproductive.

Trolling, putting out purposely incorrect information or outrageous viewpoints to watch other people correct you or get emotionally upset by your message, can obviously lead to conflict, though some see it as fun.

CONFLICT RESOLUTION STAGES

Before trying to resolve a conflict, you need to prepare. Conflict resolution is an extremely important communication experience, and you don't want to enter it without adequate thought. Here are a few suggestions for preparing for resolving conflict.

Try to fight in private. When you air your conflicts in front of others, you create a variety of other problems. You may not be willing to be totally honest when third parties are present; you may feel you have to save face and therefore must win the fight at all costs. This may lead you to use strategies to win the argument rather than to resolve the conflict. You may become so absorbed by the image that others will have of you that you forget you have a relationship problem that needs to be resolved. Also, you run the risk of embarrassing your partner in front of others, and this embarrassment may create resentment and hostility.

Be sure you're each ready to fight. Although conflicts arise at the most inopportune times, you can choose the time to resolve them. Confronting your partner when she or he comes home after a hard day of work may not be the right time for resolving a conflict. Make sure you're both relatively free of other problems and ready to deal with the conflict at hand.

Know what you're fighting about. Sometimes people in a relationship become so hurt and angry that they lash out at the other person just to vent their own frustration. The problem at the center of the conflict (for example, the uncapped toothpaste tube) is merely an excuse to express anger. Any attempt to resolve this "problem" will be doomed to failure because the problem addressed is not what is causing the conflict. Instead, the underlying hostility, anger, and frustration need to be addressed.

Fight about problems that can be solved. Fighting about past behaviors or about family members or situations over which you have no control solves nothing; instead, it creates additional difficulties. Any attempt at resolution will fail because the problems are incapable of being solved. Often such conflicts are concealed attempts at expressing one's frustration or dissatisfaction.

Now that you're prepared for the conflict resolution interaction, refer to the model in Figure 13.1 on page 318. It identifies the steps that will help you navigate through this process.

Define the Conflict

Your first and most essential step is to define the conflict. Here are several techniques to keep in mind.

- *Define both content and relationship issues.* Define the obvious content issues (who should do the dishes, who should take the kids to school) as well as the underlying relationship issues (who has been avoiding household responsibilities, whose time is more valuable).

- *Define the problem in specific terms.* Conflict defined in the abstract is difficult to deal with and resolve. It's one thing for a husband to say that his wife is "cold and unfeeling" and quite another to say that she does not call him at the office, kiss him when he comes home, or hold his hand when they're at a party. These behaviors can be agreed on and dealt with, but the abstract "cold and unfeeling" remains elusive.

- *Focus on the present.* Avoid **gunnysacking**—a term derived from the large burlap bag called a gunnysack—the practice of storing up grievances so they may be unloaded at another time, for example, the birthday you forgot or the time you arrived late for dinner are all thrown at you. Often, when one person gunnysacks, the other person gunnysacks. The result is two people dumping their stored-up grievances on one another with no real attention to the present problem.

- *Empathize.* Try to understand the nature of the conflict from the other person's point of view. Why is your partner disturbed that you're not doing the dishes? Why

TRY IT!
Apply your knowledge about defining the conflict; go to **www. ablongman.com/devito**.

Stages in Conflict Resolution
This model of conflict resolution is essentially John Dewey's problem-solving sequence. The assumption made here is that a conflict to be resolved is essentially a problem to be solved and follows the same general sequence. As you read about this problem/conflict-solving sequence, try visualizing a specific conflict and how these several steps might help you resolve it.

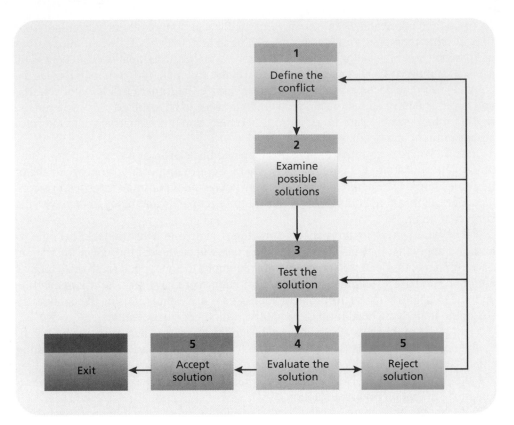

is your neighbor complaining about taking the kids to school? Once you have empathically understood the other person's feelings, validate those feelings when appropriate. If your partner is hurt or angry and you believe such feelings are legitimate and justified, say so: "You have a right to be angry; I shouldn't have said what I did about your mother. I'm sorry. But I still don't want to go on vacation with her." In expressing validation, you're not necessarily expressing agreement; you're merely stating that your partner has feelings that you recognize as legitimate.

■ *Avoid mind reading.* Don't try to read the other person's mind. Ask questions to make sure you understand the problem as the other person is experiencing it. Ask directly and simply: "Why are you insisting that I take the dog out now when I have to call three clients before nine o'clock?"

The example in the next section will help us work through the remaining steps. This conflict revolves around Pat's not wanting to socialize with Chris's friends. Chris is devoted to them, but Pat actively dislikes them. Chris thinks they're wonderful and exciting; Pat thinks they're unpleasant and boring.

Examine Possible Solutions

WEB EXPLORATION
To learn more about examining possible solutions, go to www. ablongman.com/devito.

Most conflicts can probably be resolved through a variety of solutions. Here are a few suggestions. Brainstorm by yourself or with your partner. Try not to inhibit or censor yourself or your partner as you generate these potential solutions. Once you have proposed a variety of solutions, look especially for solutions that will enable both parties to win—to get something each wants. Avoid win–lose solutions, in which one wins and one loses. They will cause difficulty for the relationship by engendering frustration and resentment.

Carefully weigh the costs and the rewards that each solution entails. Most solutions will involve costs to one or both parties. Seek solutions in which the costs and the rewards will be evenly shared. For example, among the solutions that Pat and Chris might identify are these:

1. Chris should not interact with these friends anymore.
2. Pat should interact with Chris's friends.
3. Chris should see these friends without Pat.

Clearly solutions 1 and 2 are win–lose solutions. In solution 1, Pat wins and Chris loses; in 2, Chris wins and Pat loses. Solution 3 has some possibilities. Both might win and neither must necessarily lose. This potential solution, then, needs to be looked at more closely.

Test the Solution

First, test the solution mentally. How does it feel now? How will it feel tomorrow? Are you comfortable with it? Would Pat be comfortable with Chris's socializing with these friends alone? Some of Chris's friends are attractive; would this cause difficulty for Pat and Chris's relationship? Will Chris give people too much to gossip about? Will Chris feel guilty? Will Chris enjoy these friends without Pat?

Second, test the solution in practice. Put the solution into operation. How does it work? If it doesn't work, then discard it and try another solution. Give each solution a fair chance, but don't hang on to a solution when it's clear that it won't resolve the conflict.

Perhaps Chris might go out without Pat once to test this solution. How was it? Did these friends think there was something wrong with Chris's relationship with Pat? Did Chris feel guilty? Did Chris enjoy this new experience? How did Pat feel? Did Pat feel jealous? Lonely? Abandoned?

Evaluate the Solution

Did the solution help resolve the conflict? Is the situation better now than it was before the solution was tried? Share your feelings and evaluations of the solution.

Pat and Chris now need to share their perceptions of this possible solution. Would they be comfortable with this solution on a monthly basis? Is the solution worth the costs each will pay? Are the costs and rewards evenly distributed? Might other solutions be more effective?

Critical-thinking pioneer Edward deBono (1987) suggests that in analyzing problems, you use six "thinking hats" as a way of seeking different perspectives. With each hat you look at the problem from a different angle.

- *The fact hat* focuses attention on the facts and figures that bear on the problem. For example, how can Pat learn more about the rewards that Chris gets from friends? How can Chris learn why Pat doesn't like these great friends?
- *The feeling hat* focuses attention on the emotional responses to the problem. How does Pat feel when Chris goes out with these friends? How does Chris feel when Pat refuses to meet them?
- *The negative argument hat* asks you to become the devil's advocate. How might this relationship deteriorate if Chris continues seeing these friends without Pat or if Pat resists interacting with Chris's friends?

■ *The positive benefits hat* asks you to look at the upside. What are the opportunities that Chris's seeing friends without Pat might yield? What benefits might Pat and Chris get from this new arrangement?

■ *The creative new idea hat* focuses on new ways of looking at the problem. In what other ways can Pat and Chris look at this problem? What other possible solutions might they consider?

■ *The control of thinking hat* helps you analyze what you're doing; it asks you to reflect on your own thinking. Have Pat and Chris adequately defined the problem? Are they focusing too much on insignificant issues? Have they given enough attention to possible negative effects?

Accept or Reject the Solution

If you accept the solution, you're ready to put it into more permanent operation. Let's say that Pat is actually quite happy with the solution. Pat was able to use that time to visit college friends. The next time Chris goes out with the friends Pat doesn't like, Pat intends to go out with some friends from college. Chris feels pretty good about seeing friends without Pat. Chris explains that they have both decided to see their friends separately and both are comfortable with this decision. If, however, either Pat or Chris felt unhappy with this solution, they would have to try out another solution or perhaps go back and redefine the problem and seek other ways to resolve it.

Even after the conflict is resolved, there is still work to be done. Often after one conflict is supposedly settled, another conflict will emerge because, for example, one person feels that harm was done to them and they need to retaliate and take revenge in order to restore their own self-worth (Kim & Smith, 1993). So it's especially important

A S K *the Researcher*

How Might Mediation Help?

My partner and I have had many conflicts recently and can't seem to talk with one another like we used to. We're wondering if we should ask a third party—a mediator—to give us some insight into our problems and to get us communicating again. What can a mediator do for us?

For relationship and communication breakdowns, a mediator may be a good starting point. The mediator can assist the two of you by providing a neutral and private environment for discussing the concerns that each of you has. The mediator is trained to help both of you to clarify your issues, to brainstorm possibilities about those issues, and to help you create a plan that works for both of you. You and your partner are the ones who decide if and how you will resolve your conflict. The mediator will not tell you what to do. What the mediator will do is help you talk with each other, listen and hear each other, and see each other's perspectives while clarifying your own thoughts. Keep in mind that mediation is not therapy or counseling. The focus in mediation is to help you listen, hear and be heard, and to communicate with each other so that you can decide what is important to both of you, and how you might resolve the difficulties.

Jean Civikly-Powell (Ph.D., Florida State University) is a University of New Mexico Presidential Teaching Fellow, Director of the Faculty Dispute Resolution program and Professor Emerita, Department of Communication and Journalism, and a mediator. jcivikly@unm.edu (Reprinted by permission of Dr. Jean Civikly-Powell.)

 What types of issues are likely to cause conflict between coworkers on the job? How are these issues similar to and different from those that lead to conflict between life partners at home?

that the conflict be resolved and not allowed to generate other, perhaps more significant conflicts.

Learn from the conflict and from the process you went through in trying to resolve it. For example, can you identify the fight strategies that merely aggravated the situation? Do you or your partner need a cooling-off period? Can you tell when minor issues are going to escalate into major arguments? Does avoidance make matters worse? What issues are particularly disturbing and likely to cause difficulties? Can they be avoided?

Keep the conflict in perspective. Be careful not to blow it out of proportion to the extent that you begin to define your relationship in terms of conflict. Avoid the tendency to see disagreement as inevitably leading to major blowups. Conflicts in most relationships actually occupy a very small percentage of the couple's time, and yet, in recollection, they often loom extremely large. Also, don't allow the conflict to undermine your own or your partner's self-esteem. Don't view yourself, your partner, or your relationship as failures just because you had an argument or even lots of arguments.

Attack your negative feelings. Negative feelings frequently arise after an interpersonal conflict. Most often they arise because unfair fight strategies were used to undermine the other person—for example, personal rejection, manipulation, or force. Resolve to avoid such unfair tactics in the future, but at the same time let go of guilt, of blame, for yourself and your partner. If you think it would help, discuss these feelings with your partner or even a therapist. Apologize for anything you did wrong. Hopefully, your partner will do likewise. After all, both parties are usually responsible for the conflict (Coleman, 2002).

Increase the exchange of rewards and cherishing behaviors to demonstrate your positive feelings and to show you're over the conflict and want the relationship to survive and flourish.

CONFLICT MANAGEMENT STRATEGIES

Your conflict management strategies will be influenced by a variety of considerations. For example, the short- and long-term goals you wish to achieve will influence what strategies seem appropriate. If you just want to save the date you are on, you might want to simply give in and ignore any difficulty. On the other hand, if you want to build a long-term relationship, you might want to fully analyze the cause of the problem and look for win–win strategies.

Similarly, your cognitive assessment of the situation will exert powerful influence. For example, your attitudes and beliefs about what is fair and equitable will influence your readiness to acknowledge the fairness in the other person's position. Your assessment of the likely effects of various strategies will influence the ones you select to argue with your supervisor.

A wide variety of conflict resolution skills has already been covered. For example, active listening is a skill that has wide application in conflict situations (see Chapter 5). Similarly, using I-messages rather than accusatory you-messages will contribute to effective interpersonal conflict resolution (Noller & Fitzpatrick, 1993). Of course, the characteristics of interpersonal competence (covered in the Increasing Effectiveness boxes throughout the text) are clear and effective conflict resolution techniques. The following discussion identifies additional strategies, the unproductive strategies that should be avoided as well as their productive counterparts. Recent research finds that using productive conflict strategies can have lots of beneficial effects (Weitzman & Weitzman, 2000; Weitzman, 2001).

Avoidance and Fighting Actively

Avoidance may involve actual physical flight: For example, leaving the scene of the conflict (walking out of the apartment or going to another part of the office), falling asleep, or blasting the stereo to drown out all conversation. It may also take the form of emotional or intellectual avoidance, whereby you leave the conflict psychologically by not dealing with the issues raised. Not surprisingly, as avoidance increases, relationship satisfaction decreases (Meeks, Hendrick, & Hendrick, 1998). This does not mean that taking time out to "cool off" is not a useful first strategy. Sometimes it is. When conflict is waged through e-mail, for example, this is an easy-to-use and often effective strategy. By delaying your response until you've had time to think things out more logically and calmly, you'll be better able to respond constructively and to address possible resolutions to the conflict and get the relationship back to a less hostile stage.

Nonnegotiation is a special type of avoidance. Here you refuse to discuss the conflict or to listen to the other person's argument. At times, this nonnegotiation takes the form of hammering away at one's own point of view until the other person gives in.

Instead of avoiding the issues, consider taking an active role in your interpersonal conflicts. If you wish to resolve conflicts, you need to confront them actively. Involve yourself on both sides of the communication exchange. Be an active participant as a speaker and as a listener; voice your own feelings and listen carefully to your partner's feelings.

Another part of active fighting involves the avoidance of silencers. **Silencers** are conflict techniques that literally silence the other individual. Among the wide variety that exists, one frequently used silencer is crying. When a person is unable to deal with a conflict or when winning seems unlikely, he or she may cry and thus silence the other person. Another silencer is to feign extreme emotionalism—to yell and scream and pretend to be losing control of oneself. Still another is to develop some physical reaction—headaches and shortness of breath are probably the most popular. One of the major problems with silencers is that you can never be certain whether they're strategies to win the argument or real physical reactions to which you should pay attention. Regardless of what we do, however, the conflict remains unexamined and unresolved.

Still another part of active fighting involves taking responsibility for your thoughts and feelings. For example, when you disagree with your partner or find fault with her or his behavior, take responsibility for these feelings. Say, for example, "I disagree with . . ." or "I don't like it when you . . ." Avoid statements that deny your responsibility, such as "Everybody thinks you're wrong about . . ." or "Chris thinks you shouldn't . . ."

Force and Talk

When confronted with conflict, many people prefer not to deal with the issues but rather to force their position on the other person. The **force** may be emotional or physical. In either case, however, the issues are avoided, and the person who "wins" is the one who exerts the most force. This is the technique of warring nations, children, and even some normally sensible adults. It seems also to be the technique of those who are dissatisfied with the power they perceive themselves to have in a relationship (Ronfeldt, Kimerling, & Arias, 1998).

More than 50 percent of single and married couples reported that they had experienced physical violence in their relationship. If we add symbolic violence (for example, threatening to hit the other person or throwing something), the percentages are above 60 percent for singles and above 70 percent for marrieds (Marshall & Rose, 1987). In another study, 47 percent of a sample of 410 college students reported some experience with violence in a dating relationship (Deal & Wampler, 1986). In most cases, the violence was reciprocal—each person in the relationship used violence.

The only real alternative to force is talk. The qualities of openness, empathy, and positiveness (discussed in the Increasing Effecitveness boxes), for example, are suitable starting points. In addition, be sure to listen actively and openly. This may be especially difficult in conflict situations where tempers may run high and where you may find yourself attacked or at least disagreed with. Here are some suggestions for talking and listening more effectively in the conflict situation.

Act the role of the listener. Also, think as a listener. Turn off the television, stereo, or computer; face the other person. Devote your total attention to what the other person

View point One of the most puzzling findings on violence is that many victims interpret it as a sign of love. For some reason, they see being beaten or verbally abused as a sign that their partner is fully in love with them. Also, many victims blame themselves for the violence instead of blaming their partners (Gelles & Cornell, 1985). Why do you think this is so? What part does force or violence play in your own interpersonal relationship conflicts?

is saying. Make sure you understand what the person is saying and feeling. One way to make sure is obviously to ask questions. Another way is to paraphrase what the other person is saying and ask for confirmation: "You feel that if we pooled our money and didn't have separate savings accounts that you'd feel the relationship would be a more equitable one. Is that the way you feel?"

Express your support or empathy for what the other person is saying and feeling: "I can understand how you feel. I know I control the finances and that can create a feeling of inequality." If appropriate, indicate your agreement: "You're right to be disturbed."

State your thoughts and feelings on the issue as objectively as you can; if you disagree with what the other person said, then say so: "My problem is that when we did have equal access to the finances, you ran up so many bills that we still haven't recovered. To be honest with you, I'm worried the same thing will happen again."

Face-Detracting and Face-Enhancing Strategies

Face-detracting or face-attacking orientation involves treating the other person as incompetent or untrustworthy, as unable or bad (Donahue & Kolt, 1992). Such attacks can vary from mildly embarrassing the other person to severely damaging his or her ego or reputation. So be especially careful to avoid "fighting words"—words that are sure to escalate the conflict rather than help to resolve it. Words like *stupid, liar,* and *bitch* as well

Violence and the Media

Does violence in the media lead to violent acts by viewers? And if it does, should violence on television, in movies, in video games, and in music be censored? Most of the research on media violence has focused on television (and to a lesser extent on films). But increasingly video games and music are being examined for their violent content and potential influence on children. For example, a study of Nintendo and Sega Genesis video games showed that approximately 80 percent of the games included aggression or violence as an essential part of the strategy (Dietz, 1998).

Generally research (Rodman, 2001; Bok, 1998) finds that violence in the media can:

■ Teach young people how to be violent; it can teach them the techniques of violence.
■ Give people (especially children) role models to emulate. In many Indian films, for example, violence against women is eroticized; males are encouraged to identify with those heroes who use violence to win women. In interviews Indian males revealed that they felt that the depiction of male–female relationships in films paral-

leled what they felt was the ideal male–female relationship (Derne, 1999).
■ Desensitize people to the violence around them, which, often, is not as extreme as they regularly see on television and in the movies.
■ Make viewers afraid of becoming victims of violence.
■ Create a desire for greater depiction of increased violence and is perhaps the reason why films have become increasingly violent over the years.

The extent to which media violence contributes to actual violence, however, has yet to be determined. Family and social factors, developmental and affective disorders, and substance abuse, for example, seem to interact with exposure to media violence to produce violent behavior (Withecomb, 1997).

Follow Up   How do you feel about violence in the media? Has it influenced your own interpersonal relationships? Has it influenced the interpersonal relationships of those you know; if yes, how?

as words like *always* and *never* (as in "you always do . . ." or "you never . . .") invariably create additional problems. When such attacks become extreme, they may be similar to verbal aggressiveness—a tactic explained in the next section.

One popular, but destructive, face-detracting strategy is **beltlining** (Bach & Wyden, 1968). Much like fighters in a ring, each of us has a "beltline." When you hit below it, you can inflict serious injury. When you hit above the belt, however, the person is able to absorb the blow. With most interpersonal relationships, especially those of long standing, you know where the beltline is. You know, for example, that to hit Pat with the inability to have children is to hit below the belt. You know that to hit Chris with the failure to get a permanent job is to hit below the belt. This type of face-detracting strategy causes all persons involved added problems. Keep blows to areas your opponent can absorb and handle.

Face-enhancing techniques involve helping the other person to maintain a positive image, an image as competent and trustworthy, able and good. Even when you get what you want, say at bargaining, it's wise to help the other person retain positive face because it makes it less likely that future conflicts will arise (Donahue & Kolt, 1992). Not surprisingly, people are more likely to make a greater effort to support the listener's "face" if they like the listener than if they don't (Meyer, 1994).

Generally, collectivist cultures place great emphasis on face, especially on maintaining a positive image in public. Face is generally less crucial in individualist cultures such as the United States. Consequently, collectivist peoples are less likely to use conflict strategies such as blame and personal rejection, since these are likely to result in a loss of face. Many collectivists are more likely to use strategies that preserve and enhance one's public image. Those from individualist cultures that favor more open discussion of conflict might be more apt to use argumentativeness and to fight actively. If you're from a collective culture, you're more likely to prefer mediation and bargaining as conflict resolution strategies than would those from individualist cultures who prefer a more adversarial and confrontational conflict style (Leung, 1987; Berry, Poortinga, Segall, & Dasen, 1992). But be careful that you don't think of all individualistic or collectivist cultures as similar. For example, Germans had more face concerns than Americans, although both are individualistic cultures. And Chinese had more face concerns than Japanese, although both are collectivist cultures (Oetzel, Ting-Toomey, Masumoto, Yokochi, Pan, Takai, & Wilcox, 2001).

Confirming the other person's definition of self (Chapter 7), avoiding attack and blame, and using excuses and apologies as appropriate are some generally useful face-enhancing strategies.

Verbal Aggressiveness and Argumentativeness

An especially interesting perspective on conflict is emerging from the work on verbal aggressiveness and argumentativeness (Infante & Rancer, 1982; Infante & Wigley, 1986; Infante, 1988; Rancer, 1998). Understanding these concepts will help in understanding some of the reasons things go wrong and some of the ways in which you can use conflict to actually improve your relationships.

Verbal Aggressiveness   **Verbal aggressiveness** is a method of winning an argument by inflicting psychological pain, by attacking the other person's self-concept. It's a type of disconfirmation (and the opposite of confirmation) in that it seeks to discredit the individual's view of self (see Chapter 7). To explore this tendency further, take the self-test on verbal aggressiveness.

TRY IT!
Apply your insights into verbal aggressiveness; go to **www.ablongman. com/devito**.

TEST YOURSELF   *How Verbally Aggressive Are You?*

This scale is designed to measure how people try to obtain compliance from others. For each statement, indicate the extent to which you feel it's true for you in your attempts to influence others. Use the following scale: 1 = almost never true, 2 = rarely true, 3 = occasionally true, 4 = often true, and 5 = almost always true.

_____ 1. I am extremely careful to avoid attacking individuals' intelligence when I attack their ideas.

_____ 2. When individuals are very stubborn, I use insults to soften the stubbornness.

_____ 3. I try very hard to avoid having other people feel bad about themselves when I try to influence them.

_____ 4. When people refuse to do a task I know is important, without good reason, I tell them they are unreasonable.

_____ 5. When others do things I regard as stupid, I try to be extremely gentle with them.

_____ 6. If individuals I am trying to influence really deserve it, I attack their character.

_____ 7. When people behave in ways that are in very poor taste, I insult them in order to shock them into proper behavior.

_____ 8. I try to make people feel good about themselves even when their ideas are stupid.

_____ 9. When people simply will not budge on a matter of importance, I lose my temper and say rather strong things to them.

_____ 10. When people criticize my shortcomings, I take it in good humor and do not try to get back at them.

_____ 11. When individuals insult me, I get a lot of pleasure out of really telling them off.

_____ 12. When I dislike individuals greatly, I try not to show it in what I say or how I say it.

_____ 13. I like poking fun at people who do things which are very stupid in order to stimulate their intelligence.

_____ 14. When I attack a person's ideas, I try not to damage their self-concepts.

_____ 15. When I try to influence people, I make a great effort not to offend them.

_____ 16. When people do things which are mean or cruel, I attack their character in order to help correct their behavior.

_____ 17. I refuse to participate in arguments when they involve personal attacks.

_____ 18. When nothing seems to work in trying to influence others, I yell and scream in order to get some movement from them.

_____ 19. When I am not able to refute others' positions, I try to make them feel defensive in order to weaken their positions.

_____ 20. When an argument shifts to personal attacks, I try very hard to change the subject.

▶ **How did you do?**   In order to compute your verbal aggressiveness score, follow these steps:

1. Add your scores on items 2, 4, 6, 7, 9, 11, 13, 16, 18, and 19.
2. Add your scores on items 1, 3, 5, 8, 10, 12, 14, 15, 17, and 20.
3. Subtract the sum obtained in step 2 from 60.
4. To compute your verbal aggressiveness score, add the total obtained in step 1 to the result obtained in step 3.

If you scored between 59 and 100, you're high in verbal aggressiveness; if you scored between 39 and 58, you're moderate in verbal aggressiveness; and if you scored between 20 and 38, you're low in verbal aggressiveness. In looking over your responses, make special note of the characteristics identified in the 20 statements that refer to the tendency to act verbally aggressive. Note those inappropriate behaviors that you're especially prone to commit. High agreement (4s or 5s) with statements 2, 4, 6, 7, 9, 11, 13, 16, 18, and 19 and low agreement (1s and 2s) with statements 1, 3, 5, 8, 10, 12, 14, 15, 17, and 20 will help you highlight any significant verbal aggressiveness you might have.

❱ **What will you do?**   Because verbal aggressiveness is likely to seriously reduce interpersonal effectiveness, you probably want to reduce your tendencies to respond aggressively. Review the times when you acted verbally aggressive. What effect did such actions have on your subsequent interaction? What effect did they have on your relationship with the other person? What alternative ways of getting your point across might you have used? Might these have proved more effective? Perhaps the most general suggestion for reducing verbal aggressiveness is to increase your argumentativeness.

From "Verbal Aggressiveness: An Interpersonal Model and Measure" by Dominic Infante and C. J. Wrigley. *Communication Monographs 53*, 1986, pp. 61–69. Reprinted by permission of the Speech Communication Association.

Character attack, perhaps because it's extremely effective in inflicting psychological pain, is the most popular tactic of verbal aggressiveness. Other tactics include attacking the person's abilities, background, and physical appearance; cursing; teasing; ridiculing; threatening; swearing; and using various nonverbal emblems (Infante, Sabourin, Rudd, & Shannon, 1990).

Some researchers have argued that "unless aroused by verbal aggression, a hostile disposition remains latent in the form of unexpressed anger" (Infante, Chandler, & Rudd, 1989). There is some evidence to show that people in violent relationships are

A S K *the Researcher*

Bridging the Gap

I'm a police officer charged with the responsibility of improving relationships between the police department and the community. Are there any insights you can offer from your work on argumentativeness and verbal aggressiveness that may help me create a more comfortable and more cordial atmosphere between these two groups?

Argumentativeness involves defending positions on controversial issues, while attacking the positions that other people take on the issues. Verbal aggressiveness involves attacking the self-concept of others, instead of, or in addition to, their position on controversial issues, in order to inflict psychological pain, humiliation, embarrassment, and other negative feelings. Some recommendations which may prevent or reduce verbal aggression include making people aware of situations and behaviors which are likely to stimulate verbal aggression, such as personal rejection, "hitting below the belt," nonnegotiation, and gunnysacking.

Teach people to deal with conflict through argumentativeness, helping them to argue in a relaxed, friendly, and attentive way. Teach people that if the verbal aggression continues, they can stop communicating. Make sure that people understand exactly what they're arguing about. Allow the other person to speak without interruption, try to use a calm delivery, allow the opponent to save face, and reaffirm the adversary's sense of competence.

Andrew S. Rancer (Ph.D., Kent State University) is a professor of communication in the School of Communication at the University of Akron, where he teaches courses in interpersonal communication, communication theory, research methods, and training methods in communication. His research centers on the aggressive communication traits of argumentativeness and verbal aggressiveness. He also acts as a consultant to business and industry. andre11@akron.edu (Reprinted by permission of Dr. Andrew S. Rancer.)

View point   Persons with disabilities are often singled out for verbal abuse and physical violence and are often ignored when they complain (Roeher Institute, 1995). What do you think contributes to abuse against persons with disabilities? Are these the same factors that contribute to abuse against women, against newly arrived immigrants, and against gay men and lesbians?

more often verbally aggressive than people in nonviolent relationships (Sutter & Martin, 1998).

Because verbal aggressiveness does not help to resolve conflicts, results in loss of credibility for the person using it, and actually increases the credibility of the target of the aggressiveness, you may wonder why people act aggressively (Infante, Hartley, Martin, Higgins, et al., 1992; Infante, Riddle, Horvath, & Tumlin, 1992).

Communicating with an affirming style (for example, smiling, pleasant facial expression, touching, physical closeness, eye contact, nodding, warm and sincere voice, vocal variety) leads others to perceive less verbal aggression in an interaction than when communicating with a nonaffirming style. The assumption people seem to make is that if your actions are affirming, then your messages are also, and if your actions are nonaffirming, then your messages are also (Infante, Rancer, & Jordan, 1996).

Argumentativeness   Contrary to popular usage, the term **argumentativeness** refers to a quality to be cultivated rather than avoided. Argumentativeness is your willingness to argue for a point of view, your tendency to speak your mind on significant issues. It's the preferred alternative to verbal aggressiveness. Before reading about ways to increase your argumentativeness, take the self-test "How Argumentative Are You?"

TEST YOURSELF   *How Argumentative Are You?*

This questionnaire contains statements about controversial issues. Indicate how often each statement is true for you personally according to the following scale: 1 = almost never true, 2 = rarely true, 3 = occasionally true, 4 = often true, and 5 = almost always true.

_____ 1. While in an argument, I worry that the person I am arguing with will form a negative impression of me.

_____ 2. Arguing over controversial issues improves my intelligence.

_____ 3. I enjoy avoiding arguments.

_____ 4. I am energetic and enthusiastic when I argue.

_____ 5. Once I finish an argument, I promise myself that I will not get into another.

_____ 6. Arguing with a person creates more problems for me than it solves.

_____ 7. I have a pleasant, good feeling when I win a point in an argument.

_____ 8. When I finish arguing with someone, I feel nervous and upset.

_____ 9. I enjoy a good argument over a controversial issue.

_____ 10. I get an unpleasant feeling when I realize I am about to get into an argument.

_____ 11. I enjoy defending my point of view on an issue.

_____ 12. I am happy when I keep an argument from happening.

_____ 13. I do not like to miss the opportunity to argue a controversial issue.

_____ 14. I prefer being with people who rarely disagree with me.

_____ 15. I consider an argument an exciting intellectual challenge.

_____ 16. I find myself unable to think of effective points during an argument.

_____ 17. I feel refreshed and satisfied after an argument on a controversial issue.

_____ 18. I have the ability to do well in an argument.

_____ 19. I try to avoid getting into arguments.

_____ 20. I feel excitement when I expect that a conversation I am in is leading to an argument.

▶ **How did you do?**   To compute your argumentativeness score follow these steps:

1. Add your scores on items 2, 4, 7, 9, 11, 13, 15, 17, 18, and 20.
2. Add 60 to the sum obtained in step 1.
3. Add your scores on items 1, 3, 5, 6, 8, 10, 12, 14, 16, and 19.
4. To compute your argumentativeness score, subtract the total obtained in step 3 from the total obtained in step 2.

The following guidelines will help you interpret your score: Scores between 73 and 100 indicate high argumentativeness; scores between 56 and 72 indicate moderate argumentativeness; and scores between 20 and 55 indicate low argumentativeness.

Generally, those who score high in argumentativeness have a strong tendency to state their position on controversial issues and argue against the positions of others. A high scorer sees arguing as exciting, intellectually challenging, and as an opportunity to win a kind of context.

The moderately argumentative person possesses some of the qualities of the high argumentative person and some of the qualities of the low argumentative person. The person who scores low in argumentativeness tries to prevent arguments. This person experiences satisfaction, not from arguing, but from avoiding arguments. The low argumentative person sees arguing as unpleasant and unsatisfying. Not surprisingly this person has little confidence in his or her ability to argue effectively.

❱ **What will you do?**   The researchers who developed this test note that both high and low argumentatives may experience communication difficulties. The high argumentative, for example, may argue needlessly, too often, and too forcefully. The low argumentative, on the other hand, may avoid taking a stand even when it seems necessary. Persons scoring somewhere in the middle are probably the more interpersonally skilled and adaptable, arguing when it is necessary but avoiding arguments that are needless and repetitive. Does your experience support this observation? What specific actions might you take to improve your argumentativeness?

From Dominic Infante and Andrew Rancer, "A Conceptualization and Measure of Argumentativeness" *Journal of Personality Assessment 46* (1982): 72–80. Copyright 1982 Lawrence Erlbaum Associates, Inc. Reprinted by permission of Lawrence Erlbaum Associates, Inc., and the authors.

At this point you may wish to examine your own behavior and ask yourself how argumentative you are. The following are suggestions for cultivating argumentativeness, hopefully most are already part of your communication behavior (Infante, 1988). If any are not a part of your conflict behavior, consider how you can make them a part.

Do you

1. Treat disagreements as objectively as possible? Do you avoid assuming that because someone takes issue with your position or your interpretation that they're attacking you as a person?
2. Avoid attacking the other person (rather than the person's arguments) even if this would give you a tactical advantage? Center your arguments on issues rather than personalities?
3. Reaffirm the other person's sense of competence? Compliment the other person as appropriate?
4. Avoid interrupting? Allow the other person to state her or his position fully before you respond?

ETHICS in Interpersonal Communication

Ethical Fighting

Throughout this chapter, a distinction was made between effective and ineffective conflict strategies. But all communication strategies also have an ethical dimension and so we need to look at the ethical implications of conflict resolution strategies.

■ Does conflict avoidance have an ethical dimension? For example, is it unethical for one relationship partner to refuse to discuss disagreements?

■ Is there an instance when physical force to influence another person

might be ethical? Can you identify a situation in which it would be appropriate for someone with greater physical strength to overpower another to force them to accept his or her point of view?

■ Are face-detracting strategies inherently unethical or might it be appropriate to use them in certain situations; which situations?

■ What are the ethical implications of verbal aggressiveness?

What would you do? *At your high-powered and highly stressful job you sometimes use cocaine with your colleagues. This happens several times a month, and you don't use drugs of any kind at any other times. Your partner—who you know hates drugs and people who use any recreational drugs—asks you if you take drugs. Because it's such a limited use, but mostly because you know that admitting this will cause a huge conflict in a relationship already having difficulties, you wonder if you can ethically lie about this.*

5. Stress equality and stress the similarities that you have with the other person (see the Increasing Effectiveness box on page 314)? Stress your areas of agreement before attacking the disagreements?

6. Express interest in the other person's position, attitude, and point of view?

7. Avoid presenting your arguments too emotionally? Avoid using a loud voice or interjecting vulgar expressions that will prove offensive and eventually ineffective?

8. Allow the other person to save face? Never humiliate the other person?

REVIEWING   Key Terms and Concepts in Interpersonal Conflict

This chapter examined interpersonal conflict, one possible model to follow in trying to resolve conflicts, and some of the popular productive and unproductive conflict strategies.

Nature of Conflict

What is interpersonal conflict?

■ Interpersonal conflict is a disagreement between connected individuals who each want something that is incompatible with what the other wants.

■ Interpersonal conflict is neither good nor bad, but depending on how the disagreements are resolved, the conflict can strengthen or weaken a relationship.

■ Conflict can center on matters external to the relationship and on relationship issues such as who's the boss.

■ Conflict and the strategies used to resolve it are heavily influenced by culture.

■ Before the conflict: Try to fight in private, fight when you're ready, know what you're fighting about, and fight about problems that can be solved.

■ After the conflict: Learn something from the conflict, keep the conflict in perspective, attack your negative feelings, and increase the exchange of rewards.

Conflict Resolution Stages

How do you go about resolving a conflict or solving a problem?

■ Define the conflict: Define the content and relationship issues in specific terms, avoiding gunnysacking and mind-reading, and try to empathize with the other person.

■ Examine the possible solutions: Try to identify as many solutions as possible, look for win–win solutions, and carefully weigh the costs and rewards of each solution.

■ Test the solution mentally and in practice to see if it works.

■ Evaluate the tested solution from a variety of perspectives.

■ Accept the solution and integrate it into your behavior. Or reject the solution and begin again, for example, defining the problem differently or looking in other directions for possible solutions.

Conflict Management Strategies

What are some of the strategies that people use that may help or hinder resolving the conflict?

■ Become an active participant in the conflict; don't avoid the issues or the arguments of the other person.

■ Use talk to discuss the issues rather than trying to force the other person to accept your position.

■ Try to enhance the self-esteem, the face, of the person you're arguing with; avoid strategies that may cause the other person to lose face.

■ Argue the issues, focusing as objectively as possible on the points of disagreement; avoid being verbally aggressive or attacking the other person.

APPLYING   Key Terms and Concepts in Interpersonal Conflict

1. Which characters from television frequently demonstrate verbal aggressiveness? Which characters frequently demonstrate argumentativeness? What distinguishes these types of characters?

2. Recall a recent conflict that you tried to resolve. Did you follow (at least generally) the five stages identified in the model presented in this chapter? If not, can you identify the steps you did follow?

3. Men generally score higher in argumentativeness (and in verbal aggressiveness) than women. Men are also more apt to be perceived (by both men and women) as more argumentative and verbally aggressive than women (Nicotera & Rancer, 1994). Why do you think this is so?

4. What changes would you like to see your relational partners (friends, family members, romantic partners) make in their own verbal aggressiveness and argumentativeness? What might you do to more effectively regulate your own verbal aggressiveness and argumentativeness?

5. Visit some game websites (for example, **http://www. gamesdomain.co.uk** or **http://www.gamepen.com/ yellowpages/**) and examine the rules of the games. What kinds of conflict strategies do these game rules embody?

6. Have you ever witnessed or been a party to beltlining? What happened? What could have been done differently to make resolving the conflict easier?

7. Have you ever been accused of failing to see what the "real" conflict is about? Were you accused of misunderstanding the content conflict or the relationship conflict?

8. How might failing to appreciate gender and cultural variations in approaches to conflict lead you to misread the verbal and nonverbal cues of the other person? Can you imagine an experience where this could happen?

EXPERIENCING Key Terms and Concepts in Interpersonal Conflict

Go to www.ablongman.com/devito.

These experiences focus on interpersonal conflict, especially on understanding the nature of conflict and how you can more effectively resolve and manage conflict.

(1) **Analyzing a Conflict Episode** provides an opportunity to think critically about the messages used in a conflict interaction. (2) **Dealing with Conflict Starters** looks at some of the messages that often begin conflicts. (3) **Generating Win–Win Solutions** provides opportunities to experiment with strategies that can make conflict and its resolution more effective.

Research
Navigator.com

RESEARCHING with Research Navigator Key Terms and Concepts in Interpersonal Conflict

Go to http://www.researchnavigator.com.

Reading an article.

Read a popular or scholarly article on conflict, its nature, the stages of conflict resolution, or conflict strategies. On the basis of this article what can you add to the discussion presented here?

Investigating key terms.

Investigate one of the key terms discussed in this chapter (for example, conflict, interpersonal conflict, intergroup conflict, aggressiveness, argumentativeness, competition and collaboration, or conflict avoidance). What additional insights can you provide?

Finding answers.

Try finding answers to one of the following questions or design a research study to answer it.

■ Are men or women more likely to use avoidance (or blame, force, manipulation, ridicule, silencers, beltlining, gunnysacking, or personal rejection) as a romantic conflict strategy?
■ Are people with high self-esteem likely to have more or fewer interpersonal conflicts than those with low self-esteem?
■ Are high argumentative people more satisfied with their communication than are those who are high in verbal aggressiveness?
■ Are more educated people more likely to use argumentativeness than less educated people?

14 Power in Interpersonal Relationships

The Lord of the Rings: The Fellowship of the Ring (2001)

Communication is power.
Those who have mastered
its effective use can
change their own
experience of the world
and the world's
experience of them.

—Anthony Robbins

Principles of Power
Types of Power
Communicating Power

*Y*ou see the use of a wide variety *of powers throughout* The Lord of the Rings. *The types of power discussed here are different from those wielded by Gandalf or by the Ring; the types of power considered here are those that derive largely from your verbal and nonverbal messages. In this chapter we look at the principles of interpersonal power, the types or bases of power, and how you can communicate your own power and empower others more effectively.*

PRINCIPLES OF POWER

Power influences what you do, when you do it, and with whom. It influences your choice of friends, your romantic and family relationships—and how successful you feel they are. Interpersonal power is what enables one person to control the behavior of the other. Thus, if A has power over B, then A, by virtue of this power—through either its exercise or the threat of its being exercised—can control B's behaviors. Power in interpersonal relationships may best be introduced by a discussion of some of its most important principles. These principles explain how power operates interpersonally and offer insight on how you can more effectively manage power.

Some People Are More Powerful Than Others

In the United States, all people are considered equal under the law and therefore equal in their entitlement to education, legal protection, and freedom of speech. But all people are not equal when it comes to just about everything else. Some are born into wealth, others into poverty. Some are born physically strong, good-looking, and healthy; others are born weak, less attractive, and with a variety of inherited illnesses.

A S K *the* **Researcher**

Managing Emotions

People have told me I'm overly emotional, and it's made me anxious about my new job, which I'm starting next month. I want to appear the picture of the cool, totally in control individual. Any suggestions for controlling my emotions and projecting this confident and powerful image?

If your response is due to the situation (you feel anxious and over-emotional in new, highly evaluative settings), you can probably function more effectively by maintaining a "problem-focus." Keep your thoughts and plans focused on the job problems (what are the standards for productivity, when do we have staff meetings) and don't get trapped into an "emotion-focus" (my heart's pounding, I look like a fool). If your response is driven by your personality (you're just an anxious, nervous person), things are a little more complicated. The "problem-focus" is still an excellent strategy, but in this case, it can be much more difficult to ignore your emotional response because this is who you are. If you find that you cannot produce the smooth communication (even with a problem-focus), you might want to consider clinical help. No, you're not crazy or mentally ill, but your anxiety is clearly interfering with your skilled performance. Several effective treatments for social anxiety exist and may help you learn to cope more effectively.

Melanie Booth-Butterfield (Ph.D., University of Missouri) is a professor of communication studies at West Virginia University. Her teaching concentrations include interpersonal communication, social issues associated with communication, and health communication; among her research interests are health communication, emotion and cognition, and related interpersonal communication topics. mbooth@wvu.edu Steven Booth-Butterfield (Ed.D., West Virginia University) is the chief of the Health Communication Research Branch of the National Institute for Occupational Safety and Health. His teaching focuses on media effects, influence and persuasion, and health communication. His research areas include health communication, influence and persuasion, and emotion and cognition related to communication. drsbb@mindspring.com (Reprinted by permission of Dr. Melanie Booth-Butterfield and Dr. Steven Booth-Butterfield.)

The Knowledge Gap

Knowledge is power. And the lack of knowledge means a lack of power. An interesting view of this relationship is addressed in the knowledge gap hypothesis. This hypothesis refers to the difference in knowledge between one group and another and the influence of the media in widening this gap (Tichenor, Donohue, & Olien, 1970; Viswanath et al., 2000; Viswanath & Finnegan, 1995; Mastin, 1998; Grabe, Lang, Zhou, & Bolls, 2000).

Knowledge, however, is expensive and not everyone has equal access to it. This is especially true as we live more of our lives in cyberspace. The new communication technologies—computers, CD-ROMs, the Internet, satellite and cable television, for example—are major ways for gaining information. The better educated have the money to own and the skills to master the new technologies and thus acquire more information. The less educated don't have the money to own or the skills to master the new technologies and thus cannot as easily acquire more information, creating and expanding the knowledge gap, the "digital divide" (Severin & Tankard, 2001). A particularly clear example of this is seen in the educational level of Internet users (UCLA Internet Report, 2000):

- 31% of those with less than a high school education use the Internet
- 53% of high school graduates use the Internet
- 70% of those with some college education use the Internet
- 86% of college graduates and those with advanced degrees use the Internet

You can also see the knowledge gap when you compare cultures. Developed countries, for example, have the new technologies in their schools and offices and many people can afford to buy their own computers and satellite systems. Access to the new technologies helps these countries develop even further. Undeveloped countries, with little or no access to such technologies, cannot experience the same gain in knowledge and information as those who have this technological access.

Follow Up   Do you see the knowledge gap hypothesis operating in your community or school? Can you see it in different cultures with which you're familiar?

Some people are born into power, and some of those who are not born powerful learn to be so. In short, some people control and others are controlled. Of course, the world is not quite that simple; some exert power in certain areas, some in others. Some exert power in many areas, some in just a few.

Some People Are More Machiavellian Than Others

Before reading about this fascinating concept, take the self-test "How Machiavellian Are You?" It focuses on your beliefs about how easily you think people can be manipulated.

WEB EXPLORATION
To learn more about Machiavellian behavior, go to **www.ablongman. com/devito**.

TEST YOURSELF   *How Machiavellian Are You?*

For each statement, record the number on the following scale that most closely represents your attitude: 1 = disagree a lot, 2 = disagree a little, 3 = neutral, 4 = agree a bit, 5 = agree a lot.

_____ 1. The best way to handle people is to tell them what they want to hear.
_____ 2. When you ask someone to do something for you, it is best to give the real reasons rather than giving reasons that might carry more weight.
_____ 3. Anyone who completely trusts anyone else is asking for trouble.
_____ 4. It is hard to get ahead without cutting corners here and there.

_____ 5. It is safest to assume that all people have a vicious streak and it will come out when they are given a chance.

_____ 6. One should take action only when sure it is morally right.

_____ 7. Most people are basically good and kind.

_____ 8. There is no excuse for lying to someone.

_____ 9. Most people forget more easily the death of their parents than the loss of their property.

_____ 10. Generally speaking, people won't work hard unless they're forced to.

▶ **How did you do?**   To compute your Mach score follow these steps:

1. Reverse the scores on items 2, 6, 7, and 8 according to the following scale:

If you responded with	Change it to
5	1
4	2
3	3
2	4
1	5

2. Add all 10 scores, being sure to use the reversed numbers for 2, 6, 7, and 8.

Your Mach score is a measure of the degree to which you believe that people in general can be manipulated and not necessarily that you would or do manipulate others. If you scored somewhere between 35 and 50 you would be considered a high Mach; if you scored between 10 and 15 you would be considered a low Mach. Most of us would score in between these extremes.

▶ **What will you do?**   The concept of Machiavellianism is explained in the text. As you read the discussion try to visualize how your level of Machiavellianism influences your communication options and messages.

Niccolo Machiavelli (1469–1527) was a political philosopher and advisor who wrote his theory of political control in _The Prince._ Machiavelli argued that the prince must do whatever is necessary to rule the people; the ends justified the means. The ruler was in fact obligated to use power to gain more power and thus better achieve the desired goals (Steinfatt, 1987). The term _Machiavellian_ has thus come to refer to the techniques or tactics one person uses to control another person. Research finds significant differences between those who score high and those who score low on the Mach scale. Low Machs are more easily persuaded; high Machs are more resistant to persuasion. Low Machs are more empathic; high Machs are more logical. Low Machs are more interpersonally oriented and involved with other people; high Machs are more assertive and more controlling. Business students (especially marketing students) score higher in Machiavellianism than do nonbusiness majors (McLean & Jones, 1992).

Machiavellianism seems, in part at least, to be culturally conditioned. Individualist orientation, which favors competition and being Number One, seems more conducive to the development of Machiavellianism. Collectivist orientation, which favors cooperation and being one of a group, seems a less friendly environment for the development of Machiavellianism in its members. Some evidence of this comes from research showing that Chinese students attending a traditional Chinese (Confucian) school rated lower in Machiavellianism than similar Chinese students attending a Western-style school

(Christie, 1970). Age is also related to Machiavellianism. Younger people score significantly higher on Machiavelliansm than older people (Moore, Ward, & Katz, 1998).

Your level of Machiavellianism will influence the communication choices you make. For example, if you were a high Mach, you would be more strategic and manipulative in your self-disclosures and in your conflict-solving strategies than you would be if you were a low Mach. High Machs are generally more effective in just about all aspects studied—they even earn higher grades in communication courses that involve face-to-face interaction (Burgoon, 1971). Low Mach women, however, are preferred as dating partners by both high and low Mach men (Steinfatt, 1987).

Power Can Be Increased or Decreased

Although people differ greatly in the amount of power they wield at any time and in any specific area, everyone can increase their power in some ways. You can lift weights and increase your physical power. You can learn the techniques of negotiation and increase your power in group situations. You can learn the principles of communication and increase your persuasive power.

Power can also be decreased. Probably the most common way to lose power is by unsuccessfully trying to control another's behavior. For example, the person who threatens you with punishment and then fails to carry out the threat loses power. Another way to lose power is to allow others to control you, for example, to take unfair advantage of you. When you don't confront these power tactics of others, you lose power yourself.

Power Follows the Principle of Less Interest

In any interpersonal relationship, the person who holds the power is the one less interested in and less dependent on the rewards and punishments controlled by the other person. If, for example, Pat can walk away from the rewards Chris controls or can suffer the punishments Chris can mete out, Pat controls the relationship. If, on the other hand, Pat needs the rewards Chris controls or is unable or unwilling to suffer the punishments Chris can administer, Chris maintains the power and controls the relationship. Put differently, Chris holds the relationship power to the degree that Chris is not dependent on the rewards and punishments under Pat's control.

The more a person needs a relationship, the less power that person has in it. The less a person needs a relationship, the greater that person's power. In a love relationship, for example, the person who maintains greater power is the one who would find it easier to break up the relationship. The person who is unwilling (or unable) to break up has little power, precisely because he or she is dependent on the relationship and the rewards provided by the other person.

Not surprisingly, if you perceive your partner as having greater power than you, you would probably be more likely to avoid confrontation and to be less expressive in your criticism (Solomon & Samp, 1998).

Power Has a Cultural Dimension

Recall the concept of power distance discussed earlier (Chapter 2). There it was pointed out that cultures differ in the amount of power that exists between people and in the attitudes that people have about power, its legitimacy, and its desirability (Hofstede, 1983). In many Asian, African, and Arab cultures (as well as in many European cultures such as Italian and Greek), for example, there is a great power distance between men and women. Men have the greater power and women are expected to recognize this

View point   With special reference to the principle that the person who has less interest in the relationship maintains the greater power and influence, would you find it advantageous to have your partner believe that you cared less about the relationship and had less need for the rewards of your partner than you actually do? Do you know people who do this? Do you find this ethical?

and abide by its implications. Men, for example, make the important decisions and have the final word in any difference of opinion (Hatfield & Rapson, 1996).

In the United States the power structure is undergoing considerable changes. In many families men still have the greater power. Partly because they earn more money, they also make the more important decisions. As economic equality becomes more a reality than an ideal, this power difference may also change. In Arab cultures the man makes the more important decisions not because he earns more money, but because he is the man and men are simply given greater power.

In some of these cultures, the power difference is perpetuated by granting men greater educational opportunities. For example, although college education for women is taken for granted in most of the United States, it's the exception in many other cultures throughout the world.

In some Asian cultures, persons in positions of authority—for example, teachers—have unquestioned power. Students do not contradict, criticize, or challenge teachers. This can easily create problems in the typical multicultural classroom. Those students from cultures that teach that the teacher has unquestioned authority may have difficulty meeting the American teacher expectation that students interact critically with the material and develop interpretations of their own.

Power also bears a close relationship to interpersonal violence. For example, husbands who had less power in their relationship were more likely to be physically abusive toward their wives than husbands who had greater power (Babcock, Waltz, Jacobson, & Gottman, 1993). Further, in violent marriages the interpersonal power struggle is often characterized by unproductive and dysfunctional ways of influencing each other. For example, violent couples engage in greater blame and greater criticism of each other than do nonviolent couples (Rushe, 1996).

Power Is Frequently Used Unfairly

Although it would be nice to believe that power is wielded for the good of all, it's often used selfishly and unfairly. Here are two examples: sexual harassment and the use of power plays.

WEB EXPLORATION
To learn more about sexual harassment, go to www.ablongman.com/devito.

Sexual Harassment   One type of unfair use of power is *sexual harassment,* a form of behavior that violates Title VII of the Civil Rights Act of 1964 and as amended by the Civil Rights Act of 1991 (http://www.eeoc.gov/laws/vii.html, last modified January

15, 1997, accessed May 4, 2002). There are two general categories of sexual harassment: *quid pro quo* (a term borrowed from the Latin, which literally means, "this for that") and the creation of a hostile environment.

In quid pro quo harassment, employment opportunities (as in hiring and promotion) are dependent on the granting of sexual favors. Conversely, quid pro quo harassment also involves situations in which reprisals and various negative consequences would result from the failure to grant such sexual favors. Put more generally, quid pro quo harassment occurs when employment consequences (positive or negative) hinge on a person's response to sexual advancements.

Hostile environment harassment is much broader and includes all sexual behaviors (verbal and nonverbal) that make a worker uncomfortable. For example, putting sexually explicit pictures on the bulletin board, using sexually explicit screensavers, telling sexual jokes and stories, and using sexual and demeaning language or gestures would all constitute sexual harassment. "Sexual harassment," notes one team of researchers, "refers to conduct, typically experienced as offensive in nature, in which unwanted sexual advances are made in the context of a relationship of unequal power or authority. The victims are subjected to verbal comments of a sexual nature, unconsented touching and requests for sexual favors" (Friedman, Boumil, & Taylor, 1992). Attorneys note that under the law "sexual harassment is any unwelcome sexual advance or conduct on the job that creates an intimidating, hostile or offensive working environment" (Petrocelli & Repa, 1992).

The Equal Employment Opportunity Commission (EEOC) definition of sexual harassment sums up these two basic types. Numbers (1) and (2) refer to quid pro quo and number (3) refers to hostile environment.

> Unwelcome sexual advances, requests for sexual favors and other verbal or physical conduct of a sexual nature constitute sexual harassment when (1) submission to such conduct is made either explicitly or implicitly a term or condition of an individual's employment, (2) submission to or rejection of such conduct by an individual is used as the basis for employment decisions affecting such individual, or (3) such conduct has the purpose or effect of unreasonably interfering with an individual's work performance or creating an intimidating, hostile, or offensive working environment (Friedman, Boumil, & Taylor, 1992).

To determine whether behavior constitutes sexual harassment, ask yourself the following questions to help you assess your own situation objectively rather than emotionally (VanHyning, 1993):

1. Is it real? Does this behavior have the meaning it seems to have?
2. Is it job related? Does this behavior have something to do with or will it influence the way you do your job?
3. Did you reject this behavior? Did you make your rejection of unwanted messages clear to the other person?
4. Have these types of messages persisted? Is there a pattern, a consistency to these messages?

If you answered "yes" to all four questions then the behavior is likely to constitute sexual harassment (VanHyning, 1993).

Keep in mind three additional facts that are often misunderstood. First, either sex may sexually harass. Although most cases brought to public attention are committed by men against women, women may also harass men. Further, harassment may be committed by men against men and by women against women. Second, anyone in the organization can be guilty of sexual harassment. Although most cases of harassment involve persons in authority harassing subordinates, this is not a necessary condition. Coworkers, vendors, and even customers may be charged with sexual harassment. Third, sexual harassment is not limited to the business organization but can and does occur in schools; hospitals; and in social, religious, and political organizations.

How Can You Avoid Sexual Harassment Behaviors?   Three suggestions will help to prevent the occurrence of harassment (Bravo & Cassedy, 1992). First, begin with the assumption that coworkers are not interested in your sexual advances, sexual stories and jokes, or sexual gestures. Second, listen and watch for negative reactions to any sex-related discussion. Use the suggestions and techniques discussed throughout this book (for example, perception checking and critical listening) to become aware of such reactions. When in doubt, find out; ask questions, for example. Third, avoid saying or doing what you think your parent, partner, or child would find offensive in the behavior of someone with whom she or he worked.

What Can You Do about Sexual Harassment?   Should you encounter sexual harassment and feel the need to do something about it, consider these suggestions recommended by workers in the field (Petrocelli & Repa, 1992; Bravo & Cassedy, 1992; Rubenstein, 1993):

1. *Talk to the harasser.* Tell this person, assertively, that you do not welcome the behavior and that you find it offensive. Simply informing Fred that his sexual jokes aren't appreciated and are seen as offensive may be sufficient to make him stop this joke telling. In some instances, unfortunately, such criticism goes unheeded, and the offensive behavior continues.
2. *Collect evidence*—perhaps corroboration from others who have experienced similar harassment at the hands of the same individual or a log of the offensive behaviors.
3. *Begin with appropriate channels within the organization.* Most organizations have established channels to deal with such grievances. This step will in most cases eliminate any further harassment. In the event that it doesn't, you may consider going further.
4. *File a complaint with an organization or governmental agency or perhaps take legal action.*
5. *Don't blame yourself.* Like many who are abused, you may tend to blame yourself, feeling that you're responsible for being harassed. You aren't; however, you may need to secure emotional support from friends or perhaps from a trained professional.

Power Plays   **Power plays** are patterns (not isolated instances) of behavior that take unfair advantage of another person (Steiner, 1981). Power plays aim to rob you of your right to make your own choices, free of harassment or intimidation.

For example, in the "nobody upstairs" power play, the individual refuses to acknowledge your request, regardless of how or how many times you make it. One common form is the refusal to take no for an answer. Sometimes "nobody upstairs" takes the form of pleading ignorance of common socially accepted (but unspoken) rules, such as knocking when you enter someone's room or refraining from opening another person's mail or wallet: "I didn't know you didn't want me to look in your wallet," or "Do you want me to knock the next time I come into your room?"

View point The position argued by Claude Steiner and articulated here is that power plays are unfair. And yet, it might be argued that if you want to exert influence over another person these power plays are perfectly reasonable to use, simply because they're effective (most the time) and don't seem to violate any major ethical principle. How do you feel about this issue?

Another power play is "you owe me." Here others do something for you and then demand something in return. They remind you of what they did for you and use this to get you to do what they want.

In "yougottobekidding," one person attacks the other by saying "You've got to be kidding" or some similar phrase, not out of surprise (which is fine) but out of a desire to put your ideas down: "You can't be serious." "You can't mean that." "You didn't say what I thought you said, did you?" The intention here is to express utter disbelief in the other's statement so as to make the statement and the person seem inadequate or stupid.

The power plays discussed above are just examples. There are, of course, many others that you have no doubt met on occasion. What do you do when you recognize such a power play? One commonly employed response is to ignore the power play and allow the other person to take control. Another response is to treat the power play as an isolated instance (rather than as a pattern of behavior) and object to it. For example, you might say quite simply, "Please don't come into my room without knocking first," or "Please don't look in my wallet without permission."

A third response is a cooperative one (Steiner, 1981). In this response, you do the following:

■ *Express your feelings.* Tell the person that you're angry, annoyed, or disturbed by his or her behavior.
■ *Describe the behavior to which you object.* Tell the person—in language that describes rather than evaluates—the specific behavior you object to: For example, reading your mail, saying I owe you something, or responding to everything you say with disbelief.
■ *State a cooperative response you both can live with comfortably.* Tell the person—in a cooperative tone—what you want: For example: "I want you to knock before coming into my room." "I want you to stop telling me I owe you things." "I want you to stop ridiculing my ideas."

A cooperative response to "nobody upstairs" might go something like this: "I'm angry (*expressing feelings*) that you persist in opening my mail. You have opened my mail four

Reversing Media's Influence

Although you generally think of the media as exerting influence on you, you can also exert influence on the media—on radio, television, newspapers and magazines, film, and the Internet (Jamieson & Campbell, 2001; Postman & Powers, 1992):

■ *Register your complaints.* Write letters, e-mail, or call a television station or an advertiser expressing your views. Write to a public forum, such as a newspaper or newsgroup, or to the Federal Communication Commission or to other regulatory agencies. Use any of the variety of websites (**vote.com** is perhaps the most popular) that encourage users to voice their opinions and then forward these to the appropriate agencies.

■ *Exert group pressure.* Join with others who think the same way you do. Bring group pressure to bear on television networks, newspapers, advertisers, and manufacturers.

■ *Protest through an established organization.* There's probably an organization already established for the issue with which you're concerned. Search the Internet for relevant newsgroups, professional organizations, and chat rooms that focus on your topic.

■ *Protest with a social movement,* a technique used throughout history to gain civil rights. Forming such movements or aligning yourself with an established movement can help you secure not only a large number of petitioners but also the media coverage that might enable you to communicate your message to a large audience.

■ *Create legislative pressure.* Exert influence on the state or federal level by influencing your local political representatives (through voting, phone calls, letters, and e-mails), who will in turn influence representatives on higher levels of the political hierarchy.

Follow Up   Let's say that you're unhappy about the way in which the national and local media (television and newspapers) have treated the abortion controversy. How would you go about exerting pressure on the media to better reflect your own position in their coverage?

times this past week (*description of the behavior to which you object*). I want you to allow me to open my own mail. If there is anything in it that concerns you, I will let you know immediately" (*statement of cooperative response*).

TRY IT!
Apply your knowledge about types of power; go to **www.ablongman.com/devito**.

TYPES OF POWER

Power is present in all relationships and in all communication interchanges. But the type of power varies greatly from one situation to another and from one person to another. Here we identify six types of power: referent, legitimate, expert, information or persuasion, reward, and coercive power (French & Raven, 1968; Raven, Centers, & Rodrigues, 1975; Raven, Schwarzwald, & Koslowsky, 1998). Differences in the amount and type of power influence who makes important decisions, who will prevail in an argument, and who will control the finances.

Before reading about these types of power, consider your own powers by responding to the following questions (each of which refers to a type of power discussed below).

1. Do people wish to be like you or be identified with you? For example, do high school students look up to you as a college student or do new workers admire your recent promotion?
2. Is your position such that you often have to tell others what to do? For example, are you a manager whose position demands that you tell employees what to do or a parent whose position demands that you tell children what to do?

3. Do people realize that you have expertise in certain areas of knowledge? Do you have expertise in finance or computer software such that others turn to you for advice?
4. Do people realize that you possess the communication ability to present an argument logically and persuasively?
5. Do people see you as having the ability to give them what they want? That is, do people see you as capable of giving them the rewards they want?
6. Do people see you as having the ability to administer punishment or to withhold things they want?

These statements refer to the six major types of power, to which we now turn.

Referent Power

You have *referent power* over others when they wish to be like you or be identified with you. For example, an older brother may have power over a younger brother because the younger brother wants to be like the older one. The assumption made by the younger brother is that he will be more like his older brother if he behaves and believes as his brother does. Once he decides to do so, it takes little effort for the older brother to exert influence or power over the younger. Referent power depends greatly on attractiveness and prestige; as they increase, so does identification and, consequently, power. When you're well liked and well respected, of the same sex as the other person, and have the same attitudes and experiences as the other person, your referent power is especially great. Supervisors in the United States who had referent power were especially effective in handling subordinates, but in Bulgaria it was legitimate power (the type discussed next) that was associated with such effectiveness, underscoring the cultural dimension of power (Rahim, Antonioni, Krumov, & Ilieva, 2000).

Legitimate Power

You have *legitimate power* over others when they believe you have the right—by virtue of your position—to influence or control their behavior. Legitimate power stems from our belief that certain people should have power over us, that they have a right to influence us because of who they are. Legitimate power usually derives from the roles people occupy. Teachers are often perceived to have legitimate power, and this is doubly true for religious teachers. Parents are seen as having legitimate power over their children. Employers, judges, managers, doctors, and police officers are others who hold legitimate power in different areas.

Expert Power

You have *expert power* over others when they see you as having expertise or knowledge. Your knowledge—as seen by others—gives you expert power. Usually expert power is subject specific. For example, when you're ill, you're influenced by the recommendation of someone with expert power related to your illness— say, a doctor. But you would not be influenced by the recommendation of someone to whom you don't attribute illness-related expert power—say, the mail carrier or a plumber. You give the lawyer expert power in matters of law and psychiatrists expert power in matters of the mind, but, ideally, you don't interchange them.

Your expert power increases when you're seen as unbiased and as having nothing to gain personally from influencing others. It decreases when you're seen as biased or as having something to gain from influencing others.

Research finds that men are generally perceived to have higher levels of expert and legitimate power than women and that women are generally perceived to have higher levels of referent power than men. When it comes to exerting influence, these findings suggest, women will have greater difficulty influencing others by communicating competence and authority than will men; men, on the other hand, will have greater difficulty influencing others using their referent power (Carli, 1999).

Information or Persuasion Power

You have *information or persuasion power* over others when they see you as having the ability to communicate logically and persuasively. If others believe that you have persuasive ability, then you have persuasion power. If you're seen as possessing significant information and the ability to use that information in presenting a well-reasoned argument, then you have information power.

Reward and Coercive Powers

You have *reward power* over others if you have the ability to reward them. Rewards may be material (money, corner office, jewelry) or social (love, friendship, respect). If you're able to grant others some kind of reward, you have control over them to the extent that they want what you can give them. The degree of power you have is directly related to the desirability of the reward as seen by others. Teachers have reward power over students because they control grades, letters of recommendation, social approval, and so on. Students, in turn, have reward power over teachers because they control social approval, student evaluations of faculty, and various other rewards. Parents control rewards for children—food, television privileges, rights to the car, curfew times, and the like—and thus possess reward power.

You have *coercive power* over others when you have the ability to administer punishments or remove rewards should they not yield to your influence. Usually, if you have reward power, you also have coercive power. Teachers not only may reward with high grades, favorable letters of recommendation, and social approval but also may punish with low grades, unfavorable letters, and social disapproval. Parents may deny as well as grant privileges to their children, and hence they possess coercive as well as reward power.

The strength of coercive power depends on two factors: the magnitude of the punishment that can be administered and the likelihood that it will be administered as a result of noncompliance. When threatened by mild punishment or by punishment you think will not be administered, you're not as likely to do as directed as you would if the threatened punishment were severe and highly likely to be administered.

Reward and coercive power are opposite sides of a coin, and the consequences of using them are quite different. First, if you have reward power, you're likely to be seen as more attractive. People like those who have the power to reward them and who do in fact reward them. Coercive power, on the other hand, decreases attractiveness; people dislike those who have the power to punish them or who threaten them with punishment, whether they actually follow through or not.

Second, when you use rewards to exert power, you don't incur the same costs as when you use punishment. When you exert reward power, you're dealing with a contented and happy individual. When you use coercive punishments, however, you must be prepared to incur anger and hostility, which may well be turned against you in the future.

Third, when you give a reward, it signals that you effectively exercised power and that you gained the compliance of the other person. You give the reward because the person did as you wanted. In the exercise of coercive power, however, the reverse is

Students who see their teacher exercising coercive and legitimate power, learn less effectively and have more negative attitudes toward the course, the course content, and the teacher. Further, students are less likely to take similar courses and are less likely to perform the behaviors taught in the course (Richmond & McCroskey, 1984; Kearney et al., 1984, 1985). Coercive and legitimate power also have a negative impact when used by supervisors on subordinates in business settings (Richmond et al., 1984). On the basis of your own experience and the research presented here, what suggestions would you make to your average college instructor?

true. When you administer punishment, it shows that you have been ineffective in using the threat of coercive power and that there has been no compliance.

Fourth, when you exert coercive power, other bases of power frequently are diminished. There seems to be a boomerang effect in operation. People who exercise coercive power are seen as possessing less expert, legitimate, and referent power. Alternatively, when reward power is exerted, other bases of power increase.

You rarely find only one base of power used to influence another person. Usually, a number of power bases are used in concert. If you possess expert power, it's likely that you also possess information power and perhaps legitimate power as well. If you want to control the behavior of another person, you would probably use all three bases of power rather than rely on just one. As you can appreciate, certain individuals have a number of power bases at their disposal, whereas others seem to have few to none. This point brings us back to our first principle: Some people are more powerful than others.

Also, recognize that attempts to influence others may backfire. At times, negative power operates. Each of the six power bases may, at times, have such negative influence. For example, negative referent power occurs when a son rejects his father and wants to be his exact opposite. Negative coercive power may be seen when a child is warned against doing something under threat of punishment and then does exactly what he or she was told not to do; the threat of punishment may have made the forbidden behavior seem exciting or challenging.

COMMUNICATING POWER

You can communicate power much as you communicate any other message. Here we consider how you can communicate power through speaking, nonverbal communication, and listening as well as suggestions for gaining and resisting compliance and for empowering others.

Speaking Power

The ways in which powerfulness and powerlessness are communicated through speech have received lots of research attention (Molloy, 1981; Kleinke, 1986; Johnson, 1987). Generally, research finds that men use more powerful language forms than do women (Lakoff, 1975; Timmerman, 2002). As you consider the major characteristics of powerful and powerless speech presented below think of your own speech.

Do you avoid the following powerless forms of speech?

1. Hesitations, for example, "I *er* want to say that *ah* this one is *er* the best, *you know?*" (Hesitations make one sound unprepared and uncertain.)
2. Too many intensifiers, for example, *"Really,* this was *the greatest;* it was *truly phenomenal."* (Too many intensifiers make your speech sound the same and don't allow for intensifying what should be emphasized.)
3. Disqualifiers, for example, *"I didn't read the entire article,* but . . ." *"I didn't actually see the accident,* but . . . ." (Disqualifiers signal a lack of competence and a feeling of uncertainty.)
4. Tag questions, for example, "That was a great movie, *wasn't it?"* "She's brilliant, *don't you think?"* (Tag questions ask for another's agreement and therefore may signal your need for agreement and your own uncertainty.)
5. Self-critical statements, for example, *"I'm not very good at this." "This is my first public speech."* (Self-critical statements signal a lack of confidence and may make public your own inadequacies.)
6. Slang and vulgar expressions, for example, "##!!!///****!" *"No problem!"* (Slang and vulgarity signal low social class and hence little power.)

Nonverbal Power

Much nonverbal research has focused on the factors related to your ability to persuade and influence others (Burgoon, Buller, & Woodall, 1995). For example, clothing and other artifactual symbols of authority help you to influence others. Research shows you would be more easily influenced by people in, for example, a respected uniform than in civilian clothes.

Affirmative nodding, facial expressions, and gestures help you express your concern for the other person and for the interaction and help you establish your charisma, an essential component of credibility. Self-manipulations (playing with your hair or touching your face, for example) and backward leaning will damage your persuasiveness.

Here are some popular suggestions for communicating power nonverbally in a business situation, most of which come from Lewis (1989). As you read this list, try to provide specific examples of these suggestions and how they might work in business, at home, or at school.

■ Be sure to respond in kind to another's eyebrow flash (raising the eyebrow as a way of acknowledging another person).
■ Avoid adaptors—self, other, and object—especially when you wish to communicate confidence and control.
■ Use consistent packaging; be especially careful that your verbal and nonverbal messages don't contradict each other.
■ When sitting, select chairs you can get in and out of easily; avoid deep plush chairs that you sink into and have trouble getting out of.
■ To communicate confidence with your handshake, exert more pressure than usual and hold the grip a bit longer than normal.

- Walk slowly and deliberately. To appear hurried is to appear as without power, as if you were rushing to meet the expectations of another person who had power over you.
- Maintain eye contact. People who maintain eye contact are judged to be more at ease and less afraid to engage in meaningful interaction than those who avoid eye contact. When you break eye contact, direct your gaze downward; otherwise you'll communicate a lack of interest in the other person.
- Avoid vocalized pauses—the "ers" and "ahs"—that frequently punctuate conversations when you're not quite sure of what to say next.
- Maintain reasonably close distances between yourself and those with whom you interact. If the distance is too far, you may be seen as fearful or uninvolved. If the distance is too close, you may be seen as pushy or overly aggressive.

Listening Power

Much as you can communicate power and authority with words and nonverbal expression, you also communicate power through listening. Throughout your listening, you're communicating messages to others, and these messages comment in some way on your power.

Powerful listeners listen actively. They focus and concentrate (with no real effort) on what is being said, especially on what people say they want or need (Fisher, 1995). Listen to phrases such as "I want," "It would help if I had," or "I'm looking for." Too, respond to what others have said. For example, preface comments with "In light of what you said about," or "If you feel strongly about." Powerless listeners, on the other hand, listen passively, appear to be thinking about something else and only pretend to listen, and rarely refer to what the other person has said when they do respond.

Powerful listeners respond visibly but in moderation; an occasional nod of agreement or a facial expression that says "that's interesting" are usually sufficient. Responding with too little or too much reaction is likely to be perceived as powerless. Too little response says you aren't listening, and too much response says you aren't listening critically. Powerful listeners also use back-channeling cues—head nods and brief oral responses that say "I'm listening, I'm following you"—when appropriate. When no back-channeling cues are given, the speaker comes to wonder if the other person is really listening.

Powerful listeners maintain more focused eye contact than do those seen to have less power. In conversation, normal eye contact is intermittent—you glance at the speaker's face, then away, then back again, and so on. In a small group or public speaking situation, eye contact with the speaker is normally greater.

Adaptors—playing with your hair or a pencil—give the appearance of discomfort. Because of this, adaptors communicate a lack of power. These body movements show the listener to be more concerned with himself or herself than with the speaker. The absence of adaptors, on the other hand, makes the listener appear in control of the situation and comfortable in the role of listener.

Powerful listeners are more likely to maintain an open posture. When around a table or in an audience, they resist covering their stomach or face with their hands. Persons who maintain a defensive posture with, for example, arms crossed around their stomach may communicate a feeling of vulnerability and, hence, powerlessness.

Powerful listeners avoid interrupting the speaker in conversations or in small group situations. The reason is simple: Not interrupting is one of the rules of business communication that powerful people follow and powerless people don't. Completing the speaker's thoughts (or what the listener thinks is the speaker's thought) has a similar powerless effect.

Increasing Interpersonal Effectiveness
Interaction Management

Interaction management refers to the techniques and strategies by which you regulate and carry on an interpersonal interaction. Effective interaction management results in an interaction that's satisfying to both parties. Neither person feels ignored or on stage; each contributes to and benefits from the interpersonal exchange.

Managing Communication Interactions   Of course, this entire text is devoted to effectively managing interpersonal interactions but here are a few specific suggestions.

■ Maintain your role as speaker or listener and pass the opportunity to speak back and forth— through appropriate eye movements, vocal expressions, and body and facial gestures.

■ Keep the conversation fluent without long and awkward pauses. For example, it's been found that patients are less satisfied with their interaction with their doctor when the silence between their comments and the doctor's response is overly long (Rowland-Morin & Carroll, 1990).

■ Communicate with verbal and nonverbal messages that are consistent and reinforce one another. Avoid sending contradictory signals—for example, a nonverbal message that contradicts the verbal message.

You can also signal power through visual dominance behavior (Exline, Ellyson, & Long, 1975), a consideration mentioned in the discussion of eye communication in Chapter 8. For example, the average speaker maintains a high level of eye contact while listening and a lower level while speaking. When powerful individuals want to signal dominance, they may reverse this pattern. They may, for example, maintain a high level of eye contact while talking but a much lower level while listening.

Compliance Gaining and Compliance Resisting

The use of compliance strategies clearly illustrates the way power is exercised. **Compliance-gaining strategies** are the tactics that influence others to do what you want them to do. **Compliance-resisting strategies** are the tactics that enable you to say no and to resist another person's attempts to influence you.

Compliance-Gaining Strategies   Sixteen compliance-gaining strategies are presented in Table 14.1. In reviewing these strategies, keep in mind that compliance gaining, like all interpersonal processes, involves two people in a transaction. Reading down the list may give the impression that these strategies are one-shot affairs, with one person using the strategy and the other person complying. Actually, compliance gaining is best viewed as a transactional, back-and-forth process. Conflict, compromise, renegotiation of the goal, rejection of the strategy, and a host of other responses—in addition to simple compliance—are possible.

Compliance-Resisting Strategies   Let's say that someone you know asks you to do something you don't want to do, such as lend your term paper so this person can copy it and turn it in to another teacher. Research with college students shows that there are four principal ways of responding (McLaughlin, Cody, & Robey, 1980; O'Hair, Cody, & O'Hair, 1991).

In *identity management,* you resist by trying to manipulate the image of the person making the request. You might do this negatively or positively. In negative identity management, you might portray the person as unreasonable or unfair and say, for

Table 14.1 Compliance-Gaining Strategies

As you read this table, realize that these strategies and the responses to them depend both on the personalities of the individuals and on their unique relationships. Which strategies you use, which strategies will work for you, and which strategies will backfire all depend on who you are, who the other person is, and the interpersonal relationship between you. These compliance-gaining strategies come from the research of Marwell and Schmitt (1967, 1990; also see Miller & Parks, 1982; Dillard, 1990).

Compliance Strategy	Example
Pregiving. Pat rewards Chris and then requests compliance.	**Pat:** I'm glad you enjoyed dinner. How about going back to my place for a nightcap and whatever?
Liking. Pat is friendly in order to get Chris in a good mood so that Chris will comply with Pat's request.	**Pat:** (After cleaning up the living room and bedroom) I'd really like to relax and bowl a few games with Terry. Okay?
Promise. Pat promises to reward Chris if Chris complies with Pat's request.	**Pat:** I'll give you anything you want if you will just give me a divorce; just give me my freedom.
Threat. Pat threatens to punish Chris for noncompliance.	**Pat:** If you don't give me a divorce, you'll never see the kids again.
Aversive stimulation. Pat punishes Chris, making cessation contingent on compliance.	**Pat:** (Screams and cries and stops only when Chris complies.)
Positive expertise. Pat promises rewards for compliance because of "the nature of things."	**Pat:** If you follow the doctor's advice, you'll be fine.
Negative expertise. Pat promises punishment for noncompliance because of "the nature of things."	**Pat:** If you don't listen to the doctor, you're going to wind up back in the hospital.
Positive self-feelings. Pat promises that Chris will feel better if Chris complies with Pat's request.	**Pat:** You'll see. You'll be a lot better off without me; you'll feel better after the divorce.
Negative self-feelings. Pat promises that Chris will feel worse if Chris does not comply with Pat's request.	**Pat:** You'll hate yourself if you don't give me this divorce.
Positive altercasting. Pat argues that Chris should comply because a good person would comply.	**Pat:** Any intelligent person would grant their partner a divorce when the relationship has died.
Negative altercasting. Pat argues that Chris should comply because only a bad person would not comply.	**Pat:** Only a cruel and selfish neurotic could stand in the way of another's happiness.
Positive esteem. Pat tells Chris that people will think more highly of Chris if Chris complies with Pat's request.	**Pat:** Everyone will respect your decision to place your parents in an assisted living community.
Negative esteem. Pat tells Chris that people will think poorly of Chris if Chris does not comply with Pat's request.	**Pat:** Everyone will think that you're paranoid if you don't join the club.
Moral appeals. Pat argues that Chris should comply because it's moral to comply and immoral not to comply.	**Pat:** Any ethical person would return the mistaken overpayment.
Altruism. Pat asks Chris to comply because Pat needs this compliance (relying on Chris's desire to help).	**Pat:** I would feel so disappointed if you quit college now. Don't hurt me by quitting.
Debt. Pat asks Chris to comply because of the past favors given to Chris.	**Pat:** Look at how we sacrificed to send you to college.

example, "That's really unfair of you to ask me to compromise my ethics." Or you might tell the person that it hurts that he or she would even think you would do such a thing.

You might also use positive identity management. Here you resist complying by making the other person feel good about himself or herself. For example, you might say,

ETHICS in Interpersonal Communication

Censoring Messages and Interactions

Earlier the concept of the gatekeeper was introduced (Chapter 5) where, you'll recall, a gatekeeper was defined as a person or institution that regulates what information gets through from a source to a receiver. To the extent that information is power, the gatekeeper is an especially potent powerbroker. There are, however, also relational gatekeepers, people and institutions that encourage certain relationships and discourage or even prevent other relationships. Parents, for example, often encourage their children to play with and become friends with children from the same race, national group, or religion and discourage friendships with children from different cultures. Your friends might also exert pressure on you to date one person and not another, to associate with some people but not others. Similarly, religions may exert pressure on you to marry within your religion and make it difficult for you to marry someone of a different faith.

What would you do? *Jennifer and Colleen have been friends all through college. Recently, John has been interested in Colleen and approaches Jennifer to ask what his chances are, if Colleen likes him, and so on. John's been charged with physically abusing a former girlfriend and rumor has it that he's still married. Colleen, on the other hand, is extremely vulnerable and would probably be tempted by John's fast talk. Jennifer is convinced that John would be bad for Colleen, so she tells John that Colleen is not interested in him. Jennifer also decides not to tell Colleen anything about John's interest. Was Jennifer ethical in lying to John? Was she ethical in concealing John's expression of interest from Colleen? If you were Colleen's best friend, what would you do in this situation?*

"You know this material much better than I do; you can easily do a much better paper yourself."

Another way to resist compliance is to use *nonnegotiation,* a direct refusal to do as asked. You might simply say, "No, I don't lend my papers out."

In *negotiation,* you resist compliance by, for example, offering a compromise ("I'll let you read my paper but not copy it") or by offering to help the person in some other way ("If you write a first draft, I'll go over it and try to make some comments"). If the request is a romantic one—for example, a request to go away for a ski weekend—you might resist by discussing your feelings and proposing an alternative: For example, "Let's double date first."

Another way to resist compliance is through *justification.* Here you justify your refusal by citing possible consequences of compliance or noncompliance. For example, you might cite a negative consequence if you complied ("I'm afraid that I'd get caught, and then I'd fail the course"). Or you might cite a positive consequence of not complying ("You'll really enjoy writing this paper; it's a lot of fun").

Remember that compliance gaining and resisting—like all interpersonal communication—are transactional processes in which all elements are interdependent; each element influences each other. Your attempts to gain compliance, for example, will be influenced by the responses of the person you wish to influence. These responses in turn will influence your responses, and so on. Also, just as your relationship (its type, length, intimacy, for example) will influence the strategies you use, so will the strategies you use influence your relationship. Inappropriate strategies will have negative effects, just as positive strategies will have positive effects.

TRY IT!
Apply your insights into empowering others; go to **www.ablongman. com/devito**.

Empowering Others

Empowerment involves helping others (your relational partner, an employee, another student, a sibling) to gain increased power over themselves and their environment.

Empowerment is not just an altruistic gesture on the part of one relationship partner or of management; for many, it is a basic philosophy. The reason empowerment is so much discussed and so much a part of modern business practices is that it provides lots of benefits. Empowered people are more likely to take a more personal interest in the job or in the relationship. Empowered people will be proactive; they will act and not just react. They're more likely to take on decision-making responsibilities, are willing to take risks, and are willing to take responsibility for their actions, qualities that make re lationships and business exciting. In an interpersonal relationship (though the same would apply to a multinational organization), two empowered partners are more likely to effectively meet the challenges and difficulties most relationships will encounter.

In empowering others, try to raise their self-esteem. Resist fault-finding. It doesn't really benefit the fault-finder and certainly doesn't benefit the other person. Fault-finding disempowers others. Any criticism that is offered should be constructive. Be willing to offer your perspective, to lend an ear to a first-try singing effort, or to read a new poem. Also, avoid verbal aggressiveness and abusiveness. Resist the temptation to win an argument with unfair tactics, tactics that are going to hurt the other person.

Be open, positive, empathic, and supportive and treat the other person with an equality of respect. These, of course, are among the qualities of effectiveness that are identified in the Increasing Effectiveness boxes. Similarly, be attentive and listen actively. Attentiveness and active listening tell the other person that he or she is important. After all, what greater praise could you pay than to give another person your time and energy?

Share skills and share decision making. Be willing to relinquish control and allow the other person the freedom to make decisions. Encourage growth in all forms, academic and relational. Growth, like empowerment, is not something that a relationship has a limited supply of and that has to be parceled out. Both persons can grow and develop and both persons can be empowered. The growth and empowerment of one person enhances the growth and power of the other.

Empowering others is especially important when talking with people who are high in communication apprehension. Here are some suggestions based largely on the insights of shyness and apprehension researchers (Carducci & Zimbardo, 1996; Richmond & McCroskey, 1999).

- Don't overprotect the shy person, especially the shy child. If you constantly rush to the child's aid every time he or she experiences social anxiety, the child will never learn how to cope with it. Instead, be supportive (indirectly). Nudge, instead of push, the child (or the adult) to try out new communication situations. In this way, you can help the shy person to interact in small doses and eventually develop the self-confidence needed for more extended interaction.
- Demonstrate your understanding and empathy for the other person's shyness. Don't minimize their fear of communication situations, something those with little apprehension often do. Practice active listening, should you sense they wish to discuss their anxiety and shyness.
- Avoid making the shy person the center of attention. That is exactly what they don't want. And never make their shyness the topic of a group conversation. Saying, "Oh James; he's so bright, but he's so shy" only makes it more difficult for James to even open his mouth. At the same time, make sure that you give the shy person opportunities to speak and that you don't monopolize the conversation. For example, ask their opinions, and when appropriate, try to steer the conversation in the direction of the shy person's expertise and area of competence.

REVIEWING   Key Terms and Concepts of Power in Interpersonal Relationships

This chapter discussed the importance of power in interpersonal relationships, emphasizing the nature of power and its principles, its types, and the ways to communicate power.

Principles of Power

What is power? What principles govern the operation of power in interpersonal relationships?

■ Some people are more powerful than others; some are born to power, others learn it.

■ Some people are more Machiavellian than others; people differ in their beliefs about the extent to which people can be controlled by others.

■ Power can be increased or decreased; power is never static.

■ Power follows the principle of less interest; generally, the less interest, the greater the power.

■ Power has a cultural dimension; power is distributed differently in different cultures.

■ Power is often used unfairly, as in sexual harassment and power plays.

Types of Power

What types of power can one person have over another?

■ *Referent:* B wants to be like A.

■ *Legitimate:* B believes that A has a right to influence or control B's behavior.

■ *Expert:* B regards A as having knowledge.

■ *Information or persuasion:* B attributes to A the ability to communicate effectively.

■ *Reward:* A has the ability to reward B.

■ *Coercive:* A has the ability to punish B.

Communicating Power

How can you communicate power?

■ *Speaking power* includes, for example, avoiding hesitations, disqualifiers, and self-critical statements.

■ *Nonverbal power* includes avoiding adaptors, using consistent packaging, and avoiding excessive movements.

■ *Listening power* includes responding visibly, maintaining eye contact and an open posture, and avoiding interrupting.

■ *Compliance-gaining and compliance-resisting tactics* enable you to influence others to do as you want or enable you to resist compliance attempts of others. Compliance-gaining tactics include expressing liking, making promises, and threatening. Compliance-resisting tactics include using identity management and negotiation.

■ *Empowering* others enables them to gain power and control over themselves and over the environment. Empowering others has numerous advantages, for example, empowered people are more proactive and more responsible. Empowering others involves such strategies as being positive, avoiding verbal aggressiveness and abusiveness, and encouraging growth, and is especially helpful and most often greatly appreciated in cases of shyness or high communication apprehension.

APPLYING   Key Terms and Concepts of Power in Interpersonal Relationships

1. Whom do you consider the three most interpersonally powerful people you have ever known? Which types of power did they possess?

2. What has your culture taught you about power? When is power good? When is it bad?

3. What would you add to the discussion of sexual harassment presented here?

4. In what kinds of situations do you think it might be best to (1) ignore the power play, (2) neutralize it, and (3) employ a cooperative response?

5. Will the discussion of reward and coercive power influence your own exercise of these types of power? In what ways?

6. How satisfied are you with your command of each of these six bases of power? What might you do to increase those bases with which you're not satisfied?

7. Research shows that a salesperson's referent power had more influence than any other type of power in ensuring customer satisfaction (Zemanek, 1995). Why do you think this is so?

8. How would you evaluate your own speaking, nonverbal, and listening power? What might you do to increase your power in these areas?

9. Which of the compliance-gaining strategies do you find most effective? Which strategies work best on you?

10. How would you use compliance-gaining strategies to influence someone to go on a date with you? How would you use compliance-resisting strategies to resist someone's persistent attempts to have you go on a date?

11. Even the language of a culture may influence the extent of the knowledge gap. For example, English dominates the Internet and so the Internet is more easily accessible to people in the United States and other English-speaking countries (and also to educated people in non-English-speaking countries who speak English as a second language). Still another factor is that more than half the world's people do not use the Latin alphabet; Chinese, Japanese, Korean, and Arab people, for example, use alphabets that make software development and Internet access more difficult—at least at the present time. In what ways do you see this issue changing over the next 10 or 15 years?

EXPERIENCING   Key Terms and Concepts of Power in Interpersonal Relationships

Go to **www.ablongman.com/devito**.

These experiences focus on interpersonal power, its nature, and how it can be dealt with.

(1) **Dyadic Power** looks at selected dyads and asks you to identify the types of power that exist between them. (2) **Em-**

powering Others offers scenarios where you may effectively elect to empower other people. (3) **Power Plays** presents sit- uations where power plays are used and provides the opportu- nity to develop and discuss strategies for dealing with them.

Research Navigator.com

RESEARCHING with Research Navigator   Key Terms and Concepts of Power in Interpersonal Relationships

Go to http://www.researchnavigator.com.

Reading an article.

Read a popular or scholarly article on a principle or type of power, the ways of communicating power, or empowering others. On the basis of this article what can you add to the dis- cussion presented here?

Investigating key terms.

Investigate one of the key terms discussed in this chapter (for example, power, power plays, reward power, coercive power, empowerment, or knowledge gap). What additional insights can you provide?

Finding answers.

Try finding answers to one of the following questions or design a research study to answer it.

■ What types of power work best in the elementary or high school classroom? Which work best in the college classroom?

■ What effects does the recommended management strategy for power plays have on friendship relationships? On ro- mantic relationships?

■ Which compliance-gaining strategies work best in same-sex and opposite-sex interactions? Which are least effective?

■ Which compliance-resisting strategies work best for teen- agers resisting drugs? Which are least effective?

■ Do the women and the men at your school differ in Machi- avellianism?

Glossary of Interpersonal Communication Concepts and Skills

In the film *Alice in Wonderland* (1951), based on the works of Lewis Carroll, we hear Humpty Dumpty tell Alice, "When I use a word it means just what I choose it to mean; neither more nor less." Of course, if everyone used Humpty Dumpty's system, communication would be impossible. The meaning of a word is in both the speaker and the listener, and although their meanings are never identical, we assume that both speaker and listener have some common reference for the words used. Here, then, is the jargon of interpersonal communication, a glossary of words and meaning, concepts and skills, that should provide a basis for understanding and talking about communication.

Listed here are definitions of the technical terms of interpersonal communication—the words that are peculiar or unique to this discipline—and, where appropriate, the corresponding skills (*in italics*). These definitions and statements of skills should make new or difficult terms a bit easier to understand and should help to place the skill in context. All boldface terms within the definitions appear as separate entries in the glossary.

acculturation. The process by which your culture is modified or changed through contact with or exposure to another culture.

active listening. The process by which a listener expresses his or her understanding of the speaker's total message, including the verbal and nonverbal, the thoughts and feelings. *Listen actively by paraphrasing the speaker's meanings, expressing an understanding of and an acceptance of the speaker's feelings, and asking questions to check the accuracy of your understanding, thereby encouraging the speaker to explore further his or her feelings and thoughts and increase meaningful sharing.*

adaptors. Nonverbal behaviors that serve some kind of need—for example, scratching one's head. *Avoid adaptors that interfere with effective communication and reveal your discomfort or anxiety.*

adjustment. The principle of verbal interaction that claims that effective communication depends on the extent to which communicators share the same system of signals. *Expand the common areas between you and significant others; learn each other's system of communication signals and meanings in order to increase understanding and interpersonal communication effectiveness.*

affect displays. Movements of the facial area that convey emotional meaning such as anger, fear, and surprise.

affinity-seeking strategies. Behaviors designed to increase interpersonal attractiveness. *Use the various affinity-seeking strategies (for example, listening, openness, and dynamism), as appropriate to the interpersonal relationship and the situation, to increase your own interpersonal attractiveness.*

affirmation. The communication of support and approval. *Use affirmation to express your supportiveness and to raise esteem.*

allness. The illogical assumption that all can be known or said about a given person, issue, object, or event. *To avoid allness, end statements with an implicit "etc." ("et cetera") to indicate that more could be known and said; use terms that describe the areas between the extremes.*

alter-adaptors. Body movements you make in response to your current interactions, for example, crossing your arms over your chest when someone unpleasant approaches or moving closer to someone you like. *Become aware of and control your own alter-adaptors; become aware of the adaptors of others but be* *cautious and tentative about attributing meanings to these adaptors.*

altercasting. Placing the speaker in a specific role for a specific purpose and asking that he or she assume the perspective of this specific role, for example, "as a professor of communication, what would you say is . . . ."

ambiguity. The condition in which a message may be interpreted as having more than one meaning. *To reduce ambiguity, use language that is clear and specific, explain terms and references that may not be clear to the listener, and ask if your message is clear.*

apprehension. See **communication apprehension.**

argumentativeness. A willingness to argue for a point of view, to speak one's mind. *Cultivate your argumentativeness, your willingness to argue for what you believe: for example, by treating disagreements as objectively as possible, reaffirming the other, stressing equality, expressing interest in the other's position, and allowing the other person to save face.* Distinguished from **verbal aggressiveness.**

assertiveness. A willingness to stand up for your rights but with respect for the rights of others. *To increase assertiveness, analyze the assertive and nonassertive behaviors of yourself and others, rehearse assertive behaviors, and communicate assertively in appropriate situations.*

assimilation. A process of message distortion in which messages are reworked to conform to your own attitudes, prejudices, needs, and values. See **cultural assimilation.**

attention. The process of responding to a stimulus or stimuli; usually some consciousness of responding is implied.

attitude. A predisposition to respond for or against an object, person, or position.

attraction theory. The theory that people develop relationships on the basis of attractiveness, proximity, and similarity.

attractiveness. The degree of physical attractiveness or pleasantness in personality.

attribution. The processes involved in assigning causation or motivation to a person's behavior. *In identifying the motivation for behaviors, examine consensus, consistency, distinctiveness, and controllability. Generally, low consensus, high consistency, low distinctiveness, and high controllability identify internally motivated behavior; high consensus, low consistency, high distinctive-*

ness, and low controllability identify externally motivated behavior.

avoidance. An unproductive **interpersonal conflict** strategy in which you take mental or physical flight from the actual conflict. *Instead, take an active role in analyzing problems and in proposing workable solutions.*

back-channeling cues. Responses a listener makes to a speaker (while the speaker is speaking) that do not ask for the speaking role: For example, interjecting "I understand" or "You said what?" *Respond to back-channeling cues as appropriate to the conversation and use back-channeling cues to let the speaker know you're listening.*

barriers to intercultural communication. Those physical or psychological factors that prevent or hinder effective communication, such as ignoring differences between yourself and the culturally different, ignoring differences among the culturally different, ignoring differences in meaning, violating cultural rules and customs, and evaluating differences negatively.

behavioral synchrony. The similarity in the behavior, usually nonverbal (for example, postural stance or facial expressions) of two persons, generally, taken as an indicator of liking.

belief. Confidence in the existence or truth of something; conviction.

beltlining. An unproductive **interpersonal conflict** strategy in which one hits at the level at which the other person cannot withstand the blow. *Avoid beltlining; it makes the eventual resolution of the conflict more difficult, often creates resentment, and frequently encourages the other person to respond in kind.*

blame. An unproductive **interpersonal conflict** strategy in which we attribute the cause of the conflict to the other person or devote our energies to discovering who is the cause and avoid talking about the issues causing the conflict. *Avoid using blame to win an argument, especially with those with whom you are in close relationships.*

boundary markers. Markers that set boundaries around or divide one person's territory from another's—for example, a fence.

brainstorming. An idea-generating strategy groups use to produce as many ideas as possible by following four basic rules: strive for quantity, avoid negative evaluation, suggest ideas as wild as possible, and combine ideas that are generated.

breadth. The number of topics about which individuals in a relationship communicate.

censorship. Restrictions imposed on one's right to produce, distribute, or receive various communications.

central markers. Markers or items that are placed in a territory to reserve it for a specific person—for example, the sweater thrown over a library chair to signal that the chair is taken.

certainty. An attitude of **closed-mindedness** that creates defensiveness among communicators. *Opposed to* **provisionalism.**

channel. The vehicle or medium through which signals are sent—for example, the vocal-auditory channel.

cherishing behaviors. Small behaviors you enjoy receiving from others, especially from your relational partner—for example, a kiss before leaving for work.

civil inattention. Polite ignoring of others (after a brief sign of awareness) so as not to invade their privacy.

cliché. An expression whose overuse calls attention to itself.

closed-mindedness. An unwillingness to receive certain communication messages.

code. A set of symbols used to translate a message from one form to another.

collectivist culture. A culture in which the group's goals rather than the individual's are given greater importance and in which, for example, benevolence, tradition, and conformity are given special emphasis. *Opposed to* **individualist culture.**

color communication. The use of color to communicate different meanings; each culture seems to define the meanings colors communicate somewhat differently. *Use colors (in clothing and in room decor, for example) to convey desired meanings.*

communication. (1) The process or act of communicating; (2) the actual message or messages sent and received; (3) the study of the processes involved in the sending and receiving of messages. (The term **communicology** is suggested for the third definition.)

communication apprehension. Fear or anxiety of communicating and usually identified as either **trait apprehension** or **state apprehension.** *Manage your own communication apprehension through cognitive restructuring, systematic desensitization, and acquiring the necessary communication skills. In addition, prepare and practice for relevant communication situations, focus on success, familiarize yourself with the communication situations important to you, and try to relax. In cases of extreme communication apprehension, seek professional help.*

communicology. The study of communication, particularly the subsection concerned with human communication.

competence. "Language competence" is a speaker's ability to use the language; it is a knowledge of the elements and rules of the language. "Communication competence" generally refers to both the knowledge of communication and also to the ability to engage in communication effectively.

complementarity. A principle of **attraction** holding that you are attracted by qualities you do not possess or you wish to possess and to people who are opposite or different from yourself. *Opposed to* **similarity.**

complementary relationship. A relationship in which the behavior of one person serves as the stimulus for the complementary behavior of the other; in complementary relationships, behavioral differences are maximized.

compliance-gaining strategies. Behaviors designed to gain the agreement of others, to persuade others to do as you wish. *Useful compliance-gaining strategies include expressions of liking, promise, threat, expertise, altercasting, esteem manipulations, and moral appeals.*

compliance-resisting strategies. Behaviors directed at resisting the persuasive attempts of others. *Useful strategies in resisting compliance include identity management, nonnegotiation, negotiation, and justification.*

confidence. A belief that you are an effective and competent communicator and that you can effectively project this image when interacting with others.

confirmation. A communication pattern that acknowledges another person's presence and indicates an acceptance of this person, this person's definition of self, and the relationship as defined or viewed by this other person. Opposed to **rejection** and **disconfirmation.** *To confirm, acknowledge the presence and the contributions of the other person and at the same time avoid any sign of ignoring or avoiding the other person.*

conflict. A disagreement or difference of opinion; a form of competition in which one person tries to bring a rival to surrender; a situation in which one person's behaviors are directed at preventing something or at interfering with or harming another individual. See also **interpersonal conflict.**

congruence. A condition in which both verbal and nonverbal behaviors reinforce each other.

connotation. The feeling or emotional aspect of meaning, generally viewed as consisting of the evaluative (for example, good–bad), potency (strong–weak), and activity (fast–slow) dimensions. Opposed to **denotation.**

consistency. A process that influences you to maintain balance in your **perception** of messages or people; a process that makes you see what you expect to see and to be uncomfortable when your perceptions run contrary to expectations. *Recognize the human tendency to seek and to see consistency even where it does not exist—to see friends as all positive and enemies as all negative, for example.*

content and relationship dimensions. Two aspects to which messages may refer: the world external to both speaker and listener (content) and the connections existing between the individuals who are interacting (relationship).

context. The physical, psychological, social, cultural, and temporal environment in which communication takes place. *Assess the context in which messages are communicated and interpret the messages accordingly; avoid seeing messages as independent of context.*

conversation. Two-person communication usually following five stages: opening, feedforward, business, feedback, and closing.

conversational management. The management of the way in which messages are exchanged in **conversation.** *Respond to conversational turn cues from the other person, and use conversational cues to signal your own desire to exchange (or maintain) speaker or listener roles.*

conversational maxims. Principles that are followed in **conversation** to ensure that the goal of the conversation is achieved. *Since these maxims differ from one culture to another, be sure you understand the maxims operating in the culture in which you're communicating.*

conversational turns. The process of passing the speaker and listener roles during conversation. *Become sensitive to and respond appropriately to conversational turn cues, such as turn-maintaining, turn-yielding, turn-requesting, and turn-denying cues.*

cooperation. An interpersonal process by which individuals work together for a common end; the pooling of efforts to produce a mutually desired outcome.

credibility. The degree to which you see a person to be believable; competence, character, and charisma (dynamism) are its major dimensions.

critical thinking. The process of logically evaluating reasons and evidence and reaching a judgment on the basis of this analysis.

cultural assimilation. The process by which a person's culture is given up and he or she takes on the values and beliefs of another culture as when, for example, an immigrant gives up his or her native culture to become a member of a new adopted culture.

cultural display. Signs that communicate one's cultural identification, for example, clothing or religious jewelry.

cultural rules. Rules that are specific to a given culture. *Respond to messages according to the cultural rules of the sender; avoid interpreting the messages of others exclusively through the perspective of your own culture in order to prevent misinterpretation of the intended meanings.*

cultural time. The meanings given to the ways time is treated in a particular culture.

culture shock. The psychological reaction of feeling lost or anxious when you're in a culture very different from your own.

date. An **extensional device** used to emphasize the notion of constant change and symbolized by a subscript: for example, John Smith$_{1986}$ is not John Smith$_{1996}$.

decoder. Something that takes a message in one form (for example, sound waves) and translates it into another form (for example, nerve impulses) from which meaning can be formulated. In human communication, the decoder is the auditory mechanism; in electronic communication, the decoder is, for example, the telephone earpiece. *Decoding is the process of extracting a message from a code—for example, translating speech sounds into nerve impulses. See also* **encoder.**

defensiveness. An attitude of an individual or an atmosphere in a group characterized by threats, fear, and domination; messages evidencing evaluation, control, strategy, neutrality, superiority, and certainty are thought to lead to defensiveness. *Opposed to* **supportiveness.**

delayed reaction. A reaction that is consciously delayed while the situation is analyzed and possible choices for communication are evaluated. *Generally delayed reactions will prove more effective than knee-jerk responses.*

denial. One of the obstacles to the expression of emotion; the process by which you deny your emotions to yourself or to others.

denotation. The objective or descriptive meaning of a word; the meaning you'd find in a dictionary. *Opposed to* **connotation.**

depenetration. A reversal of **penetration;** a condition in which the **breadth** and **depth** of a relationship decrease.

depth. The degree to which the inner personality—the inner core of an individual—is penetrated in interpersonal interaction.

determinism, principle of. The principle of verbal interaction that holds that all verbalizations are to some extent purposeful, that there is a reason for every verbalization.

dialogue. A form of **communication** in which each person is both speaker and listener; communication characterized by involvement, concern, and respect for the other person. *Opposed to* **monologue.**

diffused time orientation. A point of view in which time is considered in approximate rather than exact terms; opposed to *displaced time orientation.* An agreement to meet at 12 o'clock means around 12, perhaps somewhere between 11:30 and 12:30.

direct speech. Speech in which the speaker's intentions are stated clearly and directly. *Use direct requests and responses (1) to encourage compromise, (2) to acknowledge responsibility for your own feelings and desires, and (3) to state your own desires honestly so as to encourage honesty, openness, and supportiveness in others.*

disclaimer. Statement that asks the listener to receive what you say without its reflecting negatively on you. *Use disclaimers when you think your future messages might offend your listeners, but avoid using them if they may not be accepted by your listeners (they may raise the very doubts you wish to put to rest).*

disconfirmation. The process by which one ignores or denies the right of the individual even to define himself or herself. *Opposed to* **rejection** and **confirmation.**

displaced time orientation. A perspective in which time is viewed in very precise terms; opposed to *diffused time orientation.* An agreement to meet at 12 o'clock means 12 o'clock and no later.

downward communication. Communication sent from the higher levels of the hierarchy to the lower levels—for example, messages sent by managers to workers or from deans to faculty members.

dyadic coalition. A two-person group formed from some larger group to achieve a particular goal.

dyadic communication. Two-person communication.

dyadic consciousness. An awareness on the part of the participants that an interpersonal relationship or pairing exists between them; distinguished from situations in which two individuals are together but do not see themselves as a unit or twosome.

dyadic effect. The tendency for the behaviors of one person to stimulate similar behaviors in the other interactant; often used to refer to the tendency of one person's self-disclosures to prompt the other to also self-disclose. *Be responsive to the dyadic effect; if it's not operating (when you think it should be) ask yourself why.*

dyadic primacy. The significance or centrality of the two-person group, even when there are many more people interacting.

ear markers. Markers that identify an item as belonging to a specific person—for example, a nameplate on a desk or initials on a briefcase.

effect. The outcome or consequence of an action or behavior; communication is assumed always to have some effect.

emblems. Nonverbal behaviors that directly translate words or phrases—for example, the signs for "OK" and "peace."

emotional communication. The expression of feelings—for example, feelings of guilt, happiness, or sorrow. *Before expressing your emotions, understand them, decide whether you wish to express them, and assess your communication options. In expressing your emotions, describe your feelings as accurately as possible, identify the reasons for them, anchor your feelings and their expression to the present time, and own your feelings.*

empathy. The feeling of another person's feeling; the capacity to feel or perceive something as does another person. *In expressing empathy, demonstrate active involvement through appropriate facial expressions and gestures, focus your concentration (maintaining eye contact and physical closeness), reflect back the feelings you think are being experienced, and self-disclose as appropriate.*

encoder. Something that takes a message in one form (for example, nerve impulses) and translates it into another form (for example, sound waves). In human communication, the encoder is the speaking mechanism; in electronic communication, the encoder is, for example, the telephone mouthpiece. *Encoding* is the process of putting a message into a code—for example, translating nerve impulses into speech sounds. *See also* **decoder.**

enculturation. The process by which culture is transmitted from one generation to another.

E-prime. A form of the language that omits the verb "to be" except when used as an auxiliary or in statements of existence. Designed to eliminate the tendency toward **projection.**

equality. An attitude that recognizes that each individual in a communication interaction is equal, that no one is superior to any other; encourages supportiveness. *Opposed to* **superiority.** *To communicate with equality, talk neither down nor up to others but as equals, share speaking and listening turns, and recognize that all parties in communication have something to say.*

equilibrium theory. A theory of **proxemics** holding that intimacy and physical closeness are positively related; as a relationship becomes more intimate, the individuals will maintain shorter distances between themselves.

equity theory. A theory claming that the two people in a relationship experience relational satisfaction when there is an equal distribution of rewards and costs between them.

etc. (et cetera). An **extensional device** used to emphasize the notion of infinite complexity; because you can never know all about anything, any statement about the world or an event must end with an explicit or implicit "etc." *Use the implicit or explicit "etc." to remind yourself and others that there's more to be known, more to be said.*

ethics. The branch of philosophy that deals with the rightness or wrongness of actions; the study of moral values; in communication, the morality of message behavior.

ethnocentrism. The tendency to see others and their behaviors through your own cultural filters, often as distortions of your own behaviors; the tendency to evaluate the values and beliefs of your own culture more positively than those of another culture.

euphemism. A polite word or phrase used to substitute for some taboo or less polite term or phrase.

evaluating. A process whereby a value is placed on some person, object, or event. *Avoid premature evaluation; amass evidence before making evaluations, especially of other people.*

excuse. An explanation designed to lessen the negative consequences of something done or said. *Avoid excessive excuse making; too many excuses may backfire and create image problems.*

expectancy violations theory. A theory of **proxemics** holding that people have a certain expectancy for space relationships. When that is violated (a person stands too close to you, or a romantic partner maintains abnormally large distances from you), the relationship comes into clearer focus and you wonder why this "normal distance" is being violated.

expressiveness. A quality of interpersonal effectiveness; genuine involvement in speaking and listening, conveyed verbally and nonverbally. *Communicate involvement and interest in the interaction by providing appropriate feedback, by assuming responsibility for your thoughts and feelings and your role as speaker and listener, and by appropriately using variety and flexibility in voice and bodily action.*

extensional devices. Linguistic devices proposed by Alfred Korzybski to make language a more accurate means for talking about the world. The extensional devices include **etc., date, index, hyphen,** and **quotes.**

extensional orientation. A point of view in which primary consideration is given to the world of experience and only secondary consideration is given to labels. *Opposed to* **intensional orientation.**

facial feedback hypothesis. The hypothesis or theory that your facial expressions can produce physiological and emotional effects.

facial management techniques. Techniques used to mask certain emotions and to emphasize others, for example, intensifying your expression of happiness to make a friend feel good about a promotion.

fact–inference confusion. A misevaluation in which one makes an inference, regards it as a fact, and acts upon it as if it were a fact. *Distinguish facts from inferences; respond to inferences as inferences, not as facts.*

factual statement. A statement made by the observer after observation and limited to what is observed. *Opposed to* **inferential statement.**

family. A group of people who consider themselves related and connected to one another and for whom the actions of one have consequences for others.

feedback. Information that is given back to the source. Feedback may come from the source's own messages (as when you hear what you're saying) or from the receiver(s) in the form of applause, yawning, puzzled looks, questions, letters to the editor of a newspaper, or increased or decreased subscriptions to a magazine. *Give clear feedback to others, and respond to others' feedback, either through corrective measures or by continuing current performance, to increase communication efficiency and satisfaction.* See also **negative feedback, positive feedback.**

feedforward. Information that is sent prior to the regular messages, telling the listener something about what is to follow; messages that are prefatory to more central messages. *In using feedforward, be brief, use it sparingly, and follow through on your feedforward promises.*

feminine culture. A culture in which both men and women are encouraged to be modest, oriented to maintaining the quality of life, and tender. Feminine cultures emphasize the quality of life and so socialize their people to be modest and to emphasize close interpersonal relationships. *Opposed to* **masculine culture.**

flexibility. The ability to adjust communication strategies and skills on the basis of the unique situation.

force. An unproductive **conflict** strategy in which you try to win an argument by physically overpowering the other person either by threat or by actual behavior.

friendship. An interpersonal relationship between two persons that is mutually productive, established and maintained through perceived mutual free choice, and characterized by mutual positive regard. *Adjust your verbal and nonverbal communication as appropriate to the stages of your various friendships. Learn the rules that govern your friendships; follow them or risk damaging the relationship.*

General Semantics. The study of the relationships among language, thought, and behavior.

gossip. Oral or written **communication** about someone not present, some third party, usually about matters that are private to this third party. *Avoid gossip that breaches confidentiality, is known to be false, and is unnecessarily invasive.*

grapevine messages. Messages that do not follow any formal organizational structures; office-related gossip.

gunnysacking. An unproductive **conflict** strategy of storing up grievances—as if in a gunnysack—and holding them in readiness to dump on the person with whom one is in conflict.

halo effect. The tendency to generalize a person's virtue or expertise from one area to other areas.

haptics. Technical term for the study of touch or **tactile communication.**

heterosexist language. Language that denigrates lesbians and gay men.

high-context culture. A culture in which much of the information in communication messages is left implied; it's "understood," it's considered to be in the context or in the person rather than explicitly coded in the verbal messages. **Collectivist cultures** are generally high context. *Opposed to* **low-context culture.**

home field advantage. The increased power that comes from being in your own territory.

hyphen. An **extensional device** used to illustrate that what may be separated verbally may not be separable on the event level or on the nonverbal level; although you may talk about body and mind as if they were separable, in reality they're better referred to as body-mind.

illustrators. Nonverbal behaviors that accompany and literally illustrate verbal messages—for example, upward movements of the head and hand that accompany the verbal "It's up there."

I-messages. Messages in which the speaker accepts responsibility for personal thoughts and behaviors; messages in which the speaker's point of view is stated explicitly. *Opposed to* **you-messages.**

immediacy. A quality of interpersonal effectiveness; a sense of contact and togetherness; a feeling of interest and liking for the other person. *To communicate immediacy use inclusive terms, give appropriate and* *supportive feedback, maintain eye contact, use an open body posture, and maintain physical closeness.*

implicit personality theory. A theory of personality, complete with rules about what characteristics go with what other characteristics, that you maintain and through which you perceive others. *Be conscious of your implicit personality theories; avoid drawing firm conclusions (treat them as hypotheses) about other people on the basis of these theories.*

inclusion. The principle of verbal interaction holding that all members should be a part of (included in) the interaction. *Include everyone present in the interaction (both verbally and nonverbally) so you do not exclude or offend others or fail to profit from their contributions.*

index. An extensional device used to emphasize the assumption that no two things are the same; symbolized by a subscript—for example, even though two people may both be politicians, politician$_{1 \text{ [Smith]}}$ is not politician$_{2 \text{ [Jones]}}$.

indirect speech. Speech that hides the speaker's true intentions; speech in which requests and observations are made indirectly. *Use indirect speech (1) to express a desire without insulting or offending anyone, (2) to ask for compliments in a socially acceptable manner, and (3) to disagree without being disagreeable.*

indiscrimination. A misevaluation caused by categorizing people, events, or objects into a particular class and responding to them only as members of the class; a failure to recognize that each individual is unique. *To avoid indiscrimination, **index** your terms and statements to emphasize that each person and event is unique; avoid treating all individuals the same way because they are covered by the same label or term.*

individualist culture. A culture in which the individual's rather than the group's goals and preferences are given greater importance. *Opposed to **collectivist culture.***

inevitability. A principle of communication holding that communication cannot be avoided; all behavior in an interactional setting is communication.

inferential statement. A statement that can be made by anyone, is not limited to what is observed, and can be made at any time. See also **factual statement.**

informal time terms. Terms that are approximate rather than exact, for example, "soon," "early," and "in a while." *Recognize that informal time terms are often*

the cause of interpersonal difficulties; when misunderstanding is likely, use more precise terms.

information overload. A condition in which the amount or complexity of information is too great to be dealt with effectively by an individual, group, or organization.

in-group talk. Talk about a subject or in a vocabulary that some group members understand and others do not; has the effect of excluding those who don't understand.

insulation. A reaction to **territorial encroachment** in which you erect some sort of barrier between yourself and the invaders, for example, a stone wall around your property, an unlisted phone number, or "caller ID"—all of which allow you to separate yourself from would-be invaders.

intensional orientation. A point of view in which primary consideration is given to the way things are labeled and only secondary consideration (if any) to the world of experience. *Respond first to things; avoid responding to labels as if they were things; do not let labels distort your perception of the world. Opposed to* **extensional orientation.**

interaction management. A quality of interpersonal effectiveness in which the interaction is controlled and managed to the satisfaction of both parties; effectively managing conversational turns, fluency, and message consistency. *Manage the interaction to the satisfaction of both parties by sharing the roles of speaker and listener, avoiding long and awkward silences, and being consistent in your verbal and nonverbal messages.*

intercultural communication. Communication that takes place between persons of different cultures or persons who have different cultural beliefs, values, or ways of behaving.

interpersonal communication. Communication between two persons or among a small group of persons and distinguished from public or mass communication; communication of a personal nature and distinguished from impersonal communication; communication between or among connected persons or those involved in a close relationship.

interpersonal conflict. A disagreement between two connected persons. *To manage interpersonal conflict more productively: (1) become an active participant; don't avoid the issues; (2) use talk rather than force; (3) enhance the self-esteem, the face, of the person you're arguing with; (4) be supportive of the other person; and (5)* *focus as objectively as possible on the points of disagreement; avoid attacking the other person.*

interpersonal effectiveness. The ability to accomplish one's interpersonal goals; interpersonal communication that is satisfying to both individuals.

interpersonal perception. The **perception** of people; the processes through which you interpret and evaluate people and their behavior.

intimacy. The closest interpersonal relationship; usually used to denote a close primary relationship.

intimacy claims. Obligations incurred by virtue of being in a close and intimate relationship. *Reduce the intensity of intimacy claims when things get rough; give each other space as appropriate.*

intimate distance. The closest distance in **proxemics,** ranging from touching to 18 inches.

intrapersonal communication. Communication with oneself.

irreversibility. A principle of communication holding that communication cannot be reversed; once something has been communicated, it cannot be uncommunicated. *To prevent resentment and ill feeling, avoid saying things (for example, in anger) or making commitments that you may wish to retract; you won't be able to.*

jargon. The technical language of any specialized group, often a professional class, which is unintelligible to individuals not belonging to the group; shop talk. This glossary is an example of the jargon of a part of the communication field.

Johari window. A diagram of the four selves (open, blind, hidden, and unknown).

kinesics. The study of the communicative dimensions of facial and bodily movements.

language. The rules of syntax, semantics, and phonology by which sentences are created and understood; **a language** refers to the sentences that can be created in any language, for example, English, Bantu, or Italian.

lateral communication. Communication between equals—manager to manager, worker to worker.

leave-taking cues. Verbal and nonverbal signals that indicate a desire to terminate a conversation. *Become sensitive to the leave-taking cues of others and communicate your own leave-taking desires tactfully so as not to insult or offend others.*

leveling. A process of message distortion in which the number of details in a message is reduced as the message gets repeated from one person to another.

listening. An active process of receiving aural stimuli consisting of five stages: receiving, understanding, remembering, evaluating, and responding. *Adjust your listening perspective, as the situation warrants, between active and passive, judgmental and nonjudgmental, surface and depth, empathic and objective, and active and inactive listening.*

loving. An interpersonal process in which you feel a closeness, a caring, a warmth, and an excitement for another person.

low-context culture. A culture in which most of the information in communication is explicitly stated in the verbal message, rather than left implied or assumed to be "understood." Low-context cultures are usually **individualistic cultures.** *Opposed to* **high-context culture.**

Machiavellianism. The belief that people can be manipulated easily; often used to refer to the techniques or tactics one person uses to control another.

manipulation. An unproductive **conflict** strategy that avoids open conflict; instead, attempts are made to divert the conflict by being especially charming and getting the other person into a noncombative frame of mind.

markers. Devices that signify that a certain territory belongs to a particular person. *Become sensitive to the markers of others and learn to use these markers to define your own territories and to communicate the desired impression. See also* **boundary markers, central markers,** *and* **ear markers.**

masculine culture. A culture in which men are viewed as assertive, oriented to material success, and strong; women on the other hand are viewed as modest, focused on the quality of life, and tender. Masculine cultures emphasize success and so socialize their people to be assertive, ambitious, and competitive. *Opposed to* **feminine culture.**

matching hypothesis. An assumption that you date and mate with people who are similar to yourself—who match you—in physical attractiveness.

meaningfulness. A principle of **perception** that assumes that the behavior of people is sensible, stems from some logical antecedent, and is therefore meaningful rather than meaningless.

mentoring relationship. A relationship in which an experienced individual helps to train one who is less experienced: For example, an accomplished teacher might mentor one who is newly arrived or who has never taught before.

mere exposure hypothesis. The theory that repeated or prolonged exposure to a stimulus may result in a change in attitude toward the stimulus object, generally in the direction of increased positiveness.

message overload. A condition that occurs when the channel capacity is exceeded, when you get so many messages that you simply can't deal effectively with them.

messages. Signals or combinations of signals that serve as **stimuli** for a receiver.

metacommunication. Communication about communication. *Metacommunicate to ensure understanding of the other person's thoughts and feelings: Give clear feedforward, explain feelings as well as thoughts, paraphrase your own complex thoughts, and ask questions.*

metalanguage. Language that refers to language. See **metamessage.**

metamessage. A message that makes reference to another message: For example, the statements "Did I make myself clear?" or "That's a lie" are metamessages because they refer to other messages. *Use metamessages to clarify your understanding of what another thinks and feels.*

mindfulness and mindlessness. States of relative awareness. In a mindful state, you are aware of the logic and rationality of your behaviors and the logical connections existing among elements. In a mindless state, you're unaware of this logic and rationality. *Be mindful when applying the principles of interpersonal communication. Increase mindfulness by creating and re-creating categories, being open to new information and points of view, and being careful of relying too heavily on first impressions.*

mixed messages. Messages that communicate two different and often contradictory meanings: for example, a message that asks for two different (often incompatible) responses such as "leave me alone" and "show me more attention." Often, one meaning (usually the socially acceptable meaning) is communicated verbally and the other (usually the less socially acceptable meaning) nonverbally. *Avoid emitting mixed messages by focusing clearly on your purposes when communicating and by increasing conscious control over*

your verbal and nonverbal behaviors. Detect mixed messages in other people's communications and avoid being placed in double-bind situations by seeking clarification from the sender.

model. A representation of an object or process.

monochronic. A view of time in which things are done sequentially; one thing is scheduled at a time. *Opposed to* **polychronic.**

monologue. A form of **communication** in which one person speaks and the other listens; there's no real interaction among participants. *Opposed to* **dialogue.**

negative feedback. Feedback that serves a corrective function by informing the source that his or her message is not being received in the way intended. Looks of boredom, shouts of disagreement, letters critical of newspaper policy, and teachers' instructions on how better to approach a problem would be examples of negative feedback and would (ideally) serve to redirect the speaker's behavior.

networking. Connecting with people who can help you accomplish a goal or help you find information related to your goal, for example, finding a job.

neutrality. A response pattern lacking in personal involvement; encourages defensiveness. *Opposed to* **empathy.**

noise. Anything that interferes with your receiving a message as the source intended the message to be received. Noise is present in communication to the extent that the message received is not the message sent. *Combat the effects of physical, physiological, psychological, and semantic noise by eliminating or lessening the sources of physical noise, securing agreement on meanings, and interacting with an open mind in order to increase communication accuracy.*

nonallness. A point of view holding that you can never know all about anything and that what you know, say, or hear is only a part of what there is to know, say, or hear.

nonnegotiation. An unproductive **conflict** strategy in which the individual refuses to discuss the conflict or to listen to the other person.

nonverbal communication. Communication without words; communication by means of space, gestures, facial expressions, touching, vocal variation, and silence, for example.

nonverbal dominance. Nonverbal behavior that allows one person to achieve psychological dominance over another. *Resist (as sender and receiver) nonverbal expressions of dominance when they are inappropriate—for example, when they are sexist or unethical.*

object-adaptors. Movements that involve your manipulation of some object: For example, punching holes in a styrofoam coffee cup, clicking a ballpoint pen, or chewing on a pencil. *Generally, object-adaptors communicate discomfort and a lack of control over the communication situation and so are best avoided.*

object language. Language used to communicate about objects, events, and relations in the world (rather than about words as in **metalanguage**).

olfactory communication. Communication by smell.

openness. A quality of interpersonal effectiveness encompassing (1) a willingness to interact openly with others, to self-disclose as appropriate; (2) a willingness to react honestly to incoming stimuli; and (3) a willingness to own one's feelings and thoughts.

opinion. A tentative conclusion concerning some object, person, or event.

other-orientation. A quality of interpersonal effectiveness involving attentiveness, interest, and concern for the other person. *Convey concern for and interest in the other person by means of empathic responses, appropriate feedback, and active-listening responses.*

other-talk. Talk about the listener or some third party. *Opposed to* **self-talk.**

outing. The process whereby a person's affectional orientation is made public by another person without the gay man or lesbian's consent.

owning feelings. The process by which you take responsibility for your own feelings instead of attributing them to others. *Own your feelings by using I-messages and acknowledging responsibility for your own thoughts and feelings to increase honest sharing.*

paralanguage. The vocal (but nonverbal) aspect of speech. Paralanguage consists of voice qualities (for example, pitch range, resonance, tempo), vocal characterizers (laughing or crying, yelling or whispering), vocal qualifiers (intensity, pitch height), and vocal segregates ("uh-uh," meaning "no," or "sh," meaning "silence"). *Vary paralinguistic elements, such as rate, volume, and stress, to add variety and emphasis to your communications, and be responsive to the meanings*

communicated by others' variation of paralanguage features.

passive listening. Listening that is attentive and supportive but occurs without talking and without directing the speaker in any nonverbal way; also used negatively to refer to inattentive and uninvolved listening.

pause. A silent period in the normally fluent stream of speech. Pauses are of two types: filled pauses (interruptions in speech that are filled with such vocalizations as "er" or "um") and unfilled pauses (silences of unusually long duration).

perception. The process by which you become aware of objects and events through your senses.

perception checking. The process of verifying your understanding of some message, situation, or feeling. *Use perception checking to get more information about your impressions by describing what you think is happening and asking whether this is correct or in error.*

perceptual accentuation. A process that leads you to see what you expect or want to see—for example, seeing people you like as better looking and smarter than people you don't like. *Be aware of the influence your own needs, wants, and expectations have on perceptions; recognize that what you perceive is a function both of what exists in reality and what is going on inside your own head.*

personal distance. The second-closest distance in **proxemics,** ranging from 18 inches to 4 feet.

personal rejection. An unproductive **conflict** strategy in which you withhold love and affection and seek to win the argument by getting the other person to break down under this withdrawal.

persuasion. The process of influencing attitudes and behavior.

phatic communion. Communication that is primarily social; communication designed to open the channels of communication rather than to communicate something about the external world; "Hello" and "How are you?" in everyday interaction are examples.

pitch. The highness or lowness of the vocal tone.

polarization. A form of fallacious reasoning by which only two extremes are considered; also referred to as "black-or-white" and "either-or" thinking or two-valued orientation. *Use middle terms and qualifiers when describing the world; avoid talking in terms of extremes (for example, good and bad) in order to describe reality more accurately.*

politeness. Communication that most people would consider to represent "good manners."

polychronic. A view of time in which several things may be scheduled or engaged in at the same time. *Opposed to* **monochronic** time orientation.

positive feedback. Feedback that supports or reinforces the continuation of behavior along the same lines in which it is already proceeding—for example, applause during a speech encourages the speaker to continue speaking this way.

positiveness. A characteristic of effective communication involving positive attitudes toward oneself and toward the interpersonal interaction and to expressing these attitudes (as in complimenting) to others along with acceptance and approval. *Verbally and nonverbally communicate positiveness with, for example, smiles, positive facial expressions, attentive gestures, positive verbal expressions, and the elimination of negative appraisals.*

power. The ability to influence or control the behavior of another person; A has power over B when A can influence or control B's behavior; an inevitable part of interpersonal relationships. *Communicate power through forceful speech, avoidance of weak modifiers and excessive body movement, and demonstration of knowledge, preparation, and organization in the matters at hand.*

power plays. Consistent patterns of behavior in which one person tries to control the behavior of another. *In combating power plays use an effective management strategy, for example, express your feelings, describe the behavior you object to, and state a cooperative response.*

primacy–recency. Primacy refers to giving more importance to that which occurs first; recency refers to giving more importance to that which occurs last (that is, most recently).

primary affect displays. The communication of the six primary emotions: happiness, surprise, fear, anger, sadness, and disgust/contempt.

primary relationship. The relationship between two people that they consider their most (or one of their most) important: for example, the relationship between husband and wife or domestic partners.

primary territories. Areas that you consider your exclusive preserve, such as your room or office.

process. Ongoing activity; communication is referred to as a process to emphasize that it's always changing, always in motion.

projection. A psychological process whereby you attribute characteristics or feelings of your own to others; often used to refer to the process whereby you attribute your faults to others.

pronouncements. Statements made to sound authoritative and that therefore imply that the speaker is in a position of authority and that the listener is in a childlike or learner role.

protection theory. A theory of **proxemics** holding that people establish a body-buffer zone to protect themselves from unwanted closeness, touching, or attack.

provisionalism. An attitude of open-mindedness that leads to the development of a supportive relationship and atmosphere; opposed to **certainty.**

proxemics. The study of the communicative function of space; the study of how people unconsciously structure their space—the distance between people in their interactions, the organization of space in homes and offices, and even the design of cities.

proximity. As a principle of **perception,** the tendency to perceive people or events that are physically close as belonging together or representing some unit; physical closeness—one of the qualities influencing interpersonal attraction. *Use proximity to make inferences about connections among messages and people.*

psychological time. The importance you place on past, present, or future time. *Recognize the significance of your own time orientation to your ultimate success, and make whatever adjustments you think desirable.*

public distance. The farthest distance in **proxemics,** ranging from 12 feet to more than 25 feet.

public territories. Areas that are open to all people—for example, restaurants or parks.

punctuation. The breaking up of continuous communication sequences into short sequences with identifiable beginnings and endings or stimuli and responses. *See the sequence of events punctuated from perspectives other than just your own as a way to increase empathy and mutual understanding.*

pupil dilation. The extent to which the pupil of the eye is expanded; generally large pupils indicate positive reactions.

pupillometrics. The study of communication through changes in the size of the pupils of the eyes.

Pygmalion effect. The condition in which you make a prediction of success, act as if it is true, and thereby make it come true (for example, acting toward students as if they'll be successful influences them to become successful); a type of **self-fulfilling prophecy.**

quality maxim. A principle of **conversation** that holds that speakers cooperate by saying what they think is true and by not saying what they think is false.

quantity maxim. A principle of **conversation** that holds that speakers cooperate by being only as informative as necessary to communicate their intended meanings.

quotes. An **extensional device** to emphasize that a word or phrase is being used in a special sense and should therefore be given special attention.

racist language. Language that denigrates, demeans, or is derogatory toward members of a particular race.

rate. The speed with which you speak, generally measured in words per minute. *Use variations in rate to increase communication efficiency and persuasiveness as appropriate.*

receiver. Any person or thing that takes in messages. Receivers may be individuals listening to or reading a message, a group of persons hearing a speech, a scattered television audience, or machines that store information.

reconciliation strategies. Behaviors designed to repair a broken relationship. *In reconciling, try using such strategies as third-party intervention, tacit persistence, and mutual interaction to patch up a broken relationship.*

regulators. Nonverbal behaviors that regulate, monitor, or control the communications of another person.

rejection. A response to an individual that acknowledges another person but expresses disagreement. *Opposed to* **confirmation** *and* **disconfirmation.**

relation maxim. A principle of **cooperation** in **conversation** that holds that speakers communicate by talking about what is relevant and by not talking about what isn't.

relationship communication. Communication between or among intimates or those in close relationships; used by some theorists as synonymous with interpersonal communication.

relationship deterioration. The stage of a relationship during which the connecting bonds between the partners weaken and the partners begin drifting apart.

relationship development. The initial or beginning stage of a relationship; the stage at which two people begin to form an interpersonal relationship.

relationship dialectics theory. A theory that describes relationships along a series of opposites representing competing desires or motivations, such as the desire for autonomy and the desire to belong to someone, for novelty and predictability, and for closedness and openness.

relationship dissolution. The termination or end of an interpersonal relationship. *If the relationship ends: (1) break the loneliness–depression cycle, (2) take time out to get to know yourself as an individual, (3) bolster your self-esteem, (4) remove or avoid uncomfortable symbols that may remind you of your past relationship and may make you uncomfortable, (5) seek the support of friends and relatives, and (6) avoid repeating negative patterns.*

relationship maintenance. A stage of relationship stability in which the relationship does not progress or deteriorate significantly; a continuation as opposed to a dissolution (or an intensification) of a relationship. *Use appropriate maintenance strategies (for example, openness, sharing joint activities, and acting positively) to maintain a valued relationship.*

relationship messages. Messages that comment on the relationship between the speakers rather than on matters external to them. *Recognize and respond to relationship as well as content messages in order to ensure a more complete understanding of the messages intended.*

relationship repair. A relationship stage in which one or both parties seek to improve the relationship. *If you wish to preserve or repair a deteriorating relationship, take positive action by recognizing the problem, engaging in productive conflict resolution, posing possible solutions, affirming each other, integrating solutions into normal behavior, and taking risks.*

resemblance. As a principle of **perception,** the tendency to perceive people or events that are similar in appearance as belonging together.

response. Any bit of overt or covert behavior.

role. The part an individual plays in a group; an individual's function or expected behavior.

rule of perception. A principle followed in organizing and making sense of perceptions; for example, the rule of proximity helps you perceive physically close people or things as belonging together, as a couple or unit.

rules theory. A theory that describes relationships as interactions governed by a series of rules that a couple agrees to follow. When the rules are followed, the relationship is maintained; when they are broken, the relationship experiences difficulty.

schemata. Ways of organizing perceptions; mental templates or structures that help you organize the millions of items of information you come into contact with every day as well as those you already have in memory; general ideas about people (for Pat and Chris, for Japanese, for Baptists, for New Yorkers), for yourself (your qualities, abilities, liabilities), or social roles (what's a police officer, professor, or multimillionaire CEO like).

script. A type of schema; an organized body of information about some action, event, or procedure; a general idea of how some event should play out or unfold, the rules governing the events, and their sequence.

secondary territories. Areas that do not belong to you but that you've occupied and are therefore associated with you—for example, the seat you normally take in class.

selective exposure. A principle that states that listeners actively seek out information that supports their opinions and actively avoid information that contradicts their existing opinions, beliefs, attitudes, and values.

self-acceptance. Being satisfied with yourself, your virtues and vices, your abilities and limitations.

self-adaptors. Movements that usually satisfy a physical need, especially to make you more comfortable: For example, scratching your head to relieve an itch, moistening your lips because they feel dry, or pushing your hair out of your eyes. *Because these often communicate your nervousness or discomfort, they are best avoided.*

self-attribution. A process through which you seek to account for and understand the reasons and motivations for your own behaviors.

self-awareness. The degree to which you know yourself. *Increase self-awareness by asking yourself about yourself and listening to others; actively seek information about yourself from others by carefully observing their interactions with you and by asking relevant questions. See yourself from different perspectives (see your different selves), and increase your open self.*

self-concept. Your self-image; the view your have of who you are.

self-disclosure. The process of revealing something about yourself to another; usually used to refer to information that you'd normally keep hidden. *Self-disclose to improve the relationship, when it's appropriate, when there's an opportunity for open responses, and when you're willing to risk the burdens that self-disclosure might entail. In responding to self-disclosures, listen actively, support and reinforce the discloser, keep the disclosures confidential, and don't use the disclosures against the person.*

self-esteem. The value you place on yourself; your self-evaluation; usually used to refer to the positive value placed on oneself. *Increase your self-esteem by attacking destructive beliefs, engaging in self-affirmation, seeking out nourishing people, and working on projects that will result in success.*

self-fulfilling prophecy. The situation in which you make a prediction or prophecy and fulfill it yourself—for example, expecting a person to be hostile, you act in a hostile manner toward this person and in doing so elicit hostile behavior in the person, thus confirming your prophecy that the person is hostile. *Carefully examine your perceptions when they conform too closely to your expectations; check to make sure that you're seeing what exists in real life, not just in your expectations or predictions.*

self-monitoring. The manipulation of the image you present to others in interpersonal interactions so as to give the most favorable impression of yourself. *Monitor your verbal and nonverbal behavior as appropriate to communicate the desired impression.*

self-serving bias. A bias that operates in the self-attribution process and leads you to take credit for the positive consequences and to deny responsibility for the negative consequences of your behaviors. *In examining the causes of your own behavior, beware of the tendency to attribute negative behaviors to external factors and positive behaviors to internal factors. In self-examinations, ask whether and how the self-serving bias might be operating.*

self-talk. Talk about yourself. *Balance talk about yourself with talk about the other; avoid excessive self-talk or extreme avoidance of self-talk to encourage equal sharing and interpersonal satisfaction. Opposed to* **other-talk.**

semantics. The area of language study concerned with meaning.

sexist language. Language derogatory to one sex, generally women.

sexual harassment. Unsolicited and unwanted verbal or nonverbal sexual messages. *If confronted with sexual harassment, consider talking to the harasser, collecting evidence, using appropriate channels within the organization, or filing a complaint. Avoid any indication of sexual harassment by beginning with the assumption that others at work are not interested in sexual advances and stories; listen for negative reactions to any sexually explicit discussions; and avoid behaviors you think might prove offensive.*

sharpening. A process of message distortion in which the details of messages, when repeated, are crystallized and heightened.

shyness. The condition of discomfort and uneasiness in interpersonal situations.

signal and noise, relativity of. The principle of verbal interaction that holds that what is signal (meaningful) and what is noise (interference) is relative to the communication analyst, the participants, and the context.

signal reaction. A conditioned response to a signal; a response to some signal that is immediate rather than delayed. *Opposed to* **delayed reaction.**

silence. The absence of vocal communication; often misunderstood to refer to the absence of communication. *Use silence to communicate feelings or to prevent communication about certain topics. Interpret silences of others in their cultural context.*

silencers. A tactic (such as crying) that literally silences your opponent—an unproductive **conflict** strategy.

similarity. A principle of **attraction** holding that you're attracted to qualities similar to those you yourself possess and to people who are similar to yourself; opposed to **complementarity.**

social comparison processes. The processes by which you compare yourself (for example, your abilities, opinions, and values) with others and then assess and evaluate yourself on the basis of the comparison; one of the sources of **self-concept.**

social distance. The third farthest distance in **proxemics,** ranging from 4 feet to 12 feet; the distance at which business is usually conducted.

social exchange theory. A theory hypothesizing that you develop profitable relationships (those in which your rewards are greater than your costs) and that you avoid or terminate unprofitable relationships (those in which your costs exceed your rewards).

social penetration theory. A theory concerned with relationship development from the superficial to the intimate levels (**depth**) and from few to many areas of interpersonal interaction (**breadth**). *See also* **depenetration.**

source. Any person or thing that creates messages: for example, an individual speaking, writing, or gesturing, or a computer solving a problem.

speech. Messages conveyed via a vocal-auditory channel.

spontaneity. The communication pattern in which you say what you're thinking without attempting to develop strategies for control; encourages **supportiveness;** opposed to **strategy.**

stability. The principle of **perception** that refers to the fact that your perceptions of things and of people are relatively consistent with your previous conceptions.

state apprehension. Communication apprehension for specific types of communication situations—for example, public speaking or interview situations. *Opposed to* **trait apprehension.**

static evaluation. An orientation that fails to recognize that the world is constantly changing; an attitude that sees people and events as fixed rather than as ever changing. *Date your statements (mentally or actually) to emphasize the likelihood of change.*

status. The relative level one occupies in a hierarchy; status always involves a comparison, and thus your status is only relative to the status of another. In the United States, occupation, financial position, age, and educational level are significant determinants of social status.

stereotype. In communication, a fixed impression of a group of people through which we then perceive specific individuals; stereotypes are most often negative (Martians are stupid, uneducated, and dirty) but may also be positive (Venusians are scientific, industrious, and helpful). *Avoid stereotyping others; instead, see and respond to each individual as a unique individual.*

stimuli. Any external or internal changes that impinge on or arouse an organism. (*Stimulus* is the singular form of this term.)

stimulus–response models of communication. Models of communication that assume that the process of communication is linear, beginning with a stimulus that then leads to a response.

strategy. The use of some plan for control of other members of a communication interaction that guides your communications; often encourages **defensiveness;** opposed to **spontaneity.**

subjectivity. The principle of **perception** that refers to the fact that your perceptions are not objective but are influenced by your wants and needs, expectations and predictions.

superiority. A point of view or attitude that assumes that others are not equal to yourself; encourages **defensiveness;** opposed to **equality.**

supportiveness. An attitude of an individual or an atmosphere in a group that is characterized by openness, absence of fear, and a genuine feeling of equality. *Exhibit supportiveness to others by being descriptive rather than evaluative, spontaneous rather than strategic, and provisional rather than certain. Opposed to* **defensiveness.**

symmetrical relationship. A relation between two or more persons in which one person's behavior serves as a stimulus for the same type of behavior in the other person(s), for example, a relationship in which anger in one person encourages anger in another person or in which a critical comment by one person leads the other person to respond in kind.

taboo. Forbidden; culturally censored. Taboo language is language that is frowned upon by "polite society." Topics and specific words may be considered taboo—for example, death, sex, certain forms of illness, and various words denoting sexual activities and excretory functions. *Substitute more socially acceptable expressions or euphemisms where and when appropriate.*

tactile communication. Communication by touch; communication received by the skin. *Use touch when appropriate to express positive effect, playfulness, control, and ritualistic meanings and to serve task-related functions, but avoid touching that may be unwelcomed.*

temporal communication. The messages that your time orientation and treatment of time communicates.

territorial encroachment. The trespassing on, use of, or appropriation of one person's territory by another. *Generally, avoid territorial encroachment; give others the space they need; remember, for example, that*

people who are angry or disturbed need more space than usual.

territoriality. A possessive or ownership reaction to an area of space or to particular objects. *Establish and maintain territory nonverbally by marking or otherwise indicating temporary or permanent ownership. Become sensitive to the territorial behavior of others.*

theory. A general statement or principle applicable to a number of related phenomena.

touch avoidance. The tendency to avoid touching and being touched by others. *Recognize that some people may prefer to avoid touching and being touched. Avoid drawing too many conclusions about people form the way they treat interpersonal touching.*

trait apprehension. Communication apprehension generally; a fear of communication situations regardless of their specific form. *Opposed to* **state apprehension.**

transactional. A point of view that sees communication as an ongoing process in which all elements are interdependent and influence each other.

uncertainty reduction theory. Applied to interpersonal relationships, the theory holds that as relationships develop, uncertainty is reduced; relationship development is seen as a process of reducing uncertainty about one another.

universal of interpersonal communication. A feature of communication common to all interpersonal communication acts.

unproductive conflict strategies. Ways of engaging in conflict that generally prove counterproductive, for example, **avoidance, force, blame, silencers, gunnysacking, manipulation, personal rejection,** and **beltlining.**

upward communication. Communication sent from the lower levels of the hierarchy to the upper levels— for example, line worker to manager, faculty member to dean.

value. Relative worth of an object; a quality that makes something desirable or undesirable; ideals or customs about which we have emotional responses, whether positive or negative.

verbal aggressiveness. A method of winning an argument by attacking the other person's **self-concept.** Avoid inflicting psychological pain on the other person to win an argument.

visual dominance. The use of your eyes to maintain a superior or dominant position: For example, when making an especially important point, you might look intently at the other person. *Use visual dominance behavior when you wish to emphasize certain messages.*

voice qualities. Aspects of **paralanguage**—specifically, pitch range, vocal lip control, glottis control, pitch control, articulation control, rhythm control, resonance, and tempo.

volume. The relative loudness of the voice.

you-messages. Messages in which you deny responsibility for your own thoughts and behaviors; messages that attribute your **perception** to another person; messages of blame. *Opposed to* **I-messages.**

Bibliography

Acor, A. A. (2001). Employers' perceptions of persons with body art and an experimental test regarding eyebrow piercing. Ph.D. dissertation, Marquette University. *Dissertation Abstracts International: Second B: The Sciences and Engineering* 61, 3885.

Acuff, F. L. (1993). *How to negotiate anything with anyone anywhere around the world.* New York: American Management Association.

Adrianson, L. (2001). Gender and computer-mediated communication: Group processes in problem solving. *Computers in Human Behavior* 17, 71–94.

Alberti, R., & Emmons, M. (2001). *Your perfect right: Assertiveness and equality in your life and relationships,* 8th ed. Atascadero, CA: Impact.

Alberti, R. E., ed. (1977). *Assertiveness: Innovations, applications, issues.* San Luis Obispo, CA: Impact.

Alessandra, T. (1986). How to listen effectively. *Speaking of success* (Video Tape Series). San Diego, CA: Levitz Sommer Productions.

Allen, M., Bourhis, J., Emmers-Sommer, T., & Sahlstein, E. (1998). Reducing dating anxiety: A meta-analysis. *Communication Reports* 11, 49–55.

Altman, I. (1975). *The environment and social behavior.* Monterey, CA: Brooks/Cole.

Altman, I., & Taylor, D. (1973). *Social penetration: The development of interpersonal relationships.* New York: Holt, Rinehart & Winston.

Amato, P. R. (1994). The impact of divorce on men and women in India and the United States. *Journal of Comparative Family Studies* 25, 207–221.

Andersen, P. A. (1991). Explaining intercultural differences in nonverbal communication. In *Intercultural communication: A reader,* 6th ed., L. A. Samovar & R. E. Porter (eds.). Belmont, CA: Wadsworth, pp. 286–296.

Andersen, P. A., & Leibowitz, K. (1978). The development and nature of the construct touch avoidance. *Environmental Psychology and Nonverbal Behavior* 3, 89–106. Reprinted in DeVito & Hecht (1990).

Angier, N. (1995a). Powerhouse of senses: Smell, at last, gets its due, *New York Times* (February 14), C1, C6.

Angier, N. (1995b). Scientists mull role of empathy in man and beast. *New York Times* (May 9), C1, C6.

Argyle, M. (1986). Rules for social relationships in four cultures. *Australian Journal of Psychology* 38, 309–318.

Argyle, M. (1988). *Bodily communication,* 2d ed. New York: Methuen.

Argyle, M., & Dean, J. (1965). Eye contact, distance and affiliation. *Sociometry* 28, 289–304.

Argyle, M., & Henderson, M. (1984). The rules of friendship. *Journal of Social and Personal Relationships* 1, 211–237.

Argyle, M., & Henderson, M. (1985). *The anatomy of relationships: And the rules and skills needed to manage them successfully.* London: Heinemann.

Argyle, M., Henderson, M., Bond, M., Iizuka, Y., et al. (1986). Cross-cultural variations in relationship rules. *International Journal of Psychology* 21, 287–315.

Argyle, M., & Ingham, R. (1972). Gaze, mutual gaze, and distance. *Semiotica* 1, 32–49.

Aronson, E., Wilson, T. D., & Akert, R. M. (1999). *Social psychology,* 3d ed. Boston: Allyn & Bacon.

Aronson, J., Cohen, J., & Nail, P. (1998). Self-affirmation theory: An update and appraisal. In *Cognitive dissonance theory: Revival with revisions and controversies,* E. Harmon-Jones & J. S. Mills (eds.). Washington, DC: American Psychological Association.

Asch, S. (1946). Forming impressions of personality. *Journal of Abnormal and Social Psychology* 41, 258–290.

Ashcraft, M. H. (1998). *Fundamentals of cognition.* New York: Longman.

Ashe, D. D., & McCutcheon, L. E. (2001). Shyness, loneliness, and attitude toward celebrities. *Current Research in Social Psychology* 6 (9).

Aspinwall, L. G., & Taylor, S. E. (1993). Effects of social comparison direction, threat, and self-esteem on affect, evaluation, and expected success. *Journal of Personality and Social Psychology* 64, 708–722.

Aune, R. K., & Kikuchi, T. (1993). Effects of language intensity similarity on perceptions of credibility, relational attributions, and persuasion. *Journal of Language and Social Psychology* 12, 224–238.

Authier, J., & Gustafson, K. (1982). Microtraining: Focusing on specific skills. In *Interpersonal helping skills: A guide to training methods, programs, and resources,* E. K. Marshall, P. D. Kurtz, and Associates (eds.). San Francisco: Jossey-Bass, pp. 93–130.

Axtell, R. E. (1990). *Do's and taboos of hosting international visitors.* New York: Wiley.

Axtell, R. E. (1994). *Do's and taboos around the world,* 3d ed. New York: Wiley.

Ayres, J. (1983). Strategies to maintain relationships: Their identification and perceived usage. *Communication Quarterly* 31, 62–67.

Ayres, J., Ayres, D. M., Grudzinskas, G., Hopf, T., Kelly, E., & Wilcox, A. K. (1995). A component analysis of performance visualization. *Communication Reports* 8, 185–192.

Ayres, J., & Hopf, T. (1993). *Coping with speech anxiety.* Norwood, NJ: Ablex.

Ayres, J., & Hopf, T. (1995). An assessment of the role of communication apprehension in communicating with the terminally ill. *Communication Research Reports* 12, 227–234.

Ayres, J., Hopf, T., & Ayres, D. M. (1994). An examination of whether imaging ability enhances the effectiveness of an intervention designed to reduce speech anxiety. *Communication Education* 43 (July), 252–258.

Babcock, J. C, Waltz, J., Jacobson, N. S., & Gottman, J. M. (1993). Power and violence: The relation between communication patterns, power discrepancies, and domestic violence. *Journal of Marriage and the Family* 60 (February), 70–78.

Bach, G. R., & Wyden, P. (1968). *The intimate enemy.* New York: Avon.

Baird, J. E., Jr. (1977). *The dynamics of organizational communication.* New York: Harper & Row.

Banks, S. P., Altendorf, D. M., Greene, J. O., & Cody, M. J. (1987). An examination of relationship disengagement: Perceptions, breakup strategies, and outcomes. *Western Journal of Speech Communication* 51, 19–41.

Baringer, D. K., & McCroskey, J. C. (2000). Immediacy in the classroom: Student immediacy. *Communication Education* 49, 178–186.

Barker, L. L. (1990). *Communication,* 5th ed. Englewood Cliffs, NJ: Prentice-Hall.

Barker, L. L., Edwards, R., Gaines, C., Gladney, K., & Holley, F. (1980). An investigation of proportional time spent in various communication activities by college students. *Journal of Applied Communication Research* 8, 101–109.

Barna, L. M. (1997). Stumbling blocks in intercultural communication. In *Intercultural communication: A reader,* 7th ed., L. A. Samovar & R. E. Porter (eds.). Belmont, CA: Wadsworth, pp. 337–346.

Barnlund, D. C. (1975). Communicative styles in two cultures: Japan and the United States. In *Organization of behavior in face-to-face interaction,* R. Kendon, M. Harris, & M. R. Key (eds.). The Hague: Mouton.

Barnlund, D. C. (1989). *Communicative styles of Japanese and Americans: Images and realities.* Belmont, CA: Wadsworth.

Baron, R. (1990). Countering the effects of destructive criticism: The relative efficacy of four interventions. *Journal of Applied Psychology* 75 (3), 235–245.

Barrett, L., & Godfrey, T. (1988). Listening. *Person Centered Review* 3 (November), 410–425.

Bartholomew, K. (1990). Avoidance of intimacy: An attachment perspective. *Journal of Social and Personal Relationships* 7, 147–178.

Basso, K. H. (1972). To give up on words: Silence in Apache culture. In *Language and social context,* Pier Paolo Giglioli (ed.). New York: Penguin.

Bateson, G. (1972). *Steps to an ecology of mind.* New York: Ballantine.

Battaglia, D. M., Richard, F. D., Datteri, D. L., & Lord, C. G. (1998). Breaking up is (relatively) easy to do: A script for the dissolution of close relationships. *Journal of Social and Personal Relationships* 15, 829–845.

Baumeister, R. F., Bushman, B. J., & Campbell, W. K. (2000). Self-esteem, narcissism, and aggression: Does violence result from low self-esteem or from threatened egotism? *Current Directions in Psychological Science* 9 (February), 26–29.

Bavelas, J. B. (1990). Can one not communicate? Behaving and communicating: A reply to Motley. *Western Journal of Speech Communication* 54, 593–602.

Baxter, L. A. (1983). Relationship disengagement: An examination of the reversal hypothesis. *Western Journal of Speech Communication* 47, 85–98.

Baxter, L. A. (1984). An investigation of compliance-gaining as politeness. *Human Communication Research* 10, 427–456.

Baxter, L. A. (1986). Gender differences in the heterosexual relationship rules embedded in break-up accounts. *Journal of Social and Personal Relationships* 3, 289–306.

Baxter, L. A. (1988). A dialectical perspective on communication strategies in relationship development. In *Handbook of personal relationships,* S. W. Duck (ed.). New York: Wiley.

Baxter, L. A. (1990). Dialectical contradictions in relationship development. *Journal of Social and Personal Relationships* 7, 69–88.

Baxter, L. A., & Bullis, C. (1986). Turning points in developing romantic relationships. *Human Communication Research* 12, 469–493.

Baxter, L. A., Dun, T., & Sahlstein, E. (2001). Rules for relating communicated among social network members. *Journal of Social and Personal Relationships* 18, 173–199.

Baxter, L. A., & Simon, E. P. (1993). Relationship maintenance strategies and dialectical contradictions in personal relationships. *Journal of Social and Personal Relationships* 10, 225–242.

Baxter, L. A., & Wilmot, W. W. (1984). Secret tests: Social strategies for acquiring information about the state of the relationship. *Human Communication Research* 11, 171–201.

Beach, W. A. (1990). On (not) observing behavior interactionally. *Western Journal of Speech Communication* 54, 603–612.

Beatty, M. (1988). Situational and predispositional correlates of public speaking anxiety. *Communication Education* 37, 28–39.

Beck, A. T. (1988). *Love is never enough.* New York: Harper & Row.

Bell, R. A., & Buerkel-Rothfuss, N. L. (1990). S(he) loves me, s(he) loves me not: Predictors of relational information-seeking in courtship and beyond. *Communication Quarterly* 38, 64–82.

Bell, R. A., & Daly, J. A. (1984). The affinity-seeking function of communication. *Communication Monographs* 51, 91–115.

Bennett, M. (1990). Children's understanding of the mitigating function of disclaimers. *Journal of Social Psychology* 130, 29–37.

Berg, J. H., & Archer, R. L. (1983). The disclosure-liking relationship. *Human Communication Research* 10, 269–281.

Berger, C. R., & Bradac, J. J. (1982). *Language and social knowledge: Uncertainty in interpersonal relations.* London: Edward Arnold.

Berger, C. R., & Calabrese, R. J. (1975). Some explorations in initial interaction and beyond: Toward a theory of interpersonal communication. *Human Communication Research* 1, 99–112.

Berger, P. L., & Luckmann, T. (1980). *The social construction of reality.* New York: Irvington.

Berman, J. J., Murphy-Berman, V., & Singh, P. (1985). Cross-cultural similarities and differences in perceptions of fairness. *Journal of Cross-Cultural Psychology* 16, 55–67.

Bernstein, W. M., Stephan, W. G., & Davis, M. H. (1979). Explaining attributions for achievement: A path analytic approach. *Journal of Personality and Social Psychology* 37, 1810–1821.

Berry, J. W., Poortinga, Y. H., Segall, M. H., & Dasen, P. R. (1992). *Cross-cultural psychology: Research and applications.* Cambridge: Cambridge University Press.

Berscheid, E. (1985). Interpersonal attraction. In *Handbook of social psychology,* G. Lindzey & E. Aronson (eds.). New York: Random House, pp. 413–484.

Berscheid, E., & Reis, H. T. (1998). Attraction and close relationships. In *The handbook of social psychology,* 4th ed., Vol. 2, D. Gilbert, S. Fiske, & G. Lindzey (eds.). New York: W. H. Freeman, pp. 193–281.

Bierhoff, H. W., & Klein, R. (1991). Dimensionen der Liebe: Entwicklung einer Deutschsprachigen Skala zur Erfassung von Liebesstilen. *Zeitschrift for Differentielle und Diagnostische Psychologie* 12, 53–71.

Bippus, A., & Daly, J. A. (1999). What do people think causes stage fright? Naive attributions about the reasons for public speaking anxiety. *Communication Education* 48, 63–72.

Bishop, J. E. (1993). New research suggests that romance begins by falling nose over heels in love. *Wall Street Journal* (April 7), B1.

Black, H. K. (1999). A sense of the sacred: Altering or enhancing the self-portrait in older age? *Narrative Inquiry* 9, 327–345.

Blieszner, R., & Adams, R. G. (1992). *Adult friendship.* Thousand Oaks, CA: Sage.

Blood, R. O., Jr. (1973). Resolving family conflicts. In *Conflict resolution through communication,* F. E. Jandt (ed.). New York: Harper & Row, pp. 221–239.

Blumstein, P., & Schwartz, P. (1983). *American couples: Money, work, sex.* New York: Morrow.

Bochner, A. (1984). The functions of human communication in interpersonal bonding. In *Handbook of rhetorical and communication theory,* C. C. Arnold & J. W. Bowers (eds.). Boston: Allyn & Bacon, pp. 544–621.

Bochner, A., & Kelly, C. (1974). Interpersonal competence: Rationale, philosophy, and implementation of a conceptual framework. *Communication Education* 23, 279–301.

Bochner, S. (1994). Cross-cultural differences in the self-concept: A test of Hofstede's individualism/collectivism distinction. *Journal of Cross-Cultural Psychology* 25, 273–283.

Bochner, S., & Hesketh, B. (1994). Power distance, individualism/collectivism, and job-related attitudes in a culturally diverse work group. *Journal of Cross-Cultural Psychology* 25, 233–257.

Bodon, J., Powell, L., & Hickson III, M. (1999). Critiques of gatekeeping in scholarly journals: An analysis of perceptions and data. *Journal of the Association for Communication Administration* 28 (May), 60–70.

Bok, S. (1978). *Lying: Moral choice in public and private life.* New York: Pantheon.

Bok, S. (1983). *Secrets.* New York: Vintage.

Bok, S. (1998). *Mayhem: Violence as public entertainment.* Reading, MA: Perseus Books.

Boneva, B., Kraut, R., & Frohlich, D. (2001). Using e-mail for personal relationships: The difference gender makes. *American Behavioral Scientist* 45, 530–549.

Booth-Butterfield, M. (1998). Measurement of communication flexibility: Working adults vs. college students. *Communication Research Reports* 15, 365–369.

Borden, G. A. (1991). *Cultural orientation: An approach to understanding intercultural communication.* Englewood Cliffs, NJ: Prentice-Hall.

Bosmajian, H. (1974). *The language of oppression.* Washington, DC: Public Affairs Press.

Bower, B. (2001). Self-illusions come back to bite students. *Science News* 159, 148.

Bravo, E., & Cassedy, E. (1992). *The 9 to 5 guide to combating sexual harassment.* New York: Wiley.

Breidenstein-Cutspec, P., & Goering, E. (1989). Exploring cultural diversity: A network analysis of the communicative correlates of shyness within the black culture. *Communication Research Reports* 6, 37–46.

Bresnahan, M. I., & Cai, D. H. (1996). Gender and aggression in the recognition of interruption. *Discourse Processes* 21, 171–189.

Bridges, C. R. (1996). The characteristics of career achievement perceived by African American college administrators. *Journal of Black Studies* 26, 748–767.

Briton, N. J., & Hall, J. A. (1995). Beliefs about female and male nonverbal communication. *Sex Roles* 32, 79–90.

Briton, N. J., & Hall, J. A. (1995). Gender-based expectancies and observer judgments of smiling. *Journal of Nonverbal Behavior* 19, 49–65.

Brody, J. F. (1994). Notions of beauty transcend culture, new study suggests. *New York Times* (March 21), A14.

Brougher, T. (1982). *A way with words.* Chicago: Nelson-Hall.

Brown, C. T., & Keller, P. W. (1979). *Monologue to dialogue: An exploration of interpersonal communication,* 2nd ed. Englewood Cliffs, NJ: Prentice-Hall.

Brown, P. (1980). How and why are women more polite: Some evidence from a Mayan community. In *Women and language in literature and society,* S. McConnell-Ginet, R. Borker, & M. Furman (eds.). New York: Praeger, pp. 111–136.

Brown, P., & Levinson, S. C. (1988). *Politeness: Some universals of language usage.* Cambridge: Cambridge University Press.

Brownell, J. (1987). Listening: The toughest management skill. *Cornell Hotel and Restaurant Administration Quarterly* 27, 64–71.

Brownell, J. (2002). *Listening: Attitudes, principles, and skills,* 2nd ed. Boston: Allyn & Bacon.

Buber, M. (1958). *I and thou,* 2nd ed. New York: Scribner's.

Bugental, J., & Zelen, S. (1950). Investigations into the "self-concept." I. The W-A-Y technique. *Journal of Personality* 18, 483–498.

Bull, R., & Rumsey, N. (1988). *The social psychology of facial appearance.* New York: Springer-Verlag.

Buller, D. B., LePoire, B. A., Aune, R. K., & Eloy, S. (1992). Social perceptions as mediators of the effect of speech rate similarity on compliance. *Human Communication Research* 19, 286–311.

Bumby, K. M., & Hansen, D. J. (1997). Intimacy deficits, fear of intimacy, and loneliness among sexual offenders. *Criminal Justice and Behavior* 24, 315–331.

Burgoon, J. K. (1991). Relational message interpretations of touch, conversational distance, and posture. *Journal of Nonverbal Behavior* 15, 233–259.

Burgoon, J. K., Berger, C. R., & Waldron, V. R. (2000). Mindfulness and interpersonal communication. *Journal of Social Issues* 56, 105–127.

Burgoon, J. K., Buller, D. B., & Woodall, W. G. (1996). *Nonverbal communication: The unspoken dialogue,* 2d ed. New York: McGraw-Hill.

Burgoon, J. K., & Hale, J. L. (1988). Nonverbal expectancy violations: Model elaboration and application to immediacy behaviors. *Communication Monographs* 55, 58–79.

Burgoon, M. (1971). The relationship between willingness to manipulate others and success in two different types of basic speech communication courses. *Communication Education* 20, 178–183.

Bushman, B. J., & Baumeister, R. F. (1998). Threatened egotism, narcissism, self-esteem, and direct and displaced aggression: Does self-love or self-hate lead to violence? *Journal of Personality and Social Psychology* 75, 219–229.

Buss, D. M., & Schmitt, D. P. (1993). Sexual strategies theory: An evolutionary perspective on human mating. *Psychological Review* 100, 204–232.

Butler, P. E. (1981). *Talking to yourself: Learning the language of self-support.* New York: Harper & Row.

Byers, E. S., & Demmons, S. (1999). Sexual satisfaction and sexual self-disclosure within dating relationships. *Journal of Sex Research* 36, 180–189.

Cabello, B., & Terrell, R. (1994). Making students feel like family: How teachers create warm and caring classroom climates. *Journal of Classroom Interaction* 29, 17–23.

Cai, D. A., & Fink, E. L. (2002). Conflict style differences between individualists and collectivists. *Communication Monographs* 69 (March), 67–87.

Camden, C., Motley, M. T., & Wilson, A. (1984). White lies in interpersonal communication: A taxonomy and preliminary investigation of social motivations. *Western Journal of Speech Communication* 48, 309–325.

Canary, D. J., Cupach, W. R., & Messman, S. J. (1995). *Relationship conflict: Conflict in parent-child, friendship, and romantic relationships.* Thousand Oaks, CA: Sage.

Canary, D. J., & Hause, K. S. (1993). Is there any reason to research sex differences in communication? *Communication Quarterly* 41, 129–144.

Canary, D. J., & Stafford, L. (1994). Maintaining relationships through strategic and routine interaction. In *Communication and relational maintenance,* D. J. Canary & L. Stafford (eds.). New York: Academic Press.

Canary, D. J., Stafford, L., Hause, K. S., & Wallace, L. A. (1993). An inductive analysis of relational maintenance strategies: Comparisons among lovers, relatives, friends, and others. *Communication Research Reports* 10, 5–14.

Cappella, J. N. (1993). The facial feedback hypothesis in human interaction: Review and speculation. *Journal of Language and Social Psychology* 12, 13–29.

Carducci, B. J., with Zimbardo, P. G. (1995). Are you shy? *Psychology Today* 28, 34–41, 64–70, 78–82.

Carli, L. L. (1999). Gender, interpersonal power, and social influence. *Journal of Social Issues* 55 (spring), 81–99.

Carlock, C. J., ed. (1999). *Enhancing self-esteem,* 3d ed. Philadelphia, PA: Accelerated Development, Inc.

Carroll, D. W. (1994). *Psychology of language,* 2d ed. Pacific Grove, CA: Brooks/Cole.

Cashdan, E. (2001). Ethnocentrism and xenophobia: A cross-cultural study. *Current Anthropology* 42, 760–765.

Castleberry, S. B., & Shepherd, C. D. (1993). Effective interpersonal listening and personal selling. *Journal of Personal Selling and Sales Management* 13, 35–49.

Cawthon, S. W. (2001). Teaching strategies in inclusive classrooms with deaf students. *Journal of Deaf Studies and Deaf Education* 6, 212–225.

Chadwick-Jones, J. K. (1976). *Social exchange theory: Its structure and influence in social psychology.* New York: Academic Press.

Chaney, R. H., Givens, C. A., Aoki, M. F., & Gombiner, M. L. (1989). Pupillary responses in recognizing awareness in persons with profound mental retardation. *Perceptual and Motor Skills* 69, 523–528.

Chang, H., & Holt, G. R. (1996). The changing Chinese interpersonal world: Popular themes in interpersonal communication books in modern Taiwan. *Communication Quarterly* 44, 85–106.

Chanowitz, B., & Langer, E. (1981). Premature cognitive commitment. *Journal of Personality and Social Psychology* 41, 1051–1063.

Chen, G. (1992). Differences in self-disclosure patterns among Americans versus Chinese: A comparative study. Paper presented at the annual meeting of the Eastern Communication Association, Portland, ME.

Cheney, G., & Tompkins, P. K. (1987). Coming to terms with organizational identification and commitment. *Central States Speech Journal* 38, 1–15.

Chesebro, J. L., & McCroskey, J. C. (1998). The relationship of teacher clarity and teacher immediacy with students' experiences of state receiver apprehension. *Communication Quarterly* 46, 446–456.

Christians, C. G. & Traber, M., eds. (1997). *Communication ethics and universal values.* Urbana, IL: University of Illinois Press.

Christie, R. (1970). Scale construction. In *Studies in Machiavellianism*, R. Christie & F. L. Geis (eds.). New York: Academic Press, pp. 35–52.

Chung, L. C., & Ting-Toomey, S. (1999). Ethnic identity and relational expectations among Asian Americans. *Communication Research Reports* 16 (spring), 157–166.

Clark, R. A. (1991). *Studying interpersonal communication: The research experience.* Thousand Oaks, CA: Sage.

Clement, D. A., & Frandsen, K. D. (1976). On conceptual and empirical treatments of feedback in human communication. *Communication Monographs* 43, 11–28.

Cline, M. G. (1956). The influence of social context on the perception of faces. *Journal of Personality* 2, 142–185.

Cody, M. J. (1982). A typology of disengagement strategies and an examination of the role intimacy, reactions to inequity, and relational problems play in strategy selection. *Communication Monographs* 49, 148–170.

Cohen, J. (2002). An e-mail affliction: The long goodbye. *New York Times* (May 9), G6.

Cole, T., & Leets, L. (1999). Attachment styles and intimate television viewing: Insecurely forming relationships in a parasocial way. *Journal of Social and Personal Relationships* 16 (August), 495–511.

Coleman, P. (2002). *How to say it for couples: Communicating with tenderness, openness, and honesty.* Paramus, NJ: Prentice-Hall.

Collier, M. J. (1991). Conflict competence within African, Mexican, and Anglo American friendships. In *Cross-cultural interpersonal communication,* S. Ting-Toomey & F. Korzenny (eds.). Thousand Oaks, CA: Sage, pp. 132–154.

Collins, J. E., & Clark, L. F. (1989). Responsibility and rumination: The trouble with understanding the dissolution of a relationship. *Social Cognition* 7, 152–173.

Collins, N. L., & Miller, L. C. (1994). Self-disclosure and liking: A meta-analytic review. *Psychological Bulletin* 116 (November): 457–475.

Cooley, C. H. (1922). *Human nature and the social order.* Rev. ed. New York: Scribner's.

Coon, C. A., & Schwanenflugel, P. J. (1996). Evaluation of interruption behavior by naive encoders. *Discourse Processes* 22, 1–24.

Cooper, A., & Sportolari, L. (1997). Romance in cyberspace: Understanding online attraction. *Journal of Sex Education and Therapy* 22, 7–14.

Coover, G. E., & Murphy, S. T. (2000). The communicated self: Exploring the interaction between self and social context. *Human Communication Research* 26, 125–147.

Cornwell, B., & Lundgren, D. C. (2001). Love on the Internet: Involvement and misrepresentation in romantic relationships in cyberspace vs. realspace. *Computers in Human Behavior* 17, 197–211.

Counts, D. A., Brown, J. K., & Campbell, J. C. (1992). *Sanctions and sanctuary: Cultural perspectives on the beating of wives.* Boulder, CO: Westview Press.

Crohn, J. (1995). *Mixed matches: How to create successful interracial, interethnic, and interfaith relationships.* New York: Fawcett.

Cross, E. E., & Madson, L. (1997). Models of the self: Self-construals and gender. *Psychological Bulletin* 122, 5–37.

Crusco, A. H., & Wetzel, C. G. (1984). The Midas touch: The effects of interpersonal touch on restaurant tipping. *Personality and Social Psychology Bulletin* 10, 512–517.

Dainton, M., & Stafford, L. (1993). Routine maintenance behaviors: A comparison of relationship type, partner similarity, and sex differences. *Journal of Social and Personal Relationships* 10, 255–272.

Davis, F. (1973). *Inside intuition.* New York: New American Library.

Davis, M. S. (1973). *Intimate relations.* New York: Free Press.

Davison, W. P. (1983). The third-person effect and the differential impact in negative political advertising. *Journalism Quarterly* 68, 680–688.

Deal, J. E., & Wampler, K. S. (1986). Dating violence: The primacy of previous experience. *Journal of Social and Personal Relationships* 3, 457–471.

Deaux, K., & LaFrance, M. (1998). Gender. In *The handbook of social psychology,* 4th ed., Vol. 1, D. Gilbert, S. Fiske, & G. Lindzey (eds.). New York: Freeman, pp. 788–828.

deBono, E. (1987). *The six thinking hats.* New York: Penguin.

DeCecco, J. (1988). Obligation versus aspiration. In *Gay relationships,* J. DeCecco (ed.). New York: Harrington Park Press.

DeFrancisco, V. (1991). The sound of silence: How men silence women in marital relations. *Discourse and Society* 2, 413–423.

Delia, J. G. (1977). Constructivism and the study of human communication. *Quarterly Journal of Speech* 63, 66–83.

Delia, J. G., O'Keefe, B. J., & O'Keefe, D. J. (1982). The constructivist approach to communication. In *Human communication theory: Comparative essays,* Frank E. X. Dance (ed.). New York: Harper & Row, pp. 147–191.

Derlega, V. J., Winstead, B. A., Wong, P. T. P., & Hunter, S. (1985). Gender effects in an initial encounter: A case where men exceed women in disclosure. *Journal of Social and Personal Relationships* 2, 25–44.

Derlega, V. J., Winstead, B. A., Wong, P. T. P., & Greenspan, M. (1987). Self-disclosure and relationship development: An attributional analysis. In *Interpersonal processes: New directions in communication research,* M. E. Roloff, & G. R. Miller (eds.). Thousand Oaks, CA: Sage, pp. 172–187.

Derne, S. (1999). Making sex violent: Love as force in recent Hindi films. *Violence Against Women* 5 (May), 548–575.

DeVito, J. A., ed. (1981). *Communication: Concepts and processes,* 3d ed. Englewood Cliffs, NJ: Prentice-Hall.

DeVito, J. A. (1989) *The nonverbal communication workbook.* Prospect Heights, IL: Waveland Press.

DeVries, M. A. (1994). *Internationally yours: Writing and communicating successfully in today's global marketplace.* Boston: Houghton Mifflin.

Dietz, T. L. (1998). An examination of violence and gender role portrayals in video games: Implications for gender socialization and aggressive behavior. *Sex Roles* 38 (March), 425–442.

Dillard, J. P., ed. (1990). *Seeking compliance: The production of interpersonal influence messages.* Scottsdale, AZ: Gorsuch Scarisbrick.

Dindia, K., & Baxter, L. A. (1987). Strategies for maintaining and repairing marital relationships. *Journal of Social and Personal Relationships* 4, 143–158.

Dindia, K., & Fitzpatrick, M. A. (1985). Marital communication: Three approaches compared. In *Understanding personal relationships: An interdisciplinary approach,* S. Duck & D. Perlman (eds.). Thousand Oaks, CA: Sage, pp. 137–158.

Dion, K., Berscheid, E., & Walster, E. (1972). What is beautiful is good. *Journal of Personality and Social Psychology* 24, 285–290.

Dion, K. K., & Dion, K. L. (1993a). Individualistic and collectivist perspectives on gender and the cultural context of love and intimacy. *Journal of Social Issues* 49, 53–69.

Dion, K. L., & Dion, K. K. (1993b). Gender and ethnocultural comparisons in styles of love. *Psychology of Women Quarterly* 17, 464–473.

Dion, K. K., & Dion, K. L. (1996). Cultural perspectives on romantic love. *Personal Relationships* 3, 5–17.

Dittman, D. A. (1997). Reexamining curriculum. *The Cornell Hotel and Restaurant Administration Quarterly* 38, 3.

Dolgin, K. G., Meyer, L., & Schwartz, J. (1991). Effects of gender, target's gender, topic, and self-esteem on disclosure to best and middling friends. *Sex Roles* 25, 311–329.

Dominick, J. R. (2000). *The dynamics of mass communication,* 6th ed. New York: McGraw-Hill.

Donahue, W. A., with Kolt, R. (1992). *Managing interpersonal conflict.* Thousand Oaks, CA: Sage.

Dosey, M., & Meisels, M. (1976). Personal space and self-protection. *Journal of Personality and Social Psychology* 38, 959–965.

Douglas, W. (1994). The acquaintanceship process: An examination of uncertainty, information seeking, and social attraction during initial conversation. *Communication Research* 21, 154–176.

Dovidio, J. F., Gaertner, S. E., Kawakami, K., & Hodson, G. (2002). Why can't we just get along? Interpersonal biases and interracial distrust. *Cultural Diversity and Ethnic Minority Psychology* 8, 88–102.

Drass, K. A. (1986). The effect of gender identity on conversation. *Social Psychology Quarterly* 49, 294–301.

Dresser, N. (1996). *Multicultural manners: New rules of etiquette for a changing society.* New York: Wiley.

Drews, D. R., Allison, C. K., & Probst, J. R. (2000). Behavioral and self-concept differences in tattooed and nontattooed college students. *Psychological Reports* 86, 475–481.

Dreyfuss, H. (1971). *Symbol sourcebook.* New York: McGraw-Hill.

Drummond, K., & Hopper, R. (1993). Acknowledgment tokens in series. *Communication Reports* 6, 47–53.

Dsilva, M., & Whyte, L. O. (1998). Cultural differences in conflict styles: Vietnamese refugees and established residents. *The Howard Journal of Communication* 9, 57–68.

Duck, S. (1986). *Human relationships.* Thousand Oaks, CA: Sage.

Duncan, B. L., & Rock, J. W. (1991). *Overcoming relationship impasses: Ways to initiate change when your partner won't help.* New York: Plenum Press/Insight Books.

Duncan, S. D., Jr. (1972). Some signals and rules for taking speaking turns in conversation. *Journal of Personality and Social Psychology* 23, 283–292.

Duran, R. L., & Kelly, L. (1988). The influence of communicative competence on perceived task, social, and physical attraction. *Communication Quarterly* 36, 41–49.

Eckstein, D., & Goldman, A. (2001). The couple's gender-based communication questionnaire (CGCQ). *Family Journal: Counseling and Therapy for Couples and Families* 9, 62–74.

Eden, D. (1992). Leadership and expectations: Pygmalion effects and other self-fulfilling prophecies in organizations. *Leadership Quarterly* 3 (winter), 271–305.

Eden, D. (1997). Leadership and expectations: Pygmalion effects and other self-fulfilling prophecies in organizations. In *Leadership: Understanding the dynamics of power and influence in organizations,* R. P. Vecchio (ed.). Notre Dame, IN: University of Notre Dame Press, pp. 177–193.

Edwards, R., & Bello, R. (2001). Interpretations of messages: The influence of equivocation, face-concerns, and ego-involvement. *Human Communication Research* 27, 597–631.

Ehrenhaus, P. (1988). Silence and symbolic expression. *Communication Monographs* 55, 41–57.

Einstein, E. (1995). Success or sabotage: Which self-fulfilling prophecy will the stepfamily create? In *Understanding stepfamilies: Implications for assessment and treatment,* D. K. Huntley (ed.). Alexandria, VA: American Counseling Association.

Ekman, P. (1985). *Telling lies: Clues to deceit in the marketplace, politics, and marriage.* New York: Norton.

Ekman, P., & Friesen, W. V. (1969). The repertoire of nonverbal behavior: Categories, origins, usage, and coding. *Semiotica* 1, 49–98.

Ekman, P., Friesen, W. V., & Ellsworth, P. (1972). *Emotion in the human face: Guidelines for research and an integration of findings.* New York: Pergamon Press.

Elfenbein, H. A., & Ambady, N. (2002). Is there an in-group advantage in emotion recognition? *Psychological Bulletin* 128, 243–249.

Ellis, A. (1988). *How to stubbornly refuse to make yourself miserable about anything, yes anything.* Secaucus, NJ: Lyle Stuart.

Ellis, A., & Harper, R. A. (1975). *A new guide to rational living.* Hollywood, CA: Wilshire Books.

Elmes, M. B., & Gemmill, G. (1990). The psychodynamics of mindlessness and dissent in small groups. *Small Group Research* 21, 28–44.

Epstein, R. M., & Hundert, E. M. (2002). Defining and assessing professional competence. *JAMA: Journal of the American Medical Association* 287, 226–235.

Exline, R. V., Ellyson, S. L., & Long, B. (1975). Visual behavior as an aspect of power role relationships. In *Nonverbal communication of aggression,* P. Pliner, L. Krames, & T. Alloway (eds.). New York: Plenum Press.

Feeley, T. H., & deTurck, M. A. (1995). Global cue usage in behavioral lie detection. *Communication Quarterly* 43, 420–430.

Fehr, B., & Broughton, R. (2001). Gender and personality differences in concepts of love: An interpersonal theory analysis. *Personal Relationships* 8, 115–136.

Fengler, A. P. (1974). Romantic love in courtship: Divergent paths of male and female students. *Journal of Comparative Family Studies* 5, 134–139.

Fernald, C. D. (1995). When in London. . . : Differences in disability language preferences among English-speaking countries. *Mental Retardation* 33, 99–103.

Fesko, S. L. (2001). Disclosure of HIV status in the workplace: Considerations and strategies. *Health and Social Work* 26 (November), 235–244.

Festinger, L., Schachter, S., & Back, K. W. (1950). *Social pressures in informal groups: A study of human factors in housing.* New York: Harper & Row.

Fischer, C. S., & Oliker, S. J. (1983). A research note on friendship, gender, and the life cycle. *Social Forces* 62, 124–133.

Fisher, D. (1995). *People power: 12 power principles to enrich your business, career, and personal networks.* Austin, TX: Bard & Stephen.

Fitzpatrick, M. A. (1983). Predicting couples' communication from couples' self-reports. In *Communication yearbook 7,* R. N. Bostrom (cd.). Thousand Oaks, CA: Sage, pp. 49–82.

Fitzpatrick, M. A. (1988). *Between husbands and wives: Communication in marriage.* Thousand Oaks, CA: Sage.

Fitzpatrick, M. A. (1991). Sex differences in marital conflict: Social psychophysiological versus cognitive explanations. *Text* 11, 341–364.

Floyd, J. J. (1985). *Listening: A practical approach.* Glenview, IL: Scott, Foresman.

Fodor, I. G., & Collier, J. C. (2001). Assertiveness and conflict resolution: An integrated Gestalt/cognitive behavioral model for working with urban adolescents. In *The heart of development: Vol. II: Adolescence: Gestalt approaches to working with children, adolescents and their worlds,* M. McConville & G. Wheeler (eds.), Cambridge, ME: Analytic Press, pp. 214–252.

Folkerts, J., & Lacy, S. (2001). *The media in your life: An introduction to mass communication,* 2nd ed. Boston: Allyn & Bacon.

Forbes, G. B. (2001). College students with tattoos and piercings: Motives, family experiences, personality factors, and perception by others. *Psychological Reports* 89, 774–786.

Foster, D. A. (2002). *Global etiquette guide to Mexico and Latin America.* New York: Wiley.

Fox, M., Gibbs, M., & Auerbach, D. (1985). Age and gender dimensions of friendship. *Psychology of Women Quarterly* 9, 489–501.

Franklin, C. W., & Mizell, C. A. (1995). Some factors influencing success among African-American men: A preliminary study. *Journal of Men's Studies* 3, 191–204.

Fraser, B. (1990). Perspectives on politeness. *Journal of Pragmatics* 14, 219–236.

Frazier, P. A., & Cook, S. W. (1993). Correlates of distress following heterosexual relationship dissolution. *Journal of Social and Personal Relationships* 10, 55–67.

Freedman, J. (1978). *Happy people: What happiness is, who has it, and why.* New York: Ballantine.

French, J. R. P., Jr., & Raven, B. (1968). The bases of social power. In *Group dynamics: Research and theory,* 3d ed., D. Cartwright & A. Zander (eds.). New York: Harper & Row, pp. 259–269.

Frentz, T. (1976). A general approach to episodic structure. Paper presented at the Western Speech Association Convention, San Francisco. Cited in Reardon (1987).

Fresko, S. L. (2001). Disclosure of HIV status in the workplace: Considerations and strategies. *Health & Social Work* 25, 235–244.

Friedman, J., Boumil, M. M., & Taylor, B. E. (1992). *Sexual harassment.* Deerfield Beach, FL: Health Communications, Inc.

Frone, M. R. (2000). Interpersonal conflict at work and psychological outcomes: Testing a model among young workers. *Journal of Occupational Health Psychology* 5, 246–255.

Fuller, L. K. (1995). *Media-mediated relationships: Straight and gay, mainstream and alternative perspectives.* New York: Harrington Park Press.

Furlow, F. B. (1996). The smell of love. *Psychology Today* 29, 38–45.

Furnham, A., & Bochner, S. (1986). *Culture shock: Psychological reactions to unfamiliar environments.* New York: Methuen.

Galvin, K., & Brommel, B. J. (2000). *Family communication: Cohesion and change,* 5th ed. Boston: Allyn & Bacon.

Gamson, J. (1998). Publicity traps: Television talk shows and lesbian, gay, bisexual, and transgender visibility. *Sexualities* 1 (February):11–41.

Gangestad, S., & Snyder, M. (1985). To carve nature at its joints: On the existence of discrete classes in personality. *Psychological Review* 92, 317–349.

Gao, G., & Gudykunst, W. B. (1995). Attributional confidence, perceived similarity, and network involvement in Chinese and American romantic relationships. *Communication Quarterly* 43, 431–445.

Gelfand, M. J., Nishii, L. H., Holcombe, K. M., Dyer, N., Ohbuchi, K., & Fukuno, M. (2001). Cultural influences on cognitive representations of conflict: Interpretations of conflict episodes in the United States and Japan. *Journal of Applied Psychology* 86, 1059–1074.

Gelles, R., & Cornell, C. (1985). *Intimate violence in families.* Thousand Oaks, CA: Sage.

Georgas, J., et al. (2001). Functional relationships in the nuclear and extended family: A 16-culture study. *International Journal of Psychology* 36, 289–300.

Gerbner, G., Gross, L. P., Morgan, M., & Signorielli, N. (1980). The 'Mainstreaming' of America: Violence profile No. 11. *Journal of Communication* 30, 10–29.

Gergen, K. J., Greenberg, M. S., and Willis, R. H. (1980). *Social exchange: Advances in theory and research.* New York: Plenum Press.

Gibb, J. (1961). Defensive communication. *Journal of Communication* 11, 141–148.

Giles, H., Mulac, A., Bradac, J. J., & Johnson, P. (1987). Speech accommodation theory: The first decade and beyond. In *Communication yearbook 10,* M. L. McLaughlin (ed.). Thousand Oaks, CA: Sage, pp. 13–48.

Glucksberg, S., & Danks, J. H. (1975). *Experimental psycholinguistics: An introduction.* Hillsdale, NJ: Erlbaum.

Goffman, E. (1967). *Interaction ritual: Essays on face-to-face behavior.* New York: Pantheon.

Goffman, E. (1971). *Relations in public: Microstudies of the public order.* New York: Harper Colophon.

Goldin-Meadow, S., Nusbaum, H., Kelly, S. D., & Wagner, S. (2001) Gesture—Psychological aspects. *Psychological Science* 12, 516–522.

Goleman, D. (1992). Studies find no disadvantage in growing up in a gay home. *New York Times* (December 2), C14.

Goleman, D. (1995a). *Emotional intelligence.* New York: Bantam.

Goleman, D. (1995b). For man and beast, language of love shares many traits. *New York Times* (February 14), C1, C9.

Gonzalez, A., & Zimbardo, P. G. (1985). Time in perspective. *Psychology Today* 19, 20–26. Reprinted in DeVito & Hecht (1990).

Gonzenbach, W. J., King, C., & Jablonski, P. (1999). Homosexuals and the military: An analysis of the spiral of silence. *Howard Journal of Communication* 10 (October-December), 281–296.

Goodwin, R., & Findlay, C. (1997). "We were just fated together" . . . Chinese love and the concept of *yuan* in England and Hong Kong. *Personal Relationships* 4, 85–92.

Goodwin, R., & Lee, I. (1994). Taboo topics among Chinese and English friends: A cross-cultural comparison. *Journal of Cross-Cultural Psychology* 25, 325–338.

Gordon, T. (1975). *P.E.T.: Parent effectiveness training.* New York: New American Library.

Gottman, J. M. (1993). *What predicts divorce: The relationships between marital processes and marital outcomes.* Hillsdale, NJ: Erlbaum.

Gottman, J. M. (1994). *Why marriages succeed or fail.* New York: Simon and Schuster.

Gottman, J. M., & Carrere, S. (1994). Why can't men and women get along? Developmental roots and marital inequities. In D. J. Canary and L. Stafford (eds.). *Communication and relational maintenance,* San Diego, CA: Academic Press, pp. 203–229.

Gottman, J. M., Coan, J., Carrere, S., & Swanson, C. (1998). Predicting marital happiness and stability from newlywed interactions. *Journal of Marriage and the Family* 60, 5–22.

Gould, S. J. (1995). No more "wretched refuse." *New York Times* (June 7), A27.

Grabe, M. E., Lang, A., Zhou, S., Bolls, P. D. (2000). Cognitive access to negatively arousing news: An experimental investigation of the knowledge gap.

Journal of Consulting and Clinical Psychology 61 (February), 40–50.

Graham, E. E. (1994). Interpersonal communication motives scale. In *Communication research measures: A sourcebook,* R. B. Rubin, P. Palmgreen, & H. E. Sypher (eds.). New York: Guilford, pp. 211–216.

Graham, E. E., Barbato, C. A., & Perse, E. M. (1993). The interpersonal communication motives model. *Communication Quarterly* 41, 172–186.

Graham, J. A., & Argyle, M. (1975). The effects of different patterns of gaze, combined with different facial expressions, on impression formation. *Journal of Movement Studies* 1, 178–182.

Graham, J. A., Bitti, P. R., & Argyle, M. (1975). A cross-cultural study of the communication of emotion by facial and gestural cues. *Journal of Human Movement Studies* 1, 68–77.

Greif, E. B. (1980). Sex differences in parent-child conversations. *Women's Studies International Quarterly* 3, 253–258.

Grice, H. P. (1975). Logic and conversation. In *Syntax and semantics,* Vol. 3, *Speech acts,* P. Cole & J. L. Morgan (eds.). New York: Seminar Press, pp. 41–58.

Griffin, E. (2000). *A first look at communication theory,* 3d ed. New York: McGraw-Hill.

Griffin, E., & Sparks, G. G. (1990). Friends forever: A longitudinal exploration of intimacy in same-sex friends and platonic pairs. *Journal of Social and Personal Relationships* 7, 29–46.

Gross, L. (1991). The contested closet: The ethics and politics of outing. *Critical Studies in Mass Communication* 8, 352–388.

Gu, Y. (1990). Polite phenomena in modern Chinese. *Journal of Pragmatics* 14, 237–257.

Gudykunst, W. B., ed. (1983). *Intercultural communication theory: Current perspectives.* Thousand Oaks, CA: Sage.

Gudykunst, W. B. (1989). Culture and the development of interpersonal relationships. In *Communication yearbook 12,* J. A. Anderson (ed.). Thousand Oaks, CA: Sage, pp. 315–354.

Gudykunst, W. B. (1991). *Bridging differences: Effective intergroup communication.* Newbury Park, CA: Sage.

Gudykunst, W. B. (1993). Toward a theory of effective interpersonal and intergroup communication: An anxiety/uncertainty management (AUM) perspec-

tive. In *Intercultural communication competence,* R. L. Wiseman (ed.). Thousand Oaks, CA: Sage.

Gudykunst, W. B. (1994). *Bridging differences: Effective intergroup communication,* 2d ed. Thousand Oaks, CA: Sage.

Gudykunst, W. B., & Kim, Y. W. (1992). *Communicating with strangers: An approach to intercultural communication,* 2d ed. New York: Random House.

Gudykunst, W. B., & Nishida, T. (1984). Individual and cultural influence on uncertainty reduction. *Communication Monographs* 51, 23–36.

Gudykunst, W. B., Nishida, T., & Chua, E. (1987). Perceptions of social penetration in Japanese-North American dyads. *International Journal of Intercultural Relations* 11, 171–189.

Gudykunst, W. B., & Ting-Toomey, S., with Chua, E. (1988). *Culture and interpersonal communication.* Thousand Oaks, CA: Sage.

Gudykunst, W. B., Yang, S., & Nishida, T. (1985). A cross-cultural test of uncertainty reduction theory: Comparisons of acquaintance, friend, and dating relationships in Japan, Korea, and the United States. *Human Communication Research* 11, 407–454.

Guerrero, L. K. (1997). Nonverbal involvement across interactions with same-sex friends, opposite-sex friends, and romantic partners: Consistency or change? *Journal of Social and Personal Relationships* 14, 31–58.

Guerrero, L. K., & Andersen, P. A. (1991). The waxing and waning of relational intimacy: Touch as a function of relational stage, gender and touch avoidance. *Journal of Social and Personal Relationships* 8, 147–165.

Guerrero, L. K., & Andersen, P. A. (1994). Patterns of matching and initiation: Touch behavior and touch avoidance across romantic relationship stages. *Journal of Nonverbal Behavior* 18, 137–153.

Guerrero, L. K., DeVito, J. A., & Hecht, M. L., eds. (1999). *The nonverbal communication reader: Classic and contemporary readings.* Prospect Heights, IL: Waveland Press.

Guerrero, L. K., Eloy, S. V., & Wabnik, A. I. (1993). Linking maintenance strategies to relationship development and disengagement: A reconceptualization. *Journal of Social and Personal Relationships* 10, 273–282.

Haar, B. F., & Krabe, B. (1999). Strategies for resolving interpersonal conflicts in adolescence: A German-

Indonesian comparison. *Journal of Cross-Cultural Psychology* 30, 667–683.

Haferkamp, C. J. (1991/1992). Orientations to conflict: Gender, attributes, resolution strategies, and self-monitoring. *Current Psychology: Research and Reviews* 10, 227–240.

Haga, Y. (1988). Traits de langage et caractere japonais. *Cahiers de Sociologie Economique et Culturelle* 9, 105–109.

Hall, E. T. (1959). *The silent language.* Garden City, NY: Doubleday.

Hall, E. T. (1963). System for the notation of proxemic behavior. *American Anthropologist* 65, 1003–1026.

Hall, E. T. (1966). *The hidden dimension.* Garden City, NY: Doubleday.

Hall, E. T. (1976). *Beyond culture.* Garden City, NY: Anchor Press.

Hall, E. T. (1983). *The dance of life: The other dimension of time.* New York: Anchor Books/Doubleday.

Hall, E. T., & Hall, M. R. (1987). *Hidden differences: Doing business with the Japanese.* New York: Anchor Books.

Hall, J. A. (1984). *Nonverbal sex differences.* Baltimore: Johns Hopkins University Press.

Hammer, M. R. (1986). The influence of ethnic and attitude similarity on initial social penetration. In *Interethnic communication: Current research,* Y. Y. Kim (ed.), *International and Intercultural Communication Annual* 10, 225–237.

Han, S., & Shavitt, S. (1994). Persuasion and culture: Advertising appeals in individualistic and collectivistic societies. *Journal of Experimental Social Psychology* 30, 326–350.

Haney, W. (1973). *Communication and organizational behavior: Text and cases,* 3d ed. Homewood, IL: Irwin.

Harrell, W. A. (1990). Husband's masculinity, wife's power, and marital conflict. *Social Behavior and Personality* 18, 207–215.

Harris, J. (1995). Educational telecomputing projects: Interpersonal exchanges. *Computing Teacher* 22 (March): 60–64.

Harris, M. (1993). *Culture, people, nature: An introduction to general anthropology,* 6th ed. Boston: Allyn & Bacon.

Hart, F. (1990). The construction of masculinity in men's friendships: Misogyny, heterosexism and homophobia. *Resources for Feminist Research* 19, 60–67.

Hart, R. P., & Burks, D. M. (1972). Rhetorical sensitivity and social interaction. *Communication Monographs* 39, 75–91.

Hart, R. P., Carlson, R. E., & Eadie, W. F. (1980). Attitudes toward communication and the assessment of rhetorical sensitivity. *Communication Monographs* 47, 1–22.

Harvey, J. H., Flanary, R., & Morgan, M. (1986). Vivid memories of vivid loves gone by. *Journal of Social and Personal Relationships* 3, 359–373.

Hasart, J. K., & Hutchinson, K. L. (1993). The effects of eyeglasses on perceptions of interpersonal attraction. *Journal of Social Behavior and Personality* 8, 521–528.

Hasegawa, T., & Gudykunst, W. B. (1998). Silence in Japan and the United States. *Journal of Cross-Cultural Psychology* 29, 668–684.

Hatfield, E., & Rapson, R. L. (1992). Similarity and attraction in close relationships. *Communication Monographs* 59, 209–212.

Hatfield, E., & Rapson, R. L. (1996). *Love and sex: Cross-cultural perspectives.* Boston: Allyn & Bacon.

Hayakawa, S. I., & Hayakawa, A. R. (1989). *Language in thought and action,* 5th ed. New York: Harcourt Brace Jovanovich.

Hays, R. B. (1989). The day-to-day functioning of close versus casual friendships. *Journal of Social and Personal Relationships* 6, 21–37.

Heasley, J. B. S., Babbitt, C. E., & Burbach, H. J. (1995). The role of social context in students' anticipatory reaction to a "fighting word." *Sociological Focus* 27, 281–283.

Hecht, M. L., Collier, M. J., & Ribeau, S. (1993). *African American communication: Ethnic identity and cultural interpretation.* Thousand Oaks, CA: Sage.

Hendrick, C., & Hendrick, S. (1990). A relationship-specific version of the love attitudes scale. In *Handbook of replication research in the behavioral and social sciences* (special issue), J. W. Heulip (ed.), *Journal of Social Behavior and Personality* 5, 239–254.

Hendrick, C., Hendrick, S., Foote, F. H., & Slapion-Foote, M. J. (1984). Do men and women love differently? *Journal of Social and Personal Relationships* 1, 177–195.

Henley, N. M. (1977). *Body politics: Power, sex, and nonverbal communication.* Englewood Cliffs, NJ: Prentice-Hall.

Hensley, W. E. (1996). A theory of the valenced other: The intersection of the looking-glass-self and social penetration. *Social Behavior and Personality* 24, 293–308.

Hess, E. H. (1975). *The tell-tale eye.* New York: Van Nostrand Reinhold.

Hess, E. H., Seltzer, A. L., & Schlien, J. M. (1965). Pupil response of hetero- and homosexual males to pictures of men and women: A pilot study. *Journal of Abnormal Psychology* 70, 165–168.

Hess, U., Kappas, A., McHugo, G. J., Lanzetta, J. T., et al. (1992). The facilitative effect of facial expression on the self-generation of emotion. *International Journal of Psychophysiology* 12, 251–265.

Hewitt, J. P. (1998). *The myth of self-esteem: Finding happiness and solving problems in America.* New York: St. Martin's Press.

Hewitt, J. P., & Stokes, R. (1975). Disclaimers. *American Sociological Review* 40, 1–11.

Hoffner, C., et al. (2001). The third-person effect in perceptions of the influence of television violence. *Journal of Communication* 51 (June), 283–299.

Hofstede, G. (1983). National culture revisited. *Behavior Science Research* 18, 285–305.

Hofstede, G. (1997). *Cultures and organizations: Software of the mind.* New York: McGraw-Hill.

Hofstede, G., ed. (1998). *Masculinity and femininity: The taboo dimension of national cultures.* Thousand Oaks, CA: Sage.

Hoft, N. L. (1995). *International technical communication: How to export information about high technology.* New York: Wiley.

Holden, J. M. (1991). The most frequent personality priority pairings in marriage and marriage counseling. *Individual Psychology Journal of Adlerian Theory, Research, and Practice* 47, 392–398.

Holmes, J. (1986). Compliments and compliment responses in New Zealand English. *Anthropological Linguistics* 28, 485–508.

Holmes, J. (1995). *Women, men and politeness.* New York: Longman.

Honeycutt, J. (1986). A model of marital functioning based on an attraction paradigm and social penetration dimensions. *Journal of Marriage and the Family* 48, 51–59.

Hopper, R., Knapp, M. L., & Scott, L. (1981). Couples' personal idioms: Exploring intimate talk. *Journal of Communication* 31, 23–33.

Hosman, L. A. (1989). The evaluative consequences of hedges, hesitations, and intensifiers: Powerful and powerless speech styles. *Human Communication Research* 15, 383–406.

How Americans Communicate (1999). http://www.natcom.org/Research/Roper/how_Americans_communicate.htm.

Howard, P. E. N., Rainie, L., & Jones, S. (2001). Days and nights on the Internet: The impact of a diffusing technology. *American Behavioral Scientist* 45, 383–404.

Huston, M., & Schwartz, P. (1995). The relationships of lesbians and gay men. In *Under-studied relationships: Off the beaten track,* J. T. Wood, & S. Duck (eds.). Thousand Oaks, CA: Sage, pp. 89–121.

Infante, D. A. (1988). *Arguing constructively.* Prospect Heights, IL: Waveland Press.

Infante, D. A., Chandler, T. A., & Rudd, J. E. (1989). Test of an argumentative skill deficiency model of interspousal violence. *Communication Monographs* 56, 163–177.

Infante, D. A., Hartley, K. C., Martin, M. M., Higgins, M. A., Bruning, S. D., & Hur, G. (1992). Initiating and reciprocating verbal aggression: Effects on credibility and credited valid arguments. *Communication Studies* 43, 182–190.

Infante, D. A., & Rancer, A. S. (1982). A conceptualization and measure of argumentativeness. *Journal of Personality Assessment* 46, 72–80.

Infante, D. A., Rancer, A. S., & Jordan, F. F. (1996). Affirming and nonaffirming style, dyad sex, and the perception of argumentation and verbal aggression in an interpersonal dispute. *Human Communication Research* 22, 315–334.

Infante, D. A., Rancer, A. S., & Womack, D. F. (1996). *Building communication theory,* 3d ed. Prospect Heights, IL: Waveland Press.

Infante, D. A., Riddle, B. L., Horvath, C. L., & Tumlin, S. A. (1992). Verbal aggressiveness: Messages and reasons. *Communication Quarterly* 40, 116–126.

Infante, D. A., Sabourin, T. C., Rudd, J. E., & Shannon, E. A. (1990). Verbal aggression in violent and nonviolent marital disputes. *Communication Quarterly* 38, 361–371.

Infante, D. A., & Wigley, C. J. (1986). Verbal aggressiveness: An interpersonal model and measure. *Communication Monographs* 53, 61–69.

Ingram, M. P. B. (1998). A study of transformative aspects of career change experiences and implications for current models of career development, Ph.D. dissertation, Texas A&M University. *Dissertation Abstracts International Section A: Humanities and Social Sciences* 58, 4156.

Insel, P. M., & Jacobson, L. F., eds. (1975). *What do you expect? An inquiry into self-fulfilling prophecies.* Menlo Park, CA: Cummings.

Iverson, J. M., & Goldin-Meadow, S., eds. (1999). *The nature and functions of gesture in children's communication.* San Francisco: Jossey-Bass.

Ivy, D. K., & Backlund, P. (2000). *Exploring genderspeak: Personal effectiveness in gender communication,* 2d ed. New York: McGraw-Hill.

Jackson, L. A., & Ervin, K. S. (1992). Height stereotypes of women and men: The liabilities of shortness for both sexes. *Journal of Social Psychology* 132, 433–445.

Jacobson, D. (1999). Impression formation in cyberspace: Online expectations and offline experiences in text-based virtual communities. *Journal of Computer Mediated Communication* 5, np.

Jaksa, J. A., & Pritchard, M. S. (1994). *Communication ethics: Methods of analysis,* 2d ed. Belmont, CA: Wadsworth.

James, D. L. (1995). *The executive guide to Asia-Pacific communications.* New York: Kodansha International.

Jamieson, K. H., & Campbell, K. K. (2001). *The interplay of influence,* 5th ed. Belmont, CA: Wadsworth.

Jandt, F. E. (1995). *Intercultural communication.* Thousand Oaks, CA: Sage.

Jandt, F. E. (2001). *Intercultural communication,* 3d ed. Thousand Oaks, CA: Sage.

Jandt, F. E., & Nemnich, M. B. (1995). *Using the Internet in your job search.* Indianapolis, IN: Jist Works, Inc.

Janus, S. S., & Janus, C. L. (1993). *The Janus report on sexual behavior.* New York: Wiley.

Jaworski, A. (1993). *The power of silence: Social and pragmatic perspectives.* Thousand Oaks, CA: Sage.

Johannesen, R. L. (2001). *Ethics in human communication,* 5th ed. Prospect Heights, IL: Waveland Press.

Johansson, W., & Percy, W. A. (1994). *Outing: Shattering the conspiracy of silence.* New York: Harrington Park Press.

Johnson, C. E. (1987). An introduction to powerful and powerless talk in the classroom. *Communication Education* 36, 167–172.

Johnson, F. L., & Aries, E. J. (1983). The talk of women friends. *Women's Studies International Forum* 6, 353–361.

Johnson, S. D., & Bechler, C. (1998). Examining the relationship between listening effectiveness and leadership emergence: Perceptions, behaviors, and recall. *Small Group Research* 29, 452–471.

Joinson, A. N. (2001). Self-disclosure in computer-mediated communication: The role of self-awareness and visual anonymity. *European Journal of Social Psychology* 31, 177–192.

Jones, S. (1986). Sex differences in touch communication. *Western Journal of Speech Communication* 50, 227–241.

Jones, S., & Yarbrough, A. E. (1985). A naturalistic study of the meanings of touch. *Communication Monographs* 52, 19–56. A version of this paper appears in DeVito & Hecht (1990).

Jourard, S. M. (1968). *Disclosing man to himself.* New York: Van Nostrand Reinhold.

Jourard, S. M. (1971a). *Self-disclosure.* New York: Wiley.

Jourard, S. M. (1971b). *The transparent self.* Rev. ed. New York: Van Nostrand Reinhold.

Kanner, B. (1989). Color schemes. *New York Magazine* (April 3), 22–23.

Kapoor, S., Wolfe, A., & Blue, J. (1995). Universal values structure and individualism-collectivism: A U.S. test. *Communication Research Reports* 12, 112–123.

Kassing, J. W. (1997). Development of the intercultural willingness to communicate scale. *Communication Research Reports* 14, 399–407.

Kearney, P., Plax, T. G., Richmond, V. P., & McCroskey, J. C. (1984). Power in the classroom IV: Alternatives to discipline. In *Communication yearbook 8,* R. N. Bostrom (ed.). Thousand Oaks, CA: Sage, pp. 724–746.

Kearney, P., Plax, T. G., Richmond, V. P., & McCroskey, J. C. (1985). Power in the classroom III: Teacher communication techniques and messages. *Communication Education* 34, 19–28.

Keating, C. F., Mazur, A., & Segall, M. H. (1977). Facial gestures which influence the perception of status. *Sociometry* 40, 374–378.

Kennedy, C. W., & Camden, C. T. (1988). A new look at interruptions. *Western Journal of Speech Communication* 47, 45–58.

Keyes, K., Jr., & Keyes, P. (1987). *Gathering power through insight and love.* St. Mary, KY: Living Love.

Keyes, R. (1980). *The height of your life.* New York: Warner Books.

Kim, M., & Sharkey, W. F. (1995). Independent and interdependent construals of self: Explaining cultural patterns of interpersonal communication in multicultural organizational settings. *Communication Quarterly* 43, 20–38.

Kim, S. H., & Smith, R. H. (1993). Revenge and conflict escalation. *Negotiation Journal* 9, 37–43.

Kim, Y. Y. (1991). Intercultural communication competence. In *Cross-cultural interpersonal communication,* S. Ting-Toomey & F. Korzenny (eds.). Thousand Oaks, CA: Sage, pp. 259–275.

Kirkpatrick, C., & Caplow, T. (1945). Courtship in a group of Minnesota students. *American Journal of Sociology* 51, 114–125.

Kivik, P. K. (1998). What silence says: Communicative style and identity. *Trames* 2 (1), 66–90.

Kleinfield, N. R. (1992). The smell of money. *New York Times* (October 25), 1, 8.

Kleinke, C. L. (1986). *Meeting and understanding people.* New York: W. H. Freeman.

Klineberg, O., & Hull, W. F. (1979). *At a foreign university: An international study of adaptation and coping.* New York: Praeger.

Knapp, M. L., Ellis, D., & Williams, B. A. (1980). Perceptions of communication behavior associated with relationship terms. *Communication Monographs* 47, 262–278.

Knapp, M. L., & Hall, J. (2002). *Nonverbal behavior in human interaction,* 3d ed. New York: Holt, Rinehart & Winston.

Knapp, M. L., & Taylor, E. H. (1994). Commitment and its communication in romantic relationships. In *Perspectives on close relationships,* A. L. Weber & J. H. Harvey (eds.). Boston: Allyn & Bacon, pp. 153–175.

Knapp, M. L., & Vangelisti, A. (2000). *Interpersonal communication and human relationships,* 4th ed. Boston: Allyn & Bacon.

Knobloch, L. K., & Solomon, D. H. (1999). Measuring the sources and content of relational uncertainty. *Communication Studies* 50 (winter), 261–278.

Knox, D., Daniels, V., Sturdivant, L., & Zusman, M. E. (2001). College student use of the Internet for mate selection. *College Student Journal* 35, 158–160.

Kochman, T. (1981). *Black and white: Styles in conflict.* Chicago: University of Chicago Press.

Komarovsky, M. (1964). *Blue collar marriage.* New York: Random House.

Korda, M. (1975). *Power! How to get it, how to use it.* New York: Ballantine.

Korzybski, A. (1933). *Science and sanity.* Lakeville, CT: The International Non-Aristotelian Library.

Kramer, R. (1997). Leading by listening: An empirical test of Carl Rogers's theory of human relationship using interpersonal assessments of leaders by followers. *Dissertation Abstracts, International Section A. Humanities and Social Sciences* 58, 514.

Kraut, R., et al. (1999). Internet paradox. *American Psychologist* 53, 1017–1031.

Krebs, G. L. (1989). *Organizational communication,* 2d ed. Boston: Allyn & Bacon.

Kurdek, L. A. (1994). Areas of conflict for gay, lesbian, and heterosexual couples: What couples argue about influences relationship satisfaction. *Journal of Marriage and the Family* 56, 923–934.

Kurdek, L. A. (1995). Developmental changes in relationship quality in gay and lesbian cohabiting couples. *Developmental Psychology* 31, 86–93.

Laing, M. (1993). Gossip: Does it play a role in the socialization of nurses? *Journal of Nursing Scholarship* 25, 37–43.

Lakoff, R. (1975). *Language and women's place.* New York: Harper & Row.

Langer, E. J. (1989). *Mindfulness.* Reading, MA: Addison-Wesley.

Lantz, A. (2001). Meetings in a distributed group of experts: Comparing face-to-face, chat and collaborative virtual environments. *Behaviour and Information Technology* 20, 111–117.

Lanzetta, J. T., Cartwright-Smith, J., & Kleck, R. E. (1976). Effects of nonverbal dissimulations on emotional experience and autonomic arousal. *Journal of Personality and Social Psychology* 33, 354–370.

Laroche, C., & deGrace, G. R. (1997). Factors of satisfaction associated with happiness in adults. *Canadian Journal of Counseling* 31, 275–286.

Larsen, R. J., Kasimatis, M., & Frey, K. (1992). Facilitating the furrowed brow: An unobtrusive test of the facial feedback hypothesis applied to unpleasant affect. *Cognition and Emotion* 6, 321–338.

Lau, I., Chiu, C., & Hong, Y. (2001). I know what you know: Assumptions about others' knowledge and their effects on message construction. *Social Cognition* 19, 587–600.

Lea, M., & Spears, R. (1995). Love at first byte? Building personal relationships over computer networks. In *Under-studied relationships: Off the beaten track,* J. T. Wood & S. Duck (eds.). Thousand Oaks, CA: Sage, pp. 197–233.

Leaper, C., Carson, M., Baker, C., Holliday, H., et al. (1995). Self-disclosure and listener verbal support in same-gender and cross-gender friends' conversations. *Sex Roles* 33, 387–404.

Leaper, C., & Holliday, H. (1995). Gossip in same-gender and cross-gender friends' conversations. *Personal Relationships* 2, 237–246.

Leathers, D. G. (1997). *Successful nonverbal communication: Principles and applications,* 3d ed. New York: Macmillan.

Lederer, W. J. (1984). *Creating a good relationship.* New York: Norton.

Lederer, W. J., & Jackson, D. D. (1968). *The mirages of marriage.* New York: Norton.

Lee, A. M., & Lee, E. B. (1972). *The fine art of propaganda.* San Francisco: International Society for General Semantics.

Lee, A. M., & Lee, E. B. (1995). The iconography of propaganda analysis. *ETC.: A Review of General Semantics* 52 (spring), 13–17.

Lee, F. (1993). Being polite and keeping MUM: How bad news is communicated in organizational hierarchies. *Journal of Applied Social Psychology* 23, 1124–1149.

Lee, H. O., & Boster, F. J. (1992). Collectivism-individualism in perceptions of speech rate: A cross-cultural comparison. *Journal of Cross-Cultural Psychology* 23, 377–388.

Lee, J. A. (1976). *The colors of love.* New York: Bantam.

Lee, K. (2000). Information overload threatens employee productivity. *Employee Benefit News* (November 1), p. 1.

Lemieux, R., & Hale, J. L. (1999). Intimacy, passion, and commitment in young romantic relationships: Successfully measuring the triangular theory of love. *Psychological Reports* 85, 497–503.

Lemieux, R., & Hale, J. L. (2001). Intimacy, passion, and commitment among married individuals: Further testing of the triangular theory of love. *Psychological Reports* 89, 25–26.

Leon, J. J., Philbrick, J. L., Parra, F., Escobedo, E., et al. (1994). Love styles among university students in Mexico. *Psychological Reports* 74, 307–310.

Leung, K. (1987). Some determinants of reactions to procedural models for conflict resolution: A cross-national study. *Journal of Personality and Social Psychology* 53, 898–908.

Leung, K. (1988). Some determinants of conflict avoidance. *Journal of Cross-Cultural Psychology* 19, 125–136.

Lever, J. (1995). The 1995 Advocate survey of sexuality and relationships: The women, lesbian sex survey. *The Advocate* 687/688, 22–30.

Levine, D. (2000). Virtual attraction: What rocks your boat. *CyberPsychology and Behavior* 3, 565–573.

LeVine, R., Bartlett, K. (1984). Pace of life, punctuality, and coronary heart disease in six countries. *Journal of Cross-Cultural Psychology* 15, 233–255.

LeVine, R., Sato, S., Hashimoto, T., & Verma, J. (1994). Love and marriage in eleven cultures. Unpublished manuscript. California State University, Fresno, cited in Hatfield & Rapson (1996).

Lewin, K. (1947). *Human relations.* New York: Harper & Row.

Lewis, D. (1989). *The secret language of success.* New York: Carroll & Graf.

Lewis, P. H. (1995). The new Internet gatekeepers. *New York Times* (November 13), D1, D6.

Lindblom, K. (2001). Cooperating with Grice: A cross-disciplinary metaperspective on uses of Grice's cooperative principle. *Journal of Pragmatics* 33, 1601–1623.

Lindeman, M., Harakka, T., & Keltikangas-Jarvinen, L. (1997). Age and gender differences in adolescents' reactions to conflict situations: Aggression, prosociality, and withdrawal. *Journal of Youth and Adolescence* 26, 339–351.

Littlejohn, S. W. (1996). *Theories of human communication,* 6th ed. Belmont, CA: Wadsworth.

Lloyd, S. R. (2001). *Developing positive assertiveness,* 3d ed. Menlo Park, CA: Crisp Publications.

Lu, L., & Shih, J. B. (1997). Sources of happiness: A qualitative approach. *Journal of Social Psychology* 137, 181–188.

Luft, J. (1969). *Of human interaction.* Palo Alto, CA: Mayfield.

Luft, J. (1984). *Group processes: An introduction to group dynamics,* 3d ed. Palo Alto, CA: Mayfield.

Lujansky, H., & Mikula, G. (1983). Can equity theory explain the quality and stability of romantic relationships? *British Journal of Social Psychology* 22, 101–112.

Lukens, J. (1978). Ethnocentric speech. *Ethnic Groups* 2, 35–53.

Lurie, A. (1983). *The language of clothes.* New York: Vintage.

Lustig, M. W., & Koester, J. (1999). *Intercultural competence: Interpersonal communication across cultures,* 3d ed. Boston: Allyn & Bacon.

Ma, K. (1996). *The modern Madame Butterfly: Fantasy and reality in Japanese cross-cultural relationships.* Rutland, VT: Charles E. Tuttle.

Ma, R. (1992). The role of unofficial intermediaries in interpersonal conflicts in the Chinese culture. *Communication Quarterly* 40, 269–278.

Mackey, R. A., Diemer, M. A., & O'Brien, B. A. (2000). Psychological intimacy in the lasting relationships of heterosexual and same-gender couples. *Sex Roles* 43, 201–227.

MacLachlan, J. (1979). What people really think of fast talkers. *Psychology Today* 13, 113–117.

Maggio, R. (1997). *Talking about people: A guide to fair and accurate language.* Phoenix, AZ: Oryx Press.

Main, F., & Oliver, R. (1988). Complementary, symmetrical, and parallel personality priorities as indicators of marital adjustment. *Individual Psychology Journal of Adlerian Theory, Research, and Practice* 44, 324–332.

Malandro, L. A., Barker, L. L., & Barker, D. A. (1989). *Nonverbal communication,* 2d ed. New York: Random House.

Malinowski, B. (1923). The problem of meaning in primitive languages. In *The Meaning of Meaning,* C. K. Ogden & I. A. Richards (eds.). New York: Harcourt Brace Jovanovich, pp. 296–336.

Manes, J., & Wolfson, N. (1981). The compliment formula. In *Conversational Routine,* Florian Coulmas (ed.). The Hague: Mouton, pp. 115–132.

Mao, L. R. (1994). Beyond politeness theory: "Face" revisited and renewed. *Journal of Pragmatics* 21, 451–486.

Markway, B. G., Carmin, C. N., Pollard, C. A., & Flynn, T. (1992). *Dying of embarrassment: Help for social anxiety and phobia.* Oakland, CA: New Harbinger Publications.

Marsh, P. (1988). *Eye to eye: How people interact.* Topside, MA: Salem House.

Marshall, E. (1983). *Eye language: Understanding the eloquent eye.* New York: New Trend.

Marshall, L. L., & Rose, P. (1987). Gender, stress, and violence in the adult relationships of a sample of college students. *Journal of Social and Personal Relationships* 4, 229–316.

Marston, P. J., Hecht, M. L., & Robers, T. (1987). True love ways: The subjective experience and communication of romantic love. *Journal of Personal and Social Relationships* 4, 387–407.

Martin, G. N. (1998). Human electroencephalographic (EEG) response to olfactory stimulation: Two experiments using the aroma of food. *International Journal of Psychophysiology* 30, 287–302.

Martin, M. M., & Anderson, C. M. (1995). Roommate similarity: Are roommates who are similar in their communication traits more satisfied? *Communication Research Reports* 12, 46–52.

Martin, M. M., & Anderson, C. M. (1998). The cognitive flexibility scale: Three validity studies. *Communication Reports* 11 (winter), 1–9.

Martin, M. M., & Rubin, R. B. (1995). A new measure of cognitive flexibility. *Psychological Reports* 76, 623–626.

Marwell, G., & Schmitt, D. R. (1967). Dimensions of compliance-gaining behavior: An empirical analysis. *Sociometry* 39, 350–364.

Marwell, G., & Schmitt, D. R. (1990). An introduction. In *Seeking compliance: The production of interpersonal influence messages,* J. P. Dillard (ed.). Scottsdale, AZ.: Gorsuch Scarisbrick, pp. 3–5.

Masheter, C., & Harris, L. M. (1986). From divorce to friendship: A study of dialectic relationship development. *Journal of Social and Personal Relationships* 3, 177–189.

Maslow, A., & Mintz, N. L. (1956). Effects of esthetic surroundings: I. Initial effects of three esthetic conditions upon perceiving energy and well-being in faces. *Journal of Psychology* 41, 247–254.

Mastin, T. (1998). Employees' understanding of employer-sponsored retirement plans: A knowledge gap perspective. *Public Relations Review* 24 (winter), 521–534.

Matsumoto, D. (1991). Cultural influences on facial expressions of emotion. *Southern Communication Journal* 56, 128–137.

Matsumoto, D. (1994). *People: Psychology from a cultural perspective.* Pacific Grove, CA: Brooks/Cole.

Matsumoto, D. (1996). *Culture and psychology.* Pacific Grove, CA: Brooks/Cole.

Matsumoto, D., & Kudoh, T. (1993). American-Japanese cultural differences in attributions of personality based on smiles. *Journal of Nonverbal Behavior* 17, 231–243.

Maynard, H. E. (1963). How to become a better premise detective. *Public Relations Journal* 19, 20–22.

McBroom, W. H., & Reed, F. W. (1992). Toward a reconceptualization of attitude-behavior consistency. Special Issue. Theoretical advances in social psychology. *Social Psychology Quarterly* 55, 205–216.

McCroskey, J. C. (1997). *Introduction to rhetorical communication,* 7th ed. Englewood Cliffs, NJ: Prentice-Hall.

McCroskey, J. C., Booth-Butterfield, S., & Payne, S. K. (1989). The impact of communication apprehension on college student retention and success. *Communication Quarterly* 37, 100–107.

McCroskey, J. C., & Daly, J., eds. (1987). *Personality and interpersonal communication.* Thousand Oaks, CA: Sage.

McCroskey, J. C., & Richmond, V. P. (1990). Willingness to communicate: Differing cultural perspectives. *Southern Communication Journal* 56, 72–77.

McCroskey, J. C., & Wheeless, L. (1976). *Introduction to human communication.* Boston: Allyn & Bacon.

McGill, M. E. (1985). *The McGill report on male intimacy.* New York: Harper & Row.

McLaughlin, M. L. (1984). *Conversation: How talk is organized.* Thousand Oaks, CA: Sage.

McLaughlin, M. L., Cody, M. L., & Robey, C. S. (1980). Situational influences on the selection of strategies to resist compliance-gaining attempts. *Human Communication Research* 1, 14–36.

McLean, P. A., & Jones, B. D. (1992). Machiavellianism and business education. *Psychological Reports* 71, 57–58.

McLoyd, V. C., & Wilson, L. (1992). Telling them like it is: The role of economic and environmental factors in single mothers' discussions with their children. *American Journal of Community Psychology* 20, 419–444.

McNamee, S., & Gergen, K. J., eds. (1999). *Relational responsibility: Resources for sustainable dialogue.* Thousand Oaks, CA: Sage.

McNatt, D. B. (2001). Ancient Pygmalion joins contemporary management: A meta-analysis of the result. *Journal of Applied Psychology* 85, 314–322.

Meeks, B. S., Hendrick, S. S., & Hendrick, C. (1998). Communication, love and relationship satisfaction. *Journal of Social and Personal Relationships* 15, 755–773.

Merton, R. K. (1957). *Social theory and social structure.* New York: Free Press.

Messick, R. M., & Cook, K. S., eds. (1983). *Equity theory: Psychological and sociological perspectives.* New York: Praeger.

Messmer, M. (1999). Skills for a new millennium: Accounting and financial professionals. *Strategic Finance Magazine* (August), 10ff.

Metts, S. (1989). An exploratory investigation of deception in close relationships. *Journal of Social and Personal Relationships* 6, 159–179.

Metz, M. E., Rosser, B. R., & Strapko, N. (1994). Differences in conflict resolution styles among heterosexual, gay, and lesbian couples. *Journal of Sex Research* 31, 293–308.

Meyer, J. R. (1994). Effect of situational features on the likelihood of addressing face needs in requests. *Southern Communication Journal* 59, 240–254.

Midooka, K. (1990). Characteristics of Japanese style communication. *Media, Culture and Society* 12, 477–489.

Miller, G. R., & Parks, M. R. (1982). Communication in dissolving relationships. In *Personal relationships 4. Dissolving personal relationships,* S. Duck (ed.). New York: Academic Press, pp. 127–154.

Miller, J. G. (1984). Culture and the development of everyday social explanation. *Journal of Personality and Social Psychology* 46, 961–978.

Miller, M. J., & Wilcox, C. T. (1986). Measuring perceived hassles and uplifts among the elderly. *Journal of Human Behavior and Learning* 3, 38–46.

Miller, S., & Weckert, J. (2000). Privacy, the workplace and the Internet. *Journal of Business Ethics* 28, 255–266.

Mintz, N. L. (1956). Effects of esthetic surroundings: II. Prolonged and repeated experience in a beautiful and ugly room. *Journal of Psychology* 41, 459–466.

Moen, P., Jim, J. E., & Hofmeister, H. (2001). Couples' work/retirement transitions, gender, and marital quality. *Social Psychology Quarterly* 64, 55–71.

Moghaddam, F. M., Taylor, D. M., & Wright, S. C. (1993). *Social psychology in cross cultural perspective.* New York: W. H. Freeman.

Mole, J. (1990). *When in Rome . . . A business guide to cultures and customs in 12 European nations.* New York: American Management Association.

Mole, J. (1998). *Mind your manners: Managing business cultures in Europe.* London: Nicholas Brealey Publishing.

Molloy, J. (1981). *Molloy's live for success.* New York: Bantam.

Moon, D. G. (1966). Concepts of "culture": Implications for intercultural communication research. *Communication Quarterly* 44, 70–84.

Moore, A., Masterson, J. T., Christophel, D. M., & Shea, K. A. (1996). College teacher immediacy and student ratings of instruction. *Communication Education* 45, 29–39.

Moore, S., Ward, M., & Katz, B. (1998). Machiavellianism and tolerance of ambiguity. *Psychological Reports* 82, 415–418.

Moreland, R. L., & Beach, R. (1992). Exposure effects in the classroom: The development of affinity among students. *Journal of Experimental Social Psychology* 28, 255–276.

Morgan, M., & Shanahan, J. (1991). Television and the cultivation of political attitudes in Argentina. *Journal of Communication* 41 (winter), 70–84.

Morreale, S. P., Osborn, M. M., & Pearson, J. C. (2000). Why communication is important: A rationale for the centrality of the study of communication. *Journal of the Association for Communication Administration* 29 (January), 1–25.

Morrill, C. (1992). Vengeance among executives. *Virginia Review of Sociology* 1, 51–76.

Morris, D. (1977). *Manwatching: A field guide to human behavior.* New York: Abrams.

Morrow, G. D., Clark, E. M., & Brock, K. F. (1995). Individual and partner love styles: Implications for the quality of romantic involvements. *Journal of Social and Personal Relationships* 12, 363–387.

Motley, M. T. (1990a). On whether one can(not) not communicate: An examination via traditional communication postulates. *Western Journal of Speech Communication* 54, 1–20.

Motley, M. T. (1990b). Communication as interaction: A reply to Beach and Bavelas. *Western Journal of Speech Communication* 54, 613–623.

Murstein, B. I., Merighi, J. R., & Vyse, S. A. (1991). Love styles in the United States and France: A cross-cultural comparison. *Journal of Social and Clinical Psychology* 10, 37–46.

Myers, S. A. (1995). Student perceptions of teacher affinity-seeking and classroom climate. *Communication Research Reports* 12, 192–199.

Naifeh, S., & Smith, G. W. (1984). *Why can't men open up? Overcoming men's fear of intimacy.* New York: Clarkson N. Potter.

Neimeyer, R. A., & Mitchell, K. A. (1988). Similarity and attraction: A longitudinal study. *Journal of Social and Personal Relationships* 5, 131–148.

Neimeyer, R. A., & Neimeyer, G. J. (1983). Structural similarity in the acquaintance process. *Journal of Social and Clinical Psychology* 1, 146–154.

Nelson, G. L., Al Batal, M., & El Bakary, W. (2002). Directness vs. indirectness: Egyptian Arabic and U.S. English communication style. *International Journal of Intercultural Relations* 26, 39–57.

Neugarten, B. (1979). Time, age, and the life cycle. *American Journal of Psychiatry* 136, 887–894.

Neuliep, J. W., & McCroskey, J. C. (1997). The development of a U.S. and generalized ethnocentrism scale. *Communication Research Reports* 14, 385–398.

Nice, M. L., & Katzev, R. (1998). Internet romances: The frequency and nature of romantic online relationships. *CyberPsychology and Behavior* 1, 217–223.

Nicotera, A. M., & Rancer, A. S. (1994). The influence of sex on self-perceptions and social stereotyping of aggressive communication predispositions. *Western Journal of Communication* 58, 283–307.

Noelle-Neumann, E. (1973). Return to the concept of powerful mass media. In *Studies in broadcasting: An international annual of broadcasting science,* H. Eguchi & K. Sata (eds.). Tokyo: Nippon Hoso Kyokai, pp. 67–112.

Noelle-Neumann, E. (1980). Mass media and social change in developed societies. In *Mass communication review yearbook,* Vol. 1, G. C. Wilhoit & H. de Bock (eds.). Thousand Oaks, CA: Sage, pp. 657–678.

Noelle-Neumann, E. (1991). The theory of public opinion: The concept of the spiral of silence. *Communication yearbook/14,* J. A. Anderson (ed.). Thousand Oaks, CA: Sage, pp. 256–287.

Noller, P., & Fitzpatrick, M. A. (1993). *Communication in family relationships.* Englewood Cliffs, NJ: Prentice-Hall.

Nordhaus-Bike, A. M. (1999). Learning to lead. *Hospitals & Health Networks* 73, 28ff.

Norton, R., & Warnick, B. (1976). Assertiveness as a communication construct. *Human Communication Research* 3, 62–66.

Ober, C., Weitkamp, L. R., Cox, N., Dytch, H., Kostyu, D., & Elias, S. (1997). *American Journal of Human Genetics* 61, 494–496.

Oberg, K. (1960). Cultural shock: Adjustment to new cultural environments. *Practical Anthropology* 7, 177–182.

Oetzel, J., Ting-Toomey, S., Masumoto, T., Yokochi, Y., Pan, X., Takai, J., & Wilcox, R. (2001). Face and facework in conflict: A cross-cultural comparison of China, Germany, Japan, and the United States. *Communication Monographs* 68, 235–258.

O'Hair, M. J., Cody, M. J., & O'Hair, D. (1991). The impact of situational dimensions on compliance-resisting strategies: A comparison of methods. *Communication Quarterly* 39, 226–240.

Olaniran, B. A. (1994). Group performance in computer-mediated and face-to-face communication media. *Management Communication Quarterly* 7, 256–281.

Olson, E. (2002). Switzerland tells its men: Wash that pot! Mop that floor! *New York Times,* A14.

Palmer, M. T. (1989). Controlling conversations: Turns, topics, and interpersonal control. *Communication Monographs* 56, 1–18.

Papa, M. J., & Natalle, E. J. (1989). Gender, strategy selection, and discussion satisfaction in interpersonal conflict. *Western Journal of Speech Communication* 53, 260–272.

Parker, R. G., & Parrott, R. (1995). Patterns of self-disclosure across social support networks: Elderly, middle-aged, and young adults. *International Journal of Aging and Human Development* 41, 281–297.

Parks, M. R. (1995). Webs of influence in interpersonal relationships. In *Communication and social influence processes,* C. R. Berger & M. E. Burgoon (eds.). East Lansing: Michigan State University Press, pp. 155–178.

Parks, M. R., & Floyd, K. (1996). Making friends in cyberspace. *Journal of Communication* 46, 80–97.

Parks, M. R., & Roberts, L. D. (1998). "Making MOOsic": The development of personal relationships online and a comparison to their off-line counterparts. *Journal of Social and Personal Relationships* 15, 517–537.

Pasley, K., Kerpelman, J., & Guilbert, D. E. (2001). Gendered conflict, identity disruption, and marital instability: Expanding Gottman's model. *Journal of Personal and Social Relationships* 18, 5–27.

Patton, T. O. (2001). Ally McBeal and her homies: The reification of White stereotypes of the other. *Journal of Black Studies* 32, 229–260.

Paul, A. M. (2001). Self-help: Shattering the myths. *Psychology Today* 34, 60ff.

Payne, K. E. (2001). *Different but equal: Communication between the sexes.* Westport, CT: Praeger.

Pearson, J. C. (1993). *Communication in the family,* 2d ed. Boston: Allyn & Bacon.

Pearson, J. C., & Spitzberg, B. H. (1990). *Interpersonal communication: Concepts, components, and contexts,* 2d ed. Dubuque, IA: William C. Brown.

Pearson, J. C., Turner, L. H., & Todd-Mancillas, W. (1991). *Gender and communication,* 2d ed. Dubuque, IA: William C. Brown.

Pearson, J. C., West, R., & Turner, L. H. (1995). *Gender and communication,* 3d ed. Dubuque, IA: William C. Brown.

Penfield, J., ed. (1987). *Women and language in transition.* Albany: State University of New York Press.

Pennebacker, J. W. (1991). *Opening up: The healing power of confiding in others.* New York: Morrow.

Peplau, L. A. (1988). Research on homosexual couples: An overview. In *Gay relationships,* J. DeCecco (ed.). New York: Harrington Park Press, pp. 33–40.

Perse, E. M., & Rubin, R. B. (1989). Attribution in social and parasocial relationships. *Communication Research* 16 (February), 59–77.

Petrocelli, W., & Repa, B. K. (1992). *Sexual harassment on the job.* Berkeley, CA: Nolo Press.

Phlegar, P. (1995). *Love online: A practical guide to digital dating.* Reading, MA: Addison-Welsey.

Pierce, C. A., & Aguinis, H. (2001). A framework for investigating the link between workplace romance and sexual harassment. *Group and Organization Management* 26, 206–229.

Pilkington, C. J., & Richardson, D. R. (1988). Perceptions of risk in intimacy. *Journal of Social and Personal Relationships* 5, 503–508.

Pilkington, C. J., & Woods, S. P. (1999). Risk in intimacy as a chronically accessible schema. *Journal of Social and Personal Relationships* 16, 249–263.

Pinker, S. (1994). *The language instinct: How the mind creates language.* New York: Morrow.

Piot, C. D. (1993). Secrecy, ambiguity, and the everyday in Kabre culture. *American Anthropologist* 95, 353–370.

Pollack, A. (1995). A cyberspace front in a multicultural war. *New York Times* (August 7), D1, D4.

Pollack, A. (1996). Happy in the East (^—^) or smiling (:—) in the West. *New York Times* (August 12), D5.

Porter, R. H., & Moore, J. D. (1981). Human kin recognition by olfactory cues. *Physiology and Behavior* 27, 493–495.

Porter, S., Birt, A. R., Juille, J. C., & Lehman, D. R. (2000). Negotiating false memories: Interviewer and rememberer characteristics relate to memory distortion. *Psychological Science* 11 (November), 507–510.

Postman, N., & Powers, S. (1992). *How to watch TV news.* New York: Penguin.

Potter, W. J. (1986). Perceived reality and the cultivation hypothesis. *Journal of Broadcasting and Electronic Media* 30, 159–174.

Potter, W. J., & Chang, I. C. (1990). Television exposure measures and the cultivation hypothesis. *Journal of Broadcasting and Electronic Media* 34, 313–333.

Powers, W. G., & Love, D. E. (2000). Communication apprehension in the dating partner context. *Communication Research Reports* 17, 221–228.

Pratkanis, A., & Aronson, E. (1991). *Age of propaganda: The everyday use and abuse of persuasion.* New York: W. H. Freeman.

Prins, K. S., Buunk, B. P., & Van Yperen, N. W. (1994). Equity, normative disapproval, and extramarital sex. *Journal of Social and Personal Relationships* 10, 39–53.

Prosky, P. S. (1992). Complementary and symmetrical couples. *Family Therapy* 19, 215–221.

Prusank, D. T., Duran, R. L., & DeLillo, D. A. (1993). Interpersonal relationships in women's magazines: Dating and relating in the 1970s and 1980s. *Journal of Social and Personal Relationships* 10, 307–320.

Purnell, R. B. (1982). Teaching them to curse: A study of certain types of inherent racial bias in language pedagogy and practices. *Phylon* 43, 231–241.

Rabinowitz, F. E. (1991). The male-to-male embrace: Breaking the touch taboo in a men's therapy group. *Journal of Counseling and Development* 69, 574–576.

Radford, M. H., Mann, L., Ohta, Y., & Nakane, Y. (1993). Differences between Australian and Japanese students in decisional self-esteem, decisional stress, and coping styles. *Journal of Cross-Cultural Psychology* 24, 284–297.

Rahim, M. A., Antonioni, D., Krumov, J., & Ilieva, S. (2000). Power, conflict, and effectiveness: A cross-cultural study in the United States and Bulgaria. *European Psychologist* 5, 28–33.

Rancer, A. S. (1998). Argumentativeness. In *Communication and Personality: Trait Perspectives,* J. C. McCroskey, J. A. Daly, M. M. Martin, & M. J. Beatty (eds.). Cresskill, NJ: Hampton Press, pp. 149–170.

Rancer, A. S., Kosberg, R. L., & Baukus, R. A. (1992). Beliefs about arguing as predictors of trait argumentativeness: Implications for training in argument and conflict management. *Communication Education* 41, 375–387.

Raney, R. F. (2000). Study finds Internet of social benefit to users. *New York Times* (May 11), G7.

Rankin, P. (1929). Listening ability. *Proceedings of the Ohio State Educational Conference's Ninth Annual Session.*

Rappaport, H., Enrich, K., & Wilson, A. (1985). Relation between ego identity and temporal perspective.

Journal of Personality and Social Psychology 48, 1609–1620.

Raven, B., Centers, C., & Rodrigues, A. (1975). The bases of conjugal power. In *Power in families,* R. E. Cromwell & D. H. Olson (eds.). New York: Halsted Press, pp. 217–234.

Raven, B. H., Schwarzwald, J., & Koslowsky, M. (1998). Conceptualizing and measuring a power/interaction model of interpersonal influence. *Journal of Applied Social Psychology* 28, 307–332.

Rawlins, W. K. (1983). Negotiating close friendship: The dialectic of conjunctive freedoms. *Human Communication Research* 9, 255–266.

Reardon, K. K. (1987). *Where minds meet: Interpersonal communication.* Belmont, CA: Wadsworth.

Rector, M., & Neiva, E. (1996). Communication and personal relationships in Brazil. In *Communication in personal relationships across cultures,* W. B. Gudykunst, S. Ting-Toomey, & T. Nishida (eds.). Thousand Oaks, CA: Sage, pp. 156–173.

Regan, P. C., Kocan, E. R., & Whitlock, T. (1998). Ain't love grand! A prototype analysis of the concept of romantic love. *Journal of Social and Personal Relationships* 15, 411–420.

Reik, T. (1944). *A psychologist looks at love.* New York: Rinehart.

Reisman, J. (1979). *Anatomy of friendship.* Lexington, MA: Lewis.

Reisman, J. M. (1981). Adult friendships. In *Personal relationships. 2: Developing personal relationships,* S. Duck & R. Gilmour (eds.). New York: Academic Press, pp. 205–230.

Rezabeck, L. L., & Cochenour, J. J. (1995). Emoticons: Visual cues for computer-mediated communication. In *Imagery and Visual Literacy: Selected Readings from the Annual Conference of the International Visual Literacy Association* (Tempe, Arizona, October 12–16). Eric Document No. ED380096.

Rich, A. L. (1974). *Interracial communication.* New York: Harper & Row.

Richards, I. A. (1951). Communication between men: The meaning of language. In *Cybernetics, Transactions of the Eighth Conference,* Heinz von Foerster (ed.).

Richmond, V. P., Davis, L. M., Saylor, K., & McCroskey, J. C. (1984). Power strategies in organizations: Communication techniques and messages. *Human Communication Research* 11, 85–108.

Richmond, V. P., & McCroskey, J. C. (1984). Power in the classroom II: Power and learning. *Communication Education* 33, 125–136.

Richmond, V. P., & McCroskey, J. C. (1999). *Communication: Apprehension, avoidance, and effectiveness,* 5th ed. Boston: Allyn & Bacon.

Riggio, R. E. (1987). *The charisma quotient.* New York: Dodd, Mead.

Rockwell, P., Buller, D. B., & Burgoon, J. K. (1997). The voice of deceit: Refining and expanding vocal cues to deception. *Communication Research Reports* 14, 451–459.

Rodman, G. (2001). *Making sense of media: An introduction to mass communication.* Boston: Allyn & Bacon.

Roeher Institute (1995). *Harm's way: The many faces of violence and abuse against persons with disabilities.* North York (Ontario): Roeher Institute.

Roger, D., & Nesshoever, W. (1987). Individual differences in dyadic conversational strategies: A further study. *British Journal of Social Psychology* 26, 247–255.

Rogers, C. (1970). *Carl Rogers on encounter groups.* New York: Harrow Books.

Rogers, C., & Farson, R. (1981). Active listening. In *Communication: Concepts and Processes,* 3d ed., J. DeVito (ed.). Englewood Cliffs, NJ: Prentice-Hall, pp. 137–147.

Rogers, E. M. (1995). *Diffusion of innovations,* 4th ed. New York: Free Press.

Rohlfing, M. E. (1995). "Doesn't anybody stay in one place anymore?" An exploration of the under-studied phenomenon of long-distance relationships. In *Under-studied relationships: Off the beaten track,* J. T. Wood & S. Duck (eds.). Thousand Oaks, CA: Sage, pp. 173–196.

Rokach, A. (1998). The relation of cultural background to the causes of loneliness. *Journal of Social and Clinical Psychology* 17, 75–88.

Rokach, A., & Brock, H. (1995). The effects of gender, marital status, and the chronicity and immediacy of loneliness. *Journal of Social Behavior and Personality* 19, 833–848.

Rollman, J. B., Krug, K., & Parente, F. (2000). The chat room phenomenon: Reciprocal communication in cyberspace. *CyberPsychology and Behavior* 3, 161–166.

Ronfeldt, H. M., Kimerling, R., & Arias, I. (1998). Satisfaction with relationship power and the perpetration of dating violence. *Journal of Marriage and the Family* 60 (February), 70–78.

Rosen, E. (1998). Think like a shrink. *Psychology Today* (October), 54–59.

Rosenbaum, M. E. (1986). The repulsion hypothesis. On the nondevelopment of relationships. *Journal of Personality and Social Psychology* 51, 1156–1166.

Rosenfeld, L. (1979). Self-disclosure avoidance: Why I am afraid to tell you who I am. *Communication Monographs* 46, 63–74.

Rosengren, A., et al. (1993). Stressful life events, social support, and mortality in men born in 1933. *British Medical Journal* (October 19). Cited in Goleman (1995a).

Rosenthal, R., & Jacobson, L. (1968). *Pygmalion in the classroom*. New York: Holt, Rinehart & Winston.

Ross, J. L. (1995). Conversational pitchbacks: Helping couples bat 1000 in the game of communications. *Journal of Family Psychotherapy* 6, 83–86.

Rothblum, E. D., & Bond, L. A. (1996). *Preventing heterosexism and homophobia*. Thousand Oaks, CA: Sage.

Rowatt, W. C., Cunningham, M. R., & Druen, P. B. (1999). Lying to get a date: The effect of facial physical attractiveness on the willingness to deceive prospective dating partners. *Journal of Social and Personal Relationships* 16, 209–223.

Rowland-Morin, P. A., & Carroll, J. G. (1990). Verbal communication skills and patient satisfaction: A study of doctor-patient interviews. *Evaluation and the Health Professions* 13, 168–185.

Ruben, B. D. (1985). Human communication and cross-cultural effectiveness. In *Intercultural Communication: A Reader,* 4th ed., L. A. Samovar & R. E. Porter (eds.). Belmont, CA: Wadsworth, pp. 338–346.

Rubenstein, C. (1993). Fighting sexual harassment in schools. *New York Times* (June 10), C8.

Rubin, A., Pearse, E., & Powell, R. (1985). Loneliness, parasocial interaction, and local television news viewing. *Human Communication Research* 12, 155–180.

Rubin, D. C., Groth, E., & Goldsmith, D. J. (1984). Olfactory cues of autobiographical memory. *American Journal of Psychology* 97, 493–507.

Rubin, R. B., Fernandez-Collado, C., & Hernandez-Sampieri, R. (1992). A cross-cultural examination of interpersonal communication motives in Mexico and the United States. *International Journal of Intercultural Relations* 16, 145–157.

Rubin, R. B., & Graham, E. E. (1988). Communication correlates of college success: An exploratory investigation. *Communication Education* 37, 14–27.

Rubin, R. B., & Martin, M. M. (1994). Development of a measure of interpersonal communication competence. *Communication Research Reports* 11, 33–44.

Rubin, R. B., & McHugh, M. (1987). Development of parasocial interaction relationships. *Journal of Broadcasting and Electronic Media* 31, 279–292.

Rubin, R. B., & Nevins, R. J. (1988). *The road trip: An interpersonal adventure.* Prospect Heights, IL: Waveland Press.

Rubin, R. B., Perse, E. M., & Barbato, C. A. (1988). Conceptualization and measurement of interpersonal communication motives. *Human Communication Research* 14, 602–628.

Rubin, R. B., & Rubin, A. M. (1992). Antecedents of interpersonal communication motivation. *Communication Quarterly* 40, 315–317.

Rubin, Z. (1973). *Liking and loving: An invitation to social psychology.* New York: Holt, Rinehart & Winston.

Ruggiero, T. E. (2000). Uses and gratifications theory in the 21st century. *Mass Communication and Society* 3 (winter), 3–37.

Rundquist, S. (1992). Indirectness: A gender study of flouting Grice's maxims. *Journal of Pragmatics* 18, 431–449.

Rusbult, C. E., & Buunk, B. P. (1993). Commitment processes in close relationships: An interdependence analysis. *Journal of Social and Personal Relationships* 10, 175–204.

Rushe, R. H. (1996). Tactics of power and influence in violent marriages. *Dissertation abstracts international: Section B: The Sciences and Engineering* (University of Washington), 57, 1453.

Sabatelli, R. M., & Pearce, J. (1986). Exploring marital expectations. *Journal of Social and Personal Relationships* 3, 307–321.

Sabath, A. M. (1999). *International business etiquette: Asia and the Pacific Rim.* Franklin Lakes, NJ: Career Press.

Sabath, A. M. (1999). *International business etiquette in Europe: What you need to know to conduct business abroad with charm and savvy.* New York: Career Press.

Salminen, S., & Glad, T. (1992). The role of gender in helping behavior. *Journal of Social Psychology* 132, 131–133.

Samovar, L. A., & Porter, R. E., eds. (1991). *Communication between cultures.* Belmont, CA: Wadsworth.

Samter, W., & Cupach, W. R. (1998). Friendly fire: Topics variations in conflict among same- and cross-sex friends. *Communication Studies* 49, 121–138.

Sanders, J. A., Wiseman, R. L., & Matz, S. I. (1991). Uncertainty reduction in acquaintance relationships in Ghana and the United States. In *Cross-cultural interpersonal communication,* S. Ting-Toomey & F. Korzenny (eds.). Thousand Oaks, CA: Sage, pp. 79–98.

Sapadin, L. A. (1988). Friendship and gender: Perspectives of professional men and women. *Journal of Social and Personal Relationships* 5, 387–403.

Sarwer, D. B., Kalichman, S. C., Johnson, J. R., Early, J., et al. (1993). Sexual aggression and love styles: An exploratory study. *Archives of Sexual Behavior* 22, 265–275.

Satir, V. (1983). *Conjoint Family Therapy,* 3d ed. Palo Alto, CA: Science and Behavior Books.

Scandura, T. (1992). Mentorship and career mobility: An empirical investigation. *Journal of Organizational Behavior* 13, 169–174.

Schaap, C., Buunk, B., & Kerkstra, A. (1988). Marital conflict resolution. In *Perspectives on marital interaction,* P. Noller & M. A. Fitzpatrick (eds.). Philadelphia: Multilingual Matters, pp. 203–244.

Schafer, R. B., & Keith, P. M. (1980). Equity and depression among married couples. *Social Psychology Quarterly* 43, 430–435.

Scheetz, L. P. (1995). *Recruiting trends 1995–1996. A study of 527 businesses, industries, and governmental agencies employing new college graduates.* East Lansing: Collegiate Employment Research Institute, Michigan State University.

Schegloff, E. (1982). Discourses as an interactional achievement: Some uses of "uh huh" and other things that come between sentences. In *Georgetown University roundtable on language and linguistics,* Deborah Tannen (ed.). Washington, DC: Georgetown University Press, pp. 71–93.

Scheufele, D. A., & Moy, P. (2000). Twenty-five years of the spiral of silence: A conceptual review and empirical outlook. *International Journal of Public Opinion Research* 12 (spring), 3–28.

Schmidt, T. O., & Cornelius, R. R. (1987). Self-disclosure in everyday life. *Journal of Social and Personal Relationships* 4, 365–373.

Schoeneman, T. J., & Rubanowitz, E. E. (1985). Attributions in the advice columns: Actors and observers, causes and reasons. *Personality and Social Psychology Bulletin* 11, 315–325.

Schramm, W., & Porter, W. E. (1982). *Men, women, messages and media: Understanding human communication.* New York: Harper & Row.

Schuter, R. (1990). The centrality of culture. *Southern Communication Journal* 55, 237–249.

Schutz, A. (1999). It was your fault! Self-serving biases in autobiographical accounts of conflicts in married couples. *Journal of Social and Personal Relationships* 16, 193–208.

Schwartz, M., and the Task Force on Bias-Free Language of the Association of American University Presses (1995). *Guidelines for bias-free writing.* Bloomington: Indiana University Press.

Sergios, P. A., & Cody, J. (1985). Physical attractiveness and social assertiveness skills in male homosexual dating behavior and partner selection. *Journal of Social Psychology* 125, 505–514.

Severin, W. J. & Tankard, J. W., Jr. (2001). *Communication theories: Origins, methods, and uses in the mass media.* Boston: Allyn & Bacon.

Shaffer, D. R., Pegalis, L. J., & Bazzini, D. G. (1996). When boy meets girl (revisited): Gender, gender role orientation, and prospect of future interaction as determinants of self-disclosure among same- and opposite-sex acquaintances. *Personality and Social Psychology Bulletin* 22, 495–506.

Shannon, J. (1987). Don't smile when you say that. *Executive Female* 10, 33, 43. Reprinted in DeVito & Hecht (1990), pp. 115–117.

Sharkey, W. F., & Stafford, L. (1990). Turn-taking resources employed by congenitally blind conversers. *Communication Studies* 41, 161–182.

Sheppard, J. A., & Strathman, A. J. (1989). Attractiveness and height: The role of stature in dating preferences, frequency of dating, and perceptions of attractiveness. *Personality and Social Psychology* 15, 617–627.

Shibazaki, K., & Brennan, K. A. (1998). When birds of different features flock together: A preliminary comparison of intra-ethnic and inter-ethnic dating relationships. *Journal of Social and Personal Relationships* 15, 248–256.

Siavelis, R. L., & Lamke, L. K. (1992). Instrumentalness and expressiveness: Predictors of heterosexual relationship satisfaction. *Sex Roles* 26, 149–159.

Siegert, J. R., & Stamp, G. H. (1994). "Our first big fight" as a milestone in the development of close relationships. *Communication Monographs* 61, 345–360.

Signorielli, N., & Lears, M. (1992). Children, television, and concepts about chores: Attitudes and behaviors. *Sex Roles* 27 (August), 157–170.

Signorile, M. (1993). *Queer in America: Sex, the media, and the closets of power.* New York: Random House.

Silverman, T. (2001). Expanding community: The Internet and relational theory. *Community, Work and Family* 4, 231–237.

Simpson, J. A. (1987). The dissolution of romantic relationships: Factors involved in relationship stability and emotional distress. *Journal of Personality and Social Psychology* 53, 683–692.

Singelis, T. M. (1994). The measurement of independent and interdependent self-construals. *Personality and Social Psychology Bulletin* 20, 580–591.

Slade, M. (1995). We forgot to write a headline. But it's not our fault. *New York Times* (February 19), 5.

Smith, C. S. (2002). Beware of green hats in China and other cross-cultural faux pas. *The New York Times* (April, 30), C11.

Smith, S. M., & Shaffer, D. R. (1991). Celerity and cajolery: Rapid speech may promote or inhibit persuasion through its impact on message elaboration. *Personality and Social Psychology Bulletin* 17 (December), 663–669.

Smith, S. M., & Shaffer, D. R. (1995). Speed of speech and persuasion: Evidence for multiple effects. *Personality and Social Psychology Bulletin* 21 (October), 1051–1060.

Smoreda, Z., & Licoppe, C. (2000). Gender-specific use of the domestic telephone. *Social Psychology Quarterly* 63, 238–252.

Snyder, C. R. (1984). Excuses, excuses. *Psychology Today* 18, 50–55.

Snyder, C. R., Higgins, R. L., and Stucky, R. J. (1983). *Excuses: Masquerades in search of grace.* New York: Wiley.

Snyder, M. (1987). *Public appearances, private realities.* New York: W. H. Freeman.

Snyder, M. (1992). A gender-informed model of couple and family therapy: Relationship enhancement therapy. *Contemporary Family Therapy: An International Journal* 14 (February), 15–31.

Solomon, D. H., & Samp, J. A. (1998). Power and problem appraisal: Perceptual foundations of the chilling effect in dating relationships. *Journal of Social and Personal Relationships* 15, 191–209.

Solomon, G. B., Striegel, D. A., Eliot, J. F., Heon, S. N., et al. (1996). The self-fulfilling prophecy in college basketball: Implications for effective coaching. *Journal of Applied Sport Psychology* 8, 44–59.

Sommer, K. L., Williams, K. D., Ciarocco, N. J., & Baumeister, R. F. (2001). When silence speaks louder than words: Explorations into the intrapsychic and interpersonal consequences of social ostracism. *Basic and Applied Social Psychology* 23, 225–243.

Sorenson, P. S., Hawkins, K., & Sorenson, R. L. (1995). Gender, psychological type and conflict style preference. *Management Communication Quarterly* 9, 115–126.

Spencer, T. (1993). A new approach to assessing self-disclosure in conversation. Paper presented at the Annual Convention of the Western Speech Communication Association, Albuquerque, New Mexico.

Spencer, T. (1994). Transforming relationships through everyday talk. In *The Dynamics of Relationships: Vol. 4. Understanding Relationships,* S. Duck (ed.). Thousand Oaks, CA: Sage.

Spitzberg, B. H. (1991). Intercultural communication competence. In *Intercultural communication: A reader,* L. A. Samovar & R. E. Porter (eds.). Belmont, CA: Wadsworth, pp. 353–365.

Spitzberg, B. H., & Cupach, W. R. (1984). *Interpersonal communication competence.* Thousand Oaks, CA: Sage.

Spitzberg, B. H., & Cupach, W. R. (1989). *Handbook of interpersonal competence research.* New York: Springer-Verlag.

Spitzberg, B. H., & Hecht, M. L. (1984). A component model of relational competence. *Human Communication Research* 10, 575–599.

Sprecher, S. (1987). The effects of self-disclosure given and received on affection for an intimate partner and stability of the relationship. *Journal of Social and Personal Relationships* 4, 115–127.

Sprecher, S. (2001). Equity and social exchange in dating couples: Associations with satisfaction, commitment, and stability. *Journal of Marriage and the Family* 63 (August), 599–613.

Sprecher, S., & Metts, S. (1989). Development of the "Romantic Beliefs Scale" and examination of the effects of gender and gender-role orientation. *Journal of Social and Personal Relationships* 6, 387–411.

Sprecher, S., & Schwartz, P. (1994). Equity and balance in the exchange of contributions in close relationships. In *Entitlement and the affectional bond: Justice in close relationships,* M. J. Lerner & G. Mikula (eds.). New York: Plenum, pp. 11–42.

Stafford, L., Kline, S. L., & Dimmick, J. (1999). Home e-mail: Relational maintenance and gratification opportunities. *Journal of Broadcasting and Electronic Media* 43, 659–669.

Staines, G. L., Pottick, K. J., & Fudge, D. A. (1986). Wives' employment and husbands' attitudes toward work and life. *Journal of Applied Psychology* 71, 118–128.

Steil, L. K., Barker, L. L., & Watson, K. W. (1983). *Effective listening: Key to your success.* Reading, MA: Addison-Wesley.

Steiner, C. (1981). *The other side of power.* New York: Grove.

Steinfatt, T. M. (1987). Personality and communication: Classic approaches. In *Personality and interpersonal communication,* J. C. McCroskey & J. A. Daly (eds.). Thousand Oaks, CA: Sage, pp. 42–126.

Stephan, W. G., & Stephan, C. W. (1985). Intergroup anxiety. *Journal of Social Issues* 41, 157–175.

Stephens, G. K., & Greer, C. R. (1995). Doing business in Mexico: Understanding cultural differences. *Organizational Dynamics* 24, 39–55.

Stern, J. A. (1992). The eye blink: Affective and cognitive influences. In *Anxiety: Recent developments in cognitive, psychophysiological, and health research,* D. G. Forgays, T. Sosnowski, & K. Wrzesniewski (eds.). Washington, DC: Hemisphere Publishing, pp. 109–128.

Sternberg, R. J. (1986). A triangular theory of love. *Psychological Review* 93, 119–135.

Sternberg, R. J. (1988). *The triangle of love: Intimacy, passion, commitment.* New York: Basic Books.

Strecker, I. (1993). Cultural variations in the concept of "face." *Multilingua* 12, 119–141.

Sutter, D. L., & Martin, M. M. (1998). Verbal aggression during disengagement of dating relationships. *Communication Research Reports* 15, 318–326.

Szapocznik, J. (1995). Research on disclosure of HIV status: Cultural evolution finds an ally in science. *Health Psychology* 14, 4–5.

Tannen, D. (1990). *You just don't understand: Women and men in conversation.* New York: Morrow.

Tannen, D. (1994a). *Gender and discourse.* New York: Oxford University Press.

Tannen, D. (1994b). *Talking from 9 to 5.* New York: Morrow.

Taraban, C. B., & Hendrick, C. (1995). Personality perceptions associated with six styles of love. *Journal of Social and Personal Relationships* 12, 453–461.

Tardiff, T. (2001). Learning to say "no" in Chinese. *Early Education and Development* 12, 303–323.

Taylor, D. M., & Jaggi, V. (1974). Ethnocentrism and causal attribution in a South Indian context. *Journal of Cross-Cultural Psychology* 5, 162–171.

Thelen, M. H., Sherman, M. D., & Borst, T. S. (1998). Fear of intimacy and attachment among rape survivors. *Behavior Modification* 22, 108–116.

Thibaut, J. W., & Kelley, H. H. (1959). *The social psychology of groups.* New York: Wiley. Reissued (1986). New Brunswick, NJ: Transaction Books.

Thomlison, D. (1982). *Toward interpersonal dialogue.* New York: Longman.

Thompson, C. A., & Klopf, D. W. (1991). An analysis of social style among disparate cultures. *Communication Research Reports* 8, 65–72.

Thompson, C. A., Klopf, D. W., & Ishii, S. (1991). A comparison of social style between Japanese and Americans. *Communication Research Reports* 8, 165–172.

Tichenor, P. J., Donohue, G. A., & Olien, C. N. (1970). Mass media flow and differential growth in knowledge. *Public Opinion Quarterly* 34, 159–170.

Timmerman, L. J. (2002). Comparing the production of power in language on the basis of sex. In *Interpersonal communication research: Advances through meta-analysis,* M. Allen & R. W. Preiss (eds.). Mahwah, NJ: Erlbaum, pp. 73–88.

Ting-Toomey, S. (1981). Ethnic identity and close friendship in Chinese-American college students. *International Journal of Intercultural Relations* 5, 383–406.

Ting-Toomey, S. (1985). Toward a theory of conflict and culture. *International and Intercultural Communication Annual* 9, 71–86.

Ting-Toomey, S. (1986). Conflict communication styles in black and white subjective cultures. In *Interethnic communication: Current research,* Y. Y. Kim (ed.). Thousand Oaks, CA: Sage, pp. 75 88.

Tinsley, C. H., & Brett, J. M. (2001). Managing workplace conflict in the United States and Hong Kong. *Organizational Behavior and Human Decision Processes* 85, 360–381.

Titlow, K. I., Rackoff, J. E., & Emanuel, E. J. (1999). What will it take to restore patient trust? *Business & Health* 17 (6A), 61–64.

TMA Journal 19 (July/Aug 1999), p. 53.

Tolhuizen, J. H. (1986). Perceiving communication indicators of evolutionary changes in friendship. *Southern Speech Communication Journal* 52, 69–91.

Tolhuizen, J. H. (1989). Communication strategies for intensifying dating relationships: Identification, use, and structure. *Journal of Social and Personal Relationships* 6, 413–434.

Trager, G. L. (1958). Paralanguage: A first approximation. *Studies in Linguistics* 13, 1–12.

Trager, G. L. (1961). The typology of paralanguage. *Anthropological Linguistics* 3, 17–21.

Trower, P. (1981). Social skill disorder. In *Personal Relationships* 3, S. Duck & R. Gilmour (eds.). New York: Academic Press, pp. 97–110.

Tschann, J. M. (1988). Self-disclosure in adult friendship: Gender and marital status differences. *Journal of Social and Personal Relationships* 5, 65–81.

Ueleke, W., et al. (1983). Inequity resolving behavior as a response to inequity in a hypothetical marital relationship. *A Quarterly Journal of Human Behavior* 20, 4–8.

Unger, F. L. (2001). Speech directed at able-bodied adults, disabled adults, and disabled adults with speech impairments. *Dissertation Abstracts International: Second B: The Sciences and Engineering,* 62, 1146.

Uris, A. (1986). *101 of the greatest ideas in management.* New York: Wiley.

VanHyning, M. (1993). *Crossed signals: How to say no to sexual harassment.* Los Angeles: Infotrends Press.

Varonis, E. M., & Gass, S. M. (1985). Miscommunication in native/nonnative conversation. *Language in Society* 14, 327–343.

Veenendall, T. L., & Feinstein, M. C. (1995). *Let's talk about relationships: Cases in study.* Prospect Heights, IL: Waveland Press.

Velting, D. M. (1999). Personality and negative expectations: Trait structure of the Beck Hopelessness Scale. *Personality and Individual Differences* 26, 913–921.

Vergeer, M., Lubbers, M., & Scheepers, P. (2000). Exposure to newspapers and attitudes toward ethnic minorities. *Howard Journal of Communication* 11 (April-June), 127–143.

Victor, D. (1992). *International business communication.* New York: HarperCollins.

Viswanath, K., & Finnegan, J. R., Jr. (1995). The knowledge-gap hypothesis: Twenty-five years later. In *Communication Yearbook/19,* B. R. Burleson (ed.). Thousand Oaks, CA: Sage.

Viswanath, K., Kahn, E., Finnegan, J. R., Hertog, J., et al. (2000). Motivation and the knowledge gap: Effects of a campaign to reduce diet-related cancer risk. *Communication Research* 27 (February), 3–26.

Von Hassell, M. (1993). Issei women: Silences and fields of power. *Feminist Studies* 19, 549–569.

von Tetzchner, S., & Jensen, K. (1999). Interacting with people who have severe communication problems: Ethical considerations. *International Journal of Disability, Development and Education* 46 (December), 453–462.

Wade, N. (2002). Scent of a man is linked to a woman's selection. *New York Times* (January 22), F2.

Walster, E., Walster, G. W., & Berscheid, E. (1978). *Equity: Theory and research.* Boston: Allyn & Bacon.

Walster, E., Walster, G. W., & Traupman, J. (1978). Equity and premarital sex. *Journal of Personality and Social Psychology* 36, 82–92.

Watzlawick, P. (1977). *How real is real? Confusion, disinformation, communication: An anecdotal introduction to communications theory.* New York: Vintage.

Watzlawick, P. (1978). *The language of change: Elements of therapeutic communication.* New York: Basic Books.

Watzlawick, P., Beavin, J. H., & Jackson, D. D. (1967). *Pragmatics of human communication: A study of interactional patterns, pathologies, and paradoxes.* New York: Norton.

Weathers, M. D., Frank, E. M., & Spell, L. A. (2002). Differences in the communication of affect: Members of the same race versus members of a different race. *Journal of Black Psychology* 28, 66–77.

Weigel, D. J., & Ballard-Reisch, D. S. (1999). Using paired data to test models of relational maintenance and marital quality. *Journal of Social and Personal Relationships* 16, 175–191.

Weinberg, H. L. (1959). *Levels of knowing and existence.* New York: Harper & Row.

Weiner, B., Amirkhan, J., Folkes, V. S., & Verette, J. A. (1987). An attributional analysis of excuse giving: Studies of a naive theory of emotion. *Journal of Personality and Social Psychology* 52, 316–324.

Weinstein, E. A., & Deutschberger, P. (1963). Some dimensions of altercasting. *Sociometry* 26, 454–466.

Weitzman, P. F. (2001). Young adult women resolving interpersonal conflicts. *Journal of Adult Development* 8, 61–67.

Weitzman, P. F., & Weitzman, E. A. (2000). Interpersonal negotiation strategies in a sample of older women. *Journal of Clinical Geropsychology* 6, 41–51.

Werner, E. K. (1975). *A study of communication time.* M.A. Thesis, University of Maryland, College Park. Cited in Wolvin & Coakley (1982).

Wertz, D. C., Sorenson, J. R., & Heeren, T. C. (1988). Can't get no (dis)satisfaction: Professional satisfaction with professional-client encounters. *Work and Occupations* 15, 36–54.

West, C., & Zimmerman, D. H. (1977). Women's place in everyday talk: Reflections on parent-child interaction. *Social Problems* 24, 521–529.

Westefeld, J. S., & Liddell, D. (1982). Coping with long-distance relationships. *Journal of College Student Personnel* 23, 550–551.

Westwood, R. I., Tang, F. F., & Kirkbride, P. S. (1992). Chinese conflict behavior: Cultural antecedents and behavioral consequences. *Organizational Development Journal* 10, 13–19.

Wetzel, P. J. (1988). Are "powerless" communication strategies the Japanese norm? *Language in Society* 17, 555–564.

Wheeless, L. R., & Grotz, J. (1977). The measurement of trust and its relationship to self-disclosure. *Human Communication Research* 3, 250–257.

Whitty, M., & Gavin, J. (2001). Age/sex/location: Uncovering the social cues in the development of online relationships. *CyberPsychology and Behavior* 4, 623–630.

Wiederman, M. W., & Hurd, C. (1999). Extradyadic involvement during dating. *Journal of Social and Personal Relationships* 16, 265–274.

Wiemann, J. M. (1977). Explication and test of a model of communicative competence. *Human Communication Research* 3, 195–213.

Wilkins, B. M., & Andersen, P. A. (1991). Gender differences and similarities in management communication: A meta-analysis. *Management Communication Quarterly* 5, 6–35.

Wilmot, W. W. (1999). *Relational communication.* New York: McGraw-Hill.

Wilson, J. H., & Taylor, K. W. (2001). Professor immediacy as behaviors associated with liking students. *Teaching of Psychology* 28, 136–138.

Winquist, L. A., Mohr, C. D., Kenny, D. A. (1998). The female positivity effect in the perception of others. *Journal of Research in Personality* 32, 370–388.

Withecomb, J. (1997). Causes of violence in children. *Journal of Mental Health* 6 (October), 433–442.

Witt, P. L., & Wheeless, L. R. (2001). An experimental study of teachers' verbal and nonverbal immediacy and students' affective and cognitive learning. *Communication Education* 50, 327–342.

Wolfson, N. (1988). The bulge: A theory of speech behaviour and social distance. In *Second language discourse: A textbook of current research,* J. Fine (ed.). Norwood, NJ: Ablex.

Wolpe, J. (1958). *Psychotherapy by reciprocal inhibition.* Stanford, CA: Stanford University Press.

Wolvin, A. D., & Coakley, C. G. (1996). *Listening.* Dubuque, IA: William C. Brown.

Won-Doornink, Myong-Jin (1991). Self-disclosure and reciprocity in South Korean and U.S. male dyads. In *Cross-cultural interpersonal communication,* S. Ting-Toomey & F. Korzenny (eds.). Thousand Oaks, CA: Sage, pp. 116–131.

Wood, J. T. (1994). *Gendered lives: Communication, gender, and culture.* Belmont, CA: Wadsworth.

Wright, J. W., & Hosman, L. A. (1983). Language style and sex bias in the courtroom: The effects of male and female use of hedges and intensifiers on impression formation. *Southern Speech Communication Journal* 48, 137–152.

Wright, P. H. (1978). Toward a theory of friendship based on a conception of self. *Human Communication Research* 4, 196–207.

Wright, P. H. (1984). Self-referent motivation and the intrinsic quality of friendship. *Journal of Social and Personal Relationships* 1, 115–130.

Wright, P. H. (1988). Interpreting research on gender differences in friendship: A case for moderation and a plea for caution. *Journal of Social and Personal Relationships* 5, 367–373.

Yau-fair Ho, D., Chan, S. F., Peng, S., & Ng, A. K. (2001). The dialogical self: Converging East-West constructions. *Culture and Psychology* 7, 393–408.

Yela, C. (2000). Predictors of and factors related to loving and sexual satisfaction for men and women. *European Review of Applied Psychology* 50, 235–243.

Yun, H. (1976). The Korean personality and treatment considerations. *Social Casework* 57, 173–178.

Zajonc, R. B. (1968). Attitudinal effects of mere exposure. *Journal of Personality and Social Psychology Monograph* Suppl. 9, no. 2, pt. 2.

Zemanek, J. E. (1995). How salespersons' use of a power base can affect customers' satisfaction in a social system: An empirical examination. *Psychological Reports* 76 (February), 211–218.

Zimbardo, P. A. (1977). *Shyness: What it is and what to do about it.* Reading, MA: Addison-Wesley.

Zimmer, T. A. (1986). Premarital anxieties. *Journal of Social and Personal Relationships* 3, 149–159.

Zimmerman, D. H., & West, C. (1975). Sex roles, interruptions and silences in conversations. In *Language and sex: Differences and dominance,* B. Thorne & N. Henley (eds.). Rowley, MA: Newbury House.

Zmuda, R. A. (2001). Improving doctor/patient communications. http://thehealthchannel.com/. Accessed September 6, 2001.

Zuckerman, M., Klorman, R., Larrance, D. T., & Spiegel, N. H. (1981). Facial, autonomic, and subjective components of emotion: The facial feedback hypothesis versus the externalizer-internalizer distinction. *Journal of Personality and Social Psychology* 41, 929–944.

Zunin, L. M., & Zunin, N. B. (1972). *Contact: The first four minutes.* Los Angeles: Nash.

Credits

ADDITIONAL TEXT CREDITS

Page 37: Reprinted from *International Journal of Intercultural Relations 5*, Ting-Toomey, "Ethnic identity and close friendship in Chinese-American college students," pp. 383–406. Copyright © 1981. Used with permission from Elsevier Science.

Page 83: From Powers & Love, "Communication Apprehension in the Dating Partner Context," *Communication Research Reports 17*, 221–228, 2000. Used by permission of Eastern Communication Association.

PHOTO CREDITS

Page 1: Photo by 20th Century Fox/Zuma Press. © Copyright 2000 by Courtesy of 20th Century Fox; 14: E. Agostin/Getty Images; 18: Helen Norman/Corbis; 26: Chuck Savage/Corbis; 35: Photo by Columbia Pictures/Zuma Press. © Copyright 2000 by Courtesy of Columbia Pictures; 42: Dee Snider/The Image Works; 47: AP/Wide World Photos; 54: Paul Conklin/PhotoEdit; 62: The Kobal Collection; 69: Richard Hutchings/Photo Researchers; 75: Superstock, Inc.; 83: AP/Wide World Photos; 90: The Kobal Collection; 93: John Coletti/Stock Boston; 98: AP/Wide World Photos; 110: Ariel Skelley/Corbis; 113: The Kobal Collection; 118: The Everett Collection; 123: Jeff Greenberg/PhotoEdit; 129: Robert Brenner/PhotoEdit; 133: The Everett Collection; 141: Gary A. Conner/Index Stock Imagery, Inc.; 143: David Young-Wolff/PhotoEdit; 147: Photofest; 154:The Everett Collection; 156: Bob Daemmirch/The Image Works; 168: Reuters NewMedia Inc./Corbis; 175: Robert Maass/Corbis; 180: The Kobal Collection; 183: The Kobal Collection; 190: Myrleen Ferguson/PhotoEdit; 206: Michael N. Paras/Corbis; 211: Demmie Todd/The Everett Collection; 216: Mark Burnett/Stock Boston; 222: The Kobal Collection; 228: Jeff Greenberg/PhotoEdit; 233: The Everett Collection; 239: Gary A. Conner/PhotoEdit; 245: Rick Gerharter/Impact Visuals; 247: Mary Kate Denny/PhotoEdit; 252: Photo by Columbia Pictures/Zumma Press © Copyright 2001 by Courtesy of Columbia Pictures; 255: David Joel/Stone/Getty Images; 258: Bruce Ayres/Stone/Getty Images; 269: Joseph Nettis/Photo Researchers; 280: The Everett Collection; 289: Photofest; 293: Esbin-Anderson/The Image Works; 301: Superstock, Inc.; 309: The Kobal Collection; 321: Bob Daemmrich/The Image Works; 323: Index Stock Imagery, Inc.; 328: David R. Frazier Photolibrary, Inc.; 333: Photo by P. Vinet/New Line Cinema/Zuma Press. © Copyright 2002 by Courtesy of New Line Cinema; 338: Jim Whitmer Photography; 341: Ariel Skelley/Corbis; 345: Gary Conner/PhotoEdit.

Index

Note: Italicized letters *f* and *t* following page numbers indicate figures and tables, respectively.